BRITANNICA JUNIOR ENCYCLOPÆDIA

For Boys and Girls

$$\frac{12}{PQ}$$

Prepared under the supervision of the editors of ENCYCLOPÆDIA BRITANNICA

William Benton, *Publisher*

ENCYCLOPÆDIA BRITANNICA, INC.

Chicago   London   Toronto   Geneva   Sydney   Tokyo   Manila

KEY TO PRONUNCIATION

It is of especial importance that an encyclopaedia for children give the pronunciation where the boy or girl might go astray. In all such instances the pronunciation in BRITANNICA JUNIOR ENCYCLOPÆDIA is clearly marked. The accent is shown by the mark (′). The sounds for the different letters, when not self-evident, are as follows:

ā as in *pale*	ē as in *her*	ou as in *out*	ṅ (nasal) as in French *bon*
â as in *care*	ī as in *mice*	ū as in *use*	th as in *think*
ă as in *bat*	ĭ as in *tin*	ŭ as in *run*	ŧh as in *thee*
ä as in *farm*	ō as in *cold*	ṳ as in *pull*	ṯ as in *picture* (Sound varies
á as in *task*	ŏ as in *not*	ü as in French *début*, German *über*	from *t* to *ch*)
a̱ as in *ball*	ô as in *for*	g (always hard) as in *gay*	ẕ as in *pleasure* (Sound varies
ē as in *be*	oi as in *oil*	j for *g* as in *gentle*	from *z* to *zh*)
ĕ as in *met*	ōō as in *loot*	K for *ch* as in German *Bach* or Scottish *loch*	

Printed in the U.S.A.

THE UNIVERSITY
OF CHICAGO

BRITANNICA JUNIOR ENCYCLOPÆDIA IS PUB-
LISHED WITH THE EDITORIAL ADVICE OF THE
FACULTIES OF THE UNIVERSITY OF CHICAGO
AND THE UNIVERSITY LABORATORY SCHOOLS

•

Let knowledge grow from more to more and thus be human life enriched

The Pyramids of Giza were old 1,000 years before the birth of Christ. These wondrous feats of engineering, built as tombs for ancient kings of Egypt, stand in the valley of the Nile southwest of Cairo. See PYRAMID.

PACIFIC (*pä sĭf'ĭk*) **COASTAL REGION, UNITED STATES,** is the westernmost part of the country. It includes the states of California, Oregon, and Washington. This region stretches from the Mexican border to Canada and extends inland from the Pacific Ocean to the Southwestern and Rocky Mountain regions of the United States. The landscape changes considerably through the long north-south distance. The climate also varies from the generally moist, cool weather of the Canadian border to the hot, dry summers and mild winters of southern California. There also are great differences of climate at various elevations through the region. Manufacturing, fruit and vegetable farming, lumbering, fishing, mining, and tourism are important activities of the Pacific Coastal Region.

Southern California

North of Los Angeles, several ranges of east-west mountains separate southern California from the rest of the Pacific Coastal Region. The northernmost of these are the Tehachapi Mountains, which form the southern end of the Central Valley of California. To the southeast of the Tehachapis is the dry Mohave Desert. Between the Mohave Desert and the Pacific Ocean are a series of mountain ranges and valleys. Farther south are the Imperial and Coachella valleys, well-known for their irrigated crops of lettuce, carrots, cotton, alfalfa, sugar beets, and citrus fruits. The Salton Sea, between the two valleys, was created by the floodwaters of the Colorado River. In the southwestern corner of California is San Diego, known for its aircraft and missile industries and as a great naval base and military center. It is the gateway to Lower California, Mexico.

North of San Diego along the coast is the Los Angeles–Long Beach area, the largest population and manufacturing center of the West Coast. Los Angeles itself is the third largest city of the United States, after New York City and Chicago. Its metropolitan area, however, ranks second only to New York City. Los Angeles' Hollywood district is the movie capital of the world. The transportation equipment industry, including aircraft, employs more peo-

ple than any other industry. Other leading industries include oil refining, electronics, metal refining, and fish processing. Tuna and related species from the Pacific are the chief fish catches. Los Angeles also is a major port and transportation center.

The Los Angeles area, like the rest of southern California, is quite dry. Agriculture and industry in the area must depend on waters diverted from the Colorado River and from the Sierra Nevada Mountains. Farms around Los Angeles produce dairy products, vegetables, and citrus fruits.

Mountains and Highlands

The landforms of the Pacific Coastal Region north of the Tehachapi Mountains roughly resemble the letter H. There is no coastal plain along the Pacific, and the Coast Ranges form the western side of the H. The Sierra Nevada and Cascade Mountains form the eastern side. The Klamath Mountains along the Oregon-California border make the crossbar of the H.

The Cascades have a number of high volcanic cones, such as Lassen Peak and Mounts Rainier, Adams, Hood, and Shasta. The famous Crater Lake of Oregon is in the Cascades. Continuing south of the Cascades is the Sierra Nevada. This high range slopes gradually to the west but steeply to the east. Mount Whitney, 14,495 feet high, is the highest point in the conterminous United States. Less than 100 miles to the east is the lowest point, Death Valley, which is 282 feet below sea level. The Sierra Nevada and Cascades have notable forests, and they receive the rainfall and snowfall that are used to irrigate valleys to the west. Tourists are attracted yearly to the scenic beauty of these ranges, including their volcanic cones and lakes, and the great national parks—Lassen Volcanic, Kings Canyon, Crater Lake, Sequoia, and Yosemite.

East of the Cascades and Sierras are portions of the dry Columbia Plateau and the Great Basin. The Columbia Plateau in Washington is known for its great wheat fields and for apple orchards. At the northern edge of the plateau,

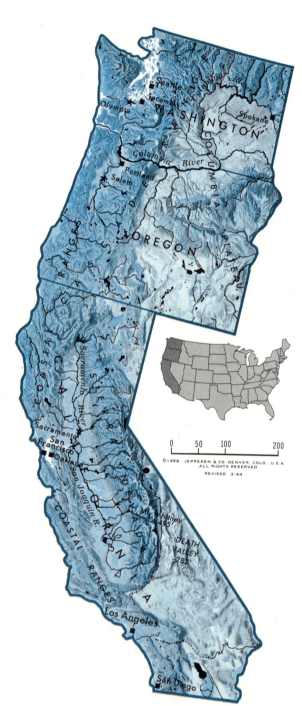

the Grand Coulee Dam on the Columbia River provides hydroelectricity and irrigation for the northeastern part of the region.

Valleys and Cities

South of the Klamath Mountains is the Central Valley of California, the largest lowland of the region. It is drained into San Francisco Bay by the Sacramento and San Joaquin rivers. North of the Klamath are the Willamette Valley of Oregon and the Columbia River Valley and Puget Sound area of Washington. The Columbia River, the sound, and San Francisco Bay are the three major coastal inlets to the region's interior.

The Central Valley is known for its cotton, grapes, rice, wheat, fruits, and vegetables. The valley was the site of the great Gold Rush of 1848 and 1849. Sacramento, capital of California; Fresno; and Bakersfield, in an oil-field area, are leading cities of the valley.

The San Francisco Bay area is the main trade center for products of the Central Valley. Around the bay has grown the sixth largest metropolitan area of the United States. San Francisco is the leading seaport on the Pacific Coast, and the San Francisco–Oakland area is a leading U.S. manufacturing region. Food processing, metal production, clothing, paper, chemicals, and transportation equipment are among the major industries. San Francisco is a major financial and insurance hub.

The Willamette and Puget Sound lowlands are much cooler and more humid than the Central Valley. They produce grains, dairy products, and fruits and vegetables. Portland, located near the junction of the Willamette and Columbia rivers, is the major city of Oregon. Reflecting Oregon's leadership in lumbering, Portland has many industries related to wood and wood products, as well as food processing, metalworking, and textile industries. Seattle, Spokane, and Tacoma are the major cities of Washington. Seattle and Tacoma are centers for the lumber industry, food processing, and the manufacture of transportation equipment. Spokane is a mining and agricultural center. (See the separate articles on cities, states, and geographic features of the Pacific Coastal Region.)

PACIFIC ISLANDS. The Pacific is the largest and deepest ocean. It covers one-third of the surface of the earth, and contains more than half the earth's water. Scattered across the western and central parts of this ocean are thousands of islands.

Some islands lie close to the continents on both sides of the Pacific, and have rocks, plants, animals, and people much like those found on the nearby continent. A chain of high islands of this type extends along the eastern coast of Asia. These are the Kuril Islands, Japan, the Ryukyu Islands, and Taiwan (Formosa) (see JAPAN; TAIWAN). South of Taiwan is a group of more than 7,000 islands, the Philippines. (See PHILIPPINES, REPUBLIC OF THE.) South of the Philippines is Indonesia. (See INDONESIA.) New Guinea, which is twice as large as the state of California and the second largest island in the world, lies between Indonesia and Australia. (See NEW GUINEA.) Australia is a continent and is not called an island. More than 1,000 miles east of Australia is New Zealand, a member of the Commonwealth of Nations. (See NEW ZEALAND.)

Other islands in the Pacific are really part of North America. The Aleutians form a chain reaching southwestward from Alaska. (See ALASKA.) The southern part of Alaska and the western coast of Canada are bordered by islands, and there are small islands off the coast of California and Mexico. The Galapagos Islands and a few smaller islands are a part of South America. (See ECUADOR.)

The Pacific islands described in this article are farther out in the Pacific Ocean. They have little to do with nearby continents. Geographers divide these islands into three great groups, called Polynesia, Micronesia, and Melanesia. The grouping of the islands is largely on the basis of the peoples who inhabit them, who are of three different types. However, the islands themselves differ somewhat in form, structure, kinds of rocks, and plant and animal life. The names of these groups come from Greek words. Polynesia means "many islands"; Micronesia means "little islands"; Melanesia means "black islands," and refers to the dark skins of the inhabitants.

Polynesia

The islands of Polynesia lie within a large triangle in the central Pacific. The corners of this area are marked by the Hawaiian Islands on the north, Easter Island on the east, and Tonga on the west. The Maori people of New Zealand are Polynesians, having migrated there from the Society Islands as early as A.D. 900. Except for the relation of these people, however, New Zealand has little in common with the other Polynesian islands.

The islands of Polynesia are the summits of volcanic mountains that rise steeply from the floor of the Pacific Ocean. Most of the mountain peaks have to be more than three miles high just to become islands. Many of these peaks have been carved off near the surface of the ocean and are capped over by reefs. Reefs are made up of the skeletons of marine plants and animals, cemented together by lime from the sea water. Reefs can live and grow only under water near the surface of the sea. Pieces of reef rock break off and are cast up on the reef surface to form low, sandy islands.

In some places, reefs have been pushed upward by great earth forces to form raised reef islands. A number of the islands of Polynesia, especially the larger ones, have volcanic peaks high above sea level. These peaks have been built up by flow upon flow of lava and ash that was thrown off by the erupting volcanoes. The island of Hawaii has the greatest elevations. The island slopes upward from the floor of the ocean to the twin summits of Mauna Kea and Mauna Loa, a total height of about 32,000 feet. The summit of Mauna Kea is 13,796 feet above sea level and is the highest elevation in the mid-Pacific. The floor of the ocean on both sides is more than 18,000 feet below sea level.

Many of the islands of Polynesia form chains. The Hawaiian Islands chain is more than 1,600 miles long. The Society Islands, of which Tahiti is the largest and highest, form another chain, and Samoa yet another. These chains of islands are really partly submerged ranges of volcanic mountains, only the highest peaks of which are visible above the sea. There are several other such mountain ranges that run diagonally across the central Pacific; only a few of their peaks reach the surface.

Micronesia

The islands of Micronesia are all west of the International Date Line, where, as one goes westward, one day changes to the next. Nearly all of the Micronesian islands lie north of the Equator, and most are very small. There are about 2,200 islands in Micronesia, but their land area is much smaller than that of Long Island, New York. The dozen largest islands together have an area of 740 square miles. The other 2,188 share the remaining 275 square miles among them, averaging only 80 acres each. These Micronesian islands are scattered over an area of ocean larger than the United States.

About 1,700 of the islets are strewn along the reef rims of 70 atolls. An atoll is a somewhat circular or angular rim of reef, surrounding a shallow lagoon. All around, outside the reef, is deep water. The reef material is coral, consisting of the limy skeletons of marine animals.

(See CORAL.) There is very little fresh water on an atoll, even where there is plenty of rainfall. There are no valuable minerals. The soil is made up of coral sand and rock, and is not fertile. Only a few kinds of plants grow readily on atolls. Life is hard for the people who live on them. There are atolls in Polynesia, more actually than in Micronesia; but Polynesia has more and larger high islands.

Melanesia

Many millions of years ago the southeastern corner of Asia extended far out into the Pacific, about to where the islands of Fiji are today. As centuries went by, this land mass broke up into groups of large, high islands. These islands are now called Melanesia. In the "young" islands of Polynesia, which were made by volcanoes during the past few million years, there are no large deposits of precious metals. The much older islands of Melanesia have large amounts of valuable ores such as chrome, nickel, manganese, iron, and even gold. Their rich soils

Pacific islands showing three main ethnic groups.

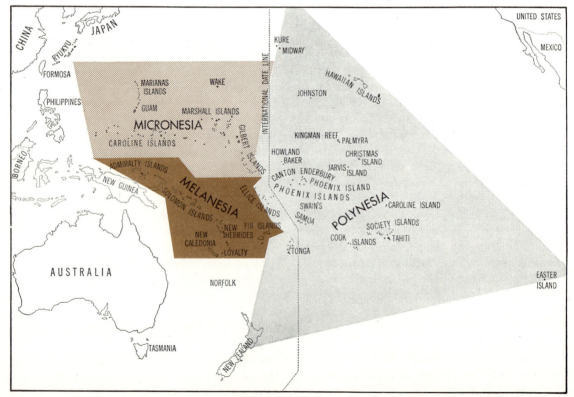

support fine forests and gardens.

All of the islands of Melanesia are west of the International Date Line and south of the Equator. They extend westward to include New Britain and Manus but do not include New Guinea. There are some low, sandy islands in and along the edge of Melanesia, even a few atolls; but most of the islands are large and high.

Peoples of the Pacific

The ancestors of all of the native peoples who live on Pacific islands are thought to have come from Asia in groups, one after another. In modern times, some of them have intermarried with peoples from Europe and America.

It was perhaps several thousand years B.C. when those who later were the natives of Australia went from Asia east to New Guinea and then south into the great continent of Australia. Although these people have black skin, they do not have kinky hair and are not thought to be closely related to modern Negroes.

Many centuries later another people with black skin occupied the southern islands of Melanesia as far eastward, at least, as New Caledonia. They had kinky hair and were more like Negroes. Today they are found chiefly in the interior of New Guinea, and are called Papuans.

Much later, but still long before the Christian era, another Negroid people pushed the earlier Papuans back into the interior of New Guinea and the larger islands of Melanesia, and occupied the coasts themselves. They had a higher culture than the earlier arrivals, and cultivated food plants, which they had brought with them from Indonesia. They were great fishermen. In time, they sailed their outrigger canoes throughout Melanesia. They are called Melanesians, the "black islanders."

The next immigrants from Asia were again of a different type. They did not have black skin or kinky hair. They settled the atolls and small islands of Micronesia. Today there are about 100,000 descendants of these Micronesians. They are not very tall, but they are an active, wiry, and happy people. Half of them live on the islands of the Trust Territory. The Trust

Official U.S. Coast Guard Photo from Ewing Galloway

A group of native Papuan children at a mission in New Guinea are delighted with the candy being given them.

Territory consists of islands which belonged to Germany before World War I, then to Japan, and which were placed in the care of the United States after World War II. Another quarter of the Micronesians live on the United States island of Guam. The rest live in the Gilbert Islands, a colony of Great Britain. The people in one part of Micronesia do not understand the language of those in another. Many of the young people of the Trust Territory talk Japanese, because they went to Japanese schools.

This group of native children in Guam are enjoying their homemade wagon.

Ewing Galloway

The older people remember a little German. Now they are all being taught English.

The last native people to arrive in the Pacific were the Polynesians. Their ancestors may have started out from somewhere in Asia as a tribe of light-skinned people. This tribe migrated southeastward into Indonesia, where they intermarried with the brown-skinned people of those islands and with Mongolianlike people who came down the eastern coast of Asia from the North. Their descendants migrated once more.

They were fearless seamen and knew how to sail large double canoes or catamarans. In small groups—men, women, and children, with their dogs, pigs, chickens, and also a few useful plants—they set out to the east in their canoes. In time, after long voyages, they settled many islands of Polynesia. Important centers of culture developed in Samoa and the Society Islands. From these islands, between the 10th and 13th centuries A.D., parties of young chiefs and priests sailed out to conquer and teach the peoples of surrounding islands, and to colonize new island groups. From Samoa parties went south to Tonga and north to the Tokelau and Ellice Islands. Some even made their home on islands far to the west in Melanesia and southern Micronesia. From the Society Islands parties went eastward to the Tuamotu Islands and

Fishing boats are lined up along the bank in Tahiti while the nets hang from the trees to dry.

Pix

Mangareva, south to the Austral Islands, southwest to the Cook Islands and on to New Zealand, northeast to the Marquesas, and north to Hawaii. From either the Marquesas or Mangareva colonists probably settled Easter Island.

The Climate of the Pacific

The Pacific has a variety of climates in its various parts, but there is small range of temperature in the inhabited portions, between the Tropics of Cancer and Capricorn. It never gets very cold at sea level because the sun stays so nearly overhead. It never gets very hot because there are cooling winds from the sea.

There are two great systems of winds across this area. In the eastern Pacific are the trade winds. In the western Pacific are seasonal winds called monsoons. The northeast trade winds blow across the part of Polynesia north of the Equator, and also across eastern Micronesia. The southeast trade winds blow across the Polynesian islands south of the Equator, and also across eastern Melanesia. The western islands of Micronesia and Melanesia lie in the path of the monsoons. These winds blow from Australia toward Asia from May to September, and from Asia toward Australia from October to April.

The ocean currents in the Pacific are produced by the winds and help to regulate the temperature. The warm Japan Current, for example, helps to keep the Bonin Islands from becoming too cold.

The distribution of rainfall is the most variable part of the Pacific climate, both from one area to another and from year to year. There are alternate bands of wet and dry islands across the central Pacific. These are related in some way to the manner in which the two sets of trade winds meet. High islands, against which the trades and monsoons blow, have wet and dry sides. The side toward the wind receives the most rain.

Tropical cyclones occur in the central and western Pacific, both north and south of the Equator, but seldom right on it. North of the Equator these violent whirling storms, known as typhoons, are most frequent between July and November. South of the Equator they are most frequent between December and April. They may vary in diameter from 25 to 500 miles; winds may reach a velocity of 150 or more miles an hour. Typhoons do great damage, especially to houses and coconut groves on low islands, where waves may wash right over the islands.

The Hawaiian Chain

The Pacific islands nearest North America are the Hawaiian Islands. Most of the islands are part of the state of Hawaii. (See HAWAII; HONOLULU.)

To the northwest of the eight largest Hawaiian islands, the group continues in a chain of smaller islands, rocks, reefs, and atolls. These islands are the nesting places for large numbers of sea birds and are the stopping place for many birds which nest in Alaska and other northern lands during the short summer. In 1909 these northwestern islands were set aside as the Hawaiian Islands Bird Reservation.

The only part of these "leeward" Hawaiian Islands inhabited by people are the Midway Islands. They lie about 1,300 miles northwest of Honolulu, and get their name from the fact that they are midway between the United States and Asia. The group is an atoll, about 20 miles around the lagoon. Just inside the enclosing reef, on the south side, are two low islands of sand and reef rock. These were unknown to the Hawaiians in olden days. They were discovered and claimed for the United States in 1859. It was planned to use them as a coaling station on the steamship route between California and Asia, but the plan was never carried out, for it was too difficult to dredge a safe harbor. Midway Islands were placed under the jurisdiction of the United States Navy, January 20, 1903, and a cable relay station was built in 1904.

When flying from Honolulu to Midway most of the tiny dots of land and broad reefs may be observed, for they are in nearly a straight line. After leaving Honolulu International Airport on the island of Oahu, Pearl Harbor, famous naval base, appears. Later the large green island of Kauai is seen, the slopes of its 5,170-foot central mountain peak covered with forest and hidden by clouds. To the southwest are the bare slopes of smaller and drier Niihau Island, then Nihoa (Bird Island), and later, Necker Island. Then, 500 miles from Honolulu, is French Frigate Shoal—a dozen sand piles and a rocky pinnacle protected by a curve of reef. These are all that remain of what long ago was another high island. One of the sand islets was enlarged during World War II to form a landing strip for fighter planes—like a stationary aircraft carrier. Gardner Pinnacles, two rocks with slopes too steep even for nesting birds, mark the end of the high islands. Beyond are only reefs and sand islets: Laysan, Lisianski, Pearl and Hermes Reef (an atoll), and then Midway Islands. Beyond Midway is only Kure, another atoll, with low scrub and sea birds. From Kure to Japan is 2,470 miles, and there are no islands between.

Wake, the Trust Territory, and Islands to the North

The airport nearest Midway is 1,185 miles to the southwest, on Wake Island. Wake is a form of atoll, a V-shaped group of three small, sandy

A native New Caledonian is guiding down the river some of the huge mahogany logs gathered on the island.

Signal Corps Photo from James Sawders

islands, with a reef across the open end of the V, closing the shallow lagoon. It became a possession of the United States in 1898, during the war with Spain. Wake remained little known to Americans until Pan American World Airways established a base there in 1935.

South and west of Wake are the Micronesian islands of the Marshall, Caroline, and Mariana groups. Guam, the largest of these, has been a United States possession since 1898. The United Nations placed the rest of the islands under the care of the United States as a trust territory in 1947.

The islands of the Trust Territory were discovered by early Spanish navigators. Spain sold them to Germany after the Spanish-American War, the Japanese captured them from Germany during World War I, and United States forces captured them during World War II.

The Marshall Islands consist of 27 atolls and 5 single low islands. Two of the atolls, Bikini and Eniwetok, have been the scene of United States atomic bomb tests, and all of their inhabitants have been taken to other islands. Jaluit Atoll in the southern Marshalls was the important center for trade and administration during the German and Japanese eras. It was badly damaged by bombing during World War II. The most important American center is Majuro Atoll.

Guam is at the southern end of a great submerged range of volcanic mountains which stretches northward to Tokyo, Japan, 1,565 miles away. Fourteen islands—mountain peaks which rise above the sea—north of Guam and Guam itself are the Mariana Islands. (See GUAM.)

Largest and best-known of the Marianas north of Guam are Rota, Tinian, and Saipan. Thousands of Japanese migrated to these islands after World War I to raise sugar cane and other tropical crops. They were all sent back to Japan after World War II. The United States built extensive airfields on Tinian and Saipan. The ten Mariana Islands north of Saipan are small, steep volcanic cones, some of them barren and at times active volcanoes.

North of the Marianas the islands of the mountain chain belonged to Japan before World War II. After the war they were administered by the United States.

Of these islands, the three nearest the Marianas are called the Volcano Islands. The middle, largest, and most famous of the Volcano Islands is Sulphur Island or Iwo Jima. Beyond the Volcanoes to the north are the Bonin Islands. They consist of four volcanic islands of moderate size, and a dozen smaller ones. The Bonins are high and rocky, with little flat land which can be cultivated. Yet several thousand Japanese, mostly fishermen, lived on them. Before the arrival of the Japanese there were a few inhabitants who were the descendants of settlers from America, Hawaii, and other lands. All of the Japanese people were sent back to Japan after World War II, but the descendants of the firstcomers were later allowed to return. The Volcano and Bonin Islands were returned to the Japanese by the United States in 1968.

The rest of the islands to the north, about a dozen in number, are called the Islands of Izu. They are inhabited by the Japanese.

In valleys near this great undersea mountain range are some of the deepest spots in the Pacific Ocean. Challenger Depth, in the Mariana Trench at its southern end, reaches a depth of 36,201 feet, the earth's greatest known ocean depth. Ramapo Deep, east of the southern Izu Islands, has a depth of 34,038 feet. The individual islands in the area were built up by volcanic action from the crest of this wrinkle. A new island was seen and photographed by airmen, as a mass of steaming lava, in the southern Izu group in 1946. It afterward disappeared beneath the waves.

To the south of Guam and the Marshall Islands are the Caroline Islands, another part of the United States Trust Territory. The Carolines are scattered along a narrow band of ocean 2,000 miles long, just north of the Equator. They include 31 atolls, 11 single low islands, and 5 groups of high islands. The high island groups, from west to east, are called Palau, Yap, Truk, Ponape, and Kusaie. There are good airfields on all of these except Kusaie.

Palau consists of about 340 islands scattered along a ridge 100 miles long, with reefs on both sides. At the northeast end is a miniature atoll, Kayangel Islands. In the midst of the Palau group is Babelthuap Island, largest in the Carolines (153 square miles). Bauxite, from which aluminum is made, is mined near the northern end of Babelthuap. There is also rich soil for farming along large streams. Southwest of Babelthuap is the small island of Koror, used by the Germans and Japanese as the center of commerce and government because of its good harbors. The islands south of Koror are of raised reef formation. Some are so high and rugged that no one lives on them, although they are covered with dense forest. Others are lower and smoother. Of these, Peleliu and Angaur have rich deposits of phosphate rock which have been mined extensively.

Three hundred miles northeast of Koror is Yap, a compact group of four large islands and a dozen smaller ones, all connected by a sheet of reef. There are only narrow, shallow passages between the islands, at the heads of deep passes through the reef. The people of Yap, unlike the progressive people of Palau, do not want to become "civilized." They dislike clothes; they like to live the way their ancestors lived. They show wealth by having great stone disks, as high as 10 or 12 feet, standing in front of their houses. These stone disks were quarried, long ago, on an island in Palau and taken to Yap on rafts. When a Yap family has to pay a debt to another, a disk is rolled over in front of the other family's house.

Truk is a group of a dozen small, high islands and many smaller islets in a broad lagoon, surrounded by a barrier reef. It is not an atoll, although the barrier reef, with about 40 small sand islets scattered along it, looks exactly like an atoll's rim. Long ago this may have been a single, large, high, volcanic island, surrounded by a fringing reef. Wind and rain carved the dome into a dozen peaks. Meanwhile the whole mass slowly sank until the peaks became separate islands. As it sank, the fringing reef built itself upward until it became a barrier reef. The Japanese built airfields and fortified Truk heavily. The Americans have a school there where teachers are trained. There is a small atoll, Kuop, close outside the southern side of the barrier reef.

Ponape is a large volcanic island. Close around it are about 25 small islets, all enclosed by a barrier reef, with deep water between. It has a very heavy rainfall and rich soil, dense forests, and even large streams. Japanese farmers started to grow manioc and other tropical crops on Ponape, and also developed a fine botanical garden of introduced plants. United States scientists hope to continue these projects. Ponape was an important center during the German period, but the Germans did not get along well with the Ponapean people.

Kusaie is a rugged volcanic island, 2,064 feet high. Very heavy rainfall and fertile soil have produced thick forests on its central mountain mass. The shore, like those of Ponape and Truk, is fringed with mangrove swamps, behind which thickets of coconut palms, breadfruit, and other trees grow on the narrow coastal plain. Some small islets, connected with the main island by reefs, lie close to the east side. Kusaie has long been a center for missionary enterprise, and all of the people are Christians.

Gilbert and Ellice Islands

East of the Carolines and south of the Marshalls are the 11 atolls and 5 low single islands of the Gilbert group. These are inhabited by Micronesian people much like the Marshall Islanders. The Gilbert Islands are quite dry and unproductive. Now that wars have ceased and health conditions have been improved, the population of each island has increased so much that it is hard to find enough food and water for all. The water is very brackish, so that most people would prefer to drink coconut water, but there are not enough coconuts to go around. People have had to move to the uninhabited Phoenix Islands, or to seek work on coconut plantations on Fanning, Washington, and Christmas Atolls.

Southeast of the Gilbert Islands are the Ellice Islands, nine more atolls. The Ellice Islands are much like those of the Gilbert group, except that there is more rainfall, so that life is a little easier. Ellice Islanders are a Polynesian people, more like the Samoans than like their neighbors of the Gilberts.

West of the Gilberts are two raised reef islands, Ocean and Nauru. They lie just south of the Equator. Both have rich deposits of phosphate, which has been mined extensively, first by the Germans and later by the British. The native inhabitants are much like those of the Gilbert and Marshall Islands. So much of the soil on Ocean Island was dug up to get the phosphate that the native people finally moved away to an island in Fiji. The phosphate on Ocean and Nauru is dug and shipped mainly by Chinese laborers from Hong Kong. The native people on both islands are given a royalty for the phosphate and are getting quite wealthy, but they are losing their land. Nauru used to belong to Germany. For a time it was a United Nations trusteeship, administered by Australia, before becoming an independent island country in 1968.

All of these islands (except Nauru), even those in the Phoenix and Line (Equatorial) Islands where the Gilbert people have gone to live and work, make up the Gilbert and Ellice Islands Colony of Great Britain. On the low islands the only exports are copra and a few native handicrafts. Copra is the dried kernel of the coconut, from which coconut oil is made. The oil is used in making some kinds of soap and butter substitute.

American Polynesia

Lying between Hawaii and Samoa in the central Pacific are about 35 sandy islands and atolls, most of which were discovered by whalers early in the 19th century. Some of the whalers were British, but most were from New England ports. They discovered guano on these low, dry islands. Guano is a grayish, powdery material which is formed from the interaction between coral sand and the droppings of sea birds. It contains phosphate and ammonium compounds and is a valuable fertilizer. Americans interested in digging and shipping this guano applied to the United States Congress, and in 1856 were given permission to claim unoccupied islands in the name of the United States for the purpose of removing guano. Claims were filed to about 48 islands under the Guano Act. Only about 30 of these islands can be identified today, and not all of them were occupied by guano

diggers, but there was so much activity in the central Pacific by United States guano companies that a German geographer, in 1859, called the whole area "American Polynesia."

The principal islands from which guano was dug were Phoenix, Enderbury, and McKean, in the Phoenix group, and Howland, Baker, and Jarvis, along the Equator. Many sailing ships were wrecked on the treacherous reefs which surround the islands. From 1859 to about 1879 guano digging was done for Americans by Hawaiians and other islanders. After the United States companies left, a British company took over the digging between 1883 and 1891. Other islands were worked by British interests, especially Malden Island, for 70 years, until about 1930. Most of these islands were uninhabited. Native people lived only on the three atolls of the Tokelau (or Union) group, and on five atolls north of the Cook group. The British government annexed all the islands not otherwise claimed, but nobody paid much attention to any of them until 1928, when Sir Charles Kingsford-Smith flew the monoplane "Southern Cross" from Oakland, California, to Australia by way of Hawaii and Fiji. Then there was a sudden scramble for tiny steppingstones across the central Pacific, to use as emergency landing places and weather stations. The United States established small parties on Jarvis, Howland, and Baker in 1935, and on Canton and Enderbury in 1938. Meanwhile, in 1937, a British party had been placed on Canton Island. Diplomats in Washington and London got together, and in April 1939, agreed to joint use of Canton and Enderbury Islands for 50 years.

Pan American Airways pioneered the air route from Hawaii to New Zealand in 1939, building a hotel on Canton and dredging the lagoon for use of seaplanes.

During World War II airfields were built on Johnston, Baker, Canton, Tongareva (Penrhyn), Christmas, and Palmyra Islands. Some of these are still used by military and commercial planes.

Eastern Islands of the South Pacific

There are very few ships and fewer planes which visit the islands of the South Pacific. Two or three times a year a French freighter visits the French islands. An occasional British freighter collects copra from British islands. A ship from New Zealand visits the Cook Islands, Samoa, Fiji, and Tonga about once a month. Other ships and planes go to Nauru and islands in Melanesia from Australia. Lack of transportation is one of the great problems of the South Pacific islands; crops cannot be sold if there is no way to get them to a market.

Easter Island is a small, isolated, barren volcanic island in the east. Most of the people who live on Easter came from Chile, to which the island belongs. (See EASTER ISLAND.)

About 1,400 miles west of Easter is Pitcairn Island, largest of four small islets which belong to Great Britain. Descendants of the mutineers of the English ship *Bounty* and their Tahitian wives live on Pitcairn. They sell oranges and vegetables to passengers on ships which occasionally come near the island. In recent years they have made money for their school and public buildings from the sale of their postage stamps to collectors all over the world. Nobody lives on the other three islands. Two of them are low atolls, called Ducie and Oeno; the other, Henderson, is a raised reef island. Although they are from 65 to 290 miles away, parties from Pitcairn visit these three islands to get coconuts and timber.

The five groups of islands which lie next west of Pitcairn are colonies of France, called French Polynesia. The groups are called the Marquesas Islands, Austral Islands, Tuamotu Archipelago, Mangareva, and the Society Islands. Tahiti is one of the Society Islands.

Mangareva (or the Gambier Islands) consists of four inhabited volcanic islands and several islets, 330 miles west-northwest of Pitcairn. They are surrounded by a 40-mile barrier reef. The hills are covered with "sword grass," so-called because the leaves have sharp edges. The people raise fruits and vegetables and catch fish for their food. To earn money, they dive for pearls.

It is 1,100 miles from Mangareva to Tahiti. Over this distance are scattered the 76 low atolls of the Tuamotu Archipelago. Some of these atolls have lagoons so wide that a person standing on one side cannot see the coconut palms on the islets on the opposite side. Only one island in the entire group rises more than about 25 feet above the sea; it is Makatea, the island closest to Tahiti. It has valuable deposits of phosphate, in places 40 feet thick, much of which is dug and shipped away to be used as fertilizer. Violent hurricanes do great damage to coconut groves and houses on the low atolls. At times waves sweep right over the reef rims and sandy islets.

Tahiti is the largest of the 14 Society Islands. Five of these islands are low atolls, and the rest are of volcanic origin. Tahiti is a luxuriant island. Its 7,339-foot mountains have been carved into sharp peaks and ridges by heavy rainfall. Nearly one-half of all the people in French Polynesia live on Tahiti. One-half of these 36,000 people live in Papeete, the largest town and the commercial and political center of the whole area. Stores, hotels, clubs, churches, a hospital, and a bank line the shore of Papeete's good harbor, which is inside a barrier reef. Much of the business is controlled by Frenchmen, who have lived in these islands for many years and intermarried with the Tahitian women.

The ten volcanic Marquesas Islands lie about 900 miles northeast of Tahiti. The climate is healthful, but the fine native people are dying off. Early explorers estimated that there were more than 100,000 people in the Marquesas. Today the population has declined to 4,000. The decrease began with constant wars between rival tribes; it has been hastened by foreign diseases against which the people had no resistance.

To the south of the Society Islands are the half dozen volcanic Austral Islands and the rugged island of Rapa. One of the Austral Islands, Tubuai, was discovered by Captain Cook in 1777. Another, Raivavae, is noted for its stone statues. Rapa has a deep natural harbor between cliffs. It is farther south than any other island in this area, and enjoys a cool climate.

Rarotonga is the highest and most important of the five larger Cook Islands. Three smaller islands and seven atolls, widely scattered to the north, are also in this group, which was named for the British explorer, Captain James Cook.

English missionaries visited all the Cook Islands and taught the people to be Christians. This led to British protection in 1888. In 1901 the islanders became the special care of New Zealand. Fine citrus fruit and tomatoes are raised on the larger islands, but the ranchers have trouble getting them to market. They may have hundreds of cases of fruit ready to ship, but if the sea is too rough for the monthly ship to stop, the fruit is left to rot on the pier. The people living on the atolls export only copra.

Niue Island was called "Savage Island" by Captain Cook in 1774, because the native people were so hostile. Their descendants, however, are very peaceful. They live on an oval, raised reef island and grow bananas and dry copra to earn money. Although this island is 580 miles from Rarotonga it is included with the Cook Island administration of New Zealand.

Samoa and Tonga

Samoa is a chain of islands, like the Hawaiian chain on a small scale. At the west end is the largest and youngest island, Savaii. Lava flowed from its volcanoes as recently as 1911. At the eastern end of the chain is a ring of reef, called Rose Atoll. Five islands to the east of 171 degrees longitude are governed by the United States. The islands to the west form the Independent State of Western Samoa. New Zealand troops took them from the Germans in World War I. The Germans wanted the islands, especially Upolu, to grow tropical crops. (See SAMOA.) Swains Island, which is part of American Samoa, is an oval ring of sand-covered reef a mile across; a doughnut of land around a shallow lagoon which has no connection with the sea. Because of heavy rainfall, the lagoon water has become almost fresh enough to drink. The ring of land is covered with about 800 acres of coconut palms, among which are scattered taro patches, bananas, and a few native trees. This island was settled in 1856 by an American named Eli Jennings and his Samoan wife. His son asked the secretary of state to let Swains Island become part of the United States, and this was permitted by Congress in 1925. Swains Island is now owned by the grandson of Jennings. He allows about 100 to 200 people from the near-by Tokelau Islands, where his wife was born, to live there and harvest his copra.

About 250 miles west of Savaii, Samoa, lies Wallis or Uvea Island. Two other islands, Futuna and Alofi, are about 125 miles southwest of Wallis. These three islands and some smaller ones are governed by France as the French overseas territory, Wallis and Futuna. The inhabitants of Wallis export copra and trochus shell. They would raise good crops of coffee and cocoa, if they could get them to a market. Futuna and Alofi together are called the Horne Islands. The population of the overseas territory of Wallis and Futuna is 9,000 (1967 estimate).

Just as Captain Cook called Niue "Savage Island," so he called Tonga the "Friendly Islands." The islands of Tonga lie in two chains. One is made up of volcanic peaks, some of which are active volcanoes. The other chain consists of raised reef islands. One of the peaks, called Falcon Island, is repeatedly built up of volcanic ash, only to be washed away again. The Tongans are the only island people in the Pacific to remain a free and independent nation. They have their own queen, Salote (which means Charlotte in Tongan). The Queen's father, King George Tupou II, made a "treaty of friendship" with Great Britain. Under this treaty Great Britain sees that foreign nations do not interfere with Tonga and keeps an eye on island finances. Tonga has no public debt, but instead has a large surplus, well invested. Foreigners are not invited to settle on any of the 160 islands of the kingdom. A few of the islands have had recent lava flows, but most of them are fertile. Bananas, pineapples, melons, and sweet potatoes are shipped to New Zealand, and large quantities of copra are sent to Great Britain, Canada, and the United States. With money from these exports the Tongans can buy many modern conveniences and have fine schools. The population is increasing; all are given land and help in making homes. There is plenty to eat.

Fiji, New Caledonia, and the New Hebrides

The two main islands of Fiji are about 500 miles west of Tonga. They are called Viti Levu ("large Fiji") and Vanua Levu ("large island").

Photos, Ewing Galloway

The Pacific Islands differ widely in size and appearance.

These islands contain ancient "continental" rocks and are near the eastern edge of the ancient Melanesian "continent." Besides these there are about 250 other, smaller Fiji islands, including the isolated island of Rotuma. All of the Fijis are governed by the British.

A curve of islands called the Lau Islands lies midway between Viti Levu and Tonga. These islands used to be the battleground between Tongans and Fijians. After Fiji became a British colony in 1874 peace was established. Now the dark Fijians, with bushy hair, and the lighter-skinned Polynesian people from Tonga live peacefully side by side in villages in many of the Lau Islands. On the main islands of Fiji there is more friction. Years ago, British planters imported people from India to work on their plantations. After working for a few years, these thrifty Indians got farms of their own or started little shops, and raised large families. Today there are more Indians in Fiji than there are Fijians, and the easy-going islanders find the competition very hard to meet. (See FIJI ISLANDS.)

Far west of Fiji there is a round, pincushion-like island, densely wooded. This is Mare, southeasternmost of the Loyalty Islands. The Loyalty Islands, along with the island of New Caledonia, make up the overseas territory of

France which is called New Caledonia. Mare looks small from the air, but is 20 miles across and has 3,000 inhabitants. Far to the northwest is Lifu, a larger island of the Loyalty group, with twice as many persons. An atoll called Uvea, not to be confused with Wallis Island, is another of the Loyalty Islands. Although small in land area, Uvea is very fertile and supports 2,000 persons. The people of these islands raise taro, yams, bananas, vegetables, and coconuts for food. They also raise pigs to sell, and they catch many fish. So many of the men are hired as sailors that there are always more women than men on the islands.

New Caledonia is one of the largest and richest islands in the Pacific. Its chief city, Noumea, is the capital of the territory of New Caledonia. The island is more than 240 miles long but only about 30 miles wide. A reef parallels each side of it and extends many miles beyond in both directions, enclosing small islands. The Isle of Pines lies about 30 miles from the southeast end.

The main island has two mountain ranges, between which are wooded valleys. The moist trade winds blow against the east side of the island and drop their rain; by the time they get over the crest of the mountains all the moisture is gone. The western slopes are steep and nearly bare of trees. The highest peaks are

Mount Panie (5,413 feet) near the northern end of the island and Mount Humboldt (5,361 feet) near the southern end. The mountains are rich in ores of nickel, chrome, cobalt, manganese, iron, copper, lead, and gold. Mining of nickel, which is purer there than anywhere else in the world, is the big business of the island. Much chrome is also mined, and cobalt formerly was. Many cattle roam the dry lowland on the western side of New Caledonia, and there is a large meat-packing plant toward the northern end of the west coast. Coconut groves on the eastern side furnish much copra. Coffee is an important export.

The first European to sight New Caledonia was Captain Cook, in 1774. The purple of the mountains reminded him of Scotland, so he named the island New Caledonia, which means New Scotland. In 1853, while Britain was busy in Europe and the Near East, a French warship dropped anchor at the Isle of Pines and the captain took formal possession of all of New Caledonia. France used the island as a penal colony for years. Many persons sent there were political prisoners of good character and education. Their descendants established good schools, including a college in Noumea. During World War II the island remained loyal to Free France, the government of General Charles de Gaulle, and was protected by a large United States garrison. The United States Army headquarters near Noumea are now the headquarters for the South Pacific Commission. This commission is made up of representatives of the six nations which administer Pacific island groups, Australia, France, the Netherlands, New Zealand, the United Kingdom, and the United States. The commission employs experts who are trying to improve the health, economy, and social conditions of the people of the Pacific Islands.

The people of New Caledonia are Melanesians, like the people of Fiji and the New Hebrides. Some of them also look like the Papuans of New Guinea, and a few, especially in the Loyalty Islands, are much like Polynesians. They are called Kanakas. There is also a European population, many of whose members live in Noumea. Some Europeans own large farms and mines. They have brought workmen, chiefly from Asia, to do the manual work. New Caledonia's population is 94,000 (1968 estimate).

Noumea, with its fine harbor, is only about 900 miles east of Australia. A large trade has developed between New Caledonia and Australia, and ships and planes travel back and forth regularly between them.

The southernmost of the New Hebrides Islands are 250 miles northeast of Noumea. This chain of islands continues northward for 500 miles, with the Banks, Torres, and Santa Cruz groups at its northern end. Only a dozen of the 70 islands of the New Hebrides group are very large. Espiritu Santo (1,500 square miles) is the largest, and Malekula (450 square miles) is next in size. The town of Vila, on Efate Island, near the center of the group, is the capital and chief port of the colony. The government headquarters, which are half French and half British, are in Vila. The French government is under the high commissioner of the French islands, at Noumea, New Caledonia; and the British government is under the high commissioner for the (British) western Pacific, at Suva, Fiji. This joint form of government is neither very popular nor very economical, since every office is duplicated but neither nation wants to give up its rights. The Banks and Torres islands are also under this government, but the Santa Cruz group is governed with the British Solomon Islands. The New Hebrides islands are hot, sultry, and covered with dense jungle. Most of the rainfall comes in summer from November to April. The rain and the mud, together with disease-carrying mosquitoes, make this season disagreeable and unhealthful. The people are mostly Melanesians, with black skin, thick lips, and woolly hair. Formerly they were savage, but missionary schools have helped to make them more friendly. Now the government, both French and English, is helping with education. Some of the native people on Efate are taller than the Melanesians, with lighter skin and more interest in education and business.

Although there was little fighting in or near the New Hebrides during World War II, thousands of servicemen, with fine equipment, mo-

Courtesy (above right) British Information Services, (below left) United Nations; photos, (above left, below right) Black Star, (left) Ewing Galloway

In the Pacific Islands the people are equally at home on the water (above left) and on the land (above right). They attend churches (left) which they have built themselves. Most of them have been converted to Christianity. After World War II many more free schools (below left) were opened. The Pacific islanders, although they may use more modern methods, still keep their old art designs alive in their work (below right).

tion pictures, and a desire for souvenirs, were stationed on the islands. They brought great prosperity to some of the islanders and Europeans, especially on Efate and Espiritu Santo. The population of New Hebrides is 56,000.

Throughout all these high islands, the New Hebrides, New Caledonia, and Fiji, there are many colorful birds. There are fruit pigeons, parrots, kingfishers, thrushes, noisy starlings, and little songbirds with red and green plumage. There are also snakes and lizards, most of them harmless; there are fruit bats but few other mammals except introduced pigs and, in places, deer.

Coconut palms are numerous and copra is an important export. Fiji and the New Hebrides produce sugar cane, cotton, bananas, rice, pineapples, coffee, and cacao. The products of some of these are important exports.

Solomon Islands, Bismarck Archipelago, and Islands East of New Guinea

Northwestward from the New Hebrides and Santa Cruz groups lie the Solomon Islands. These form a double chain of about eight large, mountainous islands and many smaller ones, surrounded by reefs. The islands of Bougainville and Buka, with various smaller ones, including atolls to the north (total area 4,100 square miles), were captured by the British from Germany in World War I. They are a trust territory of Australia, along with the Bismarck Archipelago and part of New Guinea. The rest of the Solomon Islands, the Santa Cruz Islands, and other small islands to the south and east (area 11,500 square miles) make up the British Solomon Islands Protectorate. Largest of these are Choiseul, Santa Isabel, Malaita, New Georgia, Guadalcanal, and San Cristobal.

During the military occupation of the Solomons in World War II these islands were explored, mapped, and photographed. Airfields were carved from the jungle and ports were developed along the mangrove-fringed coasts. The fertile soil should make possible the growing of tropical crops, and there are mineral resources, largely undeveloped. Most of the people in the Solomon Islands are Melanesians.

Waagenaar from Pix

A Fiji Island policeman with the special comb he uses to keep his hair arranged.

They have had the reputation of being fierce head-hunters. As they have become better known and have been better treated, however, they are found to be loyal, industrious, and friendly.

North of New Guinea, in the Bismarck Sea, are the two large, mountainous islands called New Britain and New Ireland. Near them are a number of smaller islands, their total area about 17,900 square miles. To the west of these are the Admiralty Islands, the largest of which is Manus Island. Taken together, these islands make up the Bismarck Archipelago. They, together with northeastern New Guinea, were taken from Germany during World War I, and are a trust territory assigned to Australia. The monsoon climate, with its heavy, seasonal rainfall, helps the growing of tropical crops on the islands. Coconut groves are abundant, furnishing much copra.

Off eastern New Guinea are several small island groups. They are inhabited by Melanesians and are governed by Australia as part of Papua, the southeastern part of New Guinea Island. The D'Entrecasteaux group lies north of the eastern end of New Guinea. The volcanoes which built the largest of these, Fergusson Island, have stopped pouring out lava, but hot springs and geysers are still found. To the north are the smaller Trobriand Islands, formed of raised reef. Some of the people on the Trobriands are much like Polynesians. To the east is Woodlark Island, where deposits of gold have been found. East of Woodlark is an atoll, called the Laughlin group. Off the southeastern tip of New Guinea lie the scattered islets and reefs of the Louisiade Archipelago.

World War II helped to make the world, and especially the United States, aware of the Pacific area. The six nations which administer the Pacific island territories had found that they could be allies in war. Now they are trying to be good neighbors in peace.

PACIFIC OCEAN. The Pacific Ocean is the largest and deepest of the world's oceans. It has an area of 64,000,000 square miles. The Pacific and its adjacent seas cover more than one-third the surface of the earth. Its area is greater than the total of all land surfaces in the world. At its greatest width, from Panama to Mindanao, the Pacific measures 10,600 miles —almost half the distance around the earth. It extends from the Bering Straits to Antarctica, a distance of 9,060 miles.

Among the larger seas bordering the Pacific are: Bering Sea, Sea of Okhotsk, Sea of Japan, Yellow Sea, East China Sea, South China Sea, Coral Sea, Tasman Sea, and the Gulf of California. Many other small seas separate the islands of Indonesia and the Philippines.

The chief rivers draining into the Pacific or its adjoining seas are the Yangtze, the Amur, the Hwang Ho, the Mekong, the Yukon, the Colorado, and the Columbia.

The Pacific Ocean links the Americas with Asia, Australia, and New Zealand. Hawaii is the chief refueling station on transpacific air and sea routes. Because of the great distances across the Pacific, most passenger travel is by air. Most cargo is carried by sea. The Pacific sea routes are most used by Japan and the United States.

Commercial fishing is important chiefly in the North Pacific where salmon, halibut, mackerel, and sardines are caught. From Oregon south to the waters off Central America tuna is the chief commercial fish. In the tropical waters of the Pacific are shellfish, crabs, shrimps, clams, oysters, and prawns. Pearl fishing, or the search for pearl-bearing oysters, is carried on in shallow waters.

Winds of the Pacific

The surface conditions of the ocean change with latitude. A belt near the Equator has very little wind. It is called the doldrums, or equatorial calms. (See WIND.) North and south of the doldrums is the trade wind belt. Although the trade winds are usually warm and gentle, violent storms called typhoons begin in this belt. (See STORM.) Beginning about latitude 40 degrees is the belt of westerly winds. This belt often has storms and high seas followed by fair weather. The surface of the Pacific is not often calm in the higher latitudes.

Currents of the Pacific

Within the ocean are great circular water movements called currents or drifts. Currents are close to the surface and flow at a speed of two to four miles an hour. They affect the temperature of the air above them, and thus have a great effect on the climate of nearby land. (See CLIMATE.)

The currents move in a clockwise direction in the North Pacific. In the South Pacific they move counterclockwise. Warm currents flowing away from the Equator are cooled as they meet Arctic currents. Thus, the currents returning to the Equator are generally cold. A famous warm current flowing northward past the coast of Japan is known as the Kuroshio or Japan Current. It is met by the cold Kamchatka Current, which flows southward past Japan. The Japan Current then turns eastward, crossing the ocean as the North Pacific Drift. A branch of the North Pacific Drift flows past the west coast of the United States as the cold California Current. In the southern hemisphere the cold Peru or Humboldt Current flows northward past the coast of Chile and Peru,

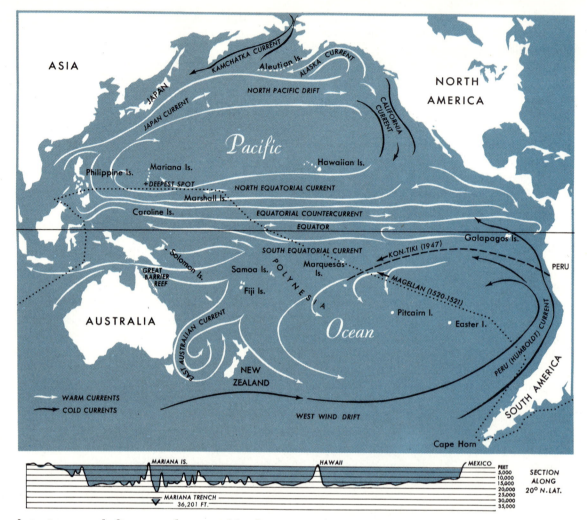

bringing a cool climate to the coastal lands.

About five degrees north of the Equator is the equatorial countercurrent. This current flows from the Philippines to Central America at a speed of about two miles an hour.

Islands

Thousands of islands are scattered in the Pacific Ocean. It is thought that the islands near the continental shores, such as the Japanese islands, the Philippines, the Marianas, New Guinea, the Solomons, New Hebrides, most of the Fiji Islands, and New Zealand, may once have been part of the Asian and Australian continents. For this reason, most of the islands of the western Pacific are called Continental Islands.

The islands of the central Pacific are known as Oceanic Islands, for they are of volcanic or coral origin. They are the tops of undersea mountains, which rise from the ocean floor. Among the many oceanic islands are the Hawaiian Islands, the Marshalls, the Carolines, the Cook Islands, the Tuamotus, and the Marquesas Islands. Some of them rise from depths of 18,000 feet. Coral islands are formed from the skeletons of tiny sea animals called coral polyps. The coral builds up on the slopes of undersea mountains. (See GREAT BARRIER REEF; CORAL.)

The Ocean Floor

By means of depth soundings, scientists are mapping the ocean floor. They have found undersea plains and mountains. The floor of the eastern Pacific, they have discovered, is fairly level at a depth of nearly 18,000 feet. For this reason there are very few islands in the eastern Pacific. A broad platform, at a depth of about 13,000 feet, is west of South America. From this platform rises lonely Easter Island, the Juan Fernandez and Galapagos Islands. (See PACIFIC ISLANDS.)

Along the edge of the continents are undersea trenches of great depth. The greatest known depth in the world is the Challenger Depth in the Mariana Trench. It is 200 miles southwest of Guam in the western Pacific. A depth of 36,201 feet has been found there. Other deep trenches are near Japan, the Philippine Islands, and the Tonga-Kermadec Islands. Depths greater than 33,000 feet have been recorded in each.

Exploration

The Pacific was the last of the world's oceans to be known to Europeans. Marco Polo had seen the Pacific in the 13th century. In 1513 the Spanish explorer Balboa crossed the Isthmus of Panama and sighted the "Great South Sea," as it was called then. This discovery led to Ferdinand Magellan's famous voyage across the Pacific in 1520–1521. (See MAGELLAN, FERDINAND.)

The greatest Pacific explorer was an Englishman, Captain James Cook. Cook led three Pacific expeditions between 1768 and 1779. By the time of his death in 1779, most of the Pacific's islands were correctly mapped. (See COOK, JAMES.)

PADEREWSKI (pä′dĕ rĕf′skē), IGNACE (ē nyás′) JAN (yän) (1860–1941), was a great pianist and composer. He was also a statesman and a leader in Poland's struggle for freedom.

Paderewski was born in a small village in Podolia, a section of Poland then part of the Russian empire. As a small child he showed a great interest in music. When he was 12 years old, he went to Warsaw to study at the music conservatory. Later he studied in Germany and in Austria.

In 1887 Paderewski gave his first piano re-

Culver Service
Ignace Jan Paderewski.

citals in Europe. He was an immediate success. Four years later he toured the United States. His opera *Manru* was performed in Europe in 1901. From that time on Paderewski was noted as a composer as well as a pianist.

Through his concerts Paderewski collected a great deal of money for the Polish Relief Fund. During World War I he gave recitals, delivered speeches, and discussed political problems, all to help Poland. He returned to his native country to serve as premier during 1919.

When Germany conquered Poland in 1939, Paderewski gave up his music career. The Polish government was set up in France, and he was elected president of the exiled government. He served in that office until his death.

Some of Paderewski's many piano compositions are "Danses Polonaises," the "Concerto in A Minor," and the "Minuet in G."

PAINE (pān), THOMAS (1737–1809), was a writer who helped persuade the American colonies to declare their independence from England.

Paine was born in Thetford, England. At 13, he had to leave school to work. For more than 20 years he worked as a sailor, a teacher, and a tax collector. During this time he read a great deal and educated himself. In London, Paine met Benjamin Franklin, who suggested that he go to the colonies in America. When Paine came to the colonies he carried with him

Thomas Paine.
Brown Bros.

a recommendation from Franklin.

After Paine arrived in Philadelphia, he earned his living by editing a magazine. In January 1776 he became part of the independence movement when he published *Common Sense*. In this pamphlet he spoke strongly against King George III and called on the peoples of the colonies to revolt and set up a republic. Fighting had already begun in Massachusetts, but most of the colonists were not sure whether they wanted independence. *Common Sense* changed many minds. (See DECLARATION OF INDEPENDENCE.)

During the American Revolution, Paine wrote pamphlets which he called the *Crisis* papers. When the war was going against the colonists, the *Crisis* papers gave many people the courage to keep fighting. Paine joined the army in 1776 and the next year he became secretary to the congressional committee on foreign affairs. He also continued his writing. *Public Good*, published in 1780, called for a convention to set up a strong central government.

After the war, New York state gave him a farm in New Rochelle. In 1787 he returned to England, hoping to persuade the people of England and France to form republics. In 1791 he published the first part of *Rights of Man*, which defended the French Revolution and his own ideas on government. Paine believed that people should elect their rulers. He also believed that the most important job of government was to protect the rights of the people and that a government should try to end poverty. *Rights of Man* made Paine unpopular in England and he fled to France.

In France Paine was made an honorary citizen and in 1792 was elected to the French Convention. Once again, his honesty hurt him. Paine criticized the execution of King Louis XVI. This made him the enemy of Maximilien Robespierre, the leader of the government, and he was thrown in prison. While in prison he wrote *Age of Reason,* an attack on many religions of his time.

In 1794 James Monroe, United States minister to France, asked the French to release Paine. In 1802 he returned to the United States.

PAINT, VARNISH, AND LACQUER (lăk'ēr).

The outside of a house is covered with paint, the interior woodwork with enamel, and floors with varnish. Fingernails may be covered with nail polish—a typical lacquer. Antifouling paints are used to kill or keep away barnacles that like to attach themselves to the bottoms of ships. Fire-resisting paints prevent the quick spread of fire.

These materials—paint, enamel, varnish, and lacquer—are called surface coatings. They serve two very useful purposes. They protect the surfaces of objects, and they make the objects colorful and attractive.

In recent years the use of paint to bring color into homes has increased. Walls, furniture, toys, and even the handles of kitchen utensils, are painted in sparkling colors. Appliances such as refrigerators, stoves, vacuum cleaners, and electric fans are now made in a wide variety of colors.

What Is in Paint

Paint is a mixture of solids in a vehicle. The *vehicle* or liquid is that part of the paint which carries the solids and helps them spread on the surface being painted. The *solids* are white or colored powders called pigments.

The vehicle usually is a combination of natural or synthetic gums and drying oils. Pigments give paint its color. They also make it opaque, which means that the surface to which the paint is applied cannot be seen through the paint. Thus one color of paint may be used over another.

Examples of white pigment used in paint are titanium dioxide, made from ilmenite ore; zinc oxide, made from zinc; and white lead, made from pig lead. Some colored pigments are Prussian blue, made from iron; para and toluidine reds, refined from chemicals; chrome yellow, made from lead; and carbon black and lampblack, which result from burning gas or petroleum. In addition to giving paint its color, some pigments can also keep metals from rusting. Among them are red lead, lead chromate, and zinc chromate.

Linseed, soybean, castor, and tung oils are typical drying oils used in paint. They absorb oxygen when they are spread in a thin film and brought into contact with air. Natural or synthetic gums, combined with the oils, help bind the pigment particles together. In addition, they make the paint last longer, give it resistance to acids and alkalies, and make it easier to apply.

A thinner or solvent is usually added to the mixture to make the paint fluid enough to spread easily. Driers made from cobalt, lead, or manganese usually are added to speed the drying of the oils.

These materials are the ones found in most paints. Actually there are thousands of raw materials used in paint. This great variety is necessary to make the many different kinds of paints, enamels, varnishes, and lacquers needed. It takes many different kinds of surface coatings to serve the home owner, the industrial plant, and the thousands of other persons and organizations that use paint.

In the early days of paint manufacture only a few raw materials were used. Among these were white lead, linseed oil, turpentine, and a few colors. Today the paint manufacturing industry is considered part of the chemical industry. It is closely related to the rubber and plastics industries. Chemistry has developed many new raw materials, and from them many new kinds of paint are made.

Some Newer Paints

One of the best-known of the newer types of paint, introduced nationally about 1950, is synthetic latex paint. There are many such paints. Among the latex paints, the so-called *rubber-base* paint is very widely used. It is called "rubber-base" because among the raw materials in it are the same chemicals that are used in making synthetic rubber. This type of paint is especially popular for decorating interior walls.

Other latex paints contain other chemical combinations. These are usually named for one or more of the chemicals used in making them.

Latex-type paints are easy to apply, dry quickly, and the painted surface is easily washed after the paint has dried. One coat is enough for most surfaces. Two coats may be applied in one day if necessary.

The thinner used in these paints is water. As a result, they are fairly odorless, and the painting tools can be cleaned with soap and water. For paints in which the solvent is mineral spirits or turpentine, these solvents must be used to clean tools and wipe up spots and splatters.

Another very popular type of paint is known as *alkyd* paint. The word "alkyd" comes from the names of its principal parts—alcohol and acid. An alkyd is a synthetic resin, comparable and superior to those resins nature provides from fossilized vegetable and animal matter. Alkyd, more properly called "alkyd resin," has been used in paint making since the early 1930's. It was not widely known until about 1950.

A surface coating made from alkyd resins lasts a long time, resists weather, sunlight, and abuse, and is washable. It may give either a glossy finish, like that of enamel, or a flat, nonglossy finish. Many alkyd paints are almost completely free from odor because of the odorless type of thinner or solvent used in making them.

How Paint Is Made

In a typical paint plant the first step in making paint is to mix together carefully measured amounts of dry pigments and oils or resin solutions. This makes a heavy paste. The paste is then sent to the grinding mills. These mills are usually on the floor below the mixing room so that the paste may flow to the mills by gravity.

Grinding of the paste is necessary to spread each particle of pigment, white or colored, throughout the paste. The grinding also makes the paste extremely smooth. One type of mill used for this purpose is the high-speed roller mill, with three, four, or five powerful steel rollers. The rollers run at different speeds, shearing or grinding the paste as it is forced between them.

The ground paste, as smooth as soft butter, flows from the mill into a tank, usually in a room below the mill. There the various oils and thinners are added and mixed throughout the paste. At this time, too, the paint is shaded

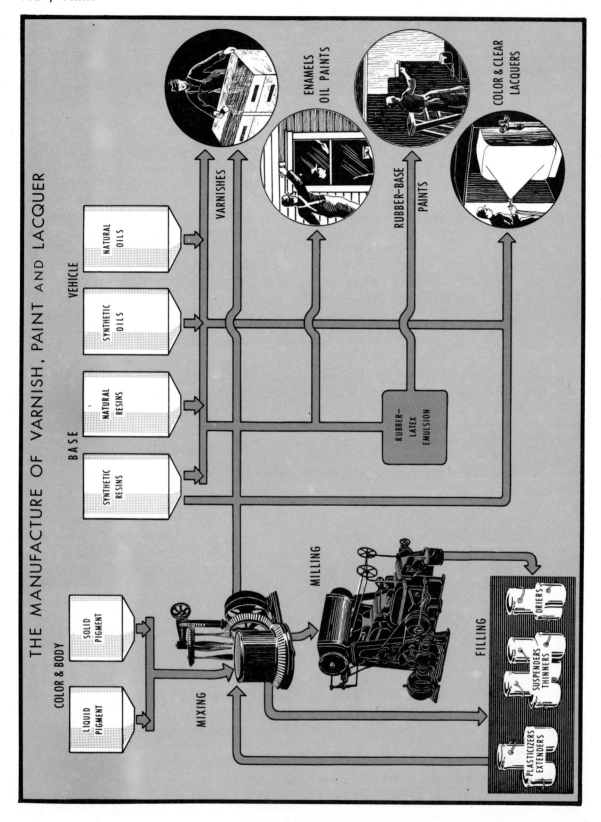

THE MANUFACTURE OF VARNISH, PAINT AND LACQUER

COLOR & BODY

LIQUID PIGMENT

SOLID PIGMENT

BASE

SYNTHETIC RESINS

NATURAL RESINS

VEHICLE

SYNTHETIC OILS

NATURAL OILS

RUBBER–LATEX EMULSION

VARNISHES

ENAMELS OIL PAINTS

RUBBER-BASE PAINTS

COLOR & CLEAR LACQUERS

MIXING

MILLING

FILLING

PLASTICIZERS EXTENDERS

SUSPENDERS THINNERS

DRIERS

by adding color to make it the exact shade desired. The paint is then tested against rigidly controlled standards. Corrections are made, if necessary, to insure uniformity. Then the paint flows from the tanks to the container-filling machines.

Another method of manufacture makes use of the ball mill. This type of mill is simply a large, horizontal, steel tank. It contains tons of steel or porcelain balls, about as big as marbles. All the raw materials in the paint are poured into the tank. Then the tank is made to revolve. As it does so, the balls tumble about, and crush, grind, and stir the materials into a smooth mixture. When the grinding is finished, the paint is ready to be thinned down, shaded, and tested. The advantage of this type of mill is that most of the raw materials—pigments, solvents, oils, and driers—may be mixed together in the mill at one time.

No matter how a batch of paint is made, the quality of the paint is carefully controlled in the process. Some products must pass through a centrifuge, a machine similar to a cream separator, which throws out any foreign or unground particles. Some paints must be strained several times through silk strainers. Still others must be forced by pressure through other strainers. All this is done before the paint is put into cans.

How Paint Is Applied

The familiar paintbrush is still widely used to apply paint. However, for painting interior walls, particularly, the paint roller has become very popular. This is simply a hollow roller, covered with a suitable fabric and set on an axle attached to a handle. It rolls the paint onto the wall.

Paint rollers can be used with any kind of paint. They spread the paint quickly and evenly and do away with the possibility of brush marks in the finished job. One type of paint roller can be used to apply patterns to a painted wall.

The paint sprayer, or spray gun, uses compressed air to "shoot" a carefully directed spray mist of paint on the surface to be painted. The sprayer is used in the automobile industry to paint cars, in the electric appliance industry to paint refrigerators and washing machines, and by commercial painters to paint large areas.

A type of paint sprayer is the aerosol paint package. This is a small can of paint which has been packaged under pressure of a gas. The top has a small valve which is pushed to allow the paint to spray from the can.

In industry, paint is often applied by dipping the object to be painted into a tank containing paint, enamel, or varnish. This is often used when many small objects are to be painted. The items are hung on a conveyor chain which carries them to the dipping tank. Still hanging from the chain, they are lowered into the paint, lifted, and drained. The chain then carries them to a drying area.

How Paints Dry

Paint dries in three ways. One is by *oxidation;* that is, the oxygen of the air combines with the oils in the paint to change the paint into a dry film. Outside house paint dries in this way, after the thinner has evaporated. So do most enamels used for interior decoration.

Heat is used to dry some paints. Many industrial finishes are dried by moving the painted objects through a baking oven after the thinner has evaporated. The heat in the oven usually comes from infrared lamps, electric coils, or gas or oil burners. It causes the molecules of the paint to grow larger and larger, which in turn makes the paint film more and more solid until it is dry. Such drying is called *polymerization.* It changes the paint into a solid film just as heating in boiling water changes an egg from a liquid to a solid state. This method of drying is often used to dry enamels on automobile bodies, refrigerators and other household appliances, toys, Venetian blinds, and other mass-produced items.

Some paints dry by *evaporation* of the thinners used in them. Shellac and lacquer dry this way. Evaporation also is part of the drying of latex paints; as the water used as a thinner evaporates, the paint forms a solid film. In this case polymerization also contributes to drying, but instead of heat, chemicals in the paint cause the change.

Varnish

Varnish is simply paint without pigment. It is a transparent or translucent liquid. The grain and color of wood that has been varnished can be seen through the surface coating.

Varnish is made by heating a mixture of tough resinous materials (usually synthetic resins) and a drying oil such as linseed or tung oil.

The high temperature melts the resin and mixes it with the oil. When this mixture is cooled, it becomes very thick and heavy. Solvent, such as petroleum spirits, is added to make the varnish thin enough to apply. Drier is also added to speed the drying of the oil.

Varnish dries somewhat by evaporation of the solvent but mainly by oxidation of the oil in which the resin is dissolved.

Shellac

Shellac is a spirit varnish. It is a solution of shellac in alcohol.

The shellac is a gummy secretion from small insects which attach themselves to certain trees that grow mainly in India. The insects, called lac insects, deposit the secretion on the tree branches. It is removed, washed, cleaned, melted, and hardened to form what is known as "orange shellac." When this is bleached, it is called "white shellac."

The shellac is then dissolved in alcohol. When the solution has been put on a surface, the alcohol evaporates into the air, and the dry, hard shellac is left as a transparent finish.

Shellac dries entirely by evaporation. As soon as the alcohol is gone, the film of shellac is dry. Speed of drying is one of the main reasons shellac is popular for use on floors and furniture. It is also easier to sand than regular varnish. When used as a first coat on hardwood floors, followed by a coat of wax, an attractive finish results.

However, shellac scratches much more easily than regular varnish. Water, alcohol, and soap and detergent solutions will make spots on shellac. The film is not so tough as varnish. Shellac, therefore, should be used on surfaces that will not be washed often and that do not get hard wear. Varnish should be used on surfaces that must withstand weather, water, and hard use.

Lacquer

Clear lacquer is transparent like varnish or shellac. It contains four basic materials. These are nitrocellulose or guncotton, which makes it fast drying, tough, and hard; resin, which gives it its adhesiveness, body, and gloss; plasticizer, which gives it flexibility; and lacquer thinner, which dissolves the first three ingredients to make a mixture that spreads easily.

To change this clear lacquer into a colored lacquer, pigments like those used in paint are added. Clear lacquer may be used as a varnish, pigmented lacquer as a paint or enamel.

Lacquer dries very quickly. As soon as the lacquer thinner has evaporated, there is left a perfectly dry and hard film. This evaporation may take as little as five minutes.

Lacquer makes a very hard and glossy finish, and it is widely used on furniture, automobiles, and decorative trinkets.

It is usually sprayed on objects because it is extremely difficult to avoid brush marks when it is brushed on.

PAINTING (pānt'ĭng). The art of painting is as old as mankind. In caves, where early man lived many thousands of years ago, there have been discovered paintings of animals as lifelike as any that have been done in the whole history of art. These were made by the people of the Old Stone Age of Europe. Perhaps they thought there was some sort of magic in picturing the animals they used for food and clothing, that by so doing they would be lucky in the hunt. Primitive peoples today like to decorate their pottery and clothing, even their bodies, with colors and designs.

Painting is the oldest as well as the most widespread of all the arts.

Egypt

The Egyptians of 2,000 to 5,000 years ago were among the first civilized people. They invented a form of picture writing called "hieroglyphic," and painted pictures on the walls of their temples. It is well worth remembering that such pictures are symbols; for one can not understand certain kinds of painting without knowing that a great deal of it is symbolic and has a hidden meaning, generally religious.

The religion of the Egyptians taught them that there was a life after death, so they painted on the walls of their tombs everything that went on in their lives, hoping to gladden the soul when it awakened. There were figures of men, women, and children with animals and boats and other objects, strung along in rows like their writing. The Egyptians also colored their sculpture. (See SCULPTURE.) Many of their works of art remain to this day and are valuable records of how these ancient people lived and thought.

Painting of the Near East

The Babylonians were also artistic. They, and later the Assyrians and the Persians, who lived in western Asia at the same time as the Egyptians, were famous for their decorated temples and palaces.

The Babylonians, too, painted their sculpture. They also made pictures out of glazed tiles which were rich, colorful, and permanent. They invented symbolic designs and patterns (the vine and the rosette, for example) which have come down to us today. Their art is called Oriental, in contrast to Western or Classical art derived from the Greeks.

Classic Art

The most artistic people of any age, except perhaps the Chinese, were the Greeks, who were at the height of their glory about 500 B.C. Their aim in painting was the imitation of life, but life in its perfect or ideal form. For example, when they illustrated the story of their national hero, Hercules, they made him faultless of figure, as godlike as possible. Their gods were very human, and were represented as ideal men and women.

The Greeks admired athletic manly beauty and painted it nude, as they observed it in their games and gymnastic exercises. The well-known story of the artist Zeuxis, who painted a bunch of grapes so naturally that the birds pecked at it, shows the Greek purpose to imitate nature as exactly as possible, but without blemishes.

We know what Greek painting was like from Roman copies, and especially from countless painted vases which are preserved in museums, and from portraits on the coffins of the dead. Like other peoples, the Greeks painted their architecture and sculpture in brilliant hues.

With Christianity, which came from the Near East, Oriental styles with their flat designs and symbolism took the place of the naturalism of Classic art.

A new kind of wall picture, based on the ancient tiles of Assyria, came into use to portray Bible stories on the walls of churches. This was mosaic painting, composed of many small blocks of brilliantly colored glass and marble, called *tesserae*, set in the plaster. (See MOSAIC.)

Medieval Art

The period from about A.D. 500 to 1500, called Medieval, was a great one for painting. In Byzantium (the Greek name for Constantinople, now Istanbul), Venice, Rome, and other capitals, the arts of fresco and of illuminating manuscripts were perfected.

Fresco is done by painting with a brush directly into the fresh (hence the name) plaster, so that when it is dry the picture is a permanent part of the wall. Fresco is best suited to buildings in sunny lands like Italy.

The illustration of manuscripts or books which is called "illumination" was practiced, along with writing, by the monks. It became a most perfect art not improved upon in modern times. The Irish monks in the seventh and eighth centuries, the Byzantine artists, and, later, the medieval artists of England, Germany, and France made exquisite letters and pictures in their scrolls, and full-page illustrations.

The Italian Renaissance

By the end of the 13th century the artists of Italy began to return to the art of the Golden Age of Greece and Rome. This return is called the Renaissance, or rebirth of Classical learning. Trade increased, cities prospered, and

From the Collection of H. M. King George VI

Anthony van Dyck's portrait of the children of King Charles I.

painters could travel and learn from each other.

Giotto di Bondone, a Florentine, was the first great painter of this new period. He began to observe nature and paint figures as if they were alive and moved about in a natural way. Although he was not successful in obtaining perfect naturalism, he nevertheless put deep human feeling into his figures. Giotto was the founder of the Florentine school. Later Masaccio gave more light and shade to figures, and Fra Angelico, Fra Filippo Lippi, and Botticelli carried the style to more complete naturalism.

In Siena, too, there was an active group of painters like Duccio, Simone Martini, and the two brothers Ambrogio and Pietro Lorenzetti, who sought gracefulness and rich pattern with not quite so much naturalism as the Florentines.

By the year 1500, interest in ancient Classic art encouraged painters like Andrea Mantegna of Padua and Antonio Pollaiuolo to illustrate the stories of the gods and heroes of Greece and Rome. Very soon Renaissance art in all its forms drew upon such subjects.

Most of the pictures of the early Renaissance were painted either in fresco or in *tempera*. Tempera is a method in which dry, powdered colors are mixed with egg and water and applied to prepared wooden panels. The result is brilliant and permanent. About the year 1487, however, Giovanni Bellini of Venice began to paint with oil on canvas. He learned this indi-

rectly from Flemish painters. He and his followers, Gentile Bellini, Carpaccio, and Titian, for example, showed the Venetian love for pageantry and rich decoration. Titian was the most famous portrait painter of his day. Tintoretto was a great painter of the Venetian school. Giorgione, another Venetian, painted dreamy, poetic scenes, often purely imaginative, which was a new idea at that time.

The three most renowned painters of the Renaissance, however, were Raphael Santi, Leonardo da Vinci, and Michelangelo Buonarroti. Raphael's painting was unexcelled for charm and naturalism; Leonardo's for deep understanding of character; and Michelangelo's for powerful studies of the human figure.

These men also reached the height of skill in other arts than painting. Leonardo was an architect, sculptor, engineer, and inventor. He was also a scientist and was among the first to experiment with oil painting.

Michelangelo, who felt that he was first of all a sculptor, painted and drew the human body. His frescoes on the ceiling of the Sistine Chapel in Rome will always remain one of the masterpieces of the art of painting.

Raphael made many models for sculptures. He also created some architectural plans and supervised some of the construction for St. Peter's in Rome.

In the later Renaissance a new style of painting gradually appeared. The continued use of oil on canvas made it possible for painters to obtain great contrast in light and shade. This is called *chiaroscuro*. Pictures painted in this style look very different from earlier ones which were more evenly lighted. Chiaroscuro spread to all countries in the 17th century. Rembrandt of Holland was the greatest to use it in obtaining the mysterious lights and shadows of his pictures.

Painting in the Netherlands

The arts follow the paths of prosperity. So the wealthy towns of Holland and Flanders, especially Bruges and Ghent, attracted the artists of the North.

The painting of Flanders was first that of the miniature, or book illustration. Throughout its history Flemish art was careful in details and for the most part very exact. The Dutch and Flemish artists liked to picture people as they really were, not idealized. Moreover, they took delight in all human activities and in nature.

The two brothers Hubert and Jan van Eyck are considered the inventors of oil painting. (See WEYDEN, ROGIER VAN DER.) They painted with glazes; that is, with thin coats of oil mixed with color, applied one over the other. This method gave brilliance and allowed exactitude. Dutch and Flemish pictures as a rule are outstanding for their clear, brilliant color. It is extraordinary that while the Van Eycks are said to be the first who painted in oil (they lived between 1366 and 1441), they were never surpassed. Their masterpiece, usually called "Adoration of the Lamb," made for the altar of the Cathedral of Ghent, is one of the treasures of the world.

Pieter Bruegel's name stands out in the long list of painters of the 16th century. Bruegel had a modern point of view, a many-sided interest in life. He painted seascapes, landscapes, winter scenes, and carnivals showing peasants whom he pictured with humor mixed with sympathy. His pictures are generally gay, brilliant, and transparent in color.

Peter Paul Rubens, a half century later, succeeded to Bruegel's fame. Not so truly Flemish, he was more a decorator in the Italian style. He covered the walls of palaces with pagan mythological subjects and the interior of churches with religious scenes.

Rubens was employed by nearly every important person of his time for portraits. His pupil, Anthony van Dyck, was almost his equal. As "Sir" Anthony, he became court painter of England and did much to establish the English school of portraiture.

Painting in Holland was somewhat different from that in Flanders. As a result of Holland's revolt against Spain and the Catholic church, Dutch artists turned their attention to domestic rather than to religious art and painted what may be called a portrait of their country. Thus Ruysdael, Hobbema, and Van Goyen painted Holland's canals, pasturelands, and windmills. Frans Hals, Jan Steen, and Rembrandt por-

trayed its citizens; and Vermeer and Pieter de Hooch its home interiors and scenes of daily life. Rembrandt is beloved for his understanding of human feeling, which he portrayed with mystery and pathos.

German Painting

In Germany, early or 15th-century painting is not unlike that of Flanders. Disturbed conditions there did not favor the arts. The Germans excelled in wood carving and carried their delight in exact realism and truthfulness in detail into their painting. The city of Nuremberg was their chief center of art. There Albrecht Durer worked about the year 1500. He was a skillful engraver, and also painted portraits, many of himself, and religious pictures. Lucas Cranach showed the German love for exactness in his portraits, which are striking in their forcefulness.

The best-known painter of Germany in the 16th century was Hans Holbein the Younger. Holbein went to England when Henry VIII was

"Pines and Rocks," by Paul Cezanne, shows how much that artist depended on brush stroke to get the desired effect of mass and depth.

Collection Museum of Modern Art, N.Y.

king and painted everybody at court. His portraits are not only truthful, but rich in design.

Spanish Painting

Spain produced a national art which is chiefly religious in character. Rich from her empire in the New World, Spain attracted artists from Italy and Flanders and other lands. Domenico Theotocopuli, called El Greco, was one of these, yet he became thoroughly Spanish. (See EL GRECO.) The Spanish people delighted especially in two things which seem to conflict with each other: religion and bullfighting. Spanish art is full of emotion and often gory in detail. Passionate emotion is what we find in the pictures of El Greco.

While most of the painters of Spain—Murillo and Zurbaran, for example—painted religious scenes, the two greatest, Velazquez and Goya, were different. Diego Velazquez is universally admired for his portraits of the little infantas or princesses of the court of Philip IV. The portraits have great naturalism and charm, yet

"The Painter and His Model" is the work of Picasso, and is an example of abstract art. The abstract picture is the opposite of the naturalistic. The artist makes no attempt to paint the figure as it appears to be; he either leaves it out entirely, confining himself to geometric patterns, or he treats the figure as part of a pattern without regard to its human likeness. He does not try to represent anything in life; hence his art is often called "nonrepresentative." Sometimes he paints one figure over another, or overlapping, so as to show the sides and the back of an object at the same time.

Courtesy The Sidney Janis Collection, New York

seem to have been executed by simple methods. Velazquez also painted realistic historical subjects and scenes from the life of the Spanish people. He must be ranked with Holbein, Titian, and Rubens as beyond national boundaries, a universal genius.

A century and a half later, when the glory of Spain had long declined, Francisco Goya arose to proclaim that the art of painting was still alive in Spain.

A forceful painter, Goya portrayed the court and the clergy with daring lack of flattery, sometimes even with ridicule. When he was allowed to paint what he pleased, children or soldiers or peasants, he did so with sincerity and sympathy.

The Rococo

Rococo is a term applied to a frivolous but beautiful style which was popular chiefly in France in the 18th century. The subjects were generally scenes of gaiety and gallantry, of leisurely aristocratic life, or of traveling actors— Pierrots and Pierrettes. Rococo paintings were used for decorating palace walls and were the vogue for a whole century. Among the foremost to create these delightful scenes were Jean Antoine Watteau, Francois Boucher, and Jean-Honore Fragonard.

English Portraiture

Mention has already been made of two foreign painters who went to England. England did not produce native painters to compare with those of other countries until William Hogarth, in the middle of the 18th century, startled the society of his day with daring illustrations of wasteful and dissolute living. He was a brilliant technician and in portraiture paved the way for a group of painters who have never been excelled.

The most noted of these painters were Sir Joshua Reynolds, Thomas Gainsborough, Sir Thomas Lawrence, and George Romney. Portraits by

Courtesy Metropolitan Museum of Art

"Spring Play in a T'ang Garden" is a detail from a silk scroll believed to have been painted by a Chinese emperor. The scroll is exhibited by the Metropolitan Museum of Art in New York City. It bears the name of Hsüan-tsung, an emperor who lived in the early 1400's.

The following series of paintings was chosen with the approval of the Metropolitan Museum of Art in New York City and the National Gallery of Art in Washington, D.C.

The pictures, which follow the story of painting throughout the world, are arranged so that the works of the early artists are at the beginning and the more modern ones at the end. Examples of most of the schools of painting described in *Britannica Junior*'s article are shown here. To see how one painter differs from another, and how the painters of one century differ from those who lived before or after them, look at the paintings as you read the article.

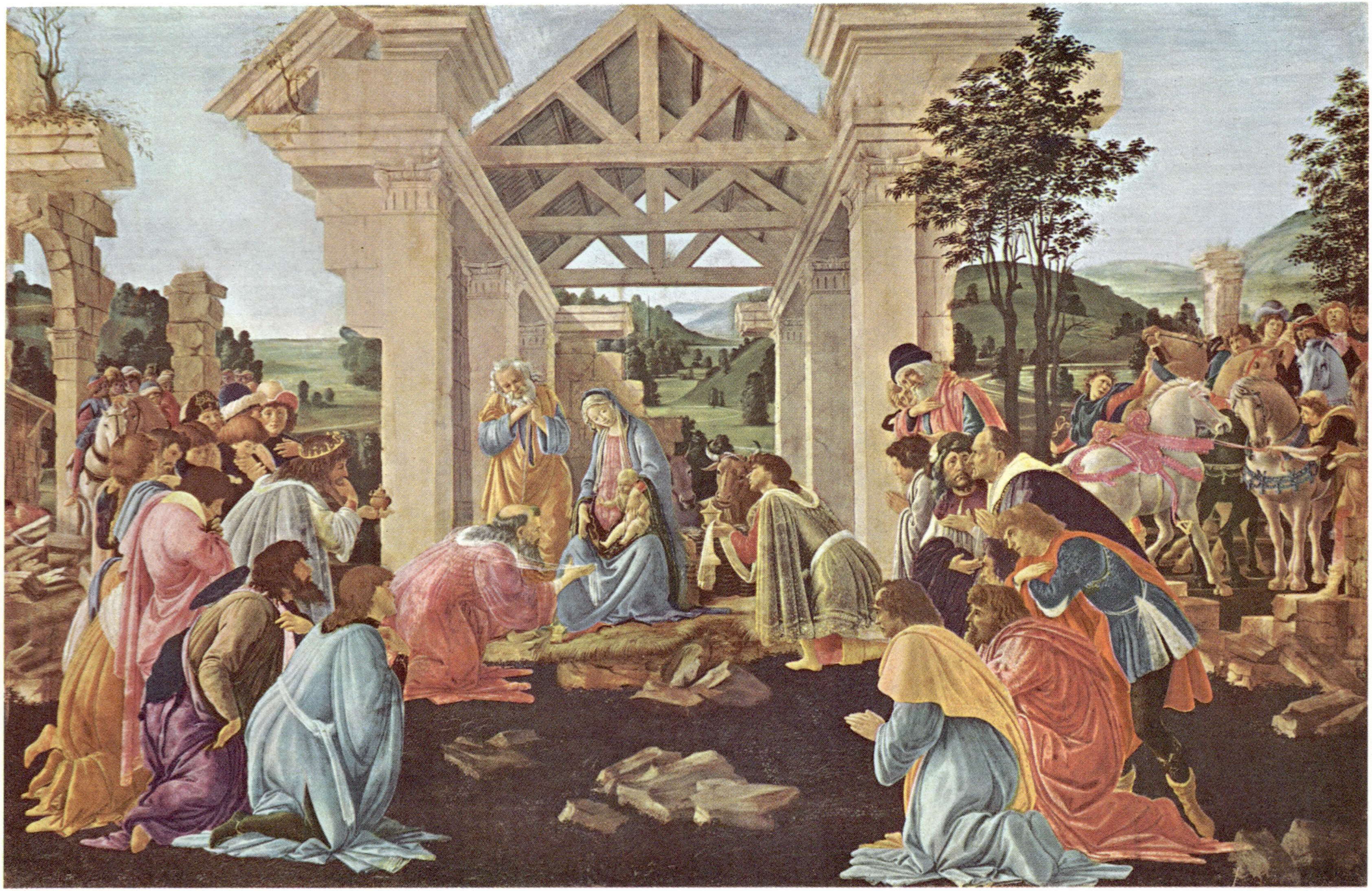

Courtesy National Gallery of Art

PLATE 2 PAINTING "The Adoration of the Magi," by Sandro Botticelli (1444–1510), is in the Mellon Collection, National Gallery of Art, Washington, D.C.

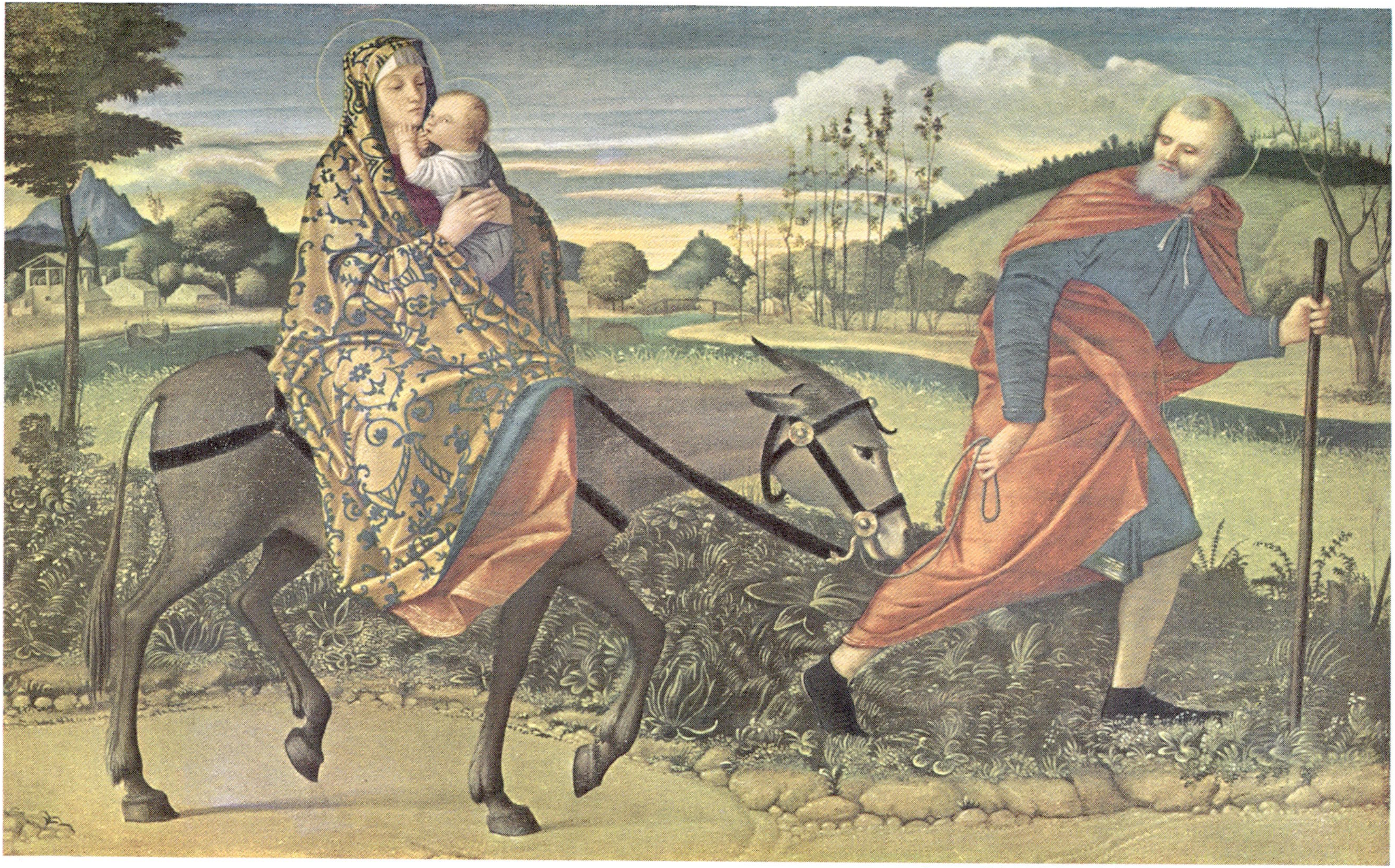

"The Flight into Egypt," by Giovanni Bellini (1430-1516).

PLATE 3   PAINTING

PLATE 4 PAINTING

"The Adoration of the Shepherds," by Giorgione (1478–1510), is in the Samuel H. Kress Collection at the National Gallery of Art, Washington, D.C.

"Christ at the Sea of Galilee," by Tintoretto, a 16th-century artist. This painting is in the Samuel H. Kress Collection at the National Gallery of Art, Washington, D.C.

PLATE 6 PAINTING

"St. George and the Dragon" by Raphael Santi (1483–1520); Mellon Collection, National Gallery of Art, Washington, D.C.

PLATE 7 PAINTING   "Ginevra Bentivoglio," by Ercole Roberti.

"Don Manuel Osorio de Zuñiga" is by Francisco Goya y Lucientes, great Spanish painter of the 18th century.

PLATE 10 PAINTING

"The Wedding Dance" by Pieter Bruegel the Elder, a 16th-century Flemish painter.

PLATE 11   PAINTING

Right: "Portrait of a Lady" by Rogier van der Weyden was painted in the 15th century. It is in the Mellon Collection, National Gallery of Art, Washington, D.C.

Left: "A Dutch Courtyard," by Pieter de Hooch, a Dutch painter of the 17th century. It is in the Mellon Collection, National Gallery of Art, Washington, D.C.

PLATE 12 PAINTING

Courtesy Metropolitan Museum of Art

"A Boy with a Lute," by the Dutch artist Frans Hals, was painted in the 17th century.

"Young Girl at an Open Half-Door" was painted by Rembrandt, a Dutch artist of the 17th century.

PLATE 14 PAINTING

"The Artist in His Studio" is a painting by Jan Vermeer, Dutch artist of the 17th century. This painting is in the Kunsthistorisches Museum in Vienna, Austria.

"Italian Comedians," by Antoine Watteau (1684-1721), is in the Samuel H. Kress Collection at the National Gallery of Art, Washington, D.C. Watteau liked to paint gay people.

PLATE 15   PAINTING

"A Game of Hot Cockles," by Jean-Honore Fragonard (1732–1806), fashionable painter during the reign of Louis XV. Samuel H. Kress Collection, National Gallery of Art, Washington, D.C.

PLATE 16   PAINTING

"A Prince Riding an Elephant," detail from an album signed "Work of Khemdaran." Khemdaran was an artist in India during the reign of Akbar (1556–1605).

"View at Hampstead Heath" was painted by John Constable (1776–1837), an English landscape artist.

"The Blue Boy" is a portrait of Jonathan Buttall by the English painter Thomas Gainsborough (1727–1788).

PLATE 19   PAINTING   "A Girl with a Watering Can," by Auguste Renoir.

PLATE 20 PAINTING

"Third Class Carriage" was painted by Honore Daumier, a French artist of the 19th century.

"Fatata Te Miti," by Paul Gauguin (1848–1903); National Gallery of Art, Washington, D.C. (Chester Dale Collection, Loan).

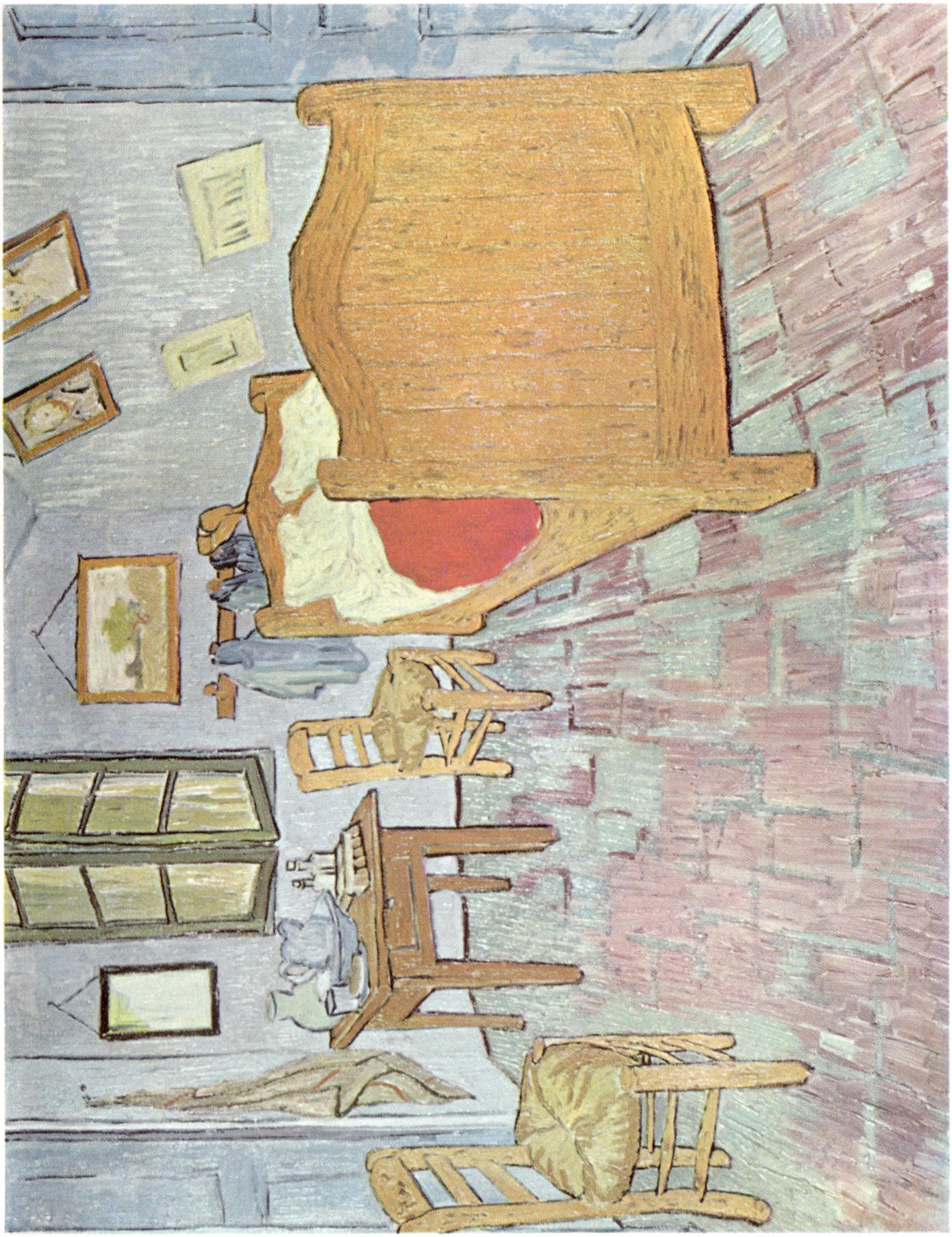

"Bedroom at Arles" is by Vincent van Gogh, an artist of the 19th century.

Courtesy The Art Institute of Chicago

PLATE 23 PAINTING "Ballet Girls on the Stage" is by the 19th-century French artist Hilaire Degas.

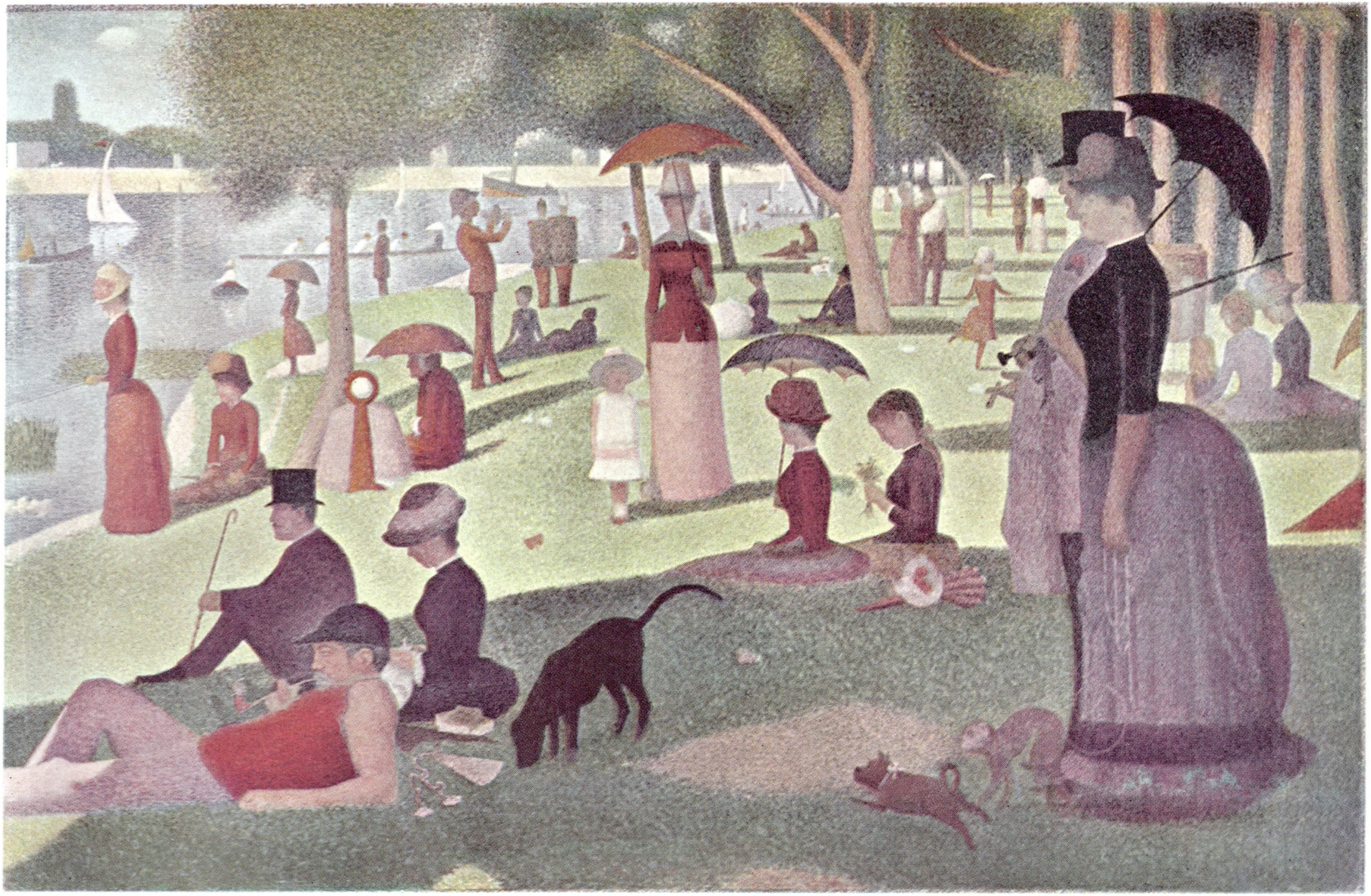

Courtesy The Art Institute of Chicago

PLATE 24 PAINTING

"Sunday Afternoon on the Island of La Grande Jatte" was painted by the French artist Georges Seurat (1859–1891).

"The Red Cross Knight," by John Singleton Copley (1738–1815); National Gallery of Art, Washington, D.C. (Gift of Mrs. Gordon Dexter.)

George Inness (1825–1894), a United States artist, painted this picture which he called "Peace and Plenty." It is in the Metropolitan Museum of Art, New York City.

PLATE 26   PAINTING

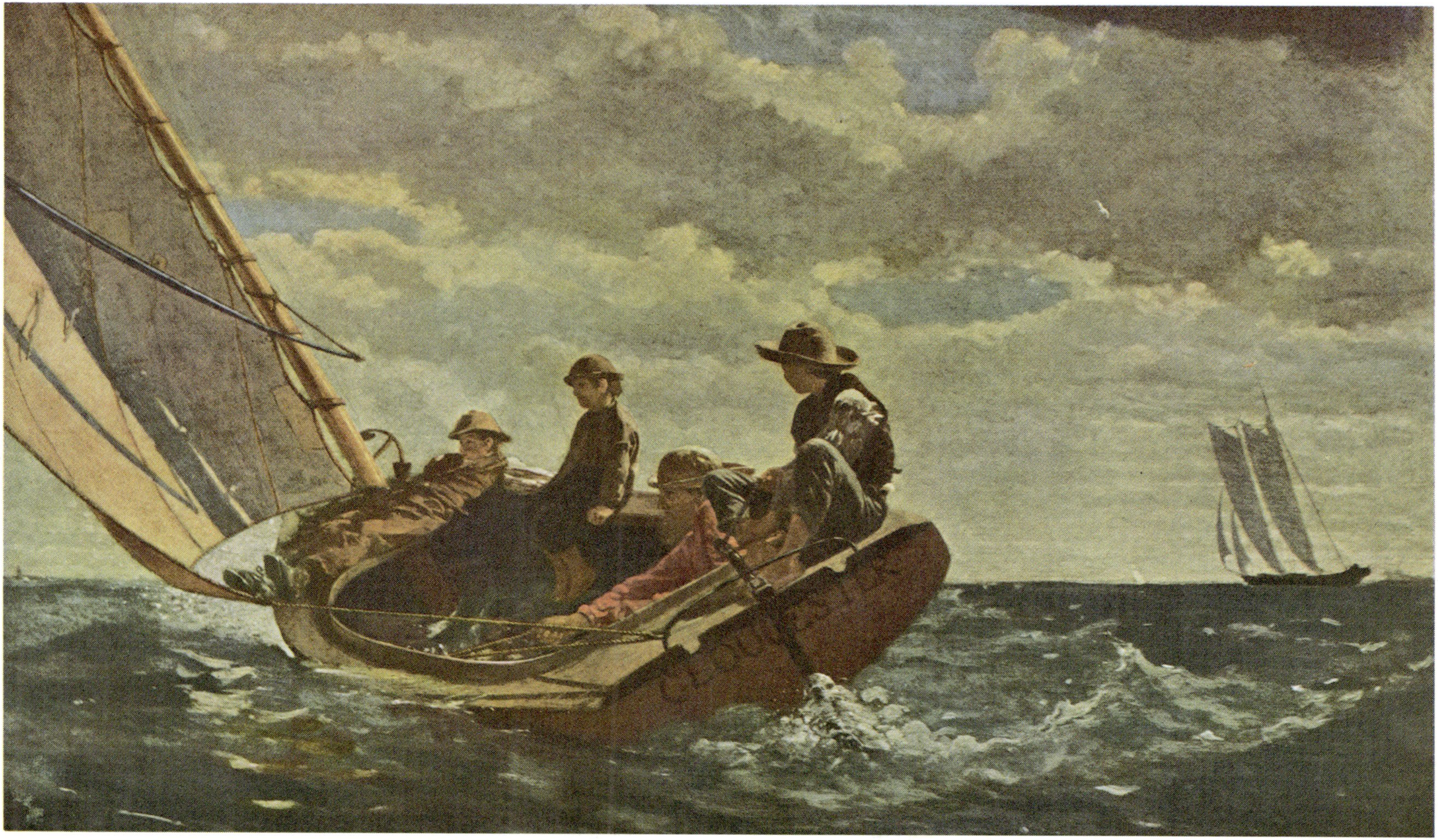

Courtesy National Gallery of Art, Washington, D.C. (Gift of W. L. and May T. Mellon Foundation)

"Breezing Up," by Winslow Homer (1836–1910); National Gallery of Art, Washington, D.C.

PLATE 27 PAINTING

PLATE 28 PAINTING

Courtesy of the Metropolitan Museum of Art

"Moonlight Marine" by Albert P. Ryder, a United States painter who died in 1917. One of Ryder's favorite subjects was a boat on a moonlit sea. His paintings began to crack even in his lifetime, for Ryder did not use the best methods for preserving his work. He kept working on his pictures for many years, adding layer after layer of paint, sometimes on top of dust that had settled on them.

"Both Members of This Club," by George Bellows (1882–1925); National Gallery of Art, Washington, D.C. (Gift of Chester Dale.)

PLATE 30 PAINTING

In "Wake of the Ferry" John Sloan (1871–1951), painted a realistic scene of life in the United States.

"The Midnight Ride of Paul Revere" was painted by the United States artist Grant Wood (1892–1942).

PLATE 32 PAINTING

"Dutch Interior" by Joan Miro, a Spanish painter of the 20th century. Miro distorts things instead of painting them as they really are.

these artists have preserved for us the grace and elegance of their subjects.

Landscape Painting

A love for landscape in and for itself did not arise until the Dutch opened their eyes to its beauty in the 17th century. At the same time two Frenchmen, Nicolas Poussin and Claude Lorrain, who worked in Italy, were creating landscapes with the Italian countryside and ancient ruins for their backgrounds. Claude's pictures became so popular in England —they were purchased by English gentlemen traveling abroad—that no doubt they did much to encourage English painters to turn to landscape.

Gainsborough, best known for his portraits, painted the English countryside purely for pleasure. Then Joseph Mallord William Turner went to Italy to paint exquisite scenes of ruins, but with richer colors than Claude's. Turner also painted English subjects. He finally turned to purely imaginative work and became a colorist, a forerunner of the French Impressionists. John Constable was another English landscapist who painted with strong color as he saw it out of doors, but with greater realism than Turner.

Constable's pictures exhibited in Paris so excited a group of French artists that they decided also to go out into the country to paint. These men, Theodore Rousseau, Charles Francois Daubigny, Jules Dupre, Jules Breton, Jean Francois Millet, and others, formed the Barbizon school, so called after the village near Paris where they worked.

Corot was associated with them, but he did not live at Barbizon. His landscapes show a Classical idealism rather than the realism for which the Barbizon painters, particularly Millet, were striving.

The Various 19th-Century Styles

Until 1800 the various changes in artistic style lasted a century or more. But from 1800 on they occurred in every generation. Artists

Collection Museum of Modern Art, N.Y.

"Zapatistas," the work of the modern Mexican painter, Jose Clemente Orozco, is in the mural style. Here the painter sees the people not as individuals but as accents repeated over and over again.

more than ever before fell under the influences of their age, the upheaval of social life, the progress of industry and of scientific discoveries. The invention of the camera was a most important influence.

The French Revolution abolished the courtly style of the Rococo. Napoleon and the Republican party demanded that artists turn to patriotic and heroic subjects. Not long before, some excavations of ancient Roman cities had excited all Europe; pictures like those unearthed at Pompeii became the rage.

The painter who answered the requirements of patriotism and of this new interest in early Roman history was Jacques Louis David. He set a style which became the official or academic, which students for nearly 100 years were forced to follow. It was called *Neoclassicism,* and was based upon the study of antiquity, perfect drawing of the nude, and skillful technique. Jean Dominique Ingres was David's greatest successor.

By 1825 many artists, like Eugene Delacroix, grew tired of Classic themes and turned to romance, adventure, and tragedy for subject matter. This was *Romanticism.* The novels of Sir

Courtesy Pierre Matisse Gallery

"Harmony in Yellow," by Henri Matisse, shows the artist's interest in outline and pattern, expressed in bold line and richly contrasting color.

Walter Scott, the plays of Shakespeare, medieval legend, and even sensational contemporary events like massacres or shipwrecks, gave the Romanticists material. Their pictures were highly imaginative, emotional, and colorful.

The paintings of the Romanticists were, however, unreal. Gustave Courbet, of the following generation, was the leader of a new movement which was called *Realism.* Courbet said the railroad train was the miracle of the modern age, and so he painted railway carriages and road menders.

Honore Daumier took his subjects from the streets of Paris, the circus, and the prisons. He, like Millet, gave the workers, whether trainmen or peasants, a dignity which had been denied them in the past.

Edouard Manet was a Realist in the sense that he did not flatter the people around him; but his chief claim to attention was in his coloring.

Instead of painting always in the quiet studio light which previous artists preferred, he went out of doors like Constable and painted the pure bright colors he found there, boldly and without blending. His famous painting of a sea fight, "The Alabama and the Kearsage," which he actually saw off the coast of Normandy, was begun on the spot, out at sea.

Impressionism

A painter with a similar name and point of view was Claude Monet. However, he differed from Manet in that he was particularly interested in temporary effects of light; that is, painting things as they appear at any given moment to the artist's eye, rather than as they are known to the artist's mind. Monet experimented by painting the same haystack at different hours of the day. By means of small dots of pure color he gave the impression of what he saw; hence the term *Impressionism.* Monet and other Impressionists believed that the eye from a distance could blend these spots together and get the effect of vibrating sunlight, an effect similar to mosaic. Hilaire Edgar Degas used this method in his studies of ballet girls, often using pastel or crayon, a medium in which the impressionistic technique is especially successful. Pierre August Renoir was another who successfully used this method, which he later abandoned, in figure painting. Georges Seurat carried the dot technique (using small dots or points, hence Pointillism) to the extreme limit, but his works are valued for their luminous quality.

Postimpressionism and Later Techniques

The mosaic-like technique, however, does not produce a sense of solidity of objects such as figures or trees. Paul Cezanne tried to achieve solidity by a scientific use of the spectrum. He used yellows and oranges for the side of an object near the eye, and greens, blues, and indigo for those farther away.

Cezanne simplified his compositions by omitting all unnecessary details, and strove for forceful arrangements. In introducing abstract ideas in this way, painting not merely what he saw, but what he felt or knew about a thing, he was the forerunner of contemporary art. His style of painting is called *Postimpressionism.*

The Postimpressionists did not believe in representing things in the academic style. Perfect drawing was less important to them than the arrangement of the various parts. Henri Matisse painted boldly in flat patterns of bright colors. Paul Gauguin went to Tahiti and painted the colorful native life, with the simplest possible drawing. Vincent van Gogh painted with streaks that seem to vibrate, and he himself was so driven by fierce emotion that he could not help but make his pictures reveal what he saw and felt.

It is easy to see that these modern painters broke away from all that had gone before. They felt that the camera could do what all artists had tried to do since the days of the Greeks, and that there was no use in competing with it. On the other hand, they found in the symbolism of Egypt, the Orient, Africa, and the Pacific islands a relationship to our own day. Finally a group called the *Expressionists* decided it was better to paint in symbols, or in the abstract, which is explained in the caption of the picture on page 18, rather than in the imitation of things as they are.

"The Red Angel" is by Marc Chagall, a contemporary French artist. His work belongs to no single school of painting, although some of it resembles Surrealism.

Courtesy Pierre Matisse Gallery

Pablo Picasso, a Spaniard who lives in France, is a painter of the abstract. He tried *Cubism* (arrangements in geometric shapes, often overlapping to show several sides of an object at once) for a while. He does not represent things as they appear to be, but distorts them, as does Joan Miro. He demands that the beholder use his imagination to understand them.

A recent invention is *Surrealism,* which means "beyond realism." It is the painting of the unseen, of dreams and hallucinations. The foremost Surrealist is a Spaniard, Salvador Dali, who lives in Port Lligat, Spain.

Painting of the Far East

While all of this was happening in Europe, the Far East was developing a different type of art. It was more concerned with the line of the drawing than with the arrangement of colors. It was closely related to the pictorial writing of China, which required great skill with the brush.

It was concerned more with the creation of a poetic mood than with the clear representation of a person or a landscape. Detailed modeling of figures, perspective, and the use of chiaroscuro were always deliberately avoided.

Painting had become a great art in China by the 3rd century B.C., but all work from this period has disappeared. The oldest surviving pieces are from the 4th century A.D. Ku Kaichih, the first Chinese master, was famous for his graphic portraits.

With the Tang dynasty (618–906) Chinese painting truly matured, largely because of the work of Wu Tao-tzu. Although not one painting by this man survives, he is considered one of China's greatest painters. His landscapes seemed so real that he painted one and, it is said, disappeared by walking into its mountains. His great successor was Wang Wei, poet and painter, who perfected the so-called literary landscape.

The Sung dynasty (960–1279) carried Chinese painting to its highest glory. Zen philosophers inspired artists with a love of nature reflected in subtle ink landscapes. The Sung was followed by the Yuan dynasty (1280–1368) and the coming of the Mongols. The great artist of the transition period was Chao Meng-fu, who painted both landscapes and the horse pictures loved by the Mongol conquerors.

With the Ming dynasty (1368–1644) true inspiration died in Chinese painting. Other arts took over in China, and leadership in Oriental painting passed to Japan.

Painting in Japan is closely tied to Chinese inspirations. New works arriving from the mainland moved Japanese artists to adapt Chinese ideas to their own tastes and so to create their own art.

The earliest Japanese paintings, which are of great Buddhist figures, date from as far back as the 6th century. The Yamato and Tosa schools flourished from about the 11th century. The most important works of this period are long illustrated scrolls. The Kano school was founded by Kano Masanobu and his son, Kano Motonobu, to revive some of the techniques of Chinese landscape. At about the same time Sesshu evolved his own style and became probably the greatest of the Japanese landscapists.

The next important school grew largely from the work of Hishikawa Moronobu. From his paintings and woodblock prints featuring the life of the common people grew *Ukiyo-e*, the pictures of the floating world, the famous Japanese prints.

Many superb artists worked in this field. To list a few: Okumura Masanobu, who did many prints of actors; Suzuki Harunobu, who drew beautiful young girls; Katsukawa Shunsho, an important teacher who did actor prints, and his pupil, Katsukawa Shunko; Kitagawa Utamaro, most famous for large portrait heads; Toshusai Sharaku, a mysterious figure who did only actor prints and who worked only in the years 1794 and 1795; Katsushika Hokusai, an all-around master of many fields; and Ando Hiroshige, greatest of the landscape printers. (See HIRO-SHIGE, ANDO; HOKUSAI, KATSUSHIKA; LI PO; ORIENTAL LANGUAGES AND LITERATURE.)

There were many more, but after Hiroshige, *Ukiyo-e* and the art of Japan came more and more under Western influences and so became less typically oriental.

Kitagawa Utamaro, 18th-century artist of the *Ukiyo-e* school of Japanese painting, is most famous for his woodblock portraits of the beautiful women of Edo (now Tokyo).

Courtesy Robert H. Glauber

Mexican Art

Though far removed from other art centers, Mexico plays an important role in contemporary art. Mexicans have their own classical tradition, that of Indian cultures. Since before the time of Christopher Columbus, Aztec and Mayan artists sought their inspiration in the drama of pain and death rather than in a Greek-like ideal of physical beauty. And much pain and death came to Mexicans in the 20th century in the form of the many civil wars sparked by the Revolution of 1910.

The Mexican artist worked in the midst of a social turmoil quite unlike the secluded quiet of Parisian studios. Jose Guadalupe Posada (1851–1913), a man of the people, mirrored their viewpoint, which was also his own, in countless engravings sold in the streets by newsboys for a few pennies.

Courtesy of The Art Institute of Chicago, The Joseph Winterbotham Collection

"Woman with a Bird Cage," by the Mexican muralist and painter Rufino Tamayo, was painted in 1941. It shows the effectiveness of a certain amount of distortion in art, as well as an extraordinary sense of color.

In 1920 the successful revolution raised to power men bold enough to commission untried artists to decorate the walls of public buildings. The muralists preferred to think of themselves as artisans, or even as manual workers. (See DIEGO RIVERA.) Jose Clemente Orozco (1883–1949) started his career as a political cartoonist. He carried to his wall murals the same freedom and power with which he drew his biting cartoons. David Alfaro Siqueiros (1896–   ) presents the theme of machine versus man in murals painted in Duco, a kind of automobile paint.

In the 1930's another group of artists reacted against the specialized attitude of the muralists. Rating artistic problems over social statements, they kept their eyes on the swiftly changing international art scene. Rufino Tamayo (1899–

) invented sophisticated distortions that came close to those of the school of Paris. Nevertheless, Tamayo's Indian heritage infuses his superb sense of color with a tragic content that remains validly Mexican. Frieda Kahlo (1910–1954) refined in exquisitely small pictures a technique close to that of a miniaturist.

The present generation appraises the period of the great murals as past history, to be neither embraced nor rejected. Rafael Coronel (1932–   ) prefers muted statements. Jose Luis Cuevas (1923–   ) stamps man with a sense of despair.

United States Painting

Painting during the Colonial period in the United States followed the English closely, and was chiefly an art of portraiture. Painters like Gilbert Stuart and John Singleton Copley were as skillful as any in Europe. During the 19th century Americans went to Europe to study and, returning, eventually established a United States style based on their own cultural background. George Inness painted the landscape of New York and New Jersey with true appreciation of its beauty. Winslow Homer devoted his skill to picturing the sea and fisherfolk of New England. Albert Ryder also painted the sea, but in a dreamlike way. John Singer Sargent was the most brilliant portrait painter at the end of the 19th century, but he and James McNeill Whistler, famous for the painting popularly called "Whistler's Mother," worked abroad. George Bellows and Thomas Eakins were leaders of Realism in the United States. The work of Thomas Hart Benton, Grant Wood, and John Sloan may be mentioned as outstanding in picturing American life in the 20th century.

Much fine work being done today is in book illustrating, advertising, and mural design. In these fields artists feel they are expressing the age in which they live. Our industrial magnates, publishers, and officials are employing the best artists to work for them. More artists are active than ever before, but because they are close to us in time, it is impossible to judge them in perspective and to say which will rank with the immortals.

THESE PAINTINGS APPEAR THROUGHOUT BRITANNICA JUNIOR ENCYCLOPÆDIA:

Artist	*Painting*	*Article*
Alexander, John White	"Isabella and the Pot of Basil"	ALEXANDER, JOHN WHITE
Angelico, Fra	"The Last Judgment"	ANGELICO, FRA
Angelico, Fra	"The Annunciation"	ANNUNCIATION
Armand-Dumaresq, Charles Edouard	"Signing the Declaration of American Independence"	DECLARATION OF INDEPENDENCE
Audubon, John James	"Belted Kingfisher"	AUDUBON, JOHN JAMES
Bastien-Lepage, Jules	"Joan of Arc"	BASTIEN-LEPAGE, JULES
Bellini, Giovanni	"Doge Leonardo Loredano"	BELLINI FAMILY
Bellini, Giovanni	"The Flight into Egypt"	PAINTING
Bellows, George	"Both Members of This Club"	PAINTING
Benson, Frank Weston	"Two Boys"	BENSON, FRANK WESTON
Bingham, George Caleb	"The Jolly Flatboatmen"	PIONEER LIFE IN THE UNITED STATES
Bingham, George Caleb	"Daniel Boone Escorting a Band of Pioneers into the Western Country"	UNITED STATES
Bonheur, Rosa	"The Horse Fair"	BONHEUR, MARIE ROSALIE
Botticelli, Sandro	"Madonna and Child"	BOTTICELLI, SANDRO
Botticelli, Sandro	"The Adoration of the Magi"	PAINTING
Botticelli, Sandro	"Portrait of a Young Man"	RENAISSANCE
Boughton, George H.	"Pilgrims Going to Church"	UNITED STATES
Breton, Jules Adolphe	"The Song of the Lark"	BRETON, JULES ADOLPHE
Bruegel, Pieter, the Elder	"The Harvesters" ("The Month of July")	BRUEGEL, PIETER
Bruegel, Pieter, the Elder	"The Wedding Dance"	PAINTING
Bruegel, Pieter, the Elder	"The Parable of the Sower"	PERSPECTIVE
Cezanne, Paul	"The Basket of Apples"	CEZANNE, PAUL
Cezanne, Paul	"Pines and Rocks"	PAINTING
Chagall, Marc	"The Red Angel"	PAINTING
Chappel, Alonzo	"Drafting the Declaration of Independence"	ADAMS, JOHN
Chardin, Jean Baptiste Simeon	"The Young Governess"	CHARDIN, JEAN BAPTISTE SIMEON
Chase, William Merritt	"Carmencita"	CHASE, WILLIAM MERRITT
Ch'iu Ying	"Saying Farewell at Hsun-yang"	ORIENTAL LANGUAGES AND LITERATURE
Colman, Samuel	"Emigrant Train"	UNITED STATES
Constable, John	"View at Hampstead Heath"	PAINTING
Copley, John Singleton	"John Hancock"	HANCOCK, JOHN
Copley, John Singleton	"The Red Cross Knight"	PAINTING
Cornelisz van Amsterdam, Jacob	"The Adoration of the Magi"	MAGI, THE
Corot, Jean Baptiste Camille	"The Ferryman"	COROT, JEAN BAPTISTE CAMILLE
Correggio, Antonio Allegri da	"Holy Night"	CORREGGIO, ANTONIO ALLEGRI DA
Daumier, Honore	"The Uprising"	DAUMIER, HONORE
Daumier, Honore	"Third Class Carriage"	PAINTING
Davey, Randall	"Rainy Day at the Track"	PAINTING
Degas, Hilaire Germain Edgar	"Dancer with a Fan"	PAINTING
Deland, Clyde Osmer	"Birth of Monroe Doctrine"	MONROE, JAMES
Dietrich, Christian Wilhelm Ernst	"Christ Healing the Sick"	JESUS CHRIST
Duccio di Buoninsegna	"Christ Entering Jerusalem"	PERSPECTIVE
Durand, Asher B.	"James Madison"	MADISON, JAMES
Eeckhout, Gerbrand van den	"Isaac Blessing Jacob"	JACOB
El Greco	"The Virgin with Saint Ines and Saint Tecla"	PAINTING
El Greco	"St. Paul"	PAUL, SAINT
Fragonard, Jean-Honore	"A Game of Hot Cockles"	PAINTING
Gainsborough, Thomas	"The Blue Boy"	PAINTING
Gauguin, Paul	"The Vision After the Sermon"	GAUGUIN, PAUL

"Rainy Day at the Track," by Randall Davey (1887–1964).

PLATE 34   PAINTING

HISTORY OF PAINTING

IN SIX APPLES

1

2

5

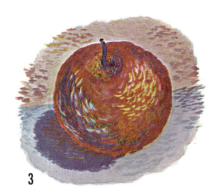

3

6

4

Continued on page 26.

HISTORY OF PAINTING IN SIX APPLES

1. A child would have no difficulty in painting a picture of an apple. First, he would paint the outline of a circle. Then, he would fill it in with red paint and add a stem. Everyone would recognize the apple, and the child would be satisfied.

2. Painters, however, know that this does not tell the whole truth about the apple. From the Italian Renaissance through the 19th century, one great concern of painters was to show apples (or heads or figures) as three-dimensional solid objects. By studying and experimenting, they found that the part of the apple closest to the light is lighter in color. Moreover, its shadow, repeating the shape of the apple, helps call attention to its roundness. The shading of color also brings out the roundness of an object. This method, developed by Leonardo da Vinci, was known as the chiaroscuro, which means light and shadow. Rembrandt carried this idea further with his dramatic shadows and mysterious lighting. Each of the Old Masters tried to develop his own individual style of showing solidity.

3. Late in the 19th century, a group of painters in Paris became interested in the scientific experiments that were being made in the field of color and light. It was pointed out that all color is the result of the way in which objects reflect light. They discovered that shadows of objects in bright sunlight are not black or brown but purple. These painters, known as Impressionists, used the entire spectrum to show the effect of light on an object. Yellow is the brightest color in the spectrum and it appears to come forward in a picture. Therefore, it was used on those parts of the apple closest to the viewer. The parts of the apple farther back in the picture were painted in small streaks or dots of darker colors. To see the apple in its true color and form, the viewer must stand some distance away.

4. Paul Cezanne began as an Impressionist but felt that the small streaks and dots of color took away from the feeling of solidity. He wanted to combine the solid forms of the Old Masters with the bright colors of the Impressionists. He painted his apples in planes, or small areas, of color. The color gradations of the planes from light to dark lead the eye around the object.

5. After the camera was invented, artists felt that it was no longer necessary to paint the apple as it actually looks. A Cubist artist paints a composition that is beautiful because of its colors, patterns, and textures. He adds what he "knows" about the apple. He may add its shape as seen from the top or when cut in half. He may emphasize its geometric shape or exaggerate the sizes of its parts.

6. A Surrealist artist paints the associations that he has with the word apple. It might remind him of the story of Adam and Eve, the snake, and the Garden of Eden. These things, while painted realistically, are unreal and dreamlike in combination.

Artist	Painting	Article
Kano Tanyu	"Confucius"	CONFUCIUS AND CONFUCIANISM
Khemdaran	"A Prince Riding an Elephant"	PAINTING
Landseer, Sir Edwin Henry	"Shoeing"	LANDSEER, SIR EDWIN HENRY
Lange, Joseph	"Wolfgang Amadeus Mozart"	MOZART, WOLFGANG AMADEUS
Lee, Doris	"Thanksgiving"	THANKSGIVING DAY
Leutze, Emanuel	"Washington Crossing the Delaware"	UNITED STATES
Liang K'ai	"Li Po"	LI PO
Lippi, Fra Filippo	"St. Lawrence Enthroned with Saints and Donors"	LIPPI, FRA FILIPPO
Lorrain, Claude	"The Ford"	LORRAIN, CLAUDE
Maccari, Cesare	"Cicero Denouncing Catiline"	LATIN LANGUAGE AND LITERATURE
Manet, Edouard	"Boy with a Sword"	MANET, EDOUARD
Matisse, Henri	"Dancer"	MATISSE, HENRI
Matisse, Henri	"Harmony in Yellow"	PAINTING
Matisse, Henri	"The Blue Window"	PERSPECTIVE
Michelangelo Buonarroti	"The Libyan Sibyl"	MICHELANGELO BUONARROTI
Michelangelo Buonarroti	"Erithraea"	RENAISSANCE
Millet, Jean Francois	"The Gleaners"	MILLET, JEAN FRANCOIS
Miro, Joan	"Dutch Interior"	PAINTING
Monet, Claude	"Bridge over Pool of Pond Lilies"	MONET, CLAUDE
Munkacsy, Mihaly	"Blind Milton Dictating *Paradise Lost* to His Daughters"	MILTON, JOHN
Murillo, Bartolome Esteban	"Moses Striking the Rock"	MOSES
Oehme, Erwin	"Council of War Convened by the Liberator on May 23, 1819, in the Village of Setenta"	BOLIVAR, SIMON
Orozco, Jose Clemente	"Zapatistas"	PAINTING
Peale, Charles Willson	"George Washington"	WASHINGTON, GEORGE
Perugino, Pietro	"The Madonna Adoring the Child"	PERUGINO, PIETRO
Picasso, Pablo	"The Painter and His Model"	PAINTING
Picasso, Pablo	"Girl Before the Mirror"	PICASSO, PABLO
Poussin, Nicolas	"Shepherds of Arcadia"	FINE ARTS
Raphael Santi	"The Sistine Madonna"	MADONNA
Raphael Santi	"St. George and the Dragon"	PAINTING
Raphael Santi	"The Marriage of the Virgin"	PERSPECTIVE
Raphael Santi	"The Alba Madonna"	RAPHAEL SANTI or SANZIO
Raphael Santi	"Bindo Altoviti"	RENAISSANCE
Rembrandt Harmensz van Rijn	"Moses Showing the Tablets of the Law to the People"	MOSES
Rembrandt Harmensz van Rijn	"Young Girl at an Open Half-Door"	PAINTING
Rembrandt Harmensz van Rijn	"Self-Portrait"	REMBRANDT HARMENSZ VAN RIJN
Renoir, Pierre Auguste	"Young Girls at the Piano"	MUSIC
Renoir, Pierre Auguste	"A Girl with a Watering Can"	PAINTING
Reynolds, Sir Joshua	"The Age of Innocence"	REYNOLDS, SIR JOSHUA
Roberti, Ercole	"Ginevra Bentivoglio"	PAINTING
Romney, George	"Lady Hamilton as Daphne"	ROMNEY, GEORGE
Rosso Fiorentino	"The Three Fates"	FINE ARTS
Rubens, Peter Paul	"The Wolf and Fox Hunt"	RUBENS, PETER PAUL
Ruysdael, Jacob van	"The Mountain Torrent"	RUYSDAEL, JACOB VAN
Ryder, Albert P.	"Moonlight Marine"	PAINTING
Salmon, Robert W.	"Boston Harbor: Long and Central Wharves"	UNITED STATES
Sargent, John Singer	"The Wyndham Sisters"	SARGENT, JOHN SINGER
Sarto, Andrea del	"Charity"	SARTO, ANDREA DEL
Savage, Edward	"The Washington Family"	UNITED STATES

Artist	Painting	Article
Seurat, Georges	"Sunday Afternoon on the Island of La Grande Jatte"	PAINTING
Sloan, John	"Wake of the Ferry"	PAINTING
Stearns, Junius Brutus	"The Adoption of the Constitution"	CONSTITUTION OF THE UNITED STATES
Stuart, Gilbert	"John Adams"	ADAMS, JOHN
Stuart, Gilbert	"George Washington"	WASHINGTON, GEORGE
Stuart, Gilbert	"Self-portrait at the age of 24"	STUART, GILBERT
Tahoma, Quincy	"Singing Warrior"	INDIANS, NORTH AMERICAN
Tamayo, Rufina	"Woman with a Bird Cage"	PAINTING
Tintoretto	"Christ at the Sea of Galilee"	PAINTING
Titian	"Man with a Glove"	TITIAN
Toulouse-Lautrec, Henri de	"In the Circus Fernando: The Ringmaster"	TOULOUSE-LAUTREC, HENRI DE
Trotter, Newbolt H.	"Held Up"	UNITED STATES
Troyon, Constant	"The Hound Pointing"	TROYON, CONSTANT
Trumbull, John	"The Signing of the Declaration of Independence"	UNITED STATES
Turner, Joseph Mallord William	"The Grand Canal, Venice"	TURNER, JOSEPH MALLORD WILLIAM
Unknown, American	"Buffalo Hunter"	ARCHERY
Van Dyck, Sir Anthony	"Portrait of the Children of King Charles I"	PAINTING
Van Dyck, Sir Anthony	"Portrait of Sir Thomas Hanmer"	VAN DYCK, SIR ANTHONY
Van Gogh, Vincent	"Bedroom at Arles"	PAINTING
Velazquez, Diego Rodriguez de Silva y	"Christ and the Pilgrims of Emmaus"	JESUS CHRIST
Velazquez, Diego Rodriguez de Silva y	"Infanta Marguerite"	VELAZQUEZ, DIEGO RODRIGUEZ DE SILVA Y
Vermeer, Jan	"The Artist in His Studio"	PAINTING
Vinci, Leonardo da	"Mona Lisa" ("La Gioconda")	VINCI, LEONARDO DA
Watteau, Antoine	"Italian Comedians"	PAINTING
Weyden, Rogier van der	"Portrait of a Lady"	PAINTING
Weyden, Rogier van der	"Christ Appearing to His Mother"	RENAISSANCE
Whistler, James Abbott McNeill	"Arrangement in Grey and Black" ("Whistler's Mother")	WHISTLER, JAMES ABBOTT McNEILL
Wood, Grant	"The Midnight Ride of Paul Revere"	PAINTING
Wyeth, Newell Convers	"Rip Van Winkle"	WYETH, NEWELL CONVERS

PAKISTAN (*păk ĭ stŏn'*), **ASIA,** is a country of southern Asia that is made up of two distinct and separate regions. The two regions, separated by India, are almost 1,100 miles apart. Before Pakistan became independent in 1947, it was a part of British-controlled India. West Pakistan, the larger of the two regions, has an area of 310,403 square miles. East Pakistan is much smaller, with an area of 55,126 square miles, but it includes more than half of the population. The official name of the country is the Republic of Pakistan.

West Pakistan is bordered by the Arabian Sea on the south, Iran on the west, Afghanistan on the north, and India on the east. Kashmir to the northeast is claimed by both Pakistan and India. The region has a variety of landforms. In the east there is a flat plain through which the Indus River and its branches flow. The plain becomes dry to the south and in some places is desertlike. The snow-capped peaks of the Himalayas and the Hindu Kush rise in the north and northwest sections of West Pakistan. Lower mountains and hills form the western border of the region. Most of West Pakistan is dry. Rainfall varies from about 4 inches a year in the south to about 40 inches in the north. Vegetation in the south is sparse, with scattered trees. In the north there is enough moisture to maintain growths of pine and oak. Animals include the deer, boar, bear, crocodile, and various waterfowl.

East Pakistan is quite different from West Pakistan in landscape and climate. Most of the land is a flat plain formed by the delta of the Ganges and Brahmaputra rivers. The plain is

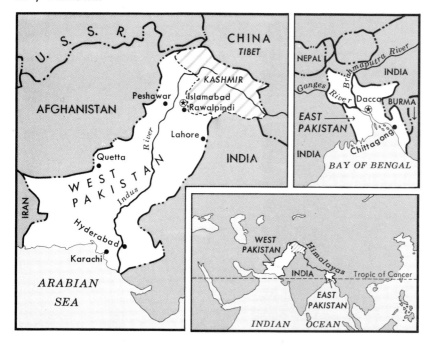

Locator map of Pakistan.

broken by the many tributaries of these rivers, which empty into the Bay of Bengal. The bay bounds East Pakistan on the south. The region's land boundaries are with India on all sides except for a short southeastern border with Burma. In the fall the rivers of East Pakistan flood, leaving a layer of fertile soil over the land that is ideal for growing rice and jute. East Pakistan has a humid tropical climate, which also aids in the growing of these crops. Rainfall in East Pakistan may vary from 50 to 135 inches a year. Evergreen vegetation covers much of the region. Among the animals of the region are the elephant, tiger, and various waterfowl. (See BENGAL.)

People

Almost 90 percent of the people of Pakistan are Muslims. Their Islamic law forbids Muslims from eating pork or drinking alcoholic beverages. It has been a Muslim custom to keep women in seclusion—a practice known as *purdah*. If they appear in public they must wear heavy veils. Among modern families, however, purdah is gradually disappearing. (See MOHAMMED AND ISLAM.)

There are wide differences in appearance, customs, and language among the various groups of people who live in Pakistan. These groups include the Bengalis, the Punjabis, the Sindhis, the Pathans, and the Baluchs. The Bengalis of East Pakistan and the Punjabis of West Pakistan are the most numerous groups.

The Bengalis are a short, dark-skinned people, most of whom are farmers. They speak their own language called Bengali. The Pun-

FACTS ABOUT PAKISTAN

CAPITAL: Islamabad (administrative capital); Ayubnagar (legislative capital).

NATIONAL ANTHEM: Qaumi Tarana ("National Anthem").

AREA: 365,529 square miles (about the size of Texas and Oregon combined): 40 percent highlands, 60 percent lowlands; 98,456 square miles of cultivated land.

POPULATION: 93,831,982 (1961); 100,762,000 (1964 estimate); 257 persons per square mile; 13 percent urban; 87 percent rural.

CHIEF LANGUAGES: Urdu, Bengali, English.

CHIEF RELIGION: Islam.

LITERACY: About 20 percent over age 5 can read and write.

MOUNTAIN RANGES: Himalayas, Hindu Kush.

HIGHEST POINT OR PEAKS (height in feet): Tirich Mir (25,236), Sad Istragh (24,170), Lunkho (22,640).

MOST IMPORTANT RIVERS: Brahmaputra, Chenab, Ganges, Indus, Sutlej.

FORM OF GOVERNMENT: Federal Republic.

HEAD OF GOVERNMENT AND CHIEF OF STATE: President.

LEGISLATURE: National Assembly.

POLITICAL DIVISIONS: 2 provinces (West Pakistan and East Pakistan).

CHIEF CITIES (1962 estimates): Karachi (2,080,000), Lahore (1,377,000), Dacca (598,000), Rawalpindi (358,000), Chittagong (376,000).

CHIEF MANUFACTURED AND MINED PRODUCTS: chemicals and chemical products, food, natural gas, tobacco, textiles.

CHIEF AGRICULTURAL PRODUCTS: *Crops,* cotton, jute, mustard, rice, sugarcane, tea, tobacco, wheat. *Livestock,* buffalo, cattle, goats, sheep.

MOST IMPORTANT HOLIDAYS: Pakistan Day, March 23; Independence Day, August 14.

FLAG: Green and white (See FLAG, *Plate 10*).

CURRENCY: Rupee; about 5 rupees equal one U.S. dollar.

jabis, who live in the Punjab section of West Pakistan, speak Punjabi. They are mainly farmers, and in appearance they are taller and lighter-skinned than the Bengalis. The Sindhis live mainly in southeastern West Pakistan, where it is hot and desertlike. Near the Indus most Sindhis are farmers. Away from the river many are herders of sheep and goats.

The Pathans are hill tribesmen of the western ranges of West Pakistan. They wander back and forth with their flocks between Afghanistan and Pakistan. In Afghanistan, the Pathans are said to make up the largest ethnic group. The Pakistani Pathans have at times asked for a separate Pathan state, but they have made little progress. They speak a language called Pashto. In the past the Pathans were fierce and warlike, going down to the plains on raids and then disappearing again into the mountains. Travelers through the Khyber Pass to Afghanistan were once in constant danger of such raids. The Pathans are now peaceful, however. Like the Pathans, the Baluchs of southwestern West Pakistan are chiefly herdsmen. Some are farmers in the oases or irrigated valleys of Baluchistan. Their language is Baluchi.

One of the official languages of Pakistan is Urdu—a mixture of Arabic, Persian, and Hindi, the official language of India. Bengali is the official language of East Pakistan and is spoken by about 55 percent of the country's population. English is also an important language and is generally spoken by well educated Pakistanis.

The largest city of Pakistan is Karachi, with a population of about 2,000,000. It is the commercial and cultural center of the country. (See KARACHI.) The country has two capitals. Islamabad, in northern West Pakistan is the administrative capital. It was especially constructed as a capital city. Before its construction Rawalpindi was the administrative capital. Ayubnagar in East Pakistan is the legislative capital. Other major cities include Lahore in West Pakistan and Chittagong and Dacca in East Pakistan.

Economy

Pakistan is basically an agricultural country. More than two-thirds of the people are engaged in farming, and more than 50 percent of the national income comes from agricultural products. Most of the cultivated land furnishes food crops, but more food must be imported to feed the population. In dry West Pakistan, farmers depend largely upon irrigation from the Indus River and its branches to grow crops. The main crop and staple food of West Pakistan is wheat. In tropical East Pakistan, rice is the main crop and staple food of the people. Jute, grown in East Pakistan, is the chief export crop. Pakistan is the world's largest jute supplier.

Other important crops include cotton, sugarcane, mustard, tea, and tobacco. The chief livestock of the country include cattle, sheep, goats, and buffalo.

Pakistan does not have well developed industries, though ambitious programs of industrial development have been started. The country is particularly poor in coal and iron ore deposits that are needed to establish a steel industry. West Pakistan has important, though limited, sources of petroleum. In its search for oil, how-

A suspension bridge suitable for light traffic spans the Gilgit River in Pakistani-controlled Kashmir. The Himalayas rise high above the river in the background.

Rene Burri-Magnum

Paul Conklin-Pix from Publix

Old and new cultures mix as automobiles, bicycles, and pedestrians jam a market street in Lahore, West Pakistan.

ever, vast fields of natural gas were discovered, which now furnish fuel for home and industry. Pakistan is not rich in minerals, and the major industries are based largely on the processing of agricultural products. Especially important is the manufacture of cotton textiles. Pakistan has become a major world producer of cotton. Jute manufacturing, which did not begin in Pakistan until 1952, has also shown good progress. Other industrial products of Pakistan include cement, sugar, cigarettes, vegetable oil, and chemicals and chemical products.

The road system in Pakistan is rather extensive, but only a small portion of it is considered first class. Rail networks provide an important means of transportation in both East and West Pakistan. Rivers are important for transportation in East Pakistan. The Pakistan International Airlines Corporation operates regular services to the Middle East, Europe, and the United States. Air services are also important in linking East and West Pakistan.

Education and Government

Extensive plans have been made for educational development in Pakistan in the 1960's. A reformed educational system is one of the country's chief goals. In the early 1960's only about 20 percent of the population more than five years of age could read and write. Schooling was neither free nor compulsory. Some advances have been made, however, particularly in the field of education for women. In the middle 1960's, Pakistan had 370 colleges and universities, the largest of which was the University of Punjab.

Pakistan is a federal republic that is governed by a National Assembly. The National Assembly is headed by a president who is both the head of government and the head of state. The country is divided into the two provinces of East and West Pakistan, each of which has its own provincial assembly and governor. The president and the members of the national and provincial assemblies are appointed by an electoral college, which represents the voters.

The constitution of Pakistan is based on the principles of Islamic social justice, and no law is allowed to be passed that would be offensive to Islam. Non-Muslims are guaranteed equal rights and freedom under the republic's constitution.

Pakistanis buy food at the open marketplace in Sialkot, West Pakistan. The country is chiefly agricultural, but food imports are needed to help feed the people.
Rene Burri-Magnum

History

The events that led up to the creation of Pakistan as a Muslim state go back to the 8th century A.D. At that time India, including what is now Pakistan, was divided into a large number of separate states. In 712, Muslim Arabs crossed the Makran coast and conquered the Sind. By the 10th century, Muslim influence had spread throughout northwest India and also to Bengal, on the eastern side of the Indian subcontinent. From the 10th through the 18th centuries a long series of invasions brought the Muslims of Persia, Afghanistan, and Turkistan into India. Between the 16th and 18th centuries the Muslim Mogul rulers brought most of India under their control. Muslim and Hindu culture existed side by side, but neither was absorbed by the other.

The British East India Company gained control of Muslim-ruled Bengal in the mid-18th century. A hundred years later British rule was extended into the Muslim northwest India.

Under the British, the fortunes and power of the Muslims became less and less. The Hindus were more numerous, and the educated ones adopted Western ways, learned English, and took part in the running of the government. Educated Muslims at first clung to their own habits and refused to adopt Western ways. Gradually most of the positions of leadership in government, business, and the professions came to be held by Hindus.

Charles Harbutt-Magnum

Beautiful mosques, Muslim houses of worship, stand throughout Pakistan. This one is in Dacca, East Pakistan.

In the first part of the 20th century, Muslims and Hindus worked side by side in a common effort to attain freedom from British rule. The Muslims, however, came to believe that independence from Britain would not in itself solve their problems. They were a minority group, and they felt that a Hindu congress would not be likely to accept Muslim views. In 1906 the All-India Muslim League was formed. Through the next 40 years it worked for Muslim rights.

The poet Sir Mohammed Iqbal first proposed the idea of a separate Muslim homeland in 1930. From then until 1947 the Muslim League, led by Mohammed Ali Jinnah, worked eagerly for the creation of Pakistan. The Hindus in India were strongly against dividing their country. In 1947, however, the British made a plan for the division of India. The Indian National Congress finally agreed to the British terms of independence. In August 1947, India and

The exquisite Juma Mosque in Lahore, West Pakistan, is noted for its huge marble court and magnificent mosaic facade. The towers of a mosque are called minarets.

Frederick Ayer III-Photo Researchers

Pakistan became separately independent countries within the Commonwealth of Nations.

The borders between India and Pakistan were established on the general basis of whether a region was Muslim or non-Muslim. One major problem was Kashmir, a region claimed by both India and Pakistan. (See KASHMIR.) Most of the people of Kashmir were Muslim, but the Hindu ruler of the province voted to join India. Fighting broke out between India and Pakistan over the Kashmir question, but was halted in 1949 by an agreement reached through the United Nations. Pakistani troops have continued to occupy the northwestern part of Kashmir, and Indian troops, the southeastern part. Pakistan controls about one-third of Kashmir, a section called Azad. Kashmir's water power resources are of particular interest to Pakistan. After another outbreak of fighting in 1965, Pakistan and India in 1966 resolved to settle their disputes by peaceful means.

The first governor general of Pakistan was Mohammad Ali Jinnah, whom Pakistanis think of as the father of their country. He died the year after Pakistan became independent. The country adopted a republican form of government in 1956. In October 1958 General Mohammad Ayub Khan became president of Pakistan. In 1962 he signed a new constitution giving the president wide powers. Dissatisfaction with Ayub's strict rule erupted into widespread public disorders in 1968 and 1969. Unrest was particularly strong among nationalistic groups in East Pakistan. In March 1969, Ayub resigned and turned over government power to General Agha Mohammad Yahya Khan. Yahya promised an eventual return to civilian rule.

PALESTINE (păl'ŭ stīn'), **ASIA,** is a region of the Middle East that includes the modern State of Israel and part of western Jordan. Since the region was divided between these two countries in 1948, the traditional name of Palestine is not officially used. The boundaries of the region have changed many times through the centuries. However, it has always included areas between the Mediterranean Sea and the United Arab Republic on the west, Lebanon and Syria on the north, Jordan on the east, and the Red

Sea on the south. Palestine is one of the oldest homes of civilized man and the site of many important historic events.

The region is often called the Holy Land because it is sacred to Jew, Christian, and Muslim. Some Jews look upon Palestine as the "Promised Land," the land promised to them in the Bible by God. Palestine is sacred to Christians because Bethlehem, the birthplace of Jesus, is located there. Other sites sacred to Christians include Jerusalem, Nazareth, and the Sea of Galilee. The Muslims have a famous mosque at Jerusalem, which ranks next to Mecca and Medina as a place of religious pilgrimage. (See JERUSALEM.)

The word *Palestine* comes from *Philistia,* the name of the coastal area where the Philistines lived during biblical times. Later Palestine came to refer to a much larger area, reaching

Palestine at the time of Christ.

north beyond the Bay of Acre and east across the Jordan River. Because of its strategic location on routes between Europe, Asia, and Africa, the region has been the object of invasion and conquest since ancient times. For hundreds of years Jerusalem was the capital city of a Hebrew kingdom founded by David and his son Solomon. Later it was conquered by a series of invaders. Between World War I and 1948 Palestine was governed by the British under mandate from the League of Nations. The mandate of Palestine included the Negev, a desert that extends southward to the Red Sea.

Among the best-known cities of Palestine is the sacred city of Jerusalem. The largest city is Tel Aviv-Jaffa, Israel, about 35 miles northwest of Jerusalem. (See TEL AVIV-JAFFA.) The largest port is Haifa, Israel. In the Negev is

In the 13th century, Crusaders built walls around the Mediterranean port of Acre to guard against Muslim attack.

Louis Goldman from Rapho Guillumette Pictures

Beersheba, Israel, which, like most of the cities in Palestine, dates from biblical times.

Land and Climate

An area with great variation in landscape, Palestine has hot, dry deserts; barren, rocky hills; rolling, irrigated farm land; and rich citrus groves. Palestine may be divided into four narrow strips, which extend from north to south. These are the coastal plains, a belt of hills, the deep Jordan Valley, and the desert.

The coastal strip is quite narrow, averaging about 12 miles wide. It is fertile country, producing the famous Jaffa oranges and other Mediterranean fruits. The narrow coastal plain widens in the south to become part of the dry Negev. East of the coast is a long belt of hills and plateaus that form the backbone of Palestine. In the north are the hills of Galilee, where Jesus grew to manhood. In central Palestine are the hills of Samaria, and to the south are the hills of Judea.

The greatest heights are found in upper Galilee, where the hills are a continuation of the mountains of Syria and Lebanon. In lower Galilee, rich soil and an adequate water supply combine to form some of the most fertile land in Palestine. Lake Tiberias (Sea of Galilee) is noted for its biblical significance. (See GALILEE.) The hills of Galilee are separated from the hills of Samaria by the fruitful Plain of Esdraelon and other irrigated plateaus and valleys. In Judea are found the famous cities of Bethlehem, Jerusalem, and Hebron, all of which date from biblical times.

Dropping off steeply from the highlands is the Jordan Valley. The Dead Sea, which also is located in the valley, is 1,302 feet below sea level. Its shoreline is the lowest spot on the Earth. (See DEAD SEA.) Few crops are grown in the valley except within reach of irrigation water from the Jordan. The valley merges in the east with the Syrian Desert and in the south with the Negev. The Jordan River empties into the Dead Sea, from which valuable mineral salts and other chemicals are obtained. In the Jordan Valley is the village of Jericho, whose walls are said to have crumbled before Joshua and the Israelites. (See JOSHUA.)

(Left) Carl Frank—Photo Researchers, (center) George Holton—Photo Researchers, (right) J. Allan Cash from Rapho Guillumette Pictures

The Church of All Nations stands at the foot of the Mount of Olives (left), traditional site of the Ascension. Nearby is the Russian Church of St. Mary Magdalene. Mosques and Christian churches are clustered together in Bethlehem, Jordan (center). Children gather near Herod's Gate (right) in the Jordanian section of Jerusalem.

The climate of Palestine is warm and dry. The winters, from November to April, are mild, with considerable rainfall. The summers, from May to October, are hot and generally without rainfall. Climate varies, however, and different crops are grown in different areas. With irrigation, the land is generally fertile throughout Palestine.

History

Scientific explorations have established that fairly well organized societies lived in Palestine as far back as 7000 B.C. Other indications of early life in Palestine came from the Egyptians, from Hebrew scholars as revealed in the Old Testament, and from the Dead Sea Scrolls. Before the Israelites became established in Palestine, civilization flourished in towns such as Beersheba, Megiddo, and Jericho. From about 1500 to about 1200 B.C., Palestine, then called Canaan, was dominated by the Egyptians. The Israelites, a confederation of Hebrew tribes, entered Canaan in about 1250 B.C. The Hebrews set up a monarchy in the land in about 1000 B.C., which later broke up into the two rival kingdoms of Israel and Judah. Kings, prophets, and judges led the Hebrew peoples during their dominance in this area.

By about the mid-6th century B.C. Hebrew political and military control of the region was considerably reduced by the invasions of foreign powers. Controlling powers in Palestine between that time and the birth of Christ included the Persians, Macedonians, Egyptians, and Romans. Through this period, the Jews, as the Hebrews were then called, rebelled several times. In A.D. 70 the Romans crushed a powerful Jewish rebellion, captured Jerusalem, and destroyed the Temple. Palestine then became the Roman province of Judaea.

The Jews fled the land through the hundreds of years that followed. In the next two thousand years Palestine was controlled by many foreign conquerors. Arabs overran Palestine in

Much of Palestine is desertlike. A desolate road winds through arid hills near Jericho (left). Bedouin tribesmen bargain for vegetables and fowl at Beersheba (right) on the fringe of the Negev desert region.

the 7th century, and the population became strongly Muslim. During the Middle Ages the Church of the Holy Sepulcher was destroyed, and the Christian states of western Europe launched the Crusades to the Holy Land. The Crusaders never succeeded in recapturing Palestine from the Muslims. In the early 16th century the Ottoman Turks conquered Palestine. The area remained within the Ottoman Empire until World War I. In 1917–1918 the British General Sir Edmund H. H. Allenby defeated the Turks, and Britain gained control of Palestine.

At the close of World War I the League of Nations declared Palestine a British mandate. Government by the British was largely confined to that part of Palestine west of the Jordan River. To the east, the region known as Transjordan was administered by the British through the Arab leader Emir Abdullah ibn-Hussein.

The Zionist movement for the establishment of a national Jewish homeland in Palestine began in the 1890's. In 1917 the Zionist movement was recognized by the British in the Balfour Declaration. In the years after 1917 the Jewish population in Palestine rose steadily through immigration. In 1925 there were about 108,000 Jews in the region, but by 1948, after partitioning, there were about 700,000 Jews.

The Zionist movement was contrary to the desires of the Arabs, who wanted an independent Arab state in Palestine. Clashes between the two groups became more and more common as Jewish immigration increased. With the rise of Hitler and anti-Semitism in Germany, Jews came to Palestine in even greater numbers. The Arabs objected to this increase and to the amount of land purchased by Jews in Palestine. Eventually, in 1939, the British restricted Jewish immigration, but immigrants were smuggled into Palestine in defiance of the British.

The British seized many of the immigrants who entered the country illegally and placed them in detention camps in other British-ruled Mediterranean areas. The largest of the camps was located on the island of Cyprus. The imprisonment of the immigrants attracted worldwide attention. Groups to resist British policy were formed by both the Jews and the Arabs, and the British were forced to increase the number of troops stationed in the area. The Jewish community developed its own government and did much to develop the country. The Arab population had no self-governing organization and depended directly on the British for public services. Arabic, Hebrew, and

Rapho Guillumette Pictures

Lake Tiberias, the Sea of Galilee, has many biblical associations. The sites along its banks include the domed Tombs of Rabbi Meir Baal Hanes and the town of Tiberias.

English were all official languages under the British mandate.

In 1946 complete independence was granted to Transjordan. The following year Great Britain asked the United Nations to consider the Palestine question. The United Nations recommended that Palestine be divided into two small countries, one Arab and one Jewish. The city of Jerusalem was to be declared an international zone under the United Nations. The Arabs turned the proposition down, however, and the Jews objected to several details. In May 1948 the British withdrew from the area, and Israel declared its independence. The neighboring states of Syria, Lebanon, Egypt,

Jordan, and Iraq joined the Arabs of Palestine to protest. As members of the Arab League, they began a series of attacks upon the Jewish community, but their forces were defeated by the Israelis. The United Nations continued in its efforts to mediate the dispute. In the fall of 1948 the UN mediator Count Folke Bernadotte was assassinated by terrorists. In 1949 his successor, Ralph Bunche, succeeded in arranging an armistice between the Arabs and the Jews. He received the Nobel Peace Prize for his work.

Palestine was divided between the Arabs and Jews according to the land each held when the war ended. Israel controlled the north Jordan Valley, Galilee, the Plain of Esdraelon, the coastal strip, and a large part of the Negev. Most of the Arab population of these areas fled to eastern Palestine or other Arab countries. The hill regions of Samaria and Judea were occupied by Arab Jordan and in 1950 were made part of that kingdom. Jerusalem was divided between Israel and Jordan.

The dispute over Palestine has continued. The Arab League united against Israel. There have been frequent raids and armed fighting along Israeli borders. Israel and the neighboring Arab countries disagree on several issues. Jordan, Syria, and Lebanon depend on irrigation for agriculture, as does Israel. The Arab countries, however, have been unwilling to co-operate in any water-conservation project involving Israel. Also, the condition of thousands of unsettled Arab refugees from Palestine, who are living in detention camps, has added to the dispute. Every proposed solution to the refugee problem has met with failure. Syria and Jordan have refused to allow survey teams to mark the boundaries of their countries with Israel. The final border is still not set. The Arab countries have no trade relations with Israel.

In November 1956, Israel fought in a brief war with Egypt. Israel captured the territory known as the Gaza Strip, which both Egypt and Israel claim. Israel also took possession of a strip of land near the Gulf of Aqaba. In March 1957, Israeli troops withdrew from the territory after United Nations troops moved in.

In June 1967 war broke out again after Egypt blockaded the Gulf of Aqaba. Israeli forces drove into Egyptian, Jordanian, and Syrian territory, causing huge Arab losses. After several days of fighting the United Nations negotiated a cease-fire and began meetings to resolve Arab-Israeli differences.

PALESTRINA (păl'ŭ strē'nä), **GIOVANNI** (jō-vän'nē) **PIERLUIGI** (pyĕr'lōō ē'jē) **DA** (dä) (1525?–1594), was an Italian composer of church music. He took his name from his birthplace, the town of Palestrina, Italy, and added it to his family name of Pierluigi.

At about the age of 12, Palestrina is known to have been a choirboy at the Santa Maria Maggiore in Rome where he probably studied music and religion. In 1544, he was organist and choirmaster at the cathedral in his native town. After his bishop became Pope, Palestrina was made choirmaster (1551) of the Julian Chapel at the Vatican. This was the first of his many papal appointments. He also served as a singer and composer for the pontifical choir and as the choir director at St. John Lateran and Santa Maria Maggiore. From 1571 until his death, Palestrina again directed the choir at the Julian Chapel.

All of Palestrina's compositions were written for the human voice without accompaniment. He produced creative work of a high standard in both secular and church music, but he is best known for the latter. He wrote at least 105 masses and much other liturgical music in many different styles and forms. He was a master of the use of counterpoint in his musical compositions. In his secular work, Palestrina's madrigals are considered equal to the best of his contemporaries.

PALISSY (pä lē sē'), **BERNARD** (bĕr när') (1510?–1589), was a French potter, natural scientist, and writer. He was born in Agen and served an apprenticeship in glass painting. After traveling around France he settled at Saintes in about 1540 where he worked as a surveyor and began experimenting in ceramics.

After working for nearly 16 years, Palissy finally produced a pure white enamel. Using this as a background, he created original ceramic designs known as *rustiques figulines*, which were based on his interest in nature. These pottery wares were molded with natural objects such as shells, snakes, leaves, rocks, and moss. They were notable for their fine colored glazes. Palissy's fame and wealth grew, and he was employed by the Constable de Montmorency to work at his chateau. In about 1556, the queen, Catherine de'Medici, summoned him to make a grotto at the palace of the Tuileries.

Unfortunately, since Palissy was a Huguenot, he suffered at various times from religious persecution, especially at the end of his life. He ceased his ceramic work to write and to lecture. Palissy's book *Discours Admirables* (1580) covers the subjects of these lectures and tells about his work in agronomy, chemistry, natural history, and the experimental method in science. Palissy died while a prisoner.

PALM (*päm*) is any plant of the family Palmae. It is of great economic importance, ranking second to the grasses. The fruit and stems of the palm provide food, and the leaves, branches, and trunks furnish wood, cane, thatch, and twine. From the bark and leaves, rugs, paper and cloth are made. The sap of some palms is made into sugar, wine, or honey. Wax, oil, tannin, and resin, are important commercial products. Of the palms, the most useful are probably the coconut, date, and sago. (See Co-CONUT PALM; DATE; SAGO.)

Most palms have straight, slender, unbranching trunks with a cluster of leaves at the top. Others have branching stems, and at least one is a trailing vine. They vary in size from a few inches to 200 feet tall. The leaves are either fan-shaped or feather-shaped, often covered with hair or spines and sometimes wax. The size of the leaf may be a few inches to more than 50 feet long. The flowers are borne in clusters near the tops of the plants. They are

The betel nut palm is cultivated in tropical Asia for its nuts.

Courtesy United Fruit Company

E. Aubert de la Rue

The Doum palm is an interesting variety of palm that grows in Tanzania, Africa.

small and usually greenish. The fruit may be the size of a bean or as large as a football, as in the case of the coconut. It may be soft and fleshy like a date, or it may have a woody covering. Palms are characterized botanically by trunks without "growth rings" and with relatively primitive flowers and seeds. The latter has only one seed leaf.

There are thought to be about 210 genera of palm with probably between 3,000 and 4,000 species. These are mostly tropical and are found in South America, Asia, Africa, Europe, the tropical islands of the Pacific Ocean, and the southern United States.

Some species are native to the United States. The stately royal palm occurs in Florida and is often used to border roads and boulevards. It is crowned with graceful feathery leaves more then ten feet long. In California and Arizona the Washington palm grows wild. The palmettos, or fan palms, which have short trunks, grow abundantly along the Gulf and Atlantic Coasts as far north as the Carolinas.

PAMPAS (*păm'păz*), **ARGENTINA,** is a vast plain that forms one of the major regions of that country. It lies east of the Andean foothills and south of Argentina's dry, scrub Chaco region. The word *pampas* comes from a Quechua Indian word meaning "plains". In a more general sense it is applied to an even greater treeless expanse that extends in Paraguay, Uruguay, and even parts of southern Brazil.

The northern end of this great plain lies in the interior of the South American continent.

In the south it ends in a cliffed coast. The pampas slopes gradually upward from southeast to northwest where it reaches elevations of more than 1,500 feet. The Argentine pampas has an area of almost 300,000 square miles. The deep, fertile soils of the region have been deposited by wind or by streams draining the eastern slopes of the Andes.

Locator map of the Pampas.

ing hunters and gatherers, unlike the farmers of the Incan domain in the central Andean highlands. They did little farming and had few domestic animals. The Spaniards in the 16th century introduced many totally new and different domesticated plants (wheat, oats, vegetables, fruits) and animals (horses, cattle, sheep, goats, pigs, chickens). Escaped cattle

Rene Burri—Magnum

Gauchos on the Argentine pampas use horse-breaking techniques similar to those of the U.S. cowboys.

The pampas is divided into two distinct climatic zones. The western portion of the pampas is known as the dry pampas. The moister eastern portion is called the humid pampas and is the most productive farming area of the entire country.

The original vegetation of much of the dry and humid pampas is thought to have been *monte*, a covering of low scrubby trees and coarse grasses. When the Spaniards first arrived in what is now Argentina in the early 1500's they saw the Indians burning the *monte* for purposes of hunting game and for warfare. The result of prolonged burnings, plus a possible reduction in rainfall over the past 1,000 to 2,000 years, was a decrease in the woody vegetation and an expansion of grasses.

The settlement of the pampas provides an excellent example of how man can change a landscape when he is motivated.

The original Indian inhabitants were wander-

and horses multiplied rapidly on the open grasslands, and the Indians learned how to ride horseback and even used their new skills to advantage in their battles with the Spaniards.

For about 300 years, Spanish settlement was concentrated in a small area surrounding Buenos Aires. The principal activity was extensive cattle raising, and income came chiefly from the sale of hides, meat, and tallow. It was the mestizo gauchos who herded the cattle and fought with the Indians in the no-man's-land beyond the area settled by the Spaniards.

In the mid-19th century long due changes in the pampas began to take place. There were several reasons for this: (1) the Indian tribes were pushed back and subdued in the campaigns of 1879–1884; (2) government sponsored immigration beginning in the 1860's provided new settlers who introduced new ideas for developing the land; (3) the growth of railways; and (4) the use of refrigerated ships beginning around 1875 and the development of a deep-water port at Buenos Aires.

Three successive waves of settlers pushed out on the heels of the border patrols into former Indian-dominated country. First the sheep ranchers dominated the pampas, followed by the cattle ranchers. Cattlemen introduced alfalfa, which increased the grazing capacity of

way for it to become one of the most productive farming areas in the world.

Most of the products of the pampas were channeled through the port of Buenos Aires, causing that city to grow into a great metropolis. About one-third of all Argentines now live in greater Buenos Aires, which has become a great Latin-American industrial center.

Rene Burri—Magnum

The flat grassy plains of the Argentine pampas have long been important as a livestock-raising region.

Sergio Larrain—Magnum

Through land reforms the pampas has become important for crop growing as well as livestock raising.

the lands by up to six times. The next group on the pampas were the farmers, who were strongly opposed by the cattlemen. Crop-growing began on a large scale in the farming colonies established around the Santa Fe area. The Argentine corn belt developed with the city of Rosario as its center.

The population of the pampas is dominated by peoples of European background. Practically all of the original peoples were eliminated or pushed back into fringe areas. The few Negroes who were brought in as slaves have long since blended into the general population. The population is heavily European in blood and in outlook. The countries that supplied most of the immigrants were Italy and Spain. It is important to note that the majority of these newcomers were, by tradition, small farmers who had little in common with the Argentine ranchers operating huge estates. These farmers first plowed the humid pampas and opened the

Cattle raising still predominates in the dry pampas to the west, but the eastern humid pampas—the economic and cultural heartland of Argentina—produces wheat, alfalfa, corn, and flax. Farmers near the urban centers specialize in fruit and vegetable production. With a large literate population and close economic and cultural ties with the rest of the world, agricultural methods on much of the pampas have been kept up-to-date. (See ARGENTINA.)

PAN (*păn*) was the ancient Greek god of huntsmen, shepherds, and later of all nature. Woods, fields, and flocks belonged to him. The Greeks believed that he stayed on earth, roaming through the mountains and valleys, playing gaily on his flute made of reeds.

Pan was generally pictured in Greek art with legs and feet like those of a goat. His upper body and face were manlike, but he had a goat's horns and ears. Pan was said to often chase

Pan had horns and the legs and ears of a goat.

after the nymphs, though they all thought him ugly and ran away.

One story tells how Pan pursued a nymph named Syrinx. After a long chase, she came to a river bank and could run no farther. Desperate, she prayed for help. The goddess Artemis heard her prayer and changed her into a bundle of reeds. Pan stood sadly, looking at the reeds and sighing, when he heard a beautiful murmuring sound as the wind blew through them. Cutting seven of the reeds in different lengths, he fastened them into the first shepherd's pipe, or syrinx. Pan learned to play so well on his pipe that once he entered a contest against Apollo, the god of music. (See MIDAS.)

Pan was considered the cause of the sudden, unreasoning terror that occurs sometimes in man and beast. This terror, or panic, was named after him.

PANAMA (păn′ŭ mä′), **CENTRAL AMERICA,** is a republic located on the narrow isthmus that connects the continents of North and South America. It is bordered on the west by Costa Rica and on the east by Colombia. The Caribbean Sea lies to the north and the Pacific Ocean to the south. Cutting across its central section is the famous Panama Canal. The official name of the country is *Republica de Panama* (Republic of Panama).

Panama extends about 480 miles in length, and varies from about 30 to 120 miles in width. Most of the economic, social, and political activities, however, are concentrated within a few miles of the canal. This focus of international trade routes makes Panama one of the great crossroads of the world.

Panama is an Indian word, but its original meaning is uncertain. It may have meant "plenty of fish" or "many butterflies," or it may have been a type of hardwood tree.

Land and Climate

A rugged backbone of hills and mountains extends the full length of the country. To the west, the Sierra de Chiriqui is a continuation of the mountains of Costa Rica. It includes the volcano Chiriqui (11,411 feet), the highest peak in Panama. Elevations are lower in central Panama and do not exceed 662 feet at the Panama Canal. East of the canal the mountains are higher again, reaching more than 6,000 feet near the Colombian border. Another highland area is the Azuero Peninsula, which extends southward into the Pacific between the Gulf of Chiriqui and the Gulf of Panama.

The climate of Panama is generally warm and humid. Temperatures average nearly 80

FACTS ABOUT PANAMA

CAPITAL: Panama city. NATIONAL ANTHEM: *Himno National de Panama* ("National Anthem of Panama").

AREA: 29,208 square miles (about the size of South Carolina); 60 percent highlands, 40 percent lowlands; 2,178 square miles of cultivated land.

POPULATION: 1,075,541 (1960); 1,243,860 (1965 estimate); 42.6 persons per square mile; 41.5 percent urban, 58.5 percent rural.

CHIEF LANGUAGE: Spanish.

CHIEF RELIGION: Roman Catholic.

LITERACY: About 78 percent over 10 years of age can read and write.

MOUNTAIN RANGES: Serrania del Darien, Cordillera de San Blas, Sierra de Chiriqui.

HIGHEST PEAK: Chiriqui (11,411 feet).

LARGEST LAKES: Gatun, Madden.

MOST IMPORTANT RIVERS: Chagres, Chepo, Tuira.

FORM OF GOVERNMENT: Republic.

HEAD OF GOVERNMENT AND CHIEF OF STATE: President.

LEGISLATURE: National Assembly.

VOTING QUALIFICATIONS: Citizens over 21 years of age may vote.

POLITICAL DIVISIONS: 9 provinces.

CHIEF CITIES: (1966 estimates) Panama (343,700), Colon (63,500).

CHIEF MANUFACTURED AND MINED PRODUCTS: Beverages, clothing and footwear, food processing, furniture, lumber, nonmetallic minerals, refined petroleum, tobacco.

CHIEF AGRICULTURAL PRODUCTS: *Crops,* bananas, beans, cacao, coconuts, corn, rice, sugarcane, tobacco, yams; *Livestock,* cattle, horses, swine.

FLAG: Colors are red, white, and blue (See FLAG, *plate 7*).

CURRENCY: Balboa; one balboa equals one U.S. dollar.

degrees Fahrenheit in the lowlands, and there is little seasonal change. Rainfall is especially heavy on the Caribbean side of the country, averaging 128 inches each year at Colon and even more on windward mountain slopes. The Pacific side receives less rain, and a distinct dry season extends from December to April.

About three-fourths of the republic is forested. A dense forest of evergreen broadleaf trees covers most of the Caribbean side. Valuable timber species include mahogany, cedar, and dyewoods. The drier Pacific side is covered by semi-deciduous forest, with patches of savanna grasslands on the coastal plains. A thick growth of mangrove forest lines the swampy areas along the Caribbean and Pacific shores.

Hundreds of rivers flow from the mountains to the coasts, but most are small. One of the most important is the Rio Chagres, which has been dammed to form Madden and Gatun lakes. It supplies hydroelectricity and much of the water used to operate the Panama Canal. Other important rivers are the Chepo and Turia.

Animal life is abundant. Included are pumas, deer, porcupines, monkeys, sloths, tapirs, and anteaters. Among the reptiles are crocodiles, lizards, snakes, and turtles. Birds include her-

ons, parrots, and macaws. Fish abound in the rivers and the neighboring oceans.

People

More than 85 percent of the Panamanian people live on the Pacific side, especially near the canal and on the coastal lowlands westward to the Costa Rican border. About 42 percent of the population is urban. Panama city is the capital and largest urban center, with more than 343,700 inhabitants. (See PANAMA, PANAMA). Colon, the next largest city, has about 63,500 people. Other important towns include David and La Chorrera.

The isthmus was first occupied by tribes of Indians, who were later conquered by the Spaniards. Today more than half of the Panamanians are *mestizos*, people of mixed Spanish and Indian ancestry. Tribal Indians form less than 10 percent of the total population. People of unmixed European ancestry are slightly more numerous and reside mostly in the larger cities.

Negro slaves were brought in during the 16th century, and free Negroes from the West Indies came after 1850 to work in building the railroad and canal. Their descendants form about 13 percent of the total population. United States citizens live and work chiefly in the Canal Zone, while Orientals engage in commerce related to the canal. About 93 percent of the Panamanians are Roman Catholic, but complete freedom of religion is guaranteed by the constitution.

Spanish is the official language and is spoken by nearly everyone, but English is also widely used. Other languages include French, Italian, and Chinese. Indians in remote areas speak their native dialects.

Central Panama has long been exposed to cultural influences from all over the world. In Panama city and Colon life is similar to that in large cities of most other countries. Rural areas are often considered to be more truly Panamanian. There, Spanish culture flourishes, with African and Indian influences.

Traditional costumes include the beautiful *pollera*, worn by women. It consists of a voluminous embroidered skirt and a blouse of exquisite lace. The *montuno* is a long, straight blouse worn by men that almost covers their

of revenue is the annual payment of $1,930,000 by the United States for rental of the Canal Zone. A large volume of business is also done by Panamanian merchants who sell imported and domestic goods to buyers in the zone. (See PANAMA CANAL.) A free trade zone at Colon is still another source of income and employment.

Agriculture supports more than half of the labor force. Yet, less than 25 percent of Panama's area is in farms, the rest being mostly mountain, forest, and swamp. Almost two-thirds of the farmers have no title to the land they cultivate. Government property is extensive, as are some private estates.

Farmland is devoted largely to pasture, and only about 7 percent is in crops. Cattle total more than 800,000 head. Most are beef animals, but some dairying has developed near the larger cities. Basic food crops include rice,

Farmers cultivate fertile valleys in the Chiriqui Highlands of western Panama (left). Along Colon's promenade, Paseo Centenario, stands the city's noted statue of Columbus (left center). Panama City workers load bananas (right center), a chief Panamanian export. Choco Indians (right) make their way through a banana grove.

(Left) Tim Kantor from Rapho Guillumette Pictures, (left center) Ewing Galloway, (right center) Carl Frank—Photo Researchers, Inc., (right) Wide World

knee-length trousers. Traditional costumes now appear mostly during special celebrations, or fiestas. The largest and most famous fiesta is the pre-Lenten *Carnaval* in Panama city.

Economy

The economic life of Panama centers around the canal. One of the republic's largest sources

corn, and beans. Tobacco, fruit, sugarcane, and vegetables are also grown.

The principal commercial crops are bananas, coffee, sugarcane, and cacao. About 7,800,000 stems of bananas were exported in 1964, mostly from plantations in western Panama near the Caribbean and Pacific coasts. Coffee is harvested on many small farms in the western highlands. Sugar production has been increasing, but cacao production has declined.

The industrial census of 1964 reported 1,370 manufacturing establishments, most of them engaged in food processing. Other manufactures include cigarettes, clothing, furniture, lumber, clay products, and cement. A large refinery near Colon processes crude petroleum imported from Venezuela.

Fishing is well-developed, and shrimp exports bring considerable income to the country. Tourism, forestry, and mining are also important. Minerals that have been produced in commercial quantities include gold, copper, manganese, salt, stone, clay, and sand.

Panama's foreign trade is primarily with the United States, western Europe, and Japan. Since establishment of the refinery at Colon in 1961, petroleum products have rivaled bananas as the country's leading export. Shrimp, coffee, sugar, and cacao are other important exports. Major imports include machinery, food products, chemicals, and crude petroleum.

Parks provide play areas in Panama City. Palm trees and tiled roofs are prominent.
Paul Almasy

The republic is served by many air and steamship lines. Tocumen Airport, near Panama city, is a center for international air traffic. Smaller airports are served by four national airlines. There are several small seaports in western Panama, but most of the country's trade is through the Canal Zone ports of Balboa and Cristobal. The merchant fleet of Panama, mostly foreign-owned, is among the largest in the world.

Land transportation is best developed in central Panama but is being expanded in other areas. The road system totals about 3,900 miles, of which about 1,000 miles are improved. The Pan-American Highway links Panama with the other Central American countries. (See PAN-AMERICAN HIGHWAY.) Three isolated railroad lines total 152 miles. The most important one connects Panama city with Colon. Navigable waterways include the 51-mile Panama Canal and about 125 miles of rivers.

Education and Government

Education in Panama is free and compulsory for children between ages 7 and 15. In addition to primary and secondary schools, there are craft, trade, and professional schools. The principal institution of higher education is the National University of Panama, which occupies a new campus near Panama city. Altogether the country has about 1,800 schools, with an enrollment of about 265,000 students.

Panama is governed under the constitution of 1946, which provides for freedom of speech, religion, and assembly. The government is composed of executive, legislative, and judicial branches, and all Panamanians 21 years of age and over have the right to vote.

The president is elected by popular ballot for a four-year term and cannot be re-elected within eight years after his first term expires. Two vice-presidents are elected for four-year terms, and a cabinet of seven ministers is appointed by the president. Governors of Panama's nine provinces, and all city mayors, are also appointed by the president. The legislature is a one-house National Assembly.

The government was controlled from 1952 to 1960 by the National Patriotic Coalition Party of Colonel Jose Antonio Remon. In 1960 Roberto Chiari became president. In 1964 he was succeeded by Marco A. Robles. Arnulfo Arias was elected as Robles' successor in October 1968, but he was overthrown immediately after inauguration by a military coup. Colonel Jose M. Pinilla became provisional president.

History

The original Indians of Panama were mostly of the Cuna, Guaymi, and Choco groups. European influence began in 1501, when Rodrigo de Bastidas sailed along the north coast of Panama. The following year Christopher Columbus explored the entire Caribbean coast of Central

America, claiming the land for Spain. In 1513 Vasco Nunez de Balboa discovered the Pacific Ocean, after a difficult march across the isthmus.

Francisco Pizarro sailed from Panama in his conquest of Peru, and Panama soon became a center of great wealth and trade. Treasures arriving from the west coast of South America were transported across the isthmus from Panama city on the Pacific side to Porto Bello or Nombre de Dios on the Caribbean. From there they were carried by Spanish galleons to Europe. Attacks by pirates such as the famous Francis Drake and Henry Morgan were frequent, but the trade continued.

Panama remained under Spanish control until 1821, when it joined the newly independent confederation of Gran Colombia. From then until 1903 it remained part of Colombia, except during brief periods of revolt.

The need for improved transportation across the isthmus became evident at an early date. The first transcontinental railroad, built between Panama city and Colon, was opened in 1855.

By the late 19th century a number of countries became interested in the construction of an interoceanic canal. When the United States failed to secure the desired treaty with Colombia, it gave assistance to a bloodless revolution that erupted in Panama. Independence was declared in 1903, and the United States obtained the rights to construct the canal. The first president of the new republic was Manuel Amador Guerrero.

Panama entered World War II in December 1941 against Germany, Italy, and Japan. Since the war, a continuing conflict has developed with the United States over the status of the Canal Zone. Although the zone is leased permanently to the United States, Panama has sought to establish greater sovereignty over the zone and to obtain a greater share of revenues from the canal. The Panamanian flag was flown in the zone beside the United States flag for the first time in 1960, but additional demands resulted in the outbreak of riots in 1964. In late 1964 U.S. President Lyndon B. Johnson proposed that a new canal agreement be negotiated.

PANAMA, PANAMA, is the capital and largest city of the republic. It borders the Bay of Panama, near the Pacific entrance to the Panama Canal, and it is served by the Canal Zone port of Balboa. Attractions include the National Palace, the Presidential Palace, the Palace of Justice, the ruins of Old Panama, historic churches, the National Musuem, and the University of Panama.

The most important activities center around government and commerce, but there are also many small industries. Products include foods, beverages, shoes, clothing, clay and cement products, lumber, and furniture.

Old Panama was a tiny fishing village until established as a seat of government in 1519. It flourished on trade between Spain and western South America, becoming one of the great Spanish colonial cities. In 1671 it was destroyed by the pirate Henry Morgan.

The new city of Panama was founded nearby in 1673. It grew slowly until selected as the national capital in 1903. The population is 343,700 (1966 estimate).

PANAMA CANAL, CENTRAL AMERICA, is a great international waterway connecting the Atlantic and Pacific oceans through the Isthmus of Panama. It lies entirely within the Canal Zone, which is controlled by the United States. The zone is bordered on the east and west by the Republic of Panama.

The canal is located near the geographical center of the Western Hemisphere and is a vital link in the world's ocean trade routes. About 11,000 ships pass through its locks each year. It saves millions of dollars in shipping costs by reducing the distances that goods must travel by sea.

Land Features of the Canal Zone

The Canal Zone extends about five miles on either side of the canal and includes 557 square miles of land and water. It is generally hilly to mountainous, with little level land. Elevations range from sea level to more than 1,200 feet. The climate is warm and humid, and forests cover much of the land.

The canal itself is almost 51 miles long and

at least 300 feet wide in the channels, with a minimum depth of 39 feet. Because of the alignment and structure of the isthmus, the canal was built in a northwest-southeast direction. This put the Atlantic entrance 27 miles farther west than the Pacific entrance.

Lush, tropical vegetation flanks the Panama Canal's Pedro Miguel Locks. These locks raise northbound ships 31 feet from Miraflores Lake to the Gaillard Cut.

Canal installations include three sets of twin locks; each lock is about 110 feet wide and 1,000 feet long. Ships entering from the Atlantic are raised 85 feet in three steps at the Gatun Locks. They then cross Gatun Lake for 23 miles and pass the Continental Divide in the 8-mile Gaillard Cut. Farther on they are lowered 85 feet in three steps to the level of the Pacific Ocean. One step is at the Pedro Miguel Locks, and two are at Miraflores Locks. Dams on the Chagres River create Madden Lake reservoir and the much larger Gatun Lake.

Trade and Transportation

Cargo from all over the world passes through the canal, but more than half of the tonnage moves to or from the United States. Other areas sending large volumes of trade through the canal are eastern Asia, western South America, and western Europe. By the mid-1960's about 350,000 ships, carrying nearly 1½ billion tons of cargo, had used the canal.

Modern port facilities have been constructed at Cristobal on the Atlantic side and at Balboa on the Pacific. Land transportation is also well-developed. The Panama Railroad runs alongside the canal for 47 miles, and there are a number of paved roads. The Inter-American Highway crosses the canal near Panama city over a one-mile-long bridge. There are also several airfields for defense purposes.

Canal Zone Organization

Many of the residents are U.S. citizens, with employment provided by the Canal Zone Government, the Panama Canal Company, and the U.S. armed forces. In addition, many Panamanians are employed and reside either in the zone or nearby in Panama. Cities of the zone are small. They include Balboa, Rainbow City, Gamboa, and Paraiso—all with populations of more than 3,000. Balboa Heights is the administrative center.

Agriculture, industry, mining, or commercial activities not directly related to canal operations are prohibited within the zone. Several enterprises, however, have developed as part of the general canal functions.

Life in the zone is in many ways similar to that in the United States. English is the chief language, although Spanish is also spoken. The unit of currency is the U.S. dollar. Public education in the zone extends from kindergarten through college and is based on U.S. standards. The school system is divided into two parts. One part is organized for students having U.S. citizenship, the other for noncitizens.

The Canal Zone Government administers services normally provided by state and local governments. The governor of the zone is appointed by the president of the United States, with approval by the Senate. The governor also serves as president of the Panama Canal Company, which administers the business affairs of the zone. Management of the company is by a 13-member board of directors, appointed by the secretary of the Army.

The Canal Zone Government and the Panama

Canal Company are supervised by the president of the United States, who delegates his authority to the secretary of the Army.

History

The idea of a canal across the isthmus occurred to early explorers, and in the early 1500's the king of Spain ordered studies to be undertaken. For the next several centuries, the world's principal maritime countries considered various plans and canal routes. Spain was especially interested during the colonial period, when the isthmus was an obstacle to the flow of treasure from Peru. The California Gold Rush stirred U.S. interest after 1849. The first actual digging, however, was begun by the French.

An international congress was held in Paris, France, in 1879 to consider plans for canal construction. The one chosen was that of the French engineer, Ferdinand de Lesseps, successful builder of the Suez Canal. A company was formed, and rights were obtained from the Republic of Colombia to build a canal across its province of Panama. Digging began in 1881. The effort failed, however, because of unhealthful living conditions in the area and the mismanagement of funds. More than 22,000 canal workers died within eight years, mostly from disease.

The United States became vitally interested in canal projects during the Spanish-American War of 1898. Negotiations with Colombia, however, were unsuccessful. In 1902 the U.S. Congress passed the Spooner Act, the basic law for construction of the Panama Canal. It authorized purchase of the French equipment and the Panama Railroad for $40,000,000. Then a revolution broke out in Panama, and independence from Colombia was declared in 1903. Dealing directly with Panama, the United States acquired permanent use of the Canal Zone for a payment of $10,000,000 plus an annual rental charge.

Construction of the Panama Canal was directed primarily by John F. Stevens and George W. Goethals. It was one of the greatest engineering achievements in history. As many as 65,000 men were employed at one time, and more than 200,000,000 cubic yards of rock and dirt were moved. Sanitary measures were taken that made the Canal Zone one of the most healthful places in the tropics. The sailing distance from New York City, N.Y., to San Francisco, Calif., was reduced by almost 8,000 miles. The waterway was opened August 15, 1914, after a net construction cost of $380 million.

By 1965 the canal was being operated at full capacity, and some ships were too large to pass through its locks. Improvements were being made to the canal, and alternate canal routes were again considered in the area from Mexico to Colombia, including Panama.

Through the 1950's and 1960's, Panama demanded more concessions from the United States for its zone privileges. In 1955 the United States raised the annual payment to Panama to $1,930,000. In 1964 the United States permitted the Panamanian flag to be flown in the zone alongside the U.S. flag. Nevertheless, Panamanians rioted in 1964 over U.S. policy in the zone, and riots continued to occur in 1965 and 1966. (See PANAMA, CENTRAL AMERICA.) The Canal Zone population in 1960 was 42,122.

PAN-AMERICAN HIGHWAY is a road system that connects the capitals and major cities of South and Central America and is linked to the road systems of the United States and Canada. By the mid-1960's it was possible for a traveller to go by automobile all the way from Fairbanks, Alaska, to within a few hundred miles of the Colombian border. At that point a ferry is used to connect the Central and South American portions of the highway. The Central American part of the highway is also called the Inter-American Highway. The Pan-American Highway has helped the economies of the countries through which it passes and has been valuable to travellers and tourists.

The idea for building a Pan-American Highway goes back more than a hundred years. In one of the earliest moves toward inter-American travel, the First International Conference of American States in 1889 began a project for building a Pan-American Railway. The railroad was never built, but at the Fifth International Congress in 1923 a proposal was made to study the possibilities of a Pan-American Highway. In 1925 the Pan-American Highway Congress was established as a permanent institution. The congress is now a part of the Organization of American States. Great progress on the highway was made in the 1930's and by the early 1940's more than 60 percent was completed.

The Pan-American Highway is designed to provide a continuous roadway through Central and South America that is linked to the U.S. highway system.

World War II spurred the road-building activity, and by the end of the war only some of the toughest sections remained to be completed. These sections were finished one by one through the 1950's and early 1960's and by 1963 only one gap needed to be closed to connect a single highway system through Central and South America. This gap was the Darien region on the Panama-Colombia border. It was estimated that a road through this 500-mile-long region of jungle would be completed by 1970.

The Pan-American Highway is really a number of roads. The country using the highway decides upon the additional roads within its boundaries that will make up part of the total highway system. The United States has given considerable financial aid to those countries that could not otherwise afford road building. United States finances and engineers are involved in the planning of the road through the Darien region.

Not all of the Pan-American Highway is paved, and in some places it is not passable in bad weather. Nevertheless, a trip on the Pan-American Highway covering the entire road network would take a traveller over some 28,000 miles of road. The trip would be varied and interesting. The traveller would pass through the deserts of northern Mexico and the tropical rain forests in Central America. He would go through passes 16,000 feet high in the Andes Mountains of Peru, through the deserts and green valleys of Chile, and across the vast Argentine pampas. He would also visit great

cities such as Mexico City; Guatemala City; Santiago, Chile; Montevideo, Uruguay; Buenos Aires, Argentina; and Rio de Janeiro, Brazil.

The highway has opened up new pioneer areas and has assured more people of access to markets for their products. Most of the intercountry traffic on the highway, however, has been limited to tourists and occasional trucks. Each country uses the highway mostly for commerce only within its own boundaries because of the tariff barriers between many of the countries.

PANCREAS (păng′ krē ŭs) is a gland found in most animals with backbones. In the human being it is six to seven inches in length. It lies

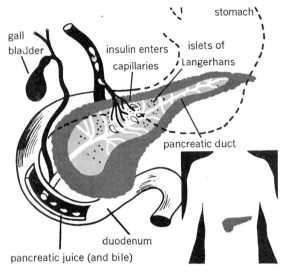

Pancreatic juice passes through the pancreatic duct into the intestine. The islets of Langerhans secrete insulin directly into the bloodstream to aid in using sugar.

against the stomach with its broad end, or head, in the curve of the duodenum, the first part of the small intestine. The pancreas aids in the digestion of foods, and it produces the vital hormone insulin.

When partly digested food enters the duodenum the pancreas pours in its secretions. These are trypsin to complete the digestion of proteins; amylase to digest starches and sugars; and lipase to digest fats. (See DIGESTION AND DIGESTIVE SYSTEM.)

The pancreas has nests of tiny cells scattered throughout. They are called islets (small islands) of Langerhans, named after the man who first described them. They produce the important hormone insulin. They are ductless glands emptying straight into the blood. (See GLAND.)

It is possible to live without the pancreas if necessary. The intestine can take over the digestive process, and insulin can be given by injection.

PANDA (pan' da) is either of two species of mammals of the family Procyonidae, the same family to which raccoons belong. The more familiar of the two is the giant panda (*Ailuropoda melanoleuca*). This animal may reach a length of about five feet and weigh between

240 and 275 pounds. It resembles a bear in shape because of its short legs and tail, small rounded ears, large paws, and massive head. The thick fur is usually white on the head and back, with black legs, ears, and eye patches and a band of black extending from the forelegs across the shoulders.

The giant panda generally lives alone in the high mountain forests of Szechwan, Shenshan, and Kansu provinces of China. Although it can climb when in danger, the panda remains mostly on the ground, finding shelter in caves and hollow trees.

Giant pandas feed mainly on bamboo shoots and roots, but occasionally they eat other plants such as crocuses, irises, and grasses. Although they are classified as carnivorous mammals, they seldom eat meat.

The giant panda first became known to Europeans in 1869 when a French missionary, Pere David, received two of the animals from hunters in China. Little more was heard about the animal until Theodore, Jr., and Kermit Roosevelt brought a dead one to the United States in 1929. The first live giant panda was brought to the United States in 1937 by Ruth Harkness. It lived in the Brookfield Zoo in Chicago, Illinois, for 16 months. Since then, about a dozen giant pandas have been brought to other zoos. Because the home of giant pandas lies only within Communist-controlled areas, no new specimens are being added to Western zoos, so these animals are rapidly disappearing. They are also becoming rare in the wild. One of the main reasons is probably because only one cub is born each year.

The other species of panda is known as the lesser panda (*Ailurus fulgens*). This animal looks a bit like a raccoon, with a head and body length of only about two feet and a bushy, lightly ringed tail about 18 inches long. The soft, thick fur shades from deep chestnut brown to rust, with white markings around the eyes, muzzle, and ears. There are scent glands beneath the tail from which the animal can give off a musky odor when excited.

Lesser pandas are found in northern Burma, Sikkim, and Nepal as well as the areas inhabited by the giant pandas. They are most

The giant panda (a cub shown at left) is native to China's mainland. Only a few are in captivity.

International News Photos

active at night. They prefer to spend the day curled up asleep in a tree.

Lesser pandas feed mainly on fruits and vegetables such as bamboo, acorns, and grasses. Occasionally, they eat eggs, small birds, or mice. Usually only one or two young are born per year. These animals generally live and travel in small family groups.

PANDORA (*păn dŏr′ ä*) was the first woman in the world, according to Greek mythology. Zeus, king of the gods, was angry because Prometheus had given the blessing of fire to men. (See PROMETHEUS.) Determined to balance this good, Zeus created Pandora to bring trouble to men. Each of the gods gave Pandora a gift; they included beauty, music, charm, and gracefulness. That is why she was called Pandora, or "having all gifts."

When Pandora opened her box, all the evils and miseries of mankind escaped.

Pandora was taken to the home of Epimetheus, a Titan, or giant, who had befriended man. He was the brother of Prometheus. At once Epimetheus fell in love with Pandora. Forgetting his brother's warning that only harm could come if he accepted a gift from the gods, Epimetheus decided to marry her.

When Pandora arrived, she brought with her a box from the gods, which they warned her never to open. It contained every kind of misery and evil. Pandora was curious, however, and lifted the lid. Out flew all the plagues, sorrows, and misfortunes to torment mankind ever after. Luckily, one good thing remained in the box. This was *hope*. With hope, said the Greeks, man was able to find life bearable, no matter what his problems.

PANSY (*păn′zē*) is a garden flower belonging to the genus *Viola* of the violet family (Violaceae). The pansy has been cultivated in so many forms for so long that its origin is not known. The many lovely pansies found in gardens are varieties that have been developed by gardeners. They are nothing like any known

J. Horace McFarland Company

The velvety blossoms of some pansy varieties resemble faces.

wild plant. Nevertheless, the pansy is thought to be a cultivated form of a European weed, *Viola tricolor*. The garden pansy is therefore designated *V. tricolor hortensis*.

Pansy blossoms vary in color from white, through yellows, brownish reds, purples, to purple-black. Some are of a single color except for a golden spot at the center. Many have three of the petals with spots of a contrasting color, causing the flower to resemble a face.

These flowers seldom grow more than five inches tall, but they make colorful borders and beds for spring gardens. Pansies do best in somewhat sandy but rich soil. They may continue to bloom through the hot summer weather, but they grow and flower most abundantly in spring or early autumn when the weather is more moist and cool. In regions where summers are cool they continue through that season also. Where winters are not too severe, seeds may be sown in the autumn, and the plants wintered out of doors. The seeds may also be sown early in spring indoors. The young plants should be transferred to the outside as soon as weather permits. They come into flower soon after planting. Flowering pansy plants may also be purchased.

PAPACY (*pā′pä sē*) is the office of the pope of the Roman Catholic church. More generally, the papacy is thought of as the whole system of the central government of the Roman Catholic church and its historic continuity.

In the early days of Christianity the name "pope" (from the Latin word *papa,* meaning "father") was used to refer to any bishop or priest, as it is still used among Russian Christians. Later, however, after the division of the Roman Empire, the Western church restricted the term to the bishop of Rome. In 998 the archbishop of Milan was forbidden to call himself pope, and in 1073 Pope Gregory VII forbade anyone but the bishop of Rome to use the title.

John XXIII was pope from 1958 to 1963.

United Press International

Roman Catholics believe that the apostle St. Peter went to Rome and there established himself as bishop. The bishopric came to be known as the Apostolic See (seat) or the See of Peter. The bishops of Rome (popes) who succeeded him were regarded as carrying on the sacred mission that Jesus Christ had entrusted to the apostle. Thus began what is called the papacy. (See PETER, SAINT; ROMAN CATHOLIC CHURCH.)

The early popes were directly concerned with only a small number of Christians. During the first three centuries of its existence, the Christian church was practically a secret organization because of the widespread persecution by the Roman authorities and others. One result of this was that the local, individual Christian communities managed their own affairs to a great extent. Much evidence exists, however, that even in those early times the general authority of the bishop of Rome was recognized by the other churches. In the 4th century the emperor Constantine I recognized Christianity as the religion of the whole Roman Empire. He moved the capital of the Empire to the city of Byzantium (later Constantinople; now Istanbul, Turkey), but Rome, the place of Peter's death and burial, remained the seat of government of the Catholic church, as it is to this day.

The first general (or ecumenical) council of the church was held at Nicaea in 325, near Constantinople. Like most of the early general councils, it was called by the emperor, but the pope was represented by two priests, and his special position in the church was recognized.

The second general council (at Constantinople) in 381 stated that the authority of the bishop, or patriarch, of Constantinople was second to that of the bishop of Rome. At the fourth general council (at Chalcedon, a suburb of Constantinople) in 451, an attempt was made to relate the authority of the pope of Rome and of the patriarch of Constantinople to the importance of those two cities. In other words, in its famous Twenty-eighth Canon, the Council of Chalcedon tried to say that the pope of Rome held the first place in the church simply because he was bishop of the city that was for so long the seat of the government of the Roman Empire. From this it would then follow that the bishop of Constantinople, the new capital of the Empire, should also have a special place in the church. The Roman popes were willing to recognize the bishop of Constantinople as a patriarch on the same level as the patriarchs of the ancient sees of Jerusalem, Antioch, and Alexandria. They refused, however, to ratify the Twenty-eighth Canon of Chalcedon because they did not feel that their own importance in the church in any way depended on the political importance of the city over which they presided as bishops.

By that time the Roman Empire had divided into Eastern and Western parts. The pre-eminent position of the pope of Rome came to be more and more clearly recognized by the church of the West, and the split between the Eastern and Western churches became wider. This split became definite and permanent in 1054, when Michael Cerularius, the patriarch of Constantinople, and his followers were excommunicated from the Roman church. Despite many attempts on both sides to heal the breech, particularly by efforts of the second Council of Lyons (1274) and of the Council of Ferrara-Florence (1439), it remains to the present day. From time to time certain relatively small bodies of Eastern Christians have reunited with the Roman church. However, the vast majority of Eastern Christians, usually known as Orthodox, remain separated from the Roman Catholic church. (See EASTERN ORTHODOX CHURCHES.)

While the Eastern Roman Empire was flourishing, for much of the time the only stable and important power in the Western Empire was the papacy. This was one important factor in the growth of papal power and influence. Another was the energetic action of such popes as St. Gregory I (590–604), St. Gregory VII (1073–1085), and Innocent III (1198–1216). (See individual biographies.) Gradually the popes acquired extensive territories over which they ruled as temporal sovereigns. This, however, deeply involved the papacy in purely political matters and often brought the papacy and governmental leaders into conflict. These States of the Church (Papal States) were finally completely taken over by the new kingdom of Italy in 1870. From then until 1929 the popes

U.P.I. Compix

The seat of the papacy is Vatican City. Its main square, fronting St. Peter's Basilica, is frequently crowded on church holidays and other special occasions.

confined themselves to the Vatican as "prisoners." This unsatisfactory state of affairs was brought to an end by the Lateran Treaty (1929) with Italy. By this treaty the pope is recognized as completely independent and sovereign over Vatican City. (See VATICAN CITY.)

The supremacy of the pope over the entire Roman Catholic church has been acknowledged from the earliest times. Throughout most of the Middle Ages the struggle to justify the pope's independence in governing the church was long and bitter. Even to the present day traces of these ancient difficulties remain in a number of places. Some governments, for example, have the right to exercise some control over choice of bishops. Also, at the Council of Constance (1414–1418), the question of the superiority of a general council over the pope was raised. With great difficulty, the question was finally settled in favor of the superiority of the pope over a general council.

The Reformation of the 16th century was largely concerned with whether or not the papacy was a necessary feature of the basic constitution of the church as founded by Jesus Christ. (See REFORMATION.) Protestants say that it is not, while Roman Catholics insist that it is.

In 1870 the First Vatican Council issued a clear and detailed decree dealing with the position of the pope. The decree states that when the pope acts in his official capacity as head of the entire church, he is incapable of making a mistake in teachings concerning Christian faith or morals. The Second Vatican Council (1962–1965) issued many decrees. One of the most important concerned the relationship with other faiths.

In the earliest times the bishop of Rome was elected to his office by the Christians of the city. Gradually, however, the right of election was restricted to the members of the Sacred College of Cardinals. At the present time the election of a pope is regulated by precise and detailed rules. One of these states that the election take place in conclave (a Latin word meaning "with a key"), which means that the cardinals are carefully locked up in a specified place to ensure that there will be no outside interference in the election.

In his general government of the church, the pope is assisted by a large organization called the Curia Romana. It is made of several congregations. One of these, the Congregation for the Doctrine of the Faith, is responsible for all matters concerning the faith. The Congregation for the Propagation of the Faith supervises all the missionary activities of the church. Other congregations deal with matters of divine worship (the Congregation of Sacred Rites); higher education, especially of the clergy (the Congregation of Universities and Seminaries); and others. In the Curia Romana are also three tribunals, or courts, and a number of offices. The principal members of all these bodies are cardinals, but they are assisted in their work by a large number of consultors and other officials of various ranks. In 1967, Pope Paul VI reorganized the structure of the Curia Romana and changed the rules for tenure of its members.

List of the Popes

St., prefixed to a name in the list below, indicates that the pope in question is venerated by Roman Catholics as a saint. The Arabic numerals which follow each pope's name indicate the years of his reign. The dates for the popes of the first two centuries cannot be exactly determined. If a name has been borne by more than one pope, this is indicated by Roman numerals. The popes in capitals and small capitals, such as JOHN XXIII, have individual articles in *Britannica Junior Encyclopædia.*

First Century
ST. PETER, ?–67
St. Linus, 67–76
St. Anacletus, 76–88
ST. CLEMENT I, 88–97
St. Evaristus, 97–105
Second Century
St. Alexander I, 105–115
St. Sixtus I, 115–125
St. Telesphorus, 125–136
St. Hyginus, 136–140
St. Pius I, 140–155
St. Anicetus, 155–166
St. Soter, 166–175
St. Eleutherius, 175–189
St. Victor I, 189–199
Third Century
St. Zephyrinus, 199–217
St. Callistus I, 217–222
St. Urban I, 222–230
St. Pontian, 230–235
St. Anterus, 235–236
St. Fabian, 236–250
St. Cornelius, 251–253
St. Lucius I, 253–254
St. Stephen I, 254–257
St. Sixtus II, 257–258
St. Dionysius, 259–268
St. Felix I, 269–274
St. Eutychian, 275–283
St. Gaius, 283–296

St. Marcellinus, 296–304
Fourth Century
St. Marcellus I, 308–309
St. Eusebius, 309 (310?)
St. Miltiades, 311–314
St. Sylvester I, 314–335
St. Marcus, 336
St. Julius I, 337–352
Liberius, 352–366
St. Damasus I, 366–384
St. Siricius, 384–399
St. Anastasius I, 399–401
Fifth Century
ST. INNOCENT I, 401–417
St. Zozimus, 417–418
St. Boniface I, 418–422
St. Celestine I, 422–432
St. Sixtus III, 432–440
ST. LEO I, 440–461
St. Hilary, 461–468
St. Simplicius, 468–483
St. Felix III (II), 483–492
St. Gelasius I, 492–496
Anastasius II, 496–498
St. Symmachus, 498–514
Sixth Century
St. Hormisdas, 514–523
St. John I, 523–526
St. Felix IV (III), 526–530
Boniface II, 530–532
John II, 533–535

St. Agapitus I, 535–536
St. Silverius, 536–537
Vigilius, 537–555
Pelagius I, 556–561
John III, 561–574
Benedict I, 575–579
Pelagius II, 579–590
ST. GREGORY I, 590–604
Seventh Century
Sabinianus, 604–606
Boniface III, 607
St. Boniface IV, 608–615
St. Deusdedit, 615–618*
Boniface V, 619–625
Honorius I, 625–638
Severinus, 640
John IV, 640–642
Theodore I, 642–649
St. Martin I, 649–655†
St. Eugene I, 654–657
St. Vitalian, 657–672
Adeodatus, 672–676*
Donus, 676–678
St. Agatho, 678–681
St. Leo II, 682–683
St. Benedict II, 684–685
John V, 685–686
Conon, 686–687
St. Sergius I, 687–701
Eighth Century
John VI, 701–705

John VII, 705–707
Sisinnius, 708
Constantine, 708–715
St. Gregory II, 715–731
St. Gregory III, 731–741
St. Zachary, 741–752
Stephen II, 752‡
Stephen II (III), 752–757
St. Paul I, 757–767
Stephen III (IV), 768–772
ADRIAN I, 772–795
ST. LEO III, 795–816
Ninth Century
Stephen IV (V), 816–817
St. Paschal I, 817–824
Eugene II, 824–827
Valentine, 827
Gregory IV, 827–844
Sergius II, 844–847
ST. LEO IV, 847–855
Benedict III, 855–858
St. Nicholas I, 858–867
Adrian II, 867–872
John VIII, 872–882
Marinus I, 882–884§
St. Adrian III, 884–885
Stephen V (VI), 885–891
Formosus, 891–896
Boniface VI, 896
Stephen VI (VII), 896–897
Romanus, 897
Theodore II, 897
John IX, 898–900
Tenth Century
Benedict IV, 900–903
Leo V, 903
Sergius III, 904–911
Anastasius III, 911–913
Landus, 913–914
John X, 914–928
Leo VI, 928
Stephen VII (VIII), 928–931
John XI, 931–935
Leo VII, 936–939
Stephen VIII (IX), 939–942
Marinus II, 942–946§
Agapitus II, 946–955
John XII, 955–964
Leo VIII, 963–965‖
Benedict V, 964–966‖
John XIII, 965–972
Benedict VI, 973–974
Benedict VII, 974–983
John XIV, 983–984
John XV, 985–996
Gregory V, 996–999
Sylvester II, 999–1003
Eleventh Century
John XVII, 1003
John XVIII, 1004–09
Sergius IV, 1009–12
Benedict VIII, 1012–24
John XIX, 1024–32
Benedict IX, 1032–44¶

Sylvester III, 1045
Benedict IX, 1045¶
Gregory VI, 1045–46
Clement II, 1046–47
Benedict IX, 1047–48¶
Damasus II, 1048
St. Leo IX, 1049–54
Victor II, 1055–57
Stephen IX (X), 1057–58
Nicholas II, 1059–61
Alexander II, 1061–73
ST. GREGORY VII, 1073–85
Victor III, 1086–87
Urban II, 1088–99
Paschal II, 1099–1118
Twelfth Century
Gelasius II, 1118–19
Callistus II, 1119–24
Honorius II, 1124–30
Innocent II, 1130–43
Celestine II, 1143–44
Lucius II, 1144–45
Eugene III, 1145–53
Anastasius IV, 1153–54
ADRIAN IV, 1154–59
ALEXANDER III, 1159–81
Lucius III, 1181–85
Urban III, 1185–87
Gregory VIII, 1187
Clement III, 1187–91
Celestine III, 1191–98
INNOCENT III, 1198–1216
Thirteenth Century
Honorius III, 1216–27
Gregory IX, 1227–41
Celestine IV, 1241
INNOCENT IV, 1243–54
Alexander IV, 1254–61
Urban IV, 1261–64
Clement IV, 1265–68
Gregory X, 1271–76
Innocent V, 1276
Adrian V, 1276
John XXI, 1276–77 ♀
Nicholas III, 1277–80
Martin IV, 1281–85
Honorius IV, 1285–87
Nicholas IV, 1288–92
St. Celestine V, 1294
BONIFACE VIII, 1294–1303
Fourteenth Century
Benedict XI, 1303–04
Clement V, 1305–14
John XXII, 1316–34
Benedict XII, 1334–42
Clement VI, 1342–52
Innocent VI, 1352–62
Urban V, 1362–70
Gregory XI, 1370–78
Urban VI, 1378–89
BONIFACE IX, 1389–1404
Fifteenth Century
Innocent VII, 1404–06
Gregory XII, 1406–15

Martin V, 1417–31
Eugene IV, 1431–47
Nicholas V, 1447–55
Callistus III, 1455–58
PIUS II, 1458–64
PAUL II, 1464–71
SIXTUS IV, 1471–84
Innocent VIII, 1484–92
ALEXANDER VI, 1492–1503
Sixteenth Century
Pius III, 1503
JULIUS II, 1503–13
LEO X, 1513–21
Adrian VI, 1522–23
CLEMENT VII, 1523–34
PAUL III, 1534–49
Julius III, 1550–55
Marcellus II, 1555
PAUL IV, 1555–59
PIUS IV, 1559–65
St. Pius V, 1566–72
GREGORY XIII, 1572–85
SIXTUS V, 1585–90
Urban VII, 1590
Gregory XIV, 1590–91
Innocent IX, 1591
CLEMENT VIII, 1592–1605
Seventeenth Century
Leo XI, 1605
Paul V, 1605–21
Gregory XV, 1621–23
Urban VIII, 1623–44
Innocent X, 1644–55
Alexander VII, 1655–67
Clement IX, 1667–69
Clement X, 1670–76
INNOCENT XI, 1676–89
Alexander VIII, 1689–91
Innocent XII, 1691–1700
Eighteenth Century
Clement XI, 1700–21
Innocent XIII, 1721–24
Benedict XIII, 1724–30
Clement XII, 1730–40
BENEDICT XIV, 1740–58
Clement XIII, 1758–69
CLEMENT XIV, 1769–74
PIUS VI, 1775–99
Nineteenth Century
PIUS VII, 1800–23
Leo XII, 1823–29
Pius VIII, 1829–30
Gregory XVI, 1831–46
PIUS IX, 1846–78
LEO XIII, 1878–1903
Twentieth Century
ST. PIUS X, 1903–14
BENEDICT XV, 1914–22
PIUS XI, 1922–39
PIUS XII, 1939–58
JOHN XXIII, 1958–63
PAUL VI, 1963–

°Deusdedit and Adeodatus are sometimes listed Adeodatus I and Adeodatus II.
†St. Martin I was dethroned in 653 and died in exile in 655.
‡Stephen II died before his consecration as bishop of Rome, therefore he was never officially a pope.
§Marinus I and Marinus II are sometimes listed Martin II and Martin III.
‖Rival popes; one or the other may be regarded as an antipope.
¶Benedict IX was pope three times.
♀There was no John XX.
♂Victor IV did not recognize his predecessor, Victor IV.

PAPER (pā′pēr) is thin, matted sheets of fiber made from wood pulp, straw, rags, or other fibrous material. It is commonly used for writing or printing upon or for wrapping.

Paper gets its name from papyrus, a sheet made by pressing together the core material, or pith, of the Egyptian papyrus plant. (See PAPYRUS.) Papyrus as a writing material was first developed about 4,000 years ago in Egypt. It was not until 2,000 years later, or just about the time of Jesus Christ, that paper, as it is known today, was invented in China. The inventor, a scholar named Ts'ai Lun, served as an official in the court of Emperor Ho Ti. Ts'ai Lun probably mixed mulberry bark, hemp, and rags, beat them into a pulp, and mixed this pulp in water to separate the fibers. The fibers were then matted into a sheet by lifting them out of the water on a screen with a shaking motion. After the water was pressed from the sheets they were hung in the sun to dry. The basic principle of papermaking is the same today.

The Arab world learned papermaking from the Chinese sometime in the 8th century. The Chinese technique of papermaking did not reach Europe until the 12th century, however, when the Moors of North Africa introduced it into Spain. Somehow along the route from the Orient, the method for making paper from wood was lost. Until the early 1800's, paper was made in the Western world only from rags and cloth. Each sheet was individually turned out by dipping a screen into a vat of water-suspended fibers and filtering the water away

This old Egyptian *Book of the Dead* was written on a roll of papyrus, the forerunner of paper. This writing material was made by pressing layers of pithy strips of the papyrus plant into sheets or scrolls.

The Oriental Institute

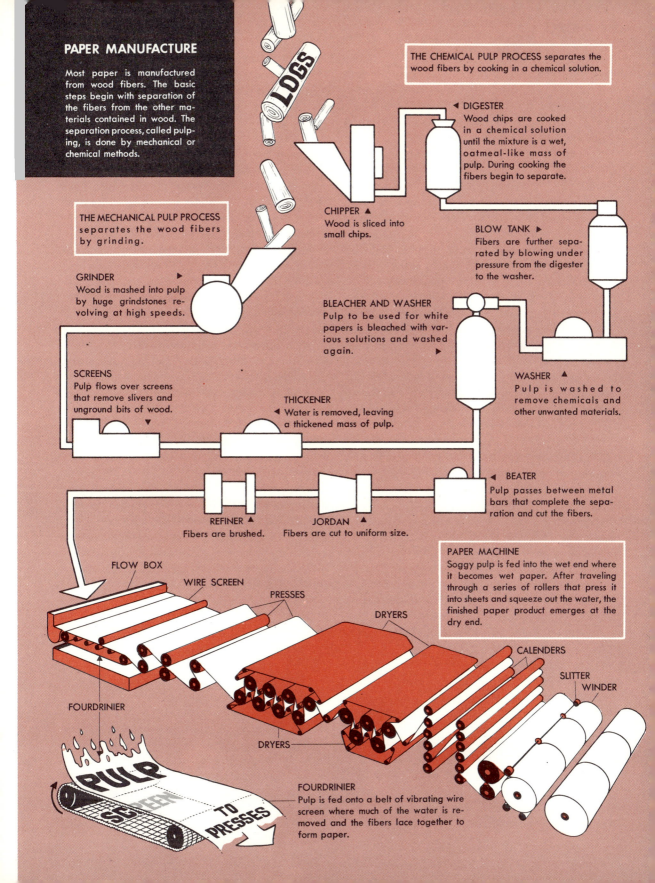

PAPER MANUFACTURE

Most paper is manufactured from wood fibers. The basic steps begin with separation of the fibers from the other materials contained in wood. The separation process, called pulping, is done by mechanical or chemical methods.

LOGS

THE CHEMICAL PULP PROCESS separates the wood fibers by cooking in a chemical solution.

◄ DIGESTER
Wood chips are cooked in a chemical solution until the mixture is a wet, oatmeal-like mass of pulp. During cooking the fibers begin to separate.

CHIPPER ▲
Wood is sliced into small chips.

THE MECHANICAL PULP PROCESS separates the wood fibers by grinding.

BLOW TANK ►
Fibers are further separated by blowing under pressure from the digester to the washer.

GRINDER ►
Wood is mashed into pulp by huge grindstones revolving at high speeds.

BLEACHER AND WASHER
Pulp to be used for white papers is bleached with various solutions and washed again. ►

WASHER ▲
Pulp is washed to remove chemicals and other unwanted materials.

SCREENS
Pulp flows over screens that remove slivers and unground bits of wood. ▼

THICKENER
◄ Water is removed, leaving a thickened mass of pulp.

◄ BEATER
Pulp passes between metal bars that complete the separation and cut the fibers.

REFINER ▲
Fibers are brushed.

JORDAN ▲
Fibers are cut to uniform size.

PAPER MACHINE
Soggy pulp is fed into the wet end where it becomes wet paper. After traveling through a series of rollers that press it into sheets and squeeze out the water, the finished paper product emerges at the dry end.

FLOW BOX

WIRE SCREEN

PRESSES

DRYERS

CALENDERS

SLITTER

WINDER

FOURDRINIER

DRYERS

PULP

SCREEN

TO PRESSES

FOURDRINIER
Pulp is fed onto a belt of vibrating wire screen where much of the water is removed and the fibers lace together to form paper.

from the fibers. A good worker could produce 750 sheets a day. It was an expensive, tedious process that could not fill the urgent demand for paper.

In 1799, paper production went from the hand to the machine. Nicholas Louis Robert, a clerk at a papermaking mill in Essonnes, France, patented a plan for a machine that replaced hand dipping and produced paper in a continuous roll. Basically, the machine was a large, endless wire screen that was turned by hand to filter the pulp.

Robert was unable to gain support for his idea in France, so he sold the patents, which sometime later became the property of Henry and Sealy Fourdrinier of England. The Fourdrinier brothers built a practical machine, but it failed to provide inexpensive, plentiful paper. The problem of papermaking was in securing raw materials. Rags were still being used, and they were expensive and limited in quantity.

Nearly a hundred years earlier, in 1719, Rene de Reaumur, a French scientist, had pointed to a solution. He noticed wasps using minute fibers of wood to make nests, the texture of which resembled paper. From his observations Reaumur concluded that man should use wood in papermaking. His suggestion was ignored until 1850 when Friedrich Gottlob Keller of Germany read his treatise and developed a machine for grinding wood into fibers. In 1851 the Englishmen Hugh Burgess and Charles Watt advanced mechanized papermaking another step by inventing a chemical pulping process. Then, in 1865, B. C. Tilghman, a United States scientist, solved a major chemical problem with his discovery of the sulfite process for dissolving unwanted resins in wood.

In the 1860's a wood-grinding machine was imported from Germany to Stockbridge, Massachusetts, and the age of economical, mass-produced paper, made from a raw material in plentiful supply, began in the United States. As a result newspapers multiplied and more, less-expensive magazines were published. The school slate vanished, giving way to notebooks and lined paper. Paperback five-and-ten-cent novels were rolled from the presses. Mills in Boston, Massachusetts, alone produced 75 million paper shirt collars a year.

Papermaking changed from an individual art to an industrial art that is dependent on teamwork between managers, technicians, and researchers. At the same time, paper itself changed from a primarily cultural product used for newspapers, books, and writing paper to a basic product, like steel, that could be used for many purposes. Wrapping paper and bags filled a need in the marketing of merchandise. Drugs, toilet articles, foodstuffs, and hundreds of other products were dressed in attractive wrappers and cartons. Signs and posters appeared across the country. Fiber boxes became more important in the economy and gradually replaced heavy wooden crates.

Without low-cost and plentiful paper and paperboard, mass production, mass packaging, and mass shipping could never have developed to the degree that it has. Paper manufacturing is now an important industry. Each person in the United States uses more than 530 pounds of paper each year. Approximately 40 percent is used in the form of paperboard (stiff paper used in such things as boxes); 18 percent as newsprint; 12 percent as books and magazines; 10 percent as coarse paper (such as heavy wrapping paper); 9 percent as building materials; 6 percent as tissue; 4 percent as fine paper (such as writing paper); and 1 percent as miscellaneous items. Large amounts of paper are also manufactured and used in Canada, Japan, Sweden, the U.S.S.R., Finland, Germany, and the United Kingdom.

Paper Manufacture

Although paper may be made from nearly any kind of vegetable fiber, 95 per cent of the paper made in the United States comes from wood. Other common plants from which paper is made throughout the world are cotton, straw, flax, jute, bamboo, and sugar cane bagasse (stalks left over from the sugar-making process). Various paper products are made from these fibers. Straw, for example, is used to make wallboard, jute to make wrapping paper, and flax to make cigarette papers. The highest quality papers are made from rags.

Wood is composed of billions of small cellu-

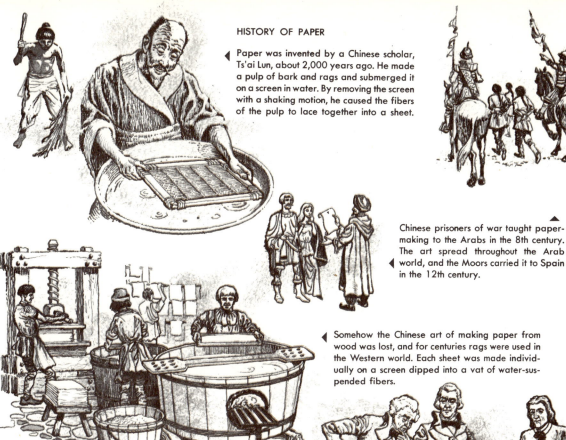

HISTORY OF PAPER

◄ Paper was invented by a Chinese scholar, Ts'ai Lun, about 2,000 years ago. He made a pulp of bark and rags and submerged it on a screen in water. By removing the screen with a shaking motion, he caused the fibers of the pulp to lace together into a sheet.

▲
Chinese prisoners of war taught paper-making to the Arabs in the 8th century. The art spread throughout the Arab world, and the Moors carried it to Spain in the 12th century.

◄ Somehow the Chinese art of making paper from wood was lost, and for centuries rags were used in the Western world. Each sheet was made individually on a screen dipped into a vat of water-suspended fibers.

▲
In the early 1800's, Henry and Sealy Fourdrinier developed a machine that made paper in a continuous roll.

lose fibers that are bound together by a gluelike substance called lignin. (See CELLULOSE.) The tree's sap and resins flow through the fibers. In order to manufacture paper, the fibers must be separated from these other materials of the wood. This is done by a process called pulping, and the crude fiber material that results is called pulp. Pulping is done by mechanical or chemical methods.

The mechanical method consists of rubbing the wood against huge grindstones that revolve at high speeds. The resulting product is called mechanical, or groundwood, pulp. Paper made from groundwood pulp lacks the strength of paper made from most chemical pulps, but it is useful in high-speed printing. Most newsprint (paper on which newspapers are printed) throughout the world is made from groundwood pulp.

The chemical method of pulp making involves cooking the wood in one of several different

In the middle 1800's, papermaking from wood was developed, and the ▼ chemical process of pulping wood was discovered.

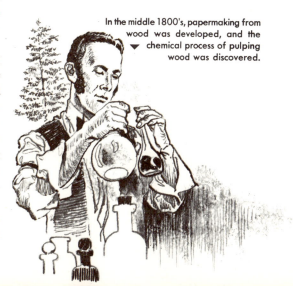

chemical solutions in order to separate the fibers from the sap, resins, lignin, and other matter. The resulting product is called chemical pulp. The kind of solution used depends on the kind of pulp desired. Cooking in sulfate solution, for example, is used for making kraft papers for use as grocery bags and wrapping for packages.

The pulpwood logs are first sliced into small chips, about one inch square and one-eighth inch thick, and then fed into large vats called digesters. These digesters are three or four stories high. The chips and chemicals are steamed in them until the mixture is reduced to a wet, oatmeal-like mass. During this cooking, the fibers are freed from the lignin and suspended in water.

The pulp is blown from the digesters under pressure to further separate the fibers. The fibers are washed to remove the chemicals and other materials and then sent to the beaters. Pulp to be used for white papers is bleached white before entering the beaters. In the beater the pulp passes between sets of metal bars, or knives, that complete the separation of the fibers, reduce the fibers to proper length, and fray their edges so they will cling together when formed into a sheet. Added during the beating are color, size (which makes finished paper water resistant), and whatever other chemicals are required to make a specific type of paper.

After beating, the pulp flows to the Jordan, a type of refiner, where the fibers are cut to uniform size. Then the pulp flows to other refiners where the fibers are brushed to further improve their ability to cling together in a sheet.

In this refined condition, the pulp, which is at this point 99 per cent water, is fed into the papermaking machine. It is run onto an endless belt of mesh screen at what is referred to as the wet end of the machine. This screen is called the Fourdrinier wire. Through a constant side-to-side vibration of the screen the fibers are interlaced and much of the water is taken out.

The paper leaves the wire and enters the drying section of the paper machine. Traveling at speeds sometimes faster than 2,000 feet per minute, it winds through a long series of steam-heated cylinders called dryers. At this point the last of the water is removed by heat, pressure, and suction.

After drying, the procedure again differs according to the type of paper being made. Many papers go through a process called calendering, which provides a smooth finish by ironing the sheets between heavy, polished rollers. Others pass through tubs of chemicals that furnish additional coatings. The product that comes from the dry end of the paper machine, regardless of the finish, is in large rolls that are sent to converting plants to be made into thousands of different useful products.

PAPYRUS (*pä pī'rŭs*) is a reed plant of the family Cyperaceae, or sedges. It is also the name given to an ancient writing material made from the plant.

The papyrus plant grows mainly in northern Africa and southern Europe. It is an aquatic plant that takes root in marshes or in the mud under shallow water. Only the roots are submerged. The height of the plant ranges from 3 to 15 feet. The stems are soft. At the base they are sometimes as large as a man's wrist. At the tops of the stems are drooping, slender branches.

The papyrus plant, or paper reed, has tall, thin, almost leafless stalks.

John H. Gerard

Papyrus was first developed into a writing material by the Egyptians about 4,000 years ago. Pliny, the Roman historian, tells in his *Natural History* how this material was made. The pith, or core, of the stem was cut into lengthwise strips. These were laid side by side, and across them at right angles another layer of strips was placed. The layers were stuck together with muddy water from the Nile River or, some historians believe, with a special paste. The sheets were then dried in the sun and hammered or rolled flat.

At one time papyrus writing material was one of Egypt's chief articles of commerce. Its use spread throughout the ancient world. Parchment finally replaced papyrus for important documents.

The plant had other uses as well. The slender stalks were woven into baskets. The thicker stalks were made into mats and sails. The pith was eaten raw or cooked, and it could be dried and used for fuel.

PARACHUTE (*păr' ŭ shoot*) is an umbrellalike device for dropping man or his goods through the air slowly enough to prevent injury or damage upon impact with the ground. The shape of the parachute greatly resists the flow of air around it. This resistance counteracts the downward pull of gravity. The speed at which the parachute descends, then, is usually slow enough to assure a safe landing. Parachute drops usually are made from a plane.

Parachutes, or chutes as they are often called, are also used to decelerate, or slow down, horizontal movement. For example, certain planes use them after touching down on short runways. High-speed racing cars sometimes use them for braking at the end of a run.

Provisions for victims of floods or other disasters are sometimes dropped by parachute. Parachutes are also used by fire fighters as a quick means of reaching forest fires in roadless areas. Spacecraft that re-enter the Earth's atmosphere make their final descent by parachute.

Skydiving is a sport in which the parachute is the principal piece of equipment. Skydivers jump from planes for hundreds or thousands of feet before opening the parachute. Often the skydiver's objective is to land on a small target.

The idea of the parachute is centuries old. Leonardo da Vinci of Italy sketched a parachute in his notebook in 1514. Fausto Veranzio, another Italian, published in 1595 a drawing of a workable parachute. Not until the 18th century, however, were parachutes successfully used. Louis Sebastian Lenormand of France parachuted from a tower. In 1797 Andre Jacques Garnerin, also of France, parachuted from a balloon that was more than 2,000 feet aloft.

It was not until the 20th century, with the development of the airplane, that the parachute began to come into practical use. The first successful parachute jump from a plane was made by Captain Albert Berry of the U.S. Army in 1912. Near the end of World War I parachutes were used by German fliers to escape from disabled aircraft.

Parachutes at that time were usually packed in open baskets attached to the outside of the planes. This arrangement was unsatisfactory, however, because a chute sometimes became entangled on the outside of the plane. The seat-pack type of parachute, strapped to the jumper's body, was adopted by the U.S. Army in 1919. In 1922 it became compulsory to wear them during flights. A backpack type, worn on the upper back, and a chest-pack type were also introduced.

Paratroops, or parachute troops, were used by armies on both sides of the conflict during World War II. These troops, as well as their tanks, artillery, motor vehicles, and other equipment, were landed by parachute with surprising speed and effectiveness.

The U.S. paratrooper wears two nylon parachutes: a main chute, on the back, and a reserve chute, on the chest. The reserve chute, which has a diameter of 24 feet, is never used unless the main chute, with a diameter of 35 feet, fails to open or to function properly.

The backpack, containing the main chute, is attached to the jumper's body by means of straps that pass around the shoulders and the upper thighs. These straps are joined at the chest. The chest pack, containing the reserve chute, is hooked to the harness of the main chute.

Parachutes have two types of opening devices: the static line and the rip cord. The static line is a cord 17 feet long. One end of it is tied with string to the vent at the top of the parachute canopy. The other end is attached to the inside of the plane. After the jumper has dropped a short distance, the static line pulls the parachute out of the pack. When it is out all the way, the string breaks. The static line stays attached to the plane as the jumper falls free. The chute

Parachutes used in the sport of skydiving are opened with the aid of small pilot chutes. Partially open panels help to reduce the strain caused when the parachute opens.

The parafoil is an experimental parachute that works much like an airplane wing. It glides to Earth at an angle, rather than descending vertically.

High-speed aircraft sometimes use drag parachutes to help reduce speed and shorten the landing run. The U.S. Air Force B-47, above, uses a 32-foot diameter chute.

Experimental high-speed cars and certain types of racing cars also use braking parachutes to reduce their speed and stop more quickly.

The Main Parts of a Parachute

canopy

panel

vent

suspension line

riser

reserve parachute

billows open in less than one second after the jumper has left the plane. A rip cord chute is opened by the jumper at any time after he has left the plane. When the rip cord handle is pulled, an umbrella-size pilot chute is released from the pack. It inflates and drags out the canopy, which also inflates. Suspension lines, attached to the skirt, or edge, of the canopy, lead to four risers that extend from the harness.

The angle and direction of parachute descent can be controlled partially by pulling down on one or two of the risers. Air is spilled out of the chute on the side opposite that which is being pulled. The chute then tends to slip in the direction of those suspension lines affected.

PARAGUAY (*păr′ŭ gwĭ′*, or *păr′ŭ gwā′*), **SOUTH AMERICA,** is a landlocked republic in the interior of the continent. It is bordered on the northeast by Brazil, on the northwest by Bolivia, and on the south, west, and east by Argentina.

No part of the country lies less than 600 miles from the ocean and Paraguay must depend on neighboring countries for its ocean shipping. This situation has strongly influenced the country's political and economic life.

Landscape and Climate

The country is divided into two contrasting regions, separated by the Paraguay River. Eastern Paraguay is a rolling, hilly plateau, with fertile soil. The area is largely covered with hardwood forests and grasses. Most of the people live in the eastern region, and economic activity is concentrated there. The other region, the Chaco Boreal, is a flat plain that becomes desert-like in the northwest. The Chaco Boreal is Paraguay's part of the Gran Chaco, a region of lowlands that extends into Argentina and Bolivia. The Chaco Boreal varies in vegetation, with dense jungle growth, swampy lowlands, and some isolated forests. Quebracho trees in the area yield a tanning extract that is a major export. Quebracho extraction and livestock raising are major activities of the Chaco.

There are no mountains in Paraguay. The highest elevations range from 1,000 to 3,000 feet and are located near the Brazilian and Argentine borders.

Rivers form most of the country's boundaries and are its most important avenues of commercial transportation. The two large rivers, the Paraguay and the Parana, are navigable. The Parana River (known as Alto or Upper Parana until it joins the Paraguay River) flows south from Brazil to form 400 miles of Paraguay's boundaries. It flows westward to its junction with the Paraguay River and continues southward to Argentina and the Atlantic Ocean.

The Paraguay River also rises in Brazil, flowing south to form part of Paraguay's border with that country. It then cuts Paraguay into its two main regions and, finally, forms some of the border with Argentina. The Pilcomayo River, which separates Paraguay from Argentina, flows southeastward across the Chaco. During rainy periods, it floods, as do other Chaco rivers.

In general, Paraguay has a pleasant, subtropical climate with mild temperatures averaging 88 degrees Fahrenheit in the summer and 59 degrees Fahrenheit in the winter. The seasons are re-

FACTS ABOUT PARAGUAY

CAPITAL: Asuncion. **NATIONAL ANTHEM:** *Himno Nacional de Paraguay* ("National Anthem of Paraguay").
AREA: 157,047 square miles.
POPULATION: 1,816,890 (1962); 2,161,000 (1967 estimate); 12 persons per square mile; 36 percent urban; 64 percent rural.
CHIEF LANGUAGES: Spanish, Guarani. **CHIEF RELIGION:** Roman Catholic.
LITERACY: About 74 percent of the people can read and write.
HIGHEST POINT: Cerro Leon (3,280 feet).
LARGEST LAKE: Lake Ypoa.
MOST IMPORTANT RIVERS: Paraguay, Parana.

FORM OF GOVERNMENT: Republic.
CHIEF OF STATE and HEAD OF GOVERNMENT: President.
LEGISLATURE: House of Representatives and Senate.
POLITICAL DIVISIONS: 16 departamentos, 1 federal district.
CHIEF CITIES: (1966 estimates) Asuncion (370,800), Encarnacion (25,400), Concepcion (24,600), Villarrica (21,800).
CHIEF MANUFACTURED AND MINED PRODUCTS: Cotton leather, wood, nut oils, processed meat, quebracho extract.
CHIEF AGRICULTURAL PRODUCTS: *Crops,* cotton, fruit, sugarcane, tobacco; *livestock,* cattle.
FLAG: Colors, red, white, and blue. (See FLAG.)
CURRENCY: Guarani; 126 guaranis are equal to one U.S. dollar.

versed from those of countries of the Northern Hemisphere; thus December and January are summer months, and June and July are winter months. The average yearly rainfall is 59 inches, but this varies regionally. Rainfall is highest in the east, near the Brazilian border, and lowest toward the west.

People

Most Paraguayans are a mixed race of Guarani Indian and Spaniard. Spanish is the official language, but Guarani, an Indian language, is spoken by most Paraguayans outside the cities. The country is largely Roman Catholic. One exception to this is the Mennonite colony of 2,100 square miles in the Chaco. The Mennonite immigrants were assured freedom to practice their religion. These people have opened a part of the Chaco to diversified agriculture.

The capital and only large city of the country is Asuncion. Almost one-sixth of all Paraguayans live there. (See ASUNCION.) Provincial cities, all with small populations, are Villarrica, Concepcion, Encarnacion, and Coronel Oviedo.

The Economy

Paraguay is economically underdeveloped and poverty is widespread. During the late 1960's, the average amount of money earned annually by a Paraguayan was less than $200.

Agriculture. Most of the people are employed in agriculture. They practice subsistence farming, cattle raising, and forestry production. Despite the large areas available for crop production, only about 5 percent of the land is under cultivation.

The major agricultural crops are corn, cassava (a staple food of the Paraguayan diet), sugarcane, rice, tobacco, cotton, vegetable and nut oils, and citrus fruits. Petitgrain oil, distilled from sour-orange leaves and used as a base for perfumes, and yerba maté (Paraguayan tea) are specialty products. Despite the availability of land and a low population density, the country must supplement its food supply with imports. The most extensive use of the land is for cattle pasture. Meat and hides are important exports.

Industry. Paraguay fought the Chaco War against Bolivia to assure its claim to a part of the Gran Chaco and the petroleum deposits that were thought to be there. By the mid-1960's, however, oil explorations had failed to develop a producing well inside the Paraguayan border. Coal and minerals have not been found in amounts great enough to pay for their extraction.

Industries in Paraguay have been mainly limited to the processing

Locator map of Paraguay.

Courtesy (below right) Office of Inter-American Affairs; photos, (left) Theodorus Verbeek—Pix from Publix, (above right) Davis Pratt—Rapho Guillumette

Fishermen cast their nets into one of Paraguay's numerous rivers, left. The architecture of the Government Palace in Asuncion, above right, reflects the country's Spanish colonial tradition. A crane hoists a quebracho log, below right, to be processed in the nearby mill. Quebracho timber and its tanning extracts are major exports.

of raw materials for export. The major ones are meat processing, timber processing, quebracho tannin extraction, cotton ginning, and the extraction of various seed oils. Cotton textiles and domestic consumer goods are also manufactured.

The major fuel within the country is wood, which largely powers the locomotives, steamboats, and the steam boilers in industry. The government, however, plans to increase the output of hydroelectric power. Paraguay has a great water-power potential on the Parana River and its tributaries, about 200 miles east of Asuncion.

Foreign Trade. Paraguay has no seacoast and, until the late 1960's, had only one route to the sea: the Parana River through Argentina. Access through Brazil has been difficult, but a land route to the sea has been opened. Paraguay's trade has been mostly with Argentina, the United States, and Western Europe. Paraguayan imports include agricultural products, machinery, petroleum, chemicals, and textiles. Important exports are meat and hides, wood, tobacco, cotton, quebracho extract, and vegetable and nut oils.

Transportation

The Parana River is navigable for small ocean liners as far as Asuncion and Concepcion. The trip, however, is difficult and costly. Small river steamers go upstream as far as Corumba, Brazil.

Paraguay's central location favors the development of Asuncion's International Airport. Railroad transportation is limited chiefly to a line from Asuncion to Encarnacion, where connections with the Argentine railroad are made.

Several important road projects have been completed and others started, chiefly with the help of foreign aid. The Trans-Chaco Highway, leading northwest into Bolivia, was opened in

1964 as part of the Pan-American Highway System. A bridge over the Parana River connects roads between the city of Asuncion and the Brazilian coastal city of Paranagua. This provides Paraguay with an overland route to the sea, which makes the country less dependent on the water route through Argentina. Free ports at both Santos and Paranagua in Brazil are available for Paraguay's use.

Education

By the mid-1960's Paraguay had made some progress in developing the educational system. Elementary education is free and compulsory for children between the ages of 7 and 14. There are not, however, enough schools to make full enrollment possible. Secondary education is neither free nor compulsory. Lack of funds, poor transportation, and isolation make attendance impossible in many areas. Higher education and adult education are available to some of the people. The National University of Paraguay, founded in 1889, in Asuncion, is the center of higher learning.

Government

Paraguay is a republic. The president is elected by popular vote for five years and can be re-elected. He appoints an advisory council of state. The legislative branch is composed of a chamber of representatives and—since 1968—a senate. A supreme court and local judges make up the judicial branch. Paraguay, however, has often had presidents who exercised power great enough to control the legislative and judicial branches and disregard the constitution. The Colorado party has dominated political affairs.

History

The first Europeans to explore the site of Paraguay are believed to have been Alejo Garcia, in about 1524, and Sebastian Cabot in 1526. Cabot sailed up the Parana and established a post that was soon overrun by Indians. About 11 years later, Asuncion was founded; it became the first permanent settlement in the interior of South America. Indian troubles continued until 1608 when Jesuit missionaries took the Indians under their protection in missions. The Guarani tribes were encouraged to settle near the missions, where they were taught farming and cattle raising.

The missions became prosperous and stable communities. The landowners and government officials, however, grew envious of their prosperity. The landowners desired the fruitful lands of the missions and the cheap Indian labor. As a result, the Jesuits were expelled in 1767. The mission communities in the outlying sections of the country fell apart and the Indians drifted to the central area around Asuncion. The Indians did not wish to return to their shifting, patch agriculture. Instead they became attached to the large estates through a feudal type of arrangement.

After 1776, Paraguay became a province of the Viceroyalty of La Plata. The viceroyalty also included present-day Argentina, Uruguay, and part of Bolivia. In 1810, Paraguay refused to join Argentina in its struggle for independence from Spain but, in 1811, overthrew Spanish rule in its own bloodless revolt. This marked the beginning of a period of isolation from its neighbors. A series of dictators ruled the country from 1814 until 1870. Jose Gaspar Rodriguez Francia ruled the country from 1814 to 1840. He governed with a strong hand, but developed agriculture and industry and left the country stronger than ever before. Carlos Antonio Lopez ruled from 1840 to 1862. In contrast to Francia, he attempted to cultivate relations with the outside world. Paraguay became recognized as an independent country, education was promoted, and transportation and communication lines were developed. Lopez was succeeded by his son, Francisco Solano Lopez, who led the country into the disastrous War of the Triple Alliance against Brazil, Uruguay, and Argentina. The war lasted five years, leaving Paraguay devastated and with only half its former population.

During the next 65 years, Paraguay made slow progress. In 1932, a boundary dispute with Bolivia led to another costly conflict, the Chaco War. After three years, a peace settlement awarded Paraguay most of the disputed territory. The campaign, however, took more than 40,000 lives and left the victorious country exhausted.

From 1940 to 1948, Higinio Morinigo was

dictator of Paraguay. He was followed by four presidents between 1948 and 1950 who attained office through coups. Federico Chavez assumed control in 1949 but was overthrown in 1954 by General Alfredo Stroessner, who had strong army backing. Afterward Stroessner served as president, but he ruled as a dictator. In the late 1960's he permitted some political reform.

PARASITE (*păr'ä sĭt*) **AND SAPROPHYTE** (*săp'rō fĭt*). A parasite is a plant or animal that lives with, in, or on another living organism. The other organism is called the *host*. A saprophyte is an organism that lives on dead or decaying matter.

All living things depend on one another. However, certain plants and animals could not live at all if they did not live together with a certain other kind of living thing. Very often, one of these partners is a parasite. The parasite takes from the host and gives it nothing in return. The name for this relationship is parasitism.

A parasite may be either a plant or an animal; and it may live off either a plant or an animal. Sometimes a parasite can live with many types of hosts, but more often it can live only with one or a few different types of hosts.

Sometimes the parasite kills its host by taking too much of the nourishment the host needs. Or it may give off substances which poison the host, making the host weak and sick. This may be unfortunate for the parasite because it depends upon the host in order to live. Unless it finds another host, it will die too.

A parasite may live on after its animal host dies if the flesh of the host is eaten by another animal. The parasite then may enter the other animal and use it as the host. A certain species of threadworm found in dogs can pass from the female dog upon which it lives to the unborn young inside the mother. In this way it goes from one generation of dogs to the next. Certain parasitic germs are carried by insects from one animal to another.

Nearly all forms of parasitic life produce large numbers of young and are very tough. If this were not true the destruction they cause would destroy them too.

Plants That Are Parasites

Many diseases of animals are caused by parasitic plants that cannot be seen except under a powerful microscope. These parasites are bacterial germs. Other parasitic bacteria cause diseases of plants, such as the black rot of cabbage, bean blight, fire blight of pear, and crown gall of apple. Bacteria are very dangerous as parasites because they are easily carried from place to place; they can stand heat, cold, and dryness; and they quickly increase in numbers. (See BACTERIA; BLIGHT AND ROT; PLANT DISEASE.)

A little higher in the plant kingdom are found the other fungus parasites. These plants do not have seeds but reproduce by tiny spores. Ringworm in man is not caused by a worm but by one of these plant parasites. Rusts, mildews, some blights, and smuts are parasitic fungi that attack plants. (See FUNGUS; FUNGUS INFECTION.) Mushrooms are also fungi. A few are parasitic, but most are saprophytic.

Seed plants that are parasites are not common. This is perhaps because most seed plants are able to make their own food in sunlight,

This tree, the host, has been killed by mistletoe, the parasite. Insert: Close-up of mistletoe.

J. Horace McFarland Company, Chicago Natural History Museum

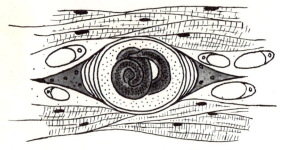

A parasite that harms its host is the trichina, which causes the disease called trichinosis. Here we see an adult worm (about 41 times life size) curled up in a cyst in a human muscle, ready to be transferred to a new host.

and so do not have to live on other things. However, the climbing dodder and the common mistletoe are both parasites which grow on other plants. They feed off their hosts through sucking or absorbing organs, which pierce the tissues of the host. These plants have lost part or all of their green coloring matter (chlorophyll), which they use to manufacture their food. They have become parasites.

Animals That Are Parasites

Among animals, as among plants, the most important parasites are the smallest ones. These are microscopic, single-celled animals called protozoa. (See PROTOZOA.) Often they cannot stand extremes of temperature and dryness as bacteria can. Therefore they have come to depend upon some animal, such as an insect, to carry them to a host. The protozoan that causes African sleeping sickness is carried by the tsetse fly. The malaria parasite is carried by the female Anopheles mosquito. (See MALARIA; SLEEPING SICKNESS.) In such diseases the parasite is not simply carried from one host to another the way the typhoid bacteria are carried on the hairy feet of the housefly. These parasites actually live part of their life in the insect, which is their second host. Yaws, recurrent fever, and amoebic dysentery are other human diseases caused by protozoa.

Another important group of animal parasites are the worms. Trichinosis, a disease of pigs, rats, and human beings, is caused by a roundworm, trichina. This worm enters the body when a person eats poorly cooked pork. Hookworm disease is caused by a worm that gets into

the body through tiny cuts in the feet. (See HOOKWORM.) The tapeworm is sometimes more than ten feet in length. It lives in the intestines, after entering the body through the eating of infected meat or fish. (See TAPEWORM.) The stomach worms of sheep, dog worms, and the liver fluke of sheep, cows, and pigs are worm parasites.

Higher in the animal kingdom than the protozoa and worms are the insects and mite parasites. One of these is the botfly, the larvae of which live in the stomachs, skins, or noses of horses and sheep and other hoofed animals. Fleas, ticks, and lice are all parasites.

Parasitic plants must not be confused with *saprophytes*, plants that get their food from dead plants and animals or lifeless products of living things. Examples of saprophytes are bacteria of decay, mushrooms, bread mold, and the bacteria that sour milk and wine and create flavor and aroma in cheese.

Saprophytes, which cause decay, are for the most part very useful organisms. They change dead material into substances that living things can use as food. Without saprophytes higher plants and animals would soon disappear from the earth. The saprophytes set free the elements and simple compounds that would otherwise be tied up in dead bodies of plants and animals.

Symbiosis and Commensalism

Sometimes a plant or animal lives co-operatively with another plant or animal. Each supplies something which the other needs, and each gets something in return. In such cases, the two are called *symbionts*, or those-who-live-together. Such a partner relationship is called *symbiosis*.

An example of symbiosis is the case of certain bacteria that live on the roots of such plants as beans,

The tick attaches itself to another animal and sucks its blood. This is a magnified picture of a tick on a human arm.

John H. Gerard

clover, and alfalfa. These bacteria take free nitrogen gas out of the air and make it into nitrates that can be absorbed and used by plants in manufacturing food. The bean plant supplies water, minerals, manufactured sugar and starch, and also protection for the bacteria. (See LEGUME, PULSE, or PEA FAMILY.)

It is not always easy to tell the difference between symbiosis and commensalism. *Commensalism*, however, is a relationship in which one of the partners is helped and the other is neither helped nor harmed. The parasite benefits, but the host is unaffected. Some very small crabs, for example, live under an oyster's shell. They eat the oyster's food and use his shell for protection, but do not harm the oyster.

PARENT (*par'ŭnt*)-**TEACHER** (*tē'chĕr*) **AS-SOCIATIONS** (*ŭ sō'sē ā'shŭnz* or *ŭ sō'shē ā'-shŭnz*) (PTA) are local groups in membership with the National Congress of Parents and Teachers (National PTA). The largest organization of volunteers in the world, the National PTA has more than 11 million members. There are more than 44,000 local PTA's in 52 branches. Included are branches for the 50 states, the District of Columbia, and the European Congress of American Parents and Teachers (PTA's for military dependents' schools in Europe). PTA's on U.S. military installations abroad are in membership directly with the National PTA.

The organization was founded in Washington, D.C., in 1897 as the National Congress of Mothers. The founders, Mrs. Alice McLellan Birney and Mrs. Phoebe Apperson Hearst, wanted to improve the welfare of all children. Throughout its history, this goal has remained the chief purpose of the PTA. Anyone interested in children may become a PTA member.

The objects of the National PTA are to promote the welfare of children and youth; to secure laws for their protection; to raise the standards of home life; to bring home and school into closer relationship; and to develop united action by educators and the general public in behalf of the physical, mental, social, and spiritual education of every child.

The National PTA supplies program material and publications to member groups. It conducts courses in universities and colleges on the techniques of administering local parent-teacher groups. It holds conferences and other meetings to keep its members informed and to train leaders.

National, state, and local organizations carry on their work through committees. The committees work in such fields of child welfare as character and spiritual education, citizenship, services for exceptional children, health, international relations, juvenile protection, legislation, mental health, parent and family life education, reading and library service, recreation, safety, and school education.

Officers of the National PTA are elected at an annual convention. National PTA publications include *The PTA Magazine* and the *National PTA Bulletin*.

PARIS (*păr'ĭs*), in Greek mythology, was a son of Priam, the king of Troy. Before Paris was born, his mother, Hecuba, dreamed that her son would bring harm to Troy. To avoid this danger, Priam sent Paris to the mountains to live like a shepherd. He married a lovely nymph named Oenone.

One day three goddesses appeared before Zeus (Jupiter), the supreme ruler of the universe. They were Hera (Juno), queen of the gods; Athena (Minerva), goddess of wisdom; and Aphrodite (Venus), goddess of beauty. Each of the goddesses claimed that she should be given a golden apple marked "For the Fairest." They asked Zeus to choose the winner, but he told them instead to consult Paris. Each goddess offered Paris a wonderful gift if he would choose her. Hera promised to make Paris ruler over all Europe and Asia. Athena promised that she would make him a great soldier who would lead the Trojans to victory over the Greeks. Aphrodite promised him that he would win the most beautiful woman in the world. Paris decided to choose Aphrodite's offer. This choice is called the Judgment of Paris.

Aphrodite took Paris to Sparta, in Greece, to the home of King Menelaus. Menelaus' wife, Helen, was the most beautiful woman in the world. When Menelaus was away from home, Paris took Helen with him to his father's palace in Troy. The Greeks demanded that Helen be returned to Greece, but the Trojans refused, thus causing the Trojan War. (See TROY.)

During the fighting, Paris was about to be overcome by Menelaus when Aphrodite helped him escape. Later he shot an arrow that killed the Greek hero Achilles. Paris himself was wounded, and he begged to be carried to Oenone, who could cure him. Oenone, angry because Paris had left her, refused. Paris died, and Oenone killed herself.

After ten years of terrible fighting, the war ended, and Troy was destroyed. The warning about Paris had come true.

PARIS (*păr'ĭs*), **FRANCE,** is one of the largest and most beautiful cities of the world. No other city in France can compare to Paris. It is to that country what New York City, Washington, D.C., Detroit, and Chicago combined are to the United States. Not only is Paris the capital of France, but it is also the main center of industry, commerce, finance, and transportation. The city ranks as the third largest French port.

Paris grew as a trade and industrial center because of its ideal location as a crossroads city on the Seine River. Early kings lived there, and eventually it became the center of a kingdom and an empire. People were attracted to the city as it developed wealth and prestige. Today, Paris with its suburbs is the world's seventh largest metropolitan area. About one of every six Frenchmen live there.

Paris is a romantic and exciting city. Its great spirit of freedom has historically attracted artists and intellectuals. It has long been a world center of culture and learning. Tourists flock there every year to enjoy the city's art, its fine foods,

Kent—Pix from Publix

The famed Eiffel Tower, which has become the symbol of Paris, can be seen from almost every section of the city. From the monumental statues at the entrance to the Jardin des Tuileries, it is visible across the Place de la Concorde.

and its charm. The beauty of Paris has been widely heralded in song and story. To describe the city, people often use a well-known phrase: "Paris is like a beautiful woman."

Description

Paris is located in the heart of northern France, about 100 miles southeast of the English Channel. The city spreads out over a level plain on both sides of the Seine River just north of the Seine's juncture with the Marne River. Paris proper covers an area of about 40 square miles, but the metropolitan area, which includes much of the surrounding departments, is several times that size. The Seine divides Paris into two parts that are known as the Left Bank and the Right Bank. The Left Bank is mostly to the south, and the Right Bank is mostly to the north.

The Ile de la Cite—a small island in the Seine—is called the birthplace of Paris. On it are many of the city's oldest and most famous buildings. The medieval Notre-Dame Cathedral, begun in 1163, is one of the most famous landmarks of Paris. Another church, the Sainte Chapelle, is noted for its magnificent stained-glass windows. The Palais de Justice contains the Conciergerie, the famous prison where Marie Antoinette, Maximilien Robespierre, and other notables of the French Revolution were imprisoned.

Near the Ile de la Cite, on the Right Bank, is a large square. For eight centuries this was the site of Les Halles, the chief food and flower markets of Paris. In 1969 the various markets were moved to new locations outside the city. To the east and near the river is the Place de la Bastille, another of the huge open squares so typical of Paris. There stood the grim Bastille prison, which was destroyed during the French Revolution. (See BASTILLE.)

The quays (wharves) of the Left Bank and of the Ile Saint-Louis (another island in the Seine River) are among the oldest sights of Paris. On both sides of the Seine, quays are bordered by picturesque houses, some of them more than 200 years old. Against the wall that borders the Seine are hundreds of stalls that have second-hand books for sale.

Opposite the Ile de la Cite on the Left Bank is the Place Saint-Michel. From it the broad Boulevard Saint-Michel runs up a low hill that marks the Latin Quarter. This part of the city has long been the home of students who attend the University of Paris. Nearby is the Pantheon, burial place of famous Frenchmen such as Victor Hugo, Jean Jacques Rousseau, Voltaire, Emile Zola, and Saint Genevieve, the patron saint of Paris. Bordering the Boulevard Saint-Michel on the west is the Palais du Luxembourg. The Council of the Republic, which replaced the French Senate in 1946, meets in the palace.

Running parallel to the Seine is the stately Boulevard Saint-Germain, once the most fashionable street of Paris. It is still inhabited by a few of the old, noble families of France. The boulevard leads to the Palais Bourbon. This building is the seat of the National Assembly of the French government.

On the Right Bank of the Seine is the Place de la Concorde, the central square of Paris. To the west, on the Left Bank, is the domed Hotel des Invalides, founded in 1670 by Louis XIV as a home for disabled veterans. It contains the tomb of Napoleon Bonaparte. Farther west along the Seine is a green open area, the Champ de Mars. From it the lofty Eiffel Tower rises high above the Paris skyline. It was erected for the Paris Exposition of 1889, and, with its television mast, is 1,056 feet high. It is especially outstanding because Paris law forbids other tall structures. Except for the tower, Paris buildings must conform in size, color, and design.

Across the river, the long, broad Avenue des Champs-Elysees runs from the Place de la Concorde to the Place de l'Etoile. At the center of the Place de l'Etoile stands the massive Arc de Triomphe, which Napoleon I had erected to commemorate his victories. Under the monument is the tomb of France's unknown soldier. An eternal flame burns over the tomb.

The Seine, with its islands and many bridges, divides the city of Paris into two sections— the Right Bank and the Left Bank.

Philippe Johnsson

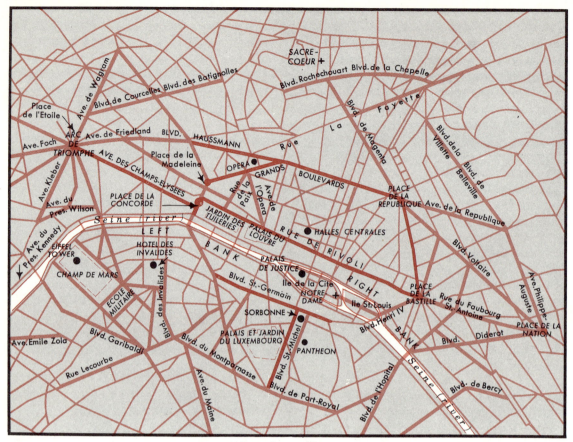

Map of central Paris.

East of the Place de la Concorde is the Jardin des Tuileries, alongside which is the Rue de Rivoli, an arcaded street lined with shops. The Palais des Tuileries, residence of French royalty, was burned during the Paris Commune of 1871. East of the Jardin des Tuileries is the old Palais du Louvre, converted in 1793 to a museum of art. North of the gardens is the Place Vendome. This spacious square has a central column on which stands a statue of Napoleon I. The Rue de la Paix, one of the best-known shopping streets in the world, runs from the Place Vendome to the Place de l'Opera. To the west is the Palais de l'Elysee, home of the French presidents.

Among the more popular tourist routes in Paris are the broad, curving Grands Boulevards. The boulevards are really sections of one street, each with its own name. The street runs from the Place de la Madeleine to the Place de la Bastille. The first section is the Boulevard de la Madeleine, named for one of the most famous Paris churches. The Boulevard des Capucines comes next and crosses the Place de l'Opera. The Avenue de l'Opera is the heart of the main financial and commercial section of Paris. In this area are the Bank of France and the Stock Exchange.

To the north the ground slopes sharply up to the Montmartre district, famous for its narrow side streets and its many picturesque nightclubs and cabarets. The colorful Place Pigalle is a popular entertainment center in the district. Montmartre is also known as a traditional residence of writers and painters. At the highest part of Montmartre is Sacre-Coeur, a white stone church. Many tourists visit this site to enjoy the magnificent view it presents of all Paris.

Throughout Paris there are green squares, broad sidewalks, open-air cafes, and long curving streets lined with gray houses.

People and Culture

By the 14th century, Paris had become the most populated city of France. The kings of France made their homes in Paris, and the city grew rapidly. In the 17th century the population rose to more than 500,000, and by the 1850's the population rose to more than one million. In the early 1960's Paris had almost three million residents, or about four times as many as the next largest French city, Marseille.

The beauty and romance of Paris attract thousands of foreigners yearly. Many of these are tourists, but some also go there to live. Paris has about 300,000 registered non-French residents and thousands more who are citizens of French Community countries.

Art and Theater. The Louvre is probably the most famous art museum in the world. Its huge collection includes Leonardo da Vinci's "Mona Lisa," one of the world's most valuable paintings. The highly prized Greek sculpture "Venus de Milo" is also in the Louvre. Paris is world famous for its musical and dramatic productions. The Opera (National Academy of Music) on the Right Bank was founded in 1669–1671. Ballets are also performed at the Opera. Another theater, the Opera

Arc de Triomphe.

Montmartre.

Comique, offers lighter musical shows. French classical drama is presented by the Theatre Francais, or Comedie Francaise, formed in 1681. The Opera, Opera Comique, and Theatre Francais are all run by the state.

Education. The University of Paris, established in the 1200's, is one of Europe's oldest universities. It is usually referred to as the Sorbonne, after Robert de Sorbon, who founded one of its colleges in the 13th century. It is by far the largest university in France. More than 70,000 students attend the schools of law, medicine, letters, sciences, and pharmacy. Its main buildings are in the Latin Quarter of the Left Bank. The university library has about four million volumes.

Notre-Dame Cathedral.

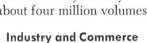

Industry and Commerce

Paris is the dynamic heart of French industrial and business life. It is the country's chief banking center, its leading dealer in foreign trade, and its major producer of clothing and books. Paris also supplies most of France's automobiles, airplanes, and motion pictures.

The city has long been known for specialized industries that demand skill and fine taste. A Paris label on a luxury item—such as perfume—has come to mean the best in quality and style. Paris is also considered the world's fashion center for women's clothing. Tourism, however, is the city's main income producer.

Parisian industry falls into two zones. There is an area of light industries in the central city and a belt of heavier industries in the suburbs. In the outer belt are manufacturing plants where automobiles, chemicals, and metal, petroleum, and rubber products are made. In the city proper are the lighter industries that

The Byzantine-domed Sacre-Coeur on the Right Bank of the Seine occupies the highest point in Paris.

History

During the time of Roman conquest, the Ile de la Cite became important because it provided an easy place to cross the Seine. An early route from the Mediterranean Sea led through the island to the English Channel coast in the north. On the island a small fishing village called Lutetia grew up. The Romans fortified Lutetia, and eventually it became known as Paris, after the Parisii tribe who lived in that part of France. It was not until A.D. 987, when the Capets became the ruling family of France, that Paris became the capital. By the 14th century, Paris had become the most populous city of France and was rapidly spreading on both banks of the Seine. At various times walls were built to protect the city from attack. The walls are gone now, but their locations are marked by a series of boulevards.

Paris, because of its importance, has been under siege many times. While under Roman control, the town was practically destroyed by barbarians. It was again devastated by Nor-

require less space, and demand the skilled workers. Furniture, clothing, jewelry, perfume, optical equipment, leather goods, musical instruments, and drugs are among the products made in the central city. Most important French firms have their main offices in Paris.

Paris is the French hub of transportation. The chief highways, railroads, and waterways of France all lead to Paris. Seven major railroads have large stations there. The Seine River and several canals have quays where coal, coke, oil, wood, grain, and wine are handled. Air lines link Paris with the world's great cities. The principal airports are Le Bourget, 6 miles north of the city, and Orly, 12 miles to the south.

Government

Paris, with its suburbs, makes up most of the Seine Department of France. The prefect, or administrative head, of the department also heads the Paris city government. The Paris Municipal Council is elected every six years and is composed of 90 councilors. The Municipal Council is also part of the larger General Council of the Seine. Unlike other French departments, the prefect does not control the police force. The city has a separate prefect of police.

At almost any time of day and evening some of the local residents can be seen fishing along the quiet Seine River.

man raids in the 9th century. During the Hundred Years' War, Paris fell into British hands from about 1422 to 1436. Joan of Arc tried but failed to recapture the city in 1429. The violent French Revolution erupted first in Paris in 1789. During the Franco-Prussian War (1870–1871) Paris was attacked and again captured.

Though Paris has been attacked many times, its beauty has grown through the ages. Many of the city's oldest buildings date from the Renaissance. The Louvre was improved during this period, and the first theater, a hospital, and the Palais des Tuileries were built. Under Louis XIII and Cardinal Richelieu, in the 17th century, streets were improved and the Ile Saint-Louis was developed. In the 1700's Paris spread to almost its modern limits.

Perhaps the city's greatest progress came during the 19th century. Napoleon I, in the early 1800's, laid plans for many improvements, but few of these were carried out during his lifetime. Napoleon III (1852–1870) and Baron Georges Haussmann, a prefect of the Seine Department, together gave modern Paris much of its beauty. Under their administration broad new avenues were built, a new sewer system was developed, and the great parks—the Bois de Boulogne and the Bois de Vincennes—were added. In 1900 the Metropolitan Railway (the Metro) was built, providing Paris with an efficient subway.

In the 20th century, Paris twice more came under siege. In World War I, a German invasion was averted by the First Battle of the Marne. The fighting came so close to the city that Paris taxicabs and buses were used to rush soldiers to the front. The drivers were regarded as heroes for their gallant action. The city, however, suffered considerable damage from shelling. World War II, which began in September 1939, struck Paris with terrifying suddenness. In June 1940 Nazi tanks raced toward the city and airplanes bombed the suburbs. The French government declared Paris an open (nonmilitary) city to save it from destruction. The German occupation that followed lasted four years and brought many hardships. The Germans seized all manufacturing plants and the French were forced to work for them.

Paris was the headquarters for Nazi collaborators, but it also became a center of French resistance. The resistance forces, aided by American and French troops, liberated Paris in August 1944. Violence did not occur again until the 1950's and 1960's when Algeria was seeking its independence from France. Anti-independence terrorists set off bombs and rioted in protest.

Paris has a population of 2,779,935 (1962 census). The Paris metropolitan area has a population of approximately 7,750,000.

(See also FRANCE, EUROPE.)

PARKMAN (pärk′män), **FRANCIS** (1823–1893), was a U.S. historian. He was born in Boston, Massachusetts, the son of a minister.

As a boy, Parkman enjoyed walking in the forest and developed a love of nature. In 1844 he graduated from Harvard University. Two years later, he and a friend took a trip along the Oregon Trail in wild and unsettled country. (See TRAILS, U.S. HISTORIC.) Parkman lived for a while with a band of Sioux Indians, and his skill as a horseman and a rifleman won their respect. His travels led to a popular book, *The Oregon Trail*, which was published in 1849.

Parkman was never again to return to the frontier that he loved so much. He suffered from poor health for the rest of his life. His eyes were so weak that he had to have people read to him. For a long period, his writing averaged only six lines a day.

In spite of his handicap, however, Parkman was determined to write. He invented a machine that so supported his hand that he could write with his eyes closed. The result of his determination was 11 books about the history of the American frontier. These include books about the French explorers and the struggle between the British and the French for control of North America. During periods when Parkman was too sick to write, he worked in his garden. As a result, he became an expert on roses and a teacher of horticulture.

PARLIAMENT (pär′li ment), originally meaning "talk," gradually came to mean a group of persons assembled for a conference. It is now

The Palace of Westminster's huge Gothic clock tower with its famous bell, Big Ben (left), has become the visual symbol of England's Parliament. In 1958, for the first time, a state opening of Parliament was photographed and televised (below); Queen Elizabeth II officiated.

(Left) J. Allan Cash, (below) Central Press Photos Ltd.

most commonly known as the name of the law-making body of the United Kingdom of Great Britain and Northern Ireland.

The beginnings of the English Parliament may be traced to the Witan of the Anglo-Saxon kings of Britain. This body, also known as the Witenagemot, was a council made up of the wise men of the realm, mainly the nobles and the clergy. The members were not elected. The king was the chief power, but the Witan could elect and depose the king, and he did not perform an act of state without its advice and approval. Originally, each of the various kingdoms of Britain held such a council. After the land was united into a single realm in the 9th century, the Witan became a national assembly.

Following the Norman Conquest of Britain in 1066, the Witan was transformed into a feudal council. It was composed of officers of state, clergy, and feudal landlords that the king chose to summon. With his council the king discussed affairs of state.

Kings continued to summon these conferences in the following years. During the reign of Henry III, they came to be called parliaments. After a time the knights were also included among those summoned. It was not until 1265 that representatives of the common man were invited to join in the conferences. In that year Simon de Montfort, the leader of the revolt against Henry III, called a national assembly that included representatives from the boroughs of England. This parliament, however, was not truly representative because most of the delegates were selected from De Montfort's supporters. (See MONTFORT, SIMON DE.)

Henry's successor, Edward I, summoned several parliaments. The most important was the

Model Parliament of 1295. This parliament was truly representative and became the model for future parliaments. The lords spiritual (clergy) and temporal (barons) were summoned, and every sheriff was directed to have elected two knights from each shire, two citizens from each city, and two burgesses from each borough. Thus, all three divisions of medieval society—the commons, the nobles, and the clergy—were represented in the Model Parliament.

The purpose of the early English parliamentary sessions was to strike a bargain between the king, who needed money, and his subjects, who had complaints. Gradually Parliament took from the king the right to levy taxes without its approval. With this power Parliament's authority grew. It was able to make and unmake kings, and by the 15th century it was no longer a meeting dismissed as soon as some particular business was completed. It had become a permanent and important body, with the lords and commons meeting as two separate houses.

Parliament no longer merely offered advice and presented petitions to the king. By the 17th century it had come forward as a critic of the king and challenged his authority. The English Civil War (1642–1651) was fought to decide whether government was to be by the king himself or by the king and Parliament. Charles I and his royalist supporters were defeated in the war by Oliver Cromwell, the leader of the parliamentary forces. Cromwell, however, failed to settle the relationship between the authority of the crown and the authority of the representative national assembly. The question was not settled until 1689 when the Bill of Rights assured that Parliament was supreme. (See CROMWELL, OLIVER; ENGLAND.)

In 1714 George I of the House of Hanover came to the throne of England. (See HANOVER, HOUSE OF.) Because he had little knowledge of the English language and little interest in England, he left the government to his ministers. As a result three parliamentary institutions developed—the party system, the cabinet government, and the prime ministership.

The French Revolution in 1789, with its emphasis on the rights of the individual, influenced the progress of Parliament. The Reform Bill of 1832 marked the beginning of more equal voting rights for the people of England. By this legislation the new middle class that was emerging as a result of the Industrial Revolution was able to share in the government. Similar reform legislation was passed in the following years until all adults—regardless of sex, status, or creed—were given the privilege of voting.

As the English parliamentary democracy developed, traditional practices and institutions had to change to keep pace with the developments. The House of Lords, whose members are not elected, had to be adjusted into a governmental system based on elected representatives. Originally the House of Lords was the more powerful of the two chambers of Parliament. It was able to control the majority of seats in the House of Commons. But as more people were given the right to vote, this control was lost.

The House of Commons thus acquired equal power and eventually even more power. The House of Lords, however, could refuse to pass legislation submitted to it by the House of Commons. The result was often deadlock. In 1909 the House of Lords rejected the Finance Bill. This brought about legislation in 1911 that greatly reduced the powers of the upper house. The House of Lords may now delay legislation, but proposals may become law without its approval.

The more than 900 members of the House of Lords are temporal peers, who have received their titles by inheritance or appointment by the Crown, and spiritual peers, the bishops and archbishops. All peers and peeresses 21 years of age and over may sit in the House of Lords.

The House of Commons is limited by law to 630 members. The members are elected from each of the country's districts, or constituencies. Women may be elected to the House of Commons.

England's government operates on a two-party system. The two principal parties are the Conservative and the Labour. Elections are held when Parliament has been dissolved at the end of five years, or when the Crown dissolves it on the advice of the ministers. The party that wins a majority in the election gains control of the government, and the leader of the majority party becomes prime minister. He chooses his cabinet from among the members of his party. The party out of power acts as the opposition. The leader of the opposition appoints a "shadow cabinet" of men who are ready to take over the cabinet whenever their party regains control of the government. When that occurs the leader of the opposition becomes prime minister. Peers may not sit in the House of Commons. Commoners, therefore, usually hold the positions of party leadership. (See CABINET; DEMOCRACY; POLITICAL PARTIES; and for information on parliaments in other countries, see the sections on government in the individual country articles.)

PARLIAMENTARY (*pär'lĭ mĕn'tä rē*) **LAW** is the body of rules of order and procedure that govern organizations and assemblies. When people come together for meetings to carry on business, they need rules to control the proceedings. If the number of people is small, there may be no need for rules. The group may reach decisions without debate or controversy. When the number is large, however, many different opinions may be represented. In order for each person to have a fair chance to express himself, the meeting must be controlled by a set of rules. Sometimes the rules are called parliamentary procedure or rules of order. They make up parliamentary law. The name comes from the English Parliament, where the rules developed with the process of making laws.

The English colonists in America brought these rules with them. In the colonial assemblies and town meetings English parliamentary law was followed. When the Congress of the United States of America was established, English parliamentary law was applied to the manner of conducting the business of lawmaking. Because the newly formed government was a republic and not a monarchy, certain changes had to be made to fit the new order.

Parliamentary law brought order and control to public meetings. It was adopted, therefore, for use in private meetings of clubs, societies, and other groups. The purposes of public and private meetings differ; therefore, differences occur in the proceedings. Lawmaking bodies are usually quite formal in procedure. The chairman or presiding officer makes rulings that are strictly in accord with parliamentary law. Private groups usually are less formal. Rules for their meetings are largely uniform in the United States. Generally, they include the following:

1. A chairman presides over the meeting. He may be the elected president of the group, or he may be a member selected to conduct at that particular meeting.
2. A secretary keeps a written record, called minutes, of what is done at the meeting.
3. If money is involved, there will be a treasurer.
4. If the membership is large, there may be a sergeant at arms who keeps order.
5. There may be one or more vice-presidents who will act in the absence of the president.
6. The chairman may appoint a committee of three or more members to look into matters of interest and to report to the gathering at a later meeting.
7. Anyone who wants to speak obtains the floor by standing and saying, "Mr. President," "Mr. Chairman," or whatever is the proper address to the person in charge of the meeting. This speaker should give his own name. The presiding officer recognizes him by saying his name or by nodding to him. Then he alone may speak without interruption.
8. A motion to take action or express opinion brings business before the meeting; for example, "I move that the club hold a stamp exhibit." This is a main motion, or one that introduces a subject, and normally takes six steps for completion:
   a) Member makes a motion.
   b) Another member seconds (supports) motion.
   c) Chairman restates motion.
   d) Chairman calls for debate.
   e) Chairman calls for a vote by saying, "All in favor of this motion say, 'Aye'; opposed, 'No'"; voting may also be by a show of hands or, in important cases, by secret written ballots.
   f) Chairman announces the result.

This motion must be disposed of before any other main motion may be made. In addition to the main motion mentioned above, there are other (secondary) motions that may greatly affect a motion before the group. For example, a motion to amend is to change the wording of a motion and may actually change the intention of the first motion. To postpone is to put decision off until later in that meeting or until the next one. To commit, or to table, is to hold the motion until a committee of members gives it further study or recommends that it be brought before the meeting again. Usually a majority vote in favor of or against a motion will determine its fate. In matters of great importance, the rules may require a two-thirds vote to support a motion.

A club may select its own rules. These are the bylaws. To cover situations that may arise outside of its own special bylaws, a book on parliamentary law should be adopted as parliamentary authority. In most group meetings, the order of business is almost always conducted in the following manner:

1. Meeting called to order by the chairman
2. Reading (by the secretary) and approval (by the group) of the minutes of the last meeting
3. Reports of officer (as, for example, a report by the treasurer)
4. Reports of committees
5. Unfinished business (as, for example, motions that had been postponed or tabled or sent to committee at a previous meeting)
6. New business
7. Plans for the future
8. Adjournment

Most organizations have a written constitution, and in it will be found the name and the purpose of the group. The constitution may also state the qualifications of members and tell what officers are to be elected. Sometimes the constitution is accompanied by a set of bylaws for the guidance and control of the officers and members.

Briefly stated, either the constitution or the bylaws should give:

1. The name of the group
2. Object
3. Members and dues
4. Officers and their duties
5. Place and time of meetings
6. Parliamentary authority to be followed

PARRISH (*păr'ish*), **MAXFIELD** (1870–1966), was a U.S. artist and illustrator. His work is easy to recognize because of its warm, rich tones and glowing, vivid colors. One shade of particularly intense blue often seen in his paintings is now known as "Parrish blue." Parrish was born in Philadelphia, Pennsylvania, the son of Stephen Parrish, an etcher. He studied art at the Pennsylvania Academy of Fine Arts and was also a pupil of the illustrator Howard Pyle at Drexel Institute in Philadelphia. He was an associate member of the National Academy and won many prizes and awards.

Parrish's illustrations range in subject matter from popular Western stories to John Keats's poems. Among the books he has illustrated for boys and girls are Kenneth Grahame's *Dream Days* and Eugene Field's *Poems of Childhood*, in which his delicately whimsical pictures capture the beauty and simplicity of the poetry. Often elaborate, his pictures reveal great attention to detail, and much gentle humor. His illustrations for the *Arabian Nights* show a world of romance and imagination. Parrish also designed bookplates and painted some interesting mural decorations. His work is widely known because it has been used frequently as illustrations for calendars.

PARROT (*păr'ŭt*) is any one of several species of the family of birds known as Psittacidae. This family is made up of more than 300 species, including parakeets, cockatoos, cockatiels, lories, lorikeets, macaws, lovebirds, and budgerigars. The distinguishing characteristics of these birds are a hooked bill, a large head, a short neck, and strong, grasping feet. The feet have two toes pointing forward and two backward.

Most parrots are brightly colored and noisy. They live in treetops throughout most of the tropics of the Southern Hemisphere. In the Western Hemisphere they are found as far north as northern Mexico. Members of the family vary in size from the $3\frac{1}{2}$-inch pygmy parrots of the South Pacific to the macaws of South America, which reach a length of 40 inches. (See BIRD, *Plates 20–22.*)

Since ancient times, parrots have been popular as pets. Many parrots can be taught to perform tricks and to "talk"; that is, they can produce sounds imitating words spoken by the human voice, although they do not know the meaning of such sounds. Many of these birds also have the ability to hold food in one foot and bite pieces off, using the foot as a person uses a hand. Among the best-known parrots to be tamed are the yellow-headed Amazon parrot and the African gray parrot. These are both excellent mimics. They are similar in size and shape, both being a little over a foot in length with short, rounded or squared tails. The Amazon parrot is mostly green with blue and red markings on the wings and a bright yellow head. The African gray parrot is colored in soft tones of gray with a bare, white face and bright red tail. Another popular cage bird of this family is the little budgie, or budgerigar. This is a true parakeet native to Australia. It is about seven inches long and has a long, tapering tail. Budgies have been bred in various colors, although the wild birds are usually green with a blue tail.

Among the loveliest members of the family are the cockatoos. These birds inhabit the jungles of the Australian region of the South Pacific. They range in size from about 15 to 32 inches. They have crests of feathers on their heads that they can raise or lower at will. Most of these birds are white, tinged with soft pinks or sulfur yellows. The largest of the cockatoos is the great black cockatoo. It has a strong, sharply pointed beak and bare, pink

The yellow and blue macaw, about 33 inches long, has a harsh, screaming call. It is noted for its power of flight.

cheeks. These cheeks "blush" bright red when the bird becomes excited.

The largest and gaudiest members of the parrot family are the macaws of Mexico and of Central and South America. The most familiar are the large scarlet macaw and the yellow and blue macaw often seen in zoos. All macaws have large, strong bills and long, tapering tails. The tail of the red and green macaw when fully developed is more than two feet long.

The only parrot native to the United States is the Carolina parakeet. Until recently this bird was found in the forests of the southern and central United States. In the early 19th century, large flocks of these yellowish-green, orange-faced birds caused a great deal of damage to grain and fruit crops throughout the South and Midwest. As a result, they were hunted and killed by the thousands. The last ones were seen in the early 1920's in the Everglades of Florida.

Lovebirds are small, pointed-tailed parrots native to Africa and Madagascar. They are much quieter than the rest of the parrots. When caged, they prefer to huddle together in pairs. In the wild state, these birds usually travel in large flocks, often damaging grain crops.

Parrots suffer from a virus disease called psittacosis, or "parrot fever." This disease is also carried by turkeys and pigeons. It can be transmitted to humans, sometimes resulting in serious illness. Antibiotics, however, give promise of controlling the disease.

Parrots in general are hardy and long lived. Their life span in the wild state is not known, but some caged birds frequently live for more than 50 years. One is recorded to have reached 80 years of age. Although they are tropical birds, they can live well in temperate and even cold climates. Sailors have long been fond of their companionship on shipboard. In their native forests they usually live in large flocks. They feed mostly on fruits, nuts, and other vegetation. Occasionally they eat insects and worms. Their strong bills are useful for cracking nuts and cutting pieces from fruits.

Parrots usually nest in holes in trees or in crevices between rocks. The number of their round, shiny white eggs varies with the species. The average is from three to five. The young birds hatch in about three weeks and are cared for by both parents for two to three months.

PARSLEY (*pärs'lē*), or *Petroselinum crispum*, is an herb of the family Umbelliferae, to which celery and carrots also belong. The plant is a biennial. It is native to the Mediterranean countries, although it is commonly cultivated throughout most of the world.

J. Horace McFarland Company

Parsley, a hardy herb, has dark green, frilled leaves.

There are two kinds of parsley. One, turnip-rooted parsley, is grown for its edible roots. It is cultivated mainly in Europe. The other kind is grown for its frilled, decorative leaves, which are used as a flavoring or trimming for food. The leaves grow in a rosette during the early stages and rarely reach more than six inches above the ground. The plant is usually picked young. If it matures, however, it may grow to a height of six feet and produce small, yellowish blossoms.

PARSNIP (*pärs'nĭp*), or *Pastinaca sativa*, one of the winter vegetables, is a biennial plant of the Umbelliferae family. Carrots and parsley also belong to this family.

The parsnip plant is native to Eurasia. It has fernlike leaves and fleshy, white, tapering roots. The root is the part that is eaten. It is sometimes 18 inches long, with a sweet taste and an aromatic smell. The roots are eaten boiled, baked, stewed, or fried and are sometimes made into marmalade and wine. They are also excellent cattle food.

Parsnip seeds should be planted in the spring, in deep, rich, but light soil. The roots may be dug in October or November. They may be left in the ground until needed, however, since their flavor is improved by frost. To obtain seeds, the roots are left in the ground

Courtesy Burpee Seeds

The parsnip root (left) has been valued as a vegetable since Roman times. The cultivated rows of parsnip plants (right) have blossomed and seeded.

until the next year, when tiny, pale yellow blossoms develop and produce seeds.

PASCAL (*pás kál'*), **BLAISE** (*blāz*) (1623–1662), a French mathematician, scientist, and religious writer, was born in Clermont-Ferrand, France. As a boy Pascal studied mathematics and proved he had exceptional skill in the subject. At age 16 he wrote the "Essay on Conics," a treatise on geometry that impressed even the great mathematician Rene Descartes.

Between 1642 and 1644 Pascal constructed an adding machine. This invention made him famous among his contemporaries. Among other accomplishments in mathematics, he helped develop the theory of probability.

Pascal also made important contributions to physics. In 1643 an Italian scientist, Evangelista Torricelli, developed the first mercury barometer, thereby showing that air exerts pressure. Pascal advanced Torricelli's principles further, proving that atmospheric weight decreases as altitude increases.

He also formulated an important principle known since as Pascal's Law. It states that if pressure is increased anywhere on the surface of a fluid in a closed container, the pressure will be carried without loss in all directions. The hydraulic brake works by this principle.

From 1646 on, Pascal became increasingly concerned with religious matters. He was a Catholic but was converted to Jansenism. To defend the teachings of his new religion he wrote "Provincial Letters." The following year he started a large work explaining the truth of Christianity. Though it was unfinished at his death, the existing fragments of it were published as *Pensées* ("Thoughts"). It depicts man as meaningless without God, and asserts that faith rather than reason leads man to salvation.

PASSIONFLOWER (*păsh'ŭn flou'ēr*) is a plant of the family Passifloraceae. There are more than 400 species of passionflowers. They grow in the warmest southern and western areas of the United States and in tropical areas of South America, Asia, Australia, and other parts of the world.

The passionflower is a climbing or trailing vine. It was given its name by early explorers who saw in it a symbol of the Crucifixion of Jesus Christ. The three pistils, at the center of the blossom, represent the nails used on the cross. The five stamens represent Christ's five wounds. The ten sepals and petals represent the faithful disciples, with Judas and Peter

The passionflower blossom has a bright, fringed corona.

J. Horace McFarland Company

missing. The beautiful fringed corona represents the crown of thorns.

In spite of the sacred tradition built around the passionflower, it is better known in its native regions by its common name of maypop. The flowers are generally purplish-white. A large scarlet-flowered variety is grown as an ornamental vine. There is also a yellow one.

The fruit of some passionflowers is the size of a small apple and is edible. One kind of passionflower is raised commercially in southern California. A refreshing drink is made from the pulp and juice of its fruit.

PASSION (*păsh'ŭn*) **PLAY** (*plā*) is a drama depicting the Passion, or suffering, of Jesus Christ. Passion plays are mystery plays (dramas based on events in the Bible). They usually dramatize Christ's life from the time of the Last Supper to His death. (See JESUS CHRIST.)

Passion plays were first presented some time in the Middle Ages. They were introduced in the Roman Catholic Church by priests who acted in the plays and presented them in Latin for Christmas and Easter. During the 15th and 16th centuries they were given by laymen in the languages of the people. In England the plays were presented on wagon stages that were moved from one place to another. In France the actors performed on stationary stages built in village squares or marketplaces. Passion plays were also given in Spain, and Spanish conquerors introduced the plays into the New World.

In 1633 the village of Oberammergau, Germany, was stricken by a dreadful plague. When the plague ended the grateful inhabitants vowed to present a Passion play every tenth year. The first performance was given in 1634. The Oberammergau Passion Play has become a world-famous event. It is seen by visitors from all parts of the world. The actors in the production, numbering about 700, are chosen from the villagers of Oberammergau. They are dedicated to the Passion play, and they consider the performances sacred.

In the United States various groups present Passion plays. Two of the most outstanding are the Zion Passion Play and the Black Hills Passion Play. In Zion, Illinois, the play opens with the Sermon on the Mount and follows the life of Christ as He wandered with His disciples. It closes with Christ's Resurrection and Ascension. The Black Hills Passion Play, given in Spearfish, South Dakota, was first known in the United States as the Luenen Passion Play. It became a permanent company when Josef Meier, seventh member of his family to play Christ, settled in Spearfish in 1939. This Passion play tells the events of the last seven days of the life of Christ.

The Ascension scene is one of the high points of the Black Hills Passion Play that is held annually in Spearfish, South Dakota.

Closely related to the Passion and other mystery plays were the miracle plays, which presented incidents in the lives of the saints. Morality plays were also popular during the Middle Ages. In these plays actors portrayed roles such as Charity, Vice, and Love and acted out a story. The best-known morality play is *Everyman*, which appeared in England sometime in the 16th century. From these plays modern drama developed. Early in the 13th century, laymen as well as priests began to write plays, and gradually nonreligious as well as religious themes were used.

PASSOVER (*pàs′ō′vẽr*) is the Jewish festival of freedom that celebrates the Exodus of the ancient Israelites from Egypt. The festival is called Pesach by the Jews. The story of Passover is told in the Book of Exodus in the Bible. An Israelite leader, Moses, demanded that Pharaoh allow the Jews to leave Egypt. When Pharaoh refused, Moses warned that God would bring plagues upon Egypt. (See Moses.) The festival is called Passover because the angel of death "passed over" the houses of the Israelites to spare their firstborn children from harm. The Egyptian firstborn, however, were killed. After this terrible plague, the Israelites were released.

According to the Book of Exodus, every Israelite in Egypt set aside a lamb on the 10th day of Nisan, the first month of spring. The lamb was kept until the 14th day of the month and then killed. The blood was sprinkled on the doorposts of the Israelite homes as a sign for the angel of death to pass by. The lamb was roasted and eaten, and the Israelites prepared to leave Egypt in haste after the plague of the firstborn. The lamb later became known as the Paschal lamb.

Passover is now celebrated for eight days beginning with the eve of the 15th day of Nisan. Reform, or liberal, Jews observe the holiday for seven days. During the entire festival, matzah, or unleavened bread, is eaten. This is a reminder that the Israelites baked unleavened bread because they were in a rush to escape from Egypt. Passover is also called the Feast of Unleavened Bread in the Bible.

Passover is chiefly a home festival. On the first two nights a Seder, or order of service, is arranged at mealtime. Reform Jews hold the Seder only on the first night. This is one of the most colorful and important family occasions in the Jewish calendar. The family reads from a special prayer book called Haggadah, or narrative, which tells the story of the slavery and freedom of the Israelites. The foods on the

Seder table are symbolic ones. In addition to the unleavened bread, there is also a roasted shank bone, which is a reminder of the Paschal lamb, and bitter herbs, which recall the bitterness of the Egyptian slavery.

The description of the Last Supper in the New Testament corresponds to that of the Paschal meal. Good Friday was originally called Pascha, or Passover. At first, Easter and Passover were observed at the same time. By the 4th century the church calendar was changed, so the two holidays rarely begin on the same day.

PASSPORT (*pàs′pōrt*) is a travel document issued to nationals of a country by the government of that country. A national is either a citizen or a person who, although not a citizen, owes permanent allegiance to and is entitled to the protection of a country. (See CITIZENSHIP.) A United States passport identifies the bearer as a U.S. national and entitles him to the protection of the U.S. government while abroad. The passport requests officials of foreign governments to permit the bearer to travel or stay in their countries and, in case of need, to give him all lawful aid and protection. A passport is not required for brief tourist travel between the United States and most countries in North, Central, and South America. A citizen, however, is required by travel control regulations to have a passport to travel outside those areas.

The word passport comes from two French words, *passer*, meaning "to pass," and *port*, meaning "harbor." The earliest passports or documents of identification were issued to individuals and also to ships that desired safe passage in and out of foreign ports. They are no longer issued to ships, however.

Passports have been issued by the U.S. secretary of state since the founding of the country. The earliest record of such a document is July 8, 1796. Congress passed legislation in 1803 and 1815 to allow the secretary to continue to issue passports under his general authority to conduct foreign relations. Until 1856, however, they continued to be issued also by governors of states and even mayors of cities. In that year a law was passed restricting the issuance of passports to federal authorities. They are now issued by the Passport Office, which is in the Department of State, and by U.S. embassies and consulates in foreign countries. The basic passport law now in effect was passed in 1856.

An application for a passport in the United States must be made in person before a clerk of a federal court or state court having naturalization jurisdiction, or at one of the passport agencies in Boston, Massachusetts; Chicago; Los Angeles, California; Miami, Florida; New Orleans, Louisiana; New York City; Philadelphia, Pennsylvania; San Francisco, California; Seattle, Washington; Washington, D.C.; and Honolulu, Hawaii.

With his application a passport applicant must submit two recent, signed photographs, $2\frac{1}{2}$ inches square. A citizen born in the United States must furnish proof of birth by submitting a previously issued passport or one in which he was included, or a birth certificate. If no birth record exists, a baptismal certificate or a certified copy of the record of baptism, census records, newspaper files, school records, or affidavits of persons having personal knowledge of the birth may be accepted. A naturalized citizen must present his naturalization certificate.

An applicant must satisfactorily establish his identity to the Clerk of Court or Passport Agent through personal knowledge, an acceptable document of identification, or by an identifying witness who has known him at least two years and is a U.S. citizen. A U.S. passport is good for three years. It may be renewed once to be valid for the remainder of a five-year period from the original date of issue.

A visa is an endorsement of a passport by a foreign country, stating that the bearer may visit there under specific conditions.

PASTEUR (*päs tēr′*), **LOUIS** (1822–1895), a French chemist, proved that infectious diseases are caused by bacteria. Pasteur, the son of a tanner, was born in Dole, France. He studied chemistry at the Ecole Normale and the Sorbonne in Paris. Then, in 1867, he became professor of chemistry at the Sorbonne.

Up to this time the spontaneous generation theory was generally accepted by scientists. According to this theory, living things could result from nonliving things. Pasteur's experiments presented final proof that all living things must be reproduced by other living things. Out of his experiments came ideas that he developed into invaluable contributions to the health and well-being of humanity.

Some of Pasteur's first experiments were made with alcoholic liquors that had fermented, or soured. With a microscope he saw that tiny rod-shaped germs had entered the "diseased" liquor from the air. By heating the liquor, Pasteur destroyed these germs.

Louis Pasteur.

Beginning in the early 1850's, the silkworm farmers of southern France were troubled by an epidemic of disease that was killing the silkworms and threatening to destroy the entire French silk industry. In 1865 Pasteur went on an official government mission to investigate the disease. After making a number of tests, he found that the tiny specks that appeared on the diseased worms were parasites. He not only discovered the causes of the disease, but he also found methods for preventing its spread.

In 1880 Pasteur turned his attention to diseases of animals. He developed preventions and cures for cholera in fowls, and anthrax in sheep and cattle. Through his effort to make animals immune to these diseases, he worked out the principle of inoculation. He introduced weakened germs of the deadly diseases into the bodies of healthy animals. Animals treated in this manner were able to resist the diseases against which they were inoculated. Pasteur went on to prove that infectious diseases in man can also be prevented. He began the work that led to the isolation of the germs of diphtheria, cholera, lockjaw, tuberculosis, and other diseases. (See GERMS AND DISEASE; IMMUNITY AND RESISTANCE TO DISEASE.)

Continuing his experiments, Pasteur began to look for a way to prevent rabies. He found that rabies, or hydrophobia, could be prevented by inoculation. He injected the virus of the deadly disease into rabbits and found that it attacked the brain and spinal cord. After the animals died, he dried their spinal cords. The longer they dried, the less virulent, or deadly, the infected matter in the cord became. Pasteur's preventive treatment of a person bitten by a rabid animal consists of injections prepared from the spinal cords. The patient's body reacts, building up resistance, so that it throws off the actual attack when it comes. (See RABIES.)

Pasteurization is a process that stops the growth of germs in milk and other liquids by heating. This process was originated by, and named for, Pasteur. In honor of his life work, the Institut Pasteur was founded in Paris in 1888 by the French government. Pasteur was director of the Institut until his death.

PATENT (*păt′ĕnt*) is a grant by a government of certain exclusive rights to an inventor in exchange for making his invention public. A patent in the United States is granted for 17 years. During this period the inventor having a patent can prevent others from making, using, or selling his invention without his consent. After this period the patent expires, and the invention can be used by anyone.

To be considered for patenting, an invention must fall into one of several categories: manufactured product; composition of matter; process; machine; plant; or design. For example, a new type parachute made from a synthetic fiber is a manufactured product. The synthetic fiber alone comes under composition of matter. The combination of steps for making the synthetic fiber is a process. The equipment for producing the parachute is in the machine category. A new variety of rose is in the plant category and a new drapery pattern is in the design category.

Regardless of the category, the invention must be new and useful and not an obvious way of doing something in order to be patented. An inventor may file his own application for a patent, but usually the filing is done by a patent lawyer or patent agent who is registered to practice before the Patent Office.

The U.S. Constitution (Article I, Section 8) gives Congress the power to grant patents in order to "promote the Progress of Science and useful Arts. . . ." The patent system does this in a number of ways. Before an inventor can get a patent, he must disclose the details of his invention—how it is made, what it does, and how it works—to the Patent Office. Patents thus discourage secrecy, and the information about the invention becomes an important part of the technical literature used by scientists and engineers in solving technical problems.

A patented product may bring to the patent owner the profit necessary for continuing the search for new and improved products. The profit enables companies to support organized research programs. With a patent an individual inventor or a small company may enter a market dominated by large companies. No matter how large or powerful the competing companies are, they cannot copy the patented products of others without permission. For these reasons patents are often the foundation of new businesses.

The patent system also encourages new inventions and investment of money to produce them. When patented products are successful, others often want to compete with the products. To do so, they must create new products that do not infringe the patents. They may invent products that are superior or less expensive.

The U.S. Patent Office, an agency under the Department of Commerce in Washington, D.C., is responsible for administering the patent laws and the trademark laws. (See TRADEMARK.) The commissioner of patents is appointed by the president. In the Patent Office are more than 1,000 patent examiners, all of whom are engineers, chemists, or persons with other technical training. Many are also lawyers. These examiners study applications in their specialized fields to determine whether the applicant has followed the rules and the patent laws.

An important part of the examiner's work is to find out what has been done before in the field of the invention. To do this the examiner must search through the patent files.

The files list more than three million U.S. patents. A patent is not granted if an invention was known, used, patented, or described in a printed publication more than one year before the patent was sought.

The idea of patents is not new. As early as the 14th century, British monarchs granted exclusive privileges to stimulate commerce and industry. Patents were granted in colonial America as early as 1641. In 1790 the first U.S. patent law was passed. After major changes in 1793 and 1836, the patent laws remained basically unchanged until 1952. At that time they underwent a general modernization.

Most countries of the civilized world have patent systems to encourage creativeness. Many of these countries, including the United States, belong to the International Convention for the Protection of Industrial Property. The terms of the convention give inventors who are filing for patents in one country certain filing privileges in other countries. Many persons are seeking to broaden the convention's terms in order to meet the needs of modern society.

PATRICK (păt′rĭk), **SAINT** (389?–461), "Apostle to the Irish," was born in either Britain or Gaul (France), the son of a British deacon, Calpurnius. At 16 years of age he was taken by raiders to Ireland, where as a slave he worked as a shepherd for six years. After seeing a vision one day, he escaped, walked hundreds of miles to a ship, and sailed back to Gaul. The seamen were starving, and, after reaching Gaul, Patrick prayed for food, and the sailors found a herd of swine.

He returned to his family. In another vision, he was told to convert Ireland. He studied in the Lérins, an island group in the Mediterranean Sea, then went to Auxerre, Gaul, where he was ordained a deacon. Fourteen years later he was sent to assist Palladius, the first bishop in Ireland. In 432, when Palladius died, Patrick was made bishop by St. Germanus.

He preached extensively, establishing many churches and religious communities. He was invited to the court of the High King Leoghaire. The druids constantly fought him, but it is said that he defeated them by miracles and his "breastplate," which warded off druid spells. His effective missionary work gained tolerance for Christianity and converted some of the royal family.

In about 442 he visited Rome. Two years later he founded the Cathedral Church of Armagh. This church became an important center for the Irish church and a source of learning for Anglo-Saxon scholars. In Ireland he organized the scattered Christian groups in the north. He converted many pagans in the west and, in general, brought Ireland closer to the Roman Catholic church. He helped raise the standards of scholarship by encouraging the study of Latin.

His *Confessions* (c. 450), a defense against his detractors, and his Letter to Coroticus are the basic sources for information about his life. Other accounts of his life are full of miracles, such as the legendary one that he drove the snakes out of Ireland.

His following has not lessened since his death. His feast day is celebrated on the anniversary of his death, March 17, by the Irish throughout the world.

PATRIOTIC (*pā′trĭ ŏt′ĭk*) **SOCIETIES** (*sō sī′ĕ-tĭz*), **UNITED STATES,** are organizations formed for one or more of the following purposes: (1) to commemorate historical events; (2) to care for documents and places important in U.S. history; (3) to help war veterans; and (4) to spread the ideals of freedom and liberty and teach good citizenship.

The oldest patriotic society in the United States is the Society of the Cincinnati, founded in 1783. George Washington was chosen as its first president. Its purpose was to help the officers who had fought together in the American Revolution to keep the friendships they had made and to aid them and their families in case of need. When a member dies, his membership goes to his eldest son. If there are no sons, it goes to the next heir. In this way the society has been kept alive.

Other societies commemorate events in the early history of the United States. The General Society of Mayflower Descendants was founded in 1897. Its members are direct descendants of those who sailed on the *Mayflower*. The mem-

bers of the General Society of Colonial Wars, founded in 1893, are men whose ancestors fought honorably in any of the colonial wars. A similar group is the Order of the Founders and Patriots of America. The National Society of Colonial Dames of America, founded in 1892, includes women who can claim an ancestor who lived in one of the colonies before 1776.

Some patriotic groups stem from the American Revolution. The Daughters of the American Revolution (D.A.R.) was organized in 1890. Its members are women who can trace their ancestry from soldiers, sailors, and other patriots who helped the American colonies win freedom from England. Other groups of the same kind are the Daughters of the Revolution, founded in 1891; the Sons of the American Revolution, founded in 1889; and the Sons of the Revolution, founded in 1883.

The War of 1812 also inspired organizations. The General Society of the War of 1812, founded in 1814, includes men whose ancestors fought in the war. The United States Daughters of 1812, founded in 1892, is a similar society for women.

After the U.S. Civil War several other patriotic societies were founded. One of these was the Grand Army of the Republic (G.A.R.), founded in 1866. Among its members were honorably discharged soldiers who had served with the Union forces. Its aim was to cherish the memory of those who had died for the Union, to care for needy survivors, and to aid widows and orphans.

The observation of Memorial Day is partly the work of the G.A.R. The organization also worked for laws to increase soldiers' pensions. The National Woman's Relief Corps worked with the men's group. When the last Union soldier died in 1956, the G.A.R. no longer existed because membership was not passed on to others in a family.

Societies also have been organized to preserve the traditions and memories of the Confederate States of America and to aid the Confederate veterans and their dependents. The United Daughters of the Confederacy was organized in 1894. The members, relatives of men who were connected with the Confederacy or who fought for it, founded homes for Confederate veterans, their widows, and their orphans. The United Confederate Veterans, founded in 1889, included men who served in the Confederate Army and Navy. Their sons may belong to the United Sons of Confederate Veterans, founded in 1896.

Soldiers who fought in the Spanish-American War formed the United Spanish War Veterans, founded in 1899. Naval officers and men who have received the Naval Medal of Honor, and also their sons, may join the Naval Order of the United States, founded in 1890. The Military Order of Foreign Wars of the United States, founded in 1894, is open to men and their sons who served in any of the foreign wars of the United States. The same men may join the Veterans of Foreign Wars of the U.S.A. (V.F.W.), founded in 1899.

Perhaps the best known of all patriotic societies is the American Legion. It was organized in 1919 under a congressional charter. Although originally a World War I organization, it is now open to all men who served in the U.S. forces during World Wars I and II and the Korean War, either at home or abroad. It is also open to U.S. citizens who were in the Allied armies.

This society was organized to continue the friendships made in service. However, the legion also has other aims. It is very active in teaching citizenship to young people. The legion has built community centers, athletic fields, and medical clinics. It also actively works for veterans' pensions and benefits, and education. Membership totals about three million. The American Legion Auxiliary, a women's organization, helps in legion activities.

Besides the many national societies, there are a number of local and state groups that help preserve historical sites.

PATTON (*păt"n*), GEORGE SMITH (1885–1945), a United States general during World War II, is famous for his daring strategy in tank warfare. Tough and colorful, he was nicknamed "Old Blood and Guts." He often wore a special white helmet and carried two pearl-handled pistols.

Patton was born in San Gabriel, California. He graduated from the United States Military Academy at West Point, New York, in 1909 and then served with cavalry units. In 1916–1917 he served as aide to General John Pershing in the army expedition into Mexico to capture the Mexican bandit chief Francisco (Pancho) Villa.

George Smith Patton.

Patton commanded the 304th Tank Brigade in the World War I battle at St. Mihiel, and was wounded in the Messe-Argonne battle. In the years between the two world wars, Patton served with various units. He also graduated from the Cavalry School (Fort Riley, Kansas), the Command and General Staff School, and the Army War College.

During World War II, Patton and his troops fought in three major battle areas: North Africa, Sicily, and Europe. In the invasion of North Africa, General Patton commanded the U.S. Fifth Army. After the victory the armored corps was reinforced for the invasion of Sicily and was renamed the U.S. Seventh Army. The British Eighth Army under General Sir Bernard Montgomery and the U.S. Seventh Army under General Patton landed on Sicily, July 10, 1943. On the morning of the 17th, General Patton entered Palermo, and Sicily fell.

In July 1944 he was placed in command of the U.S. Third Army in Europe. His greatest military success came when he led that army in a great sweep against the Germans. From August 1944 to Germany's surrender on May 8, 1945, the Third Army fought in France, Belgium, Luxembourg, Austria, and Czechoslovakia.

After the war, Patton served with the U.S. Army of Occupation in Europe. He died in Germany as the result of an automobile accident. He is buried in a U.S. Third Army cemetery at Hamm, Luxembourg. His book *War as I Knew It* tells of his military experiences.

PAUL (*păl*), **SAINT** (? –A.D. 64/65), the leading missionary of early Christianity, was a Jew born in Tarsus, Asia Minor, in the 1st century. Paul (his Jewish name was Saul) founded Christian churches throughout Asia Minor and Greece, possibly even in Spain. He is the leading figure in the biblical book of The Acts of the Apostles.

Educated a Pharisee, Paul—"the Apostle to the Gentiles," as he called himself—was originally an enemy of Christianity. He wrote that he was a consenting witness to the stoning of Stephen. He persecuted Christians in Jerusalem so effectively that he was sent by the Jews to persecute a young Christian church in Damascus. On the journey, he saw a vision of Christ, who spoke to him: "Saul, Saul, why do you persecute me?" For three days Paul remained blinded from the vision and had to be led into Damascus. Jesus then appeared to Ananias and told him to find Saul, "for he is a chosen instrument of mine to carry my name before the Gentiles and kings and the sons of Israel."

Paul regained his sight, was baptized, and began to proclaim that Jesus was the Messiah. The Jews immediately tried to kill him, but he escaped in a basket lowered from the city walls of Damascus.

After a period of meditation in Arabia, Paul returned to Jerusalem, where he convinced the suspicious Christians that he had seen Jesus in a vision and that he had been converted. The rest of his life he devoted to the building of the Christian church. Because of his missionary activity, he suffered many persecutions, lashings, and arrests by Roman authorities. During three extensive journeys in the Mediterranean area, he was able to establish Christianity throughout the known world.

Paul's first missionary journey began about A.D 45. He was accompanied by Barnabas and by Barnabas' nephew John Mark, who later left the two other men in Perga. The three sailed from Antioch to Cyprus. From Cyprus they sailed to Asia Minor, visiting the provinces of Pamphylia, Pisidia, and Laconia, and such towns as Perga, Antioch, Iconium, Lystra, and Derbe. Then they retraced their steps and sailed to Antioch, bypassing Cyprus.

On his second journey Paul was accompanied by Silas and later by Timothy. He revisited places where he had been on the first journey. In addition he entered Europe (Macedonia) for the first time. In Athens Paul delivered a famous speech to the Athenians on Mars Hill.

The third missionary journey took Paul into the general area of Galatia and Phrygia. In Ephesus, a center for the worship of the pagan goddess Diana, Paul remained over two years converting many and meeting opposition from those who favored the worship of Diana.

Back in Jerusalem, Paul was seized by the Jews, who believed that he was a traitor, preaching a false doctrine. He was rescued by Roman soldiers from the temple mob. Paul addressed his accusers and was then removed to Caesarea by the Romans when a plot to murder him was discovered. He remained under arrest for two years. When a new Roman governor assumed office in Palestine, the Jews again tried to bring Paul to trial. He asserted his Roman citizenship and asked for a trial in Rome.

After a sea voyage and a shipwreck Paul reached Rome. For two years he preached

"Saint Paul" by El Greco.

Collection City Art Museum of St. Louis

Christianity "unhindered." He may have been tried and acquitted, tried and executed, or never tried at all. Tradition says that he was beheaded in Rome. Paul's place in history is impressive. He was a thinker of the first order, and modern civilization owes him an immeasurable debt.

PAUL (Popes). Of the six popes who took the name Paul, the most important were:

PAUL II (pope, 1464–1471), or Pietro Barbo, was a Venetian born in 1417. He actively opposed the Humanists because of their paganism. He excommunicated the king of Bohemia in 1466 and worked in vain for a crusade against the Turks.

PAUL III (pope, 1534–1549), or Alessandro Farnese, was born in Tuscany in 1468. He was educated at Rome and Florence in the court of Lorenzo the Magnificent. He promoted church reform and appointed men as cardinals who were virtuous and brilliant. He established ecclesiastical commissions to draw up reform plans. He favored new orders, especially the Jesuits. In 1542 he restored the Inquisition against those who opposed the church. His opposition to Protestantism and his excommunication of Henry VIII alienated England from Rome. He fought for the general council that opened at Trent in 1545. He was a friend of art and scholarship, enriched the Vatican library, and made Michelangelo the architect in chief of St. Peter's.

PAUL IV (pope, 1555–1559), or Giovanni Pietro Caraffa, was born to a distinguished Neapolitan family in 1476. He was the first of the Counter-Reformation popes. Early in his career he sought reforms within the church. In 1520 he served on the commission that dealt with Martin Luther. He was nearly 80 years old when elected pope, and his popularity declined after his quarrels with Mary Tudor and with Spain.

Pope Paul VI.

Wide World

PAUL V (pope, 1605–1621), or Camillo Borghese, was born in Rome in 1552. He tried to enforce the decrees of the Council of Trent and tried in vain to reestablish the Roman church in Russia. He completed St. Peter's, extended the Vatican library, and arranged for missions in Africa and Canada.

PAUL VI (pope, 1963–   ), or Giovanni Battista Montini, was born at Concesio, Italy, in 1897. He attended the pontifical seminary in Milan and both the Pontifical Gregorian University and the pontifical ecclesiastical academy in Rome. He was a member of the Vatican Secretariat of State from 1922 to 1954, except for a few months spent in Warsaw, Poland, as a diplomatic representative of the papacy. In 1954 he was made archbishop of Milan. Elevated to the College of Cardinals in 1958, he was elected pope in 1963 upon the death of Pope John XXIII. The next year he made a pilgrimage to the Holy Land and met in Jerusalem with Athenagorus I, patriarch of Constantinople. In a historic trip to the United States in 1965, he addressed the United Nations General Assembly with a plea for world peace. In 1968 he became the first reigning pope to visit Latin America.

PAVLOV (*pà′vlôf*), **IVAN PETROVICH** (*pyĭtrô′vyĭch*) (1849–1936), was a Russian physiologist noted for his experiments on blood circulation, digestion, and conditioned reflexes.

Pavlov was born in Ryazan, Russia. He entered a seminary, but his scientific interests led him away from the priesthood. In 1870 he entered the University of St. Petersburg (now Leningrad State University). During the next decade, he became involved with work on animal nerve physiology. In 1883 he earned the degree of Doctor of Medicine from the Military Medical Academy in St. Petersburg. After conducting animal research in St. Petersburg and in Germany, he returned to the academy and became professor of physiology in 1895.

Pavlov's most famous experiments were with the salivation of dogs. He demonstrated that some reflexes develop as a result of training. He called these reflexes conditioned reflexes as opposed to inborn, or inherited, reflexes.

To investigate conditioned reflexes, Pavlov rang a bell each time he fed his dogs. The dogs salivated when presented with the food. Eventually, after several feedings accompanied by the sound of a bell, the dogs salivated when they heard the bell even when they received no food. Thus he had conditioned his dogs to respond to the sound of the bell. Pavlov wrote of his experiments and theories in *The Work of the Digestive Glands* and *Conditioned Reflexes and Psychiatry*.

Continuing his work, Pavlov attempted to link complicated workings of the mind with conditioning. He believed that his conditioning principles could be used to solve the problems of psychiatry. During his life Pavlov received many honors, both in his own country and abroad. Among them was the 1904 Nobel Prize for physiology or medicine, which was awarded to him for his important studies of digestion.

PAVLOVA (*pà′vlô vŭ*), **ANNA** (1885–1931), was the most famous ballet dancer in the world during her lifetime. Her dance *The Dying Swan* is one of the best-known dances in the history of ballet. It was composed especially for her by Michel Fokine, a choreographer, or dance designer.

Pavlova was born in St. Petersburg, Russia, of Polish parents. When she was eight years old, her mother took her to see her first ballet, Peter Tchaikovsky's *The Sleeping Beauty*. Instantly she decided to become a dancer. She began her training at the Imperial Ballet School in St. Petersburg at the age of ten. The training was long and hard, but by the time she was 20 she was prima ballerina, or leading dancer, of the Imperial Ballet.

In 1909 Pavlova left Russia to join a new ballet company in Paris under the leadership of Sergei Diaghilev. Her partner there was the finest male dancer of modern times, Vaslav Nijinsky. Their most famous performances were in the ballet *Les Sylphides* by the choreographer Fokine. Pavlova studied under Enrico Cecchetti, who continued as her teacher to the end of her life.

In 1910 Pavlova went to London, where she was an instant success. She then formed her own company and traveled all over the world. She took the art of ballet to many places where it was unknown. She was especially popular in North and South America. Pavlova's husband, Victor Dandré, a Russian lawyer, was the manager of her ballet company.

Before World War I, Pavlova and her husband bought Ivy House, a pleasant home outside London, where she gave ballet lessons. During the war, she went on tour throughout the world in order to brighten the lives of people everywhere. Others of her famous dances were *Les Papillons, Autumn Bacchanal, The Magic Flute,* and *Invitation to the Dance*.

She died of pneumonia at The Hague, Netherlands.

PEA (*pē*) is a plant of the family Leguminosae. Clover, vetch, and beans also belong to the family, which includes about 13,000 species. (See LEGUME, PULSE, OR PEA FAMILY.)

The common garden pea (*Pisum sativum*), also called the English pea, is grown for its edible seeds. It is a trailing or climbing plant with

The long green pods of the pea plant contain the round green seeds that are popular as a vegetable the world over.

J. Horace McFarland Company

white or purple flowers. Each pod, from two to four inches long, contains from two to ten globular-shaped seeds. The seeds are commonly green but are yellow, cream, or brown in some varieties. They may be smooth or wrinkled.

The garden pea is thought to have originated in Asia. It is an old plant. Seeds have been found on the sites of the Swiss lake dwellings, dating back to the Bronze Age of about 5,000 years ago. The plant has spread over the world. It is a cool season plant that cannot withstand hot weather or extreme cold. Several excellent varieties have been developed in England. In the United States, peas are no longer widely grown for fresh markets. Instead, most peas are shelled and shipped to food processing plants, where they are canned or frozen.

The sweet pea (*Lathyrus odoratus*) is closely related to the garden pea. It is grown mainly for its lovely, fragrant flowers. Several other members of the legume family are also called peas. They include the chick-pea, the Spanish pea, the cowpea, and the pigeon pea.

Peas are rich in vitamins and proteins, and they are an important table vegetable in every country where they are grown. The pea plant was used by Gregor Mendel in the 19th century for his famous experiments in heredity. (See MENDEL, GREGOR JOHANN.)

PEACE (*pēs*) **CORPS** (*kōr*) is an agency of the United States government that is made up of volunteers who live and work in foreign countries. Its members teach in schools, work as nurses and doctors in hospitals, build roads and houses, work on farms, and do many other jobs that help people in countries that are not so developed as the United States. The Peace Corps was established to provide these countries with skilled manpower and to promote world peace and better understanding between the people of the United States and peoples of other countries.

President John F. Kennedy established the United States Peace Corps on March 1, 1961. He appointed R. Sargent Shriver, Jr., to be director. During the first year of the corps' existence, many foreign governments invited volunteers to their countries. Thousands of Americans applied for service in the Peace Corps. More than 700 of the most qualified were chosen, trained, and sent abroad during the first year. The first groups of volunteers went to Ghana and Tanganyika in Africa and to Colombia in South America.

The first experimental projects were so successful that the U.S. Congress passed a bill in September 1961 that officially authorized the U.S. Peace Corps as an agency of the federal government. In the Peace Corps Act, Congress declared that the basic purposes were:

"To promote world peace and friendship . . . which shall make available to interested countries and areas men and women of the United States qualified for service

Courtesy Peace Corps—Paul Conklin

Typical of the many volunteers now serving abroad with the Peace Corps is this agricultural extension worker in Pokhara—a village in the Nepalese Himalayas.

abroad and willing to serve, under conditions of hardship if necessary, to help the peoples of such countries and areas in meeting their needs for trained manpower, and to help promote a better understanding of the American people on the part of the peoples served and a better understanding of other peoples on the part of the American people."

Applicants for the Peace Corps must be at least 18 years old and in good health. Because there is no upper age limit many older people in their 60's and 70's have qualified. More than 70 percent of all Peace Corps volunteers are college graduates. Neither a college degree nor a high school diploma is required, however. Volunteers usually serve for two years. They receive an allowance that permits them to live on the same level as their counterparts in the host country.

Before the volunteers are sent overseas, they train for eight weeks or more at a U.S. college or university chosen by the Peace Corps. The volunteers train together as a group. They learn the language of the country in which they will work, and they study the history, geography, government, and culture of that country. They practice improving their skills and refresh their knowledge of U.S. history and government. Health, physical education, and special training for each assignment are also a part of the training.

Peace Corps volunteers perform many different functions. They work on jobs, ranging from sewing clothes and driving tractors to teaching school. About 60 per cent of the volunteers teach—in elementary schools, in high schools, and some in colleges. They teach many different subjects, usually in the English language because English is used in many schools of Africa and Asia.

Next to teaching, the second greatest number of volunteers work in what are called "community development" projects. The volunteers are sent to small towns as well as big cities in the host countries. They live with the people, earn their confidence, and learn how the people wish to improve their lives. The volunteers help the people work on projects. These projects include such things as building a small school or health clinic, digging a well or installing electrical and plumbing systems. Most of the Peace Corps community development projects are in Latin America.

By the end of 1967, there were 14,000 Peace Corps volunteers serving in 58 countries. It is expected that 50,000 persons will have served abroad as members of the Peace Corps by 1970.

PEACH (*pēch*) is the fruit of the tree *Prunus persica* of the same family as plums, cherries, apricots, and other stone fruits.

The peach tree is cultivated mainly for its fruit. It is usually a small tree, from 10 to 25 feet in height. It blossoms early in the season, even before the leaves appear. Its lovely, fragrant flowers are usually pink or white, and sometimes the tree is cultivated only as an

The peach tree (right) has fragrant, pink or white blossoms (left top) and round, white, yellow, or red fruit (left bottom).

Courtesy Ohio Agricultural Experiment Station

ornamental plant. One peach is produced from each flower. The fruit may be white, yellow, or red. The skin is usually fuzzy, but there are smooth-skinned peaches called nectarines. The hard interior of the fruit is called the stone, and inside of it is the seed. In some varieties of peaches, called freestones, the flesh of the fruit slips easily away from the stone. In cling-stones, the flesh holds tightly to the stone.

The peach is thought to be native to China. References to it are found in Chinese writings of the 5th century B.C. It was probably introduced into Europe by the ancient Greeks and Romans. The trees were taken to Mexico by the early Spanish explorers, and from Mexico the plants spread to the United States.

Several countries cultivate commercial peach crops. Among the leading commercial producers are the United States, Italy, and France. Commercial crops are also grown in the Republic of South Africa and Australia. In the United States the leading producing states are California, South Carolina, Georgia, Pennsylvania, New Jersey, and Michigan.

The peach tree thrives in temperate climates. Some varieties are able to withstand low temperatures, but most cannot survive in areas that experience heavy frosts. On the other hand, the tree does not produce well in areas where the winter is too mild.

The seeds of peaches are planted in late summer. They are allowed to grow during the following winter and spring, after which the tiny shoot is grafted on the root stock of a sturdier variety. The grafts are stored or allowed to lie dormant until the following spring when the grafted bud begins to grow. (See GRAFTING).

Many insects and diseases attack peaches. To control fungi, such as mildew and blight, and to ward off insects, peach farmers must spray their trees with fungicides and insecticides. Trees infected with a virus, such as the ring spot, must be uprooted and burned.

PEACOCK (pē′kŏk) is a male peafowl. The female is a peahen. Peafowl are birds of the pheasant family (Phasianidae).

The peacock is noted for his colorful plumage. The head, neck, and breast of the common peacock (*Pavo cristatus*) are metallic blue-purple with glints of greenish-gold. The feathers of the back are green, and those of the wings are blue, black, and copper colored. The

Although most male peacocks have plumage of blue, green, and gold, a white variety, as this one, is common in captivity.

Ewing Galloway

head bears a crest of slender feathers of similar metallic hues. The peacock's magnificent train is an extension of the feathers just above the tail. The train is colored in iridescent blues, greens, and golds, and is often longer than the bird itself. Some of its feathers are tipped with patterns resembling eyes. The train is raised and held in a fanlike display by the stiff feathers' of the bird's true tail. The peacock uses this gorgeous plumage to attract a mate.

Adult peacocks with their sweeping trains average about seven feet in length. The peahen is slightly smaller than the cock and does not have a long, colorful train. Her plumage is mostly brown, with accents of green and white on breast and tail. She lays four to six whitish, sometimes spotted, eggs.

The common peafowl is native to India and Ceylon but is a familiar sight in zoos and parks throughout the world. They are usually kept for ornamental purposes, but their meat and eggs are eaten in certain areas. Roast peafowl was regarded as a delicacy in Roman and Medieval times.

The less familiar species is the Javan peacock (*Pavo muticus*), which inhabits jungles from Burma to Java. It is similar to the common peafowl in size and form, but its head, neck, and breast are green rather than blue-purple, and the feathers of its crest are webbed or connected rather than individual. The cry of both species is harsh and rather unpleasant.

PEANUT (*pē'nŭt*) is the seed of the plant *Arachis hypogaea* of the family Leguminosae. This plant grows erect to a height of about $1\frac{1}{2}$ feet, or it may spread along the ground like a vine. The peanut (also sometimes called groundnut, earthnut, monkey-nut, or goober nut) develops in a pod, or papery shell, that grows beneath the ground.

There are several varieties of the peanut plant. Some of them have seeds that are small and round, while others have large seeds that may be elongated or flattened. The color of the coat surrounding the seed varies from white to pink and purple. Some varieties have one- or two-seeded pods; still others may have four

or five seeds in a pod.

Peanuts develop in an unusual manner. After the flowers wither, they produce stalklike organs, or pegs, that reach into the ground. The ends of the pegs enlarge, forming pods that contain seeds. The seeds mature in the pods, and when ripe, the pods are dug out of the soil.

The peanut is native to South America. It has been found in prehistoric graves at Ancan, Peru, along with pottery decorated with peanut designs. From there the plant apparently was carried to Africa and then to the United States.

J. Horace McFarland Company

Tiny, rounded nodules on the roots of the peanut plant help it take nitrogen from the air.

Today the peanut is grown commercially in the southern United States, from Florida to California, and as far north as Washington, D.C. It is also cultivated in Latin America, Asia, and Africa. Common varieties are the large-podded, red-skinned Virginia peanut and the smaller Spanish peanut.

Given at least a five-month frost-free season, the peanut grows well. Although it is a tropical plant, it can survive long dry periods. But moisture is necessary for flower development.

Peanuts are planted late in the spring and are dug by machinery before frost comes. After the vines are dried, the peanuts are removed by machine. Peanuts, like other legumes, such as peas and beans, enrich the soil with nitrogen.

In addition to the millions of pounds of peanuts grown in the United States, many are imported from the Orient. Great quantities are crushed for oil. Before the peanut oil industry was established, peanuts were not important in world trade. They were roasted in the shell and sold for immediate food use. Peanut oil is now used in shortenings, oleomargarines, soaps, and salad oils. It may also be made into glycerine for munitions. Choice nuts are usually not crushed for oil but are saved for other food purposes. Millions of pounds are made into peanut butter, sold as salted and roasted nuts, or put into candy.

The skins and stems are used to feed cattle. The hulls are used as filler in cleaning compounds, linoleum, dynamite, and paperboard. Flour is made from the peanut meal residue and used in breads. Other peanut products are face powders, rubber substitutes, dyes, and printing inks. Many of these products were experimentally produced by the agricultural scientist George Washington Carver. (See CARVER, GEORGE WASHINGTON.)

PEAR (pãr) is the fruit of any of several species of trees of the family Rosaceae, genus *pyrus*. Like its close relative the apple, the pear fruit develops on a tree. The pear tree resembles the apple tree, although it is generally more upright. The trees are colorful in the spring with snowy white or pink blossoms about one inch across. Although pear trees generally are small, some grow more than 60 feet high and have trunks more than one foot in diameter. The leaves are two to four inches long, rounded at the base and pointed at the tip.

Pears are round in shape, tapering toward the stem, and have cores. They vary in color from yellowish-green to yellowish-brown. The many varieties of pears spring mainly from two species: the European pear (*Pyrus communis*) and the oriental pear (*Pyrus pyrifolia*). The popular Bartlett pear of the United States (called the Williams pear in Europe) is a variety of the European pear. The Kieffer pear is also widely grown. Other varieties include the Coyenne du Comice, the Buerre Bosc, and the Anjou.

The pear tree is subject to injury by insects and diseases. It is attacked by the codling moth, the pear leaf blister mite and several other insects. Leaf spot is a fungus growth that forms on the fruit and the young twigs. The most

serious threat to pears in the United States is fire blight, a bacterial disease that attacks the interior of the plant. Most oriental pears are more resistant to blight than European pears. Hybrid pears are formed by crossing the hardy oriental pears with the European pears.

The pear is a common food in many parts of the world. It is native to southern Europe and Asia, but it is now cultivated in many parts of the world where the climate is temperate. Although the pear is mentioned in Greek writings of the 10th century B.C., it was not until little more than a hundred years ago that it was widely cultivated.

Like those of the apple, seedlings of pears are first grown in nurseries. After one or two years they are transplanted to orchards. The fruit is picked when mature but still hard and green. It is then stored in cool storerooms to ripen. After being sorted and wrapped, the fruit is usually shipped in boxes or barrels to fresh fruit markets or to food processing plants.

Important pear-producing countries are the United States, France, West Germany, Italy, and Switzerland. In Europe, pears are raised

The pear tree (right) has tiny, white or pink blossoms (left top) and elongated, globular fruit (left bottom).

Courtesy (right) Ohio Agricultural Experiment Station; photos, (left top) Roche, (left bottom) J. Horace McFarland Company

mainly in yards and on lands used for grazing and other purposes. In the United States however, pears are commonly produced in large orchards. The main areas of production are in California, Oregon, and Washington, New York and Michigan. In Canada, Ontario is the major pear-producing area.

PEARL (*pĕrl*) is a valuable gem that is produced by certain mollusks. It is an attractive concretion, or solid mass, that takes shape within the body of a mollusk. All mollusks with shells are capable of producing these concretions, but only those that line their shells with nacre, or mother-of-pearl, produce true pearls. The most important saltwater mollusks that produce pearls belong to the genus *Pinctada* (or *Meleagrina*). Freshwater mollusks that produce pearls belong to the genus *Unio*. Edible oysters (genus *Ostrea*) do not produce pearls of any value. (See MOLLUSK.)

Pearls are formed in nature when a small foreign object, such as a particle of sand, works its way through the mantle, which is the layer of tissue that separates the body of the mollusk from its shell. The outer edge of this mantle contains cells that secrete materials to build the shell. When the foreign object has penetrated the mantle, it often carries with it some shell-building cells. In their new position within the body of the mollusk, these cells continue their shell-building action and coat the foreign object with layers of nacre. Nacre is a lustrous, iridescent material that gives a pearl its beauty. Mollusks that do not line their shells with nacre usually form black, purple, or white concretions that lack luster and have no value.

The most valuable pearls are those that are ball shaped and lustrous and have delicate surface coloring. The iridescence of this coloring is the pearl's orient. In addition to the usual cream-colored or white pearls, valuable black, pink, gray, yellow, and green ones are found.

Pearls also occur in various shapes. Sometimes the foreign object entering the mollusk becomes lodged in muscle tissue. The resistance from the muscle fibers causes an irregular-shaped pearl to form. This is called a baroque pearl. When the foreign object does not

penetrate far enough beyond the shell, the pearl forms attached to the shell. The result is a half sphere, flat on one side, called

Pearls are formed in various shapes, such as round (above), baroque (left), and pear-shaped (below).

Courtesy Imperial Pearl Syndicate, Inc.

a blister pearl.

The major sources of valuable saltwater pearls are the Persian Gulf; the Gulf of Mannar, between India and Ceylon; the South Pacific Ocean, especially near the Tuamotu Archipelago; the waters off Australia; and the waters of the Caribbean Sea off Margarita Island. Some pearls have also been found in the Gulf of California and the Gulf of Mexico. The pearls of the Persian Gulf are the most highly prized.

Lovely pearls are found in freshwater mollusks in the rivers of middle western and eastern United States, as well as in Great Britain and Germany. These pearls usually occur in a wider color range than the saltwater variety. A lack of supply and difficulty in matching colors have made freshwater pearls considerably less important than saltwater pearls.

The life span of a Persian Gulf mollusk is about 12 to 15 years. The best time to remove the pearl is several years before the expected time of death. A healthy, younger mollusk usually deposits more even and attractive layers of nacre than an aging mollusk. The outer layers deposited by an older mollusk tend to be less colorful and perhaps irregular. In wild pearl fishing, as compared with the cultured pearl industry, the age of the mollusk is not known exactly, so all adult shells are brought to the surface for pearl extraction. Natural pearls are found only in a few mollusks.

In the production of cultured pearls, the mollusks are protected in submerged wire cages until they reach 3½ years of age. At that time they are removed from the water, and a bead of mother-of-pearl is inserted into the body, together with a small piece of shell-building material from the outer edge of the mantle. The mollusks are returned to the water for approximately another 3½ years, after which they are brought to the surface, and the pearls are removed. Most of the pearls are bleached, dyed, and graded for use in necklaces or other jewelry pieces.

The production of cultured pearls from saltwater mollusks is a major industry in Japan. There are also cultured pearl stations in Burma and Australia, but in Japan production has been perfected. Japan now has a freshwater cultured pearl industry as well. Freshwater mollusks do not require a mother-of-pearl bead. A piece of shell-building material is used instead.

Pearls are not durable. They may be discolored by skin acids or by heat. Cultured pearls are least durable because they often have only a thin coating of nacre.

PEARL HARBOR, HAWAII, is a large, well-protected inlet of the Pacific Ocean on the southern coast of Oahu Island. This excellent deepwater harbor is about seven miles from Honolulu, the state capital. It is an important naval base and the headquarters of U.S. military forces in the Pacific area.

Two peninsulas extend into the harbor and divide it into three bays. Among the naval facilities around the harbor and on tiny Fords Island (in the east bay) are dry docks, refueling and supply piers, training and communications buildings, administrative offices, and a submarine base. Hawaii's location makes the harbor especially important as a refueling and supply point for ships crossing the Pacific and as an outpost of U.S. defense.

By a treaty with Hawaii in 1887, the United States was permitted to use the harbor as a repair and fueling station. Maps of the harbor were first drawn in 1897. Congress approved construction of the naval base in 1908.

Pearl Harbor was the site of a Japanese surprise attack, Sunday morning, December 7, 1941. The attack brought the United States into World War II. Beginning at about 7:55 A.M.

Photos, Courtesy U.S. Navy

The U.S.S. Arizona Memorial (above) has been built over the partly submerged battleship U.S.S. Arizona in Pearl Harbor, just off the Navy Supply Center (left) at Oahu, Hawaii. It honors those who died in the Japanese surprise attack, December 7, 1941, of whom 1,103 were killed aboard the Arizona.

that morning, the first of a series of air attacks was launched from enemy aircraft carriers 200 miles northwest of Oahu. By about 9:45 the fighting was over. It had been a great Japanese victory. Although nearly 100 U.S. ships were in Pearl Harbor at the time, the chief targets were the 8 battleships and the aircraft on the island. During the short raid more than 2,000 men were killed, 16 ships were sunk or damaged, and about 150 planes were destroyed. The Japanese losses amounted to about 95 men, 29 airplanes, and several midget submarines. A large share of the U.S. casualties were sailors aboard the battleship *Arizona*, which blew up and sank. After the attack the harbor facilities were rebuilt, and many of the ships were repaired and used during the war.

PEARSON (*pĭr's'n*), **LESTER BOWLES** (*bōlz*) (1897–   ), 19th prime minister of Canada and a leader of the Canadian Liberal party, was born in Toronto, Ontario. He entered Victoria College of the University of Toronto in 1913 and received his degree in 1919, after serving in World War I. Following graduate studies at St. John's College, Oxford University, he taught history at the University of Toronto.

In 1928 Pearson's career in the diplomatic service began when he became first secretary in the Canadian Department of External Affairs. From 1935 to 1941 he served in London, England, as first secretary in the office of the High Commissioner for Canada. During World War II he served in the embassy in Washington, D.C., becoming Canadian ambassador to the United States in 1945.

Lester Bowles Pearson.

In 1948 he was elected a member of Parliament from Algoma East in northern Ontario Province. From 1948 to 1957 he was Secretary of State for External Affairs in the cabinet of

Prime Minister Louis S. St. Laurent. He succeeded St. Laurent as leader of the Liberal party in 1958.

In 1957 Pearson was awarded the Nobel Prize for peace for his part in settling the Suez crisis. The resolution that he presented to the United Nations—which stated that the United Kingdom, France, and Israel were to withdraw from Egyptian territory and be replaced by a United Nations emergency force—was accepted, and peace was restored to the area.

In 1963 Pearson criticized the Conservative government's foreign policy, especially the refusal to accept U.S. controlled nuclear arms. He became prime minister that same year and held the office until 1968.

PEARY (*pĭr'ē*), **ROBERT EDWIN** (*ĕd'wĭn*) (1856–1920), discovered the North Pole on April 6, 1909. He was born at Cresson, Pennsylvania, on May 6, 1856. After he graduated from Bowdoin College, Brunswick, Maine, he joined the Civil Engineer Corps of the U.S. Navy. He decided to be a polar explorer after a trip to Greenland in 1886. Between 1891 and 1908 he led five expeditions to Greenland, and used it as a base for reaching the pole.

Peary's trip to the North Pole made use of all his Arctic experience. His ship, the *Roosevelt*, was specially built for Arctic work. On the actual trip a large group set out from Cape Columbia in Grant Land with as much equipment as they could carry. A small advance party selected the route and marked the trail. At intervals small parts of the main party turned back with only enough supplies to reach the base, leaving the others fully provisioned. Finally only Peary, Matthew Henson, and four Eskimos were left to make the last dash of 140 miles to the pole. After reaching it, they remained for about 30 hours, taking observations and recording scientific data.

Peary proved Greenland was an island and learned a great deal about the Eskimos. Information was collected on the polar seas, tides, and winds. Peary made soundings within five miles of the pole which failed to touch bottom at 9,000 feet and proved the North Pole to be in the center of a vast sea covered with ice. His expeditions are described in *Northward Over the Great Ice, Nearest the Pole, The North Pole,* and *Secrets of Polar Travel.*

PECAN (*pē kăn'*). The pecan is one of the most popular nuts in the United States. The tree is native only in the United States. It is the only native nut tree extensively grown in orchards, located chiefly in the southern states, Arizona, California, and Oregon. Georgia is the leading pecan state.

The pecan tree is one of about 15 hickories that are native to the United States. The wild tree grows as much as 150 feet tall, and six to seven feet in diameter. Its large leaves are made up of 9 to 17 tapering leaflets. The tree bears two types of flowers: those from which nuts develop (pistillate); and pollen-bearing (staminate) flowers. The nuts grow inside a thin husk of four parts. They ripen from October to December. Nuts from different trees differ in size, thickness of shell, and flavor.

Until about 1900 most of the pecan crop came

Photos, J. Horace McFarland Co.
Above: A cluster of pecan nuts on the tree. Insert: The shucks removed, and the nut cut open showing the kernel.

from wild trees. Many nuts from wild trees still are harvested. The finest quality nuts are from the southern orchards. Budded or grafted varieties of trees are grown in most orchards. They produce the so-called paper-shelled pecans, large nuts with sweet kernels and thin shells.

After harvest, ripe nuts are dried and cured, sorted and graded. They are sold in the shell or as shelled nuts. The nuts have high food value as they are rich in fat and a good source of certain vitamins, calcium, phosphorus, and iron. Pecans were used as food by American Indians. The early white settlers also used them as food for themselves and for their hogs.

Pecan wood is too brittle to be of much value. Some tannin is taken out of shells collected at pecan-cracking factories.

The trees are sometimes planted around homes or along streets and roads.

PECCARY (*pĕk'ä rē*), an American animal of the swine family. It is sometimes called wild pig, musk hog or javelina. It is not a true pig but is related to it.

Peccaries squeal and grunt. Their snout and body build is piglike; but their tusks turn downward. They have only three toes on the hind foot instead of four, and no visible tail. On their backs, they have a musk gland which gives off a strong and unpleasant odor. Sometimes they live in hollow tree trunks or in a thicket, where they give birth to their young.

Although peccaries will eat almost anything, they prefer nuts, grain, and vegetables. Herds of peccaries sometimes uproot whole fields. They kill all kinds of small animals, including snakes.

There are two kinds of peccaries. Both are grayish black with a mane of stiff black hairs down their back. The collared peccary has a grayish white band from its shoulder to its chest. It is about three feet long and it weighs about 50 pounds. It is found from southern Texas, New Mexico and Arizona down through South America.

The white lipped peccary has a band of white from its chin almost to its eye. It is larger than the collared peccary and lives in Central

Courtesy National Zoological Park, Smithsonian Institution

The short-necked, fat body of this collared peccary resembles a half-grown pig. It is about three feet long.

and South America.

Peccaries are killed for their skins which are used in making gloves and jackets. Some people eat them for food.

PECOS (*pā'kŏs*) **BILL** was the legendary hero of the cowboys in the western United States. As cowboys sat around their campfires, they made up stories about their hero. He did all the things they could not do.

When Bill was four years old, he fell into the Pecos River. The wagon carrying his father, mother, and 17 brothers and sisters went on. But a grandfather coyote found him. Pecos Bill learned to howl like a coyote and to talk with the other animals and birds.

One day his brother discovered Bill and took him back to the ranch. First Bill scared an old steer out of his skin and made some clothes. Then he fought a mountain lion until the lion agreed to be his cow pony. Later he captured a beautiful horse called Lightning.

Pecos Bill invented the lariat. With it he could bring down a flying eagle. He could rope a thousand cattle at one time. When it got very hot in Texas, Bill roped part of the Rio Grande to water his cows. Once he threw the lariat over a cyclone and saved his ranch.

When Pecos Bill decided to fence in his land, he sent for the prairie dogs. They quickly dug the holes and Bill stuck a frozen rattlesnake in each one. Then he stretched a wire hung with cactus thorns along the rattlesnake posts. This was the first barbed-wire fence.

PEDRO (*pā'drō*), **DOM** [EMPERORS OF BRAZIL]. Brazil had only two emperors. Both of them were named Dom Pedro. They ruled from 1822 until 1889 when Brazil became a Federal Republic.

DOM PEDRO I (1798–1834) was born in Portugal. When he was nine, his father, later to become King John VI of Portugal, fled to Brazil to escape capture by Napoleon. Brazil was then a Portuguese colony. In 1821 King John returned to Portugal. He left Dom Pedro, then 22 years old, as ruler of the colony.

The *Cortes*, the ruling body of Portugal, ordered Dom Pedro to return also. Instead, in January 1822, he gave in to the Brazilian people's request that he remain. The following September he declared Brazil an independent country. On December 1, 1822, he was crowned emperor of Brazil. (See BRAZIL, *The Independence Movement* and *The Empire*.)

Even with this fine start, Dom Pedro's rule was a time of trouble, for his dictatorial character made him many enemies. Uprisings broke out over the country. Uruguay, then a part of Brazil, rebelled and gained independence. In 1831, when Dom Pedro learned that the army had deserted him, he gave up the throne in favor of his five-year-old son, Dom Pedro de Alcantara, and returned to Portugal, where he died three years later.

DOM PEDRO II (1825–1891). During Dom Pedro's childhood, the government of Brazil was run by a group of men called a regency. Before he came of age there were more revolts against the regency rule. On July 18, 1841, at the age of 16, Dom Pedro was crowned emperor of Brazil. He became a very strong and popular king. Order was established by 1846. Dom Pedro traveled to Europe and the United States. When he returned, he worked to develop his country's resources. He helped the growth of railroads, industries, schools, and a free press. Immigration was welcomed and slavery ended.

However, certain groups (the church, army, and slaveholders) plotted against the emperor. On November 15, 1889, they revolted and declared Brazil a Federal Republic. Dom Pedro was forced to leave the country he had ruled for almost 50 years. He died in exile in Paris two years later.

PEEL (*pēl*), **SIR ROBERT** (1788–1850), spent his life serving the government of England. He was born in Lancashire, England and attended Harrow and Oxford. Peel was only 21 when he was elected to the House of Commons.

At the age of 24, Peel was appointed to his first important government job, secretary for Ireland. He started the first regular police force there. In 1821 he became home secretary, that is, he was in charge of affairs for England. At that time the laws dealing with punishment for crimes were very unfair. He is still remembered because he changed many of them. He also set up the first London police force. The London police are still called "bobbies," a nickname for Robert, Peel's first name. (See POLICE).

In 1826 Peel became leader of the House of Commons. Earlier he had believed that Roman Catholics should not be allowed to vote or be elected to any job in the government. However, in 1829 he helped to pass a law that gave them these rights.

As leader of the Tory party, Peel served as prime minister in 1834–1835. He and his followers in the Tory party called themselves "Conservatives," the name that party still uses.

In 1841 Peel again became prime minister. He worked hard to do away with the Corn Laws, and it is for this that he is best known. The Corn Laws put an extra tax on grain that came into England from other countries. Without these taxes, foreign grain was cheaper than English grain. Peel felt that low cost grain was needed to save many people from starvation. Most Englishmen, except farmers and landowners, were glad to have the Corn Laws removed. But most of Peel's party were farmers and landowners, and they were very angry with him. They forced him to resign as prime minister in 1846. The last four years of his life he worked with the Whigs, the opposition party.

PEGASUS (*pĕg'ä sŭs*) was the flying horse in Greek mythology. Two different stories tell about his birth. One story says that he was the son of Poseidon, the god of the sea, and Me-

dusa, a horrible monster with snakes instead of hair. The other story says that when a great hero, Perseus, cut off Medusa's head, Pegasus sprang from her blood.

Athena (Minerva), the goddess of wisdom, caught Pegasus and tamed him. She gave him to the Muses, the nine goddesses of music and poetry. One time Pegasus stamped on the ground of Helicon, the mountain where the Muses lived. His hoof print opened a fountain, called Hippocrene.

Athena gave a golden bridle to a great hero, Bellerophon, to use in taming Pegasus. With the help of Pegasus, Bellerophon was able to kill the fire-breathing monster Chimera, which was part lion, part goat, and part dragon. But when Bellerophon tried to ride to heaven, Pegasus reared and threw him off. Pegasus continued on to heaven where he lives as a constellation of stars. (See the drawings in CONSTELLATION.)

PEKING (*pē king*), **CHINA,** is the capital and second largest city of the People's Republic of China. During the period from 1928 to 1949 the city was called Peiping.

Peking is on the North China plain, 80 miles inland from the Gulf of Po Hai which opens into the Yellow Sea. The city is the starting point of an important land route to Mongolia and northwest China. Railroads and air lines connect Peking with other major cities of China. Peking is a transportation center, and its industries include the manufacture of railway rolling stock. Other industries are an iron and steelworks and factories processing wool, hides, and food products.

Within Peking's Outer Wall is a nest of cities, each at one time walled. The Tatar or Inner City is to the north and the Chinese or Outer City is to the south. Within the Tatar City was the Imperial City, which, in turn, housed the innermost walled area, the Forbidden City. Once the residence of China's emperors, this area is now the site of many government buildings. In recent decades the city has expanded beyond the area of the Outer Wall.

Peking through the ages has become the greatest center of learning and art in China.

煙霞天成

OROC

The former Summer Palace, about eight miles from Peking, is built around a lake. This is a section of a covered walk, with its intricate ornaments, and decorations in blue, green, vermilion, and gold.

Located there are many of China's leading universities, including Peking (formerly Yenching) University, People's University, and Tsinghua University, and numerous specialized technical institutes.

Decaying architectural treasures reflect the former glory of Imperial Peking. Within the Forbidden City is the Palace of the Son of Heaven, once the residence of emperors but now a museum. The famous Temple of Heaven, with its sacred Altar of Heaven is in the Chinese City, and the Lama Temple is in the Tatar City. These and the Temple of Agriculture, the Five-towered Pagoda, and the former Summer Palace all attract many visitors.

The earliest record of a city on Peking's site dates from about 200 B.C. Following its capture by the Tatars in A.D. 920, Peiping first became a great capital. The city's greatest period, however, was under Mongol rule (1267–1368), when it became the headquarters of the Mongol emperor Kublai Khan. Peking con-

tinued as the capital of China down to the 20th century.

Only after the Boxer Rebellion in 1900 were foreigners permitted to enter either the Forbidden City or the Imperial City. At that time a special area, the Legation Quarter, was set aside as the residence of all foreigners. China was proclaimed a republic in 1911. After that the Forbidden and Imperial cities, as well as the Manchu emperors' Summer Palace, eight miles to the south, were opened to public view. Peking was used as the early capital of the Chinese Republic, but in 1928 the capital was transferred by the Nationalist government to Nanking. Peking was then renamed Peiping. The Sino-Japanese War, 1937–1945, began in Peiping, when Japanese soldiers fired at the Chinese army on the outskirts of the city. From then until the end of World War II Peiping was occupied by the Japanese. In 1945 it came under Chinese control again. The city fell to the Chinese Communists in 1949. The Communists made the city the capital of China once more and again named it Peking. The metropolitan population is 6,800,000 (1962 estimate).

PELICAN (*pĕl′ĭ kăn*). A large pouch is suspended from the pelican's long bill. This odd pouch gives the bird an unusual appearance. Pelicans belong to the order of birds which includes cormorants, gannets, boobies, man-of-war birds, and other fishers of the sea. Their family is the Pelecanidae, of which there are some six species. They are widely scattered in the Temperate and Tropic regions. Two species are found in North America.

Pelicans are large birds. They range in length from four feet to nearly six feet and have wing spreads which may reach ten feet.

The bill of a large pelican is about 18 inches long. The pouch, which is attached to the bill, runs nearly its entire length. This bill gives to the bird a solemn, self-satisfied look as it stands on the shore.

The pouch is used somewhat in the manner of a scoop-net to catch fish, which are carried

The white pelican's body is about five feet long and pure white with black quills on the wings.

home in it to the nestlings.

The white pelican is about five feet long, with a wing spread of nine feet. It is found in flatter, western parts of Canada and the United States. In spite of its queer-looking head, it is a handsome bird. It is pure white except for the black, primary wing feathers and the straw-shaded wing coverts. The pouch, when stretched out, will hold a gallon or more of water. This pelican is rarely seen along the Atlantic Coast.

The brown pelican is slightly smaller. It is found in the West Indies, along the Gulf Coast, and from British Columbia to Chile. Its color is a dull brown, darker above than below. Its head is white, tinged with yellow on the crown. The white reaches part of the way down the side of the neck in a narrow, well-marked line, and gives way to seal-brown on hind neck and lower neck. In winter most of the neck is white.

Pelicans make their nests on the ground. The parent birds first scrape up a low mound of earth. On this they build a rude nest of sticks and weeds. Two to three, or occasionally four, chalky-white eggs are laid. The birds nest together in large colonies because they like company. Partly because of their oversized bills, they are awkward walkers. Their flight is a combination of flapping and sailing. In spite of their large bodies they make good speed for considerable distances. White pelicans work in groups to drive schools of fish into shallow water. They do not dive but catch fish while swimming.

When fishing the brown pelican dives down and scoops a fish near the surface of the water. Then as the pelican rises, it turns its beak and pouch sidewise to get rid of the excess water in the pouch. Sometimes, at the proper moment, a gull will seize the fish from the slightly open bill and fly away. The pelican will not chase its stolen prey, but resumes fishing.

PEN (*pĕn*). One of the most important contributions to the development of civilization was the art of writing. The pen has been one of the tools by which man has recorded his thoughts and deeds.

Before a real pen was first made, there were many other writing tools. Early man used pointed flints to scratch records and pictures on cave walls, rocks, or bones. He also learned to dip his index finger in plant juice or the blood of an animal and to use his finger as a "pen." Later he tried lumps of earth and pieces of chalk. He made lines on clay tablets with bone tools. The Chinese always painted their letters with a fine camel's-hair brush.

One of the first real pens was made by the Egyptians. They fastened a piece of copper, similar to a modern steel pen point, to the end of a hollow stem. The first letter handwriting was done by the Greeks nearly 2,000 years before Christ. They used a stylus of metal, bone, or ivory, and wrote on wax-coated tablets.

Later still a split pen was fashioned from hollow, tubelike grasses. It was called the *calamus, arundo,* or *juncus.* Before it could be

Left: Ornate Venetian glass dip-type pen. Center: A painting shows a clerk of the Middle Ages writing a letter for a rich merchant. He uses a sharp reed. Right: A modern ball-point pen. Bottom: Japanese writing outfit of 100 years ago consists of a strong metal brush holder, a fine brush, and an attached inkhorn with a lid. The holder at the left shows how it was carried at the writer's belt; the small ivory carving and cord were looped under the belt.

Courtesy (left, center) Parker Pen Company, (right) Parker Pen Company, photo, Webster-Chicago Corp., (bottom) Smithsonian Institution

used to write on papyrus, it was dipped into a form of ink.

When paper was introduced in the Middle Ages, man learned that the tail or wing feathers of a goose, crow, or swan could be made into a serviceable pen. The tip was pointed and split so that the ink could flow down the pen channel to the paper. The word "pen" itself comes from the Latin "penna" meaning feather. Even though a feather point did not last long, the quill type of pen was man's standard writing instrument for a thousand years.

Records show that steel pens were made in England as early as 1780 by a split-ring maker named Samuel Harrison. But it took 40 years for steel pens to come into popularity. In 1830 James Perry took out a patent to make steel pens more flexible. He cut a center hole and one or more slits in each side of the pen's center slit to direct the flow of ink.

The modern writing instrument is the fountain pen. It was first manufactured in the United States during the 1880's. The point or nib, usually made of 14-carat gold, is tipped with osmiridium or iridium. These are smooth, hard metals which enable the pen to write without scratching. The barrel holds a supply of ink and usually is made of hard rubber or synthetic, durable plastic. In some pens this barrel contains a rubber sack which is compressed by a lever or plunger and released to draw ink up into the container. In other fountain pens the pistonlike plunger has to be pushed up and down several times in order to fill it. No sack is then necessary.

Quill pens were used for many centuries. A quill was sharpened with a small "pen" knife. Sand from a shaker was spread on the ink to dry it quickly.

Courtesy Parker Pen Company

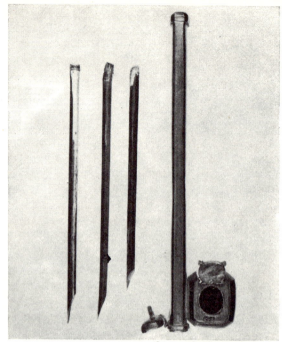

Courtesy Smithsonian Institution

A Syrian writing set, complete with metal penholder, attached inkpot, and a number of reeds pointed and split for use.

Another type of pen is the stylographic pen first made in the 19th century. The nib is replaced by a needle valve. When pressed, this serves to release the ink in the barrel.

The ball-point pen is a 20th-century invention. The writing point is a tiny ball of chrome steel about $\frac{1}{25}$ inch in diameter. The ball sits in a socket and revolves as it is dragged across any writing surface. It picks up the ink from an inner reservoir.

To work properly the pen must be made with microscopic accuracy.

PENCIL (*pĕn'sĭl* or *pĕn's'l*). A "lead" pencil contains not lead but a mineral substance called graphite.

Graphite, like lead, leaves a mark when drawn across paper. Because of this it is called "black lead"; hence the name *lead pencil*.

In pencil manufacture dried ground graphite is mixed with clay and water. The more clay, the harder the pencil will be; the more graphite, the softer the pencil. After the mixture reaches a doughy consistency, it passes through a forming press. It emerges as a thin sleek rope. This is straightened out, cut into lengths, dried, and put into huge ovens to bake.

Meanwhile the pencil case has been prepared. The wood, either red cedar or pine, is shaped in halves and grooved to hold the lead. After the finished leads are inserted in the grooves, the halves of the pencil are glued together. A saw cuts the lead-filled slats into individual pencils, and a shaping machine gives the surface a smooth finish.

Colored pencils are made of kaolin mixed with waxes, gums, and coloring matter. Often they are encased in paper wrapped spirally around the lead. The pencil is "sharpened" by unwinding the paper. Copying and ink pencils are made of a mixture of aniline dye, graphite, and China clay. In carpenters' and markers' pencils, graphite is combined with wax or tallow. In "automatic" pencils the lead is held in a small metal tube inside the shell of the pencil. The lead is pushed out or pulled in by means of a plunger operated by a screw mechanism.

The United States, Great Britain, and Germany lead the world in pencil manufacture.

PENDULUM (*pĕn′dū lŭm*). Galileo Galilei, the great scientist of the 16th century, saw a hanging lamp swinging at the end of a chain in the cathedral of Pisa in Italy. He noticed its regular motion. He found that the time for one complete swing or vibration was always the same, whether the lamp had a large swing or a small one. This discovery led to one of man's most useful inventions—the pendulum clock.

A pendulum is a weight mounted to swing freely at the end of a cord, chain, or rod. Whenever the weight is moved to one side or the other and released, it swings toward its position of rest, which is directly below the support. Its momentum, however, carries it past this point and out on the other side. Then it swings back and repeats the movement, covering slightly less distance on each swing, until the friction of the air and in the point of support finally brings it to rest.

The important feature is that the time, or *period*, of one complete swing is the same whether the weight is light or heavy. The pe-

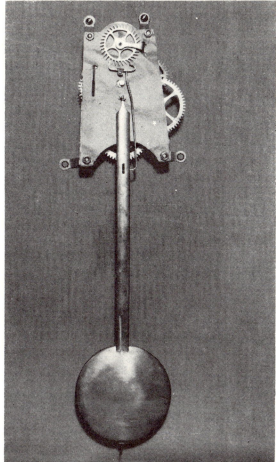

Courtesy W. Barclay Stephens, M.D., Hon. Curator of Horology, California Academy of Sciences

Clock pendulum. The rod and bob are made of a metal which does not contract or expand greatly when the temperature changes.

riod of vibration does not depend on the material of the *bob* as the weight is called. The time taken for its swing depends upon the pull of gravity and the length of the supporting string or rod. This makes the pendulum useful, for example, in regulating clocks. (See CLOCK AND WATCH.) The period is changed by any change in the length of the string or rod. The longer the pendulum the longer its time of vibration,—that is, the slower it moves.

To regulate a pendulum clock the bob is moved upward with the adjusting nut to make the clock run faster. If the clock is running too fast, the bob is lowered slightly to make it go slower.

The rods of clock pendulums, which are usually made of metal, expand in the heat of summer and contract in winter. This change in length would make the clock inaccurate unless it was avoided by means of a *compensated* pendulum. One type of compensated pendulum is made of alternating brass and steel rods, with adjoining rods fastened first at the top, then at the bottom. Since some expand upward, and others downward, the length of the pendulum as a whole is not changed. Pendulums are also made of invar, an alloy of nickel and steel, that is not much affected by changes in temperature. For long simple (uncompensated) pendulum rods wood is better as it expands less than metal.

There are several types of pendulums other than the swinging one described above. A weight hung on a coil spring will move up and down for quite a length of time when depressed and then released. A disk or heavy bob hung from a light wire or thin flat spring and then twisted well will untwist on being released, twist in the other direction, and untwist again. This is called a *torsion* pendulum.

All types of pendulums have been used to control *escapements* in clocks. In escapement a tiny push is given to the pendulum—enough to overcome the friction so the pendulum does not run down in its swing until the spring or weight that supplies energy to the escapement runs down. Thus, clocks that run 24 hours, a week, a month, or even a year (anniversary clocks) are possible.

The word pendulum is almost always used in connection with a clock or timekeeper. However, there is another type of pendulum known as the *Foucault* pendulum. This pendulum has no time-telling function, nor has its rate of swing any bearing. It is only the direction or plane of its swing which is important.

The Foucault pendulum gets its name from Jean Bernard Leon Foucault, a French physicist and astronomer. He demonstrated visually the rotation of the earth making use of a pendulum for the purpose.

Foucault made a public demonstration which attracted world-wide attention in the spring of 1851 in Paris, France. From the dome of the Pantheon he hung a wire pendulum 213 feet long with a ball at the lower end weighing about 100 pounds. The purpose of this exceedingly long pendulum was to show that a ball (pendulum bob), once started, would

A Foucault pendulum at the California Academy of Sciences, San Francisco, California, showing the dial, the 175-pound ball, or bob, and a portion of the suspending cable, which has its point of suspension 40 feet above.

Courtesy California Academy of Sciences, Golden Gate Park, San Francisco, Calif.

swing forth and back for several hours before another impulse was required. When a suspended body, like the pendulum bob, is once started it will swing in the same direction or plane, unless changed by some other force, regardless of the earth's rotation. This is one of the fundamental laws of physics. The turning at the point of suspension will not affect the direction of the swinging pendulum.

On the floor of the Pantheon a large compass dial, showing the north-south and east-west directions, was placed directly below the suspended pendulum. The pendulum ball was then given a north-south motion. After an hour or two it was noted that the pendulum apparently had changed its swing in a clockwise direction. This was not so, however. The rotation of the earth caused the illusion of change of direction.

PENGUIN (*pĕn'gwĭn* or *pĕng'wĭn*). Penguins are water birds that live along the Antarctic continent and islands. They are found as far north as Peru or southern Brazil, the Galapagos Islands, southwest Africa, New Zealand, and southern Australia. The island of South Georgia is a favorite breeding place for penguins.

There are 17 species of penguins. The emperor penguin is the largest and the rarest. Yet the emperor, as well as the king and the Adelie, are among those species best known. The sizes of penguins vary from around 16 inches for some species to 4 feet for others.

Their bodies are long and usually oval in shape. Their plumage covers their entire bodies and is made of small scalelike feathers. It looks like a man's evening dress of black coat and white shirt front. Their wings look like flippers and have no quills. The wings are useless for flight but are used for swimming and diving. Penguins are expert swimmers and are very graceful in the water. They catch and eat small fish. Penguins usually sit in an upright position on land. King and emperor penguins even hatch their single egg while erect. The male and the female take turns in the hatching process.

The king penguins are about 38 inches long. They travel in groups. They look very dignified

H. Armstrong Roberts

Emperor penguins may be nearly four feet tall.

but are quite quarrelsome. King penguins are natural buglers. They sometimes stretch to their full height and send clear notes a great distance.

The Adelie penguins are smaller, plumper birds and are more sociable. These penguins have a great deal of curiosity. If an observer stands very still, they may surround him, sitting quietly and staring steadily at him.

PENN (*pĕn*), **WILLIAM** (1644–1718), was the English Quaker leader who founded the colony of Pennsylvania.

Born in London, Penn was the son of Admiral Sir William Penn. Even as a boy he was very religious. In 1662 he was expelled from Oxford because he spoke and wrote things that did not agree with the teachings of the Anglican Church.

In 1666 Penn went to Ireland to manage some of his father's estates. Earlier he had been strongly influenced at Oxford by the Quaker preacher, Thomas Loe. In Ireland Penn attended meetings of the Society of Friends (Quakers) and spent some time in prison for his actions at religious meetings. By the time he returned to England in 1667, he was an active Quaker.

Two years later he was imprisoned in the Tower of London for his writings and preaching. There he began writing *No Cross, No Crown* which attacked luxury, frivolity, and economic oppression. After his father died in 1670 Penn traveled through Germany and Holland teaching the Quaker religion. For about ten years he devoted himself to preaching and writing in favor of religious freedom and political rights.

By 1677 the Quakers had acquired as a colony more than half of West Jersey in America. Penn, one of the trustees of the property, helped to draw up a charter for the colony that gave the settlers freedom of religion, trial by jury, and an elected assembly. (See NEW JERSEY.)

Brown Brothers

William Penn.

In 1681 Charles II gave Penn a tract of land in America in payment of a debt owed his father. It was named Pennsylvania in honor of Penn's father. The next year Penn acquired the area of Delaware as an addition to his Pennsylvania grant. He then left for America with a group of settlers.

In America he planned the city of Philadelphia and set up a council elected by the people to help him govern the colony. He advertised in Europe inviting people of all religions to settle in Pennsylvania, and offered land at a low price to farmers and workers. He visited Indian tribes and made agreements to pay just prices for their lands. Because the Indians were treated fairly, the Pennsylvania colony had no trouble with the Indians until long after Penn died. (See PENNSYLVANIA.)

The colony grew quickly, but Penn remained there less than two years. Persecution of English Quakers was getting worse and in 1684 he returned to England to help them and also to settle a border conflict with Lord Baltimore of the Maryland colony. When the Duke of York

became King James II in 1685, Penn arranged for the release of about 1,300 Quakers from jail.

James II was forced off the throne by the Revolution of 1688. Because of his friendship with James II, Penn was accused of treason in 1692 and the governorship of Pennsylvania was taken from him. He was able to prove his innocence and Pennsylvania was returned to him in 1694. During this time he arranged to have a public grammar school started in Philadelphia. He also drew up the first plan for uniting the American colonies.

In 1699 he returned to Pennsylvania. In 1701 he changed the form of government of the Pennsylvania colony giving the elected Assembly more power, and giving Delaware its own Assembly. The same year he went back to England never to return. (See DELAWARE.)

Penn was important in the founding and settling of New Jersey, Pennsylvania, and Delaware. His beliefs in democratic government and religious freedom set an example for those colonies which were founded after his work was completed. (See COLONIAL BEGINNINGS IN AMERICA.)

PENNSYLVANIA (pĕn′sĭl vā′nĭ ä), **UNITED STATES,** in the northeastern part of the country, is one of the Middle Atlantic group of states. On its northern border are Lake Erie and New York; on the east is the Delaware River, separating it from New York and New Jersey; on the south are Delaware, Maryland, and West Virginia; and on the west are West Virginia and Ohio.

In 1681 King Charles II of England made a grant of land in the New World to William Penn. The land was named Pennsylvania after Penn's father, Admiral Sir William Penn. The name means "Penn's Woods."

The state is the 3rd most populous in the Union but it is only 33rd in land area. Most of its people live and work in or near Philadelphia, Pittsburgh, and Scranton. Pennsylvania is sometimes called the Steel State because almost half of all its industrial workers earn a living in this industry.

The land surface is very uneven with mountains, hills, valleys, and small plains. Elevations range from sea level at the Delaware River to more than 3,000 feet in the mountainous areas. More than half of the state is covered with forests. Generally the summers are hot, and the winters are cold.

Landscape

About one-half of the state lies in the Appalachian (or Allegheny) Plateau region. That region covers the western and northern parts of the state. Much of this area has rolling hills, but toward the east the hills blend into the Allegheny Mountains. The highest point in the state, Mount Davis (3,213 feet), is in the southern part of these mountains. The Pocono Mountains are in the northeastern part of the plateau region. On the eastern edge of the plateau is the Allegheny Front, a sharp slope that drops into the Ridge and Valley region.

The Ridge and Valley region is a part of the great Appalachian Mountain chain that stretches across the eastern part of the United States. In Pennsylvania the region runs diagonally from southwest to northeast across the state. It is made of a series of sharp, parallel mountain ridges separated by valleys, as though a giant comb had been pulled across the landscape. The Cumberland and Lebanon valleys form a part of the Great Valley of the Appalachians. (See APPALACHIAN MOUNTAINS.)

On the southeastern edge of the Ridge and Valley region is a highland region known in Pennsylvania as South Mountain. It is the northernmost part of the Blue Ridge Mountains that reach into the state from Maryland.

The southeastern part of Pennsylvania is the Piedmont region. It is a rolling area that slopes gently downward from the Ridge and Valley region until it meets the flat plains of the Delaware River in the southeastern corner of the state.

Pennsylvania's soil is as different as its land surface. The soil best suited for agriculture is found in the Piedmont and along Lake Erie. The soils of the river valleys also are fertile. However, in the mountains much of the soil is poor.

The state is drained by three major river systems: the Delaware, the Susquehanna, and the

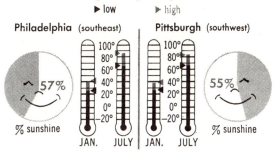

Average Daily Temperature

▶ low   ▶ high

Philadelphia (southeast)   Pittsburgh (southwest)

57%   55%

% sunshine   JAN. JULY   JAN. JULY   % sunshine

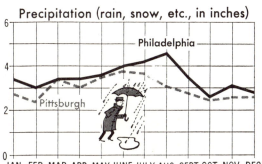

Precipitation (rain, snow, etc., in inches)

Philadelphia

Pittsburgh

JAN. FEB. MAR. APR. MAY JUNE JULY AUG. SEPT. OCT. NOV. DEC.

Ohio. The Delaware flows into Delaware Bay and the Susquehanna flows into Chesapeake Bay. The Ohio, formed at Pittsburgh, flows southwest to the Mississippi River. These rivers are natural waterways for shipping, and supply water power for homes and factories.

Pennsylvania's lakes are not large. Conneaut Lake in the west is the largest natural lake within the state. Lake Erie, on the northwestern border, connects the state with the Atlantic Ocean by way of the St. Lawrence Seaway.

More than 50 per cent of the state is covered with forests. Hardwoods, including oak, chestnut, maple, birch, hickory, hemlock and poplar, are the most common trees.

Climate

The climate varies in different sections. The southeast has a milder climate than other sections of the state. (There is also a small area of mild climate along the shore of Lake Erie.) The warmest average annual temperature, 52 degrees Fahrenheit, and the longest frost-free growing season, 170 to 200 days, are in the southeast.

Toward the north and west (in the plateau region) the climate is colder. There the aver-

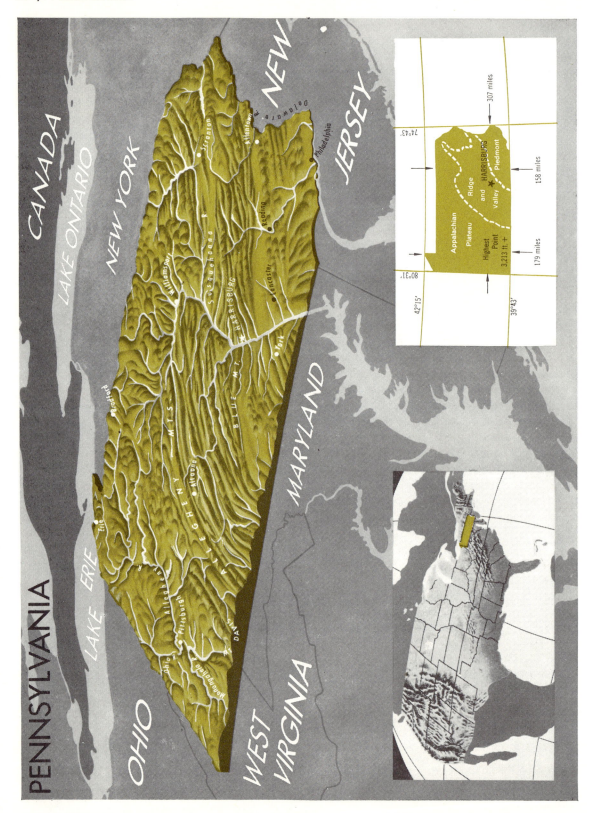

CANADA

LAKE ONTARIO

NEW YORK

NEW JERSEY

Delaware R.

Scranton

Allentown

Philadelphia

Reading

Williamsport

Susquehanna R.

HARRISBURG

Lancaster

BLUE MT.

York

Bradford

MTS.

ALLEGHENY

Altoona

Erie

LAKE ERIE

DIV.

OHIO

Allegheny

Pittsburgh

Monongahela

Ohio

PENNSYLVANIA

OHIO

WEST VIRGINIA

MARYLAND

74°43'

307 miles

42°15'

80°31'

Appalachian Plateau

Highest Point 3,213 ft.+

HARRISBURG

Ridge and Valley

Piedmont

158 miles

179 miles

39°43'

Nickname: "Keystone State"
Capital: Harrisburg
Motto: Virtue, Liberty and Independence
Date admitted to the Union: One of original 13 states
Order of admission as state: 2nd to ratify U.S. Constitution, December 12, 1787
Song: None

Mountain Laurel   Hemlock   Ruffed Grouse

Physical

AREA: 45,333 square miles, including 326 square miles of water; 1.3 per cent of total United States; 33rd state in size.

POPULATION: 11,319,366; 6.3 per cent of total United States; 3rd state in population; 249.7 persons per square mile; 71.6 per cent urban, 28.4 per cent rural.

MOUNTAIN RANGES: Appalachian System.

CHIEF MOUNTAIN PEAK (height in feet): Davis (3,213).

LARGEST LAKES: Wallenpaupack Creek Reservoir, Pymatuning, Conemaugh River Reservoir.

MOST IMPORTANT RIVERS: Allegheny, Lehigh, Monongahela, Schuylkill, Delaware, Susquehanna, Ohio.

NATIONAL PARKS AND MONUMENTS: Independence National Historical Park, 21.84 acres (established 1956).

STATE PARKS: Total of 150 including Shawnee, Cook Forest, French Creek, Crooked Creek, Hickory Run, Raccoon Creek, Laurel Hill, Ricketts Glen, Caledonia, Pine Grove Furnace.

ADDITIONAL PLACES OF INTEREST: Coudersport Ice Mine, Buck Hill Falls, Delaware Water Gap, Grand Canyon of Pennsylvania, Penn's Cave, Horseshoe Curve, Ephrata Cloisters, Fort Augusta, Gettysburg National Cemetery.

Transportation and Communication

RAILROADS: 9,154 miles of track; first railroad, Leiperville to Ridley Creek, 1809.

ROADS: Total, 108,347; surfaced, 84,030.

MOTOR VEHICLES: Total, 4,182,000; automobiles, 3,587,000; trucks and buses, 548,000.

AIRPORTS: Civil, 135.

NEWSPAPERS: 130 dailies; 385 others; first newspaper, *American Weekly Mercury*, Philadelphia, 1719.

RADIO STATIONS: 186; first station, KDKA, Pittsburgh, 1920.

TELEVISION STATIONS: 22; first station, WRCV, Philadelphia, 1941.

TELEPHONES: Total, 3,969,000; residence, 2,972,000; business, 997,000.

POST OFFICES: 2,058.

People

CHIEF CITIES: Philadelphia (2,002,512); Pittsburgh (604,332); Erie (138,440); Scranton (111,443); Allentown (108,347).

NATIONAL BACKGROUNDS: 94.7 per cent native-born; 5.3 per cent foreign-born.

CHURCH MEMBERSHIP: Of the total state population, 58.8 per cent are church members; 48 per cent Protestant (including Lutheran, 13.8 per cent; Methodist, 8.9 per cent; Presbyterian, 8.2 per cent; Christian Reformed, 3.4 per cent; Baptist, 1.8 per cent), 46.3 per cent Catholic, and 5.7 per cent Jewish.

LEADING UNIVERSITIES AND COLLEGES: University of Pennsylvania, Philadelphia; Pennsylvania State University, University Park; University of Pittsburgh, Pittsburgh; Villanova University, Villanova; Temple University, Philadelphia; Drexel Institute of Technology, Philadelphia.

MUSEUMS: Philadelphia Museum of Art, Philadelphia; Carnegie Museum, Pittsburgh; Franklin Institute, Philadelphia, transportation; University of Pennsylvania Museum, Philadelphia, anthropology; State Museum, Harrisburg, colonial exhibits.

SPECIAL SCHOOLS: State Oral School for the Deaf, Scranton; Overbrook School for the Blind, Philadelphia; Pennsylvania School for the Deaf, Philadelphia; Royer-Greaves School for the Blind, Paoli; Western Pennsylvania Schools for the Blind and the Deaf, Pittsburgh.

CORRECTIONAL AND PENAL INSTITUTIONS: Eastern State Penitentiary, Philadelphia; Western State Penitentiary, Pittsburgh; State Industrial Home for Women, Muncy; State Penitentiaries, Rockview and Graterford; State Industrial School, Camp Hill.

Government

NUMBER OF U.S. SENATORS: 2.

NUMBER OF U.S. REPRESENTATIVES: 27.

NUMBER OF STATE SENATORS: 50. **TERM:** 4 years.

NUMBER OF STATE REPRESENTATIVES: 203. **TERM:** 2 years.

STATE LEGISLATURE CONVENES: January, each year.

SESSION LIMIT: None.

CONSTITUTION ADOPTED: 1873.

GOVERNOR'S TERM: 4 years. He may not succeed himself.

NUMBER OF COUNTIES: 67.

VOTING QUALIFICATIONS: Age 21; residence in state 1 year, in district 2 months.

STATE HOLIDAYS: Lincoln's Birthday, February 12; Good Friday; Memorial Day, May 30; Flag Day, June 14; Columbus Day, October 12.

ANNUAL STATE EVENTS: Mummers' Parade, Philadelphia, January 1; Pennsylvania Farm Show, Harrisburg, January; Maple Festival, Somerset County, March; Pennsylvania Folk Festival, Kutztown, July; Dutch Days, Hershey, August.

Historic Events

1609—Henry Hudson explores Delaware Bay.

1616—Cornelius Hendricksen sails up Delaware River.

1643—Swedish settlement on Tinicum Island near Philadelphia.

1655—Dutch take over New Sweden.

1664—England takes Dutch lands.

1681—William Penn receives grant for Pennsylvania area.

1754—French capture English forts in Pennsylvania during French and Indian War.

1763—Pontiac leads Indians in attacks on English forts.

1774—First Continental Congress meets at Philadelphia.

1776—Declaration of Independence signed in Philadelphia.

1777—British capture Philadelphia.

1787—Constitutional Convention meets at Philadelphia; Pennsylvania ratifies U.S. Constitution.

1846—Wilmot Proviso designed by David Wilmot.

1863—Confederate forces defeated at Battle of Gettysburg during the American Civil War.

1938—Congress of Industrial Organizations (C.I.O.) held its first convention at Pittsburgh.

1940—Pennsylvania Turnpike opens.

1955—Polio vaccine is developed by Dr. Jonas Salk in Pittsburgh.

1957—Atomic generating station begins operation at Shippingport.

Courtesy Standard Oil Company (New Jersey)

A coal mining town in the Appalachian Mountains.

age annual temperature is 49 degrees, and the summers are shorter and the winters are longer than in the southeast. In this region the growing season ranges from 120 to 165 days. Western Pennsylvania has the state's most changeable weather. Yearly temperatures there range from zero degrees to 100 degrees. It also has the most frequent rains and snow storms.

The temperatures of the mountainous regions are usually eight to ten degrees lower than the areas of lower elevation. The average annual rainfall of the state is about 42 inches. The greatest snowfalls are in Somerset County, the state's most mountainous area, where the yearly average is 88 inches.

Animal Life and Resources

In colonial times there were many kinds of wild animals in Pennsylvania. Most of the larger ones have disappeared except bears and deer. Raccoons, squirrels, rabbits, woodchucks, and other small animals still are common. The lakes and streams are well stocked with fish. Birds such as the wild turkey, duck, ruffed grouse, quail, goose, and pheasant are found in the state.

Pennsylvania has rich mineral deposits. The state produces about one-fifth of all the coal mined in the United States. The state's coal, oil, gas, and water furnish a great deal of power not only for Pennsylvania but also for the rest of the nation. This supply of power has helped Pennsylvania to become a leading industrial state.

The People

In early times, the Delaware, Iroquois and other Indian tribes moved from the West into what is now Pennsylvania and drove out the original Indian settlers. The Iroquois went on to New York, but the Delawares remained in the area. Later the Shawnees settled in the southeast while the Eries lived in the northwest. The city of Erie and Lake Erie bear the Indian name.

In 1609 the Dutch sent explorers to North America. One was Henry Hudson. In his ship, the *Half Moon*, he discovered what is known as Delaware Bay and explored some of the Delaware River. In 1616 another Dutch explorer, Cornelis Hendricksen, sailed the Delaware River as far as the Schuylkill River.

Swedish people began the settlement of Pennsylvania. Their first settlements were started in 1638 in what is now Delaware. Five years later the Swedish governor, Johan Printz, started the first permanent white settlement in present-day Pennsylvania. This was on Tinicum Island about 20 miles south of Philadelphia. Tinicum became the capital of New Sweden, the name given the Swedish settlements along the Delaware River.

The Swedes were interested in farming. From the Indians they learned to track game and to plant corn, pumpkins, and beans. The Swedes were the first to build homes and churches and start civil government in Pennsylvania. The log homes they built started the famous log cabin tradition in America.

When William Penn was granted the Pennsylvania area, many settlers, chiefly English, Germans, and Scotch-Irish, flocked to the colony. Several shiploads of English Quakers arrived between 1682 and 1684. Englishmen also came from Virginia, Connecticut, and the other colonies. Philadelphia, Chester, and Bucks counties became strongly English with Philadelphia as the cultural center. Eastern Pennsylvania still bears marks of English Quaker life and culture.

Courtesy Pennsylvania Department of Commerce

The so-called "Pennsylvania Dutch" were not Dutch but Germans who came to America in search of religious freedom and a better way of living. By the time of the American Revolution (1775), one-third of the people of Pennsylvania

The Amish, or Pennsylvania Dutch, decorate their farm buildings with colorful designs.

were German. They settled mainly in the southeast where they farmed the rich soils. The descendants of these people are still noted for their excellent farms. Some of them continue to speak a language known as "Pennsylvania Dutch," and to follow German customs and folkways.

Before the American Revolution large numbers of Scotch-Irish also came to Pennsylvania. Unlike the Germans they became chiefly traders and manufacturers rather than farmers. They also started many schools. Their descendants still live in western Pennsylvania.

In more recent years many people have come

Where the people live.

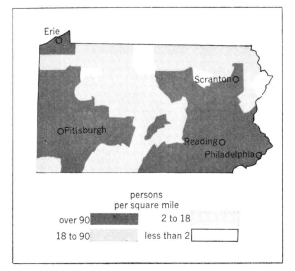

persons per square mile

over 90 ▮▮▮   2 to 18

18 to 90 ▮▮▮   less than 2 ☐

from southern and eastern Europe to work in the coal mines and steel mills of the state. More than five per cent of the total population is foreign-born. The largest number of these are Italians. People from Poland and Great Britain make up the next largest groups. Negroes make up about 7.5 per cent of the total population.

Most of the people of Pennsylvania live in the large cities and their suburbs. The southeastern corner, near Philadelphia, is the most thickly populated region. The area around Pittsburgh is also heavily settled as is the coal region of the northeast. A large part of the north central portion and some of the southern portions have few people because they are forested or are used for farming.

The greatest number of the Roman Catholics, the Negroes, and the foreign-born live in the large cities. The rural areas and smaller towns are mostly white and Protestants. More than half the Negroes of the state live in Philadelphia.

Philadelphia, the state's largest city, is the nation's fourth largest city. An important Atlantic port, it is also a great industrial and textile center. (See PHILADELPHIA.)

Pittsburgh, the second largest city, is called the "Gateway to the West." The "Steel City," as it is also called, manufactures steel, glass, aluminum, electrical goods, and food products. (See PITTSBURGH.)

PENNSYLVANIA

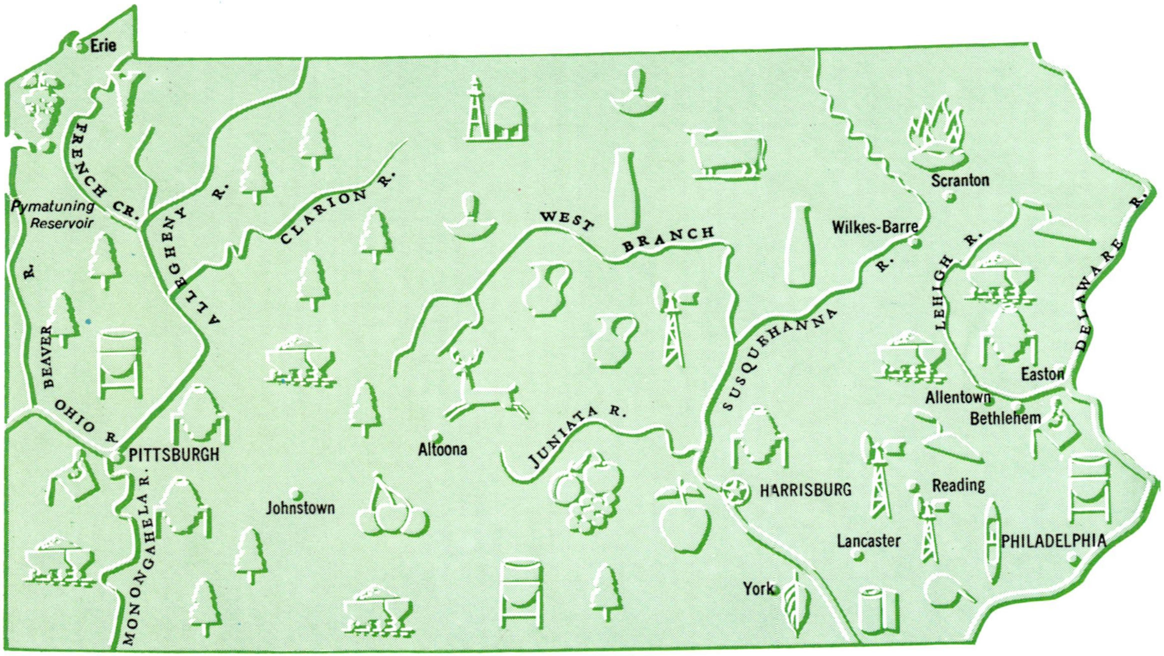

KEY TO SYMBOLS

ANTHRACITE	SMELTING
TANNING	IRON & STEEL
FORESTS	OIL REFINING
CEMENT	DAIRY PRODUCTS
GENERAL FARMING	PAPER MILLS PULP
COAL	APPLES
CANNING	CHERRIES
DRUGS & CHEMICALS	GRAPES
TEXTILES	METAL PRODUCTS
CATTLE	CLAY PRODUCTS
BIG GAME	FRUIT
TOBACCO	

LAND USE

- 56% FOREST
- 7% PASTURE & GRAZING LAND
- 26% CROPLAND
- 5% WASTELAND
- 6% BUILT-ON

VALUE OF PRODUCTS
(FIGURES IN $ MILLIONS)

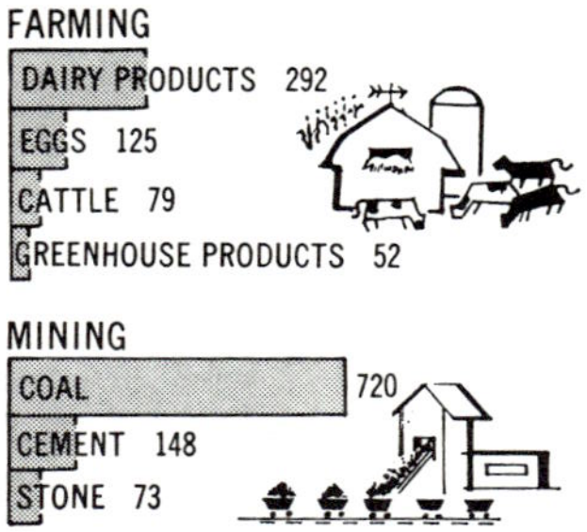

FARMING

DAIRY PRODUCTS	292
EGGS	125
CATTLE	79
GREENHOUSE PRODUCTS	52

MINING

COAL	720
CEMENT	148
STONE	73

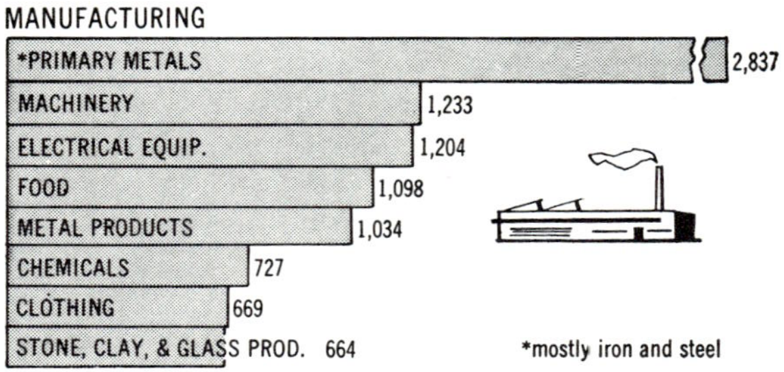

MANUFACTURING

*PRIMARY METALS	2,837
MACHINERY	1,233
ELECTRICAL EQUIP.	1,204
FOOD	1,098
METAL PRODUCTS	1,034
CHEMICALS	727
CLOTHING	669
STONE, CLAY, & GLASS PROD.	664

*mostly iron and steel

Map labels

Erie, Pymatuning Reservoir, FRENCH CR., ALLEGHENY R., CLARION R., Scranton, Wilkes-Barre, LEHIGH R., DELAWARE R., Easton, Bethlehem, Allentown, Reading, WEST BRANCH, SUSQUEHANNA, Harrisburg, Lancaster, Philadelphia, York, JUNIATA R., Altoona, Johnstown, PITTSBURGH, MONONGAHELA R., OHIO R., BEAVER R.

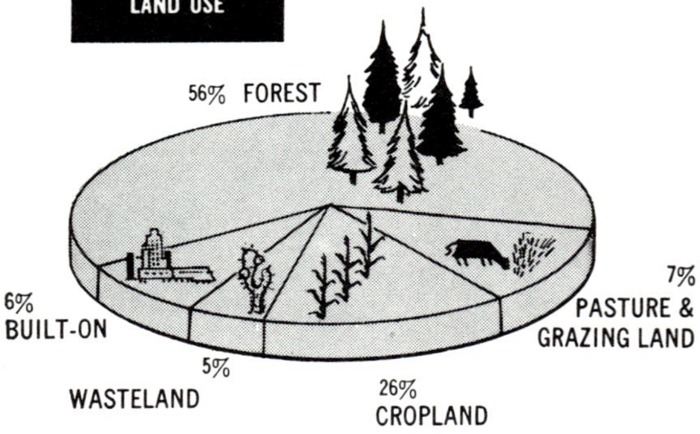

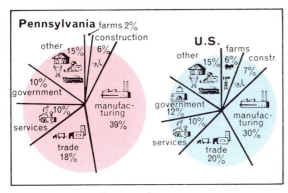

Sources of income.

Erie is the state's only lake port. It receives and ships large amounts of iron, coal, and other products such as grain and fish. The largest paper mill in the state is in Erie.

Scranton is the center of the hard coal district and a railroad center. Reading, in the middle of the "Pennsylvania Dutch" district, is a railroad center. The largest hosiery mill in the world is in one of Reading's suburbs. Allentown, also in a German area, manufactures textiles and has many cement plants. Harrisburg, the state capital, is a transportation center. (See HARRISBURG.)

How the People Make a Living

Agriculture. Almost half of the land of the state is in farms, but only about six per cent of the people live and work on farms. Although there is some farming in all counties, Lancaster County is the richest farming region in the state and one of the most important in the nation. With favorable weather conditions and good soils the farmers there are able to grow many kinds of crops.

Corn is the chief farm crop; other leading crops are oats, wheat, and potatoes. Large amounts of these are grown in Lancaster County to feed livestock. The Lancaster stockyards are the largest east of Chicago. Cigar leaf tobacco is another important crop of the area. The poultry products of nearby York County make Pennsylvania one of the nation's largest producers of eggs and chickens.

Dairying is a major farming activity in Pennsylvania. Near such cities as Philadelphia, Erie, Pittsburgh, and Harrisburg are large dairy

farms that sell their products to city dwellers. Dairy farming is especially important in the northern area where the short growing season is favorable to the pasturing of cows and the growing of hay. Surplus milk products are shipped to New York City or processed and canned in the large dairies. Most of the milk from Lebanon County is used to manufacture milk chocolate in the town of Hershey.

Pennsylvania has long ranked high nationally in the production of buckwheat. It is grown in the mountains and areas where most other crops will not grow. Buckwheat provides nectar for bees and feed for poultry, and is made into flour.

Vegetables are grown in many areas of the state and shipped fresh to nearby cities or to food processing plants. A considerable amount of all the mushrooms of the United States are grown in Chester County.

Fruit growing also is important. Pennsylvania

How the people make a living.

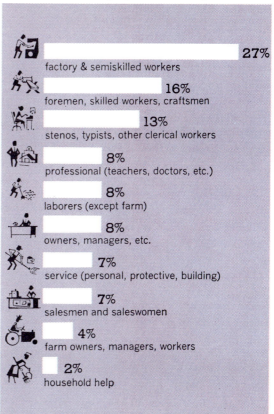

Courtesy Standard Oil Company (New Jersey)

A dairy farm in eastern Pennsylvania.

ranks as one of the leaders among the states in the production of peaches, maple syrup, grapes, apples, cherries, pears, and plums. Much of the fruit is grown in the southern part of the state, especially Franklin, York and Adams counties. However, Allegheny County in the west is also a fruit region, and grapes are raised along Lake Erie.

Mining. The minerals the state produces in large amounts—limestone, coal, iron ore, sand, cobalt, clay, oil, natural gas, slate, and stone— are used in some of the state's industries.

Fuel production outranks all other minerals. Pennsylvania ranks among the state leaders in the production of coal. It produces almost all of the anthracite (hard) coal mined in the United States. This coal is found in the northeast around Scranton, one of the largest mining cities in the nation. Anthracite coal is used for heating homes and factories.

Soft or bituminous coal of high quality is found in southern and southwestern Pennsylvania. Coal also underlies large areas of the Appalachian Plateau. The coal of the western part of the plateau is the finest for coke, the material used in making steel. About three times more soft coal than anthracite is mined.

The United States' first oil well was drilled at Titusville, Pennsylvania, in 1859. Oil has since been found in almost all of the state's western counties. The amount of oil is not as great as that found in the western states, but its quality is high. It is in great demand as machine oil, grease and other lubricants. However, the state does not produce enough oil to serve its needs, so much crude oil has to be brought from the gulf states or from Venezuela.

Natural gas is found in western Pennsylvania. Gas production has been increased by deeper drilling but there is still not enough to meet the state's needs. Therefore large amounts of it must be shipped from Texas.

Stone and clay products are produced throughout Pennsylvania. Limestone is used in the manufacture of steel, in the construction of buildings and highways, and in agriculture. Eastern Pennsylvania is the major cement producing region in the United States. In this area also are the greatest slate deposits in the country. The slate is quarried and then cut for use on roofs or blackboards. Special clays found in the state are used in many products such as tile, brick, and pottery. Chinaware produced at New Castle is among the world's finest.

Manufacturing. The availability of laborers, industrial experience, and nearness to transportation and markets have helped Pennsylvania

A steel reduction mill. Making steel is a major Pennsylvania industry.

Courtesy United States Steel Corporation

to become one of the five leading industrial states. Philadelphia and its surrounding area is the state's great manufacturing center, but plants and factories are scattered throughout the state. The leading industries in order of their importance are: metal and metal products, textile and textile products, and food processing.

Almost half of Pennsylvania's industrial workers are employed in the metals industry. Steel plants are found in almost every large city, but the mills of the Pittsburgh district produce most of the state's steel. Pennsylvania produces and uses more steel than any other state.

Courtesy Delaware River Port Authority

Although it is 88 miles from the Atlantic Ocean, the Port of Philadelphia handles more shipping than any other port in the United States except New York City.

Philadelphia is the center of the textile industry. There are also plants in several other parts of the state. They manufacture all types of clothing, carpeting, yarns, hosiery, and yard goods. The famous Stetson cowboy hats are made in Philadelphia.

Pennsylvania's rapidly growing food processing industry is a leader in the production of pretzels, ice cream, and chocolate products. It ranks high in sugar cane refining, liquors, and meat packing. In addition, many other food products are canned or frozen in the processing plants and shipped to all parts of the nation.

Many people are employed in the paper and paper printing industry. Several paper mills are in the mountains where there is a good supply of timber. However, much of the pulpwood must be imported from Canada. The major printing center is Philadelphia.

Other important manufactured products include electrical machinery, electronics equipment (such as radio and television tubes and receivers), professional and scientific instruments, watches, textile machinery, hardware, ships and boats, aluminum, brass, bronze, copper and zinc products, wire products, chemical products, leather and rubber goods, glass, and tobacco products.

Other Industries. From about 1850 to 1900 Pennsylvania was the center of the world's lumber production. Wasteful cutting and the moving of lumber companies to the thicker forests of Michigan, Wisconsin, and Minnesota caused the industry to decline. Today, however, the Department of Forests and Waters is helping to rebuild the timberlands. The industry is again becoming important, and it now employs many people.

Pennsylvania attracts many tourists. It not only has beautiful scenery but there are many sites of historical interest such as Valley Forge, Gettysburg, and Independence Hall. The largest resort and vacation area in the state is in the Poconos Mountains. Presque Isle at Erie also attracts many people.

About one out of every seven persons in Pennsylvania works in wholesale and retail trade. This includes food stores, restaurants, cafeterias, taverns, gasoline stations, hotels, department stores, and drug stores. Many others earn a living in the professional services—engineering, law, medicine, pharmacy, dentistry, ministry, teaching, and nursing.

Transportation and Communication

The Lancaster Turnpike, the first hard-surfaced highway in the United States, was built

Ken Smith

The dome of the Pennsylvania state capitol in Harrisburg is modeled after that of St. Peter's cathedral, Rome.

from Philadelphia to Lancaster between 1792 and 1796. Today the state has many miles of fine roads. The best known is the four lane Pennsylvania Turnpike, opened in 1940. It extends all the way across the state and connects the superhighways of the east with the Ohio and Indiana Turnpikes on the west.

After 1865, the railroads were the chief method of transportation. However, with more highways and air service the use of rail transportation for passenger and freight service has decreased. Now major airlines serve all the large cities of the state.

Water transportation has been important since the founding of the colony. Philadelphia is one of the greatest ports on the Atlantic Coast. Pittsburgh, at the junction of the Ohio, Monongahela, and Allegheny rivers, is another important shipping port. The Monongahela carries millions of tons of coal and coke to the steel furnaces of the Pittsburgh district. The city of Erie connects the state with the Great Lakes and the St. Lawrence Seaway.

The first newspaper published in Pennsylvania, the *American Weekly Mercury*, was started in 1719 at Philadelphia. It was one of the first newspapers published in the colonies.

In 1846 the first commercial telegraph line in the United States was opened between Philadelphia and Lancaster. It was also in Pennsylvania (Pittsburgh) that the country's first commercial radio station began operation (1920).

Government

Pennsylvania's constitution, adopted in 1873, provides for three branches of government: executive, legislative, and judicial. The governor heads the executive department; the lieutenant governor is the president of the senate. In addition to the major executive officers, 20 executive departments and many boards and commissions carry out the work of governing the state. The heads of three departments are elected: the Auditor General, the State Treasurer, and the Secretary of Internal Affairs.

The General Assembly is made up of a Senate and House of Representatives. One senator is elected from each senatorial district. The representatives are chosen from each of the counties, the number depending on the population.

The Supreme Court, the state's highest court, is made up of seven justices. Other courts of the state include the superior, county, and municipal.

Education

The state's educational program is directed by the Department of Public Instruction. The Superintendent of Public Instruction heads the department. He is also president of the State Council of Education, which advises and recommends laws concerning education.

Pennsylvania has more than 100 institutions of higher learning—more than any other state. This number includes more than 10 state colleges, plus Pennsylvania State University (at University Park), and the University of Pennsylvania (at Philadelphia, founded in 1740). The Woman's Medical College, established in 1850, was the first woman's medical school in the country. Carnegie-Mellon University, Chatham College, and the University of Pittsburgh are all Pittsburgh institutions. The number of community colleges in Pennsylvania is growing.

Medical research has been carried on by such

schools as the universities of Pennsylvania and Pittsburgh. At the University of Pittsburgh Dr. Jonas Salk developed a vaccine against poliomyelitis (infantile paralysis).

Religion

Since the American Revolution there has been a great change in the strength of religious groups in Pennsylvania. Before 1776 the strong groups were the Lutherans, Quakers, Presbyterians, Reformed churches, and the German sects. All of these churches are still strong except the Quakers, who are now a small group. The Baptists, Methodists, and Espicopalians, whose numbers were small before the Revolution, have become the largest denominations.

The greatest change has been in the number of Roman Catholics. From a few members during the colonial period the church has grown to be the largest in the state. Close to one-third of the state's present population is Roman Catholic.

Health and Welfare

The Department of Public Welfare super-

Courtesy University of Pittsburgh

Heinz Memorial Chapel (left) and the 42-story Cathedral of Learning at the University of Pittsburgh.

vises, inspects, and distributes money to all state hospitals. It also supervises homes for the aged, and private nursing homes. In 1958 it was combined with the Department of Public Assistance. It is now called the Office of Public Assistance and is a part of the Department of Public Welfare. The office provides care for the aged, dependent children, blind, needy, disabled, and, in some cases, orphans. Private agencies such as organized charities and religious organizations also help the poor and sick.

The Department of Health advises the county and local health units and enforces public health laws. It fights against water pollution, unhealthy sewage and garbage disposal, diseases, and other dangers to health.

Recreation

In addition to the parks, resort areas, and historic sites, there are many other recreational attractions in the state. There are two major league baseball teams—the Pittsburgh Pirates and the Philadelphia Phillies; and two professional football teams—the Philadelphia Eagles and the Pittsburgh Steelers.

Museums, special exhibits, concerts, and other such activities attract visitors and continue to make the state important to the country's cultural life. This importance began many

In Pittsburgh an inclined railway takes passengers up the steep bank of the Monongahela River.

Ewing Galloway

Ewing Galloway

The Delaware Water Gap where the river cuts a channel through the mountains.

years ago. Pennsylvania produced the first United States novelist to gain an international reputation, Charles Brockden Brown (1771–1810), and the first internationally known painter, Benjamin West (1738–1820). Later, another Pennsylvanian, Stephen Collins Foster (1826–1864), became famous as a composer of folk songs and ballads. Today's cultural attractions include the Philadelphia Symphony Orchestra, which is one of the finest in the world, and the Pittsburgh Symphony, which is also outstanding. An event of international importance is the Bach Festival held each May at Bethlehem.

History

The Swedish people made the first permanent settlement in what is now Pennsylvania in 1643. The Dutch captured New Sweden in 1655 and ruled it until the English took over in 1664. Under the English the administration of New Sweden was in the hands of the Duke of York, the brother of King Charles II.

On March 4, 1681, a charter was granted to William Penn naming him the proprietor of the Pennsylvania area. Penn, one of the most famous American colony builders, acquired the land that is now Delaware and added it to his

Pennsylvania grant. From the beginning the colony grew rapidly. Its success was due largely to Penn's ideas of democracy and to his ability as a wise leader and as an organizer. (See DELAWARE; PENN, WILLIAM.)

Penn's fair treatment of the Indians and his friendliness to them also was important to the colony's early success. Even though full title to the land was given to him by the King, Penn bought land from the Indians. As a result, Pennsylvania had none of the bloody experiences of the other New England colonies.

Penn's descendants did not have his ability or his ideals. They argued with the General Assembly and with the Indians. The walking purchase of 1737 was an example of trickery. In an old deed of 1686, the Delaware Indians had promised to give up as much land as a man could walk over in a day and a half. Instead of walking, Thomas Penn used runners who were able to cover more land.

Pennsylvania's geographic location played an important part during the French and Indian War (1754–1763). Western Pennsylvania became a battleground between the French and the English. Also, because of dishonest land

A lift takes skiers up Pennsylvania's Pocono Mountains.

Courtesy Pennsylvania Department of Commerce

deals in many of the colonies, the resentful Indians joined the French.

In 1754 the French captured the unfinished English Fort Prince George (now Pittsburgh) and renamed it Duquesne. The war began on May 28, 1754, when a small detachment of French soldiers from the fort were captured by George Washington near present day Uniontown, Pennsylvania. Washington's soldiers then built a stockade which they called Fort Necessity. There, on July 4, Washington was forced to surrender his fort and withdraw to Virginia. The French were then in control of western Pennsylvania.

The British general, Edward Braddock, sent to regain the lost land, was defeated on July 9, 1755. The whole west was left at the mercy of the French and Indians. This crisis caused the peaceful Quakers to lose the control of the General Assembly. Finally, in 1758, English forces drove the French from the colony. Five years later the war ended with the signing of the Treaty of Paris. (See FRENCH AND INDIAN WAR.)

The Indians, however, were still angry. The Ottawa Indian Chief, Pontiac, set up a league of many tribes to drive the English from the lands west of the mountains. In 1763, they began attacking English forts, not only in Pennsylvania but in other territories as well. (See PONTIAC.)

Colonel Henry Bouquet stopped the attacks at a battle at Bushy Run (1763) in Westmoreland County. This defeat was Pennsylvania's most important Indian battle. If Colonel Bouquet had failed, the opening of the whole Ohio River Valley for settlement would have been delayed for some time.

Meanwhile throughout the colonies, there was a growing movement to improve the English rule. An early and important colonial patriot was John Dickinson, a Philadelphia lawyer. Starting in 1767 his newspaper essays, "Letters from a Farmer in Pennsylvania," spoke out against unfair taxation. (See DICKINSON, JOHN.)

Later, when the colonial movement changed to one for independence, Philadelphia became an important meeting place. The Continental Congress first met at Carpenter's Hall and then

Courtesy Pennsylvania Department of Commerce

There are many monuments and memorials across the Gettysburg Battlefield. Above are Confederate cannon.

at State House (Independence Hall). On July 4, 1776, the Declaration of Independence was adopted. The signers of the Declaration included more men from Pennsylvania (nine) than from any other colony.

At different times during the American Revolution, Philadelphia was the capital of the new nation. Some of the most important campaigns of the war were fought in Pennsylvania. In 1777 the British invaded the state and captured Philadelphia. General George Washington tried unsuccessfully to defeat the British during the campaigns of Brandywine and Germantown. Finally Washington went into winter quarters at Valley Forge. In 1778 the British gave up Philadelphia after the tide of the war turned against them. (See REVOLUTION, AMERICAN.)

During the war the colony provided not only soldiers but its iron industry and craftsmen furnished much of the country's cannon and shot, powder, guns, and supplies. Its civilian leaders were also important. Robert Morris and Haym Salomon raised the money the new nation needed to fight the war. The world famous Philadelphian, Benjamin Franklin, persuaded France to give necessary help during the war. (See individual biographies.)

In 1787 when the new nation took its next important step, a convention of its leaders met again in Philadelphia. They met to strengthen the country's constitution, the Articles of Confederation. Instead they wrote a new constitution and among its signers were eight men from Pennsylvania (again, more signers than from any other state). Three of those men were of great importance to the Constitutional Convention: James Wilson brought up for discussion most of the major issues; Benjamin Franklin was a calm, wise voice during the difficult debates; Gouverneur Morris probably wrote much of the Constitution. Pennsylvania then became the second state to ratify the document. (See CONSTITUTION OF THE UNITED STATES; also biographies.)

During the years that followed the war, Pennsylvania became a prosperous state and continued to have an important part in the growth of the new nation. But not all of its people were pleased with the new government. In 1794 an uprising against federal taxes broke out in western Pennsylvania. Known as the Whiskey Rebellion, it was put down by order of President Washington. (See WASHINGTON, GEORGE, section on "Washington Leads the New Nation.")

Social changes were also taking place, and Pennsylvania was becoming an antislavery area. David Wilmot of Bradford County became a national figure through his Wilmot Proviso of 1846 which opposed the growth of slavery.

During the War Between the States (1861–1865), Pennsylvania's industrial and farming strength was important to the Union. Several times the state was invaded by Confederate forces. General Robert E. Lee's defeat at Gettysburg (1863) was the turning point of the war. Not only was this battle fought on Pennsylvania soil, but nearly a third of General George Meade's Union army were Pennsylvanians. Other wartime leaders from Pennsylvania were General George McClellan, Admiral David Porter, and Secretary of War Simon Cameron. (See GETTYSBURG, BATTLE OF; WAR BETWEEN THE STATES, THE.)

Most important in the state's history since the War Between the States has been the great industrial growth. Along with industry the labor movement has grown. The Congress of Industrial Organizations (C.I.O.) held its first convention at Pittsburgh in 1938.

Again in World War I the mills, factories, and shipyards of Pennsylvania turned out a flood of goods and its people added to the armed forces. But during World War II Pennsylvania's industries supplied even greater amounts of ships and other war materials, including almost one-third of the nation's steel and coal.

Since the war years the state has continued to grow. In 1957 the United State's first full-scale atomic generating station for civilian needs began operation at Shippingport near Pittsburgh. Other indications that progress would continue were the city planning programs of Pittsburgh and Philadelphia, the discovery of new natural gas deposits in Clinton and Cameron counties, a good water supply, and the growth of industries in the state.

The population of Pennsylvania in 1960 was 11,319,366.

PENSION (*pĕn′shŭn*) is the regular payment of money to a person who is physically handicapped, or has retired from active service, or who is in need. Since ancient times rulers have granted pensions to persons who gave them special services. Pensions also were often given to court favorites and to artists. This practice was continued in France until the French Revolution in 1789 and in Great Britain into the 19th century. Today most pensions go to older people, or to those who are not able to work.

Pensions were first paid by the United States government to disabled veterans of the American Revolution. Since that time the United States government has given pensions to disabled war veterans or to their dependents. In 1930 the three government bureaus that dealt with pensions and disabled soldiers were combined into one department—the Veterans Administration.

France and Britain early in the 19th century made payments to their retired civil servants. Compared with European countries, the United States was late in planning retirement income for government workers. It was not until 1920 that Congress approved a civil service pension plan for retired federal employees. Each pension is based on the number of years the person worked for the government. A part of the money is taken from the employee's salary. The rest is paid by the government.

Before that time, however, some of the states had pension plans for state employees. In 1894 New York became the first city with teachers' pensions. Today public-school teachers in nearly every part of the country receive pensions. These pensions are paid for by the state, or jointly by the state and the local government. Part of the teachers' salaries is usually paid into the pension fund.

In 1935 Congress passed the Social Security Act. This set up a system of pensions for retired workers in private industry. The Social Security system has been broadened several times to include more workers and to increase the benefits. (See SOCIAL SECURITY.)

Even before the Social Security Act was passed, many business corporations and groups, such as colleges and churches, had pension plans. The first private pension plan in industry went into effect in 1875. Many labor unions have recently included old-age pensions as part of their contracts with management. Most of these private pension plans make payments that are in addition to what persons may receive from their Social Security benefits.

A separate retirement system was set up for railroad workers by the federal Railroad Retirement Act in 1935. Today about 1,000,000 workers are covered by this act. About 265,000 workers receive old-age benefits, and 92,000 receive disability benefits. Payments go to 375,-000 dependents and survivors.

Other Countries

European countries began adopting pension plans for retired workers in the 19th century. Prussia in 1854 started a pension fund for miners, railroad workers, policemen, and firemen. The first program of old-age pensions for all workers was started in Germany in 1889. France in 1910 and Sweden in 1913 began such plans.

These early pension plans, and those of the United States Social Security Act, are based on *compulsory contributions*. The employee, and often the employer, might put a certain percentage of his wages into the pension fund. Denmark, in 1891, was the first country to have a pension plan paid for by the government entirely from general taxation. New Zealand in 1898 and Australia in 1908 adopted similar plans.

In 1946 Britain passed the National Insurance and Family Allowance acts. They were part of the system of "cradle to the grave" social security for all citizens. Workers, employers, and the government all contribute money to the pension plan. The plan provides for standard pensions, regardless of a person's earnings during his working years. The retirement age in Britain is set at 65 for men and 60 for women.

In Canada 65 and over is set as the retirement age. To be eligible a person must live in Canada at least 10 years immediately before the time he is to receive his old-age pension. The 1957 revision of the Old Age Security Act set a standard payment of $55 a month.

Some provinces of Canada allow a person over 70 to receive more, but then the province must pay the additional sum. Blind persons between 18 and 69 can receive if married up to $1,980 a year. Disabled persons over 17 and widowed mothers in need may also receive up to $55 a month.

Workers in the Communist countries of Eastern Europe do not make direct contributions to their pension systems. Since the national government sets the wages paid to all workers, it can set these wages low enough to cover the costs of retirement pay.

In 1924 Chile became the first Latin-American country to provide for retirement pensions. Between 1934 and 1936 Ecuador, Uruguay, and Peru adopted various forms of social security. The other Latin-American countries did not follow until the 1940's. Only a very few workers in these countries are eligible for retirement pensions. The largest systems in South America are found in Argentina, Brazil, and Chile. Even these do not cover as great a proportion of the people as those of the United States or Europe.

PEONY (*pē'ō nē*). Peonies belong to the buttercup family and are among the oldest of garden flowers. They have been cultivated in

J. Horace McFarland Company

Peony blossoms in several colors help to brighten late spring gardens. One plant may live 40 years.

China for more than 2,000 years. In early times their roots were used for food and in medicines, but they were prized, then as now, for their beautiful flowers. Wild ancestors of garden peonies grew in China, parts of Europe, and Asia Minor. From them have come thousands of varieties.

Most peony flowers are white or shades of pink or red. A few are yellow. The blossoms may measure eight or more inches across. Several types are known, ranging from single flowers with few petals to ball-shaped double blossoms. In northern United States they bloom in May and June. They make excellent cut flowers, and the bushy plants are attractive all summer.

Peonies are very hardy, and live without winter protection throughout the United States. Except the tree peonies (which have woody stems) the plants die down in autumn. Gardeners usually cut the stems close to the ground.

New plants are started by dividing large clumps or are grown from seed. Plants usually are set out or moved in the fall. They grow best in rich, well-drained soil with plenty of sunlight. Once well started, plants will keep growing for many years. For this reason peonies have been called the "lifetime flowers."

PEOPLE ($p\bar{e}'p'l$). The word people refers to all human beings as separate from other members of the animal kingdom. People stand upright, have a well-developed brain, the power of speech, and a hand with a thumb that is separated from the other fingers so that it can help the fingers to grasp objects firmly. It is believed that all people have a common ancestor. All people, therefore, are related to one another, making up one large family.

The scientists who study the people of the world divide the large family of man into smaller divisions called *stocks* or *races*. (See ANTHROPOLOGY.) Often the word people is used in place of these scientific terms. Thus we speak of the Mongoloid people, the Caucasoid people, and the Negroid people. (See MAN.) These terms tell what people of a different stock or race are like. Mongoloid people, for example, have medium stature, straight dark hair, dark eyes, and yellowish or brownish skin color. Mongoloid people always have these physical traits because they are inherited.

"People" is used whenever one wishes to point out differences between man and the other members of the animal kingdom. Man, for example, has developed language, by which people are able to communicate with one another. By different sounds animals can indicate a few of their feelings, but they can not talk about things and they can not communicate their thoughts.

Different groups of people speak different kinds of languages. Such expressions as "Japanese-speaking people" or "English-speaking people" divide people into groups according to the languages they speak.

People belong first to the large family of man, second to one of the groups of stocks or races, and third to one of several groups of language families. The word people is used to form the plural word *peoples*. When the word peoples is used, as in the phrase "the peoples of the world," it refers to smaller groups within the large family of man.

Meanings of the Word People

Geographers, who study the natural environment in which people live, use the word people to describe those of a geographical area, as the "jungle people" or the "mountain people." In the same way, they speak of people on a continent as the "African people," the "people of South America," and so on.

The word people is also used to mean membership in any human group. For example, it may be used in place of the word *nation*. A nation includes people who live within the same geographical boundaries, have the same government, and usually speak the same language. Thus, the "people of the United States" are the people, or citizens, of that nation. They share the same rights and duties, such as the right and the duty to serve their country.

Nations, which are made up of people, are really large family groups. They are influenced by their customs and surroundings just as the members of a family living in the same house are influenced by their surroundings. The problems different nations have in living together are much like the problems different families have in living together. In order to live at peace with others in the same family, or with other families in the same neighborhood, people must understand one another and their neighbors.

The nations within the family of man must also know something about one another. They must try to understand the many different customs and ways of thinking that are found in the world today. (See CUSTOM, SOCIAL.)

Thus, the word people may be used for both the larger family, the nation, and the smaller family groups within a nation. When a person speaks of "my people," he usually means his family, his ancestors, or the people of his nation. It may even be used to include all the people living on the planet Earth.

There are still other uses of the word people. It may refer to a people's religion, as the "Moslem people," or the "Jewish people," or the "Christian people." It can show the work people do, as "fishing people" or "agricultural people."

In the same way, it may stand for those living in a certain city, as the "people of San Francisco" or the "people of Timbuktu."

It may also stand for an idea. For example, the expression "We, the people" stands for the development of democratic ideas by the peoples of the world.

All people—all the men, women, and children who live in the world—belong to many groups. The word people may be used to show membership in any one or in all of them.

PEPPER (*pĕp′ẽr*) is a common name for several kinds of plants and for food materials taken from some of them. Black pepper was one of the first widely used spices, or food seasonings. For ages it was a profitable article of trade between Europe and India. High prices for it and other spices during the Middle Ages led to searches for new trade routes. This was partly responsible for the Portuguese discovery of a sea route to India by way of the Cape of Good Hope.

Black pepper is obtained chiefly from the small clustered berries of a climbing shrub, native to India. It is grown in tropical Asia, the East and West Indies, and the Philippines. The berries, gathered when red but not fully ripe, turn black as they dry. They are then ground or sold as whole peppercorns. White pepper is less strong in taste. It usually is prepared from fully ripened berries from which the outer coat has been removed. Singapore is the great exporting center of both white and black pepper. The United States uses about 25,000 tons per year.

Red pepper, cayenne pepper, paprika, Tabasco, pimientos, and sweet or bell peppers are all products

Green peppers add color and flavor to other foods.

J. Horace McFarland Company

of different pepper plants. These belong to the genus *Capsicum* of the nightshade family. They range in size from small berries to fruits five or six inches long. In their native countries, Central and South America, the plants are shrubs. In northern areas, they are grown as annuals. Started indoors, they are set outside after the cold weather has passed. The large, sweet-fleshed peppers are commonly eaten while still green. They are red or yellow when ripe. The hot-fleshed peppers, usually red when ripe, are used fresh or dried. These peppers are now grown in great quantities in the East and West Indies, India, Mexico, and southern United States. Evergreen pepper trees, with red or rose-colored berries, are grown for ornament in California and Florida. They are natives of South America and belong to the cashew family. They are not spice producers.

PEPYS (*pēps*, *pĕp′ĭs*, or *pĕps*), **SAMUEL** (1633–1703), became well known from the diary he kept. This diary, written between 1660 and 1669, is full of information about many important happenings in England, especially in London. Pepys wrote about the Black Death (great plague) and the terrible London fire of 1666. He told what it was like when Charles II became the new king.

He also wrote about all the little things that made up his life—what he ate for dinner, what time he went to bed, what he thought of a new play he had seen the night before. These are important to us today as they tell how people lived in 17th century England. Pepys' diary is fun to read. It is full of funny stories and interesting happenings.

Pepys wrote his diary in a secret code. Maybe this is why he could be so honest. He seemed to tell his diary everything he thought. There were six books, or volumes, of the diary. Before he died, he gave them to Magdalene College at Cambridge University, where he had studied. A translation of the code was made and Pepys' Diary was published in 1825.

For many years Pepys worked for the English Navy. He was in charge of all the Navy's records and accounts. During the great plague (1666), when most people ran away to

The Bettmann Archive

Samuel Pepys.

the country to escape the sickness, Pepys stayed bravely at his job.

In 1673 Pepys was elected to Parliament, and was re-elected several times.

At this time, England was ruled by Charles II, a Protestant. People were afraid that Charles' brother, James, a Catholic, would become king. Pepys was accused of trying to help James, and for this Pepys was arrested in 1679.

Pepys was soon able to prove that he was innocent and the charges against him were dropped. Pepys retired in 1689, four years before his death.

PERCENTAGE (*pẽr sĕn′tĭj*), or percent, means hundredths. "Sixty-two percent of the trees on this street are elms" means that of every 100 trees on the street, 62 are elms, and the other 38 are other kinds of trees. That is, sixty-two hundredths of the trees are elms. Hundredths may be written as common fractions, for example, $^{62}/_{100}$; as decimal fractions, 0.62, or as percent, 62%. Each of these figures stands for 62 parts of a whole that has 100 parts.

Percents that are more than 100 are often used to compare quantities. For every 100 children in school last year, there are 110 children in school this year. In other words, this year's enrollment is equal to 110% or $^{110}/_{100}$ or 1.1.

Both decimal fractions and common fractions can be changed to percents; and, percents can be changed to both decimal fractions and common fractions. To change a decimal fraction to a percent, the decimal fraction is multiplied by 100, by moving the decimal point two places to the right, and the percent sign is added. For example, .4 = 40%; .25 = 25%; and .375 = 37.5%. To change a common fraction to a percent, the common fraction is first changed to a decimal fraction; then the decimal fraction is changed to a percent. For example, ⅕ = .20 = 20%.

To change a percent to a decimal fraction, the percent is divided by 100, by moving the decimal point two places to the left, and dropping the percent sign. For example, 50% = .50; 62.5% = .625; and 375% = 3.75. To change a percent to a common fraction the percent is first changed to a decimal fraction and then the decimal fraction is changed to a common fraction. For example, 50% = .50 = ½; 62.5% = .625 = ⅝; and 375% = 3.75 = 3¾.

PERCH (*pẽrch*) is any of several freshwater fishes that make up the family Percidae. The family is divided into three subfamilies: those species commonly referred to as perch; the walleyes (also called walleyed pike or pike perch); and the darters. All the members are carnivorous, spiny-rayed fish with two dorsal fins.

The yellow perch (*Perca flavescens*) is found in the lakes, ponds, and streams of North America. It is a popular game fish and forms the basis of an important fishing industry in the Great Lakes region of the United States. It is a small fish, usually four to twelve inches long and weighing less than one pound. It is a brassy, yellow color with several blackish bars on the side of the body.

The European perch (*P. fluviatilis*) is found in northern Eurasia. It is similar to the yellow perch but slightly larger. It is greenish in color with dark bars.

Perch begin to spawn when three years old. They lay their eggs in the spring. A female may produce from 10,000 to 40,000 eggs. She strings them together in long bands of gelatinlike material and deposits them on water plants. A single female has been known to produce a string of eggs more than 80 inches long.

Walleyes are the largest members of the family. They reach a maximum length of three feet and may weigh as much as 25 pounds. Their identifying features are their coloring—which is olive to blue, mottled with brown or black—and their many small canine teeth. Walleyes are excellent food fish and are popular among sportsmen.

The yellow perch (top), usually from four to twelve inches long, is a popular freshwater game fish in North America. The walleyed pike (bottom), or pike perch, also a North American freshwater game fish, varies from one to three feet in length.

Darters are small, quick fish. They are usually less than four inches in length, but some reach up to nine inches. Their coloring varies greatly. Some darters are among the most brilliantly colored freshwater fish.

PERENNIAL (*pẽr ĕn′ĭ ăl*) is a plant that grows for more than two growing seasons without being replanted. Perennials grow from some part of the plant that remains alive over the winter. There are two kinds of perennials. Trees, shrubs, and vines are woody perennials. Iris, peonies, violets, dandelions, daisies, wild flowers, ferns, grass, and many weeds are herbaceous perennials.

Some perennials tend to die in a few years, but some—such as peonies, iris, and day lilies—may live for 50 or more years. They have many ways of surviving through winter. The iris, for example, produces a short creeping stem (rhizome) at the soil surface. This rhizome can withstand the cold conditions of winter. Peonies, Oriental poppies, and dandelions have large, thick roots with buds that survive the winter. Other plants, as chrysanthemums, produce new plantlets in late fall that remain dormant at the top of the soil until they grow again in spring.

All perennials grow originally from seed. Many of them, however, have some sort of branching underground stems and buds that can be separated and planted to produce new plants. By dividing clumps of these underground parts, gardeners obtain additional plants that are identical in flowers and growth. (See ANNUAL; BIENNIAL.)

PERFUME (*pĕr′fūm* or *pĕr fūm′*) is a substance that gives off a sweet-smelling aroma. Centuries ago man began to burn incense in religious ceremonies as offerings to the gods. Fragrance was thereby introduced to history, and perfume was given its name—from the Latin *per* meaning through and *fumus* meaning smoke.

Fragrance was used among the ancients in a variety of ways. They usually made perfumes from resins, balsams, leaves, spices, and the wood of such trees as sandalwood, camphor, and cinnamon.

Sometime between the 9th and 12th centuries A.D. the Arabians first distilled rose petals with water to produce rose water. From the Crusades, Western Europe came to know of Arabian fragrances. From the Orient the art of distilling flowers and spices for perfumes was taken to Italy and the rest of Europe.

The cultivation of flowers became an important industry in southern France during the 18th century. Today France continues to play an important role in the manufacture of perfume. Perfume has become tremendously popular, and the industry has grown, resulting in increased need for basic ingredients. Nearly every part of the world now contributes the flowers, grasses, spices, herbs, citrus products, woods, leaves, and animal fixatives necessary to the creation of fragrance.

Manufacture

The essential oils used in the manufacture of perfumes are extracted by five major methods:

Distillation with water is the oldest and least expensive method. The flowers are placed in a still, and the essential oil (the substance that gives a flower its color) is extracted by means of steam. Attar of rose, one of the earliest perfumes, is obtained by this method. An acre of roses yields one ton of petals. From these only a pound of essential oil can be distilled. This essence may sell for as much as $50 an ounce.

Enfleurage, whose meaning in French is enflowering, is a widely used process of extracting essential oils. Both sides of glass sheets are covered with a coating of cold grease, and the flower petals spread on them. The glass sheets are placed between wooden frames in tiers. The petals are then removed by hand and replaced several times until the fat has absorbed all the odor it can. The glass sheets are removed from the frames and washed with a solvent that separates the essential oil from the fat.

Maceration is a process similar to enfleurage, but differs in that warm grease is used. The

For thousands of years man has created fragrant substances from wood, flowers, herbs, and spices and used them for personal adornment, medicine, and religious tribute.

Modern chemistry has provided perfumers with synthetic raw materials and enabled them to lower the costs of their products. Now fragrance may be economically used in many products, some of which are soap, rubber, leather, and cosmetics.

Photo, Courtesy International Flavors & Fragrances Inc.

flowers are mixed and stirred into the fats. The mixture is then strained to separate the flowers from the fat containing the essential oil.

Extraction is a more modern method of obtaining perfume from flower petals. The flowers are placed in large tanks. A pure solvent is pumped in and left in contact with the flowers. After this process is repeated three times, the solvent has extracted the natural flower oil. The solvent is then removed by distillation, and the perfume is purified with alcohol.

Expression is a popular method of obtaining oils from citrus fruits and plants. The fruit is pressed until the oil runs out. It may be done by mechanical pressure, by hand, or by both. It takes about 1,000 pounds of fruit to yield a pound of oil.

When the essential oils have been obtained, the final product is prepared. The perfumer chooses a basic scent and builds on it by mixing, blending, and adding essential oils and fixatives. Fixatives fix or hold the fragrance together—making the perfume lasting. They are obtained from animals, mosses, and resins. Musk, a widely used fixative, comes from the male musk deer of Asia and Africa. Civet is obtained from a gland of the civet cat of Abyssinia, India, and China. Other fixatives are castor, from a gland of the beaver, and ambergris, a rare substance secreted by whales and found floating on the surface of the ocean.

To complete a perfume, the natural oils and fixatives must be diluted in alcohol. The mixture is then allowed to age. A properly aged fragrance has a more mellow and subtle fragrance than does an unaged product.

The perfume manufacturer of today faces difficult problems in obtaining the raw materials for his product. Many of these materials come from politically troubled areas, and the perfumer must face the possibility that his supply may be cut off at any time. Chemists are offering some solution to the problem. They have developed processes for the manufacture of many synthetic raw materials from such substances as coal tar and turpentine. (See COAL-TAR PRODUCTS.) The perfumer in the meantime must continue to experiment with synthetics and attempt to discover new geographical areas to supplement the dwindling supply of natural products.

Types

Fragrance takes many different forms. Perfume is the strongest, most concentrated, and most lasting. A fine perfume may contain as many as three hundred elements—a blend of natural essential oils, synthetics, and fixatives. The amount of alcohol added to the original blend determines the strength of the fragrance. Next in strength is toilet water, which is lighter and more subtle. Cologne is the lightest form of fragrance and is usually a diluted version of perfume. It is, however, less highly concentrated with perfume oils than toilet water. Sachet is a concentrated and long-lasting fragrance that comes in powders, creams, and tablets. The use of fragrance does not end with these forms. Exotic fragrances are also put in lotions, soaps, bath preparations, and candles.

PERICLES (*pĕr'ĭ klēz*) (490?–429 B.C.), a famous Greek statesman, helped make Athens the head of an empire and the center of a brilliant culture. He was of aristocratic ancestry. His father, Xanthippus, was a commander of the Athenian fleet that helped defeat the Persians at Mycale. His mother, Agariste, was the niece of Cleisthenes, an Athenian leader. Pericles was educated by some of the great men of his time, including the philosophers Zeno of Elea and Anaxagoras, and the musician Damon.

He was an inspiring leader and an intellectual man, and he sought the company of many great artists and scholars of the day. His public speeches were masterfully composed and eloquently delivered. At 30 years of age Pericles was the outstanding political figure in Athens. He received his power through the support of the people. He was elected a member of the top governing body each year but one between 461 B.C. and his death. In that position, with the approval of the people, he ran the state almost as a dictator.

Under Pericles some of the greatest Greek monuments, including the Parthenon, were built. He encouraged sculptors, writers, philosophers, and scientists. In order to promote more participation in government by the people, Pericles reduced the powers of the Areopagus, the council of nobles. The Council of the Five Hundred and the assembly of citizens (*ecclesia*) became more important. Pericles also introduced pay for service on the many jury panels. This made him popular with the poorer citizens.

Pericles was less successful in foreign affairs. In transforming the Athenian alliance of Greek states into an Athenian empire he came into conflict with powerful Sparta. Also, Athens had become wealthy through its control of trade, but in so doing it clashed with other trading states, including Corinth.

After a number of incidents, the Peloponnesian War began in 431 B.C. Pericles was confident that Athens with its wealth and strong navy could hold out inside its city walls and that its sea raids on enemy coasts would finally bring victory. He also thought the Athenian fleet would be able to bring in food supplies.

The first year of the war was uneventful. In the second year Athens suffered a terrible plague. Thousands died, and the people rose against Pericles. For the first time in 30 years he was not elected general. Pericles managed to rally the people around him, however, and was reelected in 429 B.C. Soon after this, he too became a victim of the plague. The war he had helped start dragged on for 25 years. When it ended, Athens and Sparta were exhausted.

PERIODIC (*pĭr ĭ ŏd'ĭk*) **TABLE OF THE ELEMENTS** is a unique listing of all the chemical elements in order of increasing atomic number. The elements are grouped according to similar chemical and physical properties, and the table shows the recurrence (periodicity) of those properties. (See ATOM; ELEMENT; CHEMISTRY.)

In 1869 a German chemist, Lothar Meyer, and a Russian, Dmitri Mendeleyev, made a list of all the chemical elements known at that time in order of increasing masses. By subdividing the list into groups or periods, they could see that a repetition, or recurrence, of similar chemical and physical properties occurred at

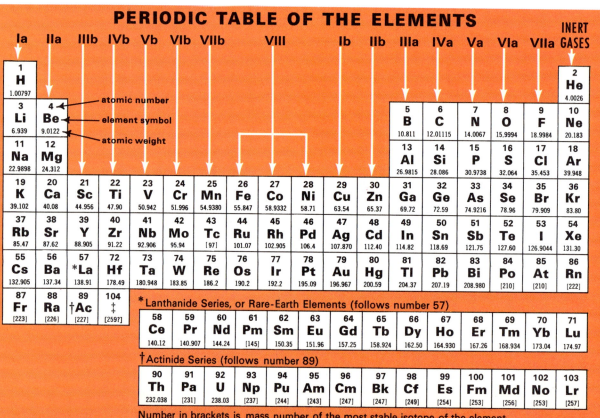

PERIODIC TABLE OF THE ELEMENTS

INERT GASES

atomic number
element symbol
atomic weight

Ia	IIa	IIIb	IVb	Vb	VIb	VIIb		VIII		Ib	IIb	IIIa	IVa	Va	VIa	VIIa	INERT GASES
1 H 1.00797																	2 He 4.0026
3 Li 6.939	4 Be 9.0122											5 B 10.811	6 C 12.01115	7 N 14.0067	8 O 15.9994	9 F 18.9984	10 Ne 20.183
11 Na 22.9898	12 Mg 24.312											13 Al 26.9815	14 Si 28.086	15 P 30.9738	16 S 32.064	17 Cl 35.453	18 Ar 39.948
19 K 39.102	20 Ca 40.08	21 Sc 44.956	22 Ti 47.90	23 V 50.942	24 Cr 51.996	25 Mn 54.9380	26 Fe 55.847	27 Co 58.9332	28 Ni 58.71	29 Cu 63.54	30 Zn 65.37	31 Ga 69.72	32 Ge 72.59	33 As 74.9216	34 Se 78.96	35 Br 79.909	36 Kr 83.80
37 Rb 85.47	38 Sr 87.62	39 Y 88.905	40 Zr 91.22	41 Nb 92.906	42 Mo 95.94	43 Tc [97]	44 Ru 101.07	45 Rh 102.905	46 Pd 106.4	47 Ag 107.870	48 Cd 112.40	49 In 114.82	50 Sn 118.69	51 Sb 121.75	52 Te 127.60	53 I 126.9044	54 Xe 131.30
55 Cs 132.905	56 Ba 137.34	57 *La 138.91	72 Hf 178.49	73 Ta 180.948	74 W 183.85	75 Re 186.2	76 Os 190.2	77 Ir 192.2	78 Pt 195.09	79 Au 196.967	80 Hg 200.59	81 Tl 204.37	82 Pb 207.19	83 Bi 208.980	84 Po [210]	85 At [210]	86 Rn [222]
87 Fr [223]	88 Ra [226]	89 †Ac [227]	104 ‡ [259?]														

*Lanthanide Series, or Rare-Earth Elements (follows number 57)

58 Ce 140.12	59 Pr 140.907	60 Nd 144.24	61 Pm [145]	62 Sm 150.35	63 Eu 151.96	64 Gd 157.25	65 Tb 158.924	66 Dy 162.50	67 Ho 164.930	68 Er 167.26	69 Tm 168.934	70 Yb 173.04	71 Lu 174.97

†Actinide Series (follows number 89)

90 Th 232.038	91 Pa [231]	92 U 238.03	93 Np [237]	94 Pu [244]	95 Am [243]	96 Cm [247]	97 Bk [247]	98 Cf [249]	99 Es [254]	100 Fm [253]	101 Md [256]	102 No [253]	103 Lr [257]

Number in brackets is mass number of the most stable isotope of the element.
‡ Element 104 not yet named.

more or less regular intervals. There were many empty places in the table into which Mendeleyev correctly assumed unknown elements would fit. Although he did not know what the missing elements were, he could predict their characteristics from the properties of the nearby known elements. For example, in 1871 Mendeleyev predicted the existence and many of the properties of germanium, which was not discovered until 1886.

The table drawn up by Mendeleyev has since been modified and expanded many times. The location of certain elements has been changed and the gaps have been filled as new elements have come to light.

In the development of the periodic table, many inconsistencies were clarified. For example, the series of elements with atomic numbers from 58 to 71, and another from 90 to 103, did not conform to the general pattern of the table. The first of these were eventually identified as the lanthanide, or rare earth, series. The others have been classified as the actinide series. (See RARE-EARTH ELEMENTS.)

Except for hydrogen, group Ia in the table is the alkali metals. Group IIa is the alkaline-earth metals; group VIIa is the halogen group. The platinum-metals family is part of group VIII. The last group at the right is the inert gases.

From the periodic table, the period law of the elements was derived. It states that the properties of the chemical elements depend on the structure of the atom and that these properties vary periodically with the atomic number of the element.

The weights in the periodic table are based on the assumption that the relative atomic weight of the most stable isotope of carbon is 12.000. Each square in the chart shows the chemical symbol of the element, its atomic whole number (the number of protons in the nucleus), and its atomic weight.

The 18 vertical columns in the table are called groups, and the elements in each group have similar properties. These similarities are repeated periodically in the horizontal rows, comprising the seven periods. All the elements in each row have the same arrangement of electrons in the various shells of the atoms.

PERISCOPE ($p\breve{e}r'\breve{i}\,sk\bar{o}p$) is an optical instrument used for viewing around obstacles. Its operation is based on the reflection of light. Light rays that enter the periscope are reflected by mirrors or glass prisms along a new path. Some periscopes magnify their field of view.

The simplest periscopes are little more than hollow tubes containing two mirrors, one at each end. The facing mirrors are parallel to each other and inclined at an angle of 45 degrees to the tube. Light entering the periscope strikes one mirror and is reflected to the other, as shown in the illustration. The second mirror reflects the image to the eye of the person using the periscope. (See LENS; MIRROR.)

In the 17th century, Johannes Hevelius (1611–1687) designed a primitive periscope, which he made out of a telescope with a doubly bent tube and mirrors. It was not until the U.S. Civil War that the periscope was put to its first prac-

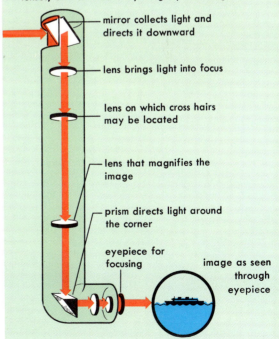

HOW A PERISCOPE WORKS

A periscope can "see" around corners because light can be made to change direction by means of mirrors and prisms. Complex periscopes can "see" around several corners; they have a prism at each corner. Usually periscopes have several lenses, one of which may magnify the image.

mirror collects light and directs it downward

lens brings light into focus

lens on which cross hairs may be located

lens that magnifies the image

prism directs light around the corner

eyepiece for focusing

image as seen through eyepiece

tical shipboard use. Thomas H. Doughty, of the Union warship *Osage*, rigged up a periscope out of steam pipe. He fitted mirrors into opposite ends of the pipe. He then attached the periscope to the gun turret so that the guns could be sighted from below. The ship was later attacked. The Confederate forces, fired upon by the concealed gun crew, were repelled.

Periscopes have many uses. They permit scientists to view the inner workings of nuclear reactors and particle accelerators. An adaptation of the periscope is used to determine distances for photography and for artillery control. Doctors are able to make internal examinations by means of special periscopes called cystoscopes and endoscopes.

HOW TO MAKE A SIMPLE PERISCOPE

Draw a pattern on cardboard as shown below. Then cut out the pattern along the heavy lines. Make the two cutouts as indicated. Glue the mirrors in place. Then fold the pattern and glue the tabs in place.

PERIWINKLE (*pĕr'ĭ wĭng'k'l*) is any of the trailing or erect plants that make up the genus *Vinca*. The genus belongs to the dogbane family (Apocynaceae). There are three common species of periwinkle. One (*V. minor*) is known by several names—lesser, creeping, running, or grave myrtle. It has small, glossy, oval leaves that remain on the plant all winter. Lesser periwinkle creeps on the soil's surface, forming mats. In early spring, blue flowers appear. It is frequently used, therefore, in cemeteries as a grave covering. Greater periwinkle (*V. major*) is a long vine with blue flowers and roundish leaves, often edged with white. It is grown by florists for window boxes. Madagascar periwinkle (*V. rosea*) is an erect plant, grown as an annual. It is usually less than 18 inches high and looks somewhat like a small bush. Red, pink, or white flowers cover the plant during the summer and fall.

Vincas, as periwinkles are also called, grow well in shady places. The vine species are grown from cuttings of the stem. The annual is grown from seeds. The vines frequently root along the stems where they touch the soil. These may be dug up and cut off to be planted elsewhere. This is called layering.

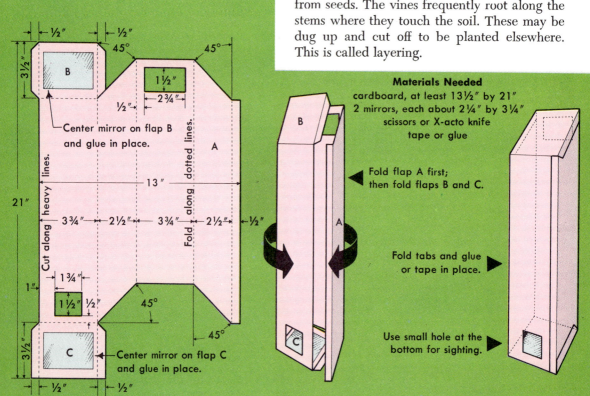

Center mirror on flap B and glue in place.

Center mirror on flap C and glue in place.

Materials Needed
cardboard, at least 13½" by 21"
2 mirrors, each about 2¼" by 3¼"
scissors or X-acto knife
tape or glue

Fold flap A first; then fold flaps B and C.

Fold tabs and glue or tape in place.

Use small hole at the bottom for sighting.

John H. Gerard

Running myrtle—also known as lesser, creeping, or grave myrtle—is one of the best known of the periwinkle plants.

Periwinkle is also the name for several types of marine snails. (See MOLLUSK.)

PERON (*pĕ rôn'*), **JUAN** (*hwän*) **DOMINGO** (*dō mēng'gō*) (1895–   ) and **EVA** (*ĕ'vä*) **MARIA** (*mä rē'ä*) **DUARTE** (*dwär'tā*) **DE** (1919–1952). Juan Peron was the dictator of Argentina from 1946 to 1955. His wife, Eva, was his active partner.

Peron was born near Lobos in Buenos Aires Province. He moved with his parents to Patagonia, then to Buenos Aires, where in 1913 he graduated from the Military College. By 1936 he had advanced to the rank of colonel in the Argentine Army. During the next few years he was sent on special missions for the Army to Chile and Italy.

Eva Duarte was born in Los Toldos, Buenos Aires Province. After two years of high school she moved to Buenos Aires and became a radio and movie actress. Her active interest in public affairs led to meetings with well-known leaders, including her future husband. They were married in 1945.

Juan Peron first came to public notice in June 1943, when a group of young Army officers took control of the government. He rose rapidly as a leader in the new government. As secretary of labor and social welfare, he laid the groundwork for his future Peronista Party. He brought labor unions under government con-

trol and did a great deal to help the underprivileged workers who were known as the "shirtless ones." He soon took over the positions of minister of war and vice-president. By 1946 he had assumed enough power through these positions and through the support of the working class to be elected president for a six-year term.

As president, Peron set up a military dictatorship. He increased government control of both social and economic life. At the same time, he won public approval of his changes by increasing wages and social-security benefits for the workers. An armament program and salary raises kept the Army loyal. To prevent opposition he closed newspapers, controlled education, and packed the Congress and Supreme Court with members of his Peronista Party. To make sure that he would remain in office, Peron changed the constitution to permit his re-election in 1951.

Eva Peron encouraged the Argentines to support her husband. She helped organize labor unions. She promoted the woman suffrage law of 1947. She gave food, money, and medicine to the needy and helped to promote better hospitals, housing, and recreation.

By 1955 Peron had made many enemies. His attacks on the Roman Catholic Church resulted in his excommunication. In September of that year his enemies in the armed forces succeeded in overthrowing him. He fled to exile in Spain. His followers have kept the Peronista Party active. (See ARGENTINA.)

Eva and Juan Peron.

PERRAULT (pĕ rō′), **CHARLES** (1628–1703), was a French scholar chiefly known today as a writer of fairy tales that have been translated from the French into almost every language. He was the son of a lawyer, and was born in 1628 in Paris. As a teen-ager he wrote poetry, but he never gained much fame in this field even though he continued to write some poetry all his life. After a bitter argument with his professor of philosophy, he and a friend left school to read every French book they could get their hands on. Then in a book called *The Aeneid,* he, his two brothers, and his friend wrote their criticisms and opinions. This was the beginning of a series of books which Charles Perrault continued to write alone, in which he tried to prove that the great French writers of his time were greater than the masters of Greece and Rome. This way of thinking aroused heated discussions among the great writers of his time.

Meanwhile, Perrault received his degree in law. From 1654 to 1664 he worked for his brother Pierre, who was a tax collector for Louis XIV. This led to his appointment as secretary or assistant to Jean Baptiste Colbert, the great financial minister of Louis XIV. As Colbert's assistant, Perrault had considerable influence over most of the outstanding writers and artists of his time. His principal job was to select and direct the artists and architects who were to construct and decorate the buildings and furnishings prepared for Louis XIV, the most extravagant of French kings.

This influential position was not only well paid but gave Perrault enough free time to write such works as *The Century of Louis XIV, Parallel of the Ancients and Moderns,* and *In Praise of the Famous Men of Louis XIV's Time.* All these books continued the battle to decide who were the greater writers, the ancients or the moderns. In 1671 Perrault was appointed to the French Academy, which was the highest honor a writer could receive.

While these books were taken seriously in Perrault's time, they are today considered of little interest. But in 1697, only six years before his death, his first book of prose fairy tales was published. It was called *Mother Goose's Tales.* Whether he was ashamed to admit he was the author or not, no one knows exactly, but he attached some false name to each of his earlier collections of children's stories. After he saw how successful they were, however, he admitted he had written them, and added many more in his own name. After more than 250 years, hundreds of new editions of these charming and witty fairy tales are still being published. The most famous ones are "Sleeping Beauty," "Little Red Riding Hood," "Bluebeard," "Puss-in-Boots," "The Fairy," "Cinderella," and "Hop o' My Thumb."

PERRY (pĕr′ē) **FAMILY** was a family whose members included U.S. Navy officers. At one time there were seven members of the family at the Naval Academy at Annapolis, Maryland. The best-known members were two brothers.

OLIVER HAZARD PERRY (1785–1819) was born in South Kingston, Rhode Island, and was the

Oliver H. Perry.

son of a naval officer. Oliver entered the Navy at the age of 14 and served in the war against the Barbary pirates. During the War of 1812 he built and commanded the United States squadron on Lake Erie. In a few months he had ten vessels ready to attack the British.

On September 10, 1813, the two fleets met. The attack was so fierce that 83 of 101 men on Perry's ship, the *Lawrence,* were injured or killed. Although his ship was crippled, Perry did not surrender. Instead, he went over the side into a small boat. While British guns fired at him, he was rowed to the *Niagara.* From there he continued the battle and forced the British to surrender. He then reported to General William Henry Harrison: "We have met the enemy and they are ours: two ships, two brigs, one schooner, and one sloop." This victory gave the United States control of Lake Erie. Perry was made a captain for this deed. (See WAR OF 1812.)

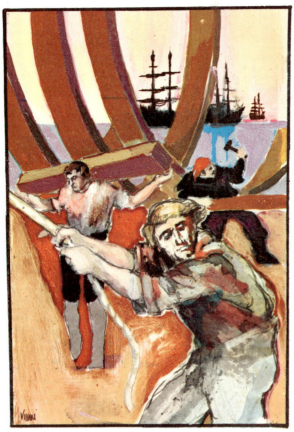

Within a few months, the men of Oliver Hazard Perry's command built and equipped ten ships with which to attack the British on Lake Erie during the War of 1812.

the *Fulton II*, the first United States war vessel run by steam. During this time he planned the *Missouri* and the *Mississippi*, the first steam frigates of the Navy. In 1841 he became commander of the New York Navy Yard. In 1843 he was sent in command of a squadron to the African coast to stop the slave trade. During the Mexican War, he was in charge of a blockade of the Mexican coast. He raided Mexico and landed General Winfield Scott's army at Veracruz. (See MEXICAN WAR.)

In March 1852, Matthew Perry was appointed commander of a naval expedition to Japan to establish diplomatic relations with the Japanese government. Until that time, the Japanese had refused to let United States and European ships visit their ports. Perry sailed into Edo Bay with a small fleet of armed boats in 1853. With a show of military power and with tactful diplomacy, he asked the Japanese to sign a treaty. He returned in 1854 for the emperor's answer, and the treaty was then signed. The treaty permitted United States trading ships to visit two ports and protected the rights of sailors shipwrecked in Japan. (See JAPAN.)

After the war he commanded the *Java* in the Mediterranean expedition of 1815–1816 against the Barbary pirates. In 1819 Perry was sent to clear West Indian waters of pirates. He became ill with yellow fever, and died at Port of Spain, Trinidad.

Matthew C. Perry.

MATTHEW CALBRAITH PERRY (1794–1858), a brother of Oliver, also was born in South Kingston, Rhode Island. He became a midshipman at 15 and served during the War of 1812. In 1826 he organized the U.S. Navy's first naval apprentice system. From 1838 to 1840 he built and commanded

PERSEPHONE (*pẽr sĕf′ō nē*) (PROSERPINA [*prō-sẽr′pĭ nä*]) was the daughter of Demeter, the goddess of good harvest in Greek mythology. Her Roman name was Proserpina. One day, Pluto, the god of the underworld, saw Persephone. He fell in love with her and carried her off to Hades, the Greek hell. (See HADES; PLUTO.) Demeter was angry and refused to bring forth a harvest. Crops would not grow and the earth became a frozen desert.

The famine became so great that Zeus, king of the gods, asked Demeter to stop being angry. She replied that she would never let the earth bear fruit until she had seen her daughter. Zeus promised to return Persephone if she had not eaten any food while in Hades. However, Pluto had Persephone eat the seeds of a pomegranate so that she would return to him.

As a result, Persephone lives for half the year in Hades, and it is winter. She sits beside Pluto, punishes the dead, and rules over ghosts. When Persephone returns, her mother brings forth flowers and green things, and spring comes.

Perseus killed the evil creature Medusa by cutting off her head. He was careful not to look at her, knowing that he would turn to stone if he beheld her face.

PERSEUS (*pẽr′sūs* or *pẽr′sē ŭs*) was a hero of Greek mythology. He was the son of Danae, the daughter of King Acrisius of Argos. An oracle predicted that a son of Danae would kill her father. Therefore, when Perseus was born, Acrisius locked Danae and her son in a chest and cast them into the sea. The chest was washed ashore on the island of Seriphos. A fisherman found it and took care of them.

Later, Polydectes, the island's evil king, wanted to marry Danae. To get rid of Perseus, he sent him to kill Medusa. Medusa had hair of serpents, a dragonlike body, and a face so horrible that all who saw her were turned to stone. (See MEDUSA.) Several gods helped Perseus. Hermes (Mercury) gave him a sword and winged sandals. Athena (Minerva) lent him her shield. Perseus flew over Medusa's island. Keeping his eye on her reflection in the shield, he swooped down and cut off her head.

On his way home he came to the kingdom of Atlas. When Atlas refused to give him shelter, Perseus held up Medusa's head. Atlas was turned into the mountain range which bears his name. (See ATLAS.) Then Perseus flew over Ethiopia, where he rescued Andromeda from her cruel father, the king, and married her.

Perseus finally reached Seriphos, but his mother had fled from the king. He burst in on a palace banquet and held up Medusa's head. The evil king and his courtiers turned to stone.

Perseus, Andromeda, and Danae returned to Argos to make peace with Acrisius. There they found that he had fled. Later Perseus was in an athletic contest. He threw a discus too far, killing a man in the crowd. The man was Acrisius. The prediction had come true. When they grew old, the gods placed Perseus, Andromeda and her mother Cassiopeia among the stars. (See the drawings in CONSTELLATION.)

PERSHING (*pẽr′shing*), **JOHN JOSEPH** (1860–1948), commanded the United States forces in Europe during World War I.

Pershing was born near Laclede, Missouri. At 17 he began to teach in a country school and earned enough money to attend a normal school. Later he passed an examination for an appointment to the United States Military Academy at West Point. He did not want an army career because he wanted to study law, but he did want an education.

After graduating from West Point in 1886, Pershing joined troops fighting Geronimo, the Apache chief. (See GERONIMO.) In 1891 he became a military instructor at the University of Nebraska in Lincoln. While at Nebraska, he graduated from the law school.

When the Spanish-American War began in 1898, Pershing resigned from teaching at West Point to fight in Cuba. His bravery won the admiration of Colonel Theodore Roosevelt. After the war the Philippines were given to the United States. In 1903 Pershing was sent to Mindanao in the Philippines where he put down the Moro tribesmen rebellion. Several years later he was appointed governor of Moro province and commander of Mindanao.

John Joseph Pershing.

During the Russo-Japanese War (1904–1905), Pershing went with the Japanese armies as an observer. In 1906 he was promoted from captain to brigadier general by President Roosevelt. To do this Roosevelt by-passed 862 other officers.

In 1913 Pershing was placed in command of the 8th brigade in San Francisco, California. Three years later the Mexican bandit chief Francisco (Pancho) Villa and his men raided a town in New Mexico. Pershing went to Mexico, where he spent many months looking for Villa, but he never caught him.

During Pershing's absence, his wife and three daughters were burned to death in a fire. Only his son survived. Although he was deeply hurt, he continued his work in Mexico.

In 1917 the United States entered World War I. Once again, higher ranking officers were bypassed, and Pershing was given command of the American Expeditionary Forces. He became the first to lead a United States army on European soil. In France Pershing organized and directed an army of 3,000,000 men. In the spring and summer of 1918, United States units were first used to stop German advances.

In September 1918, United States armies went into action near St. Mihiel and won a quick victory. Another victory, in the Argonne Forest, drove the Germans farther back. Pershing's United States divisions had helped bring victory to the Allies. (See WORLD WAR I.) His memoirs, *My Experiences in the World War* (1931), tell about his part in the war.

In 1921 Pershing became chief of staff with the rank of general of the armies. He retired in 1924 but continued to take part in military affairs. When Japan attacked Pearl Harbor in World War II, he offered his services. He was too old and sick to take a command, but General George C. Marshall, army chief of staff, often asked his advice.

PERSIA (*pĕr′zhä*) is famous as the great Achaemenid Empire of western Asia that was destroyed by Alexander the Great in 331 B.C. Persia's history began long before the Achaemenid dynasty, however, and it continues in the present kingdom of Iran.

The word *Persia* derived from the name of the southwestern province, called Persia by the Greeks, where the original Persian tribesmen settled. The word *Iran* reflects the larger grouping of Aryan, or Irani, tribes that occupied most of the areas now included within the boundaries of the modern country.

Earliest History

Men lived in Persia during both the Old and New Stone ages. They made simple tools and slowly developed agriculture and village life.

In southwestern Persia the Elamites, in conjunction with the Sumerians in the Tigris and Euphrates Valley, created a distinct culture during the third millennium B.C. By 2000 B.C. the Elamites were writing in a cuneiform script. They built great cities, such as Susa, organized armies, and developed a complex religious system.

Aryan, or Indo-European, peoples began to move into India and the Near East from the east and north by about 1500 B.C. These tribal movements continued for hundreds of years. Among major Aryan tribes that went into Persia were Medes, Persians, Parthians, Bactrians, Arians, Hyrcanians, Sogdians, and Scythians. The new invaders often displaced older non-Aryan groups.

The Medes settled in the mountains of western Persia. The Persians moved in south of them. The Medes were first mentioned in Assyrian records toward the end of the 9th century B.C. At the close of the 8th century, the great Assyrian king, Sargon, captured a Median chief.

Having established control over the Persians by the end of the 7th century, Cyaxares, king of Media, joined the Babylonians in destroying the hated Assyrians. Cyaxares went on to conquer part of Asia Minor and to create a Median empire.

Achaemenid Era

Cyrus, ruler of the Persians, rebelled against the Medes in 553 B.C. and three years later took over as king of Persia and Media. He defeated King Croesus of Lydia in Asia Minor about 546, and in 539 he conquered Babylonia. Cyrus also fought successfully in the northeastern parts of Persia. His son Cambyses conquered Egypt.

Another great ruler, Darius I, became king in 522. His invasion of Greece did not succeed, but he maintained the empire and gave it effective organization. Darius built Persepolis in the Persian homeland. Pasargadae, Susa, Ecbatana, and Babylon also remained as capitals.

After Darius, lesser Persian kings struggled to hold the empire together, but internal decay and revolt slowly weakened it. A timid Darius III was no match for Alexander the Great, who completed the destruction in 331.

Achaemenid Culture

The history of Persia in this age is learned from the records of Greek observers; from local written sources, such as Babylonian and Persian documents; and from archaeological remains. The empire was divided into about 20 provinces, or satrapies. Each satrap, usually a Persian noble, had his own army, but the king also maintained his troops throughout the empire. The king's bodyguard consisted of 1,000 men, members of a group of 10,000 soldiers known as "the Immortals." Various parts of the empire were linked together by extensive road networks. The Royal Road, with inns and a post system, ran from Susa, Persia, to Sardis, Asia Minor, a distance of about 1,500 miles.

Zoroastrianism was the official religion. Although the time of Zoroaster is not fixed, he probably lived in the late 7th and early 6th centuries B.C. He preached one god, Ahura Mazda, or Ormazd, god of light and truth; the immortality of the soul; and a final judgment. (See ZOROASTER AND ZOROASTRIANISM.) The Persians permitted peoples throughout the empire to follow their own religions, however.

The Persian, Elamite, Babylonian, Greek, and Aramaic languages were widely spoken in the empire. Many documents of the age have been preserved. Art and architecture reflect the Babylonian and Assyrian influences.

Seleucids, Parthians, Sassanids

Alexander's conquest of Persia was, in his thinking, the beginning of a new world order with a merging of Greek and Oriental culture. He married the daughter of Darius III and encouraged Macedonian and Greek soldiers to marry Persians. When he died in 323 B.C., he left no will and no successor.

Alexander's empire was split among his generals. Seleucus took over that part of western Asia that included Persia. In 247 the Seleucid ruler, Antiochus II, lost most of Persia to the aggressive Parthians, a nomadic tribe from the northeastern part of the country.

The Parthians under their great king Mithradates I, who came to the throne between 174 and 160 B.C., managed to push the Seleucids out of Persia and out of Iraq, where the Parthians established their capital at Ctesiphon.

The Persian Empire in the Achaemenid period extended from Macedonia to India.

Parthians spoke Persian, accepted Zoroastrianism, and fought Rome to a standstill.

In A.D. 224 a revolt in the province of Fars brought the new Sasanian dynasty to power. These rulers considered themselves more Persians than the Parthians. They promoted Zoroastrianism and revived Persian art and literature. They also waged war against Rome and later against the rising power of Byzantium.

Soon after the death of Mohammed (632)—who founded Islam, the Muslim religion—the Arab invasion of Persia began. In 637 and 641 the Arabs defeated large Sasanian armies. (See MOHAMMED AND ISLAM.)

Arabs, Turks, Mongols

Muslim Arab invaders completed their conquest of Iran by 651. Persia came to be ruled by Arab overlords known as the Omayyad caliphs, or "successors" to Mohammed, who were followed by the Abbasid caliphs in 750. Islam was imposed on Persia, but Persian art, architecture, and literature flourished under local rulers. The great poets Omar Khayyam and Firdousi lived in the 11th century. (See OMAR KHAYYAM.)

In 1055, Seljuk Turks from central Asia conquered Persia. In 1220 the Mongols, led by Genghis Khan, swept over Persia. In 1256 Hulagu, grandson of Genghis Khan, returned to continue the destruction.

Tamerlane and his Turkish warriors moved into Persia in 1383, bringing more destruction, but Tamerlane and his descendants also developed an appreciation for Persian culture, which they encouraged. (See TAMERLANE.)

Safavids and Qajars

Under the Safavids (1501–1736) the Shia branch of Islam was made the official religion. The Shias were in opposition to the more orthodox Sunni faith held by the Turks and by most of the Arabs. Shah Abbas (1587–1629), the outstanding ruler of the Safavids, fought successfully against the Ottoman Turks and made Isfahan one of the great cities of the world. Learning, art, and architecture prospered. After him a decline set in, and Afghan invaders destroyed the dynasty.

Courtesy Everett and Ann McNear

A richly colored 16th-century painting depicts Zal, a Persian king and folk hero, courting Rudabah, who stands on the balcony. The illustration is done in Safavid style.

In 1736 Nadir Shah came to power. He defeated the Turks and then extended his conquests to include Iraq, Afghanistan, and India, whence he brought the famous Peacock Throne.

The Qajar dynasty, of Turkish origin, was established in 1794. The 19th century and early 20th century brought Persia into increasing contact with the West. Great Britain and Russia vied for influence in oil-rich Persia. Western political ideas also came to Persia, and agitation for political freedom began. In 1906 Persia received a constitution and its first parliament.

Following World War I, shortly after the Communists had taken over in Russia, they concluded a treaty of friendship with Persia, guaranteeing nonintervention in Persian affairs. At the same time, in 1921, the weak government of the last Qajar ruler was overthrown by troops led into Tehran by Colonel Reza Khan, commander of the Persian Cossack brigade, who as Reza Shah founded the new Pahlavi dynasty a few years later. He was crowned in April 1926. (See IRAN, ASIA.)

PERSIMMON (*pĕr sĭm' ŭn*) is any tree of the genus *Diospyros* of the ebony family, Ebonaceae. The trees are well known for their fruits, called persimmons, which have an edible pulp. Because of the tannin it contains, an unripe persimmon is bitter and puckers the mouth. When the fruit is fully ripe, it is deep orange-red, wrinkled, soft, and sweet. The persimmon frequently sold in markets is the Japanese persimmon (*Diospyros kaki*). Though native to eastern Asia, it is now grown in many warm parts of the world—including Hawaii, California, and the southeastern United States. The fruits, 3 to 4 inches long and about 3 inches in diameter, somewhat resemble tomatoes in shape. Persimmons are usually eaten fresh, although puddings, jellies, pies, and ice cream may be made from them.

The native American persimmon (*Diospyros virginiana*) grows wild from central Pennsylvania

The fully ripe persimmon is orange-red, wrinkled, and quite sweet. When unripe, this fruit is extremely bitter.

John Regensburg—National Audubon Society

and central Illinois southward to the Gulf States. The tree may be 40 feet tall, but it is usually smaller or even shrubby. The fruits are about 1 to 2 inches long. Their color is orange-yellow, dark red, or sometimes blue-purple. They do not ship well, and so they are seldom seen in northern markets. The Texas persimmon (*Diospyros texana*), which grows in Texas and northern Mexico, is also a native American plant and has a black fruit about 1 inch long. Both of these North American native persimmons are important food for wildlife.

PERSPECTIVE (*pŭr spĕk' tĭv*) is the technique of showing distance, depth, and space on a flat surface. In drawing and painting, an artist faces the problem of reproducing the three-dimensional world on the flat, two-dimensional surface of paper or canvas. Engineers and architects, who are also concerned with reproducing three-dimensional objects, use the technique of mathematical perspective. They use a ruler, T square, and compass when drawing an object. The engineer is interested in reproducing the object exactly as he knows it to be, rather than as he sees it. In such drawings, objects may actually seem to be distorted. Artists, on the other hand, use visual, rather than mathematical, perspective. That is, they try to reproduce things as they appear to the human eye. Since the retina of the eye is curved, the image seen by the eye may not be an exact representation of things as they really are. There are two basic types of visual perspective, linear and aerial.

Linear perspective is based on two primary rules, or principles: the principle of converging lines and the principle of diminishing size. According to the principle of diminishing size, objects appear smaller and closer together as the distance increases from the object to the eye of the observer. On a street lined with trees of equal size, the trees nearest to the observer will appear largest. Those farther away seem to become smaller and closer together and finally seem to disappear at the horizon.

The principle of converging lines is also a basis for linear perspective. On any flat surface, one may draw three types of straight lines: vertical, horizontal, and diagonal. One horizontal

The use of linear perspective is illustrated in the painting "The Marriage of the Virgin," by Renaissance artist Raphael Santi. The feeling of distance between foreground and background is a result of the application of the principle of converging lines. The lines of the diagram indicate the painting's horizon line and vanishing point.

line is called the horizon line, or the eye level. When the diagonal lines in a drawing meet, or converge, at a single point in the center of the horizon line, that point is the vanishing point. When we view an object from a frontal position, all diagonal lines will appear to converge at a single vanishing point. We are seeing this object in one-point perspective. If, however, the same object is viewed from an angle, the perspective changes. If we view a building from a corner, for instance, the diagonal lines will meet at two separate vanishing points on the horizon line. This is angular, or two-point, perspective. Finally, if we view an object from high above or far below eye level, the perspective is three-point, angular perspective having three vanishing points. To draw the open cover of a book or a slanting roof also requires a third vanishing point. The third point will be on a line perpendicular to one of the other vanishing points.

Aerial perspective is another method of showing distance. In nature the more distant parts of a landscape appear less bright in color and less distinct in outline. In art, faraway objects are often made hazy or given a bluish-gray tone to give a feeling of distance. Another way to make objects seem to recede is to depict them in cool colors. Blue, green, and purple are examples of cool colors. They appear to be farther away. Bright colors—yellow, orange, and red, for instance—seem to come forward and make an object appear closer to the viewer.

Artists have not always known the principles of perspective. In many ancient cultures, objects and people were represented as flat shapes. In Europe in the late Middle Ages and early Renaissance, men became interested in the exact nature of the world around them. Consequently, they sought a more realistic type of art. In the attempt to reproduce things in a realistic and scientific manner, artists began to experiment

"The Parable of the Sower," painted by the Flemish artist Pieter Bruegel, is a fine example of the use of aerial perspective. In order to make the distant parts of the landscape appear to recede, Bruegel made their outlines hazy and unclear. The blue-gray color of the background contributes to the impression of depth.

Courtesy The Putman Foundation

"Christ Entering Jerusalem," below left, was painted early in the 13th century by Italian artist Duccio. His crude attempts to indicate perspective did not quite succeed. The road, for example, appears to tilt sharply. The buildings are three-dimensional, but are viewed from different angles. Henri Matisse's still life "The Blue Window" (1911), below right, dispenses with perspective altogether. The table and window are merely flat squares. The landscape, supposedly beyond the window, is actually in the same plane as the objects on the table.

Courtesy Opera Metropolitana di Siena, photo, SCALA   *Courtesy The Museum of Modern Art, New York, Abby Aldrich Rockefeller Fund*

with perspective. At first, Cimabue, Giotto, and other artists used overlapping to indicate space. In order to show a crowd of people, for instance, they would show several rows of heads, one row above the other. Renaissance artists such as Piero della Francesca, Andrea Mantegna, and Paolo Uccello formulated the rules of perspective. The use of these rules was perfected by later masters. Since the late 19th century, however, many artists have lost interest in realistic representation of nature. They have discarded the rules of perspective and interested themselves more in color and pattern.

PERU (*pŭ rōo′*), **SOUTH AMERICA,** is the third largest country of the continent. It is located on the western coast of South America and is bounded on the north by Ecuador and Colombia, on the east by Brazil and Bolivia, on the south by Chile, and on the west by the Pacific Ocean. The official name of the country is Republica del Peru (Republic of Peru). The Incas occupied much of Peru before the Spaniards came, and the country still has many Indian inhabitants.

Landscape

Peru is sharply divided into three natural regions: the coastal desert, the high Andes mountains and plateaus, and the eastern forested lowlands. These regions run parallel, in a north to south direction.

Marie Mattson

The ruins of Machu Picchu, an ancient Incan city, are located high in the Peruvian Andes. U.S. explorer Hiram Bingham discovered the long-lost city in 1911.

The coastal desert region is a narrow strip, extending from the Pacific Ocean to the base of the Andes Mountains. It comprises 11 percent of the total area of the country. The region is one of the world's driest, but irrigation has made much of it productive.

The highland region of the Andes Mountains, known by Peruvians as the *sierra*, makes up 26 percent of the country. The highlands have mountain chains with many snow-capped peaks, elevated plains, and deep ravines with fertile

A herd of llamas crosses a plateau in the Andes Mountains. Llamas, domesticated even before the time of the Incas, are still raised as beasts of burden in Peru. They can carry only light loads but can cover long distances at a stretch.

Ray Manley—Shostal

valleys. The highest mountain is Huascaran, the second highest in all of South America. In the south, volcanic landscapes are common.

East of the Andes is the largest region, the eastern lowlands, which includes about 63 percent of the area of Peru. It is part of the vast Amazon Basin. The land becomes progressively lower and flatter toward the east.

Climate

The climate of Peru is markedly different in each of these three regions. In the coastal region, the temperatures are quite moderate because of the effects of the Peru current. The current is a cold stream of ocean water, which flows northward off the coast and cools the shore. The cool waters also make the coast foggy for about ten months of the year. At the same time, however, rain rarely falls and the coast is a virtual desert.

The highland climate changes with the elevation. The higher the elevation, the colder the temperature becomes. Most of the rainfall comes from October to April. Rainfall is highest in the eastern part of the Peruvian Andes and lowest in the southern and western parts.

In the eastern lowlands, the climate is hot and wet. The average monthly temperature is about 80 degrees Fahrenheit, and the yearly rainfall is from 80 to 100 inches.

Plant Life

On the coast, most of the land is bare of plants except where groundwater is close to the surface and in the irrigated areas.

In the highlands, vegetation varies with altitude. Most of the hills and mountains are covered with shrubs and grasses, but there are few native trees. The Australian eucalyptus tree has been introduced. On the eastern slopes, which are exposed to incoming moisture-bearing winds, is a dense, jungle-like forest known as the *ceja de la montana* (eyebrow of the forest).

At left, a fishing boat, top, makes its way across the harbor at Callao, Peru's major port. Naval vessels lie anchored in the distance. Lima, center, the rapidly growing capital, lies at the foot of the Andes Mountains. Cattle are loaded up for market near the Peru-Ecuador border, below, far left. Indians sell their wares on market day in Pisac, below, near left.

In the eastern lowlands, tropical rain forests cover most of the area, although there are patches of grassland. These forests have many tree species with a dense canopy of foliage.

Animal Life

There are hundreds of species of fish in the waters off the Peruvian shore. Millions of sea birds feed on these fish. The birds deposit excrement, known as guano, on islands off the coast. Guano has a high nitrogen content, which makes it a particularly rich fertilizer.

There are few land animals on the coast, but in the highlands there are foxes, skunks, and many kinds of rodents. The domesticated guinea pig is native to Peru. Peruvian animal life includes four members of the camel family: the vicuna, guanaco, llama, and alpaca. The Andean condor, one of the world's largest flying birds, also inhabits the mountains. In the eastern lowlands animal life is abundant. There are various species of monkeys and of the cat family. Anteaters, armadillos, large rodents, bats, bright-colored birds, and numerous insects are among the other animals.

Rivers and Lakes

The Andes form a major water divide in South America. To the west of these mountains all rivers flow into the Pacific Ocean. To the east of them, the water flows into the Atlantic Ocean.

Thirty-five major east-west rivers flow into the Pacific Ocean. These are mostly short and seasonal. Some of them have little water remaining in their beds after demands for irrigation are met. The Santa River, however, flows for almost 200 miles, providing irrigation for the sugar lands. These coastal rivers are extremely important to Peru, because their valleys produce the major agricultural exports of the country.

The rivers of the Atlantic drainage are much longer and form important headwaters of the Amazon River. The major ones are the Ucayali and the Maranon. The largest lake in the country is Lake Titicaca, which Peru shares with Bolivia.

The People

Although the highland population has remained largely Indian, coastal Peru has become

FACTS ABOUT PERU

CAPITAL: Lima. NATIONAL ANTHEM: *Himno Nacional de Peru* ("National Anthem of Peru").

AREA: 496,222 square miles; one-seventh the size of the United States; 40 percent highlands, 60 percent lowlands.

POPULATION: 10,420,357 (1961); 12,011,500 (1966 estimate); 47.4 percent urban; 52.6 percent rural.

CHIEF LANGUAGES: Spanish, Quechua.

CHIEF RELIGION: Roman Catholic.

LITERACY: About 60.6 percent of the people can read and write.

MOUNTAIN RANGES: Andes.

HIGHEST PEAKS: Huascaran (22,204 ft.); Huayhuash (21,758 ft.); Carnicero (21,689 ft.).

LARGEST LAKE: Titicaca.

MOST IMPORTANT RIVERS: Amazon, Ucayali, Maranon, and Santa.

FORM OF GOVERNMENT: Republic.

HEAD OF GOVERNMENT and CHIEF OF STATE: President.

LEGISLATURE: Congress made up of a Chamber of Deputies and a Senate.

VOTING QUALIFICATIONS: Persons between the ages of 21 and 60 must vote.

POLITICAL DIVISIONS: 23 departments.

CHIEF CITIES: (1966 estimates) Lima (1,883,700), Callao (279,500), Arequipa (167,100), Trujillo (129,500), Chiclayo (127,000).

CHIEF MANUFACTURED AND MINED PRODUCTS: Coal, copper, fish meal, gold, iron ore and pig iron, lead, petroleum, silver, steel, zinc.

CHIEF AGRICULTURAL PRODUCTS: *Crops,* coffee, cotton, fruit, corn, rice, sugarcane, vegetables, wheat; *Livestock,* cattle, sheep.

FLAG: *Colors,* red and white (See FLAG).

CURRENCY: Sol; 38.70 soles are equal to one U.S. dollar.

a mixture of many races. The Spanish conquerors mixed freely with the Indians to produce the mestizo. Negro slaves were introduced in the 16th and 17th centuries, and East Asian laborers came during the 19th and early 20th centuries. In the mid-1960's, the population was about 13 percent white, 49 percent Indian, 37 percent mestizo, and 1 percent Negro and East Asian.

The differences between the major groups—white, Indian, and mestizo—are cultural as well as racial. The white population has kept many of the traditions of the Spanish colonial period, developing the distinctive *criollo,* or Creole, culture. It has also adopted modern European and North American cultural habits.

The mestizos may resemble whites in their customs and habits, or they may be culturally more like Indians, and then they are known as *cholos.* Most Indians and cholos live in the highlands, where they maintain many customs and beliefs that go back to Inca and Spanish colonial times. The Indians dress in homespun wool clothing and speak mostly their Indian languages. Cholos wear mostly factory-made clothes and speak both their Indian language and Spanish.

Most people in Peru are Roman Catholics, and the religion is supported by the state. Many Indians, however, include pagan religious practices in their lives. Spanish is the official language of Peru, but many of the Indians still speak their own languages. Quechua, the tongue of the ancient Incas, is the main Indian language, but there are others.

In the mid-1960's about 55 percent of the population lived in the highlands, 30 percent on the coast, and 15 percent in the eastern lowlands. The coastal region was increasing in population at the fastest rate. This is partly because people from the highlands migrate to the coastal cities to seek jobs and better living conditions. The largest city is Lima, the capital. No other Peruvian city approaches it in size and importance.

Locator map of Peru.

The Economy

Peru is an underdeveloped country. Most of the country's wealth is controlled by a small percentage of the population. A middle class is growing but is still small. Despite development programs, chiefly sponsored by foreign aid, most of the Peruvian people remain quite poor.

Agriculture. The majority of Peruvians make their living by farming, although only about 2 percent of the country is in crops. The irrigated valleys of the coastal region have the most productive and efficient agriculture. Sugarcane, cotton, and rice are the main crops. There are many large commercial estates in these irrigable river valleys where the yields are high.

In the highlands, farming is the major livelihood in most of the area. The farms are typically very small and farmed in a primitive manner with simple tools. Most Indians have had no desire to change their way of life and have resisted the introduction of new agricultural practices.

The Indians grow different crops at different altitudes. At very high elevations, above 12,000 feet, they grow potatoes and various native crops. Wheat, barley, and corn are planted at lower elevations, up to about 12,000 feet. In addition to small plots farmed by Indians, large estates, known as *haciendas,* are located in the highlands. Some are quite large, but few are as modern and efficient as the estates on the coast. More than 60 percent of the land in Peru is owned by only 2 percent of the landowners.

Farming in the eastern lowlands is not very productive. Soils are poor, and there are few roads on which to take the products to market. Farmers grow a variety of tropical and subtropical crops, such as bananas, coffee, and cacao.

Peru has a livestock industry of moderate size. Cattle raising is spread throughout the country, and sheep raising is important near Lake Titicaca. Llamas and alpacas are also raised, llamas as beasts of burden, and alpacas for their wool.

Industry. Peruvian industry has been historically of little economic importance, but it has developed somewhat since World War II. The processing of fish products is now the country's leading industry. Other industries make products for the small domestic market. These industries include food processing, automobile assembly, and the making of textiles, clothing, rubber, chemicals, and steel.

Mining and Power. Peru has always been an important mining country. Gold and silver have been exports since colonial times. Metals such as copper, lead, zinc, vanadium, and iron ore are now mined, chiefly by the United States-owned Cerro de Pasco Corporation. There is also some crude oil and coal production.

Hydroelectric power has been developed to supply most of the major cities and mining plants. Major opportunities, however, still exist for power development, particularly on the rivers that flow east from the Peruvian Andes.

Foreign Trade. Peru exports roughly equal proportions of mineral, agricultural, and fish products. Fish meal, a relatively new product, has shown the greatest single growth. Copper, cotton, and sugar are also important. Other products sold abroad include alpaca wool, coffee, lead, silver, and zinc. Peru imports manufactured products, including machinery, metal products, chemicals, and consumer goods. The United States, Western Europe, and Japan are the country's major trading partners.

Transportation and Communication

The development of a transportation network in Peru has always been difficult because of the rugged terrain. In all of the country in the mid-1960's, there were only three main railroads.

During the last 30 years, however, road construction has been extensive. The most important land route is the Pan-American Highway, which is the only land transportation link that runs the entire north-south length of the country.

The airplane has been significant in linking Peruvian cities. All larger towns are now served by air, and many smaller ones, especially those in the eastern lowlands, have air service.

Most of the navigable waterways in Peru are in the eastern lowlands. There the rivers are generally the only means of surface transportation.

Peru depends on oceangoing vessels, mostly from the United States-owned Grace Lines, to handle its foreign trade. Callao, on the seacoast

Cornell Capa—Magnum

Citizens of Cuzco, the largest city in the Peruvian highlands, celebrate the Roman Catholic holiday of Corpus Christi with a festival featuring a religious procession.

near Lima, is the most important port.

Education

Although elementary education is free and compulsory, many Peruvians, particularly highland Indians, cannot read and write. There are nearly 17,000 elementary schools and about 780 secondary schools. The secondary schools are mostly private. Most large cities now have an institution of higher learning. The largest is the University of San Marcos in Lima.

Government

Peru is a republic. The president is elected for six years by direct popular vote and cannot succeed himself immediately. The legislative branch is the Congress, which is made up of the Senate and the Chamber of Deputies. The judicial branch consists of the Supreme Court at Lima, as well as minor courts. Peru has had 15 constitutions. The latest was adopted in 1933.

History

Man has lived in Peru since at least 8000 B.C. Several Indian cultures developed that achieved high levels of civilization. From 2500 B.C., these ancient peoples practiced agriculture. They grew a variety of crops that are still cultivated. They also made pottery and textiles of high quality.

Beginning about A.D. 1100, the Inca Indians appeared and gradually consolidated the highlands beyond the borders of present-day Peru into an empire. They developed a highly advanced civilization. Many of the Inca achievements in agriculture and architecture are still evident in modern Peru. Machu Picchu, the ruins of an Incan city, is a well-known tourist attraction. (See INCAS.)

Pascual de Andagoya, in 1522, was the first white man to see the coast of Peru. Ten years later, Francisco Pizarro landed at what is now the town of Piura. He captured the Supreme Inca, Atahualpa, and executed the Indian leader in spite of a huge ransom paid in silver and gold. Cuzco, the Incan capital, was taken in 1533. It was the seat of Spanish power until 1535, when Lima was founded and became the capital.

In 1544, the first viceroy was appointed by the King of Spain, Charles I. The viceroyalty form of government, once established, lasted almost 300 years. Until 1776, the Viceroyalty of Lima governed Panama and all of the Spanish territories of South America except Venezuela. During the colonial period, much land was taken away from the Indians to establish estates. Many of the Indians were forced to work in the mines.

Resentment of Spanish authority developed for several reasons, including class privileges held by colonists from Spain, commercial monopolies held by Spain, and the denial of the rights of Spaniards born in Peru. The liberation of Peru from Spanish domination, however, came from outside the country. In 1821, General Jose de San Martin, an Argentine, declared Peruvian independence after he took control of Lima. It was not, however, until Simon Bolivar and Antonio Jose de Sucre liberated the highlands in 1824 that full Peruvian independence was achieved.

After independence, the republic was torn by opposing forces and anarchy reigned. A political confederation with Bolivia lasted only three years. From 1844 to 1862, General Ramon Castilla dominated Peruvian politics. Under his rule, the country achieved political stability and economic progress. Bird guano was marketed on a large scale for the first time, providing large revenues for the government. The Negro slaves were freed, and payment of tribute by the Indians was abolished. Public education, communications, and the country's military power were developed.

After Castilla left office, a period of economic depression and political disturbances

Water from the Andes Mountains flows through a canal to reach the hot, arid lands of Peru's coast. The irrigated lands have a highly productive agriculture.

followed. In 1879, the War of the Pacific with Chile broke out, ending with a Chilean victory and Peru's loss of two southern provinces.

In the early 20th century, the economy of Peru expanded greatly. Foreign investors exploited Peru's mineral resources and copper and oil production rose. Trade also increased greatly.

Peru was governed during this period by an oligarchy of rich landowners and military men. A reform movement known as Apra developed, mostly under the leadership of Victor Raul Haya de la Torre. Apra's program called for increased industrialization, help for the Indian through land reform, welfare legislation, and return of Peru's natural resources from foreign holders. Although Haya de la Torre was a favored candidate for the presidency in 1931, his opponent, an army colonel, seized power and outlawed Apra.

Political life continued to be unstable. Manuel Prado y Ugarteche held power from 1939 through World War II. Prado was a more enlightened member of the oligarchy. He developed public education, encouraged labor unions, and tried to lessen the suffering of Peru's Indians and urban workers. He held the office of president once again, from 1956 to 1962.

Political and social unrest have continued to hamper Peruvian progress. Demands for reform often have been resisted by the ruling oligarchy, who want to keep their privileged positions. The oligarchy have been traditionally opposed to the Apra reform party. Despite repression, however, the Apra party and Haya de la Torre have continued to be forces in Peruvian politics.

In 1963 Fernando Belaunde Terry became president. He undertook programs to improve Peru's economy and social conditions. In 1968 Belaunde's government was overthrown by a military coup. The constitution was suspended, and a military junta was installed headed by General Juan Velasco Alvarado, who took the post of president.

PERUGINO (*pĕr′ ŭ jē′ nō*), **PIETRO** (1446?–1523), was one of the greatest Italian artists of the Renaissance. He is known today not only as a painter of Madonnas and saints, but also as the teacher of the famous Italian artist Raphael.

(See RAPHAEL SANTI or SANZIO.)

Perugino was born Pietro di Cristoforo Vannucci, near Perugia, the city from which he took his professional name. Tradition has it that he studied with Piero della Francesca, the great master from Arezzo, Italy, who was one of the first artists to experiment with perspective. Later, Perugino was thought to have worked in Florence with Andrea del Verrocchio, the sculptor who was also a teacher of Leonardo da Vinci. In 1497 Perugino was living in Rome. There he joined other artists commissioned by Pope Sixtus IV to paint frescoes for the Sistine Chapel. Several of the Sistine frescoes were later destroyed when Michelangelo painted over them. After finishing this work Perugino went to Florence, where he worked on frescoes for the Palazzo della Signoria. While in Florence he was asked to join the committee in charge of finishing the city's cathedral. He returned to Perugia around 1500. It was there that the young Raphael may have learned his fresco technique while working as Perugino's pupil and helper.

Perugino became quite successful. He married a wealthy Florentine girl and was the father of three sons. Toward the end of his life, however, his popularity as a painter began to decline. He lost many admirers because, although the taste of his contemporaries changed, Perugino continued to paint his saints and Madonnas in the very same style. The quality of his paintings suffered as a result of this repetition. He died of the plague not far from the city of Perugia.

Perugino's paintings are characterized by orderly composition with a quiet, peaceful atmosphere. His most frequent subjects were religious scenes. Perugino's Madonnas generally have oval faces with delicate features and sweet expressions. Even the male saints seem to have this sweetness. The lakes and blue-misted mountains of Umbria, the artist's native region, are frequently shown in landscape backgrounds. Among Perugino's best-known works is the "Giving of the Keys to St. Peter," a fresco in the Sistine Chapel.

PESTALOZZI (*pěs' tŭ lät' sē*), **JOHANN** (*yō'hän*) **HEINRICH** (*hīn' rĭk*) (1746–1827), a famous Swiss educator, was responsible for many great improvements in education that occurred during the 19th century. His theories and methods were influential around the world. Pestalozzi is also remembered for his efforts to aid poor and orphaned children.

Pestalozzi was born at Zurich. He was only about 14 when he decided to devote his life to improving the condition of the poor ignorant peasants among whom he lived. At the age of 21, having tried the ministry and law, he took over 100 acres of poor land. He intended to show what improvements could be made by scientific farming. His book *The Father's Journal* tells how he brought up his son Jacob on the farm.

In 1774 he took into his home 20 needy children. He clothed, fed, and trained them. Besides their regular lessons he taught the boys farming and the girls domestic work and sewing. All of them had to spin and weave to help pay for their education. This was the beginning of vocational and manual training in schools. The children were happy and showed wonderful improvement. In 1780 Pestalozzi had to give up his school for lack of money.

He started a boarding school at Burgdorf and later transferred it to Yverdon. There children of all ages were trained. This school lasted for more than 20 years and passed through many hard times. Teachers from Europe and North America visited the schools to learn the new methods. England and the United States especially showed the influence of Pestalozzi's ideas. He and his helpers were so kind and the children were so happy that one visitor exclaimed, "This is not a school, but a family!"

PETER (*pē'tēr*), **SAINT.** Simon, as Peter was originally called, and his brother Andrew were fishermen on the Sea of Galilee. They were in partnership with James and John, the sons of Zebedee. Some believe that they had offered themselves as disciples to John the Baptist and first met Jesus Christ when He came to be baptized. They were busy at their fishing, however, when Jesus began His ministry in Galilee and summoned them to be His disciples.

From the first, Peter was an enthusiastic disciple. He wanted to understand things clearly and was continually asking questions of the Master. Because he expressed to the apostles his clear belief in the divinity of Jesus, Jesus chose Peter as the leader of the apostles and the head of His church. Jesus said He founded the church upon a rock (Matthew xvi, 18), since His name for Simon was *Cephas*, or *the rock*, which in Greek is *petra*, or *Peter*. To Peter He gave the keys of the kingdom of Heaven, a symbol always associated with St. Peter in art. Peter was one of the three disciples selected to behold the Transfiguration and to be near at hand during the Agony in the Garden of Gethsemane.

When Jesus was arrested, the angry and impulsive Peter cut off the ear of the high priest's servant. During the trial he sat outside, not wishing to desert Jesus as the others had done. But even he lost courage at the last moment, and, as Jesus had predicted, three times denied that he knew Him. Then, as the Gospel says: "Going out, he wept bitterly." He was the first apostle to whom Jesus showed Himself after the Resurrection.

Peter was the recognized head of the Christians in Jerusalem, and he and John were the leaders in early missionary work. They went to Samaria, to Joppa, and also to Caesarea where Peter received Cornelius, the first Gentile, into the church. After that, Peter remained in Jerusalem. Paul spent some time with him, learning from him the story of Jesus. Herod Agrippa imprisoned Peter, but he escaped. In A.D. 49 Peter presided at the Council of Jerusalem, which opened the church to all Gentiles.

Some writers say that Peter went to Rome, where he wrote his two Epistles between A.D. 56 and 59. Because of his presence there, Rome became the center of the Roman Catholic church. The history of the popes is traced back to Peter, the first bishop of Rome. About A.D. 67, when he refused to give up his religious ideas, he was sentenced to death by the Roman ruler. It is said he was crucified upside down, having asked that it should be done that way because he felt that he was unworthy to suffer in the same manner as his Master.

PETER I (1672–1725). Peter was a man of strong feeling and determination. He wanted to help his people but he was often brutal toward them. He was unreasonable in his religious beliefs. In spite of these things, Peter the Great, emperor of Russia, Westernized his empire and made it a great world power.

Peter was the son of Czar Alexis of the Romanov dynasty. His father died in 1676, leaving the kingdom to his oldest son, Feodor. Before his death in 1682, Feodor named Peter as his successor instead of Ivan, a half-witted brother. An uprising placed both Ivan and Peter on the throne, with Peter's half sister Sophia as regent.

In 1689 Sophia's influence was broken by Peter, who sent her to a convent, and in 1696 Ivan died. With his friends, "the jolly company," the young Czar Peter spent his nights in rounds of pleasure, and his days in exhausting work. He and his friends studied geometry and the science of fortifications. They launched a ship at Archangel which Peter had built with his own hands, thereby encouraging the development of the Russian navy.

Peter I.

In 1695 Peter attacked the Turks at Azov on the Black Sea, but he was badly beaten. In spite of defeat, he was not discouraged. He spent the winter in the Don forests, hewing timber and supervising the building of a fleet. In the spring the fleet sailed down the river. Peter commanded the galley which he had built. This second expedition was successful. Azov fell in 1696, and Peter established a naval base there. In 1697, after suppressing a revolt of musketeers with horrible cruelty, he went with an embassy to enlist the help of western Europe against the Turks. His request was denied, but he had the opportunity to travel extensively abroad. He studied gunnery at Koenigsberg, Germany, shipbuilding at Deptford, England, anatomy at Leyden, Holland, and in the Netherlands he worked for a time as an ordinary ship's carpenter. During the visit to England, Peter engaged 500 engineers and artisans to return to Russia with him. In 1698 he quelled a second revolt with great cruelty.

Peter began to carry out his plans for a Western type of civilization in Russia. He cut off the beards and mustaches of the chief nobles with his own hands. He forbade them to wear their old-fashioned costumes. He changed the beginning of the Russian year from September 1 to January 1. Schools of mathematics, hitherto unknown in Russia, were introduced. Even the church was reorganized so that Peter became its head. Whoever rebelled against his will was put to death.

Peter's next task was to open up the seas for Russian trade. Sweden, then a strong military power, held the Baltic, and Turkey held the Black Sea. In 1700 Peter made peace with Turkey, and allied himself with Denmark and Saxony. The following year he launched an attack on Sweden.

The war lasted 21 years. During the first six years Charles XII of Sweden was campaigning in Saxony and Poland, winning victories which had no great importance. Meanwhile Peter occupied Ingria, got his outlet to the sea, and founded there his new capital, St. Petersburg (now Leningrad). From 1707 to 1709 he was on the defensive, for the Swedes had invaded Russia as far as the Ukraine, but on July 8, 1709, in the Battle of Poltava, he wiped out the enemy.

His success alarmed the Turks. They joined the struggle against him, and in 1711 he had to agree to the Peace of the Pruth by which he surrendered Azov to them. In 1718 Peter sentenced his son, Crown Prince Alexis Petrovich, to death for treason, but finally pardoned him. The prince, however, died as the result of tortures. The war with Sweden ended in 1721. Sweden gave up the Baltic provinces and Russia gained access to the sea and took her place as a great power. In the same year Peter became "Emperor of All the Russias."

During the last four years of his reign he was expanding Russia in the east by war with Persia, educating his people, and improving St. Petersburg. At his death he was succeeded by his wife, Catherine I.

PETERSHAM (*pē'tēr shăm*), **MISKA** (*mĭs'kä*) (1888–1960) and **MAUD** (*môd*) (1889–   ), wrote and illustrated books for children. Their pictures for *The Rooster Crows* won the Caldecott Medal for 1946.

Miska was born in a small village in Hungary. When he was seven years old, he saved his money to buy a box of paints. He knew even then that he wanted to be an artist. He attended art school in Budapest. Often he went without meals and walked to school to save money for paints. In 1911 he went to England and in the following year to the United States.

Maud Fuller was born in Kingston, New York. Her father was a Baptist minister and Maud loved to listen to the stories told by the missionaries who visited him. She spent summers in Pennsylvania with her grandfather who was a Quaker. He told many stories of the early years of the United States. Maud attended Vassar College and the New York School of Fine Arts. Her first job was at the International Art Service where she met Miska. They were married in 1917.

The Petershams began working as a team by illustrating schoolbooks and stories by other authors. In 1929 the first book that they wrote themselves was published; it was based on Miska's life in Hungary as a boy, but was named *Miki* after the Petershams' son. *Miki and Mary*, published in 1942, tells of their son and his cousin Mary. Maud's interest in United States history is shown in the Petershams' book *Presidents of the United States*, published in 1953.

The Petershams traveled to many places for ideas for their stories and drawings. Most of their work, however, was done in their Woodstock, New York, home and studio.

PETRARCH (*pē'trärk*) (Francesco [*frän-chäs' kō*] Petrarca [*pā trär' kä*]) (1304–1374) was an Italian poet and thinker whose work marked the beginning of the Renaissance. He is best known today for the beautiful poems he wrote to a woman named Laura. But when he was alive he was known throughout Europe as a scholar, a fiery orator, and a brilliant writer.

Petrarch encouraged people to use their minds and talents. He urged wealthy men to sponsor artists, writers, and musicians. He was one of the founders of the movement called "humanism," which looked to the ancient civilizations of Greece and Rome for its inspiration. Humanism was one of the most important elements of the Renaissance, the so-called revival of learning. (See RENAISSANCE.)

Petrarch was born in Arezzo, Italy, after his father had been banished from Florence for his political beliefs. The family then moved to Avignon in France where the boy started school. He loved poetry more than all his other studies. There is a story that his father once threw his poetry books into the fire, hoping to make him study other things. Petrarch did

study law for several years. But after his father died, the poet began to work at the subject he liked.

In 1327 Petrarch saw Laura for the first time in a church in Avignon. No one knows who she really was, but for 40 years he wrote about her beauty and his love for her.

Petrarch set out on the first of his many long journeys in 1333. He visited Paris, Ghent, Liège, and Cologne. Wherever he went he did three things. He tried to meet and talk with educated men. He searched for manuscripts of works by ancient authors. He walked miles through the countryside.

He was one of the first to climb mountains just for the sake of the sport and to see the beautiful scenery. He was one of the first to collect books for his own library. He was one of the first to collect coins.

In 1337 Petrarch retired to Vaucluse, France, in a region surrounded by mountains. He lived alone, wrote poems to Laura, began a history of Rome and an epic poem about the Punic Wars. In 1340 he was invited to teach at the University of Paris. At the same time King Robert of Naples invited him to his court. Petrarch went to Naples. His poems were becoming famous, and in 1341 he went to Rome where he was given the title of poet laureate and received a laurel crown from a Roman senator.

Petrarch.

Invitations to visit rich and powerful men began to pour in. Petrarch loved fame and fashionable living. He became friendly with tyrants and stayed in their homes. He does not seem to have had any trouble reconciling these friendships with his beliefs in political freedom.

The next few years were sad ones for Petrarch. His old friends, Cardinal Colonna and King Robert, died. His brother entered a monastery and shut himself away from the world. Many friends died of the terrible plague which was sweeping through Europe and finally, in 1348, Laura herself died of the plague. Petrarch felt completely alone in the world. His inspiration was gone and he was ready to give up all work. Then, unexpectedly, he met the young poet, Boccaccio, and a new friendship was formed which lasted till Petrarch's death.

Petrarch gave his many books to the Republic of St. Mark, Venice, in 1363 and in 1369 he retired to the quiet village of Arqua. Five years later he was found dead among his beloved books and papers.

PETREL (*pĕt'rĕl*). Several kinds of the petrels are called stormy petrel and also Mother Carey's chickens. About the size of a swallow, the stormy petrels are the smallest of all web-footed birds. These hardy birds are seen over the ocean, circling about ships or close to the crests of waves. They fly for long periods and then may "walk" on the surface of the water. If a storm arises, they are forced to remain in the air day and night.

The common stormy petrel of the Antarctic is Wilson's petrel. It appears off the eastern and southern coasts of the United States during summer—which is the bird's winter season. It is sooty-black with a white rump-patch. Its wing coverts are gray. It is about seven inches long and has a short bill and long, stiltlike legs. It

The stormy petrel (about seven inches) is usually found in the North Atlantic. Its coloring, like that of the other petrels, is sooty black or brown, with touches of grayish-white.

migrates and breeds far to the south in Antarctic islands. There is usually only one white egg in the nest. It seldom goes farther north than the North Atlantic. It greets the traveler with a friendly chattering, but is not a singer.

Leach's petrel is a brownish black species of stormy petrel. It has the same general habits as the Wilson's. However, it seems to prefer the northern seas for its breeding grounds. In the summer it is found all along the shores of the Arctic Sea. It is common in the Bering Sea and in Labrador, but seldom goes farther south than Maine. It lays a single white egg. It builds its nest in holes or burrows in the ground, or in hidden spots among the rocks. The brooding bird will be completely concealed. Hundreds may gather near a given spot without being seen.

There are some 80 species of petrels, ranging all the oceans of the world, but particularly common in southern seas. The largest is the giant petrel of subantarctic islands. It is 35 inches long, while in the same regions the diving petrels measure 7 to 10 inches. The fulmars are 19 inches long; the many species of shearwaters 10 to 22 inches in length; the numerous species of subtropical "ghost" petrels 9 to 18 inches.

PETROLEUM (*pĕ trō'lē ūm*). From the last quarter of the 19th century, the petroleum industry has played a major role in the story of man's progress. From petroleum come gasoline, kerosene, fuel oils, lubricating oils and greases, wax, asphalt, and scores of other products.

Petroleum is one of the great servants of mankind. It provides light, heat, and power for automobiles, trucks, tractors, planes, and ships. Without it, nearly all our machines would stop because of friction (the rubbing of one body against another). Petroleum makes men's work easier and more productive.

The word *petroleum,* meaning "rock oil," comes from the Latin. Scientists think that petroleum was formed from plants and animals that lived ages ago in and around warm seas that covered much of the earth. As the plants and animals died, they piled up on the sea bottom. In time millions of tons of sand and mud covered them. Under pressure, the mud and

Photos, Courtesy Standard Oil Co. (N.J.)

Left: A welder mends a petroleum pipe line so that it can be used again. Right: Drilling by the rotary method. When the drill bit becomes dull, rotary men bring the drill pipe out of the hole to replace the bit.

sand changed to rock. The plants and animals turned to a dark liquid trapped in the pores of the rocks. Upheavals of the earth's crust caused parts of the old sea floor to become dry land. Some of the liquid oozed to the surface of the earth where men first noticed it.

Some Historical Facts

Petroleum, or crude oil, has been used for thousands of years. Ancient peoples, including the Egyptians and Chinese, used it as medicine. In India it was burned before the beginning of the Christian Era. It was used in ancient days to make torches and, in its heavier forms of pitch and asphaltum, to bind bricks, to waterproof baskets, and seal the seams of wooden ships. The American Indians found petroleum useful for many purposes. To hold it, they dug pits, some of which are still in existence. When white men came to America, they imitated the practice of the Indians, placing the mineral oil on the market as a cure for many ailments.

Until the middle of the 19th century men collected crude oil where it seeped naturally from the earth. Sometimes they skimmed it from the surface of streams or soaked it up in rags. Often, however, they got oil they did not want. From Colonial times in North America,

salt wells were sunk from which brine was pumped and allowed to evaporate. Frequently the brine, containing the salt from ancient seas, was mixed with petroleum and so was ruined for salt production. Oil, seeping into streams where cattle were watered, was regarded as a great nuisance.

At that time people lighted their homes with lamps in which they burned whale oil. In 1847 James Young, a Scotsman, began to distill oil from coal. In the United States Abraham Gessner developed a similar process, calling his product kerosene.

About 1850 Colonel A. C. Ferris and a little later S. M. Kier did much pioneer work on petroleum as a source of lamp oil. Then George Bissell and Jonathan Eveleth, two New York lawyers, formed a company to prospect for oil in Pennsylvania. They secured the services of Colonel E. L. Drake, a retired railroad conductor, and set him to drilling near the little town of Titusville, Pennsylvania.

On August 27, 1859, at the shallow depth of $69\frac{1}{2}$ feet, Drake struck oil. Soon, he was pumping 8 barrels a day, then 20. The petroleum was a cheaper and surer source of lamp oil than the dangerous and risky business of hunting whales. It readily found a market. Excitement

LEADING OIL-PRODUCING COUNTRIES
(Average Yearly Production)

each symbol = 100,000,000 barrels

ran high. Thousands flocked to see the Drake well. Soon the first oil rush in history was on. Farms were leased. More wells were sunk, resulting in everything from a dry hole to a gusher. Many were suddenly made rich, others became poverty stricken. Oil towns sprang up overnight. The flood of oil mounted, and refining and transportation became the problems of the hour. The age of petroleum had come.

The United States was and is the largest oil-producing nation. It supplies about one-third of the world's petroleum. The largest producing areas in the United States are in the midcontinent fields of Texas, Kansas, and Oklahoma, and in California.

Oil can be found in many places on earth, but there are four great oil regions. What is believed to be the most important oil basin of the future lies at the eastern end of the Mediterranean Sea. There are the oil fields of Iran, Iraq, southwestern Russia, Arabia, Egypt, and Rumania. The second most important region is the Caribbean Basin, including the Gulf Coast of the United States and Mexico, Colombia, and

Venezuela. The third region includes Borneo and other islands of the East Indies. The fourth, strangely enough, is believed to lie at the North Pole.

Although oil men do not know where oil is sure to be found, they do know that it is most likely to be found in rocks that used to be the bottoms of old seas. However, oil does not collect in all these rocks. It collects in places called "traps." An oil trap is not an underground "pool," as many people imagine. Rather, it consists of porous rock between layers of nonporous rock. The layers are seldom flat, but are usually tilted or folded upward. The oil collects in tiny spaces in the rock. Gas, oil, and water are often found together in a trap. Gas, being lightest, is highest in the trap. Oil, being lighter than water, comes next. Water is at the bottom.

Pressure of the gas and water pushes the oil to the surface. If these forces give out, the oil ceases to flow. Then the wells must be pumped. Pumping gas or water back into a field makes possible the recovery of petroleum in wells from which the original gas pressure has disappeared. Often in the early days of the industry, less than 20 per cent of the oil in a trap was recovered. The remainder was lost in the earth. Today, careful control of "bottom-hole" gas pressure, scientifically spaced drilling, and other conservation measures result in recovery of 80 per cent or more of the oil in a field.

How Oil Is Located

The oil hunter searches for oil traps in several ways, using scientific instruments. These instruments do not show whether or not oil actually exists at certain places. They merely help the oil hunters locate what may be an oil trap.

One of the instruments is a gravity meter. Heavy rocks pull harder, or have a greater force of gravity, than light rocks. The gravity meter gives clues to underground formations by measuring the "pull" of buried rocks. A magnetometer, which measures variations in the earth's magnetic field, may also be used to gain information on underground rock formations. The most widely used method for exploring the subsurface of the earth is to make a

Courtesy The Standard Oil Company (N.J.); photo (above) by Corsini, photo (right) by Rosskam

Above: Oil produced in Saudi Arabia is stored in a terminal on the Persian Gulf until it can be loaded into tankers. **Right:** One unit of an alkylation plant. The alkylation process produces a blending agent for high-octane fuels from waste refinery gases.

small earthquake by setting off a charge of dynamite. Then the earth's shivers, which travel faster through some types of rock than they do through others, are timed and measured.

After the scientific findings have been checked and rechecked there is just one job left. That is to drill in the most favorable spot. Colonel Drake drilled his well with a machine which repeatedly lifted and then dropped a heavy sharpened tool, punching a hole into the earth. Today most wells are rotary drilled. A rotating tool bores into the earth in much the same manner as a carpenter bores into a plank with a brace and bit.

Crude petroleum, as it comes from the well, is of little use. It must be refined. The basic refining process, distillation, is based on the fact

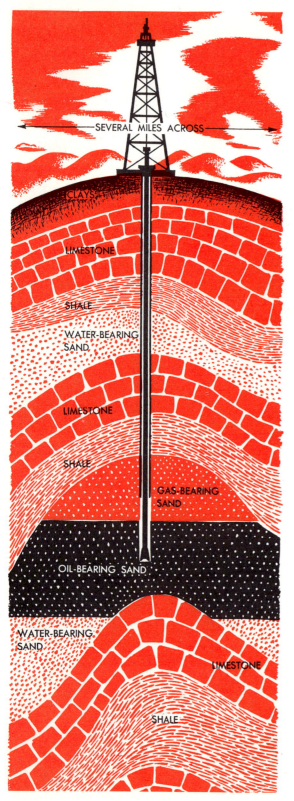

SEVERAL MILES ACROSS

CLAYS

LIMESTONE

SHALE

WATER-BEARING SAND

LIMESTONE

SHALE

GAS-BEARING SAND

OIL-BEARING SAND

WATER-BEARING SAND

LIMESTONE

SHALE

that petroleum is a mixture of many solids, liquids, and gases. The chemist calls them *hydrocarbons*, for they are chemical compounds of carbon and hydrogen. (See CARBON; OIL; WAX.)

By means of heat, distillation separates the different things nature put into crude oil. This is possible because each part of the mixture boils, or changes to a gas, at a different temperature. When crude oil is heated the first thing to leave is gasoline. It leaves in the form of a gas, which when cooled becomes gasoline again. Kerosene leaves next, and after that gas, oil and lubricating oils. Only fuel oil and asphalt are left. Refinery men call these products of distillation "fractions" or "cuts." Distillation was the first refining process. Although many other methods are also used in refining now, distillation is still the beginning of most of them.

At first the only important products from petroleum were kerosene for lamps and axle grease. The lighter ingredients, such as gasoline, were considered useless.

In time gas and electricity began to replace kerosene for lighting. Then, with the coming of the automobile gasoline became the principal petroleum product. Soon it seemed that gasoline obtained by simple distillation would be unable to meet the demand. Something had to be done. Either the output of motor fuel must be increased, or the production of cars must be limited. About this time the "cracking" process was invented. It greatly increased the amount of gasoline obtainable from petroleum.

To understand cracking it is necessary to understand that all substances on earth are built of tiny blocks called *molecules,* which in turn are made up of *atoms.* Petroleum molecules are formed of atoms of the two elements, carbon and hydrogen—but not all the molecules contain the same *number* of atoms. For example, the molecules of fuel oil contain more atoms of hydrogen and carbon and are heavier than the molecules of gasoline. In the cracking process, heat and pressure are used to crack some of the heavy molecules into lighter molecules, almost as large stones might be cracked into gravel.

This pipe and bit was drilled through different layers of the earth to a layer of oil-bearing sand.

Petroleum cracking makes it possible to produce more than twice as much gasoline from a barrel of crude oil than can be obtained by simple distillation.

Petroleum Products

Petroleum research scientists have learned a great deal about juggling the molecules of oil. They can add or subtract atoms of hydrogen almost at will. The high-octane gasoline for large modern airplanes is a very complex substance. It is made through use of the chemical processes these scientists have developed. Without this special fuel planes could not fly so far, so high, so fast, or carry so heavy a load as they do.

Gasoline, kerosene, lubricating oils, home heating oils, fuel oils for industry, bunker oils to drive great ships, and greases are not the only products from petroleum. There are hundreds of others. Your automobile may use a petroleum-base antifreeze in winter. Its paint may be made with a base derived from oil, and its tires may be made of synthetic rubber. Special cutting and stamping oils have aided in the manufacture of the car's metal parts. Petroleum products are often used to make road-paving materials, roofing, candles, paraffin, waxed paper, carbon paper, salves, chemicals, cold cream, lotions, lipsticks, linoleum, T.N.T., fly sprays, moth repellents, dry-cleaning fluids, and alcohols. A few years ago there was usually some waste gas left over when oil was refined. Today everything can be used, even the smell. Odor made from oil is often put into gas used for cooking and heating, so people will be warned by their noses when there is a leak in a gas line.

Transportation of Petroleum

Rivers of oil flow underground across the United States all the time, through big pipes. If oil is thought of as freight, then one-ninth of all the freight in the United States moves underground through oil pipe lines.

"Tankers," ships especially built to carry oil, can carry more than 6,000,000 gallons of oil at a time. Tankers carry most of the oil which moves about the world. Oil is also moved by

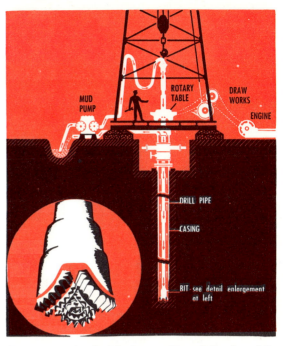

MUD PUMP
ROTARY TABLE
DRAW WORKS
ENGINE
DRILL PIPE
CASING
BIT—see detail enlargement at left

The man on the derrick gives an idea of the size of the machinery used in drilling for oil.

river barges, railroad tank cars, and tank trucks. American oil is carried everywhere—to the jungles of Africa, to the heart of China, to the islands of the sea, and to the remote places of the earth. On the backs of camels it crosses the deserts.

Some people are afraid that in the near future there will be no more oil. Oil experts figure differently. In the United States alone

The diamond core bit at left is the type used for drilling oil wells. It bored the smooth cylinder at right out of solid rock.

Acme

Courtesy Standard Oil Co. (N.J.)
An oil derrick rises out of water at the Tia Juana field located in Venezuela.

only about half the territory favorable for the discovery of oil has been even explored. The percentage of unexplored favorable land in other countries is even higher.

If the day ever comes when drillers can no longer find oil, the world can turn to other sources. Petroleum scientists can take oil from *coal,* from certain kinds of rocks known as *oil shale,* and from *tar sands.* Canada has the world's greatest supply of tar sands. However, the greatest potential supply is coal. There is enough coal to supply all the heating needs and all the oil needs for many hundreds of years.

PETUNIA (*pĕ tū′nĭ ä*). The petunia was not grown in North American or European gardens until the 19th century. It is now a favorite in flower beds and window boxes because of its easy culture, the abundance of flowers produced, and its pleasing fragrance. Its many flowers are trumpet-shaped and gaily colored. It grows best in rich, well-prepared soil and with plenty of sunshine.

The petunia belongs to the same family as the potato and tomato. It grows wild in South America. Through cultivation and selection

many kinds are now grown. The flowers of some varieties are small and trumpet-shaped. They may be not more than one inch across. Others range up to more than six inches across with their edges fringed or ruffled. Many are completely double. The petunia's flowers may be plain white, lavender, rose, deep red, or purple. Some of the cultivated varieties are marked with spots, pencil lines, and broad stripes. The plants range from tiny compact bushes to large spreading vines two or three feet long. The foliage is dark gray-green. The surface of the leaves is covered with downy, sometimes sticky hairs.

Petunias should be planted in sunny, open soil in May or they may be started indoors in

Petunia blossoms.
J. Horace McFarland Company

April. In planting care should be taken to select a particular type for a special purpose. If high-quality seed is sown, most of the plants will come true to the type specified. If poor seeds are selected, plants of many types and colors result.

PHAETHON (*fā'ĕ thŏn*). In ancient mythology Phaethon was the son of Apollo and the nymph Clymene. When Phaethon was a young boy Apollo promised to grant whatever favor he asked. Phaethon begged to be allowed to take his father's place and drive the chariot of the sun for one day. Apollo unwillingly agreed, and showed him the route across the heavens, advising him to drive neither too high nor too low.

When dawn came, Phaethon drove off. He soon lost control of the horses. They went too high and scorched the Great Bear and the Little Bear. Then they drove so low that the earth began to burn. The snow on the mountains melted, and the rivers smoked. The people of Ethiopia became black, as they have remained ever since. Finally Earth prayed to Zeus for mercy, and Zeus launched his thunderbolt against Phaethon. The boy, with his hair on fire, fell like a shooting star and plunged into the river Eridanus. His sisters, who stood weeping on the shore, were changed into poplar trees. Their tears became drops of amber.

PHALAROPE (*făl'ä rōp*). Phalaropes are nicknamed "little swimming sandpipers." They belong to the order of shore birds, which includes such larger species as gulls and auks. They are among the smallest of the group, ranging in size from 7 to 9 inches. As they inhabit the marshes and wide open spaces, it is not surprising that the birds are unknown to most persons.

The phalaropes somewhat resemble tiny ducks in appearance. They have a heavy, duck-like plumage which protects them from the icy waters. Their feet are partly webbed, and they are expert swimmers. Their food is insects and small marine life. They have proved a friend to man by devouring millions of mosquitoes. In this way the birds have been of value in man's

The phalaropes are shore birds. They have partly webbed feet and are expert swimmers. Their length is from seven to nine inches.

fight against these troublesome pests.

Unlike most birds, the female phalarope is more brightly colored than the male. It is she who does the courting of the shy male. The male builds the nest and hatches the eggs, completely reversing the accepted order of bird life. For example, in the red phalarope, which nests in the far north, the male's plumage is dull cinnamon, with a reddish breast. He does all the work. The female has an upper coat of rich brown, and underparts wine red.

Both have white patches on the cheeks, but the female's are more pronounced. They nest in hollows in the ground, with a poor lining of moss or grass.

The northern phalarope is found in both the northern parts of the Old World and the New. It is abundant in Greenland and Alaska. In summer, flocks of these birds may be seen floating idly on the surface of the water along the New England coast. They are so small that they can not be seen from any great distance. The female is richly dressed in gray and white, streaked with yellowish brown. There are patches of red and of white on the throat. The male has a dull brown back and white underparts. Both the red phalarope and northern phalarope change their plumage according to the seasons. In winter their plumage is a white and pale-brown mixture that blends with the winter landscape. Their summer shades are bright.

(1) The Lady Amherst pheasant has a ruff of feathers around the neck and its colors are rich and contrasting. (2) The ring-necked pheasant is about 34 inches long. Its color is reddish-yellow spotted with black. (3) The golden pheasant has a body streaked with red, blue, black, and yellow and is often seen in zoological parks.

PHEASANT (*fĕz'ănt*). The true pheasant is an Old World bird. The ring-necked pheasant was brought to North America from China about 1881. It has been introduced successfully in many sections of the United States. It is hunted extensively in the Dakotas. The ringneck is also well-known in Wisconsin, Montana, Wyoming, and many other states. The ring-necked pheasant is found in many lands. It is said to have been a native of China, where it was bred for centuries. The bird was known in other ancient countries and is mentioned in their writings. It was highly valued as a game bird, and served as the chief feature at banquets, especially in ancient Rome. The ring-necked pheasant is about 34 inches long when its long tail is fully grown, with a wing spread nearly as great. Its general color is a beautiful golden buff spot-

ted with black. The top of the head is greenish bronze. The sides of the head, which are bare, are scarlet. There is a bold ring of white around the neck, which gives it its name. The wing and tail coverts are a grayish-blue, the underparts greenish-black. This bird is also called the Chinese pheasant, and Chinese ringneck.

The true pheasant is strikingly colored and has a very long tail. The grouse is neutral-hued and has a short tail.

The English pheasant is about three feet long. The tail, which is slender and tapering, often measures 20 inches. Apparently this race originally had no ring around its neck. The head and neck are a clearer green. The back is orange brown. The tail and wing coverts are brownish red. The female has yellowish-brown plumage and measures about two feet.

The two species most often seen in zoological parks are the golden pheasant and the Lady Amherst. Both species were brought from the mountains of Tibet and southwestern China. The silver pheasant is also imported for display purposes. These and other species were brought into the United States and were set free in New Jersey, Maryland, and along the Delaware River. Although they were provided with food and shelter they were not to be found the following spring. Whether they migrated, or could not survive the change of climate, is not known.

The Lady Amherst is a pheasant of rich contrasting colors, metallic green, crimson, and white. It has a ruff of feathers which can be erected around the neck. Its tail is very long, even for a pheasant, being about twice as long as the body. The golden pheasant has a brilliant golden crest. Its body is mottled in scarlet, blue, black, and yellow. Its tail is not quite so long as the Lady Amherst's. A species called the peacock pheasant resembles the peacock in head, neck, and body. Its head is crested, and it has a long tail marked by beautiful plumage. The long feathers of the tail and the upper coverts are set off by colorful "eyes," somewhat like those of the peacock.

Probably the handsomest species of all is the Argus pheasant, a native of the Malayan Islands. The male of the species has the ability to extend or erect the tail, as the peacock does. It has a large ruff which extends fan-shaped around its neck. The feathers are gorgeously colored, and there is a pattern of spots at regular intervals.

Pheasants and chickens belong to the order Galliformes, or fowl-like birds. They form the family Phasianidae. There are many species, such as the ring-necked, English, Mongolian, Bohemian, Reeves, Lady Amherst, golden, and others. These birds are still bred in captivity in many parts of the world strictly as game birds. When bred in this way, the birds lose their fear of man and come at a call or whistle. Then the sportsmen in the blind can shoot them down.

In their wild state pheasants are often found at the edges of forests. They come out into the cleared lands in search of food. They are fond of fruits, berries, weed seeds, grain, and occasional grubs and insects. They prefer ground with thick undergrowth and reedy marshes. They build their nests on the ground, with eight or ten eggs for a setting. The fledglings are taught early to provide for themselves. Pheasants are easily tamed. In the countries where they flourish, wild ones have been known to come into the farmyards to feed with the fowls there.

PHEIDIAS (*fid'ĭ ăs*) (500?–432? B.C.). The greatest of the Greek sculptors, Pheidias, is known first of all for his work on the Parthenon in Athens. The gold and ivory statue of Athene which stood inside the temple was one of his most famous works. Apparently some of the Athenians were jealous of his fame and of his close friendship with Pericles. He was accused of the theft of some of the precious materials meant for the statue of Athene. When this could not be proved, the charge of sacrilege (misusing something sacred) was brought against him. It

was said that he had designed likenesses of himself and of Pericles among the reliefs which decorated the shield of the goddess. According to some accounts he died in prison in Athens. Others believe that he was banished to Elis.

Two other statues of Athene, both now lost, were made by Pheidias. The bronze Athene, also called the Athene Promachos, stood outdoors on the Acropolis, the citadel of Athens. It was well known to mariners who could see her tall spear and the crest of her hel-

Gramstorff Brothers, Inc.
This marble statue in Athens is a copy of the original Athene Parthenos, by Pheidias.

met gleaming in the sun as they sailed toward Athens. The third Athene was called the Lemnia because she was dedicated by the people of Lemnos. Probably the statue was made of bronze and showed the goddess without a helmet. It was known as "the beautiful Athene" and was especially admired for the delicate shape of the face.

What was perhaps the greatest work of Pheidias, and certainly the one most famous in his own time, was the Zeus in the temple at Olympia. It was a colossal statue filling almost the whole height of the temple. In addition to his statues of Athene for the Parthenon, Pheidias is also thought to have made many of the sculpture bas-reliefs on the frieze above its columns.

PHILADELPHIA (fĭl'ä dĕl'fĭ ä), PENNSYLVANIA, is a city in the southeastern corner of Pennsylvania on the Delaware River, where the Schuylkill River flows into the Delaware. The city is located in part on the upland Piedmont Plateau and partly on the low Atlantic coastal plain. About 95 miles northeast of Philadelphia is New York City, and 88 miles down the Delaware River lies the Atlantic Ocean. Philadelphia is one of the leading trade, industrial, cultural, and educational centers of the United States.

Industry, Trade, and Transportation

Philadelphia's growth was made possible by its nearness to coal, petroleum, water power, and other natural resources, and by its location on the north and south trade routes of the Delaware River and Atlantic Ocean. Leading industries include manufacture of textiles, carpets, clothing, paper, chemicals, glassware, and railroad cars, oil refining, metalworking, shipbuilding, sugar refining, and printing and publishing. Philadelphia is one of the leading United States cities in refined sugar production. Its oil refineries are among the oldest on the Atlantic Seaboard.

The Philadelphia industrial area accounts for about one-fifth of the United States output of finished wool textiles, lamp shades, carpets and rugs, children's dresses, refined petroleum, and refined sugar.

Philadelphia handles more shipping than any other port in the United States except New York City. About half this goods moves between Philadelphia and other United States ports. Imports of petroleum, sugar, sulfur, nitrates, iron, and manganese ore come into Philadelphia through a 40-foot-deep channel to the Atlantic. Petroleum products, coal, grain, flour, textiles, lumber, railroad equipment, and other manufactured goods are shipped out.

Philadelphia is also served by rail, air, and bus connections. The headquarters of the Pennsylvania Railroad are in Philadelphia. The Baltimore and Ohio and the Philadelphia and Reading railways have terminals in the city. Philadelphia's International Airport serves many air lines.

A large transportation system operates inside the city. The Broad Street subway runs under Broad Street for 6½ miles. The Market Street subway and elevated railroad was privately built and is connected with the Frankford elevated railroad, built and owned by the city. A spur of underground shuttle trains runs from the shopping district at Eighth and Market streets across the Benjamin Franklin Bridge to Camden, New Jersey. The bridge, built by the states of Pennsylvania and New Jersey, is one of the largest suspension bridges in the world. At Torresdale another highway bridge crosses the Delaware to Palmyra, New Jersey.

The City

From an original area about 1 mile wide and 2 miles long near the Delaware River, Philadelphia has grown until it now covers 127 square miles and includes all of Philadelphia County. William Penn named many of the east-west streets for trees—Chestnut, Walnut, Spruce, and Pine—and many of the north-south cross streets are numbered. The heart of the city is the City Hall, standing at the intersection of Broad and Market streets.

The City Hall, the tallest building in the city, was begun in 1871 and cost more than $24,000,000. The building is decorated with many kinds of sculpture and a huge clock, installed in 1899. The tower, rising to a height of more than 500 feet, is topped by a 37-foot statue of William Penn. Around the City Hall is the main business district of banks, office buildings, department stores, shops, and railway terminals. East of Broad Street to the Delaware River is the old city—the Philadelphia of William Penn and Benjamin Franklin. There are the historic shrines—Independence Hall, Congress Hall, Carpenters' Hall, Christ Church, Benjamin Franklin's tomb, etc.

Independence Hall, which stands on Chestnut Street, was completed in 1741 as the Pennsylvania State House. It was the meeting place of the Continental Congress when the Declaration of Independence was signed. It was the scene of George Washington's appointment to the command of the Continental Army, and was the place where the Articles of Confederation were signed. The Constitutional Convention framed the Constitution of the United States at Independence Hall in 1787.

The Liberty Bell, rung when the Declaration of Independence was signed, is preserved in Independence Hall. The bell was made in England in 1751, and had to be remade twice before it was hung in the belfry of the State House. Before the British occupied Philadelphia during the Revolutionary War, the Liberty Bell was moved to Allentown. It was returned to Independence Hall when the British withdrew. The bell cracked in 1835 when tolling the death of John Marshall, chief justice of the Supreme Court.

To the west of Independence Hall, at the corner of Sixth Street, stands Congress Hall. This was the capitol of the United States from 1790 to 1800. At the other end of the block, at the corner of Fifth Street, is the old City Hall. It was the home of the Supreme Court of the United States from 1791 to 1800. Near Fourth Street on Chestnut is Carpenters' Hall, where the first Continental Congress met in 1774. It was built and is still owned by the Carpenters' Company, a trade union founded in 1724.

Other historic buildings in the old part of Philadelphia are the First Bank of the United States and the Second Bank of the United States. The Second Bank building was long used as the

The new and the old in Philadelphia. Below: Logan Circle and the Philadelphia sky line. Right: Elfreth's Alley, in the original section of Philadelphia, is one of the oldest streets in the U.S.

Courtesy (right) Philadelphia Convention & Visitors Bureau; photo, (below) Ewing Galloway

Keystone View Co.

The statue in front of Independence Hall honors John Barry, U.S. naval hero.

Custom House. It is now occupied by the Carl Schurz Foundation and is a national historic shrine. Other historic places in Philadelphia include Old Swedes' Church, now Gloria Dei Episcopal Church, built 1698–1700; Christ Church, started in 1727; and St. Peter's, completed in 1761. These are the oldest of the city's more than 1,000 churches. St. George's Methodist Church is said to be the oldest Methodist church in the world, dating from 1769. Benjamin Franklin's tomb is at Fifth and Arch streets. At 239 Arch Street stands the Betsy Ross House.

Near Independence Hall is the Hall of the Philosophical Society. The American Philosophical Society, begun by Franklin in 1743, grew out of his informal debating club, the Junto, formed in 1727.

Along the Delaware River front a wide avenue runs for many miles. Several railways use tracks in the center of Delaware Avenue, from which spur tracks are connected with the many piers jutting into the river. There are more than 200 United States government, city, and privately owned piers, with modern equipment for handling the shipping of the port. In the northeast section of the city near the Delaware are shipyards, refineries, and industrial plants. This section of Philadelphia is one of the city's most rapidly growing industrial areas.

Directly north of the City Hall is the part of Philadelphia called North Philadelphia. Germantown and Chestnut Hill are two well-known residential districts in North Philadelphia. Germantown Avenue is one of Philadelphia's longest business thoroughfares. It leads to the highest point in the city, Chestnut Hill, northwest of Germantown.

Germantown has the largest number of colonial mansions in Philadelphia. One of these is "Cliveden," which was the center of struggle at the Battle of Germantown during the Revolutionary War. The Germantown Academy, whose original building dates from 1760, is still standing.

West of the Schuylkill River lies the section known as West Philadelphia. It has the largest population of any area in the city. There is much industry in the northwestern part of West Philadelphia.

In the southern part of Philadelphia are several old roadways, including Passyunk Avenue, Penrose Ferry Road, Frankford Avenue, and Old York Road.

Education and Modern Developments

The University of Pennsylvania, dating from 1740, established the first school of medicine in the American colonies. Its campus occupies a large section of West Philadelphia. The buildings of Temple University, incorporated in 1888, are in North Philadelphia. In North Philadelphia also are Gratz and Dropsie colleges.

Among other educational institutions is the

Penn Charter School, which operates under a charter dating from 1701. The Pennsylvania Academy of the Fine Arts, the oldest of its kind in the country, was founded in 1805. Other schools include the Pennsylvania Museum and School of Industrial Art, an outgrowth of the Centennial Exhibition of 1876; Drexel Institute of Technology; Philadelphia College of Pharmacy and Science, founded in 1821; Moore Institute of Art, Science, and Industry; Jefferson Medical College; Hahnemann Medical College; Women's Medical College; Philadelphia Dental College; and Girard College. The Pennsylvania School for the Deaf, established in 1821, and the Pennsylvania School for the Blind, founded in 1832, are pioneers in their fields.

There is a modern Junto in Philadelphia, founded in 1941. It is an educational society for adults and is based on the informal plan of Benjamin Franklin's debating club.

Philadelphia has always been a musical center. The Philadelphia Orchestra, founded in 1900, and the Curtis Institute of Music, established in 1924, are known throughout the world. The Philadelphia Orchestra has its home in the Academy of Music. In the summer outdoor concerts are given in Robin Hood Dell in Fairmount Park.

The Library Company of Philadelphia, founded by Franklin in 1731, is known as the Ridgway Library. The Free Library of Philadelphia, founded in 1891, is the center of a system including many Carnegie library buildings among its many branches.

At the northwestern end of the Benjamin Franklin Parkway stands the Philadelphia Museum of Art. This is one of the largest buildings in the city and one of the greatest art museums in the world. In front of it stands Rudolf Siemering's statue of George Washington on horseback, the gift of the Society of the Cincinnati. It is said to be the largest bronze sculpture in the United States.

In 1876 the Centennial Exhibition, the country's first international exposition, was held to celebrate the 100th anniversary of the Declaration of Independence. Exhibition buildings filled a large part of Fairmount Park. Among the exhibits was Alexander Graham Bell's new telephone. Exhibits sent from Old World galleries gave many Americans their first real idea of European painting and sculpture. People from many nations attended the fair. It influenced art and architecture in the United States for many years afterward.

In 1926 a Sesqui-Centennial Exposition was held in the southern section of the city. The Municipal Stadium, seating 102,000 and the scene of many Army-Navy football games, marks the spot where the 1926 exposition stood.

The Philadelphia Mint was established in 1792 and was the first United States coinage factory. It is the largest of the United States mints. Frankford Arsenal, dating from 1816, was built for the manufacture of ammunition. Fort Mifflin, on the Delaware River, is a national monument. It was rebuilt in 1930 on the site of Mud Fort, which was a scene of battle in the American Revolution.

The Philadelphia Navy Yard is on League Island and is one of the largest naval stations on the Atlantic coast. Hog Island, which during World War I became the largest shipyard in the world, has been partly included in the large International Airport.

The park system of Philadelphia covers an area of more than 11 square miles. Fairmount Park, with nearly 4,000 acres, is the largest municipal park in the United States and probably the largest in the world. It borders both banks of the Schuylkill River for 5½ miles, and extends for an even greater distance

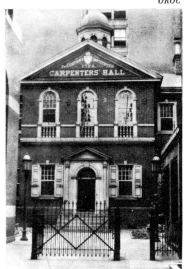

Carpenters' Hall was the meeting place of the First Continental Congress and the original headquarters for the First Bank of the United States.

OROC

along the beautiful valley of the Wissahickon Creek. Many colonial estates are included in Fairmount Park. Lovers of nature visit the Philadelphia Zoological Gardens, oldest zoo in the United States; the Academy of Natural Sciences; and the Morris Arboretum with its famous collection of Asian plants and trees.

History

Almost 40 years before William Penn founded Philadelphia, Swedish pioneers had settled on a piece of land between the Delaware and Schuylkill rivers. In 1681 the Quaker colonizer William Penn received the Pennsylvania land grant from King Charles II of England. (See PENN, WILLIAM.) Since the grant stated that a site for a large town should be laid out, Penn made plans for the new town of Philadelphia. There was to be a large square, or common, with a network of streets in parallel lines around it in a checkerboard pattern. Four small parks were to be in outlying sections at equal distances from the common. Every house was to have a plot of ground for a garden or for or-

chards. From England Penn sent his cousin, Captain William Markham, two shiploads of colonists, and commissioners to the site to lay out the town. Penn himself arrived the next year, in 1682. Philadelphia was to become a home for people who had suffered religious persecution. The founding of the town in 1682 was for Penn a Holy Experiment, and he wanted a city government which would ensure freedom of religion. Penn and other members of the Society of Friends named the town Philadelphia (meaning "city of brotherly love" in Greek).

The early settlers were Swedish. But soon came English, Irish, Welsh, and German immigrants of many different religions. Quaker influence, however, was strong, and through the centuries the Society of Friends continued to work for religious tolerance and peace. Philadelphia is often called the "Quaker City."

Philadelphia was the capital of Pennsylvania until 1799. It was also the capital of the colonies during most of the American Revolution, and capital of the United States from 1790 to 1800. Philadelphia grew rapidly from trade

Left: There are more than 1,000 churches in Philadelphia. The oldest, Old Swedes' Church, was begun in 1698. Below: Independence Hall houses the Liberty Bell, which was rung to celebrate the signing of the Declaration of Independence.

(Left) James Sawders, (below) K. F. Lutz

with the colonies and the West Indies. The city became a shipbuilding center in the early 1800's.

During colonial times, Philadelphia was the center of United States culture. At that time Benjamin Franklin was one of the city's outstanding citizens. He made an even deeper impression on Philadelphia than did its founder, William Penn. It was Franklin who suggested ways to get money to carry out city projects, including the building of the State House (Independence Hall). He suggested paving, cleaning, and lighting the streets, and helped in the formation of fire engine companies. He formed the first lending library in the colonies, started the University of Pennsylvania as an academy, and assisted in the establishment of the Pennsylvania Hospital. (See FRANKLIN, BENJAMIN.)

Until 1850 Philadelphia was the educational and publishing center of the country. Within two years after the city was settled, a school had been opened. In 1689 this school became the first public school in the colonies.

In 1685 William Bradford printed an almanac, the first book printed in the middle colonies. In 1719 his son, Andrew Bradford, published the first newspaper south of New England, the *American Weekly Mercury. Poor Richard's Almanack,* published by Benjamin Franklin from 1732 to 1757, was America's first best seller. The first American magazine was issued by the younger Bradford in 1741. Famous magazines of early America, *Godey's, Graham's,* and many others, were published in Philadelphia.

The American Anti-Slavery Society was organized in Philadelphia in 1833. The city became the scene of riots by people who opposed freeing the slaves. Until the War Between the States the people of the city were divided in opinion over the slavery question. Although the Quakers had always been opposed to slavery, Philadelphia traded heavily with the South. After war was declared, however, the city remained loyal to Pennsylvania and to the Union.

During the 19th century in Philadelphia groups of people dressed in costume during the Christmas season. They went from house to house and received cakes and candies if their identities were not guessed. From this custom came the idea of the Mummers' Parade, since 1901 a popular and colorful annual New Year's Day event.

Philadelphia is governed by a single council whose members are salaried, and is administered by a mayor and many departments and bureaus.

Philadelphia is the largest city in Pennsylvania and the fourth largest city in the United States. Its population is (1960) 2,002,512.

PHILIP (*fil'ip*) [KINGS OF FRANCE]. Six kings of France have been named Philip.

PHILIP I (1052–1108), son of Henry I and Anne of Russia, came to the throne in 1060. His mother and Count Baldwin V of Flanders acted as regents until Philip came of age in 1066. He extended his kingdom from the Seine River to the Loire River by taking advantage of the quarrels of his powerful vassals.

PHILIP II (1165–1223), known as Philip Augustus, succeeded his father Louis VII in 1180. The king made France into a European power. He began his reign by acquiring territory from Flanders. In 1187 he allied himself with the sons of Henry II of England to defeat their father in his attempt to conquer Languedoc.

When Henry died, his son and successor, Richard I, became Philip's deadliest enemy. Yet, in 1190 they set out together on the Third Crusade. Philip quarreled with Richard soon after they landed in Palestine, left their common cause, and returned to France. Before starting the expedition he had sworn not to interfere with Richard's dominions, but at once he began plotting with Richard's brother John to make trouble for the absent king. On his way home Richard was imprisoned in Germany. Philip did his best to prolong his captivity by offering money to the German emperor. Richard, however, got back to England in time, and Philip had to defend himself against a general attack on all his frontiers.

Philip also came into conflict with the papacy when he disowned his wife and married again. As a result, he was officially cut off from communion with the church by Pope Innocent III.

In 1199 the barons of Poitou revolted against their overlord John, then king of England. Philip took part in the struggle and conquered and annexed all the Angevin dominions in France. John, Otto IV of Germany, and the Count of Flanders made a last attempt to break Philip's power in 1214, but he defeated them at the Battle of Bouvines. Philip did away with some of the old feudal traditions, among other things, substituting money payment for feudal service. Under him Paris became the capital of France.

PHILIP III (1245–1285), nicknamed "the Bold," was the son of Louis IX whom he succeeded in 1270. He allowed the kingdom to be run by his relatives and his favorites.

PHILIP IV (1268–1314), nicknamed "the Fair," was the son of Philip III, whom he succeeded. He was said to be "the handsomest man in the world, but unable to do anything but stare fixedly at people without saying a word." When he once got an idea into his head he would stick to it obstinately. One idea he clung to all his life—he wanted to make the French monarch independent of the pope. In 1296 Pope Boniface VIII issued a bull forbidding the clergy to be taxed without his consent. Philip promptly made a law forbidding coin to be exported from France without the king's consent. This meant that nobody in France could pay any dues to the pope, and Boniface had to give way on the question of taxing the clergy. He resumed his attack in 1301 when Philip arrested the Bishop of Pamiers. Boniface issued a bull, or decree, which challenged the power of all kings. In reply, Philip summoned a meeting of the three estates of his realm to make sure that they would support him. The meeting was the origin of the States-General. When he was sure of their support he began his attack. In 1303 his emissary captured the Pope at Anagni and held him prisoner for three days. He was released and returned to Rome where he died a month later. The papacy fell under control of the French king. Clement V, after he became pope (1305), transferred the papal court to Avignon, France.

PHILIP V (1294?–1322), called "the Tall," was the second son of Philip IV. He seized the throne on the death of his brother and predecessor, Louis X. His succession found opposition with the party who favored Louis's daughter. But in 1317 the assembly declared that a woman might not succeed to the crown of France. Philip was a hard-working king. He did for France what Edward I had done for England, organized the army, abolished garrisons except on the frontiers, and ordered the taxes to be paid to the royal treasury instead of to the feudal barons. He was succeeded by his brother Charles IV.

PHILIP VI (1293–1350) was the first member of the House of Valois to be king of France. He was the son of Charles of Valois, youngest brother of Philip IV. He came to the throne in 1328. In August of that year he put down the revolt of the Flemings at Cassel. But Edward III of England took up the Flemish cause, claiming that he was himself the rightful successor to the French throne. This resulted in the Hundred Years' War which began in 1337. Philip's fleet was destroyed at Sluys, and his army at Crecy in 1346. But in 1348 the Black Death (see BLACK DEATH) fell on England and France and overshadowed the horror of the war. Philip was an extravagant king. He left the French treasury drained, but he acquired the province of Dauphine and the City of Montpellier for France.

PHILIP [Kings of Macedonia]. The name Philip, meaning "lover of horses," first became known to the world through the kings of Macedonia.

PHILIP I, the third king of Macedonia, is only legendary, although treated as a real person by the Greek historian Herodotus.

PHILIP II (382–336 B.C.) developed the first civilized kingdom in Europe. In 367 B.C. he was given as a hostage to the Thebans. He spent three years in Thebes, where he learned the use of the phalanx formation of infantry in war from its inventor, Epaminondas. Philip's brother, Perdiccas, had inherited the kingdom of Macedonia, but in 360 B.C. he was killed during a revolt of the hill tribes. Philip seized the throne and began to create a Macedonian national army. He conquered the hill tribes and then turned his eyes to Greece.

In 358 B.C. he took the Athenian colony Amphipolis which gave entrance to the gold mines of Mount Pangaeus, and later he founded the city of Philippi at the mines. Then two other cities fell to him. He was able to calm the suspicions of the Greeks by promising to return Amphipolis to Athens and by handing over the newly taken cities to the Olynthian Confederation. In 352 B.C. he suddenly advanced into Thessaly and Magnesia and took them and in 347 captured Olynthus.

The following year Philip passed Thermopylae, allied himself with Thebes, and crushed the Phocians.

Philip was a brilliant diplomat. By costly bribes and promises he had kept Athens from offering resistance while he made himself master of Greece. His victory over the Phocians allowed him to pose as the deliverer of Greece, for the Phocians had scandalized everyone by occupying the holy city of Delphi. In 346 B.C. he held the Pythian Games at Delphi and presided over them, thereby showing that he considered himself a Greek and not a foreign conqueror. Demosthenes, ever his enemy, accused him of destroying the liberties of Greece. But a strong party, led by Isocrates, saw him as a leader who would end the petty quarrels of the Greek cities and lead them all in a crusade against Persia.

For the next few years Philip was engaged in extending his power to the north. Although Philip was recognized as captain general of the Greeks, he was assassinated before he could complete his plans. Alexander the Great, Philip's son by the witch-woman, Olympias, succeeded him.

PHILIP III, another son, who was in Babylon at the time of Alexander's death, was acclaimed king by the Macedonian Army in 323 B.C. although he was practically an idiot. He was murdered in 317 B.C. by order of Olympias.

PHILIP IV, reigned from 297 B.C. to 296 B.C.

PHILIP V (237–179 B.C.), who reigned from 220 to 179 B.C., maintained a hopeless struggle against the Romans. He was defeated by Titus Flaminius at Cynoscephalae in 197 B.C.

PHILIP [Kings of Spain]. Five kings of Spain have borne the name of Philip.

PHILIP I (1478–1506) was a son of the Holy Roman Emperor Maximilian I. In 1496 he married Joan, daughter of Ferdinand and Isabella of Spain. Philip was crowned king of Castile in 1504 after the death of Isabella, although Ferdinand had never admitted Philip's right to the throne.

PHILIP II (1527–1598) was the son of the Emperor Charles V, who was at the same time king of Spain. Philip was brought up as a Spaniard. In 1555 he was entrusted by his father with the government of the Netherlands. In 1554 Philip married Mary, Queen of England. In 1556 Charles V abdicated. His son, Ferdinand, took the empire while to Philip were left Spain, Spanish America, the Spanish possessions in Italy, and the Netherlands. Philip's kingdom was a threat to France. England was Spain's ally by the marriage with Mary. Flanders on the north and Spain on the south aided in encircling France.

But the whole scene changed when Elizabeth came to the throne of England. Both England and the Netherlands adopted the Protestant religion. Philip was religious and nothing could shake his belief that he was the person chosen by God to punish the Protestants. Also, the English under Elizabeth were raiding Spanish ships, and France was a political enemy. Philip only added to his difficulties when he tried to enforce Catholicism in the Netherlands by war. Grave and self-possessed, he was disliked by all but the Spaniards. He was no soldier, but he was a good administrator. He ran the whole kingdom, and worked day and night reading and drafting messages. But his industry and thriftiness were his ruin. He would not trust his generals and admirals, and he would not provide them with enough money. Holland won its independence, and England shattered the armada which was sent against it in 1588. Three later armadas were unsuccessful because they were ill equipped and led by admirals whom Philip had chosen without regard to naval ability. Toward the end of his life he was tortured by dreadful skin diseases, but he never ceased working. For 50 days and nights before his death he lay in the chapel of the Escorial, surrounded by chanting monks and priests.

PHILIP III (1578–1621), son of Philip II, succeeded his father. Philip II had been fond of endless discussions and extensive writing of minutes. The Spanish administration was choked with useless paper notes and regulations. Philip III did not attempt to remedy this. He let the empire drift, and devoted himself to living a life that was as religious as that of his father.

PHILIP IV (1605–1665), son of Philip III, succeeded his father at the age of 16. He was weak and frivolous and his reign was a long story of disaster. He chose the Count of Olivares, a grossly inefficient man, as his minister, but dismissed him in 1643. He was very solemn and dignified in public, but immoral in private. He was fond of art and literature, and was the patron of Diego Rodriguez de Silva y Velasquez and Pedro Calderon de la Barca.

PHILIP V (1683–1746) was the founder of the Bourbon dynasty in Spain. Born at Versailles, he was a grandson of Louis XIV, and when the Hapsburg line died out in Spain he was named heir to the throne by Charles II of Spain. He was a courageous ruler, who fought gallantly in the War of the Spanish Succession. Unfortunately his ambition was to succeed Louis XV of France. With that object in view, he abdicated in 1724. Later he resumed the rule of Spain, but he found little success because he became mentally ill.

PHILIPPINES (fĭl′ĭ pēnz), **REPUBLIC OF THE,** is a group of more than 7,000 islands off the southeast coast of Asia in the Pacific Ocean. Most of the islands are small. The island group extends about 688 miles east and west and about 1,152 miles north and south between Formosa and Borneo. The Philippines are bounded by the South China Sea on the west and north, the Philippine Sea on the east, and the Celebes Sea on the south.

The island group was given the name Las Felipinas in 1542 by the members of a Spanish expedition which had crossed the Pacific Ocean westward from Mexico. The name honored the prince who later became King Philip II of Spain.

The Spanish ruled the Philippines until the end of the 19th century. After the Spanish-American War (1898) the United States governed the islands until they became an independent country in 1946.

Landscape

Only about 1,000 of the Philippine Islands have people on them. The others are uninhabited coral reefs or small, rocky points rising out of the ocean. The country's total area is 115,707 square miles. Luzon in the north and Mindanao in the south are the two largest islands. Together they make up about two-thirds of the area of the Philippines. The other large islands of the group include Samar, Negros, Palawan, Panay, Mindoro, Leyte, Cebu, and Bohol.

The Philippines are a part of a vast underwater mountain chain. The peaks rising above the water's surface form many of the islands. Most of the islands are mountainous with only a narrow rim of coastal plains. The mountain ridges run generally north and south. Most of the people live in the lowlands.

There are several volcanoes in the Philippines. Most of them are no longer active. Mount Apo (9,691 feet), an active volcano on Mindanao, is the highest peak in the islands. Mount Mayon (7,943 feet) in southern Luzon, noted for its almost perfect volcanic cone, is

Locator map of the Philippines.

Top Left: Manila is on the Pasig River. Right: The Legislative Building in Manila houses the Philippine Congress. Top Right: This typical Moro village is on Mindanao.

Gendreau

also active. The areas of volcanic soils are the most fertile, but good soils are also found in many of the small basins and river valleys.

The rivers are short, rapid streams. The Cagayan River on Luzon is the largest. None are navigable for any distance except the Pasig River, along which the city of Manila has grown. Of the many lakes, Laguna de Bay on Luzon is the largest. Many small bays and inlets fringe the coasts of most of the islands. Manila has the finest natural harbor in the Orient.

Climate and Vegetation

The climate of the islands is tropical except in the higher mountain areas. The moderate temperatures vary only slightly throughout the year in the lower areas. Monthly averages range from 76 to 84 degrees Fahrenheit.

Heavy rainfall is common throughout the year on the eastern sides of the islands, with the greatest amount during the winter. Monsoon winds bring heavy rains to the western portions from October to June, but there is a dry season during the remaining months. Total yearly rainfall for the east coasts is usually more than 120 inches. A few areas receive more than 250 inches. The drier western areas usually receive less than 60 inches. The northern and central islands are in the typhoon belt. Between May and early December, violent storms cause great destruction in these areas. Occasional earthquakes also cause damage.

Tropical forests of the islands contain valuable timber, such as Philippine mahogany, one of the country's leading exports. The forests also provide other hardwoods, softwoods, bamboos, rattans, and gums and resins.

Nearly 20 per cent of the country is grassland. The most common grass, "cogon," grows to about six feet. The coconut palm, found throughout the islands, yields the chief export products—coconut oil and copra—and is also a source of food, clothing and building materials, and other products.

Animal Life and Mineral Resources

Many species of wildlife live in the forests, including wild buffaloes, wild hogs, monkeys, deer, and civet cats. Hundreds of birds add color and noise to the forests. Many kinds of reptiles are found throughout the islands. The domesticated animals include cows and water buffaloes (carabaos), both of which are important as dairy animals and beasts of burden. Marine life is plentiful in the coastal waters of

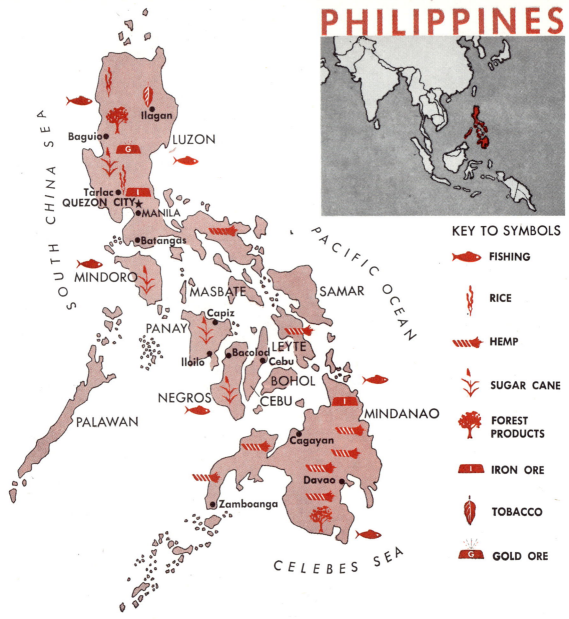

PHILIPPINES

KEY TO SYMBOLS

- FISHING
- RICE
- HEMP
- SUGAR CANE
- FOREST PRODUCTS
- IRON ORE
- TOBACCO
- GOLD ORE

Map labels: SOUTH CHINA SEA, PACIFIC OCEAN, CELEBES SEA, LUZON, Ilagan, Baguio, Tarlac, QUEZON CITY, MANILA, Batangas, MINDORO, MASBATE, SAMAR, Capiz, PANAY, LEYTE, Iloilo, Bacolod, Cebu, BOHOL, NEGROS, CEBU, PALAWAN, MINDANAO, Cagayan, Davao, Zamboanga

the islands.

The Philippines are rich in mineral resources. Gold, silver, iron ore, manganese, and chromium are exported, and copper, lead, asphalt, marble, and gypsum also are mined. The islands, however, lack large deposits of two important minerals—petroleum and high-grade coal. The lack of good coal has slowed the development of metal industries.

The People of the Philippines

The Filipinos are mainly descendants of the many groups of invaders, settlers, and traders who have traveled to the islands during the past 8,000 years. The customs, physical appearance, and languages of the people are a blend of many different backgrounds.

Primitive Negrito peoples were among the earliest inhabitants of the Philippines. They are thought to have come from some of the other Pacific islands thousands of years ago. The Negritos have very dark skin and kinky hair and are usually less than five feet tall. Today there are not more than 50,000 Negritos in

FACTS ABOUT
REPUBLIC OF THE PHILIPPINES

CAPITAL: Quezon City
NATIONAL ANTHEM: "Tierra Adorada"
("Land of the Morning")

Physical

AREA: 115,707 square miles (about 7,090 islands), including 877 square miles of water; 14,400 miles of coast line.

POPULATION: 27,087,685 (1960 census); 234 persons per square mile; about 75 per cent rural, 25 per cent urban.

MOUNTAIN RANGES: Cordillera Central, Ilocos or Malaya, Sierra Madre, Caraballo.

CHIEF MOUNTAIN PEAKS (height in feet): Apo (9,691); Mayon (7,943).

LARGEST LAKES: Laguna de Bay, Taal, Lanao, Mainit.

MOST IMPORTANT RIVERS: Cagayan, Agno, Pampanga, Pasig, Bikol.

ADDITIONAL PLACES OF INTEREST: St. Augustin's Church, Manila; Zamboanga Harbor.

Government

FORM OF GOVERNMENT: Republic.

HEAD OF GOVERNMENT AND CHIEF OF STATE: President; elected by direct popular vote for four-year term.

LEGISLATURE: Congress, including 24-member Senate and 102-member House of Representatives.

VOTING QUALIFICATIONS: Age 21; must be able to read or write Spanish, English, or a native dialect.

POLITICAL DIVISIONS: 56 provinces.

NATIONAL HOLIDAYS: New Year's Day, January 1; Easter Holidays (Holy Thursday and Good Friday); Labor Day, May 1; Independence Day, July 4; National Heroes' Day, November 30; Christmas Day, December 25; Rizal Day, December 30.

Transportation and Communication

RAILROADS: 711 miles of track.
ROADS: 21,862 miles.
MOTOR VEHICLES: 171,000.
TELEPHONES: 58,332.
RADIO STATIONS: 20.
TELEVISION STATIONS: 1.
NEWSPAPERS: 723.

People

CHIEF CITIES: Manila (1,138,611); Cebu (251,146); Davao (225,712); Basilan (155,712); Iloilo (151,266); Quezon City (397,990).

CHURCH MEMBERSHIP: 83 per cent Roman Catholic; 7.6 per cent Philippine Independent; 4.1 per cent Muslim; 2.3 per cent Protestant.

LEADING UNIVERSITIES AND COLLEGES: University of the Philippines, Quezon City; University of Santo Tomas, Manila; Far Eastern University, Manila.

IMPORTANT MUSEUMS: National Museum, Manila, anthropology and history; Santo Tomas Museum, Manila, natural history.

Economy

LEADING INDUSTRIES: Agriculture, fishing, forestry, mining, light manufacturing.

CHIEF PRODUCTS: Rice, corn, copra, coconut, sugar, copper, chromite, iron ore, logs and lumber, abaca (manila hemp).

the Philippines. They live among the rougher highlands and still use primitive ways of hunting and fishing.

The Malays are the largest racial group in the Philippines. They are a Mongoloid people with brown skin and straight black hair. Over a period of thousands of years, the Malays came in groups to the Philippines from the other Pacific islands or from the mainland of Southeast Asia. These groups settled in many parts of the islands. Their languages and customs therefore developed separately. Today 87 dialects are spoken in the Philippines, and there are more than 40 separate cultural groups. The Tagalog peoples of central and southern Luzon and the Visayan peoples of the central islands are among the largest of these groups.

Chinese and Indian traders visited the Philippines as early as 2,000 years ago. They brought new skills and ideas and also introduced Chinese and Indian racial characteristics into the physical make-up of the population. It is estimated that about 5 per cent of the people are partly of Indian origin and about 10 per cent partly Chinese.

After the Spaniards came to the Philippines in the 16th century, they converted many of the islanders to Christianity and introduced several elements of Western culture. Strong Spanish influence is still seen—particularly in dress, architecture, manners, and names. During the years of U.S. administration, the Americans influenced the islanders. Many Filipinos now speak the English language. But even with the strong Spanish and United States influence, there is a much older and deeper heritage from the mainland of Southeast Asia. It is seen especially among the farming people —in the way they work their land, build their homes, and prepare their food.

Two areas of the islands have been largely untouched by Western influences. One of these is the northern part of Luzon, where Malay tribesmen stubbornly resisted Spanish efforts to conquer them. One of the tribes, the Igorots, only recently gave up head-hunting. These northern tribesmen number about 200,000 and, for the most part, are still pagans.

The other area, more troublesome both to the

Spanish and to the United States, was the group of southern islands, including Mindanao, where the Moros live. The Moros were Malay tribesmen who were converted to the Muslim faith in the 13th century by Arab missionaries. They fiercely resisted Spanish and American rule, but gradually have grown more peaceful and cooperative.

Cities, Towns, and Villages

Most Filipinos live in villages or small towns. Often a village is simply a double row of bamboo houses facing each other along a road. About 18 per cent of the people live in cities with populations of 10,000 or more. The largest city is Manila. (See MANILA.) Quezon City, near Manila, is the capital.

Many Philippine cities and towns are laid out around a central plaza or village square. The residential areas of the cities often consist of a wide variety of housing styles. Split bamboo and wood are the most common building materials. Many Filipinos build their homes on stilts in order to keep them dry during floods that result from heavy rains.

How the People Make a Living

Agriculture. About 70 per cent of the Philippine workers are farmers. Most farms are between four and ten acres in size. Farmers plow with iron-tipped wooden plows drawn by water buffaloes. Crops are harvested by hand. Crop rotation is practiced rarely, and seldom are farmers able to afford fertilizer. As a result, even though the tropical climate and fertile soils favor agriculture, crop yields are low.

There is a surplus of farm land in the Philippines. Only about 20 per cent of the land is used for farming, although much more is suitable. Nevertheless, some farming areas are very crowded. The government is urging farmers of the crowded central islands to move to Mindanao and other less-populated islands.

Rice, the main food of the Philippines, is grown on nearly half of the cultivated land. Luzon's central plain is the largest cropped area. Corn, another important food crop, is grown on about one-fourth of the cropland. Garden crops—sweet potatoes, cassavas, and beans—peanuts, bananas, and a variety of tropical fruits are usually grown in the small plots around the farmers' houses.

Crops grown mainly for export include coconuts, sugar cane, abaca (Manila hemp), pineapples, and tobacco. Southern Luzon has large coconut plantations. The republic leads the world in the export of coconut products. In addition to crop raising, many Filipinos raise livestock—including water buffaloes, horses, hogs, cattle, goats, sheep, and poultry.

Fishing. After rice, fish is the most important food in the Philippine diet. Next to farming and livestock-raising, more Filipinos earn a living from fishing than from any other occupation. Canned tuna is the chief fish export. Many marine creatures are used for purposes other than food. Coral and shells, for example, are used for making jewelry and other decorative articles.

Manufacturing. The chief manufacturing industries in the Philippines are based on the processing of products from the farms, forests, and mines. There are rice, sugar, and palm-oil processing plants; lumber mills; leather tanneries; rope, furniture, and cigar and cigarette factories; mineral-refining plants; and food canneries.

Several government-owned cement plants, a small shipbuilding center, an iron and steel plant, a hydroelectric plant, and several thermoelectric plants are also operating. Aided by government, manufacturing has begun to grow rapidly, especially near Manila. Rubber, chemical, textile, aluminum, and enamelware plants are among the newer industries.

Handicrafts employ more workers than all the other industries together. Working at home, Philippine women turn out beautiful woven fabrics, baskets, hats, matting, and embroidery.

Transportation

Land transportation in the Philippines depends chiefly on the system of roads built during the period of U.S. administration. Nearly all back-country areas are without roads of any kind. Public buses operate on the better highways. Narrow-gauge railways serve cities on the islands of Luzon, Panay, and Cebu.

Travel between islands is usually by boat. Airlines, however, connect all the major cities and towns of the islands. Philippine Air Lines also runs regular passenger and cargo service to other countries in the Orient.

Government

The constitution of the Republic of the Philippines was adopted in 1935 and amended in 1940 and 1946. It is very similar to the Constitution of the United States in that it contains a bill of rights and divides the government into three branches. The executive branch is headed by the president and vice-president. The legislative, or law-making branch, is the Senate and the House of Representatives. The judiciary is headed by the Supreme Court.

Below the national government are the 56 provincial governments, each with a governor and an elected legislature. Cities and towns are governed by mayors and municipal councils.

Education

The Philippines has the highest literacy rate of any of the countries of Southeast Asia. More than 65 per cent of the people are able to read and write. Education is compulsory through the sixth grade and is free at all levels. The educational system is similar to that in the United States and includes elementary schools, secondary schools, and institutions of higher learning. The best-known universities are the University of the Philippines, the University of Santo Tomas (founded 1611), and the Far Eastern University.

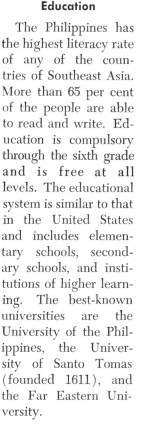

Filipino, based on Tagalog (a Malayan dialect), is the national language. English and Spanish also are recognized as official languages and are used in international trade and diplomacy.

Religion

The Republic of the Philippines is the only country in eastern Asia in which Christianity is the principal faith. Most of the church members are Roman Catholic. Some, however, are followers of the Philippine Independent church (a Catholic group that does not recognize the Roman Catholic pope as its head), Islam, and Protestantism.

The islanders celebrate many religious festivals. Christmas lasts from December 16 to January 6. Each village has a festival on the day of its patron saint and one before Lent.

History

Ferdinand Magellan is thought to have been the first European to visit the Philippines

The almost perfect cone of Mayon Volcano rises above Legaspi on southern Luzon.

Courtesy Pan American World Airways

(1521). Spain claimed the Philippines as the result of his visit, and by the end of the 16th century the Spaniards ruled nearly all of the islands. (See MAGELLAN, FERDINAND.) Hundreds of Spanish friars came to live in the Philippines to convert the people to Christianity and to teach them to live in peace.

During the 19th century open resentment flared up against the Spanish. One of the leaders of the campaign for freedom was Jose Rizal. He wrote against the dictatorial manner in which the friars ruled the villages. When the Spanish executed him on December 30, 1896, he became a national hero. Meanwhile, another Philippine leader, Emilio Aguinaldo, was organizing the people to revolt.

In 1898 the first major battle of the Spanish-American War took place in Manila Bay, where a U.S. fleet led by Commodore George Dewey defeated a Spanish fleet. (See SPANISH-AMERICAN WAR; DEWEY, GEORGE.) That same year, Spain gave up the islands to the United States in return for $20,000,000. By this time the Filipinos had declared themselves independent and made Aguinaldo president of the provisional government. Aguinaldo's forces resisted the United States occupation but were beaten in 1901, and, by 1902, peace was established in all parts of the islands except those inhabited by the Moro tribes. The Moros continued guerrilla warfare on the island of Mindanao for nearly ten years.

The United States wanted the Philippines to have self-government but realized that the people needed much help before they would be ready for independence. The United States government built schools and roads, installed sewage systems, vaccinated the people to protect them from smallpox and cholera, and drilled deep wells to provide pure drinking water.

William Howard Taft was the first civil governor of the Philippines (1900 to 1904). (See TAFT, WILLIAM HOWARD.) In 1916 the United States Congress passed the Jones Act, which gave the Philippines an elected legislature. In 1934 the Tydings-McDuffie Act set the date for Philippine independence at July 4, 1946. This act made the Philippines a commonwealth and gave it almost complete control over its own affairs. The United States kept control of defense, foreign relations, and important financial policies. Manuel Quezon, elected in 1935, was the first president of the Philippine Commonwealth.

World War II broke out in the Pacific on December 7, 1941. The Philippine Islands were one of Japan's chief objectives. On January 2, 1942, Manila was captured. (See WORLD WAR II, *War in the Pacific* and *The Return to the Philippines*.) President Manuel Quezon went to Washington, D.C., where he organized his government in exile. Upon his death in 1944, he was succeeded by Sergio Osmena, the vice-president. While the Philippines were occupied by the Japanese, U.S. and Filipino guerrillas kept resistance alive. In 1945 the Japanese were driven out.

The Philippines became independent on July 4, 1946. Manuel Roxas y Acuna was elected the first president of the new Republic of the Philippines. War damage was widespread, and the Communist-led Hukbalahaps (Huks) occupied considerable areas in Luzon and Panay. These problems were overcome, largely because of the enthusiasm of the Filipinos for their independence. Money was given by the U.S. to help repair war damage.

In 1948 President Roxas died and was succeeded by the vice-president, Elpidio Quirino. In 1949 Quirino was elected for a full four-year term. In November 1953 Ramon Magsaysay, a famous guerrilla fighter during World War II, was elected president.

Magsaysay began a widespread program of improvements for the new republic. In order to defeat the Huks, he kept the Philippine Army constantly in the field, introduced land reforms, and gave farm lands on Mindanao to all Huks who would surrender. When he was killed in an airplane accident in March 1957, Magsaysay was succeeded by the vice-president, Carlos P. Garcia. In November 1957 Garcia was elected for a four-year term, and in 1961 Diosdado Macapagal succeeded him.

In recent years the republic has made great progress. Agricultural and industrial output, national income, and the income of individual workers have been rising.

The republic was one of the original members of the United Nations. When the Korean War broke out in 1950, Philippine troops were among the first sent to serve under the United Nations command. The republic is a member of the South East Asia Treaty Organization (SEATO) defense pact, which was signed at Manila in 1954.

PHILISTINES (*fĭ lĭs'tĭnz* or *fĭl'ĭs tĭnz*). Certain people escaped when the island of Crete was sacked by the Achaeans. They settled on the southwest shore of Judaea and became known as Philistines. Amos and Jeremiah say that they came from Caphtor, a word which closely resembles the Egyptian *Keftill*, meaning *people of Crete*. They overwhelmed Syria about 1200 B.C. and were kept out of Egypt by Rameses III. In the Egyptian pictures they are shown wearing a headdress of feathers, and their appearance is more European than Semitic. Their weapons were like the Greek arms—short swords, spears, and round shields.

In the 11th century B.C., after their final defeat in Egypt, they settled on the coast of Palestine. One of their chief cities was Gaza. They made the Israelites slaves and at the Battle of Aphek captured the Ark, a chest containing the Ten Commandments. While king of Judah, David became the vassal of their king Achish. But when David became king of all Israel he managed to confine the Philistines within their frontiers. Gaza was taken by the Egyptians and given to Solomon. Thereafter the Philistines disappeared under the attacks of the Egyptians, Syrians, and Assyrians.

Delilah and the giant Goliath, whom the Jews so hated and feared, were Philistines. In modern usage Philistine means an uncultured person who is content with his present way of living and is opposed to making any change in it.

PHILOSOPHY (*fĭ lŏs'ō fē*). The word "philosophy" is formed from two Greek words, one meaning "love," the other "wisdom." It is generally supposed to have been coined by Pythagoras. (See PYTHAGORAS AND PYTHAGOREANS.) Pythagoras, when asked if he were a wise man, replied, "No, but I am a lover of wisdom." The term philosophy is used to signify man's most general efforts to understand the world in which he lives and his place in the world.

Even primitive men sought to understand the nature of the heavenly bodies, what caused the rain to fall and the grass to grow, what happened to men after their bodies died, and whether friendly or unfriendly powers were in control of the world.

But the first people of the western world whom we now describe as philosophers were a few Greeks who lived in coastal cities of the Aegean Sea during the 6th century B.C. Thales, Anaximander, and Anaximenes, all of the city of Miletus, are usually regarded as the first of the Greek philosophers. Most of the actual writings of these men have been lost. We learn from Aristotle and other later Greeks, however, that these first philosophers began their speculations by rejecting the myths and religious explanations of the universe which were current among men in their times.

The early Greek philosophers may also be regarded as the first scientists of the western world. Some of the theories of modern science, such as the theory of evolution and the theory of the atomic structure of matter, were developed in an incomplete manner by these early thinkers. The Greek philosophers differed from modern scientists, however, in their way of finding out about the world. They based all their conclusions on observations and thoughts, and did not perform experiments. All the bodies of learning which we now call "sciences" were once included in philosophy. For this reason philosophy is sometimes called the "Mother of the Sciences." Mathematics and astronomy were the first of the sciences to become independent branches of learning. Physics, chemistry, and biology later became separate studies. The studies which have most recently become independent of philosophy are sociology and psychology. The distinction between science and philosophy is much clearer now than it once was. Scientists want to discover facts, and nothing but facts, about the universe, while philosophers try to gather both facts and values. Philosophers want to know the meaning and the worth of facts. Scientists limit their study to an examination of aspects of the world which can be measured exactly. Scientists seek knowledge; philosophers seek wisdom.

The relationship between philosophy and religion is more difficult to determine than the relationship between philosophy and science. Philosophy began in the ancient Greek world as a protest against religion. It became a method of defending religious ideas during the Middle Ages. The most influential kind of philosophy during the Middle Ages was Scholasticism. The Scholastics devoted their lectures and writings chiefly to showing that the ideas of Christianity were reasonable. They wanted to show that Christian doctrines were true, not because the church said they were true, but because human reason could prove them so. During and after the Renaissance in southern Europe (see RENAISSANCE) many philosophers became very critical of the Christian religion. In modern times, whether or not a philosopher is sympathetic to any religion, he shares with religionists an interest in such human values as justice, goodness, and beauty. The religionist, however, is willing to accept many ideas on faith; that is, without rational proof or evidence from his senses. The philosopher, like the scientist, demands that ideas be supported by reason and evidence.

The development of philosophy in the western world, which excludes the speculative thought of India, China, Persia, and other oriental countries, can be divided into three historical periods: Ancient, Medieval, and Modern. The dates of these three periods cannot be definitely set. It is common to date the Ancient period from 700 B.C. to A.D. 700. This period includes the rise and fall of Greek philosophy; the changes which took place as Greek philosophy came into contact with Roman and Christian thought; and finally the fall of Rome, which left Christianity in a position of increased strength. The Medieval period lasted from 700 to 1600. During this time the Christian philosophers absorbed Aristotle's thinking and developed an unusually complete philosophy. The peak of this development was reached in the writings of St. Thomas Aquinas (1225–1274).

In the last centuries of the Medieval period the rediscovery of the Classical literature of the Greeks and the Romans, in which the enjoyment of living was emphasized, turned the attention of scholars from heaven and the afterlife to earth and this life. Their studies fostered a curiosity about man and nature which led to the development of modern science.

Divisions of Philosophy

The work of the philosophers in the modern world is twofold. On the one hand, they analyze and clarify the basic ideas of the sciences, the arts, and religion. For example, philosophers examine the idea of time in physics, of beauty in painting, and of God in religion. This is analysis. In their analytic function modern philosophers act much like Socrates did when he helped the young men of Athens to understand their own ideas. (See SOCRATES.) Philosophers also bring together ideas to form a system of thought. This is called synthesis. In their synthetic function philosophers show the relations which are possible between science, art, ethics, and religion. They try to put these ideas together in a total world view.

The studies of philosophers can be divided into six areas: logic, methodology, epistemology, metaphysics, aesthetics, and ethics.

Logic is the study of ways of thinking. Logicians examine both the sort of thinking done in mathematics (deduction) and the sort of thinking which is about facts (induction). They consider incorrect ways of thinking (fallacies of thought) and show how they can be avoided. Aristotle (384–322 B.C.) was the first and greatest logician in the western world. (See ARISTOTLE; LOGIC.)

In methodology philosophers study the ways of gaining knowledge. Philosophers usually state that there are four methods of getting knowledge: appeal to authorities; the use of reasoning powers; the use of intuitions or feelings; and experiences of the senses. Philosophers determine which ways of attaining knowledge are best for various subject matters, and the dangers and weaknesses of each method.

Epistemology is the study of how much man can know, of the differences between knowledge and opinion, and of whether things just as they are can be known or whether the act of knowing changes things. Some philosophers (Realists) have thought that man can know things exactly as they are. Others (Phenomenalists) have thought that man never knows things as they are in reality. Still others (Idealists) have said that things cannot even be said to exist except when, and as, they are known.

Metaphysics is an attempt to understand the ultimate nature of reality, to answer such questions as: Is the universe mental, or physical, or both? What are space and time? Does the universe have a purpose? Is there a God? The modern metaphysician borrows ideas for his speculations from both science and religion.

Aesthetics is the study of problems such as: What is art? What constitutes beauty in art? What is the human value of art? What are the relations between art and morality?

Ethics is concerned with the right and the good in human behavior. Many separate studies such as social philosophy, political philosophy, and philosophy of law may be regarded as part of ethics. In ethics philosophers are interested not so much in what people ought to do in various situations as they are in the careful analysis of such terms as good, right, ought, obligation, justice, state, and community.

Schools of Philosophy

Philosophers are often classified into schools. A school of philosophy consists of a certain way of thinking and certain basic ideas. The school to which a philosopher belongs depends partly upon the kind of man he is. Since the philosopher deals with values as well as facts, he is not able to keep his own desires out of his conclusions. He has more difficulty than the scientist in being unprejudiced. For these reasons philosophers do not agree as to which philosophy is the true philosophy. In fact, most philosophers doubt that there is any philosophy which can be defended as the true school of philosophy.

We shall consider eight of the principal schools or systems of philosophy. The first two, Idealism and Realism, are systems which begin as epistemological points of view. The second pair, Supernaturalism and Naturalism, are metaphysical systems. The third pair, Rationalism and Empiricism, are methodological in their origin. The last two, Pragmatism and Existentialism, may be regarded as primarily systems of value.

According to Idealistic philosophers the realities of the world are minds and the ideas which minds think. The school should probably be called "Idea-ism." Plato (428?–347 B.C.) was the first great Idealist in the western world. (See PLATO.) Plato believed that the objects we perceive, such as trees, tables, and pencils, are not real in themselves. The real tree, he said, is the Idea of tree which exists independently of all the trees we see. These Ideas of Plato also exist independently of all minds; they are not merely ideas or thoughts in a mind. Plato thought that when we look at an object and say, "This is a tree," what we mean is, "This is a particular imitation which reminds me of the Idea 'tree.'" The school of Idealism has lived through centuries and has undergone many modifications. Plotinus (205?–270), for example, believed that the Platonic Ideas are ideas in the mind of God. Bishop George Berkeley (1685–1753) thought that nothing exists except as ideas in a mind. Schopenhauer (1788–1860) singled out the act of willing as the basic reality.

According to the Realists, things have existence apart from their reality as ideas. Aristotle was the first great Realist in the western world. He was a pupil of Plato for many years, but upon the death of Plato he began to develop his own views about the world. He finally established a school in Athens in competition with Plato's famous Academy. Aristotle called his school the Lyceum. Aristotle believed that the world of physical objects has a reality of its own. Particular things, such as trees, tables, and pencils, exist apart from the Platonic Ideas. Realism, like Idealism, has been presented in many forms in the long history of its existence. St. Thomas Aquinas believed in the existence of God and the angels; Thomas Hobbes (1588–1679) believed that nothing but matter exists. Yet both were Realists.

Supernaturalism and Naturalism are in some

respects similar to Idealism and Realism. The difference is that Idealism and Realism are points of view as to the dependence or independence of realities upon minds, whereas Supernaturalism and Naturalism are metaphysical systems about the reality of God and the physical world. Supernaturalistic philosophers believe that God is a real being—usually the Supreme Being. They think of God as the Creator of the world, the Sustainer of all life, and the Source of all values. They think of man as possessing an immortal soul given to him by his Creator.

Naturalists or Materialists, as they are sometimes called, believe that the only reality is the reality of material things. They believe that we do not have to look outside the world of things which we perceive to find the causes for everything. We must not conclude from this that all Naturalists are irreligious. Some of the Naturalistic philosophers believe that God is a force which is working from within the world; others feel that the idea of God should be retained as an idea which stands for man's deepest longings for beauty and goodness. Others would remove the idea of God entirely from human thought.

Rationalism and Empiricism are schools which deal with the sources of knowledge. Rationalists believe that the mind is able to arrive at knowledge without appeal to the senses. One of the greatest of all Rationalists was Descartes (1596–1650). (See DESCARTES, RENE.) He built an entire philosophical system upon his awareness of his own thinking, expressed in his well-known statement: "I think, therefore I am."

Empiricists, on the other hand, believe that man can discover the nature of the world only through sense observations and experiments. Francis Bacon (1561–1626) was one of the first Empiricists to work out the principles of the methods used in modern science.

Two schools of philosophy have developed largely in the 20th century. Pragmatism was developed by Charles Sanders Peirce (1839–1914) and William James (1842–1910). Pragmatists, like Empiricists, hold that the world can be known only through the use of the sense organs, but the Pragmatists in addition believe that all knowledge must be tested by practical consequences. The meaning of a theory is contained in the effects the theory has when it is applied to life situations. Any theory that works well may be said to be true. Value becomes the test of truth. Pragmatism is often claimed to be a truly American philosophy.

Existentialism is a philosophy which came into prominence after World War II, although its roots can be traced back to a Danish philosopher, Soren Kierkegaard (1813–1855). The central doctrine of this school is that the existence of a thing (*that* a thing is) is distinct from and superior to the essence of a thing (*what* a thing is). In the writings of the French philosopher-playwright Jean-Paul Sartre (1905–   ), Existentialism has taken the pessimistic line that man cannot expect much value from life and therefore ought to devote his attention just to living rather than to trying to live well.

Philosophers believe their task will never be finished. They are convinced that as long as there is human life upon the earth there will continue to be interest in the examination of what is real and true and valuable in man and the universe.

PHLOX (*flŏks*). In Greek the name *phlox* means "flame." The plant is so called from the red color of one species. The colors of others range from white and pink to purple. Many species of phlox are native to the United States. They are among the most abundant and showy of all wild flowers.

One light lavender species is found commonly in moist woodlands throughout almost the whole north central and northeastern region. Another pink-flowered species grows in dense tufts on rocky ledges. Still others occur in the western states.

Diffcrent kinds of phlox may occur at high or low altitudes, in areas that are dry, or in those that are moist. Some are annuals; others are perennial.

Through many years of cultivation, hybridization, and selection, a very great variety of phlox is now grown in gardens. They are grown as annuals in many colors and forms. Others occupy places in the rock garden. Still others

J. Horace McFarland Company

The bright pink, lavender, or white blossoms of phlox are popular garden flowers because they are easily grown and cheerful in color.

are among the most brilliant and easily grown of the summer perennials. Dozens of varieties have been named. Most of them are easily grown and flower abundantly from spring to autumn.

PHOENICIA (*fē nĭsh'ĭ à*). The people of Phoenicia were the most daring of ancient sailors. They ventured far beyond the Mediterranean Sea in their galleys. By their travels they joined the old eastern civilizations of Mesopotamia, Egypt, and India with the growing power of Greece and Rome. They left few records of themselves so the little that is known about them today was learned in histories written by other nations.

The Phoenicians were the only one of the Semitic tribes to become a seafaring people. They were merchants and navigators rather than herdsmen or farmers. Their language was related to Hebrew. Originally a desert people, they were descended from the Canaanites.

Phoenicia was a strip of coast line in Syria, lying between Mount Lebanon and the Mediterranean. It was north of Palestine. Off the mountainous coast were several rocky islands that are now joined to the mainland. The great cities of Tyre and Sidon were built on two of these islands. Phoenicia was such a mountainous country that it was not suitable for agriculture, but it was well located for trade. These facts were responsible for its growth as a sea power. The Phoenicians came there from the east, perhaps from Babylon. According to one historian they founded Tyre about 2756 B.C.

History of Phoenicia

The Phoenicians were mentioned in the records of the Egyptians, who conquered them about 1600 B.C. In the 15th century B.C., when Sidon was in revolt, Tyre remained loyal to Egypt. From the middle of the 14th century down to the rise of the Assyrian empire in the 9th century B.C., Phoenicia was independent. When the Cretan civilization was destroyed by the first Greeks, Phoenicia stepped into Crete's position as the naval power of the Mediterranean. Hiram, who was king of Tyre from 970 to 936 B.C., became the friend and ally of Solomon and built him a fleet. Solomon and Hiram joined in expeditions to the east coast of Arabia. Other expeditions settled colonies on the north coast of Africa. In 814 B.C., according to tradition, Elissa (called Dido in the *Aeneid*), daughter of a king of Tyre, founded Carthage on the northern coast of Africa. (See CARTHAGE AND CARTHAGINIAN WARS.)

But already the Assyrians were pressing westward. In 868 B.C. Assur-nasir-pal II forced Phoenicia to pay tribute. Tyre was beseiged by Sennacherib in 701 B.C. but held out. Sidon fell to the Assyrians in 678 B.C., and six years later Tyre was again attacked without success. The Assyrians could ravage the whole of Phoenicia, but they could not interfere with the prosperity of Tyre.

Tyre was now at the height of its sea power. Phoenician ships collected the produce of Egypt and Babylon and carried it to the west. The East African and Indian trade went to Sheba in Arabia and thence by caravan to Tyre. A

Phoenician expedition reported having sailed south through the Indian Ocean, around the Cape of Good Hope, up the west coast of Africa, and home through the Mediterranean. Some did not believe this report because the sailors had declared that while they sailed west along the Cape of Good Hope, the midday sun was to the north of them instead of to the south. This statement is now considered good proof that they made the voyage.

The Phoenicians not only traded from east to west; they sailed out into the Atlantic and discovered some mysterious islands which they called the Cassiterides. There they mined tin and shipped it home. These were formerly believed to be the British Isles. Probably, however, the Cassiterides were the Scilly Islands off the coast of Cornwall. Tyre was not only interested in trade but in colonization as well. It founded the colony of Tarshish in what is now lower Spain, and settled Sicily, Sardinia, and Corsica.

Sidon, twin city and rival of Tyre, alternated with it in power. Unlike Tyre, Sidon's glory lay more in manufacture than in trade. Especially was it famous for its purple dyes and finespun glass.

The Phoenicians kept the secrets of their trade routes. They terrified the Greeks, who became their competitors, with tales of the dangers of the western Mediterranean. The Phoenicians never settled in Greece, but the Greek ports knew them well. They scoured the coasts of the Peloponnese for the murex, a shellfish of which the famous Tyrian dye was made. Tyre was governed by a king and a council of elders. The city was self-governed. If the king was away, the wealthy merchants did not hesitate to make war, or conclude treaties of peace. Their religion was most distasteful to the Jews. They sacrificed infants to Moloch and to Baal the sun god, and worshiped the moon goddess, Astarte. The patron god of Tyre itself was Melkarth, whom they later identified with Hercules.

Trade Rivalry with the Greeks

Nebuchadnezzar, after capturing Jerusalem, besieged Tyre from 585 to 573 B.C. without suc-cess. The Chaldeans were unable to capture it. In 538 Tyre and Sidon peacefully accepted the overlordship of the Persians. The king of Sidon ranked next to Xerxes in the Persian Empire. The Phoenician fleet fought at Salamis and in all the other engagements against the Greeks. Indeed the trade rivalry between the Greeks and the Phoenicians was one of the causes of war.

Evagoras, king of Salamis and ally of Athens, won Cyprus from them, and for several years actually held Tyre itself. In 333 B.C., after the Battle of Issus, all the Phoenician cities except Tyre surrendered to Alexander the Great. Tyre prepared for another of the great sieges of its history. It took Alexander seven months to capture it. He finally succeeded only by building a mole, or bridge of rocks, across the sea from the mainland to the island. Then he brought his catapults right up to the wall of Tyre. The Phoenicians lived on ingloriously under the successors of Alexander. In 64 B.C., Pompey annexed all Syria to the Roman Empire and the culture of the Phoenicians died out.

The harbors of Tyre and Sidon are now too shallow for traffic. Even the name *Phoenician* has disappeared.

Despite their own meager contribution the Phoenicians played a great part in history as the distributors of wealth and culture. The Greeks adopted their manner of dress and learned the alphabet from them.

PHOENIX (*fē'nĭks*), **ARIZONA,** the capital and largest city, is in the Salt River oasis in the south central part of the state. From the air it looks like an emerald green island in a great sea of dead brown rocks and sand. The Salt River Valley is a rich area of irrigation agriculture.

Crops include alfalfa, cotton, dates, citrus fruits, as well as many kinds of green vegetables. These farm products are packed in and shipped from Phoenix. The city also makes aircraft equipment, air-conditioners, and Indian novelties. One of its newest industries is electronics manufacture.

Where Phoenix stands today, an ancient people once had buildings, canals, and irrigated farm land. Some early American prospectors saw the ruins of this Indian civilization. They dreamed of rebuilding the irrigation works and again farming this desert land. Water from the Salt River was used. The new community was called Phoenix for the mythical bird that was supposed to have risen from its ashes after being burned. So Phoenix arose from the old Indian foundations, and in a short time became a modern city.

Phoenix became the capital of the Arizona territory in 1889. When Arizona was admitted as a state in 1912, it became the state capital. Phoenix is a famous resort area because the winter climate is sunny and warm. The high spot of the winter season comes the last week in March when La Fiesta del Sol (The Festival of the Sun) takes place.

Phoenix has a council-manager form of government. It had a population of 439,170 in 1960.

PHOSPHORESCENCE (fŏs′fō rĕs′ĕns). Before the true nature of phosphorescence was understood almost any substance that glowed in the dark was called phosphorescent. Today the term is used only for the glow which follows fluorescence. (See FLUORESCENCE AND FLUORESCENT LIGHT.)

Phosphorescent materials are those which glow for minutes or hours after fluorescence has

stopped. The glow slowly becomes weaker until it cannot be seen at all. It must then be excited again.

Fluorescence and phosphorescence are caused by a slight rearrangement of the molecules of the exposed material. Some of the energy is absorbed from the source of radiation.

In returning to its original state the radiated material gives off the absorbed energy in the form of light. If the return is very fast, the material may show fluorescence. If the return is slow, it will show phosphorescence (glow after the source of radiation is removed).

Many natural minerals show phosphorescence and fluorescence. The commonest of these are varieties of calcite, willemite, dacite, and fluorite.

In 1940 scientists agreed that the term "phosphorescence" should be used only for the type of luminescence (giving off of light) described above. Often, however, the glow or giving off of light is caused by a slow chemical reaction between the substance and oxygen in the air and is not a result of changes in the molecules of the material.

This type of glow is called *chemiluminescence* (the prefix *chemi-* is used to describe the cause of the luminescence). The glow of the element phosphorous is the result of this type

Left: Phosphorescent paint makes the numbers on a watch face visible at night. Center: Calcite is a natural mineral which shows phosphorescence. Right: A glass model of a tropical marine animal that gives off light.

Courtesy, (left) Elgin National Watch Company, photo by Jun Fujiti; photos, (center and right) The American Museum of Natural History

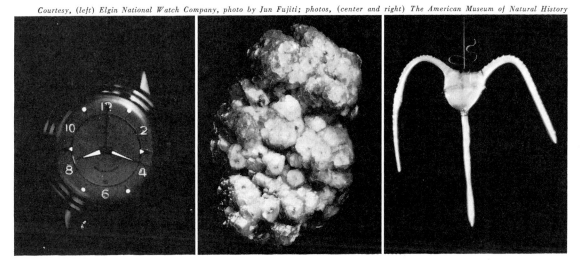

of chemical reaction. Therefore, phosphorus is not actually phosphorescent.

Many insects and marine animals are luminous (give off light) because of a chemical reaction between substances manufactured by the creatures and the oxygen in the air or water where they are found. The luminescence shown by fireflies is of this type. To show the origin of this type of light in living things the term *bioluminescence* is used.

Materials that show phosphorescence or fluorescence have many commercial uses. These include inner coatings for television picture tubes, coatings for the interiors of fluorescent lighting tubes, and for paints used in coating the numerals of watch dials. In the latter a phosphorus compound is mixed with a slightly radioactive substance which radiates the phosphorus material, causing it to glow. Phosphorescent materials may be made into fairly durable paints and markers. Good paints can be made from special zinc sulfide and strontium sulfide chemicals.

PHOSPHORUS (*fŏs′fō rŭs*). Pure phosphorus is a yellowish to white waxlike solid which is not metallic. (See CHEMISTRY.) Its weight is about twice that of water. Its chemical symbol is P and its atomic weight is 30.9738. In moist air, phosphorus slowly combines with oxygen in the air. This causes it to glow in the dark, to give off poisonous fumes that smell like garlic, and to catch fire spontaneously (without added heat).

Phosphorus is never found by itself in nature, but in combination with other elements, especially calcium. It is found in rocks and minerals bearing phosphate (phosphorus and calcium combined) and in animal bones. When white phosphorus is brought to a very high temperature in a closed container it changes to a red variety of phosphorus. This type does not glow in the dark, is not poisonous, and will not catch fire without added heat.

Phosphorus was discovered accidentally by Hennig Brand, an alchemist of Hamburg, Germany, in 1669. The discovery of this strange, fire-producing element was of great interest to the leading chemists of the day. But phosphorus was obtained with difficulty and in very small amounts from animal and vegetable remains.

In 1775, more than 100 years later, Karl Scheele, a Swedish chemist, developed a simple method of getting phosphorus from animal bones. Some uses for it were then developed. One of the early uses of phosphorus was in the first friction matches. But because white phosphorus was poisonous, nonpoisonous mixtures of phosphorus were later used in matches.

Before the middle of the 19th century it was discovered that phosphorus was one of the 20 elements needed for the healthy growth of plants and animals.

Next it was proved that each crop took phosphorus from the soil. Therefore, to keep production high, the mineral would have to be replaced. In order to do this, scientists became interested in the production of phosphorus as a plant food.

A method of getting phosphorus from phosphate rocks was soon found. Today most phosphorus comes from this source. The method now used is that of heating crushed phosphate rock, coke, and sand in an electric furnace. During the heating process phosphorus gas is given off. This is distilled to a liquid and then to solid phosphorus, which is stored under water so that it will not burn up.

Little or no phosphorus is used in pure form, but phosphorus combined with other substances has many commercial uses. Great amounts of phosphoric acid are used to treat phosphate rock for use as a fertilizer. This is done by mixing the crushed rock with the acid, which enriches it with phosphorus and makes the rock dissolve into the soil more easily. The phosphorus in the raw rock can then be absorbed by the plants.

Other minor uses include the manufacture of smoke-producing weapons for warfare, chemicals for detergents, rat poisons, safety matches, laboratory chemicals, and medicines to help the growth of bones.

PHOTOELECTRICITY (*fōt′ ŭ wŭ lĕk trĭs′ ŭt ē*) is the electrical effect produced when light strikes certain substances. The energy of the light rays separates electrons from the atoms of these sub-

PHOTOVOLTAGE

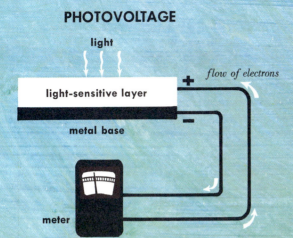

light

light-sensitive layer

metal base

+

−

flow of electrons

meter

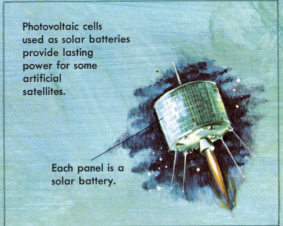

Photovoltaic cells used as solar batteries provide lasting power for some artificial satellites.

Each panel is a solar battery.

PHOTOCONDUCTION

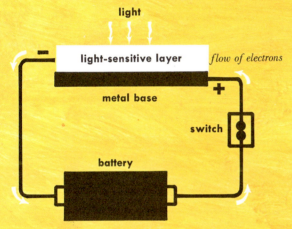

light

−

light-sensitive layer

metal base

+

flow of electrons

switch

battery

Photoconductive cells, used in automatic switches, turn on street lights when twilight fades to darkness.

PHOTOEMISSION

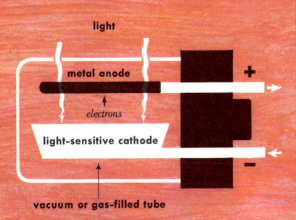

light

metal anode

+

electrons

light-sensitive cathode

−

vacuum or gas-filled tube

Photoemissive cells are used to open doors automatically. A beam of light shines on a photoelectric cell. When the beam is broken, the cell activates a circuit that starts a motor, which opens the door.

stances. The energy of the light causes the photoelectric effect. Photoelectric devices that automatically open doors, adjust camera lenses, set off burglar alarms, and perform many other functions are based on this effect.

Three principal photoelectric effects are produced: photovoltage, photoconduction, and photoemission. Which of the three effects is produced depends on how strongly the electrons are held by their atoms.

The device that puts photoelectricity to work is the photoelectric cell. Three types of cells are used, one for each effect to be produced.

The Photovoltaic Cell

The photovoltaic cell consists of a volt meter wired to a two-layered plate. One side of the plate is usually selenium, a nonmetal. The other side is metal. When light strikes the selenium, electrons pass from it to the metal side. Electrons then flow from the metal side into the wire around to the selenium, completing a circuit. The electric voltage created by this flow of electrons is registered by the volt meter. In the photovoltaic cell the atoms of the light-sensitive substance hold their electrons more firmly than in the photoconductive or photo-emissive cells. The electrons in the photovoltaic cell that are disturbed by light rays move relatively short distances.

Cameras are often equipped with photovoltaic cells that automatically set the opening of the camera lens. The energy to do this is generated by the light rays coming from the scene being photographed. The photovoltaic cell is also used in artificial satellites to convert solar energy into electric power. This power is used to transmit data about space back to Earth. As many as 10,000 cells may be used in one satellite.

The junction photodiode, a type of photovoltaic cell, uses a silicon crystal to convert light energy into electric voltage. The voltage can be amplified, or increased, to control large amounts of electric power. The junction photodiode is commonly used in computers.

The Photoconductive Cell

In the photoconductive cell the electrons of the light-sensitive material move more freely than in the photovoltaic cell. When the photoconductive cell is connected with a battery and exposed to light, a current will flow within the cell. The amount of current increases with the amount of light.

The best-known application of the photoconductive cell is the light meter used in photography. The reading on the meter tells the photographer to what opening he should set his camera lens. One type of meter shows the amount of light coming from the subject to be photographed; another type shows the amount of light falling on the subject.

The photoconductive cell is also used in automatic light switches. These switches automatically turn on when the natural daylight fades below a certain level. The same type of device is used to control furnaces. It reacts to changes in the brightness of the flame.

The Photoemissive Cell

In the photoemissive cell the electrons that are disturbed by light rays actually leave the surface of the light-sensitive material. The photoelectric cell, enclosed in a tube somewhat like a light bulb, is a phototube. The air in the tube is either pumped out, leaving a vacuum, or is replaced by an inert gas such as argon. The two-layered plate found in the other types of photoelectric cells is replaced in the phototube by two separate parts, a cathode and an anode, with a space between them. The cathode is made of light-sensitive material, usually cesium, lithium, sodium, or potassium. When light strikes the cathode, electrons jump from it to the anode, which is made of another metal. The phototube must be plugged into an external source of power in order to produce a useful current.

The phototube is used in television cameras, and in sound movie systems. The electric eye, which is a phototube, is used to automatically open doors, detect burglars, and measure air and water pollution.

The Discovery of Photoelectricity

In 1887 Heinrich Hertz discovered that ultraviolet light falling upon the metal terminals of a spark gap greatly reduces its resistance to the passage of the electrical discharge. In 1888 Wilhelm Hallwachs investigated this effect. He cleaned a zinc plate, and allowed ultraviolet light to fall upon it. Slowly the plate acquired a positive charge. Next Hallwachs charged the plate negatively and allowed light to fall upon it. Gradually it lost negative charge.

In 1889 Julius Elster and Hans Geitel discovered that metals such as sodium, potassium, rubidium, and cesium are very sensitive to visible light. In 1905 Albert Einstein showed that the number of electrons sent out of the metal depends on the strength of the light falling on the surface, but that the speed with which the electrons are ejected depends on the wave length of the light and the nature of the material.

PHOTOENGRAVING (*fō′tō ĕn grāv′ ing*) is engraving with the aid of light. It was invented by Joseph Niepce, of France, in about 1825. However, much credit for its development is given to Louis Daguerre, a famous French photographer.

Daguerre worked with Niepce and developed his own photoengraving process in 1839, six years after Niepce's death. His process provided the means of rapidly making reproductions of drawings and photographs in zinc and copper. It is this process that produces the many pictures used to make modern books, newspapers, and magazines more interesting and informative. Before engravings were perfected, illustrations in newspapers and books were crude engravings made by etching greasy designs on zinc plates. Woodcuts were also often used. Though they were beautiful and carefully done, they were costly and took a long time to make.

Photoengraving has changed all that. Today most newspapers in the United States have pictures on almost every page. A baseball player who hits a home run may be able to see his picture in the paper by the time the game is over.

The Line Engraving

Photoengraving is based on the discovery that certain chemicals, when exposed to light, will resist the actions of acids. Using these chemicals, a design is laid down on a metal plate and the plate exposed in a strong light. When acid is applied to the plate, the parts covered by the light-hardened chemicals are protected. The bare metal of the other parts is eaten away. This leaves on the plate a raised design which may be inked and printed.

The simplest form of photoengraving is made on a zinc plate from a line drawing. Examples of this are shown throughout these volumes. Briefly, the steps involved in making a line engraving are as follows:

The original drawing, known as the copy, is mounted in front of a special camera. A photograph is taken at the exact size the finished engraving is to be. The film is then taken from the camera and the negative film is developed.

The negative is a sheet of acetate covered with an emulsion, on which the image is made. It is placed on a glass plate with other line negatives, to make up a flat of several negatives, and then dried. If the negative was not turned, the proof from the engraving would have to be held up to a mirror, in order to read the type, or writing, on the proof.

The flat of turned negatives is laid tightly against a sheet of polished zinc, which has been covered with a solution that is sensitive to light. A strong light prints the negative on the zinc. Wherever the light shines through the negative, the coating on the zinc becomes insoluble, and when the zinc plate is washed, the design of the copy is left on the surface. The zinc plate is heated in an oven to cure the design or image on the plate. The plate is then cleaned chemically and placed in an etch machine containing a solution of nitric acid and special oils that etches the plate to the proper printing depth.

The zinc plate is mounted on a block of metal just thick enough to make it as high as the lead type when set up in a page of type. A proof of the engraving is taken on a hand press. If it is satisfactory, the job is complete.

The Halftone

Halftone engraving is used for photographs, wash drawings, or any design that has in it a variety of tone values. It is similar in idea to the line engraving, but there are several important differences. In the first place, the copy is photographed through a screen. This results in the whole surface being broken up into tiny dots with white spaces between. The dots in the

PHOTOENGRAVING

The line engraving is used to reproduce line drawings and other types of copy that do not have tone values. The magnified portion of the line drawing below shows how the image has been reproduced with solid, ungraded lines.

The halftone is used to reproduce photographs and other copy with tone values. The copy is photographed through a screen, which breaks up the image into tiny dots. The size and density of the dots reproduce the different tones.

Courtesy The Art Institute of Chicago

Michael Sullivan for the O.E.O.

The printing of color by the four-color process requires four filters—one for each of the three primary colors and one for black. The original color picture is photographed four times, once with each filter.

A blue-violet filter allows only yellow values to show on one negative.

A green filter allows only red values to show on the next negative.

An orange filter allows only blue values to show on the third negative.

A yellow filter allows only black values to show on the fourth negative.

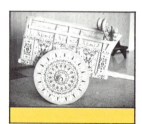

A printing plate is made from each of the four negatives. The yellow, red, blue, and black plates, in that order, print their images one over another.

yellow

yellow and red

yellow, red, and blue

yellow, red, blue, and black

Each color plate forms a halftone image because its printing surface is also made up of a dot structure. At the right is a magnified view of a four-color printed picture.

halftone illustrations on the pages of this volume may be easily examined by means of a magnifying glass. Each halftone screen that is used in the camera is formed from two pieces of clear, optically flat glass about one-eighth of an inch thick. Each of these sheets of glass is ruled with fine lines. These are cut into the surface by a machine fitted with a diamond tool, and the tiny grooves are filled in with an opaque substance to make the lines.

When the lines have been ruled upon the glass and filled in, the two sheets of glass are brought together so that the parallel lines on one cross the parallel lines of the other at right angles. The two pieces of glass are permanently bound together with transparent cement. The screens may be ruled from 55 to 400 lines to the inch, though screens of more than 150 lines are seldom used. Coarse screens (those with fewer lines) are used for printing on poorer quality paper. Halftones of 120-line screen and 133-line are widely used where good reproduction is desired.

The halftone negative, like the line negative, goes through a process of developing, turning, and printing on metal. In this case a copper plate is used instead of zinc, and iron perchloride is used for etching. The etching process is much more delicate because the tiny dots of the design are so fine they may easily be destroyed. Handwork is done on the plate to etch highlight areas more deeply, to bring out tone values, and to correct any little defects. Looked at through a magnifying glass, the finished copper halftone engraving shows raised dots in the light areas. On the dark areas it shows wells, or depressions, of various sizes where the metal has been etched to give the different tonal values.

In printing, the ink touches only the raised areas of the halftone. In this way the image with all its tonal variations is transferred to the paper.

Color engravings are made like halftones. A separate plate must be made for each color, usually yellow, red, blue, and black. The first separation of colors is made in the negatives, using filters in the camera. A violet filter cuts out red and blue and leaves yellow. A green filter cuts out yellow and blue and leaves red.

An orange filter cuts out yellow and red and leaves blue. This separation of color values in the negatives and their transfer to the copper plates is not exact. The most skillful workmanship is required by the etchers who re-etch the plates by hand. They not only must determine the tones in the different parts of each plate, but must know how the picture will look when colors are printed one over the other. Sometimes an electronic color scanner is used in color reproduction. The machine scans the original copy with a small beam of light. The light signals, separated into primary colors through filters, are changed into electrical energy by photo-multipliers. The electrical energy is then modified by a computer system to suit the requirements of the printing process and is used to create photographic negatives.

The Ben Day Process

A method for applying tones and shading to zinc engravings is the ben day process, named for its inventor, Benjamin Day. To add ben day, the artist indicates the ben day screens to be applied to his drawing. He selects patterns that are already engraved on celluloid sheets. The process of line etching is interrupted after the picture has been printed on the zinc plate. The plate at this point is taken to the ben day operator, who selects the desired screen. The zinc is first blocked off with a preparation of gum arabic except where the new tone is desired, and the ben day is inked on. The plate is washed and then continues in the processing already described. The use of the ben day process has decreased considerably in modern photoengraving shops.

Photoengraving is most often connected with letterpress, or relief, printing. However, the basic idea, using light-hardened chemicals to resist the action of acids, is used in other basic printing methods. These are lithography, or offset printing, and intaglio, or gravure process. (See LITHOGRAPHY; PRINTING.)

PHOTOGRAPHY (*fŭ tăg′ rŭ fē*) is making pictures by means of light. The word photography comes from the Greek and means "writing with light." It affects man's life in so many ways that photography must be regarded as one of the most significant of all scientific achievements.

The number of photographs taken each year in the United States totals nearly four billion. More than half of these are color photos. Motion picture cameras are owned by more than seven million amateur photographers. More than 90 percent of their pictures are taken in color. (See MOTION PICTURES.)

Uses of Photography

Photography makes possible one of the most important leisure activities of today—the cinema, or motion picture, shown in theaters and through home television sets. It is of primary importance in the transmission of news and educational material by way of television, newspapers, magazines, and books. Photography has also achieved importance as an art form. Many amateur and professional photographers take still and motion pictures primarily for their artistic value.

Photography plays an important role in science, industry, medicine, and research. Many processes and products that we depend upon would be impossible without it.

Pictures have been made from spacecraft of the other side of the moon, of the moon's surface in close-up detail, of Mars, and of Venus' cloud cover. Color photographs have been made of the Earth, showing its spherical shape, and of the Earth as seen from the moon. Special photographic plates record the light from stars the eye cannot see. Drawings of complex electronic circuits are reduced photographically to pictures no larger than the head of a pin, the lines of the drawing being reproduced in metal. These pictures become the tiny circuits used in computers and transistorized radio receivers and transmitters.

Photography is used in criminology, not only to make identification pictures, but to detect arson and identify hit-and-run drivers, and in bullet comparison photos and blood analyses. High-speed films that can be used in very dim light are used to photograph suspected criminals. Special film has been developed for use in the detection of forgeries.

In scientific research, photography is used to record what the electronic microscope sees, to analyze metals and gases, and to trace the course of electrons and cosmic rays. Infrared photographs are made from aircraft to detect disease in orchards and woodlots and to trace sources of air pollution. Similar films are used in war to detect camouflage.

In industry, photography is used for quality control, in the analysis of motions too fast for the eye to see, in testing, and in production processes. Motion pictures taken at high speed are projected at slower speeds to study the action of machinery in motion that otherwise would be a blur to the eye. Welds are inspected by X-ray photography. In business, photo processes are used to copy documents. With the use of microfilm, as many as ten thousand letters can be stored on a few rolls of film that can be held in one hand.

The labels on cans and packages are reproduced by means of photography. The pictures in magazines and newspapers are not only made by photography, but in many cases the photographic process is a step in their reproduction. (See PHOTOENGRAVING.)

In medicine, X-ray photography has become a necessity in diagnosis of body ailments and in the setting of bones. Infrared photography is also being developed as a diagnostic tool.

History of Photography

Photography was not invented by any single person. It was the result of many discoveries during hundreds of years. The principle of the camera was discovered long before a method of recording what the camera saw was found.

The camera obscura, the forerunner of the photographic camera, was developed during the period from the 11th to the 16th century. Its purpose was to show on paper an image that could be traced by hand to give accurate drawings of natural scenes. In 1558 Giovanni Battista della Porta illustrated camera principles in his book *Natural Magic*. In 1568 Daniello Barbaro fitted the camera obscura with a lens and a changeable opening to sharpen the image.

Johann Heinrich Schulze discovered in 1725 that the change in color of a mixture of silver nitrate and chalk, in sunlight, was caused by light, not heat. In 1802 Thomas Wedgwood and Sir

Humphry Davy recorded by contact printing, on paper coated with silver nitrate or silver chloride, silhouettes and images of paintings made upon glass. They could not make these prints permanent, however. Joseph N. Niepce made a crude photographic camera in 1816 from a jewel box and a simple lens. With it he made a negative image. In 1835 William Henry Fox Talbot discovered a method of rendering the camera obscura image permanent. The image was fixed on silver chloride paper by means of sodium chloride. Talbot was the first to make positives from negatives, the first to make enlargements by photography, and the first to publish (in 1844) a book illustrated with photographs.

In about 1837 the daguerreotype process was invented by Louis J. M. Daguerre. The image was recorded on a silver plate made light-sensitive with iodine. The plate was then developed in mercury vapor. In 1839 Sir John Herschel used sodium thiosulfate, or hypo, to make pictures permanent. William Talbot patented the calotype process in 1841. Frederick Scott Archer invented in 1851 the wet collodion process for making negatives. In 1861 James Clerk Maxwell reproduced a colored ribbon by the three-color additive process.

Louis Ducos du Hauron and Charles Cros independently, in 1869, published pieces on the various methods used in three-color photography. In 1871 Richard L. Maddox prepared the first gelatino-bro-mide emulsion. Eadweard Muybridge first made serial photographs of moving animals and people in 1872. He later projected them, showing motion. Hermann W. Vogel discovered in 1873 that by adding certain dyes to the emulsion, plates could be made sensitive to all colors. Early photographic materials were sensitive only to blue light.

In 1880 George Eastman began his dry plate business in Rochester, New York. The Kodak system was started in 1888 by the Eastman Dry Plate and Film Company, and a box camera was placed on the market. The camera was sold already loaded with enough film for 100 exposures. After exposure, both camera and film were returned to Rochester, where the film was removed and processed and the camera then

The camera obscura, used mostly by artists, resembled a portable room. The artist entered through a trapdoor, F, and traced over an image cast on paper by a lens in the wall. The engraving above, made in 1671, shows the inside with the top and one wall removed. The earliest known photograph was taken in 1826 by Joseph N. Niepce. Made on pewter, it shows a view from a window.

The calotype, patented by W. H. Fox Talbot in 1841, was the first photographic process in which the negative, or reverse image, was used to make a positive image. The still life of a breakfast table, above left, is a calotype taken by Talbot. The portrait of a man, above right, taken in 1849 by William and Frederick Langenheim, shows the right half of a calotype print, or positive, joined to the left half of the negative of the same photo.

reloaded and returned to the customer.

In 1889 Thomas Edison made the first motion pictures on 35-millimeter film with the transparent, flexible roll film made by the Eastman Company. In 1924 the Leica 35-millimeter camera was marketed in Germany, initiating widespread interest in candid, or unposed, photography. In 1931 the electronic flashbulb was patented in the United States. The Polaroid Land camera was introduced by Edwin H. Land in 1947. It developed and printed black-and-white pictures in 60 seconds. In the same year the David White Company marketed the first stereo camera. In 1963 Land introduced the Polaroid color camera, which developed and printed color photographs in 50 seconds.

How Film Is Made

The first series of steps in the making of photographic film is the fabrication of a flexible plastic base. This is made by treating cotton fibers or wood pulp with acetic acid. A white flaky product called cellulose acetate is formed. The cellulose acetate is then dissolved in special solvents, and a clear, thick fluid known as dope is produced.

The dope is fed evenly onto large, wide, drums. As the drums turn, heat drives off the solvent, and the dope becomes a thin, flexible, transparent sheet.

All sensitized photographic products (films and papers that are sensitive to light) are made possible by the fact that silver reacts to light by turning black. All photographic films and papers are coated with emulsions containing silver bromide.

To obtain silver nitrate, photographic manufacturers buy silver bars, or ingots. These ingots weigh 75 pounds each and are 99.97 percent pure silver. The silver is placed in nitric acid and silver nitrate crystals are formed. The silver nitrate is then mixed with gelatin and potassium bromide. The nitrate and potassium combine as potassium nitrate, which is washed away. The silver bromide crystals are left suspended in the gelatin. Because the silver crystals are sensitive to light, the coating operation must be performed under conditions of almost total darkness.

By changing the emulsion-making methods somewhat, and by adding small amounts of other chemicals, photographic manufacturers make emulsions for more than 200 kinds of film. Next, the film base is coated with the gelatin. The dry film is cut into selected widths and wound onto spools. Once packaged, the film

The first photograph made on glass was taken by Sir John Herschel in 1839. The glass was coated with silver carbonate. The scene shows an observatory.

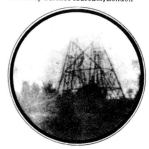

Courtesy George Eastman House Collection

The stereoscopic slide, or stereograph, is made up of two photographs taken at slightly different angles. When viewed through a stereoscope it appears as a three-dimensional image. "Pensive Man," above, was made in 1855.

is ready for use. Film can be made in sheets as well as in rolls. It can also be made in long, perforated strips for miniature and motion picture cameras. For some purposes and where extreme accuracy of size is required—as in photographic plates for astronomy—the emulsion is coated on glass plates.

Photographic papers used for printing a picture are manufactured in a manner similar to that used for films, except that the emulsion is coated on a paper. Baryta, a mixture of barium sulfate and gelatin, is put on the paper before the emulsion. This fills in the pores and provides a foundation for the emulsion.

Viewing stereographic slides became a popular amusement in the 1850's. Inexpensive stereoscopes were produced and used for viewing slides showing travel scenes and current events. The stereoscope exists today in somewhat modified form.

in such a way that no light can enter. Its only opening is filled by a lens or group of lenses that focus whatever the camera sees upon the film inside the box. The lens of the camera performs the same function as the lens of the eye. The lens opening, similar to the iris of the eye, controls the amount of light that reaches the film. (See LENS.)

The camera shutter might be compared to the eyelid. When the shutter release is pressed, the shutter blinks open momentarily. This determines the length of time that light is allowed to reach the film. Simple cameras have a shutter speed that is usually around $\frac{1}{90}$ of a second.

On the outside of the box is a film advancer knob or lever that is used to turn the film ahead for each exposure. A viewfinder on the camera shows the scene on which the camera is focused.

Cameras are often supplied with accessory equipment that aids the photographer in a variety of ways. A built-in photoelectric exposure control automatically adjusts the lens to the correct opening; zoom lenses provide close-up, wide-

How a Camera Works

When a picture is taken by any camera it is necessary that an image of the subject be focused on the light-sensitive material and that the light-sensitive material, the film, be shielded against all other light.

The camera may be thought of as a box sealed

DEVELOPING FILM NEGATIVES

In darkness the reel is loaded with film and placed in the tank. The tank is then covered.

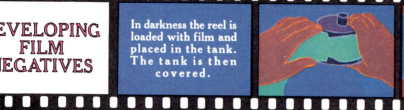

Developer is poured into the tank. The tank is rocked at intervals. The developer is then poured out.

Stop bath is poured into the tank. The tank is rocked and the stop bath poured out. These steps are then repeated with hypo.

The film is washed, dried with a soft chamois, and hung in the air to dry.

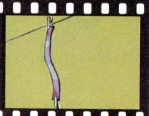

DEVELOPING CONTACT PRINTS

The negative is laid on contact paper, covered with glass, and briefly exposed to bright light.

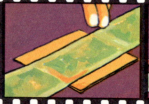

The contact print is placed successively in developer, stop bath, and fixing bath.

The prints are dried between layers of blotting paper.

angle, or telephoto effects; and battery-powered motors advance the film in still cameras as well as in motion picture cameras. (See CAMERA.)

Taking the Photograph

In taking a photograph, several simple steps are followed. First of all, a roll of film is loaded into the camera. When the shutter is briefly opened, the lens allows light to enter. At the instant the picture is taken, the light coming from the subject passes through the lens and strikes the film. Tiny silver bromide grains inside the film emulsion are thus exposed, or tagged. This is a photoelectric action, forming what is called a latent image. The change is impossible to see. Only after processing in the developer solution does the latent image become visible. The developer changes the exposed grains of silver bromide to metallic silver. The grains that have not been exposed remain unchanged and are removed in the processing. The resulting silver in the emulsion becomes the dark part of the film negative, from which positives, or prints, are made.

After the entire roll of pictures has been exposed the roll is ready for processing. From 12 to 36 exposures, or individual snapshots, are commonly made from one roll of film. The processing of film and the making of prints can be done in the home. Many amateurs enjoy darkroom work as a hobby. Several of the steps can be done in ordinary room light. Others, however, must be done either in darkness or by the light of a safelight—usually yellow green—to which photographic paper is least sensitive.

The Polaroid Land camera develops and prints within itself finished black-and-white or color photographs. The light-sensitive film lies face-to-face with the print paper in the camera. After the picture is taken, the film is advanced through rollers. Pods containing developer and fixer solutions break open, and in less than one minute a complete image has been transferred to the print paper. The sheets are taken from the camera, peeled apart, and the finished photo is removed.

Developing the Film

The developing room, or darkroom, should have a sink or a tank with running water for mixing solutions. The equipment required for developing films in a tray rather than in a tank is inexpensive, but less efficient. Some daylight load, or dayload, tanks do not require the use of a darkroom. With such tanks the film can be processed completely in ordinary room light. Other daylight tanks, not having the dayload feature, must be loaded in total darkness. After loading, the processing is completed in daylight.

The following procedure applies to film developing in a tank. The three essential solutions —the developer, the stop bath, and the fixing bath —should be prepared beforehand. A thermometer should be used to check all solution temperatures. Their temperatures should agree within five degrees. Each solution is prepared by following the manufacturers' instructions on the packages. Usually it is necessary only to dissolve a powder in water.

1. The film is loaded into the developing tank. Before loading, the film should be carefully removed (handled only by its edges) from its cartridge. It is inserted into the reel of the developing tank, and the tank cover is closed.

2. The developer is poured into the tank. The pouring holes are so arranged that light does not enter. The developer should be used at the temperature recommended on the package. If it is too warm, its action will be speeded up, and overdevelopment of the image as well as softening of the emulsion may result. Cold developers act slowly and produce weak, underdeveloped negatives. The tank should be rocked gently for 5 seconds out of every 30. After the film has been developed for the time recommended in the instructions, the developer is poured out.

3. The stop bath is poured into the tank. This solution stops film development. It also prevents excess developer from being carried over into the fixing bath. This solution, too, should be agitated occasionally. The length of time for the stop bath is given on the package. It is then poured out.

4. The fixing bath (hypo) is added. This solution should be briefly agitated as soon as it has been poured in, and again at two-minute intervals. In the hypo, the unexposed silver bromide grains on the film are removed, leaving the black silver in the gelatin emulsion. The silver forms

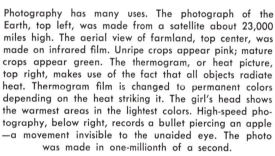

Photography has many uses. The photograph of the Earth, top left, was made from a satellite about 23,000 miles high. The aerial view of farmland, top center, was made on infrared film. Unripe crops appear pink; mature crops appear green. The thermogram, or heat picture, top right, makes use of the fact that all objects radiate heat. Thermogram film is changed to permanent colors depending on the heat striking it. The girl's head shows the warmest areas in the lightest colors. High-speed photography, below right, records a bullet piercing an apple —a movement invisible to the unaided eye. The photo was made in one-millionth of a second.

Courtesy (top left) NASA, (top center) Mark Systems, Inc., (top right) AGA, (bottom right) E G & G, Inc.

a reversed, or negative, picture. Wherever the original scene was light, there is now a grain of black silver. The film should usually remain in the hypo for about ten minutes. The hypo is then poured out.

5. The film is washed in running tap water at 65 to 70 degrees Fahrenheit. The water should run fast enough to refill the film tank every five or six minutes, but not fast enough to whip the film and cause scratches. If running water is not available, the film can be removed from the tank and soaked in a large, clean container for five minutes at a time in each of six changes of water.

6. The film is hung up to dry. Water droplets are removed by wiping the film gently with a damp chamois. The lower end of the film should be weighted to prevent the strip from curling or swinging about.

Making Contact Prints

After the developing, contact prints, commonly called prints, can be made. The image that appears on the print is the reverse of that on the developed film, or negative. Where the negative shows black the print shows white. To make prints a sheet of photographic paper is placed in contact with the negative and exposed to white light through the negative. The paper is then developed, put in a stop bath, fixed, washed in trays, and dried in much the same manner as that already described for negatives. Contact prints can be made with an inexpensive printing frame and a desk lamp. A printing box or some other type of contact printer simplifies the process. For normal negatives, the print should be exposed for about nine seconds to a 40-watt lamp at a distance of eight inches. Working under the dim light of a safelight, three solutions are used

Photographer Margaret Bourke-White provides a striking example of photojournalism with her documentary photograph taken during the disastrous Louisville flood in the depression year 1937. The hardship of the poor people lined up to receive food is contrasted sharply against the happy, prosperous family pictured on the billboard.

to process the print: the developer, the stop bath, and the fixing bath.

After the print has been exposed, it should be placed in the developer and the tray rocked gently. If correctly exposed, it should develop to the proper appearance in about one minute. If it becomes too dark in less than 45 seconds, another exposure must be made in about half the original time. If the print is too light, even after two minutes' development, the exposure should be at least doubled.

After development, the print is taken from the developer, rinsed in the stop bath for approximately 15 seconds, and placed in the fixing bath. Prints should be fixed for five to ten minutes and occasionally separated. After the fixing, prints should wash for at least one hour in running water at 65 to 70 degrees Fahrenheit. The most convenient way to dry small prints is with a blotter roll, in which the emulsion, or picture, side is placed toward a clean, lintless, linen surface.

Making Enlargements

Enlarging is the process of making big pictures from small negatives. The light from the lamphouse at the top of the enlarger is projected through the negative and through a lens down to a piece of enlarging paper, which is held flat on the baseboard by an enlarging easel. The distance from the lens to the paper determines how much the original image is enlarged. The lamphouse and the lens can be moved up and down until the desired size of enlargement is obtained.

After the enlarger is set and focused, the paper is exposed and developed in much the same manner as for a contact print.

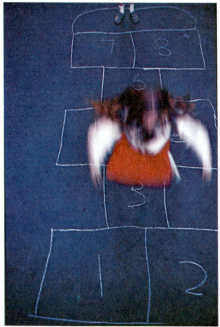

Top left, "Autumn on the Seine" by Alex J. Kovaleff, courtesy "Popular Photography"; top right, "Hopscotch" by Art Kane; center, "Rolling Ball" by Pete Turner; bottom left, "Ellen, 1965" by Marie Cosindas; bottom right, "trees & vase" by Scott Hyde.

The art photographer, like the painter, is concerned with colors, shapes, textures, and overall composition. Also like the painter, the photographer need not limit himself to the reproduction of reality. Instead, he may choose to interpret or to distort his subjects or even to convert them into abstract designs. In addition to the basic tools of camera and film, he uses varied techniques of exposure, developing, and printing. The result, as illustrated in this gallery of photographs, may be an original and distinctive work of art.

Enlarging allows for artistic judgment, since unwanted areas of a picture may be left out and only selected parts enlarged. Control can also be maintained in the darkening or fading of selected areas. To lighten an area, it is shaded from the projected image during part of the normal exposure given the rest of the print. To darken an area, it should be exposed for a longer time by shading the rest of the paper after the rest of the picture area has had the normal exposure. If this is done, the shading object should be kept in constant motion so that its own image will not be reproduced on the desired enlargement of the picture.

Color Photography

Since the beginning of photography, inventors have tried to make photographs in natural colors. Color photography had its beginning in 1861 when James Clerk Maxwell, an Englishman, demonstrated that all colors could be matched by mixing in various proportions the light of three primary colors—a pure red, a pure green, and a blue-violet. It was not until the introduction of Kodachrome film in 1935, however, that color photography became easily available to amateurs. (See COLOR.)

Modern color films have three layers of emulsion, each corresponding to one of the primary colors. In some color films, dyes replace the silver during the processing. These films must be handled in a special laboratory. In other films the dyes are incorporated in the film and are brought out during the processing. These films can be processed by the skillful amateur in his home laboratory.

Processing of color transparency film at home —a 65-minute procedure—requires less equipment than for black-and-white film. A color transparency is a direct photographic impression, like a negative, rather than a print. Usually the image on a transparency is viewed on a projection screen, like movie film.

Eight solutions as well as a thermometer are needed for the processing of transparencies. A stopwatch for timing some of the steps is also helpful. The film is loaded into a dayload tank in the same way as for black-and-white film. A first developer solution is poured into the tank and the tank is agitated for ten minutes. The developer is poured off, and the film, still in the tank, is rinsed for one minute in running water or in two changes of still water. A hardening solution is then poured into the tank and left for three minutes.

The solutions in these first steps must not vary more than $\frac{1}{2}$ degree from one another. The rest of the developing process can be done with the tank cover removed.

The remaining steps include color developing, clearing, bleaching, fixing, stabilizing, and drying. A water rinse is required between each step. For some color film reversal exposure is required, in which the film is exposed to bright light for 15 seconds.

Color negative films are also available. From these, color prints, snapshots, enlargements, and transparencies, as well as black-and-white prints may be made. Processing of the color negative film is similar to that of the color transparency film, but the making of color prints is a more complicated process, requiring a number of filters and skillful handling.

PHYSICS (*fiz'iks*) is the study of matter and energy and the interactions of the two. Everything is made of matter—in one of its three forms, or states: gas, liquid, and solid. All matter is made up of the chemical elements. (See ELEMENT; GAS; LIQUID; MATTER; PERIODIC TABLE OF THE ELEMENTS; SOLID.)

Energy, on the other hand, is what gets things done. In the sense of physics, energy is the ability to do work. There are many forms of energy: mechanical, electrical, magnetic, heat, sound, light, and nuclear. (See ATOMIC ENERGY; ELECTRICITY; ENERGY; FORCE AND MOTION; HEAT; LIGHT; MACHINE; MAGNET AND ELECTROMAGNET; SOUND.)

In early times, the men who studied physics, as well as those who studied chemistry, were known as natural, or physical, philosophers. Physics was then, as it is now, the study of nature. Early physics was not based on experiment. It was, instead, based on guesses of why things happened. Sometimes the guesses were surprisingly correct. Democritus and Leucippus, Greek philosophers of the 5th century B.C., for example, believed that matter was composed of atoms. It was not until the 19th century, however, that the atomic theory was proved to be correct.

Physics is theory and experiment. Experiments prove or disprove theories. Theories, on the other hand, form the basis for experiments. In the 19th century, physicists thought that light traveled through some "thing" called the "ether." In the early 20th century, the German physicist Albert Einstein, who later became a citizen of the United States, proved that the "ether" was just time and space. Before the present-day idea of the atom's structure, many other theories of atomic structure existed. One by one, however, experiments proved that they were not correct. Only the atom pictured by Danish physicist Niels Bohr proved to be correct. (See BOHR, NIELS; EINSTEIN, ALBERT.)

The development of mathematics allowed more and more complex theories to be set forth. Sometimes a new theory created a need for a new method of mathematics. Other times a previously unused method of mathematics became useful in a particular theory. (See MATHEMATICS.)

The development of experiments was closely related to the methods and tools of measurement. In the early days of physics, measurement units were not uniform. Eventually units were standardized. Physicists, for example, in the United States and France could measure the same thing and then compare their findings. (See MEASUREMENT; WEIGHTS AND MEASURES.)

The tools of measurement, or the instruments with which measurements are made, often were improved over several hundreds of years. The telescope used by Galileo in 1610 is quite simple when compared to the 200-inch telescope used in 1948. Other instruments, such as the mass spectrometer, which is used to identify matter by its electrical charge and weight, were unknown until the 20th century. The microscope, of course, permitted physicists to see tiny things, about which there were many theories. Later, the electron microscope allowed examination of even smaller things. Electronic instruments, of which Democritus and Leucippus knew nothing, are commonplace today. (See ATOMS, *Atomic Nuclei;* ELECTRONICS; GALILEO; MICROSCOPE; TELESCOPE.)

Many other sciences apply the principles of physics. Geophysics, for example, combines physics with geology. Biophysics combines the study of physics with biology. Engineering is applied physics.

Physics and chemistry are closely related. Sometimes it is difficult to draw a line between them. Both chemistry and physics deal with matter, but physics considers physical changes, and chemistry considers chemical changes. More often than not, the changes that occur in matter are both physical and chemical.

The burning of carbon to form carbon dioxide, for example, is a chemical change, but the heat energy produced when the change takes place is of interest to both chemists and physicists. (See CHEMISTRY.)

As in the growth of any science, there is an effort to reach general principles, or laws, that apply in all situations. Sir Isaac Newton, for example, discovered many of the laws of motion, although his work is based on the earlier work of Galileo. These laws stated for the first time the conditions that apply to all cases of motion. A physical law does not tell what men think must happen, but describes what does happen in nature. (See NEWTON, SIR ISAAC.)

The law of conservation of energy was discovered in the middle of the 19th century by German and English physicists. That law states that energy cannot be created or destroyed, but it can be transformed or changed from one form to another or passed from one object to another. Today, it is known that energy can be transformed into mass, and that mass can be transformed into energy. The present-day conservation law states that the sum of mass and energy must always remain the same. The law is now often called the law of conservation of mass-energy.

The continually developing kinetic theory of gases has done much for man's understanding of matter and many of the ways it works. It explains, for example, how gases exert pressure on the walls of vessels that contain them.

The fields of physics that were studied up to just before the 20th century are called classical physics. These included heat, light, sound, electricity, magnetism, and mechanics (mechanical energy and forces).

Modern physics may be said to have been the result of five events, all of which took place between 1895 and 1905. Two of these were theories, and three were laboratory discoveries. German physicist Max Planck (1858–1947) developed the quantum theory, and Albert Einstein, while living in Switzerland, developed the theory of relativity. The electron, one of the smallest particles of matter, was isolated by the English physicist Joseph John Thomson (1856–1940). X-rays were identified by German physicist Wilhelm Roentgen. Radioactivity was discovered by French chemist Henri Becquerel (1852–1908). (See ROENTGEN, WILHELM CONRAD.)

Although the five scientists involved were West Europeans, modern physics is the work of men and women from all over. Nobel Prizes in physics have been awarded to people of the Near East, the Orient, and the Americas.

Recent years in physics have been marked by several important branches of discovery. Cosmic rays, which come from outer space, have been found to show energies enormously greater than men had previously expected. The attack upon the atomic nucleus by atom smashers has been successful and has opened a whole new field of physics, chemistry, and medicine. Man has increased his knowledge of the structure of the atom and radioactivity. The discovery by French physicist Louis de Broglie (1892–) that all particles may also have the properties of waves has led to a new and growing field of wave mechanics. There has also been rapid growth in the fields of applied physics in communications. (See ELECTRON; RADAR; RADIATION; RADIO; TELEPHONE; TELEVISION.)

PHYSIOLOGY (fiz ē äl'ŭ jē) is a branch of biology that deals with the workings of all parts of the body. This science includes all that has been learned about cells, organs, systems, and the body as a whole.

To understand what takes place in any living body requires the knowledge of three other sciences. First, *anatomy* explains how the body is made. Second, *biochemistry* explains the chemical changes that take place in the body. Third, *physics* explains the movements of liquids, solids, or gases, the electrical currents, the exchanges of energy, and the many other mechanical actions of the body. Thus, physiology uses what is known of anatomy, adds facts of chemical and mechanical actions within the body, and presents the total picture of the behavior, or function, of the parts of the body.

An anatomist dissecting a dead animal cannot study the physiologic actions of the organs. As he looks at thin slices of the tissues through a microscope he sees only the tiny structures. He cannot tell what they did when the animal was alive except by guessing. He is studying the body with its action stopped at a certain stage. This is like stopping a moving picture to study the still picture that is there at the moment. From this one picture, it is possible to be fairly certain of what some of the actions were. The position of a man's body may show that he was running in the moving picture. The wet ground may show it was raining. However, from the one picture it is not possible to follow all of the actions.

The physiologist, on the other hand, studies the living body. He may carry out experiments on the body as a whole, such as measuring the amount of heat it gives off. He may measure some activity of an organ, or group of organs (called a system). For example, physiologists measure the time it takes for food to pass through the stomach.

Another way to study the body in action is to remove parts of organs and keep the tissue alive long enough for studies to be made. A strip of muscle kept in a liquid like the body fluids will continue to contract and the strength of the contraction can be measured.

The process of "tissue culture" allows the study of action of single cell types. Tissue culture is the growing of cells outside of the body in a natural surrounding substance. It is used to study problems such as the passage of material through the cell membrane or the growth and reproduction of the cells.

All parts of a healthy body perform in harmony with other parts. It is possible, however, to separate groups of organs which work together more closely. These groups are the systems. Two of the body's systems are the heart and blood vessels and the kidneys, ureters, bladder, and urethra. Organs are parts of a system if their physiologic actions are related. They need not be located close to each other. (See BODY.) For example, the hormones are given off by the endocrine system of glands. But, except for the thyroid and parathyroid glands, the endocrine organs lie far apart in the body. They are called a system because they are alike in what they do. They all secrete directly into the blood, and they do not have ducts leading away from the glands.

Each system has its own activities for its special functions or work. The functions of the respiratory system have to do with breathing and the exchange of gases in the whole body. Breathing is concerned with air entering into the lungs by movements of chest muscles and diaphragm. (See BREATHING.) Gases from the air enter the tiny capillaries where the oxygen becomes bound to part of the red blood cells. The oxygen-rich blood reaches other parts of the body by the working of the circulatory system. (See CIRCULATORY SYSTEM.) However, the lungs and the heart-blood vessel system have many problems in common.

The action of the heart cannot be understood without an understanding of muscle action. Heart muscle can be grown in tissue culture and its contractions watched as chemicals are added to its surroundings. But more often the heart's action is studied in the living animal or man. One instrument that does this is the electrocardiograph which traces the rhythms of the beating heart in a graphlike form on paper. These recordings (called electrocardiograms) show how the heart is working; certain differences in rhythms indicate certain defects in the heart. Other physiology studies are the action of the heart valves and the output of blood by contraction of the heart.

By observing the stomach and intestines, physiologists can measure the motion of the walls and the secretions from the lining cells. The problems of digesting foods and absorbing the digested materials into the blood and lymph are important subjects.

In the urinary tract there is need to know how fluids and salts filter from the blood in the kidneys to form urine. The flow of urine from the kidney to the bladder, its stay there and final discharge are also proper subjects for the physiologist.

In disease, one or more systems fail to work properly. A major part of the understanding of a disease is the knowledge of the changes in the physiologic action. Earlier, doctors could see certain changes and their descriptions pictured how the patient looked. They could also find by trial and error some treatments which helped. But the aim of modern medicine is to correct the physiologic action that is known to be at fault. The ability to do this has advanced rapidly in recent years. For example, hearts can now be opened and defects corrected because knowledge of heart and lung action has resulted in a mechanical "heart-lung pump." This machine can substitute for these vital organs during the operation.

Physiology, then, is an important part of medical science as well as a science in its own right. (See also articles on individual organs of the body.)

PIANO (*pĭ ăn′ō* or *pĭ ä′nō*), the name of a large stringed, musical instrument. It is not only the best-known instrument, but also the most popular with musicians. It is often played alone, but is also used to accompany a singer or another musical instrument, such as a violin.

The piano is a complicated instrument with five main parts: *keys, action, strings, plate,* and *sounding board*. A pianist strikes a key to start the action, which moves a hammer to hit a string. The strings are stretched across a heavy metal plate. When the strings vibrate, the sound waves are made fuller by the sounding board and a musical tone is produced. All of the parts fit into a case.

There are 88 wooden keys. The 52 white keys are covered with ivory. The 36 black keys are shorter than the white keys and are raised higher above the keyboard. Part of each key sticks out from the inside of the piano. A pianist need only press a key to make a musical

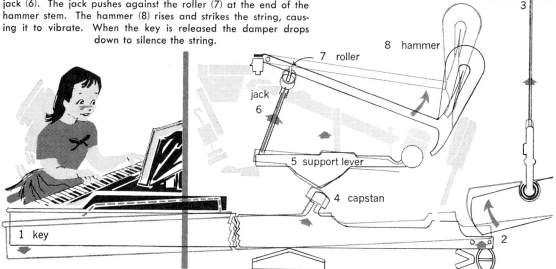

A PIANO KEY WORKS THROUGH A SERIES OF LEVERS
As the key (1) is pressed down, the other end (2) rises and lifts the damper (3) so the string is free to vibrate. At the same time the capstan (4) pushes up the support lever (5) which raises the jack (6). The jack pushes against the roller (7) at the end of the hammer stem. The hammer (8) rises and strikes the string, causing it to vibrate. When the key is released the damper drops down to silence the string.

string damper

3

8 hammer

7 roller

jack
6

5 support lever

4 capstan

1 key

2

tone. The real working of the key is hidden inside the case of the piano.

Each key acts as a lever to move a small hammer. This starts the *action* to make music. The hammer, covered with a piece of felt material, strikes a string. The strings are made of strong, steel wire. Those on the right side are short and thin for high notes. Those on the left are very long and thick for the low notes. The low-tone strings are wound with copper wire to make them heavy enough to produce the deepest tones. The middle tones are produced by two wires, and the highest tones by three wires.

For each string there is a separate key and hammer. Beneath the strings is a sounding board made of wood. It reinforces the sound so that music can be heard by a large audience. Without a sounding board the sounds would be very weak. The strings are stretched across a heavy iron plate. The plate or frame must be strong for the strings are pulled very tight. This is to make sure that a key will produce the same tone no matter how often it is struck.

A string can vibrate for a long time, with the sound becoming softer and softer. Usually a pianist does not want the sound to continue very long because he wants to strike a different

note. So a strip of felt material called a *damper* rests against each string. When a key is struck, the damper is moved away from the string and the string can vibrate. When the key is released, the damper moves back against the string and stops the vibration.

A piano has three pedals which are worked by the pianist's feet. The *sustaining* pedal holds the dampers away from the strings so that the sound continues. The *sostenuto* pedal acts the same way but only for the notes played just before the pedal is pressed down. The *soft* pedal causes the dampers to rest against part of each string so the tone is softened.

The whole piano is enclosed in a case made of wood. The wood must be seasoned or specially treated for at least three years. Then it is dried under special conditions. The two sides of the case are made of many thin strips of wood carefully bent to the proper shape and glued together. Strong pieces of wood are used for cross pieces to connect the sides. Then the sides are covered with thin, highly polished wood and the whole case is varnished.

The largest piano, a concert grand, is nine feet long. For a home a baby grand is often used. It is never more than five feet long, and there are some baby grands that are only three

Above left: The clavichord's sharp sounds are made when thin strips of brass, called tangents, are pressed against the strings. Above right: The harpsichord is larger than the clavichord and generally has two keyboards. The strings are plucked by quill or leather points when the keys are pushed down. Center right: The concert grand, the largest of all pianos, is usually almost nine feet long. Below right: The baby grand is usually between four and five feet in length. Below left: In the upright and spinet pianos, the strings are set in an up-and-down or upright position.

Courtesy (above left, right) Philip Manuel and Gavin Williamson, (center right, below left, right) Kimball Piano & Organ Company

feet long. The upright piano gets its name from the fact that the frame, sounding board, and strings are standing up. In a grand piano they are laid flat. Upright pianos are usually between three and four feet high. At one time they were more than five feet high. The smallest pianos, sometimes called spinets, may have fewer than the standard 88 keys.

Development of Pianos

Before the piano was invented there were many string instruments and some keyboard instruments. The clavichord became popular in the 15th century. The early clavichord looked like a box and was placed on a table to be played. Later, legs were added to the instrument. The clavichord has keys and strings as does a piano. The strings, struck by a metal wedge called a *tangent*, make a twanglike sound.

The harpsichord was developed in the 16th century. It looks very much like a modern grand piano but the strings are plucked by quills or pieces of leather.

The clavichord and harpsichord cannot be played loudly or softly, the sound is always the same. Because the strings are plucked, it is not possible to hold a note.

Bartolommeo Cristofori, an Italian, made the first piano about 1709. The use of hammers to strike the strings was a great improvement over earlier keyboard instruments. He named his instrument *gravecembali col piano e forte,* which means "harpsichord with loud and soft."

The piano grew in popularity as improvements were made. The upright piano was invented by John Hawkins in 1800 in Philadelphia, Pennsylvania.

In the 19th century the player piano was invented. Music for the player piano is recorded by punching holes in a roll of paper. The paper moves over a bar that also has holes. When two holes match, air can pass through both holes, moving the proper hammers to strike the strings. The air pressure is produced by pumping by either electricity or pedals. The player piano was used less after the radio was invented, but it has again become popular.

There have been many great composers of piano music. Ludwig van Beethoven was one

of the first. Robert Schumann, Frederic Chopin, and Franz Liszt are also well-known composers.

PICASSO (*pē kä'sō*), **PABLO** (*pä'vlō*) (1881–), is considered the greatest experimenter in art of his time. While his fame rests largely on his painting, he has also made important contributions in sculpture and pottery.

Picasso was born in Malaga, Spain. His father was an artist and teacher of painting. As a child, Pablo showed artistic talent. By the age of 16 he had tired of the formal education of the Barcelona and Madrid academies of art, so he set himself up as an independent artist in Barcelona.

At this time, Paris was the world center for new ideas in painting. So in 1900, at the age of 19, Picasso went to Paris. By then he had already begun to paint in the Impressionist style of using streaks of pure color. By 1903, after several trips between Spain and Paris, he

In his painting "Girl Before the Mirror" (1932), Pablo Picasso interpreted a female form in terms of a series of abstract shapes. Rather than imitate the realistic image of a person, he painted a pattern of lines and colors decorating a flat surface.

Courtesy The Museum of Modern Art, New York, Mrs. Simon Guggenheim Fund

Picasso's "Baboon and Young" (1951) reflects the artist's sense of humor.

was ready to exhibit paintings showing a style of his own. These paintings of beggars, clowns, and acrobats showed the influence of El Greco's elongated figures. But the feeling of sadness was heightened by the use of blue as the main color. Picasso's "Guitar Player" is a well-known work of this period.

This "blue" period soon gave way to a "rose" period, inspired by the drawing and color of the terra cotta vases of ancient Greece. This, in turn, gave way to a series of paintings based on the sculpture of the African Negroes, which had then become fashionable in Paris.

The painter Paul Cezanne had once said that all nature could be painted in terms of the cube, the cone, and the cylinder. This observation, and Picasso's own experiments in painting, were the origin of "Cubist" painting. Picasso's "Three Musicians" is a good example of Cubism.

Picasso experimented in many other directions—in Surrealism for a short period, in almost pure geometric patterns, in mural painting, and in sculpture. He also worked with bits of paper, pieces of wood, and scraps of cloth, a new form of art known as *collage*. Later he designed pottery plates and vases that were unique in the history of this ancient art.

PICCARD (*pē'kàr*), **AUGUSTE** (1884–1962) and **JEAN FELIX** (1884–1963), twin brothers and scientists, made record balloon flights to study the stratosphere (the upper atmosphere). Born in Basel, Switzerland, in January 1884, they were educated in the Swiss universities at Basel and at Zurich. In 1916 Jean came to the United States, and in 1931 he became a citizen. Auguste stayed in Europe.

As physicists, the Piccards were interested in the problems of man's environment. Their balloon flights were made in order to find out more about conditions in the stratosphere.

Auguste Piccard and Paul Kipfer went up to 51,961 feet over Augsburg, Germany, in May 1931. A little over a year later (August 1932), he and Max Cosyns went to 53,139 feet over Zurich, Switzerland. Starting from Dearborn, Michigan, in October 1934, Jean, with his wife Jeanette, went to 57,579 feet. They used balloons carrying lightweight, spherical gondolas enclosed and pressure-tight. (See BALLOON.)

In the late 1940's, Auguste turned to exploring below the surface of the sea. The ocean explorer, Charles William Beebe, had gone down to about 3,000 feet in his bathysphere. Auguste wanted to go much deeper.

The problem of designing a gondola for underwater exploration is almost the same as that for balloons. When aloft in balloons, scientists must be protected against very low outside pressures in air containing little oxygen. Down in the sea, the outside pressures are very high in very deep water, and there is no oxygen.

Auguste used his knowledge of gondola construction to design an undersea craft. He made his first experimental dives off Dakar, Africa, in 1948. The same year, with the help of Max Cosyns, Auguste designed and built a bathyscaphe (the "Trieste") for his undersea exploration. The bathyscaphe is a two-man submarine which can dive beneath the sea. In September of 1953, Auguste and his son Jacques reached a depth of 10,330 feet.

The United States Navy bought the "Trieste" in 1959, and in 1960 it went down in the Mariana Trench, in the Pacific, to a depth of 35,800 feet. Jacques Piccard took part in the dive. (See EXPLORATION, section on *Below the Ocean Surface*.)

PIERCE (*pĭrs*), **FRANKLIN** (1804–1869), was the 14th president of the United States. He was born November 23, 1804, at Hillsborough (now Hillsboro), New Hampshire. He was the son of General Benjamin Pierce and Anna Kendrick Pierce. General Pierce, an American Revolution hero, served 12 years in the New Hampshire legislature and was twice elected governor.

Pierce married Jane Means Appleton, daughter of a former college president. They had three sons. The first lived only three days; the second died at the age of four. The third was killed in a train wreck just after his father was elected president. These tragic deaths were a great sorrow to both Franklin and his wife. This was most true of Mrs. Pierce, whose health was very poor. She formed a strong dislike of politics and got little satisfaction from her husband's election as president.

Political Career

After Pierce graduated from Bowdoin College at Brunswick, Maine, he studied law and was admitted to the bar (1827). Pierce used his law training as a way of getting into politics. He was elected to his first public office, the New Hampshire legislature, and served from 1829 to 1833. During his last two years he was chosen Speaker of the House, a great honor for a young politician 29 years of age.

Pierce's next service was in the federal legislature. From 1833 to 1837 he was a member of the House of Representatives. Next he was chosen by the New Hampshire legislature as United States senator (1837). When he took his seat he was the youngest member of the Senate, only 32.

In 1842 Pierce resigned from the Senate and moved to Concord, New Hampshire, to practice law. When the war with Mexico started, he entered the service as a private (1847) and before a year had passed he became a brigadier general.

Pierce's next public service was as chairman of the New Hampshire constitutional convention of 1850. There his influence and hard work helped to keep out of the new constitution a provision barring Catholics from holding public office. This question had become more of a problem as the number of Irish immigrants settling in the New Hampshire towns increased. But Pierce's leadership in the fight to strike out this unfair provision was not solely for the political reasons of pleasing the Irish. He honestly believed that political discrimination on religious grounds was undemocratic and an insult to citizens of the Catholic faith.

At the Democratic National Convention of 1852, there were three leading candidates, Lewis Cass, Stephen A. Douglas, and James Buchanan. No one of them was able to get the two-thirds majority needed to be nominated. Pierce's name was entered on the 35th ballot and he was finally chosen on the 49th. William R. King of Alabama was chosen as the candidate for vice-president. The Whig party's candidates were General Winfield Scott, a Mexican War hero, and William A. Graham.

The Presidency

Pierce made a very quiet campaign, as was the custom then. Pierce won the election with 254 electoral votes to 42 for Scott. This defeat marked the end of the Whig party in national politics. (See WHIG PARTY.) When the next presidential election was held in 1856, the Democrats were opposed by the newly organized Republican party.

Vice-President King was in poor health when the time for his inauguration arrived. He had gone to Cuba for his health, and, by special act

Franklin Pierce, U.S. President, 1853–1857.

Leet Brothers Company, Inc.

of Congress, he took the oath of office in Cuba. King did not get well and returned to Alabama. Six weeks after the start of his term he died (April 18, 1853).

In his inaugural address, Pierce stated that his administration would not be afraid to have the United States add to its territory. Pierce

Underwood and Underwood

Jane Pierce.

wanted to annex (add) Cuba but did not succeed. On the disagreements between North and South over slavery, he hoped that the Compromise of 1850 would be a lasting solution. As events took place it was Pierce himself who helped reopen the quarrel by signing the Kansas-Nebraska Act of 1854.

Under President Pierce the United States made several important treaties. The first came after the visit to Japan in 1853 by Commodore Matthew C. Perry. Before that time, Japan refused to deal with most other countries. Perry presented to the Japanese a letter from President Pierce to the emperor asking for trade relations. This trip was followed by a second visit by Perry. On March 31, 1854, he signed a treaty of commerce and friendship between the United States and Japan.

The Gadsden Purchase treaty with Mexico was signed on December 30, 1853. It added to the United States a strip of land south of the Gila River to be used as a route for a railroad to the Pacific coast. The treaty also gave United States businessmen the right to build a railroad across the narrow part of Mexico known as the Isthmus of Tehuantepec. In return, the United States paid Mexico $10,000,000. (See GADSDEN PURCHASE.)

The year 1854 was an important year in the history of the United States. Violence and bloodshed started in the territory of Kansas. Abolitionists like John Brown fought against proslavery men from Missouri. (See BROWN, JOHN.) This "War in Kansas" lasted for over

four years. The issue was whether Kansas would come into the Union as a slave state or as a free state. The Kansas-Nebraska Act provided for two territories to be organized west of Missouri and Iowa. The settlers themselves were to decide whether slavery would be permitted. This plan was called "popular sovereignty" and was to be used in Utah and New Mexico territories by the Compromise of 1850. In the end Kansas was admitted as a free state in 1861. (See KANSAS-NEBRASKA ACT.)

People in the free states objected to the Kansas-Nebraska Act because it opened to slavery territory that had been closed to slavery by the Missouri Compromise of 1820. (See MISSOURI COMPROMISE.) Pierce's support of a slave state constitution for Kansas Territory was attacked by many northerners. Actually, Pierce was following what he thought was best for the whole country. Personally against slavery, he believed that saving the Union was more important than ending slavery in the United States.

The quarrel over the Kansas-Nebraska Act led to the organization of the Republican party. The new party welcomed all men who were against slavery in any new territory: antislavery Democrats, northern Whigs, and abolitionists who had been in the Liberty party. Their first state convention took place at Jackson, Michigan, on July 6, 1854. The new party frightened many friends in the Union because it was a sectional party. The Republicans had no organization and practically no members in the slave states of the South. (See REPUBLICAN PARTY.)

PIERCE'S LIFETIME

		Pierce's Term of Office (1853–1857)	
1803	Louisiana Purchase.		
1804	Pierce born.		
1824	Pierce graduates college.		
1827	Pierce becomes lawyer.		
1829	Pierce to legislature.	1853	Gadsden Purchase.
1830	1st passenger railroad.		Perry visits Japan.
1833	Pierce to Congress.	1854	Kansas-Nebraska Act.
	Nullification issue.		Republican Party
1837	Pierce to Senate.		formed.
1846	Mexican War.		Ostend Manifesto.
1850	Compromise of 1850.	1855	Sault Ste. Marie Canal.
			Panama railroad.
	PRESIDENT		1st kindergarten.
1857	Dred Scott decision.		Walker in Nicaragua.
1861	War Between the		Sumner beaten.
	States.	1856	Mississippi railroad
1869	Pierce dies.		bridge.

Pierce and many of his supporters wanted to add Cuba to the United States. In October 1854 the United States ministers to Great Britain, France, and Spain met at Ostend, Belgium, and drew up a statement known as the "Ostend Manifesto," recommending that the United States offer a very large sum to Spain for Cuba. If Spain refused this offer they said that the United States should then take Cuba by force. Pierce wanted Cuba, but he refused to use such methods.

Last Years

Pierce would have accepted a nomination for a second term as president, but the Democratic National Convention chose James Buchanan of Pennsylvania. Following the end of his term, Pierce returned to Concord, New Hampshire. With Mrs. Pierce he made a long trip to Europe. They returned to Concord in 1860, where they lived quietly.

During the U.S. Civil War, Pierce helped raise funds for the benefit of the Union army, even though he believed that the war was a mistake. Pierce died in his home on October 8, 1869.

Franklin Pierce was an honest and patriotic man. Eager to please, he did not know when to say "No." He liked to compromise and have agreement. He disliked slavery, but was also opposed to the abolitionists. He knew that the antislavery movement in the free states was causing so much trouble in the slave states that the Union was in danger. For that reason Pierce supported the Kansas-Nebraska Act to keep the South happy. But this angered enemies of slavery in the North. Every year brought war closer.

Pierce's United States

One of the most interesting events in United States history began while Pierce was in the White House. The settlement of Utah by the Mormons under the leadership of Brigham Young had started in 1847. (See YOUNG, BRIGHAM.) Many Mormons, however, did not have the money to buy horses and wagons for the 1,200-mile trip from the Missouri River to Salt Lake City. Brigham Young's plan was that two-wheeled carts, pushed by hand, would carry the supplies needed for the long overland trip. On July 20, 1856, the first handcart party left Florence, Nebraska, for Salt Lake City.

During Pierce's administration the Republican party grew quickly while southerners tried to prove that slavery was good. When Senator Charles Sumner of Massachusetts gave a speech attacking slavery and the South, he was beaten almost to death by a southern congressman. (See SUMNER, CHARLES.) Northern mobs several times freed slaves who had been arrested and were to be sent back to the South.

The nation was growing rapidly. Several important eastern railroads were completed and in 1855 a canal connecting Lake Huron and Lake Superior was opened at Sault Ste. Marie, Michigan. In later years this canal was to become the busiest in the world, with boats carrying iron ore from Minnesota to the steel-making centers on the Great Lakes. The first railroad bridge across the Mississippi River was opened in 1856. A railroad across the Isthmus of Panama cut the time of a journey from the eastern United States to the Pacific coast.

Immigration was increasing. More than 400,-000 people came to the United States in 1854. A new political party was formed, the American party, which opposed foreigners and Catholicism, the religion of most of the immigrants. It was called the Know-Nothing party because its members answered "I don't know" when asked what their party favored. The American party quickly lost its strength.

In 1855 the first kindergarten was opened in Watertown, Wisconsin. In the same year, a United States adventurer named William Walker set himself up as dictator of Nicaragua. The outstanding books of the period included Henry Thoreau's *Walden* and Walt Whitman's book of poetry, *Leaves of Grass*.

PIERRE (*pĭr*), **SOUTH DAKOTA,** the capital, is on the east bank of the Missouri River, almost in the exact center of the state. Pierre is between the eastern farming region of South Dakota and the ranch area lying west of the Missouri River. North of the city is the great Oahe Dam, which provides irrigation water, power, and flood control for the Missouri River Valley. Pierre is an important shipping and wholesale center. It has railroad shops, granite works, and other manufacturing industries. During World War II a United States Air Force Base was built east of the city.

In the early days, a fur-trading post, named Fort Pierre Chouteau, stood on the west side of the river. Its name was shortened to Fort Pierre, and then to Pierre. The little settlement grew up on the east side of the river, where a ferry crossed. During the Black Hills Gold Rush, Pierre was a stopping place for travelers before they began the long trip over the Deadwood Trail to the Black Hills. In 1889 Pierre became the capital of South Dakota.

Pierre has a commission form of government. Population (1950) 5,715, (1960) 10,088.

PIGEON (*pĭj'ŭn*) **AND DOVE** (*dŭv*). There are 289 different kinds of pigeons and doves. Ex-

cept for the polar regions and the colder parts of the temperate regions, every land has some kinds of pigeons and doves. There is no difference in meaning between the words pigeon and dove, but dove usually refers to the smaller pigeons. Both pigeons and doves are members of the family Columbidae. The smallest member of the family is about six inches long. The largest, the greater crowned pigeon of New Guinea, is about 32 inches long.

The feathers, or plumage, are soft and thick, and of many colors. There are green, yellow, blue, brown, and purple species; the markings may be of any color found in the rainbow. Many of the birds have designs, or patterns, in their feathers.

All pigeons and doves have a somewhat fleshy, platelike covering (the *cere*) at the base of the upper bill. The head and neck usually are small compared with the size of the body; the neck looks short. Legs, tails, and wings

(1) The now extinct passenger pigeon (about 16 inches); (2) mourning dove (12–13 inches); (3) the band-tailed pigeon (16 or more inches); (4) the crowned pigeon (usually more than 2 feet long); (5) the pouter pigeon; (6) the carrier, or homing, pigeon (more than 12 inches long).

vary from short to long. Unlike many other birds, male and female look alike. Most species eat seeds and fruits, although some species eat insects, worms, and snails.

Some species like to live and travel alone; others are always found in flocks. The larger species, like the crowned pigeons, are terrestrial; that is, they feed and live mainly on the ground. Most kinds live in forested areas and build their nests among the tree branches. Nests are usually built of twigs and sticks in the lower branches of the trees, on ledges, or in burrows; some species nest on the ground. One to three eggs (usually two) are laid in each nest. In most species the eggs are white, but a few species lay yellowish eggs. Both parents care for the eggs and young.

When the young are first hatched, they are fed a milky fluid by the parents. This is called "pigeon milk." It is not true milk but a liquid food formed in the *crops* of the adults and then forced up and into the mouths of the young birds. The crop is a special food-holding sack in the throat of some kinds of birds.

Domestic Pigeons

There are many kinds of domestic pigeons. Most of them came from the rock dove of Europe and Asia. Originally, these birds were bred for food but later were developed as pets.

The carrier pigeon was developed from one of the domestic breeds which could find its way back to its home from long distances. These carrier, or homing, pigeons were used to carry messages perhaps as long ago as the days of the Roman Empire. Modern armies still train homing pigeons to carry messages when other methods of communication fail or are difficult. There are now at least 200 varieties. Many are bred for their racing abilities.

The passenger pigeon is an American species that no longer exists, but it is better known than most living kinds. The history of its destruction showed the need for wise conservation practices. Before 1880 there were billions of passenger pigeons. They were killed at their nesting areas, shipped to cities by freight car, and sold at food markets for about two cents apiece. The last-known passenger pigeon died in the zoo at Cincinnati, Ohio, in 1914.

The most common member of the family today in the eastern United States is the mourning dove. This dove is about 12 inches long with gray and brownish plumage. Its name is taken from its sad song. Its gray, black, and white pointed tail makes it easy to recognize.

In the western United States and through much of Mexico a common member of the family is the band-tailed pigeon. This bird is about 14 inches long, with a banded tail of dark gray, black, and light brownish-gray color.

The domestic pigeon of city parks is sometimes called the rock dove. It has become a pest in many places because of its messy habits and the dirt it leaves around public buildings. These birds live on scraps of food found near garbage cans, and on food brought to them by people who like to watch them flock to eat. Better garbage disposal, and less feeding, would soon reduce these birds to a more reasonable number. (See BIRD, *Plate 19.*)

PIKE (*pīk*), **ZEBULON** (*zĕb'ū lŭn*) **MONT-GOMERY** (*mŏnt gŭm'ēr ē*) (1779–1813), was a soldier and explorer who explored much of the southwestern United States. Pike was born in Lamberton, New Jersey, the son of a captain in George Washington's army. In 1794 Pike joined his father's company. About five years later he became a first lieutenant.

After Louisiana was purchased from France in 1803, President Thomas Jefferson wanted the new territory explored. (See LOUISIANA PURCHASE.) While Lewis and Clark went west, Pike took a small party north in 1805. They went up the Mississippi River as far north as Cass Lake, Minnesota, and took possession of the area for the United States.

Pike then was sent to map the southern border of the Louisi-

Zebulon Pike.

Bettmann Archive

ana Purchase. He went up the Arkansas River to central Colorado, and there discovered the mountain that has since been named Pikes Peak in his honor.

While he was looking for the headwaters of the Red River, Pike found the Rio Grande and crossed into Spanish territory by mistake. When the Spanish heard about his explorations, they sent out troops to capture him. Pike was taken to Santa Fe, and then to Chihuahua, Mexico. He explained that he had not intended to cross the border, and was released in 1807. His book about his trip was published in 1810.

During the War of 1812, Pike was made a brigadier general. While leading the attack on York, Ontario, in 1813, he was killed when a powder magazine exploded.

PIKE (*pīk*) is a fish that often lurks in the weeds that fringe the edges of streams and lakes. When it decides to go after another fish, a water rat, a frog, or perhaps a duckling, it darts through the water like a long slender torpedo. It is swift and cruel and greedy. All

Pike are the swiftest in motion of any fresh-water fish when they dart after their prey or away from danger. Some are 4 feet in length and may weigh 50 pounds.

pike are good food. They are fine game fish because they are strong and fight madly to escape when hooked.

The seven species of pike form a distinct family of fresh-water fishes. They are found in Europe, Asia, and North America. All have long bodies and long heads. The large mouth is well-equipped with jaw teeth and with rows of smaller teeth on the palate and tongue. These smaller teeth can be flattened if they prevent the swallowing of a large-sized fish. Northern pike grow as long as 2 to 4 feet and weigh from 5 to 50 pounds. Their coloring is dark bluish- or greenish-gray, spotted with yellowish-white, paler to yellowish-white on the belly. They occur in northern Europe and Asia and in the northeastern United States south to the Ohio River and northwest to Alaska. They are found in shallow, weedy lakes and sluggish rivers. A large female may lay as many as 100,000 eggs in April or early May. A distinct variety of northern pike without spots, known as the silver pike, has appeared in recent years in northern Minnesota lakes.

Smaller Pikes or Pickerel

Three kinds of much smaller pikes, of little or no value as food or game fishes, are called pickerel. Scales are found over the entire gill-cover. The mud or grass pickerel is grassy olive-green. It has irregular dark wormlike wavy bars on the sides and a yellowish line along the middle of the back. The largest are about 13 inches long. They live among reeds on shallow muddy bottoms of lakes and slow streams, from southern Ontario to southern Wisconsin and Iowa south into the lower Mississippi drainage area. They eat minnows and water insects. They lay their eggs among the reeds in March and leave them to their fate. The closely-related eastern barred pickerel, and the slightly larger eastern green pike or chain pickerel, are found in the eastern and southern United States. Muskellunge also belong to the pike family. (See Muskellunge.) The so-called wall-eyed pike or pike perch is not a true pike but a member of the perch family. It is found from southern Canada and the Dakotas to North Carolina, Georgia, and Alabama.

PILGRIM (*pĭl′grĭm*) **AND PILGRIMAGE** (*pĭl′-grĭ mĭj*). In almost every part of the world are places that were connected with some great religious figure or event. It was a custom among many people to visit these places. The people were called pilgrims and the trips they took were pilgrimages.

In India the pilgrims go to the sacred river Ganges and the holy city of Benares. Every non-Mohammedan who can walk or be carried goes there. It is the hope of every pious Hindu not only to have his misdeeds washed away in the river, but to die beside it. He then hopes to have his body burned and his ashes scattered there.

In ancient Greece and ancient Rome the roads were traveled by pilgrims on their way to worship at places connected with the lives of their many gods. Christianity, from an early date, has had its pilgrimages to Palestine and Rome. If the practice of pilgrimage has had what may be called a climax, its peak seems to have been reached under Mohammedanism. Swarming shiploads, caravans, and motor cars of pilgrims go to Mecca, the holy center of Islam.

Pilgrimages to Palestine grew in popularity under the Christian church of early times, but they were outnumbered by pilgrimages to Rome. Rome had become the seat of the church and was associated with at least two of the apostles. In the Middle Ages the number of pilgrims to Palestine increased. Large pilgrimages continued even after the Holy Land was seized by unbelievers. The Knights Templars and Knights of Saint John furnished protection for the travelers. The Crusades may be regarded as armed pilgrimages. Meanwhile crowds of pilgrims in nearly every Christian land sought out the tombs, relics, and dwellings of persons of religious reputation, where miracles were said to have taken place. There were several reasons for going on pilgrimages. Many people went in order to receive partial or complete forgiveness of their sins. Others went hoping to be cured of an illness. Still others went in order to gain special favors. Henry II of England made a pilgrimage at the command of Pope Adrian IV. He went barefooted to the tomb of Thomas Becket, who was murdered in 1170. The king's example was followed by great numbers of rich and poor alike.

The pilgrim of the Middle Ages, with his gray cowl and broad-brimmed hat, his sack and staff, received a hospitality and a consideration not given to ordinary travelers. This was because of his religious mission. Chaucer, an early English writer, told of such pilgrimages in *Canterbury Tales.*

Unfortunately many a vagabond took to pilgrimage as a permanent calling. He went about doing a good business in devotional objects and relics which were not genuine.

The abuses which grew up around the idea of pilgrimage were always declared wrong by some churchmen. In about the 16th century in Europe there rose a wealthy class whose riches came from commerce. Then ridicule began to be poured out upon all pilgrims, even the honest ones. Protestantism, as the religious expression of the new era, did away with holy pilgrimages.

Pilgrimages Today

Catholicism, however, has declared that pilgrimages, rightly understood and undertaken, are deeds of religious worth. They believe that they are deserving of supernatural reward. In recent times the number of pilgrimages made with Catholic support has greatly increased. So have the number of shrines. Hardly a Catholic area in the world today is without its holy places and pilgrims. Among the shrines is the Grotto of Lourdes in France, and the Shrine of Sainte Anne de Beaupre in Quebec, Canada. Various churches have special relics that are said to be furnished with the power of granting special supernatural privileges. Meanwhile there is no decrease in the number of pilgrimages to Rome. North Americans usually speak of the first Puritan settlers in Massachusetts as pilgrims. (See MAYFLOWER and PLYMOUTH, MASSACHUSETTS.)

PIN (*pĭn*). Without modern machinery a man working by hand could make hardly one pin a day. Pins were once so valuable that when a woman married she was given "pin money."

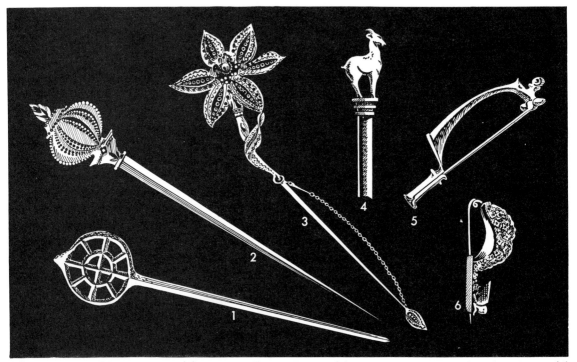

(1) A bronze pin of German origin. (2) An antique Etruscan hairpin. (3) A modern pearl filigreed pin from France. (4) Found in Pompeii, the head of this Roman hairpin is decorated with a small carved animal. (5) This antique bronze pin was a forerunner of the safety pin. (6) A gold pin of Etruscan origin.

In France the people were taxed to provide the queen with pins for her boudoir.

The earliest form of pin was doubtless a thorn. The word *pin* resembles the Latin word for thorn which is *spina*. Next pins were made of the bones of fish or animals, and later ornamental bronze pins were used.

Pins as they are now known were first made in France about the 14th century. From there they were exported to England. In 1775 the Continental Congress in the American Colonies offered a prize for the first 25 dozen domestic pins equal in quality to those imported from England. Present-day machinery, first invented in the early part of the 19th century and constantly improved, now produces several hundred pins a minute. It is estimated that only one pin out of every hundred is worn out or broken by use; the others are lost.

Usually pins are made of brass wire which is wound off a reel to the length of the pin desired. The wire is gripped by viselike jaws which allow a portion of the wire to protrude. A steel punch then flattens this projecting portion into a head. The pins are cut off and drop into slits which allow the wire to pass through, but retain the heads. Hanging thus, they are sharpened by a revolving cutter. They are then cleaned, polished, plated with tin, and packed in boxes or fed into papers by machine.

Pins range in size from the tiny, gilt entomologists' pin weighing $\frac{1}{4500}$ of an ounce, to the large blanket pin measuring $3\frac{1}{2}$ inches. United States pins are manufactured chiefly in Waterbury, Connecticut. Birmingham is the center for the industry in England. More than 100 ordinary pins per person are manufactured annually in the United States. There is also a great demand for safety pins. These are clasp pins that have guards to hold and cover the points after the pins have been pushed into place.

PINE (*pīn*). The state of Maine has chosen the clustered leaves and scaly cone of the pine tree as its official emblem. About 30 of the 90 species of pine trees are native to North America. They are found throughout the continent. The true pines form one division of a large family of resinous evergreen trees and shrubs. This family includes cedars, spruces, junipers, hemlocks, and cypresses. Many of these are incorrectly called pines. The true pine can be readily told from the rest of the family by its long, needlelike leaves which grow in bundles of from one to five. These are covered at the base by a sheath of papery scales. Its fruit is a woody, scaly cone. It varies in length from an inch to 18 inches and encloses seeds.

Pines are usually divided into two groups, the soft pines and the pitch pines. The needles of the soft pine lose their scaly sheaths when they are full-grown. The pitch pine needles always keep their sheaths. Almost all pines are valuable either for their lumber or for the turpentine, tar, and resin obtained from them. The seeds of the pinyon pine are eaten in large quantities. Many of the species are beautiful ornamental trees.

The white pine is one of the best known species in the northeastern parts of United States and Canada. Its white or pale-yellow wood is soft and easily worked and is valuable for interior work and furniture. The tree is usually more than 75 feet high and sometimes reaches a height of 200 feet. Its long, soft slender needles grow in bundles of five. Its curved cones are also long and slender. Its grayish-green bark is smooth. Although white pines grow rapidly and will thrive in many soils, they have been cut so extensively for lumber they no longer occur abundantly.

Like other pines with yellow wood the longleaf pine is valuable because its wood is hard and strong. It also supplies quantities of turpentine and resin. The longleaf pine is found along the coast from Virginia southward and westward to Texas. Its slender orange-brown trunk often towers up 100 feet. Its needles grow in clusters of three and are often 15 inches long. From them may be made a fiber used for coarse cloth and in stuffing pillows.

Somewhat similar to the longleaf pine in wood and yield of turpentine is the smaller loblolly pine which springs up in deserted fields from New Jersey to Texas. This has bright-green needles borne in clusters of three. The shortleaf pine grows over much of the same region, has short needles, and may attain a height of from 75 to 150 feet. The giants among the pines are the western sugar pine, western white pine, and western yellow pine. The sugar pine, for example, is often 200–220 feet high. The wood of these species is heavy but strong.

In eastern Canada and northeastern United States is found the red or Norway pine. This tree grows especially well on dry, sandy soils and reaches a height of from 60 to 120 feet. It has reddish-brown bark and its wood is light, strong, and pliable.

One of the loveliest of the pines is the Monterey pine of California. In young trees its branches form a dense spreading crown and its needles are a beautiful bright green. Other pines are the scrub, or jack pine of the East and the lodgepole pine of the West. The latter was given its name because the Indians used its straight slender trunks for lodge poles. The digger pine of California has edible seeds. The pinyon of the southwestern states furnish most of the supply of edible seeds.

Among the European pines one of the most

This white pine tree growing in Wisconsin is an example of a well-known species of pine found in North America.
Rutherford Platt

valuable is the Scotch pine. It has a bright red-brown bark, blunted oval cones, and needles borne in clusters of two. Its wood is used for making furniture and for shipbuilding, and it supplies turpentine. It is widely used for reforestation both in Europe and other countries. Both the Scotch pine and the black or Austrian pine, which has long dark leaves, are planted in the United States. Two other European pines are the low, flat-topped stone pine of Italy, which has sweet almond-flavored seeds, and the cembra or Swiss pine of central Europe, which also has edible seeds and produces a white oil used in cooking. The dwarf pine of the Alps grows so close to the ground that it looks more like a vine than a tree.

PINEAPPLE (*pīn′ăp″l*). Soon after their first explorations in South America the Spaniards took the pineapple back to Europe. For many

The pineapple's pointed, saw-toothed leaves are clustered in a long rosette around the fruit. The plant grows to about three feet in height.

Ewing Galloway

years after that time pineapples were carefully grown in private greenhouses and were considered a great luxury. With the development of rapid transportation it became possible to grow pineapples in the tropics and ship them to northern markets. As a result greenhouse-grown pineapple plants are now rare.

The principal pineapple fields are in the West Indies, Florida, northern Africa, Hawaii, the Azores, the Canary Islands, and Queensland, Australia. Most of the canned pineapple in United States markets comes from the Hawaiian Islands. Cultivation is much cheaper there than on the mainland of the United States. Florida produces more than any other one of the states. Small quantities are raised in Georgia, Texas, and southern California.

The fruit of the pineapple (which was given its name because it somewhat resembles a pine cone) is really a group of tightly packed small fruits. Each of these resembles a small apple. The hard outer shell corresponds to the calyxes at the ends of apples. The central core is the stem on which each individual small fruit is borne. In weight pineapples vary from 4 to 20 pounds.

The pineapple plant belongs to the Bromeliaceae family and is related to Spanish moss. It grows about three feet high and bears its fruit at any time of the year. After the fruit is mature new shoots for succeeding crops develop below it. A single plant may live and bear fruit for many years. Its pointed leaves are clustered in a close rosette. From the fibers of the leaves the natives of the Philippines weave a fine cloth, called pinya muslin.

Pineapples are rarely raised from seed. They are grown from cuttings or from the leafy crown at the top of the fruit. They must be planted in thoroughly drained soil. The sandy soil of the Florida Keys is well suited to pineapple cultivation even where there are only a few inches of soil. Sheds of laths on a framework of posts are often built over the plants to protect them from possible frost or too much heat. In the Hawaiian Islands thousands of acres are produced. The largest yields of highest quality are obtained from areas which receive abundant sunshine and where the soil is well drained. Any lack of fertility of the soil is supplied by application of fertilizers. In Hawaii most of the fruit is picked when fully mature. It is canned or made into juice. From Cuba, Florida, Mexico, and some other regions the entire fruits are shipped fresh. They are also grated, fresh-frozen, and marketed in packages. When the whole fruit is to be shipped it is usually picked before fully ripe, packed in crates, and sent to market.

PINK (*pĭngk*) is the common name of a large group of flowering plants known to botanists as *Dianthus*. Many *Dianthus* flowers are pink, but the name pink is used to describe the scalloped or "pinked" edges of the flower petals. Pinks are mostly natives of Europe and Asia, where many kinds have been cultivated in gardens for centuries.

Plants of the pink family have stems with swollen joints and leaves growing in pairs on opposite sides of the stems. Flowers of culti-

Fragrant pinks are a favorite in old-fashioned gardens.

J. Horace McFarland Company

vated pinks are white, pink, red, sometimes yellow, and often striped. They may be single or double, alone, or in clusters. Many are sweet-scented.

Cultivated pinks include the carnation, grown more in English gardens than in the United States. Other garden pinks are: fragrant cottage, or grass pinks; small-flowered, mat-forming maiden pinks; sweet-scented clove pinks; fragrant Cheddar pinks, with blue-gray foliage; scentless China pinks, often grown as annuals; and bunch pinks, such as sweet William, with closely clustered flowers.

Pinks are easy to grow in ordinary garden soil. They enjoy sunshine, but do best in temperate and cool climates. Some are annuals, but most are biennials or perennials.

Pinks are grown from seed or cuttings. Some, sweet William, for example, often self-sow and grow year after year in old gardens, or even escape to roadsides and waste places.

PIONEER (*pĭ'ō nēr'*) **LIFE IN THE UNITED STATES** describes the way people moved to, and settled, the frontier lands. It is not about a period of history but about life in new places as people moved west. "All America seems to be on the move" said an English traveler who visited the United States in 1818. He saw long lines of wagons filled with tools and household goods. The drivers urged the straining horses along muddy ruts and over rocky ledges. Beside the drivers sat their wives holding babies. Boys and girls walked alongside the wagons. Older boys on horseback drove little herds of cows, sheep, and hogs. Dogs barked with excitement. All were on the move to new homes where land was cheap, fertile, and plentiful.

One old farmer said that all the people of the United States were divided into two classes, those who went West and those who wanted to go West. From the Atlantic to the Pacific oceans it is 2,500 miles. From the Gulf of Mexico to the Canadian border it is 1,200 miles. Most of this area of nearly 3,000,-000 square miles was settled in a little over 100 years (about 1775 to 1890).

To settle such an area in so short a time

meant that a large percentage of all families moved at least once. It was not unusual for a family to move, build a cabin, clear ground, and then sell out and move again. One man who had moved 17 times said even his chickens learned how to get ready. When he called, they would come and cross their legs, waiting to be tied. Quite often the Virginia farmer, who had moved from the seacoast to the back country, had a son who lived across the mountains in Kentucky and a grandson who lived in Missouri. Had the Virginian lived long enough he would have learned that he had a great-grandson in Kansas and a great-great-grandson in Oregon.

The Frontier and Frontiersmen

The frontier, an area of cheap land and great opportunities, seemed to invite the people from along the Atlantic Coast. The eastern states sent out wave after wave of eager settlers. These pioneers blazed trails, fought Indians, built cabins, cleared fields, organized new states, and pushed on. As the frontier was changed into a settled area, restless families joined the stream of settlers and moved on to the new frontier. Thus the frontier where the pioneer lived was always moving westward. (See WESTWARD MOVEMENT.)

The first frontiersmen were the explorers and fur traders. They discovered and described new areas. Next came the soldiers who built forts and held the Indians in check. Then came government agents who bought the land from the Indians. Next came surveyors who ran lines and marked off farms. Finally, when the land was ready for sale, the settlers came in great numbers. Not everyone followed this order of settlement. Many moved west before the Indians had ceded (sold) the land or the government had surveyed it. They were "squatters" on land they did not own. Their claims were marked by gashes cut into trees and were called "tomahawk claims."

There were many kinds of frontiers. The first one was the Atlantic Coast itself. European people thought of the Atlantic Coast of North America as a frontier. Within the country the first frontier was the hilly region far back from the coast. The mountains slowed, but did not stop, the westward movement. Clearing the tree-covered plains and hills was hard work. The prairies, with their shortage of timber for houses and the high plains with their shortage of rainfall, were added troubles for the pioneers. Mountains, such as the Rockies, were hard to cross. In spite of these difficulties the pioneers moved steadily westward until they had conquered a continent.

Living conditions were not the same on all frontiers. The pioneer planter of Alabama might have a big house and many slaves. The early settler in Ohio might have to do all the work himself. The pioneer who moved to Oregon in a prairie schooner faced problems very different from those of an immigrant who went to Nebraska on the train. All frontiers were

Pioneers usually traveled in caravans for protection.

Culver Pictures, Inc.

alike in being thinly populated. They all had few conveniences. All pioneers faced separation, loneliness, hard work, and difficult living conditions. One pioneer remembered this about his early life: "It was very lonesome for several years. . . . The few seeds I was able to plant the first year yielded but little produce. We, however, raised some half-grown potatoes, some turnips, and soft corn, with which we made out to live, without suffering, till next spring, at planting time, when I planted all the seeds I had left; and . . . we had nothing to eat but leeks and cow-cabbage . . . we wore out all our shoes the first year. We had no way to get more . . . I was obliged to work and travel in the woods barefooted. . . ."[1]

A Nebraska pioneer in the 1870's later told how they ". . . had no stoves but the cook stoves, no vehicles but our farm wagons, and in these we went to church, some of them drawn by oxen." They planted corn, pumpkins, melons, and squashes the first year, he said, so ". . . while our bill of fare was not great we did not have to go hungry." Life was hard but it was good. "Many of us went barefoot in warm weather. One man said that on Sunday morning when he wished to dress for Sunday, all he had to do was to wash his feet."[2]

Good land along the seacoast was soon occupied. Land became expensive. Much of it was soon worn out by repeated crops of corn and tobacco. Great areas of fertile and cheap land were waiting on the frontier. Even though a man was fairly well off, he did not have room for his married sons on the old homestead. Thus a big family was often a reason for moving. The West was described in newspaper advertisements, booklets, and letters as a place of endless opportunities. The climate was described as pleasant and free from diseases and plagues. The pioneer was led to believe that he could get rich by buying lands which would quickly increase in value.

The poor workmen and renters along the Atlantic seaboard were urged to leave their low wages and hard conditions and become

1 From S. J. Buck and E. H. Buck, *The Planting of Civilization in Western Pennsylvania*, University of Pittsburgh Press.
2 From Walker D. Wyman, ed., "Reminiscences of a Nebraska Pioneer of the '70's," *Nebraska History*, July–Sept. 1947.

Culver Pictures, Inc.

The tough prairie sod made plowing difficult.

their own landlords on the frontier. Some of the eastern states required voters to be church members and property owners. But the newer states let all white men vote. Some restless and ambitious men moved west because they loved adventure. A few went west to escape the disgrace of having broken the law. There a man could begin life anew. On the frontier it was bad manners to ask about a person's former life.

Life on the frontier was always hard work and sometimes exciting. Cutting trees, rolling logs, plowing rocky and root-filled ground, watching for Indians, carrying goods from the distant store, caring for livestock—these and dozens of other tasks tired the strongest pioneer. Sometimes a band of Indians stole goods or killed a few settlers. Sometimes a burned cabin, a ruined crop, the death of a horse, or other disaster struck the pioneer. More often, however, he built his cabin, raised his crops, cared for his family and became a successful farmer. In many cases he expanded his farm, built a large house and lived a quite comfortable life. This settled region was then no longer the frontier, for the line of settlement had moved on.

Transportation and Communication

Pioneers moved to the frontier in a number of ways. Before the days of roads across the mountains, many went on horseback. Large packs strapped across the horse's back contained all their possessions. As soon as roads

A covered wagon, fitted for moving the pioneer family and all their possessions westward to new land.

were made, canvas-covered wagons and carts were used in great numbers. Women and children could ride in them and more goods could be taken than on horseback. Thousands of settlers floated down the Ohio River and other western streams on flatboats, houseboats, and keelboats. They carried with them goods and tools. Still others went by canal boats and on steamers across Lake Erie and Lake Michigan. The Erie Canal through upper New York State was heavily traveled. The railroads, after they were built, became the most important means of transportation for they were faster, more convenient, and cheaper. (See RAILROAD.)

The pioneer built his cabin and cleared his ground by hand. He still needed hardware, tools, dishes, and other products which he could not make. To get them he had to sell some of his corn, cotton, or tobacco. To sell crops he had to have a way to transport them to market. Therefore he wanted roads, canals, and railroads built.

Some famous roads and trails were made for the pioneers. The Wilderness Road from Virginia to Kentucky, was laid out by Daniel Boone who worked for a land company. The Cumberland Road or "Old National Road" ran across the mountains from western Maryland into western Pennsylvania and Ohio. An early turnpike ran from Philadelphia to Lancaster, both in Pennsylvania. Other roads ran on to Pittsburgh, Pennsylvania. Settlers from New England crossed the mountains to Albany, New York, and followed the route of the Erie Canal to Buffalo, New York.

In the South sandy roads ran across Georgia and Alabama. A better road was the Natchez Trace from Nashville, Tennessec, to Natchez, Mississippi. In the West the most famous trails were the Santa Fe Trail from the Missouri River to New Mexico and the Central Overland Trail to Oregon, Utah, and California. (See TRAILS, HISTORIC.)

The pioneer was interested in getting mail as well as transportation. Post offices and post roads were established promptly. Letters and newspapers did much to keep the people united even though they were scattered over wide areas. (See POSTAL SYSTEM.) The Pony Express from St. Joseph, Missouri, to Sacramento, California, was a system of fast relays carrying mail rapidly across the country. (See PONY EXPRESS.) The telegraph helped even more to tie the scattered parts of the nation together.

Land and Farming

The pioneer knew that the United States government owned the western land and would sell it on reasonable terms. Government surveyors marked off each square mile, known as a section. It contained 640 acres and might be divided into farms of 320, 160, or 80 acres each.

The government did not sell all its land directly to the settlers. In the early days a few big land companies bought large tracts and resold to settlers. Later, speculators bought large blocks of good land from the government. When this land increased in value the owners divided it into small tracts. These plats (or plots) were sold to settlers at a profit. Beginning in 1850, the government wished to encourage the building of railroads. Therefore, it gave away millions of acres to railroad companies. They, in turn, sold the land to settlers. Some railroads were so eager to sell their land that they offered free transportation to settlers.

Until 1862, the usual price of government land was two dollars or less for an acre unless sold by private land owners or speculators. The pioneer had to pay one-fourth of the cost when the deal was made. The rest he paid in annual installments. If his crop failed he was sometimes given more time. While two dollars an acre now seems like a cheap price, it was not so in those times. In addition, the pioneer had to buy equipment and travel hundreds of miles. Careful saving was necessary for a farmer from Connecticut to move to Ohio. It is doubtful if many factory workers in the East ever saved enough money to take their families out West to buy a farm.

In 1862, the Homestead Act was passed. By this law a man could own a farm if he built a house, improved the land, and stayed on it a certain time. Most land east of the Mississippi

(1) In areas where trees were plentiful, log cabins were built. (2) In places where there were no trees, the settlers built sod huts. (3) A fort or trading post often became the nucleus for a city or town. Shown here is Fort Dearborn, built where Chicago now stands.

Courtesy (2) Nebraska State Historical Society; Photo, (1) Brown Brothers, (3) Ewing Galloway

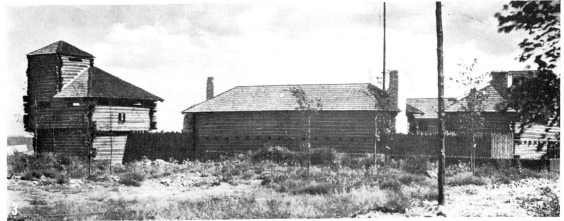

Courtesy Ohio State Museum

The log cabin, built by the pioneer himself, usually consisted of one room. Here his family cooked, ate, slept, and lived.

River and much of it as far west as the Missouri River was sold before the Homestead Act. Millions of acres farther west were given to homesteaders. (See LAND, PUBLIC.)

The pioneers used the land many ways. The most common use was farming. Corn, tobacco, cotton, and other crops were raised. Even though farming new ground was hard work, it yielded a living. (See AGRICULTURE.) In some areas the chief use of the land was to strip it of its valuable trees. In the South some farmers used the pine trees as a source of resin and turpentine. On the Great Plains immense herds of cattle were raised. Farther west, among the Rocky Mountains, sheep raising was popular. Along the Pacific Coast, cattle were raised and fruits and vegetables were grown.

Each kind of farming offered its own difficulties. Raising cotton and corn required much plowing. Raising tobacco was heavy work. The stalks had to be spread by hand to cure. The farmer, with the help of his boys, fought a constant battle against weeds, briars, and bushes. The long spring and summer days were filled with work. The harvest season was also a time of hard work. Carrying the crops to market was perhaps the greatest problem of all. Wagons were few, roads were muddy, and distances were great. Fortunate was the pioneer who lived near a river. He could then load his products on a flatboat. The coming of railroads was a great help to the pioneer. (See TRANSPORTATION.)

Houses on the Frontier

Having arrived on the frontier and secured his land, the pioneer set to work building his house. Between the Allegheny Mountains and the prairies the log cabin was the typical house. The frontiersman became very skillful in fitting the logs properly. He fastened good boards to the roof with wooden pegs. Strong doors, made without a single nail, swung on strong wooden posts. Although the log cabin was not very beautiful or comfortable, it was a fairly good protection against rain and cold.

Within a very short time some energetic

pioneer set up a sawmill and the more prosperous farmers built weather-boarded houses.
From the very first, some of the more well-
to-do pioneers, such as merchants, fur traders,
and government officials, built houses of brick
or stone. Some of these old houses are still in
good condition after more than 100 years of
use.

When the frontier reached the treeless
prairies, the pioneer could not build a log
cabin. Bringing in lumber for a board house
was too expensive. So the typical house of the
prairies and Great Plains was a sod hut. Over
a framework of poles the pioneer placed heavy
blocks of grassy sod. These houses were cool
in summer and easily warmed in winter, but
they were hard to ventilate. Water always
soaked through the thickest roof that could be
made. In the Southwest houses were made of
adobe, a mixture of wet soil and straw which
was baked in the sun.

The furnishings were crude homemade
benches, chairs, tables, and beds. The pioneer had little time to spend making beautiful
furniture. A split log with its flat surface
turned up and supported by sticks fitted into
holes served as a table or a bench. Short sections cut from a log and stood on end served
as temporary chairs. Cabinets, dressers, and
rocking chairs came later.

Indians

On some frontiers pioneers often fought the
fierce and warlike Indians. The lone farmer
worked with his gun slung on his back or
within easy reach. Some tribes made attacks
upon forts and whole towns. Lone braves attacked the scattered settlers. While these
threats and dangers were not too common, they
were always a worry.

The early settlers of Kentucky, Ohio, and
Tennessee were often attacked by Indians.
Sometimes the Indians laid siege to a fort or a
cabin. They tried to starve the defenders into
surrender. Some heroic volunteer crept
through the Indian lines and went for help.
When the new forces arrived, the Indians fled.
These brave struggles by pioneers have been
told often in song and story.

The Indians also suffered. Even though the
government paid them for their land they were
forced to sell it. Having sold their land and
agreed to move, they still did not want to leave
their old villages and hunting grounds. Sometimes they did not like the new lands to which
the government sent them. They also feared
battles with other tribes which were sure to
follow when they moved onto new lands. Thus
the Indians were pushed farther and farther
west.

The Indians were poverty-stricken and
starved. Since they were poor farmers they
had to depend largely upon fishing and hunting. As the white men cleared the forests the
game disappeared. The government paid the
Indians money and gave them food, but there
was still a great deal of suffering among them.

Although the Indians were often hostile and
warlike, they did not delay the westward
movement very much. The reasons were many.
In the first place there were too few of them.
Between the Alleghenies and the Rockies there
were, in 1825, probably no more than 200,000
Indians. In the second place they were divided
into many tribes and bands. These tribes usually failed to co-operate, and often fought one

The stage coach driver pays the toll before entering the
Maysville Turnpike, Kentucky.

Courtesy Public Roads Administration

The fiddler played lively music to which the pioneers danced. This is "The Jolly Flatboatmen," a painting by George Caleb Bingham.

another. They tried to organize against the whites several times but were defeated. Even though they had guns, they never had enough of them. The soldiers had forts and stood ready to fight. But it was starvation and disease, not bullets, that destroyed the Indian. (See INDIANS, NORTH AMERICAN.)

Frontier Government

The pioneers wanted law and order. Settlements were sometimes made before laws for governing the towns were written. In such cases the men banded together to protect themselves against robbers and other outlaws. Anti-horse-thief associations were formed to catch and execute such thieves. Anti-claim-jumping societies were formed to keep trespassers off other people's claims. Squatters organized to threaten speculators who wanted to buy the land they claimed. The speculator dared not bid if he knew he might be tarred and feathered. In the mining camps of the West, "vigilante" committees took over and handed out justice for wrong-doing. Whipping and hanging were common punishments.

As soon as a reasonable number of people moved into an area, Congress marked off the boundaries and set up a territory. The president appointed a governor, a council, and judges. The people elected a legislature and a territorial delegate to Congress. As long as the area remained a territory the people could not choose their own governor. They could not vote in presidential elections.

Some people were always eager to have the territory changed into a state. There were others who opposed statehood. They did not want to pay taxes for support of the state government, roads, and schools. But these who wanted statehood always won in the end. More than once they padded (falsified) the census record to make it appear that the territory had enough people to become a state. They carried on a campaign in the newspapers. Their delegate in Congress would try to get statehood for the territory. Finally Congress would permit the people to draw up a constitution. If Congress approved the constitution the new state was admitted into the Union.

Thus, the pioneers who went out to a wild frontier often had the satisfaction of seeing the area grow into a state. Each new state came into the Union equal to all other states. This wise policy promoted national unity. The citizen of Indiana or Idaho realized that his state had all the rights and powers of any one of the original 13 states.

Frontier states were sometimes more democratic than the older ones. For example, Kentucky, Tennessee, and Ohio provided in their first constitutions for nearly full manhood suffrage. Free Negroes were not allowed to vote. Religious and property qualifications for voting were largely removed. Wyoming, as a territory, was first to give women the right to vote. Other new states copied the same ideas. From the frontier they spread back to the older states. Frontier states usually favored spending public money for improving railroads, canals, and schools. Frontier courts were prompt in their hearings. Frontier juries believed in applying punishments quickly. The quality of government and the practice of democracy did not decline on the frontier.

Religion

For the pioneer, church attendance was a social as well as a religious custom. Six days of the week were spent on a farm. During this time the pioneer saw few persons outside his own family. On Sunday therefore, he was glad to hitch his team to the wagon and haul his wife and children, and possibly a neighbor or two, to church. If they walked, they probably carried their precious shoes until in sight of the "church-house," then put them on for the service. After the service they discussed the weather, exchanged information about crops, and gossiped with neighbors.

In the older states nearly all the people of a town or county usually belonged to the same church. The typical New Englander was a Congregationalist. The typical Pennsylvanian was a Quaker or a Presbyterian. The typical Virginian was an Episcopalian. A village or neighborhood often would have only one church. The situation on the frontier was quite different. Into each area came people from all these and from other churches. The result was that a town on the frontier might contain several churches. The fact that people of different beliefs lived side by side helped to develop religious toleration. A Congregationalist soon saw that his Methodist neighbor was honest, well-intentioned, and neighborly. Each group held to its own beliefs, and allowed others to do likewise.

In the Mississippi Valley, the Methodists and Baptists were the first to send traveling preachers to the frontier settlements. The Congregationalists and Presbyterians followed. The Catholic Church also was at the frontier.

Religion on the Midwest frontier was highly emotional. Many of the preachers were untrained. Some were eloquent. They were strongly against drunkenness, Sabbath-breaking, swearing, and not going to church. Sinners were warned to repent and accept salvation. Revival meetings with their shouting and praying were held often. Camp meetings were

After a day's work the pioneers sometimes held a dance.

(1) Commercial flatboats were a common sight along the Mississippi. (2) The whole family joined in cornhusking and other farm work. (3) Pioneer women eagerly greeted the Yankee trader, who brought news and wares from the east.

Photos, (1) Culver Service, (2, 3) Brown Brothers

popular. A platform for the preacher was erected between large trees in the woods. Planks were placed on blocks as seats for the congregation. Cabins and tents were put up and hundreds of people spent weeks at these revivals. The night meetings, held by the light of torches, were most exciting.

Those churches which preached mainly on the personal and emotional nature of religion were the most popular. The Baptists and Methodists gained thousands of converts. The Congregationalists, Presbyterians, Episcopalians, and Catholics were also active. New churches, such as the Disciples of Christ (Campbellites), Adventists, Shakers, and Mormons gained many followers.

The frontier preacher was a picturesque figure. Astride a horse he rode to the farthest church in order to bring his message. The several churches that were served by one preacher made up a circuit. The circuit rider, devout, devoted, and patient, has become the symbol of the frontier preacher.

Education

Pioneer boys and girls had few schools. Those which they did have were poor and crude. The teacher was not well trained. He spent too much time keeping order and punishing unruly students. The readers, arithmetics, and spellers were little books with small type and crude illustrations. The stories tried to teach good behavior rather than to tell an interesting story. The pupils studied out loud. The louder they read, the more praise they won from the teacher. The quiet or shy pupil whose voice was not heard was sure to be scolded by the angry teacher. To a passer-by the school must have sounded like a madhouse.

The schoolhouse was made of logs or weather-boarded planks. It was heated by a fireplace or a big, square iron stove. The seats consisted of split logs supported by wooden sticks inserted into holes in the log. The pupils wrote on slates rather than paper. The walls had no pictures. There were no school libraries. In this unattractive setting frontier children learned their simple lessons.

Pioneers who had some education wanted to

give their children a few winter terms of "schooling." Those who had never been to school had no interest in "book larnin'." The first schools were often "subscription" schools. Parents with children built a log building and hired a teacher. They paid the teacher $10 or $20 a month. Even this amount was a great hardship to them since people on the frontier had so little to sell for cash. It was common for the teacher to take part of his pay in board and room. Each family had its turn boarding the teacher. They enjoyed his company for he helped do the chores and read to them around the fireplace in the evening. On the other hand, sleeping in the loft with several children and eating some of the cooking might have seemed poor pay. Most of the early teachers in the Midwest were youths from New England seeking their fortune in the West.

For many years people felt that educating boys and girls was the responsibility of the parents. People who had no children felt that they should not have to pay to send other people's children to school. This attitude changed slowly. The change came first in the Midwest where farms were small and villages rose fast. It also came there because the federal government set aside public lands to be sold to support schools. Public schools came last in the South where plantations were large and the population more scattered. Planters educated their children but the children of small farmers grew up without much education. Free schools were built for all children in most of the western states.

The federal government gave public lands to help the schools. The states levied taxes for the schools. Agricultural and mechanical colleges were started and finally came state universities. The states were much slower in starting high schools. The need for these was met by the founding of hundreds of academies. These academies taught Latin, literature, and advanced mathematics, subjects which were not very much needed on the frontier. The requirements for girls who entered Mt. Holyoke Seminary in 1837 seem much more practical. Holyoke required that girls should be able to "kindle a fire, wash potatoes, repeat the multi-plication table" and "walk a mile a day." Most of the academies were founded and supported by the churches. Even in pioneer days the churches founded hundreds of colleges. In them preachers, teachers, lawyers, and doctors were trained. These private colleges filled a great need in United States education.

Health and Food

While the frontier was a healthful place, the people were often not very sturdy. Although food was usually plentiful, it was coarse and unappetizing. It was usually the same day after day. In the Ohio Valley, fat pork, corn bread, and coffee were the most common diet. Beans, peas, and other fresh and dried vegetables were also included. Berries, apples, plums, peaches, and pears were raised. Most of these, however, came some years after the frontier was settled. Wild game, such as squirrel, rabbit, deer, and bear could easily be shot. But their numbers began to decrease rapidly. Thus the good food found earlier on the frontier soon became scarce. The result was that the pioneer had a rather unattractive diet. When the foreign immigrants came to the frontiers of the Midwest and the Plains, they added variety to early cooking with their coffee cake, hamburgers, and coleslaw. The foods of the Southwest included Mexican and Indian dishes.

Diseases were common. The death rate among babies was very high. People in their thirties were regarded as having reached middle age. Measles, smallpox, typhoid fever, cholera, cancer, and tuberculosis carried away their victims by the thousands. A form of malaria known as the "ague" was very common. Pioneers believed it came from gases in the soil which escaped when the land was first plowed.

The medicines that were known did very little good. They often were strange mixtures of bitter herbs and whisky. The patients took such mixtures and probably suffered no more than usual. Doctors on the frontier were few. They were probably less capable than those in the older communities. They "cured" the sick by giving them herbs from the woods, or bled them to get rid of too much blood. The scientific treatment of disease had to await the coming of trained doctors. In the meantime, diseases and accidents took many lives and suffering was great. Since there were few dentists and few ways of treating teeth, a common sight on the frontier was a toothless person.

Amusements

The pioneer had little time for anything except work. It is not surprising, therefore, that the list of his amusements is very short. Games and sports of physical skill were popular. The local champion in wrestling, running, and hammer throwing won the respect of his fellow citizens. While hunting, fishing, and trapping were businesses, they were more pleasant than plowing and gardening. Log rollings, husking bees, apple peelings, and corn cuttings combined work and pleasure, especially when refreshments were served. Weddings and "house warmings" were very festive affairs. On such occasions people of all ages would do square dances for hours on end to the music of a fiddle.

The swapping of yarns and jokes at country stores, in trains, in saloons, and even in churchyards was always a source of entertainment. People read newspapers regularly even on the frontier. Books were few and magazines unknown. Once in a while a circus visited the frontier town and the showboat pulling into river towns gave drama and music to lonely boys and girls.

The pioneer had other recreation. Going to the store was an adventure for country boys and girls. Going to church was a social occasion as well as a religious duty. Even camp meetings were used for visiting and exchanging information about people, medicines, and local events. Political campaigns were also entertainment as well as instruction on the problems of the day. In spite of these pleasures, life on the frontier was often monotonous.

Effects of the Frontier

Millions of people spent their lives on the frontier. Three or four generations grew up in its hardships. This has had a great effect upon national manners, customs, and beliefs. The pioneer was impatient and direct. He was interested not so much in words as in action. Appearances, forms, and rules, he distrusted. The well-dressed, smooth-talking politician was not likely to be popular. The people were more willing to vote for one of their plain, simple neighbors. Common sense and hard work were most important. The man who ran for an elective office tried to prove that he, too, was a man of lowly birth and simple manners. If he came from a wealthy family, he sometimes spoke and dressed like a frontiersman.

The pioneer was a fierce believer in equality. Nearly everyone was equal in wealth, or rather lack of it. The frontiersman's own hard lot also led him to make fun of fine manners. He therefore had a bluntness that sometimes approached bad manners. He was suspicious of any insult to his dignity or any lack of respect for him because of his poor clothes, hard fate, and crude manners. He believed that he was as good as his neighbor, as good as the well-dressed politician, as good as the highly trained college man. His beliefs helped to produce a fundamental type of democracy in the United States. Once at a southern barn-raising, a pioneer planter came to help, bringing his slaves. He had them do the work while he gave the orders. The other settlers did not like this. After that, they had little to do with him.

The frontier liked action. The man who had just arrived soon found that his name and his past were not nearly so important as what he could do. The man who could shoot an Indian, fell a tree quickly, build a cabin skillfully, raise a good crop with poor tools, and meet the demands of his new surroundings was the man who won the respect of his neighbors. The frontier had its own standards of excellence.

The settler on the frontier was usually optimistic. This optimism naturally grew from the great progress he saw about him as the frontier developed. Looking into the future he could see the forests becoming rich farmlands or the prairies turning to cornfields. He could dream of frontier villages and rough mining camps growing into thriving cities. It was but a short step from optimism to boastfulness. The pioneer considered his region as the best place on earth. "Heaven," to a Kentuckian, "was a Kentuck of a place."

The pioneer has had great influence in the United States. People respect his heritage of democracy, honest vigor, and frank directness. Dangers and hardships sometimes brought out the best in those who might otherwise have lived quite commonplace lives.

PIPE (pīp), **TOBACCO.** Smoking tobacco is an important part of life today everywhere in the world. Before America was discovered, however, no one in Europe, or Asia, or Africa had heard of tobacco. In England the first pipe for smoking was brought there in 1586. Ralph Lane, the first governor of Virginia, gave it to Sir Walter Raleigh. Before long, however, many Englishmen must have been smoking pipes because in 1619 there was an organized group of pipe-makers in London.

Pipes like those now used seem to have been invented by the Muskogee Indians, who lived in the southeastern part of the United States. These Indian pipes were like a tube that curved at one end. The curved end was widened into a cup, or small bowl, for holding the tobacco. Traders and explorers from France, England, and the Netherlands learned to use these pipes. They then became very popular throughout northern Europe.

Another kind of pipe was made by the Indians of southern Brazil. This pipe had two pieces—a reed or a hollow tube of wood and a nutshell, which made a very tiny bowl. Traders from Portugal saw these pipes and carried them in their travels to Turkey, Persia, China, and Japan. Even today two-piece pipes with very tiny bowls are popular in Japan.

The Indians in the northern Mississippi River valley had a very special pipe. It had a large stem decorated with duck heads and eagle feathers. This pipe was called a *calumet*. It was always carried as a sign of friendship and peace whenever Indians from different tribes visited each other. That is why it is often called a peace pipe. Indians also smoked pipes for pleasure and in ceremonies to the gods.

Pipes are made of many different materials—corncobs, gourds (called calabashes), metal, wood, and clay. Clay pipes break easily, but

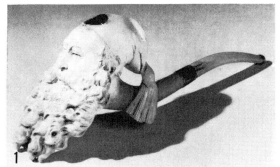

Alfred Dunhill Limited (London)

(1) A Meerschaum pipe made in France. It has a beautifully carved bowl and an amber mouthpiece. (2) A central European pipe which is still popular in Bavaria, especially among the peasants. The mouthpiece and top of the stem are made of bone, the lower stem of cherrywood, the bowl of brier. The bowl has a metal lid. It is known as the Tyrolean style. (3) An elaborately finished Persian pipe. It has a bone stem with gilt and color decoration. The bowl is made of clay. (4) A china pipe of the U.S.S.R. (5) An early 17th-century Elizabethan clay pipe. (6) Two modern pipes made from light brown brier root dug in the rocky and arid island of Sardinia. (7) A Burmese pipe made from bamboo root, with decorative fitments. (8) A pipe carved in slate by Indians of northwest America. The bowl is sunk in the middle of the top.

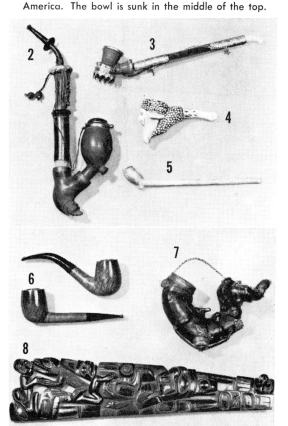

they are cheap and can easily be replaced. Very expensive and beautiful pipes are made of meerschaum, a fine white mineral, something like clay. Brier wood, which comes from very hard roots, is often used in modern pipes.

PIPELINES (pīp′līnz) are tubes used to carry liquid or gas products from one place to another. Usually they are made of steel, or concrete strengthened with steel. Those that carry products under high pressure are always made of steel in order to protect against explosions or breakage. Pipes range in size, depending on their use, from as small as 2 inches to 36 inches in diameter.

Most pipelines in the United States and other countries carry petroleum or oil products. There are several reasons for this. When oil or gas is discovered by drilling a well, it must be carried to a refinery to be processed. From there, it is sent to the consumer (the user)— either a factory, or a home, or to storage tanks. Although crude oil or gasoline can be carried in barrels, railroad tank cars, or in trucks, the cost of such transportation is very high. Because pipeline transportation is so much cheaper, the products can be sold for less money.

When a new oil or gas well is found, it is connected to a pipeline. A series of pumps or compressor stations are built along the pipe to force with pressure the oil or gas through the line. When the products reach their destination, however, the pressure is lowered. A substance like natural gas then comes out at the kitchen stove under the amount of pressure needed for cooking.

Development of Pipelines

Pipelines are not a modern invention. In ancient history the Chinese used pipelines to carry water for irrigation. However, it was not until the early 1900's that pipelines became well developed.

In 1859, at Titusville, Pennsylvania, Edwin L. Drake drilled the first oil well. For the next few years, horse-drawn wagons were used to carry the oil in barrels to refineries. Later, the barrels were carried by railroads or boats. It was not until 1865, however, that the first successful oil pipeline was built. Five miles long and two inches in diameter, this iron pipe carried 800 barrels of crude oil per day.

The first well known pipelines, called "Big Inch" and "Little Big Inch," were built during World War II (1939–1945). Before the United States entered the War (1941), petroleum products were moved from Texas and Louisiana ports to the eastern seaboard by ships and railroad tank cars. A shortage of oil developed, however, when the ships and railroads had to be used for the war. The government then decided to build two pipelines. The first line, the "Big Inch," went from Texas to Pennsylvania, with branches leading to New York and Philadelphia. It was completed in 350 days and the first oil reached the Philadelphia area in August 1943. The second line, the "Little Big Inch," went from Texas to New York. Started later and finished in less time, its first gasoline arrived at Linden, New Jersey, in March 1944. The "Big Inch" line extended a total length of 1,476 miles and the "Little Big Inch" was 1,714 miles.

After the war, there was less demand for petroleum products. The government sold the "Big Inch" and "Little Big Inch" to a natural gas company. Since then, many other pipelines have been built to carry natural gas to the east. In the last few years, natural gas pipelines have also been built to nearly every part of the United States.

In 1959 there were more than 570,000 miles of natural gas pipelines and more than 200,000 miles of lines carrying crude oil and petroleum products in the United States. It is thought that more than 75 per cent of all crude oil and 20 per cent of all products such as gasoline are carried in pipelines. There are more miles of pipeline in the United States than there are miles of railroad track.

Other uses for pipelines are also being developed. Because of lack of rain in many parts of the United States, pipelines have been laid to carry water from lakes and rivers for irrigation purposes and for drinking purposes.

In 1955 a 108-mile long pipeline was built in Ohio to transport coal. First the coal is crushed into small pieces and then mixed with water. After the coal, with the water, has been forced through the pipeline by pumps, it is dried at the other end and cut into the proper size lumps.

A large gas field was discovered in Alberta, Canada, shortly after World War II. In 1958 a 2,000-mile pipeline was completed to transport natural gas from that field to the eastern part of Canada. Pipelines have been built in all parts of the world, including North Africa, the Middle East, and the U.S.S.R. (See PETROLEUM.)

PIPIT (*pĭp′ĭt*) **AND WAGTAIL** (*wăg′tāl*), small slender birds found in most parts of the world. There are about 50 species that belong to the *Motacillidae* family. This Latin name refers to their common habit of jerking the tail whenever they run or perch. Usually, they have a long, thin, and pointed bill with a notch at the end. Because their back toe is long and curved, they can walk faster and easier than most of the smaller birds. In size, they range from five to nine inches. They eat insects and mollusks along with a little vegetable matter.

Although wagtails are mainly Old World birds, two species reach the northwestern section of the United States. Brighter in color than pipits, they vary in shades of black, gray and green with a white or yellow breast and sometimes a yellow head. The tail is longer than the wings while that of a pipit is shorter. Most wagtails live along streams or still water, but some prefer corn fields and meadows.

The nest of a wagtail is made from vegetable material and lined with hair and feathers. It is built usually in holes of trees, walls, or rocks. Two to six eggs, bluish-white or brown with yellow marks, are set in the nest. Both parents help make the nest and care for the young.

Pipits are also found all over the world, but only two species live in North America. The most common in the United States is the water pipit or titlark which has a cry that sounds like its name. Like the lark, all pipits sing while in flight. They have brown and tan bodies with dark brown streaks and spots. The open country is their favorite place to settle and they

(1) The wagtail has a slender form and is one of the most graceful of birds. (2) The American pipit is a nimble bird which resembles the lark.

build their nests on the ground. Grayish or yellowish white in color, the eggs have brown and gray markings.

PIRATE (*pī′rĭt*) **AND PIRACY** (*pī′rä sē*). Piracy is robbery at sea by men who are called pirates. Piracy is nearly as old as recorded history. As recently as 1961 a ship was boarded by "pirates." A small group of exiled Portuguese and Spanish leaders boarded the luxury liner *Santa Maria* at La Guaira, Venezuela. When they took over the ship in the Caribbean Sea, their purpose was to promote a revolt in Portugal to overthrow the government. They stopped to leave the wounded at St. Lucia Island, and then sailed out into the Atlantic Ocean. After a 63-hour chase by United States, British, and Portuguese ships and airplanes, the rebels surrendered the ship in Brazil.

Barbary Pirates

Piracy in the Mediterranean Sea began before the days of the Roman Empire. During the 16th, 17th, and 18th centuries the Mohammedans, who held the north coast of Africa, were a danger to Christians' ships. They captured passengers and sailors and sold them as slaves. These Mohammedans were called the Barbary pirates, after the Berber tribes who lived in North Africa. They formed four small countries, Morocco, Algiers, Tripoli, and Tunis. Each of these states was ruled by a *pasha* or *bey*. The pasha wanted piracy, and received part of the profits from each captured ship.

After a time the countries of Europe discovered that they could pay the robber nations to leave their ships alone. These payments were called *tribute*. England paid tribute, and as long as the American colonies belonged to her, the Barbary pirates did not attack their ships.

After the American Revolution, however, the pirates began to attack United States ships and put the seamen into slavery. The United States did not want to pay for protection, and in 1801 declared war on Tripoli. This forced the pasha to agree to leave United States ships alone. The pirates soon broke their treaty, and in 1804 Stephen Decatur led an expedition against them, but they were not completely put down until France conquered Algeria in 1830.

History of Piracy

In the Middle Ages pirates of all nationalities were a danger to coastal trade of northern Europe. Many were criminals who had fled from home and were afraid to return. They had to have friends on shore to help sell the goods they stole. In some places nobles protected them for a share in their profits.

In the 1500's and 1600's pirates sailed near the trade routes of the Spanish empire in the Americas. Thousands of Frenchmen and other Europeans had come out to lead a wild life in the West Indies. They were called buccaneers, from the French name (*bou-*

can) for the frame on which they cured meat. When they took to piracy they were also called filibusterers and freebooters.

From the 16th to the 19th century freebooters were often hired by one government to act as privateers in attacking the trade of an enemy country. Hiring of privateers started because it was hard for a government to protect its people against foreign pirates. Pirates caught by agents of their own country were usually hanged, but punishment of pirates who were citizens of a foreign country was likely to cause trouble. Therefore, a plan was worked out whereby if a merchant of one country, say England, had lost goods to pirates of another country, say France, the merchant could ask his government for a *letter of marque*. The term *marque* was a French word which meant seizure with official approval. Thus, a letter of marque was a license giving the English merchant permission to attack a French merchant ship and take from it goods equal in value to those he had lost to French pirates.

In time of war governments issued letters of marque to anyone who would offer to attack the merchant shipping of the enemy. People licensed in this way were called privateers.

Pirates attacked rich merchant ships.

Some Famous Pirates

Some famous English freebooters were licensed by their government to attack Spanish shipping even when Spain and England were not at war. Men like Sir John Hawkins, Sir Francis Drake, and Sir Henry Morgan led adventurous lives fighting to capture Spanish colonial ports and treasure ships. (See DRAKE, SIR FRANCIS; HAWKINS, SIR JOHN.)

Sir Henry Morgan was one of the best-known privateers. In 1668 he began his attacks on the Spanish for the governor of Jamaica. In a few years he had attacked and looted Porto Bello, the Cuban coast, Maracaibo, and Panama. To the Spanish he was a pirate. The English considered him a privateer. Indeed, Charles II knighted him and made him lieutenant governor of Jamaica.

As French and English colonial trade grew in value, still more pirates made their headquarters in the West Indies or along the coast of the Carolinas. The island of Tortuga, or Turtle Island, off the coast of Hispaniola, was a pirate haven. There pirates of all nationalities could get whatever they needed in the way of supplies. They could sell their plunder to the colonists of New England or the Carolinas. Many people were grateful for smuggled goods at low prices.

The island of Madagascar, off the southeast coast of Africa, was a base for pirates attacking ships in the Indian trade. The crew of the famous Captain Kidd turned to piracy after an unsuccessful expedition against these pirates. (See KIDD, WILLIAM.)

One of the most brutal pirates was Edward Teach. He was nicknamed "Blackbeard," for he had a long, bushy beard which he tied back over his ears with ribbon. He served as a privateer during the war between England and Spain, but turned to piracy when the war ended in 1713. Soon he was the terror of the Virginia and Carolina coasts. Finally the governor of Virginia sent two ships to capture him. After a fight, the pirate ship was captured, and Teach was killed.

Sometimes a captain's picture was painted on the flag at the mast of a pirate ship, but usually the pirate flag was the Jolly Roger, which showed a human skull and crossed thighbones.

Piracy began to die out when steamships came into use. The last strongholds of piracy were in the Pacific, in areas where steamships were not used. In the Malay Islands native chiefs sometimes practiced piracy on a large scale. Their boats were long galleys rowed by slaves. Much of their business was in the plunder of villages and the capture of prisoners to be sold in slave markets. British and Dutch navy patrols finally destroyed the power of the island pirates about 1860. Even today, however, there are still a few pirates along the south coast of China.

PISA (pē′zä), **ITALY.** On the banks of the Arno River in central Italy lies the city of Pisa. Eight hundred years ago Pisa had more than twice its present population. It was then the capital of a strong, independent republic, and a leading Mediterranean port. Unfortunately, Pisa lay between two ancient enemies, Genoa and Florence, and fought long and costly wars with both. A war within Genoa ended in the ruin of Pisa in 1284. In 1406, it came under the control of Florence. In 1861, the city and province of Pisa became part of the kingdom of Italy.

There is another reason for the downfall of ancient Pisa. During its golden age, the city was a seaport at the mouth of the Arno. But soil carried by the river built a delta at its mouth, and the Arno gradually pushed the delta farther and farther out into the Mediterranean. Now Pisa is seven miles from the coast.

Modern Pisa is known for the beauty of its old buildings. The walls which encircled the ancient city still stand. Near them, in the northwest corner of the city, is a famous square known as the Piazza del Duomo, which means Square of the Cathedral. In the center of the square is the black and white marble cathedral begun in 1063. In this cathedral Galileo noticed a swinging lamp set in motion by the person who was filling it, and from that event came the principle of the motion of a pendulum. (See GALILEO; PENDULUM.) To one side of the cathedral is a beautiful, old circular church called the Baptistery, and to the other side is

Philip Gendreau

The Baptistery, Cathedral, and campanile (Leaning Tower) of the famous Piazza del Duomo in Pisa.

the famous Leaning Tower of Pisa. The Leaning Tower is a campanile, or bell tower, built chiefly of white marble. It is 179 feet high and 50 feet in diameter. Its top overhangs its base about $16\frac{1}{2}$ feet. The reason for the leaning position of the building is not known.

Other well-known structures in Pisa include many buildings of the University of Pisa, one of the oldest universities in Italy. It was founded in the 14th century, and is still an important center of learning. Galileo, a native of Pisa, taught there at one time.

Pisa has some cotton mills, and carries on trade in oil and marble. Most of the people, however, live by farming the rich land in the Arno delta, and by fishing.

The population of Pisa is 62,000.

PITCHER (*pĭch'ẽr*), **MOLLY** (1754–1832), was a heroine of the American Revolution. Her real name was Mary Ludwig. Molly was born

near Trenton, New Jersey, the daughter of a farmer who had come to the colonies from Germany. In 1769, at the age of 15, Molly took a job in Philadelphia as a maid. Later that year, she married John Caspar Hays, a Philadelphia barber.

When the American Revolution began, Hays joined an artillery outfit in the colonial army. Molly returned to her father's farm, but after Hays' outfit spent a hard winter at Valley Forge, Molly joined him.

Molly was with the army during the Battle of Monmouth, fought on a hot June day in 1778. She spent much of the day carrying pitchers of water from a well to the tired and wounded soldiers on the battlefields. The soldiers called her Molly Pitcher.

Molly saw her husband fall unconscious from the heat. Quickly, she took his place in the gun crew and kept the gun going throughout the battle. For this brave action she was publicly praised by General Nathaniel Greene, and was made an honorary sergeant by George Washington.

John Hays was never healthy again. He died in 1789. Molly's second marriage was not a happy one, and she worked for many years as a washerwoman. In 1822 Pennsylvania gave her a bonus and a pension for the rest of her life.

PITT (*pĭt*), **WILLIAM** (THE ELDER AND YOUNGER). The two Pitts, father and son, were both English statesmen.

WILLIAM PITT, THE ELDER, 1ST EARL OF

CHATHAM (1708–1778), was born at Westminster and educated at Eton and at Trinity College, Oxford. He entered Parliament in 1735 and joined the opposition to Sir Robert Walpole's ministry. From the beginning he claimed to speak for the people and the colonies and soon was called the "Great Commoner." In 1746 he became paymaster general. This office was often used to make money, but Pitt gained admiration by being honest.

In the Seven Years' War with France, the English were defeated several times. Pitt became the head of the government and leader of the House of Commons in 1756. In 1757 Pitt took charge of the War Ministry. He revived the militia and reorganized the navy. His attack on France's colonies gained Canada, part of India, and other possessions for England, making it a great empire.

In 1760 George III came to the throne determined to end the war quickly, and Pitt was forced to resign. He continued to oppose England's treatment of the colonies in America. He became prime minister again in 1766. Becoming an earl made him less popular, and illness kept him from working. He resigned in 1768.

WILLIAM PITT, THE YOUNGER (1759–1806), was born in Kent and went to Cambridge when he was 14 years old. He entered Parliament at 21. In 1783, after the House of Commons passed a bill against the King's wishes, the King dismissed the ministry and made Pitt prime minister. He was not yet 25. Although most of the House was against him, he gained the support of the people. In the next election they elected representatives who were on his side.

As prime minister, Pitt made many needed changes and got rid of many useless political offices. He started a fund to pay off part of the national debt. Also he brought about a parliamentary union between England and Ireland.

In the war against Napoleon, England's strong navy destroyed French sea power. But England's weak army forced Pitt to rely on Austria and Russia on land. Napoleon's victory at Austerlitz in 1805 won France the continent. The news was a blow to Pitt, and he died soon after.

PITTSBURGH (*pĭts′bĕrg*), **PENNSYLVANIA,** is a city in the foothills of the Appalachian Mountains in the southwestern part of the state. It covers a triangular area between the Allegheny and Monongahela rivers where they join to form the Ohio River. Pittsburgh, one of the chief U.S. industrial centers, is known as "The Steel City." It is a hub of rail and water transportation. It is also a U.S. port of entry. Industry in Pittsburgh grew because it is on the path of east-west trade routes and near supplies of coal, petroleum, limestone, natural gas, and iron ore.

Industry and Trade

The Pittsburgh district is a leading iron and steel producing center of the world. Pittsburgh is a leading manufacturer of coke, aluminum, air brakes, rolled steel, glass, steel sheets, safety equipment, plumbing fixtures, electrical equipment, wire, nuts, bolts, rivets, radium and vanadium products, wrought-iron pipe, and stainless steel. It is the home of the largest tin plate mill and the largest by-product coke plant in the world.

Pittsburgh is also an important trade center. The yearly tonnage carried on its rivers—the Monongahela, Allegheny, and Ohio—is greater than the tonnage moved in any other inland river area in the world. In addition to three major railroads, there are also air lines, bus lines, and the Pennsylvania Turnpike. The Greater Pittsburgh Airport is the second largest in the world. Cable cars are used to haul passengers and freight up the city's many steep hills.

The City

The city of Pittsburgh has a sky line highlighted by factories, skyscrapers, and tall apartment buildings. A number of narrow, winding streets climb the hills and run along the river banks. Pittsburgh's rivers, lined with steel mills and factories, present a picture of a workingman's city. However, a view from the top of Mount Washington, the Gateway Center, the tower of the Gulf Building (Pittsburgh's tallest building), or the Cathedral of Learning shows a city of parks, green hills, and streets

Downtown Pittsburgh has been called the "Golden Triangle" because of its shape and the city's rich industrial heritage. The Allegheny and Monongahela rivers, crossed by many bridges, meet at the point of the triangle.

bordered with trees.

Pittsburgh has a population made up of many nationalities. Up to the 19th century the city was populated mainly by Irish and Scots. Shortly after 1800 many English settlers arrived. Large groups of Germans went to Pittsburgh during the U.S. Civil War. The rapid growth of the city's coal and steel industries during the 1880's brought in thousands of Italians, Poles, Czechs, Slovaks, Hungarians, and Russians.

The triangular-shaped chief business district, $1\frac{1}{2}$ square miles between the Monongahela and Allegheny rivers, has become the "Golden Triangle," called so because of the men who made large fortunes in Pittsburgh: Andrew Carnegie, Henry Clay Frick, Andrew Mellon, Henry Phipps, George Westinghouse, H. J. Heinz, Henry Buhl, and others. To the people of Pittsburgh they returned some of this wealth in gifts and grants: Carnegie Institute, the many Carnegie libraries, Carnegie-Mellon University, Mellon Institute of Industrial Research, Mellon Park, the Buhl Planetarium, Phipps Conserva-

tory, Heinz Memorial Chapel, Mellon Square Park, and many other schools, churches, libraries, office buildings, parks and playgrounds, museums, and monuments.

In 1945 the Allegheny Conference on Community Development began its work to gain public support and approval for community improvement projects. Since that time storage dams have been built for flood control; progress has been made in smoke control; work has gone forward to build a historical park at the western point of the triangle; slum areas have been rebuilt; roads and highways have been extended; parks have been opened; bridges are under construction; underground parking garages have been built; and many new skyscraper office buildings are being completed. In 1956 a $43,000,000 physical redevelopment program was approved that included modernization of the city's water system, street repaving and sewer improvement, and more recreation areas.

Among the institutions of higher learning in Pittsburgh are Carnegie-Mellon University (formerly Carnegie Institute of Technology); the University of Pittsburgh, with its chief building, the 42-story Cathedral of Learning; Duquesne University; and, for women, Chatham College (formerly Pennsylvania College for Women) and Mount Mercy College. There are also theological seminaries, a school for the blind, and Point Park College.

Much progress has been made in medical and industrial research. The Medical Center includes modern hospitals and clinics; and large industrial companies—United States Steel, Westinghouse, Pittsburgh Plate Glass, Koppers, Jones and Laughlin Steel, and others—support important research laboratories in the Pittsburgh metropolitan area.

Among Pittsburgh's radio and television stations are KDKA, the world's first broadcasting station, and WQED, an educational outlet. The *Pittsburgh Post-Gazette*, established in 1786 as the *Pittsburgh Gazette*, is the oldest newspaper west of the Appalachians.

The city maintains 22 parks. The zoos are in Highland Park; the conservatory, in Schenley Park; and the Allegheny Observatory, with its large refracting telescope, in Riverview Park.

History

The Indians called the narrow triangle of land between the Allegheny and Monongahela rivers Diondega, meaning "Fork." White men set up a trading post there. Trappers and traders with their pack horses followed the Indian trails and streams and cut through new passes over the Allegheny Mountains leading to the post. In time these trails became wide enough for the Pennsylvania Conestoga wagons to bring white settlers from the East. Soon the Fork became known as the "Gateway to the West." It was the last stop for supplies needed by pioneers traveling into the unknown regions of the West.

The Upper Ohio region was claimed by both the English and the French. Both fought for control of the plot of land between the rivers that was to become the city of Pittsburgh. Fort Prince George, which was built by the English, was captured by the French before it was completed. The French built their own Fort

Huge steel plants glow in heavily industrial Pittsburgh. The city's position, near coal and iron ore deposits, helped it become a leading U.S. steelmaking center.

David Corson from A. Devaney—Publix

Duquesne, which in turn was taken over by the English in 1758. Since Fort Duquesne was left in ruins by the French, it was replaced by Fort Pitt, named in honor of William Pitt, prime minister of England. After the French were driven out, Irish and Scottish settlers moved into the region.

During the American Revolution, the settlement had a population of less than 500. About that time a government boatyard was built in the village, and shipbuilding became a successful industry. In 1792 the sailboat *Western Experiment* was launched on the Monongahela River. Flatboats and keelboats were the commonest river vessels, however.

It was not until 1795 that a lasting peace with the Indians was gained by "Mad" Anthony Wayne. The village became Pitts Borough, and soon a growing manufacturing community developed. Small shops and factories, iron foundries, lumber yards, shipyards, and glass and other businesses were operating. In 1816 Pittsburgh was incorporated as a city.

A new era in transportation started in 1811 with the appearance of the first steamboat west of the Appalachian Mountains. Wooden ships were slowly replaced by ships made of iron, and Pittsburgh-made barges and stern-wheel steamers were used on rivers all over the world.

In 1845 a terrible fire destroyed 20 blocks of buildings and left 2,000 persons homeless. Flood damage at times has been serious.

During the War Between the States, Pittsburgh was one of the arsenals of the North, making ammunition and equipment for the Union army. World Wars I and II brought great increases in production.

Pittsburgh is the seat of government of Allegheny County.

It is the second largest city in Pennsylvania, with a population of (1960) 604,332.

PIUS (*pī′ŭs*). The Latin word *pius,* meaning *godly,* or *devout,* has been used as a name by 12 popes, of whom the following are the best known.

Pius II (pope, 1458–1464) was born near Siena, Italy, in 1405 and bore the name of Enea Silvio de Piccolomini. Becoming a writer of considerable fame and a man of keen political power, he was well known before he entered the priesthood. He had served the church well at the Council of Basle by healing a break between Frederick III of Germany and the papacy.

When he finally entered the church in 1446 he rose rapidly from priest to bishop, to cardinal, and then to the papal chair. His chief activity as pope lay in organizing crusades against the Turks. He died at Ancona, Italy, on the eve of embarking for the Holy Land.

Pius IV (pope, 1559–1565) was a native of Milan, Italy, where he was born in 1499. He studied medicine and law, and was sent on important diplomatic missions before he entered the church. As pope he is chiefly remembered for his work in connection with the second session of the Council of Trent (1562–1563) which drew up under his guidance the "Creed of Pius IV." It is still used today by those who take orders in, or who become converts to, the Roman Catholic church.

Pius VI (pope, 1775–1799) was born in Cesena, Italy, in 1717. Before his ordination he served as secretary to Benedict XIV. His pontificate included the stormy years of the French Revolution. After being forced to give up part of his territory to the invading Napoleon Bonaparte, he later saw Rome, Italy, entered by French troops and proclaimed a republic. Refusing to yield his temporal sovereignty, he was carried off a prisoner to Siena, to Florence, Italy, and finally to Valence, France, where he died.

Pius VII (pope, 1800–1823), like his predecessor, was born in Cesena, Italy, in the year 1740. He was a Benedictine abbot, but had been raised to the cardinalate before he became pope. The French still held Rome, but the new pope was allowed to enter the city. Later a sort of peace was set up, the French Concordat of 1801 was arranged, and Pius went to Paris to crown Napoleon emperor. In 1809 Napoleon annexed the papal states. The pope, in his turn, excommunicated Napoleon, who then arrested Pius VII and carried him off to Fontainebleau, France. Here Napoleon forced him to sign a new Concordat, which the pope later repudiated. When the emperor lost his power, the papal territory was restored and Pius returned to Rome.

PIUS IX (pope, 1846–1878) was born Giovanni Mastai-Ferretti in Senigallia, Italy, in 1792. He was from an old Italian family. He succeeded Gregory XVI as pope. Although he promptly started reforms in the government of the papal states, he was forced to leave Rome during the Italian Revolution of 1848. Later he returned and was protected by the French until they withdrew in 1869. In 1870 Rome became the capital of united Italy and the papal states were taken over. However, Pius IX refused to recognize the new government, or to accept its offer of settlement. He shut himself up in the Vatican as a voluntary prisoner.

During his reign two important church dogmas, or accepted beliefs, were established. The Immaculate Conception of the Virgin Mary was proclaimed in 1854. The doctrine of the infallibility of the pope in matters of faith and morals was defined and published by the Vatican Council in 1870.

PIUS X (pope, 1903–1914) was born Giuseppe Sarto in a humble home at Riese, Italy, in 1835. His excellent work as bishop and cardinal patriarch of Venice, Italy, led to his being elected pope. He is remembered chiefly for his efforts to promote religious fervor among the clergy and the people, and for his protests against the increasing liberality of modern views. He was canonized in 1954.

PIUS XI (pope, 1922–1939) was born Achille Ratti in Desio, Italy, near Milan, in 1857. He was educated in St. Charles's College at Milan and decided early to become a priest. He studied at the Lombard College and at the Angelico. He was ordained in 1879. In succession, he was a village curator, a professor at Milan Seminary, and prefect of the Ambrosian Library. He was also vice-prefect of the Vatican Library and canon of St. Peter's.

In 1918 Pope Benedict XV sent him to Poland, where he remained during the Bolshevik invasion. For his efforts to secure peace and relieve suffering, Poland awarded him the Order of the White Eagle. In 1921 he was made archbishop of Milan and created cardinal. He was

elected pope February 6, 1922.

Pius XI was often called the "pope of peace." He helped settle the long dispute between Italy and the papacy. On February 11, 1929, the Lateran treaty was signed. It made Vatican City independent of Italy and subject only to the rule of the pope. (See PAPACY; VATICAN CITY.)

Pius XI was opposed to communism and persecution of Jews in Germany and Italy. When World War II was about to break out, he made many pleas for peace.

PIUS XII (pope, 1939–1958) was born Eugenio Pacelli in 1876 at Rome, Italy. Ordained priest in 1899, his diplomatic abilities were early recognized. In 1917 he was sent to Munich, Germany, where he made great efforts to help end World War I. He became papal nuncio (diplomatic representative) to Germany in 1920, and was created cardinal in 1929. Appointed papal secretary of state in 1930, he worked to settle the conflicts that arose between the church and Russia, Germany, Spain, Italy, and Mexico. When he was elected pope in 1939, his major aim was to bring about a lasting peace. Although he preserved strict neutrality in the Vatican State, he repeatedly spoke against the evils of government by dictators, and outlined the necessary conditions for "a new order formed on moral principles." One of the most important acts during his reign was his pronouncement of the dogma of the Corporal Assumption of the Virgin Mary.

PIZARRO (pĭ zär'ō), **FRANCISCO** (frän thēs'-kō or frän sēs'kō) (1471?–1541). The very air of the 16th century was filled with the glamour of adventure. Francisco Pizarro, conqueror of Peru, was one of those bold men who crossed the Atlantic in search of fame and fortune. No one knows much about his boyhood except that he had a hard time, having had no one to look after him. It is known, however, that he was born in Spain, and that he was in Seville, Spain, when the news came that Christopher Columbus had discovered a rich, new world. Pizarro asked nothing better than an opportunity to trust his life and fortune to one of the many expeditions which went to investigate the discoveries of Columbus. By some means he crossed the Atlantic. Later he was with Vasco de Balboa when that daring leader first saw the Pacific Ocean. After 1517 Pizarro settled on a grant of land in Panama. An expedition returning from Andagoya brought news of a fabulously rich kingdom to the south. Pizarro determined to equip an expedition to conquer it.

In 1522, in partnership with Diego de Almagro, a soldier, and Hernando de Luque, a priest, Pizarro collected an expedition to explore the west coast of South America. While Almagro returned to Panama for supplies, Pizarro with 13 men was left stranded for months off the coast. The fierce Indians there prevented him from leaving the Island of Gallo. He lived there without ship or supplies until Almagro returned.

But he had heard more of the golden treasures of Peru and was more than ever determined on conquest. When he could not raise the army he needed in Panama, Pizarro boldly decided to return to Spain and get help from Charles V. He succeeded in becoming that emperor's favorite, was decorated with the order of Santiago and granted a coat of arms. But what pleased him most was the emperor's permission to go back to South America, conquer a large tract and establish a province to be called New Castile, where he was to rule supreme. First, however, he was required to collect a force of men by himself. When he was unable to get the required number he sailed secretly in 1530. A year later he reached Panama, whence, with 180 men, three ships, and about two dozen horses, he sailed for Peru.

Pizarro was a great leader, generous to his soldiers, but he was also treacherous and cruel. He seized the Inca ruler who came to welcome him. Pizarro later had him executed for treason, although the ruler had filled his prison cell with gold as ransom. Pizarro's reign was marred by wars with his own followers as well as with the Incas. He was finally assassinated at Lima, Peru, the city he had founded.

PLANETARIUM (*plăn'ē tār'ĭ ŭm*). A planetarium is a device for showing the motions of the planets in their orbits. In the sky, the planets look like stars, but they slowly change their po-

sitions among the stars from night to night. Mechanical devices to show these motions have been made for several centuries. The first machines had a number of small balls to represent the planets and the sun. Complicated gears controlled the motions of the balls representing the planets so that they moved around the ball representing the sun just as the real planets move around the real sun. Later models were made in the form of a hollow sphere, with holes of different sizes to represent stars of the different magnitudes. The sphere was lighted from outside and housed the device showing the motions of the planets. Some of these machines were driven by hand and some by clockwork. Most modern ones are driven by electric motors.

A different kind of planetarium, the Zeiss, was invented in Germany about 1920. The first

For many years men tried to make models of the heavens that would show the locations of the stars, planets, and moon. This instrument is the Zeiss planetarium machine, which shows the heavenly bodies as they appear in the sky. It is in the center of the Adler Planetarium in Chicago, Illinois.

Courtesy Adler Planetarium

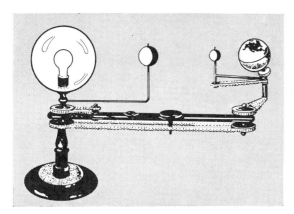

By a system of gears and chains this planetarium shows the movements and positions of the sun, Venus, Earth, and the moon.

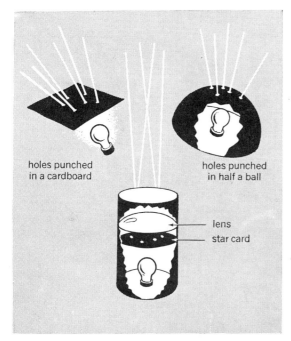

holes punched in a cardboard

holes punched in half a ball

lens
star card

The stars of a single constellation can be shown by punching holes, properly spaced, in a piece of cardboard and shining a light behind the cardboard. The beams of light passing through the cardboard will then show as stars on the wall or ceiling. Half a hollow ball punched with holes can show the whole sky. Large planetaria use many-lensed projectors like the one at the bottom. These throw very sharp images of the heavenly bodies on a curved ceiling.

Zeiss model was finished in 1924. Six Zeiss planetaria are in use in the United States, in Chicago, Illinois; Philadelphia and Pittsburgh, Pennsylvania; Los Angeles, California; New York City; and Chapel Hill, North Carolina.

Eight more are in operation elsewhere, and 11 others were destroyed in World War II. Many smaller, simpler models are in use in the United States. In 1952 the Morrison Planetarium was opened in San Francisco, California. Its projector is even more elaborate and complicated than the Zeiss. It took $4\frac{1}{2}$ years of work in instrument shops of the California Academy of Science to build.

The visitor to a modern planetarium sits in a circular theater with several hundred chairs and sees overhead a wonderfully accurate and beautiful artificial sky. At the center of this room stands the planetarium instrument, a complicated machine made up of more than 100 projectors or stereopticons. These projectors are like those used in motion-picture theaters, except that there is no motion within the separate pictures which each projector throws on the dome-shaped ceiling above the audience.

Some of the pictures show the stars, and these pictures are very carefully fitted together on the dome so that they form a single picture, a nearly perfect one of the night sky. Other projectors, like small searchlights, throw spots of light on the dome for the sun, moon, and planets. There are electric motors and very complicated gears to move these projectors to show the motions of the sun, moon, and planets among the stars. Other motors turn the whole instrument, except for its supporting framework, on different axles to produce other changes visible in the real heavens. Every object and every motion visible in the real sky without telescopes is reproduced in the planetarium sky. The heavens can be shown as seen from any place on the earth at any time in the past, present, or future. The passage of time can be speeded up so that the events of thousands of years pass in review in a few minutes. (See OBSERVATORY.)

PLANTAGENET (*plăn tăj'ĕ nĕt* or *plăn tăj'ĕ-nĭt*). A family of kings that ruled England from 1154 to 1400 were known as the Plantagenets. They belonged to the house of Anjou of France. Under the Plantagenets, the English people were united for the first time after the Norman invasion in 1066.

The counts of Anjou were among the most daring and blood thirsty barons in medieval France and England. Count Fulk V of Anjou and Henry I of England fought bitterly. (See HENRY [KINGS OF ENGLAND].) But in 1129 they patched up their quarrel by a marriage between Fulk's son Geoffrey and Henry's daughter Matilda. Geoffrey succeeded his father as count of Anjou. He was called Geoffrey Plantagenet because he wore a sprig of broom (*genet* in French) plant in his cap. When Henry I died, the English throne went to his nephew Stephen. Meanwhile Geoffrey conquered Normandy and gave it to his son Henry. When Stephen died, Henry became Henry II of England, the first Plantagenet king. He also possessed the French provinces of Anjou, Normandy, and Aquitaine.

The Normans and Saxons in England became one people under the rule of the Plantagenets, who founded both the system of law and Parliament. Henry's two sons, Richard I and John, succeeded him. (See JOHN [KING OF ENGLAND]; RICHARD [KINGS OF ENGLAND].) Other Plantagenet kings were John's son Henry III, who was beaten by the barons; Edward I, who restored order; Edward II, the only weak Plantagenet; and Edward III, who, aided by his son Edward the Black Prince, regained most of the French territory lost by John. (See EDWARD [KINGS OF ENGLAND].) The line of the Plantagenets ended with Richard II, son of the Black Prince, who died in 1400.

PLANT (*plànt*) AND PLANT BREEDING

(*brēd'ing*). Plants belong to one of the two great groups of living things. Every living thing is either a plant or an animal. Although most plants are quite different from animals, they are alike in some ways. (See BOTANY.) Both plants and animals grow, increase in size, and mature to an adult stage. Both may have accidents or injuries which damage or kill them. Both plants and animals have the power to repair many kinds of injuries. In many cases scars are left where the injury has healed.

Plants, like all living things, are able to adjust to the changes around them. They respond to touch, water, gravity, sunlight, and chemicals. A plant which has been turned upside down will grow so that the roots again point downward and the top will point toward the sun. The Mimosa plant, usually called "sensitive plant," will fold its leaves and appear to wilt when it is touched. Tendrils of the grape vine wind themselves around a wire or branch. They could not do this if they did not respond to the touch of the wire or branch. Flower petals may open and close as the sun comes and goes and plant leaves gradually turn toward the sun.

Plant and animal bodies both are made up of cells. (See CELL AND CELL THEORY.) The cells contain the living material called protoplasm. The bodies of living things are organized into different parts and each part has a certain work or function. Reproduction is one of the functions. Reproduction is much the same in higher plants and animals. There are certain parts which produce eggs and certain parts which produce sperm. Among simple plants and animals, reproduction is a very simple process. For example, yeast plants, bacteria and some forms of algae reproduce by cell division. (See REPRODUCTION.)

So we see that plants, like animals, are able to grow, repair injuries, and respond to stimuli (things or changes around them). They are able to produce—or help produce—more plants like themselves.

Plants and Animals Are Different

Although plants and animals have a great deal in common there are certain ways in which they are different from each other. When an animal has reached adult stage it no longer grows. A plant, however, continues to grow or increase in size as long as it lives. Movement is another way in which they are different. Most plants stay in the same place all their lives. They move only as they are moved about by wind and water or as they grow upward, outward or downward. They are not able to walk, run, swim or fly as are animals.

Plants become scattered over all parts of the earth as their seeds are carried from place to place. Some seeds are like wings for flying in the wind. Some have spines and hooks and catch onto animals' fur to be carried. Others can roll, float, or sail.

Most kinds of plants are green. Because they are green they are able to manufacture food out of carbon dioxide and water. Animals must depend upon green plants for their food. The green material which gives the plant its color is called chlorophyll. The chlorophyll is contained in small bodies called chloroplasts which act as the machines of the leaf. Some kinds of plants contain chlorophyll and are able to make food for themselves, but they also have so many other color pigments that the plant does not look green. (See LEAF.)

Perhaps the best way to tell a plant from an animal is to look at the cell wall. The cell walls of plants are made of a material called cellulose. Almost no animals have cellulose cell walls—their cell walls are made of membrane.

There are a few living things which in some ways are like plants and in some ways like animals. It is very difficult to find out whether a Euglena is a plant or an animal. It moves about as animals do and it is able to make its own food much as green plants do.

Plant Groups

Scientists have divided all plants into 12 main groups or divisions. In turn each group is divided into smaller groups. These divisions are made on the basis of structure. Those plants which are most alike are in the same group. Some of these plants are very simple, having only one cell in their bodies.

The common green pond scum is an algae and is one of the simplest kind of plants. (See ALGAE.) Another in the same group of plants is the fungi, which are not green and for that reason are not able to make their own food. They are called dependent plants because they must depend upon green plants for their food. Mushrooms, toadstools, wheat rust and bacteria are some of the plants which belong to the dependent plants. (A few kinds of green plants are dependent upon other green plants, and for this reason, they are called parasitic plants. Mistletoe and dodder are examples of parasitic plants which are green.)

Another group of plants is green and has leaflike structures, and tiny rootlets, but does not have stems or flowers. They are small and live where there is much moisture. Mosses and liverworts belong to this group. Ferns belong to a little higher group. They are more complicated in structure than the group to which mosses and liverworts belong. They do not have true stems, flowers or seeds.

The bodies of higher plants have roots, stems, leaves and flowers. Each of the plant parts serves a different purpose or function. Roots absorb water and minerals from the ground, as well as help to hold the plant firmly in the ground. (See ROOT.) Stems hold the leaves up to the sunlight and carry water and food materials up and down. The leaves serve as the manufacturing centers of the plant and supply the world of plants and animals with food. Flowers produce the seeds and carry on the reproductive processes of the plant.

All the plants of today are thought to have developed from the very simple green plants of long ago. The flowering plants are most complex and rank at the top of the plant kingdom.

Plant Breeding

Man and other animals have always depended upon green plants for their food. Long ago plants grew wild and people moved from place to place to find them. Since that time many kinds of plants have been domesticated (raised by man) and are grown in large quantities. All of the plants now raised came from plants that once grew wild. In most cases, however, the plants grown today are quite different from their ancestors. Plant breeders have brought about many changes as they domesticated them. These changes have made them much better for our use. For example, the tulip and iris in our gardens are much larger and more beautiful in color because of plant breeding. The many varieties of apples in our orchards are larger and more flavorful. Plant breeders made many improvements in wheat, and made it possible to produce more of it. They worked for larger grains, more of them in each head, and with better food value. They also worked for stronger stems and for resistance to plant disease. They were able to develop plants which are resistant to insect pests.

The length of time it takes for wheat to reach full growth was changed—sometimes made longer and sometimes made shorter—to suit the place in which it is raised. Improvements such as these were made in all of our food grains— rye, oats, corn, etc.

Even though two plants may have come from the same ancestor they may be quite different. There are apples of many kinds, colors and flavors but they all came from the same ancestor. Cauliflower, cabbage, Brussels sprouts, broccoli, kale and kohlrabi all came from wild cabbage and they are quite different from each other.

Plant breeders work carefully and with a purpose. They usually start by deciding upon what they want to develop. For example, they may wish to grow a seedless tomato. They then try to produce the new plant from the plants which they already have.

Plant breeders produce new varieties of plants in different ways. One of the ways is by growing hybrids. To understand hybrids it is important to know about pollination and fertilization in flowering plants. Pollination is the transfer of pollen from the stamens of one flower to the stigma of the pistil of the same flower or of another flower. It is necessary for pollination and fertilization to take place in order that seeds will be formed. Fertilization can only take place after pollination takes place. In each little pollen grain there are two tiny sperm cells. The two tiny sperm cells from the pollen grain must reach an ovule of the pistil in order that one of them may unite with the egg cell in the ovule. The union of the egg and sperm cell is fertilization. The fertilized egg cell may then develop into a tiny plant. It is easy to see the tiny plant in the bean seed, with the food stored around it. There is a firm coat or covering around both the food and baby plant.

Hybrid seeds are produced when cross pollination takes place. This happens when pollen from one kind of plant pollinates the flower of another kind of plant. Plant breeders are able to produce hybrid seeds by making sure that pollen from one kind of plant pollinates another carefully chosen plant. The hybrid plants

Joe Munroe

In growing flowers, the blossoms are covered after they have been pollinated. Without the covering, unwanted pollen from other plants, carried by the wind, would land on the blossoms.

which grow from the hybrid seeds may be quite new and unusual. Seeds from the hybrid plants usually will not grow into plants like the mother plant. To get more hybrid seeds, plant breeders must cross pollinate all over again. Much of what is known about hybridization is due to the results of experiments made by Gregor Mendel. He was the first person to experiment with heredity in plants.

Often new plants come about by accident. When this happens and their seeds grow into more of the new kind of plant—plant breeders call it a mutant. The loganberry is an example of a mutant. It grew by accident from a wild blackberry. No one knows a great deal about what causes mutants. Scientists are trying to find ways to produce useful mutants. They have tried X-ray, chemicals, and atomic radiation and have produced mutations, but have not as yet been able to control kinds of mutations. The one sure thing plant breeders can do is to watch for good mutants and help the mutants to produce more like themselves.

A very common way of getting better plants

Photos, Courtesy United States Department of Agriculture

Breeding different varieties of the same plant. Left: Pollen from one plant is collected in a paper bag. Right: The pollen is then sprinkled on the flower of another plant.

is by selection. Plant breeders carefully select seed from those plants which have the greatest number of good qualities. For example, seed corn should be selected from ears that are well filled out and have straight rows of seed. The ears of corn should be selected from fields of good strong corn plants. Selection not only means careful selection of seed but also careful selection of bulbs, roots, tubers or any other part of a plant from which new plants will grow. Improving plants by selection is very slow but some very good changes have come about in this way. Many of the cultivated plants have been improved a great deal by selection.

Certain chemicals known as growth regulators are used to improve plant growth, too. Growth regulators may be used to speed up growth or to slow it down. Others may be used to make fruits develop even though fertilization has not taken place. Still other growth regulators slow up blooming and help to prevent flowers from dropping before pollination has taken place. With growth regulators plant

breeders have been able to produce a seedless tomato, but how to produce quantities of them is still a problem. Some day there may be seedless cucumbers, seedless watermelon and many other seedless fruits.

Hybridization, mutation, selection, and using growth regulators are four important ways to get better and new kinds of plants. As time goes on scientists are sure to find other and better means of improving plant breeding.

Some plant breeders have had plants named for them. Developing a new plant is an important discovery. A new variety of plant can be patented just as new machinery inventions are patented. The government grants the patents in much the same way.

Plant breeding is an effort to get new and better kinds of plants for special purposes.

Plant Raising

Many millions of people make their living raising plants for themselves and for others. These people are called farmers or agriculturists. They prepare good seed beds, cultivate the crops while they are growing, and harvest the crops when they are ready.

Many plants are grown in great quantities. Large fields of corn and wheat are a common sight in many parts of the world. Fields of cotton and rice, orchards of fruit trees, and forests of Christmas trees are common in other parts of the world. Mushrooms, a dependent plant, are grown in many places, too.

Plants which grow where they are not wanted are called weeds. It is often hard for the farmer to keep weeds from growing. They rob the soil of its moisture and food material and may even crowd out more desirable plants. (See WEED.)

People who till the soil need to know a great deal about the soil and the plants which they are raising. Each kind of plant needs a little different care than every other kind of plant.

Agriculture is one of the world's most important occupations because everyone depends upon plants for food.

PLANT CLASSIFICATION (*klăs′ ŭ fŭ kā′ shŭn*) is the placement of a plant in a system that shows the relationships between plant groups. Classification, along with the identification and naming of plants, is a part of the branch of botany called taxonomy.

The classification system commonly in use today works in somewhat the same way as the method used by the U.S. postal service. Persons and plants are members of large and small groups. Each person has a specific address that includes the state, city or town, and street and house number. Each person also has a family name, first name, and middle name. When a letter begins its route to someone, the postman first looks at the largest group to which this person belongs—the state. He then looks at the next largest group—the city—and so on down to the smallest. Only one person could be described in this way:

State	Montana
City	Helena
Street and Number	55 Main
Family name	Smith
First name	George
Middle name	Finley

Each plant can be classified in a similar way. The groups to which a plant belongs are division, or phylum (state), class (city), order (street and number), family (family name), genus (first name), and species (middle name). The classification of *Rosa setigera* (commonly called prairie rose) is therefore:

Division	Tracheophyta
Class	Angiospermae
Order	Rosales
Family	Rosaceae
Genus	Rosa
Species	setigera

Just as each person has a distinct address, each plant has a specific classification.

The largest group in the plant kingdom to which any plant belongs is a division. Each plant is classified into one of 12 divisions, just as each person in the United States lives in one of the 50 states. Each of the 12 divisions includes plants that are thought to be more closely related to each other than they are to members of a different division. The divisions are arranged in the classification so as to indicate plant groupings of increasing complexity and to suggest the order in which the groups are believed to have developed. (See EVOLUTION.) The simplest plants are the thallophytes, which include algae and fungi and are mostly water plants or plants that live in damp places. (See ALGAE; FUNGUS.) The first land plants were the bryophytes and the psilophytes. The bryophytes are the liverworts, hornworts, and mosses. (See MOSS.) The tracheophytes, which are the vascular plants, are more advanced than the bryophytes. The tracheophytes have a vascular system for conducting food from the leaves to the roots and other parts of the plant and a vascular system for conducting water and dissolved minerals from the roots to the leaves. The tracheophytes include the psilopsids, ferns, horsetails, club mosses, and the more complex group called the seed plants. (See FERN; SEED.) The latter plants include the gymnosperms and the angiosperms. (See BOTANY, *Naming and Classifying Plants*.)

The prairie rose (*Rosa setigera*) is similar to other roses but has characteristics by which it may be distinguished from them. Each species of rose has its own name. For example, *Rosa setigera* and *Rosa canina,* or dog rose, are two different kinds of roses. All species of roses are grouped in the genus *Rosa.* The genus *Rosa* is related to other genera by similarities of flowers, fruits, and other parts. Some of these other genera are *Prunus* (peach, plum, cherry, apricot), *Malus* (apple, crabapple), *Pyrus* (pear), *Crataegus* (hawthorn), and *Rubus* (blackberry, dewberry, raspberry). These genera make up a larger group called a family.

The genera just mentioned belong to the rose family, or Rosaceae. This is a large and important family of seed plants, including more than 100 genera and about 3,200 species. In several ways it is like certain other families, especially the saxifrage (Saxifragaceae) and the legume (Leguminosae) families. These families, plus several others, make up the order Rosales. Rosales, in turn, is one of a number of orders that make up the subclass Dicotyledoneae, which includes plants with two seed leaves. This subclass and the subclass Monocotyledoneae—plants with only one seed leaf—make up the class of Angiospermae.

When classifying a new plant, a botanist first determines the division to which it belongs. He then determines the other categories in which it should be placed: subdivision, class, subclass, order, family, genus, and species, in that order. He always proceeds in the same way. For this reason, no matter where a plant is found, or by whom, it will be classified by the same method. Such a method of classification can be understood by any botanist.

One of the early systems of plant classification was made by Swedish botanist Carolus Linnaeus. (See LINNAEUS, CAROLUS.) In his system, plants were classified according to the number of stamens in the flower. One important part of the system was the double name—a genus name and a species name—given to each plant. This is known as the binomial (from *bi,* meaning "two," and *nomen,* "name") system. The genus name (*Rosa*) shows the genus to which any rose belongs, and the species name (*setigera, canina,* etc.) designates the type.

In 1859 Darwin proposed his theory of evolution. This theory has led to the understanding that members of a group, such as the roses, share many characteristics because all the members developed from the same ancestors. Botanists have attempted to develop a system of classification showing relationships based on common ancestry. In the development of such a system of classification several types of evidence have been used. One of these is the study of fossil plants—their structures and their relative ages. The living plants are compared with each other and with fossil plants in order to learn more about their relationships. On the basis of this information a system of classification has been developed. The present system of classification is subject to improvement as more knowledge of plant relationships becomes known. (See BOTANY.)

PLANT DISEASE. Plants like other living things are attacked by many diseases. Such diseases can be divided into three main groups. These groups are virus diseases; bacterial diseases; and diseases caused by some types of fungi. (See FUNGUS.) A fourth class known as nutritional diseases is sometimes made. The most difficult type of disease to fight is that caused by viruses. A virus is different from a bacterium or a fungus in that it is difficult to see even with a microscope. Most virus diseases can not be controlled by sprays, dusts, or methods of sanitation, as can many of those caused by bacteria or fungi. An example of a virus disease is the mosaic of tobacco, so-called because the leaves of the infested tobacco plant appear mottled—green and lighter green. Another virus disease is called "little cherry" because trees infected with it bear little fruits. In some areas it is a serious disease. Experiments are still being made to find a control for it, but as yet none has been found.

A good example of a bacterial disease is pear blight, which is destructive to pear trees. It is carried by bees in the spring when the trees are in bloom. It spreads rapidly down the limbs and trunk of the tree. The best ways to control it are to cut out the diseased portions as soon as they are seen, or to spray the infected trees with an antibiotic spray.

There are many diseases caused by fungi,

which attack many kinds of plants. Most fungi, at some time in their life, produce tiny bodies called spores. It is possible to control the spores by means of sprays put on the plants before the spores have a chance to spread. A protective coating is put over the plant so that the tiny filaments which the spores produce are destroyed before they have a chance to enter the plant.

Spraying is not always the best way to fight fungus diseases. Sometimes other methods are used. Control of the common rust of wheat is a good example. In the early stages of its development the stem of the wheat plant appears rusty. This rust consists of thousands of red spores ready to be scattered by the wind and enter the stems of other wheat plants. At the end of summer thicker-walled black spores take the place of the red spores. Spores produced by these must grow on the common barberry before again growing on the wheat. Therefore, getting rid of the barberry also gets rid of the rust. There are then no more spores produced which can infect the wheat. In some regions great care has been taken to get rid of the barberry wherever wheat is grown. (See RUST AND SMUT.)

The fourth kind of disease is not caused by any known organism. It is caused by a lack of proper minerals in the soil, or by high or low temperatures at which the plants are grown. Such diseases can be corrected by adding the proper fertilizers, or giving the plant the proper temperature for growing.

(For other plant diseases see BLIGHT AND ROT; MOLD AND MILDEW.)

PLASTER (*plăs'tẽr*). One of the commonest methods of finishing the walls and ceilings of rooms is to use a pasty composition called plaster. It can be applied easily and will harden into a hard, even surface that is capable of receiving any type of decoration. Before plastering, the walls and ceilings must be lined with laths of wood or metal or with gypsum lath, unless the walls are of masonry. Sometimes portland cement is used for plastering, and in some cases lime plaster is used. The type of plaster most generally used, however, is gypsum plaster (a white, powdery material). It is mixed with sand and water and applied in either two or three coats. The first or scratch coat, except on masonry, is mixed in the proportion of one part of plaster to two parts of sand and is spread evenly over the wall. Before it sets it is scratched to provide a rough surface for the second or brown coat. The first coat on masonry and the second or brown coat in all three-coat work is mixed in the proportion of one part of plaster to three parts of sand. After being applied, it is brought to an even surface and left rough to receive the finish coat. The finish coat may be a smooth, hard, white coat made of lime and gypsum plaster. Or it may be an even, sandy finish made of lime, cement, and sand, or of gypsum plaster and sand. The finish coat may be left as it is, or it may be covered with wallpaper, paint, or calcimine.

Left: Bacterial wilt of a tomato plant is an infection which attacks and destroys the inside of the stem. The whole plant wilts and dies.

Right: A fungus infection of a tomato leaf. A fungus infection usually enters from outside the leaf or the stem.

Photos, Courtesy United States Department of Agriculture

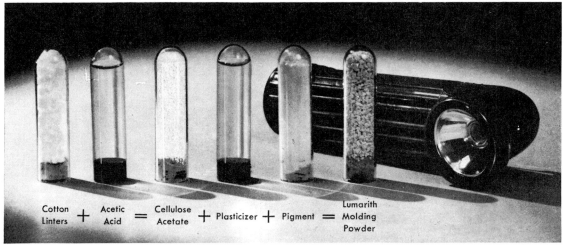

Cotton + Acetic = Cellulose + Plasticizer + Pigment = Lumarith
Linters   Acid   Acetate   Molding
Powder

Plastics are man-made materials created by putting basic raw materials (such as coal tar, cotton linters, wood pulp, bran, and skimmed milk) through a series of chemical changes, then shaping the resulting material under heat and pressure. This right-angle flashlight, for example, is a plastic product which will withstand temperatures from —40 degrees to +175 degrees Fahrenheit, and will continue to operate when submerged in water. Actually, it is made of cotton linters treated chemically and then molded into shape. The process is outlined above.

PLASTICS (*plăs'tĭks*). A wide variety of useful products is manufactured from plastics. Ten major plastics have been developed since 1907. Products manufactured from them are used widely in homes and industry. The growth of the plastics industry began during World War II.

The word plastic means "capable of being molded or modeled." When heated, plastics are somewhat like modeling clay. They can be molded into shapes which last when the material is cooled. This behavior gives them their name.

What Plastics Will Do

Like clay, plastics are easy materials to work with. With little difficulty they can be formed into complicated shapes in a wide variety of colors. Some of their specific properties make them useful in many applications.

Since plastics resist the flow of electricity, for example, they are used for the plugs on toasters and the knobs on television sets. Because they insulate against heat, plastic handles are put on cooking utensils; such handles do not become too hot to touch. As plastics are light in weight and wear well, air lines choose plastics for dishes. Some plastics are tough and

can be used to make unbreakable objects. Others can be cracked or broken when dropped or hit by a flying object.

Many products have been made possible because plastics can do things no other materials can. In a television set, for example, tube bases are made of phenolic plastic, the wire to the antenna is insulated with polyethylene, the tuner mechanism is insulated with phenolic and styrene, and the picture tube is cradled in a vinyl plastic yoke. In air-borne radar, a reinforced polyester plastic housing protects the revolving scanning device from being torn off by the wind, yet it does not interfere with radar waves going out and coming back.

Plastics have also made possible many improvements in other products. When photography was dependent on glass plates instead of film, it was a job for experts. But the camera became something everyone could use when the film was made from cellulosic plastics. A transparent vinyl film is sandwiched between two pieces of glass as a safety feature in automobile windshields. Cellulosic plastics provide football players with helmets to protect them from head injury. Vinyl, styrene, polyethylene, and phenolic plastics bring products to the public in attractive packages that protect and display the contents at the same time.

Where Plastics Come From

Organic chemistry is based on chemicals formed from carbon plus hydrogen, oxygen, or some other element. These elements are found in plants and animals and are also the building blocks of most plastics. The organic chemist combines these and other raw materials of nature to form molecules of plastics.

The molecule is the starting point in making a plastic. It is the smallest division of matter that still acts like the whole material from which it comes. Under the right conditions, the chemist causes these molecules to form a long chain, the links being the molecules. The new "long-chain" molecule acts differently from the single molecule. The molecules are said to *polymerize* when they link into chains. The whole process is called polymerization. By polymerization new materials are made. Sometimes two different types of molecules are joined to form materials called *copolymers*. A chain of two types of molecules acts differently from long chains made up of either type alone.

Something similar to polymerization takes place when fudge is made. In the first stage, when the mixture is very fluid, it can be stirred easily. When this fluid is heated, it becomes thicker and thicker. First it changes to the consistency of heavy oil, then to a molasseslike substance, and finally it becomes a barely flowing mass that will set up into hard pieces.

The hard pieces of polymer must be changed to be suitable for molding. They are ground into fine powder or made into pellets, colors are added, and chemicals are worked in to make it flexible. To some plastics plasticizers are added. These are chemicals which change a plastic that is as stiff as a blackboard into a material flexible enough for a raincoat. To other plastics fillers, such as ground wood, are added to make them stronger or more resistant to electricity or heat. The final mixture is called a commercial molding powder.

How Useful Objects Are Made

Since plastics can be made into so many varied shapes, there are a number of methods for manufacturing usable products. *Molding* is the oldest and probably the most important method. Some plastics are hardened by heat. They are called thermosetting (meaning that they are permanently set by heat) and withstand heat best. They are molded by placing a measured amount of plastic in the cavity of a mold and applying heat and pressure. When the plastic begins to flow, it completely fills the cavity and later hardens to solid form. This method, called *compression molding,* is something like making a waffle in a waffle iron.

Some plastics are softened by heat. They lose their shape at temperatures even below that of boiling water, 212 degrees Fahrenheit. These are called thermoplastic (meaning that they are changeable or plastic when heated). Thermoplastics are usually *injection molded.* The plastic is fed into a heated chamber where it is softened to a smooth-flowing, puttylike mass. Pressure is applied to squirt the material into a closed mold, where it hardens by cooling. Very complicated shapes with finely detailed surfaces can be made, and the whole process can be automatic.

Extrusion is much like injection molding except that the plastic is squeezed through an opening called a die. The plastic takes the shape of the die just the way toothpaste squeezed from the tube assumes the shape of the opening. Thermoplastics usually are extruded to make sheeting, films, tubes, rods, and fine threads.

Calendering is a process which uses rollers like giant clothes wringers. The plastic is heated by the hot rollers and is squeezed between them into flat sheets. Calenders can make plastic sheets and can be used to spread and squeeze plastic onto a fabric or paper. Only thermoplastics are calendered.

Laminating is like making giant sandwiches of plastic. In one type, layers of wood, paper, cloth, or glass mat are made up with a syrupy liquid plastic spread like paste between each layer. The sandwich is placed in a press where heat and pressure are applied to press the layers firmly together. The plastic polymerizes to form a firm bond between the other materials. In this process, called high-pressure laminating,

Courtesy "Modern Plastics Magazine"

Compression molding. A hydraulic press forces the movable section into position to compress the plastic powder into the required shape. Constant heat and great pressure are required.

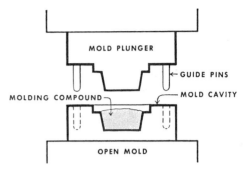

MOLD PLUNGER

GUIDE PINS

MOLDING COMPOUND

MOLD CAVITY

OPEN MOLD

Dry extrusion might be compared to a sausage grinder. The plastic in powder, granular, cube or sheet form is fed into the extruder. As it is spiraled through a heated cylinder it forms a molasseslike mass. Pressure forces it through a die which shapes it. Then it runs onto a take-off belt and is cooled.

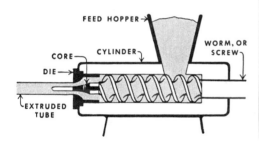

FEED HOPPER

WORM, OR SCREW

CORE   CYLINDER

DIE

EXTRUDED TUBE

Courtesy Plastics Division, Carbide and Carbon Chemicals Corporation

Injection molding transforms the material into a flowing state by the application of heat. Then the material is forced under high pressure into a cold mold where it forms the required shape.

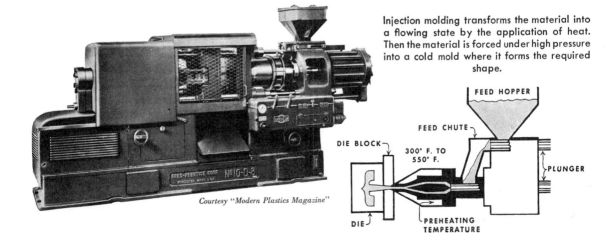

Courtesy "Modern Plastics Magazine"

FEED HOPPER

FEED CHUTE

DIE BLOCK

300° F. TO 550° F.

PLUNGER

DIE

PREHEATING TEMPERATURE

only thermosetting plastics are used.

There is another type of laminating called low-pressure laminating. In this case a plastic-saturated cloth or glass mat is placed over a mold to give the material shape. Heat and moderate pressure are then applied. Often chemicals are used to speed up the process of setting. This method is particularly useful for large objects and for shapes that could not easily be placed in a press.

Thermoplastics are also laminated. Moderate heat and pressure are used to sandwich photographs and identification cards between two transparent sheets.

Casting is a type of molding. In casting, the plastic is heated, poured into a mold, and allowed to harden. No pressure is used, the plastic taking the shape of the mold as it hardens. Casting is similar to making a cake: Batter is poured into a baking tin and the cake assumes the shape of the tin. Both major types of plastics (thermosetting and thermoplastic) can be cast.

Bag molding, blow molding, or *vacuum molding* may be used to form a sheet of plastic material. The sheet is heated and either forced over the top of a mold by air or drawn over a mold by a vacuum. Advertising displays are made in this manner.

A special way of shaping plastics is by foaming. Foamed plastics are thermoplastics to which chemicals have been added that cause a gas to be given off when the material is heated. The gas creates a foam similar to that found when yeast causes bread to rise. Plastics can be foamed in place in molds or cut into design shapes after the blocks of foam are obtained. Almost any plastic as well as foamed plastics can be machined into shape by using woodworking equipment. Since this process is expensive, it is not used a great deal.

The method used to make a plastic product is necessarily selected on the basis of the type of product, the quantity desired, and the ease with which the particular plastic can be handled. All these determine the cost of making a product.

Kinds of Plastics

Phenolics are among the oldest plastics and a very important group. The basic raw materials for making phenolic are coal, air, and water. For use in the manufacturing process, however, these ingredients are converted to phenol (carbolic acid derived from coal tar) and methanol.

Methanol is a wood alcohol. It is further changed to formaldehyde before it can be used to make phenolics. Usually the plastic is mixed with ground wood, chopped cotton or paper, asbestos, or other materials in order to obtain various physical properties.

Phenolics are long-lasting, hard, rigid, not easily burned, lightweight, and easily molded. They are available in dark colors only. The ability to stand rough usage makes phenolic a good material for vacuum cleaner parts, while the hard surface lends itself well to molded radio and television cabinets. Since phenolics are good heat insulators, they are found as handles for cooking utensils and electric irons.

Good electrical insulation properties make this plastic excellent for use in electric switch boxes, switch plates, and light plugs. The familiar washing machine agitator is usually molded of phenolic because the material has excellent moisture resistance.

The *amino* plastics, like the phenolics, are thermosetting. They include the chemically similar urea-formaldehyde and melamine-formaldehyde types.

To make *urea-formaldehyde* the manufacturer starts with ammonia to make urea. The urea is then combined with formaldehyde. This plastic is similar to the phenolics but is available in brighter colors that do not fade. It is unaffected by greases and oils and so is used for cosmetic containers. It is odorless and tasteless and therefore good for picnic ware and packaging. It also is made into buttons, novelties, and home appliance parts.

Melamine-formaldehyde is the combination of melamine (from calcium carbide and nitrogen) and formaldehyde. Melamine has bright colors, is odorless and tasteless, and has a very hard surface which resists staining and scratching.

Because melamine is scratch and stain resistant it is excellent for table and counter tops and dinnerware. Its electrical resistance makes it valuable for electrical equipment where arcs occur.

Polyethylene, made from natural gas, is wax-like in appearance, flexible even when cold, lightweight, tasteless, and odorless. In addition, it has good electrical and chemical resistance properties.

Perhaps the most familiar application of polyethylene is the squeeze bottle. It also is being used, however, for such things as a coating on paper for home freezer food wrapping, wire insulation, cold-water pipes and pipe fittings, and fresh vegetable bags.

Styrene, another important thermoplastic, is sometimes called polystyrene. This plastic is made from coal and natural gas. The coal is used in the form of another coal-tar product, benzene.

Bright colors, and transparency when it is desired, make styrene a cheerful material for the manufacture of kitchenware, toys, and wall tile. Good strength even at low temperatures makes it an ideal material for refrigerator parts, especially when its normal brittleness is decreased by using a rubbery copolymer.

Excellent electrical resistance makes styrene important for electrical equipment. The ease with which it can be molded in very minute detail, maintaining the shape of the mold on removal, has made it ideal for ship, airplane, and automobile models.

The *cellulosics* are a large group of thermoplastics. Cellulose, which is made by treating wood or cotton fibers, is the main raw material. It is combined with various chemicals to give hard materials. These are then changed by the addition of plasticizers to render more flexible products.

As a family, cellulosics are strong, can take rough use, and are transparent enough to make good semirigid packaging containers. At the same time they are good electrical insulators, are lightweight, have a hard surface, and are available in a wide range of colors.

In this category are *cellulose acetate*, which is used for packaging and toys; *cellulose nitrate*, well-known as eyeglass frames; *cellulose acetobutyrate*, used in piping and automobile steering wheels; and *ethyl cellulose*, used for tool handles.

Acetate is noted for a lack of odor and taste. Acetobutyrate is known for outdoor weathering resistance, low-temperature strength, and moisture resistance. Ethyl cellulose is the lightest of the cellulosics and is tough. Nitrate is the toughest in the category, has a hard surface, and can be made to look like marble, snakeskin, or wood grain. It is a flammable material.

The *vinyls* are made from salt, which is changed to chlorine, and either natural gas or acetylene. Acetylene comes from calcium carbide (a product of coke and limestone) and water.

There are many forms of *polyvinyl chloride*, the most important of the vinyls, and its copolymers. They can be seen as film in shower curtains, as sheeting for table mats, in a semirigid form for floor tile, as rigid material in phonograph records, and as a coating on fabric for upholstery.

The main advantages of the vinyls are durability and good electrical, water, and outdoor weathering resistance. Consequently they are widely used as wire insulation.

A special member of the group is *vinylidene chloride* or *saran*, which has excellent chemical resistance and is readily molded or extruded. This material can be used for products ranging from pipe to fabric coating, but it is most familiar as a thin film used for food wrapping. Another special member is *polyvinyl butyral*, which is the sandwich filling in laminated safety glass.

The *acrylics* are important thermoplastics made from materials derived from petroleum, coal, air, and water.

Having excellent clarity and transparency, outdoor weather resistance, and shatter resistance, acrylics can be used for partitions, shower doors, and, more familiarly, transparent aircraft canopies.

A group of important plastics in which the plastic is much like a glue used to hold other materials together is the *polyesters*, the so-called reinforced plastics. Polyesters are chemicals which can be polymerized by the use of other chemicals without the need for great heat and pressure.

To make a reinforced plastic product such as a chair, a sheet of glass fibers, paper, cotton, or other material is soaked with the plastic, then placed in a mold where it is hardened into shape. *Epoxy* plastics act much like polyesters, but even phenolics, melamines, and styrene can be reinforced.

Reinforced plastic is well suited to making large products such as boats. The reinforcing material—glass, paper, or other—adds strength to the product, but the plastic makes the surface difficult to scar. In addition, the plastic makes the product resistant to water and weather and gives it good heat and chemical resistance.

There are also many plastics that lend themselves to small specialty jobs but that are not suitable for large-volume applications. *Fluorocarbons* are noted for their use in products which must withstand heat up to the charring point of wood, 350–400 degrees Fahrenheit. *Silicones* resist water and high temperature extremely well. *Casein* plastic, made from skimmed milk, is used for buttons and buckles. These plastics are high in price or have properties which limit their use to short-run, special jobs rather than general production.

History of Plastics

Chemists knew about and had worked with plastics as early as the mid-1800's. Vinyl chloride was polymerized in 1838, styrene in 1839, acrylics in 1843, and polyester in 1847. It was during this era that chemists began to investigate the gums and resins that turned up in their experiments.

At that time there was no particular need for these synthetic materials. Other materials such as wood, metals, rubber, ivory, and hides were plentiful and well suited to the products of the time. But the world's growth and appetite for things to make life pleasanter grew faster than the raw materials could be found to make them.

The supply of ivory was first to be used up. Consequently a prize was offered to anyone who succeeded in developing a substitute for ivory. While working on the ivory project, John Wesley Hyatt and his brother Isaiah Hyatt discovered celluloid by plasticizing celluloid nitrate with camphor. They patented celluloid in 1870. This was not a good substitute for ivory because the material was inflammable, became yellow and brittle with age, and dissolved in alcohol. But it was new, tough, easily made and shaped, and resisted many chemicals.

Hyatt's discovery was most important in stimulating chemists to think about developing additional synthetic materials. In 1907 Leo Baekeland discovered the phenol-formaldehyde (phenolic) plastic which was the first entirely synthetic material to be produced in large quantities. Since that time, particularly since World War II, many new plastics have been discovered. In 1954 the industry in the United States was producing at a rate of nearly 3,000,000,000 pounds per year.

Although the research in plastics had originally been for substitutes, the discoveries were proving to be new and better substances. Plastics are not now regarded as substitutes, for they are really new materials. They may be glasslike, metallike, leatherlike, or woodlike, but they are not exactly like any of these. Plastics are not limited in application, use, or form.

PLATINUM (*plăt'ŭ num*) is a grayish, metallic, solid chemical element. Its atomic weight is 195.09, its atomic number is 78, and its chemical symbol is Pt. Few chemicals corrode platinum, and even at high temperatures it remains shiny. Its melting point is 3,216 degrees Fahrenheit. According to estimates, about half the world's platinum comes from the Ural Mountains in the U.S.S.R. Other important producers are Canada, South Africa, and the United States.

Platinum is usually found in ores often mixed with the rare metals palladium, rhodium, iridium, and osmium, which are called "platinum metals." Occasionally it is found with other metals such as gold, copper, silver, iron, chromium, and nickel.

Platinum was known in the early 16th century when it was discovered along the banks of the Rio Pinta in South America. It is used for rings and jewel settings. Being much more expensive than gold it is most commonly seen in the form of white gold which contains a little platinum or palladium. It is used a great deal for contact points where electrical circuits are open and closed. Laboratory weights and crucibles, especially those which are to contain acids, are made of platinum. It is used in instruments for exact measurement of temperature and for electrolysis. Platinum was formerly used for wires sealed into glass, as in glass bulbs. It expanded and contracted at almost the same rate as the glass. Cheaper alloys now are used. Platinum black, a mixture containing a great deal of the metal, is very valuable as a catalytic. (See CATALYSIS.)

The world production of platinum in 1942 was more than 750,000 ounces. It fell to 500,-000 ounces in 1944 because of World War II, but by the mid-1950's it increased to about 1,000,000 ounces. In 1963 about 1,530,000 ounces of the metal were produced.

PLATO (plā'tō) (428?–347 B.C.) is generally considered the greatest of Greek philosophers. He has exercised immense influence on the thought and literature of the world since his time.

His birthplace is unknown, though some say it was the island of Aegina. He came of a distinguished family and received the usual education of his class in poetry, music, oratory, and gymnastics. He is said to have distinguished himself as an athlete. Plato is thought to have written poetry until about his 20th year, when, under the influence of Socrates, he turned to philosophy. He remained with Socrates until 399 B.C., when Socrates was put to death. Plato and other followers of Socrates are said to have taken refuge in Megara, Greece. For the next ten years Plato traveled in Greece, Italy, Sicily, Egypt, northern Africa and elsewhere.

In about 387 B.C. Plato established, about one mile from Athens, his famous academy. It was an institution for philosophical education and discussion over which he presided until his death. In his travels Plato had become friends with Dion, kinsman of Dionysius, ruler of Syracuse. When Dionysius died Dion persuaded Plato to visit Syracuse in 367 B.C. in the hope that under Plato's influence Dionysius the younger

might rule Syracuse justly and wisely. The experiment failed. In consequence young Dionysius banished Dion and sold Plato into slavery. Friends immediately secured Plato's release. Still others rallied about Dion, who organized an expedition and invaded Syracuse, driving Dionysius into exile. Dion himself was assassinated and lawlessness prevailed. It is this turn of events which is thought to have saddened Plato's later life and made his later writings melancholy.

Plato's works include the *Republic,* various *Dialogues,* and the *Laws.* All of them have been written in the form of dialogue. In many of the dialogues Socrates is the chief figure. The discussions are informal, human, and written with great charm. The most famous of them are those comprising the *Republic,* in which are expounded Plato's chief political and philosophical reflections. (See PHILOSOPHY.)

Politically the *Republic* describes an ideal state in answer to a question propounded in the first book, or dialogue—what is justice? Unsatisfied with the answers which are given, including his own, Socrates proposes to investigate the true nature of justice on a larger scale by tracing the rise of a just state. The perfect state, Socrates declares, would be made up of three classes of citizens. The guardians, or rulers, would be specially educated for the duties of government and have the particular attribute of wisdom. A military class whose duty would be the defense of the state would be second. The general body of citizens would make up the third class. Art would be censored in the interests of the state. Socrates advocated the suppression of untruthful poems and plays, and also of soft, enervating forms of music. Women would receive exactly the same training and education as men. Those capable of philosophy would associate with the guardians, and those with a turn for war would share the duties of the warriors. Children would be separated from the parents and brought up in establishments operated by the state. Only in this way would it be possible to eliminate the sense of private property. On being asked how these results are to be brought about, Socrates replies that the highest political power must by one means or another be vested in philosophers, or men of wisdom.

Having concluded his description of the aristocratic, or perfect, state, Socrates criticizes the other four kinds of political government: timocracy, under which the love of honor and glory is the ruling principle; oligarchy, under which the wealthy few govern the impoverished many; democracy, under which he believed political abuses inevitably prepare the way for despotism or rule by a dictator; and tyranny, itself the rule of the despot.

Among the most eloquent of the dialogues not included in the *Republic* is the *Apology*, recording the speech made by Socrates in his own defense at the trial which preceded his execution.

PLOVER (*plŭv'ẽr* or *plō'vẽr*). Belonging to the order of shore birds and related to the snipes, the plovers have a family to themselves, the Charadriidae. There are some 60 species, found in many parts of the world along the seacoasts. Only about eight species are found in North America. They are relatively small shore birds, about 10 inches long, being plumper and stubbier than the snipes and having shorter, thicker necks. Their wings are long and pointed, as a general rule. They exhibit a wide variety of plumage, as well as change of color with the seasons. They nest on the ground and usually lay four eggs. The eggs are so mottled and spotted that it is hard to tell them from the pebbles of the beach. Even the chicks when hatched are so marked as to defy detection. A chick a day old will remain perfectly still, its instinct telling it that this affords it safety. Another peculiarity of the plover is a soft, piping whistle. It does not sound loud even close at hand but has marvelous carrying power.

The golden plover is the most beautiful of its tribe. Its back is sprinkled with dull gold and its breast is black. In winter it fades to a dull brown. While walking it bobs its head up and down in a curious manner. The most remarkable trait of these birds is their power of flight. They have been traced from the Arctic Circle down to the pampas of Argentina, a distance of almost 10,000 miles. Coming down through

The golden plover is a shore bird, about 10 inches long. They are famous for their long flights.

Canada, they will fly in great flocks, high in the air, as far as Nova Scotia. There they will fly straight south and hundreds of miles out at sea, down to and across the West Indies and on along the Brazilian coast until they reach their winter home in lower Argentina. Then in the spring they will fly north again, mostly up the Mississippi Valley, repeating their wonderful journey of almost half the distance around the globe.

The black-bellied plover has the same dark undercoat, but with upper parts black and white. A broad white stripe extends from over its eye down along its side. It also migrates for long distances and is found in both hemispheres, but it is so shy that little is known of its habits. A small flock may be noted out on the beach at low tide. At the first approach of man, a mellow cry of warning goes up from some sentinel, and off they fly.

The killdeer, another species of plover, takes its name from its cry, which sounds like *killdeer*, or *killdee*. This bird is found in both North and South America and often leaves the shore for inland feeding grounds. It likes freshly-plowed fields and will run along a furrow at a rapid gait. It will eat any grubs or worms that the plow may turn up, all the time uttering its fretful cry. It is about 10 inches long, with an olive-brown coat above, pure-white breast, and a black collar. The young, as in other plovers, are of gray shades. In the care of the young the parents are brave and quick at thinking up things to do. If danger threatens her brood, the mother bird will make use of all sorts of tricks, such as acting as though wounded herself, to distract attention. At the same time the male will fly angrily about, uttering its cry.

Probably the commonest species of plover to be found along the Atlantic Coast is the semipalmated plover. It is a small bird of very distinctive coloring, about seven inches long. Its crown and back are yellowish-brown, about the color of wet sand. Its breast is pure white. Broad bands of brown adorn its face and throat. One would think that so striking a combination would make the bird readily noticeable, but quite the reverse is true. Many a person strolling along a beach has passed very close to these birds time and again and never seen them at all. They are widely distributed in both North and South America, nesting in Alaska and on the upper shores of Canada and wintering southward.

The piping plover is about the same size and color. It is so called from its mournful note, which rings out as the bird rises swiftly from the sand and takes to the air. So closely does it resemble its sandy home that it is practically invisible until it moves. These birds are found not only along the ocean shores but also on the Great Lakes.

Other well-known species of plovers are the snowy plover, a western coast bird, and the mountain plover, an inland western bird. The ringed plovers are common in Europe, along the Mediterranean, and in Africa.

Among the ploverlike birds belonging to another family is the zick-zack, which is noted for its association with the crocodile. It picks leeches and other parasites from the crocodile's mouth and acts cautiously as a sentinel for the reptile.

PLOWS (*plouz*) AND PLOWING.

The first plow was made of a forked branch of a tree with wooden pins in the front end by which it could be pulled. Ancient carvings show that a plow of this type was used in Egypt long before the time of written history. The Egyptians seem to have covered the wearing parts with metal. In biblical times the Israelites went down "to the Philistines to sharpen every man his share and his coulter." It is believed that the primitive Egyptian plow was taken to Greece and Rome, where it was improved.

The ancient Roman farmers not only used iron plows but also they plowed deeply, with the first plowing as much as nine inches deep. The Etruscans sometimes plowed their stiff clays as many as nine times.

According to Virgil the Roman plow had a point made of two pieces of wood put together in a "V" shape and covered with iron. It is also believed that the Roman plows had moldboards to partially turn the soil if not turn it completely over. While the modified hoe, crooked stick, and wooden pick were used by many ancient farmers, others thus used iron or iron-plated plows.

The first plows were pulled by men. One or more men pulled the plow and another man forced a fork of it into the ground. Later oxen were used to pull plows.

Eventually the Roman plow was taken over by the Germans. They made few, if any, improvements in it. Plows having simple beams and wooden moldboards were in use in northern Germany as late as 1860.

A plow said to have been used in the time of William the Conqueror (about A.D. 1070) is described as being a wooden wedge covered with straps of iron. The plow cut a slice of earth, turned it, and moved it to one side. It cleared its own path and left an unobstructed furrow for the next slice.

The Dutch were among the first to make important changes in the plow. They found it necessary to give the moldboard a more perfect form and to plate it with iron. Some Dutch plows were imported into England as early as 1730.

The Dutch plow was improved by a Mr. Small of Scotland, who made the major portion of iron. Robert Ransome of England secured a patent for a major improvement of the cast-iron share of the Dutch plow in 1803. In 1840 John Howard established a plow factory in England, and about the same time a factory was estab-

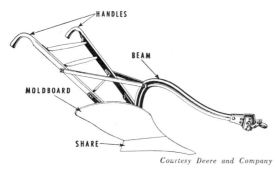

HANDLES

BEAM

MOLDBOARD

SHARE

Courtesy Deere and Company

Horse-drawn walking plow.

lished to manufacture Ransome plows.

Ignorance and superstition played a part in hindering the progress of the plow. Sir Robert Peel of Great Britain in 1835 presented a farmers' club with two of his best iron plows. They were not used, for the farmers thought that the iron plows made the weeds grow. Charles Newbold, an American inventor, met with the same difficulty. In 1797 he was granted a patent for a plow which he invented about 1780. This plow was a cast-iron plow designed particularly for work in the loose gravel soils of eastern United States.

The Newbold plow had one serious defect. In the gritty, gravelly soils of the East, its point soon wore out. When this occurred, since moldboard, share, and landside were cast in one piece, the plow was entirely worthless. Jethro Wood solved this problem by casting the bottom in sections so that the worn parts could be

Replica of ancient Egyptian plow.

Courtesy J. I. Case Co.

replaced. This improvement was made in 1819.

While attempting to introduce his cast-iron plows in the United States, Newbold found that the farmers thought the iron plows poisoned the soil and kept the crops from growing.

Early American Developments

The plow used by the early settlers in the United States was a very crude implement. To make a plow the maker would cut down a twisted tree and cut a moldboard from it. He followed the grain of the wood as nearly as possible along the shape of the moldboard. To this he nailed an old hoe blade, then straps of iron or old horse shoes to make it wear longer.

The landside of the plow was made of wood, covered with thin plates of iron on the side and bottom. The share was of iron with a hardened steel point. A coulter made of iron helped to cut heavy sod and small roots. The beam was usually a straight piece of timber, and the handles were usually cut from small crooked trees or branches.

Thomas Jefferson, the third president of the United States, used principles of mathematics in 1788 to make moldboards more efficient. This also made it possible for different persons to make plows that were alike. Some believe that this was the beginning of all the real progress that has been made in the manufacture of this important implement.

Daniel Webster built a very large and cumbersome plow in 1836. It was designed to plow 12 or more inches deep and was 12 feet long. The landside was four feet long; the bar and share were forged together, and the moldboard was of wood covered with strips of iron.

As the pioneer farmer started West he tied his plow on the side of his covered wagon. When the westward-bound settlers reached the rich, black land of the Mississippi River country they were faced with a heart-breaking problem. Their iron-patched wooden plows and cast-iron plows usually succeeded in plowing the prairie sod for the first time. They refused, however, to work the second time the soil was plowed. The rich, black earth stuck to the moldboard. Drawing such a load was almost more than horses or oxen could do. The plows were also very hard to hold in the ground. The plowman had to carry a stick or paddle to clean the moldboard. This added to the work and decreased the amount of plowing that could be done.

The problem was so serious that many settlers gave up their homesteads in disgust to return East, where they could at least make a seedbed to grow their crops. Others passed right through the prairie lands and went on to the hill country in the West.

About this time blacksmiths began fastening steel saw blades over the surfaces of the wooden moldboards. The smooth saw blade took on a polish and the black soil would slide off instead of sticking to the moldboard. Besides improving the quality of plowing, the steel plow also decreased the amount of power required to pull it.

John Deere, a blacksmith, was one of the first inventors to make a steel plow from a circular saw blade.

Through the middle of the 19th century improvements were made in the steel used in the plows. Gang plows were also built. This kind is composed of two or more plows attached together to be pulled and controlled as one plow. About 1864 a two-wheeled sulky plow was built which permitted the plowman to ride.

Besides the plow itself, next in importance to the plowman was his source of power. Just as oxen replaced men as power in primitive times, horses and mules later replaced the slow, plodding ox.

A still greater advancement came around the turn of the 20th century when the plowman could replace the horse with a steam or gasoline tractor.

The steam tractor was first used to pull farm implements about 1876. In parts of the West large steam engines pulled as many as 12 plows in a gang.

A different type of plow, the rotary plow, was made of large cupped disks. The first successful disk plows were produced about 1891. An arrangement of these disks was used to make the wheatland plow said to have been first made in Kansas. These plows were designed to mix wheat stubble with the soil to prevent

Courtesy (top, above, bottom) J. I. Case Co., (below) Deere and Company

Top: Walking plow built about 1857. Above: Sulky plow built in 1893 enabled the plowman to ride. Below: Gang plow pulled by steam tractor around 1910. Bottom: Modern disk plow.

blowing of the soil and to hold the snow for soil moisture. This type of plow was first sold in large numbers about 1927.

Another type of plow used by the early settlers in the eastern part of the United States was the shovel plow, or horse hoe. It had a beam and handles like other plows but with one large shovel instead of the regular plowshare. This plow threw the soil to both sides and was used for cultivating as well as breaking the ground.

The shovel plow was used in newly cleared land where large roots and stumps made it difficult to use the moldboard plow. A coulter, usually called a "root cutter," was fastened to the beam and extended into the soil to cut the small roots. Many a young plowman has come home with aching shinbones when tough roots, pulled tight across the coulter blade, would break, letting the ends fly back and whack the plowman across the legs. This plow was used in some hilly sections of the southeast as late as 1930.

The improvement of the internal-combustion engine brought with it the smaller tractor. One farmer with his tractor and two, three, or four plows could take care of the plowing job in fine fashion. The older type of traction engine required a crew of from three to as many as ten men to keep it in operation. The smaller tractor, being adapted to more uses, naturally made its way into farms of various sizes.

It is for these reasons that the old-type traction engine and multiple engine gang have disappeared from the farm picture.

From the crooked stick, powered by man's muscles, to the modern tractor-drawn plow is a long step. With modern equipment, a farmer can plow 25 acres in the time it took to plow 1 acre when his forefathers first started across the rich prairies.

PLUM (plŭm). A choice orchard fruit, the dark-blue, purple, red, green, or yellow plum is related to the peach, apricot, cherry, and almond. The plum belongs to the family Rosaceae. The fruit is rich in food value. It usually ranges in size from that of a cherry to a domestic hen's egg.

J. Horace McFarland Company

A cluster of plums of the Abundance variety cling to a heavily laden branch of a plum tree.

There are several wild species, and the plum in some variety will grow in almost any temperate climate.

The first white settlers in America found several kinds of wild plums, some of which have been improved by cultivating. Among these are the beach plum, the Chickasaw, "wild goose" types, and the American plum.

There are three important groups of species of plums. The European plum was brought to North America from Europe. It may have come originally from the region between the Caucasus Mountains and Persia. Varieties in this group grow best in Ontario, Canada, northeastern and central United States, and in the states bordering the Pacific. The Japanese plum is adapted to regions a little farther south and does especially well in California. The American plums belong to several species. Some of these are difficult to distinguish from others. Specific types do best in special regions. None of them is grown over great areas. Some one or more of them may be found in specific portions of the United States.

Orchard growers classify this fruit in groups.

Plums are grown and marketed to be eaten fresh or preserved. Prunes contain more sugar, have firmer flesh, and are used for drying. There are a great many varieties of both plums and prunes. Commercially a variety is grown in any special area after it has proven to produce high yields of excellent fruit in that locality. For home use many more varieties can be grown. The specific choice depends upon the grower. There are dozens of excellent kinds from which to choose.

California leads both in plum and prune production. It is followed by Oregon, Washington, New York, Pennsylvania, Missouri, and Ohio. Some plum trees tend to yield so heavily that the branches have to be thinned several times a season. This thinning allows the ripening fruit sufficient room to develop. The plums are picked when a good color and packed and shipped in lightweight baskets or crates. If they are to be dried as prunes they are allowed to remain on the trees much longer. Prunes are dried either on trays in the open air or with additional heat in specially constructed buildings. Trees of the best varieties are propagated usually by budding or by grafting.

Plums rank third in importance among United States orchard fruits following apples and peaches.

PLUMBING (plŭm'ing).

The problem of obtaining water and getting rid of wastes is ages old. There were many attempts, even in the earliest civilizations, to construct what are in modern times called plumbing installations. This name grew out of the use of lead, called *plumbum* in Latin, for most of the piping.

Disposal of wastes by having them carried along by water is such a convenient and sanitary system that it is continually being extended in its application. Now even garbage can be disposed of in that manner. The usual wastes are of such consistency that they either float or are suspended in the water.

The drainage system is designed to fit into the typical building construction. It consists of vertical lines, called stacks or risers, which at each floor branch out into horizontal lines and connect to the various fixtures. There may be one or several stacks, depending on the size of the building. They are usually collected below the lowest occupied floor, and from there led outside to the street sewer.

The plumber has to have special training and must be licensed before he can go into business. His work is carefully inspected. All plumbing installations are regulated by plumbing codes. The essence of these codes is briefly that all installations shall be "safe" and "sanitary." The piping and the fixtures must not cause harm to anyone, break easily, or chip, and should be constructed to withstand ordinary wear and tear, or even abuse. Sanitary piping and fixtures are made in such a manner that they can be kept clean easily. They must be installed so that they function properly at all times, that there is no danger of contamination, that the pure water will not come in contact with soiled water, and that the wastes, after they have been carried into the waste pipes, can not back up or create foul odors in the building.

The whole drainage system is "vented," which means that each stack is carried up above the roof to the air, and sometimes additional vents are installed. They serve the purpose of admitting or letting out air, depending on the flow conditions in the pipes. They also allow gases, which are generated in the wastes, to escape. The "trap," an S-shaped pipe under the fixture, or sometimes, as in water closets, an S-shaped channel built into the fixture, prevents these gases from escaping into the building by forming a pocket always full of water.

The many small mechanical devices on a plumbing system serve in one way or another to insure a safe and sanitary condition, and to enable the plumber to make necessary repairs and adjustments. At the bottom of the stacks can usually be found large access openings with screwed plugs. They serve as "clean-outs" in case the lines become plugged. The shape of the fixtures and the location of the supply fittings are features to safeguard the pure water supply and to keep the fixtures clean and neat. Supply fixtures, faucets, for instance, should be kept above and clear of the washbasins and tubs.

Spouts on drinking fountains are shielded

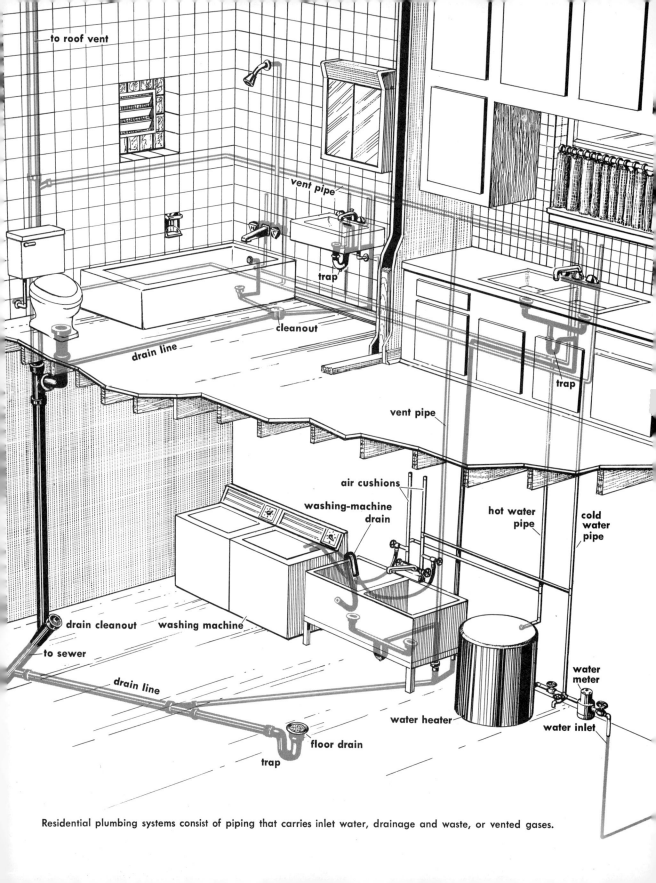

to roof vent

vent pipe

trap

cleanout

drain line

vent pipe

air cushions

washing-machine drain

hot water pipe

cold water pipe

drain cleanout

washing machine

to sewer

drain line

water meter

water heater

water inlet

floor drain

trap

trap

Residential plumbing systems consist of piping that carries inlet water, drainage and waste, or vented gases.

and produce a slanting stream to avoid contact with the mouth of the drinker.

The whole idea of sanitation and safety is carried out by the use of proper materials. All materials must be completely resistant to corrosion. The joints and connections must not be able to work loose or leak.

Waste pipes must be either screwed together, or calked by having hot lead poured into the cast-iron sockets and then hammered tight. A simpler type of joint is permitted only where the trap is connected with the fixture and where the soil pipe is connected with the water closet.

Lead pipes are extremely well adapted to plumbing, but because of their high cost and the softness of the material, they have been replaced in most cases by cast iron or galvanized steel. For water, especially hot water, brass or even copper piping is desirable. In the same manner the hot-water tanks have been improved by making them of rust-resisting alloys or copper or glass lined.

PLUTARCH (*plōō'tärk*) (46–120). Of all the ancient writers Plutarch is the most entertaining. Every age has thought that he wrote like a modern writer. This may be because every age enjoys reading about great men when the writer gives details of their private lives.

Plutarch's *Parallel Lives* contains the biographies of 50 famous Greeks and Romans. Forty-six of them go in pairs. There is a Greek general with the Roman general whom Plutarch thought was most like him. A Greek orator is placed with a Roman orator. Sometimes Plutarch wrote a little essay at the end of the two lives. In this he compared the two and tried to decide which was the greater.

Plutarch was well fitted for his work. He was a Greek who wrote in Greek but he was also a Roman citizen of consular rank. Plutarch was born at Chaeronea and was trained in philosophy at Athens. He spent some time in Rome where he may have been tutor to the young Hadrian.

When Hadrian became emperor he made Plutarch governor of Greece.

Plutarch had a deep admiration for the Greeks especially the Spartans. Plutarch's sense of humor was keen and he filled his biographies with stories about famous people. He delighted in telling about their odd habits such as a quaint trick of speech. Often he discussed the nature of eclipses or the beginning of old customs or how a word got its meaning. "But this," he says, "is more fitting for another place." The "other place" was his book of more than 60 essays called the *Opera Moralia*.

PLUTO (*plōō'tō*) **OR HADES** (*hā'dēz*). In ancient Greek mythology Pluto was the god of the underworld, also called Hades. One of the three sons of Cronus, he won his kingdom when he and his brothers, Zeus and Poseidon, drew lots for the various parts of the universe. Pluto was originally only the pitiless king of the dead. Later he came to be considered also the source of the treasures of the earth. In this sense he was a kind god.

He wore a helmet which made him invisible. Sometimes he rode in a car drawn by four coal-black horses, which he guided with golden reins. His wife Persephone, whom he had carried off by force, shared his throne in Hades. But owing to the entreaties of Demeter, her mother, she reigned in the underworld for only half the year and on earth for the other half.

Seldom did Pluto restore the dead to life. Orpheus, however, so charmed him with his music that Pluto surrendered Eurydice, the musician's wife. Aesculapius, the skillful physician, once restored a dead man to life. This made Pluto so angry that he begged Zeus to strike Aesculapius with his lightning. Zeus did so, but then set the great doctor among the gods. Pluto was called Dis in Roman mythology.

A small outer planet is named Pluto. (See Solar System.)

PLYMOUTH (*plĭm'ŭth*), **MASSACHUSETTS.** Plymouth is in southeast Massachusetts on a wide sheltered bay of the Atlantic Ocean. It is a small summer resort, tourist center, and manufacturing town about halfway between Boston (37 miles to the northeast) and Cape Cod. The town is a part of Boston's well-known "South Shore" country and is much like the Cape with its sandy beaches, colonial charm,

Courtesy Plymouth Chamber of Commerce

Plymouth Rock.

and busy summer activity. Plymouth is also a small port and the county seat of Plymouth County.

Plymouth's factories make cordage, woolens, rubber goods, and hardware. The town has the largest cordage works in the world. Yet Plymouth has remained quiet, quaint, and lovely. The 100,000 tourists who come every year still find much that suggests the life of the 17th century. Many of the old houses still stand, and Pilgrim Hall, built in 1824, contains many interesting relics.

On the shores of Plymouth Bay stands Plymouth Rock under a granite roof supported by columns. The Pilgrims are said to have stepped on this rock when they landed in 1620. Other tourist attractions are the Brewster Gardens with their beautiful statue of the Pilgrim Maid; a statue of the Indian chief Massasoit on Cole's Hill; and the National Monument to the Forefathers. This is an 80-foot shaft topped by a figure representing Faith with its upraised hand pointing to Heaven.

History

The story of Plymouth begins in 1620 with the voyage of the *Mayflower*. The ship, with its 101 passengers, dropped anchor in Cape Cod Bay. It was winter, and the captain of the *Mayflower* refused to take the chance of sailing across the sand bars and shallow water to land farther south. (See MAYFLOWER.)

In December 1620, the men who had been sent ahead to find a good harbor and place to settle decided on Plymouth. There they saw a level, sandy beach, not very wide or long, but protected by sharply rising sand hills. There were wooded hills to supply timber and some clear patches for crops. Running down to the sea was a fresh-water brook which the colonists later named Town Brook. The men cleared the land and laid out a road which they named Leyden Street. They put up a crude hut to be used by all the people until other houses could be built. A week later they brought the women and children from Cape Cod.

The first winter the Pilgrims spent in the New World was one of great hardship. It was hard work clearing the land, and there was little food. Many became ill, and many died. The following April when the *Mayflower* sailed for England half the passengers it had brought lay buried on Cole's Hill.

The men and women who remained in the tiny colony were mostly farmers and craftsmen who had very little schooling. They plowed the land and planted crops. They cut timber and traded with the friendly Indians for fish and furs. The chief of the Wampanoag Indians was Massasoit, who made a treaty of friendship with the Pilgrims that lasted for many years. The Indians taught the Pilgrims how to use the strange foods of the New World— corn, beans, and many kinds of wild game and fish. These foods were used in the first Thanksgiving dinner celebrated late in 1621.

In November of that year an English ship came with 35 more colonists but brought no food. The Pilgrims fed the newcomers and the crew and supplied the ship for its return voyage. They loaded it with lumber, sassafras, and skins as the first payment to the merchant owners who had outfitted their expedition. Later they joined Massachusetts Bay Colony and did not become a separate colony.

During the 19th century Plymouth became an active fishing and whaling port and began to build a number of manufacturing plants. The new industries brought many immigrant workers. Their descendants now make up one-fourth of the town's people. But Plymouth never grew very large. The population of Plymouth (1960) is 14,445.

PNEUMATIC (*nū măt'ĭk*) **APPLIANCES** (*à plī'-ăns ĕz*). In a Birmingham, Alabama, steel plant a large air-driven hammer suspended from an electric crane is used to break cast-iron after it is poured into molds. Its rate is a ton of iron a minute. Another type of air hammer, designed to aid in preparing wallpaper printing plates, weighs only a few ounces.

The power of compressed air was noted at a relatively early date in history, but not until the 19th century was it much employed. Important among 19th-century developments were the pneumatic tube for mail transport in city postal systems and the air brake for railway trains and cars. For a time many inventors worked on the problem of a suitable compressed air automobile, but the development of the internal combustion engine rendered this project impractical. The internal combustion engine, however, did supply a source of power for operating portable compressed air machines.

How Pneumatic Hammers Work

Pneumatic hammers are used for chipping castings and billets, cutting bolt heads and other projections in structural metal work, calking joints, riveting, and for many other jobs. A pneumatic impact drill turns its tool slightly between blows, bringing new surfaces under the attack of a cutting edge. Pneumatic hammers and drills for heavy work deliver some 2,000 strokes per minute. For light work, such as stone-dressing, hammers and drills are used which deliver 10,000 strokes per minute.

The lightest hammers have a single piston and no valves. The pressure of the air forces the piston to strike the blow and as the pressure is released the piston is sprung into place again. In larger hammers two pistons of unequal size are so arranged with a system of valve holes that the air drives the larger piston down against the tool being used. The drop in pressure operates the small piston in such a way as to open a valve which admits air to lift the piston back ready for the next blow. Pneumatic impact drills are used with pneumatic scrapers in mining.

Rotary drills for boring and reaming holes in wood or metal are driven by a tiny four-cylinder

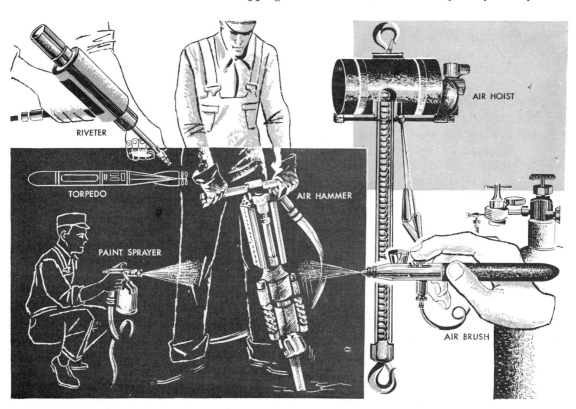

RIVETER

TORPEDO

PAINT SPRAYER

AIR HAMMER

AIR HOIST

AIR BRUSH

compressed air engine within the shaft of the tool. Compressed air is much more efficient than steam for this purpose since it loses no energy by radiation, creates little moisture, and can be transmitted economically through uninsulated flexible tubes.

Pneumatic energy is employed in sand blasting, air blast cleaning, and paint spraying. Small air brushes are used in connection with stencils for painting signs. Many presses, forging hammers, and similar types of machinery are operated by air, and air blasts are used in metal purification. (See IRON AND STEEL.)

Pneumatic conveyers find use in a wide range of enterprises, from the grain industry to the public library. Pneumatic energy drives agitators used in mixing explosive compounds, serves as a starter for Diesel engines, and lessens the formation of ice on the edges of airplane wings. Its pressure is used to prevent water from entering submarine tunnels in course of construction, to carry submarine torpedoes to their objective, and to propel bullets from small-caliber guns. In some industrial plants, locomotives are driven by compressed air. (See CAISSON; DIVING.)

PNEUMONIA (nū mō'nĭ ä), sometimes called pneumonitis, is an infection of the lung. It can be caused by a great many different germs: bacteria, viruses, or fungi. The disease develops in different ways, depending upon which germ infects the lung.

Pneumonia may be acute. That is, it may flare up suddenly and then clear up quickly, especially with the help of antibiotic drugs. The patient has fever and often chills. His white blood cells usually increase to fight the germs. He feels very sick and often has pain in his chest as he breathes. Coughing is common.

When pneumonia is caused by the bacteria pneumococcus, the germs are spread very quickly through a whole lobe of the lung. The body reacts by pouring out fluid and white blood cells into the air spaces of this lobe. This is the material that the patient may cough up. The doctor can tell by the patient's breathing, or by the sound of tapping over his chest, that a large part of the lung is filled up and without air. The X ray shows a thick shadow

throughout this lobe. This is called *lobar pneumonia* because it fills one or several lobes. Doctors refer to pneumonia by the kind of bacteria causing it because the choice of drug depends upon which bacteria it is. The course of the disease can be greatly shortened by proper antibiotic drugs. The germs die. The pus in the lung is coughed up, leaving the lung as it was before. Because of new drugs, pneumonia no longer has the high death rate that it had before 1935.

Most other germs tend to infect the lungs only after some event like measles, or whooping cough, or after an operation with general anesthesia. Streptococcus and staphylococcus are common infective bacteria. They attack only patchy areas in the lung, but are still serious. When the infection is mainly in the walls of the bronchi and lung right around them it is called *bronchopneumonia*. An example of a chronic, or long standing, pneumonia is one due to the tubercle bacillus. (See TUBERCULOSIS.)

POCAHONTAS (pō'kä hŏn'täs) (1595–1617) was an Indian princess who helped the colonists at Jamestown, Virginia. She was the daughter of Powhatan, chief of the tribes near Jamestown. Many stories have been told about her.

The best-known story is about Captain John Smith of the Virginia colony. According to Smith's story he was captured by Indians in 1608 and tied to a rock. He was about to be beaten to death when Pocahontas threw herself on him and pleaded that he be saved. (See SMITH, CAPTAIN JOHN.) Some historians do not believe this story.

In 1613 Pocahontas was captured by a British sea captain. At that time Powhatan's tribes had several English prisoners. Also they had stolen some arms and tools from the Jamestown colony. Pocahontas was to be freed when Powhatan returned the Englishmen, the arms, and the tools.

While a prisoner, she was well treated. The acting governor was pleased with her gentleness and her intelligence. He decided to give her lessons in the Christian religion. She became a Christian and was baptized with the

It was said to be Pocahontas, the 12-year-old daughter of Powhatan, who saved the life of Captain John Smith.

name of Rebecca.

While Pocahontas was at Jamestown, an English gentleman, John Rolfe, fell in love with her and asked to marry her. Both Powhatan and the English governor approved of the marriage. It led to a period of peace and good will between Powhatan and the Jamestown settlement.

In 1616 Pocahontas and her husband went to England. There she was introduced to the king and queen and was the center of much attention. Early in 1617 Pocahontas suddenly became sick and died. Her son, Thomas Rolfe, later returned to Virginia.

POE (*pō*), **EDGAR** (*ĕd'gēr*) **ALLAN** (1809–1849). One of the first detective-story writers was Edgar Allan Poe. He was also a great poet. Though his life was one of misery and tragedy he became known as one of the United States' great writers.

Poe's troubles began early, for his mother and father both died before he was three. He was brought up by Mrs. John Allan, wife of a rich tobacco merchant in Richmond, Virginia. His childhood years with the Allans, including a five-year stay in England, were probably the happiest of his whole life.

At 17 Poe entered the University of Virginia.

Although he was a good student, he soon began to gamble and lost large sums of money. Poe left school during his first year, his large debts unpaid. He began working for Allan in Richmond, but quickly tired of this and left home for Boston. He enlisted in the army, served for two years, and then with Allan's help got an appointment to the U.S. Military Academy at West Point as a cadet. In six months he decided he had had enough and refused to carry out his duties. He was court-martialed and dismissed.

In the meantime Mrs. Allan had died and his foster father decided that he had had enough of Poe. The young writer wandered to Baltimore, Maryland. He tried, without success, to find work there but was encouraged in his writing. He won a $50 prize for a story, "MS. Found in a Bottle." A friend helped him get a job with a magazine in Richmond. Poe soon became assistant editor. He held many editorial jobs during the rest of his life. But in each case he lost his position because of quarrels and his own poor habits. He married his young cousin, Virginia Clemm. His love for her was very great and Poe never recovered from her early death. Poe had wanted to become a great writer and thought that he had not. He had wanted love and understanding and now found himself alone in the world. He retreated more and more from life and spent more and more of his time in drinking. He died in Baltimore, less than two years after the death of his wife.

Poe wrote such stories as "The Fall of the House of Usher" and "The Murders in the Rue Morgue." These brought him a reputation as an excellent young writer. In 1843 he published "The Pit and the Pendulum" and "The Tell-Tale Heart." They captured the imagination of readers with the feelings of terror and horror they produced. Another story, "The Gold Bug," showed how the mind worked in solving a mystery. It started the development of the modern detective story.

Fame came to Poe with the publication of his poems, "The Raven" and "The Bells." His poetry had extraordinary qualities of rhythm and music. Like his stories, his poetry deals largely with the strange, the unreal, and the supernatural.

Photo, Brown Bros.

"Not the least obeisance made he; not a minute stopped or stayed he;
But, with mien of lord or lady, perched above my chamber door—"

From "The Raven" by Edgar Allan Poe.

His writings brought Poe fame not only in the United States but also in other countries. French writers, for example, studied his writings and were strongly influenced by Poe's interest in the human mind.

Greater fame came to Poe after his death than he ever found while alive. As a writer of unusual stories and poems, he had shown his interest in developing new ideas and forms for writing. "He had studied such mysteries of life as dreams and life after death." He had stirred the imaginations of readers with appeals to their feelings and moods. Today his influence upon literature is recognized and he holds a position as a United States author of genius.

POET (pō'ĕt or pō'ĭt) **LAUREATE** (lô'rē āt or lô'rē ĭt). In ancient days kings had court minstrels or poets to sing their praises or to write of their victories. The custom may still be said to be alive today in England in the post of poet laureate to the Court of St. James. A poet is appointed to the position and granted a certain sum of money each year. The title came from the laurel wreath with which poets and victors were once crowned.

Geoffrey Chaucer, Edmund Spenser, and other poets enjoyed royal patronage. Ben Jonson was the first to hold the post, which was created for him by James I in 1617. John Dryden, in 1670, was the first to have the title poet laureate. It was part of the duty of the early poets laureate to write poems for special state celebrations and affairs. Later, this requirement was dropped and the poet wrote only as he wished. The salaries of the office changed often. Ben Jonson's included a butt of wine. This explains why Alfred, Lord Tennyson got £72 plus £27 "in lieu of sack." Formerly appointed by the lord chamberlain, poets laureate are now chosen by the prime minister. They are still considered members of the royal household and are expected to attend levees, or receptions.

In the days of the four Georges, the post lost the high regard in which it had been held. Most of the poets were chosen for political reasons. Therefore both Thomas Gray and Sir Walter Scott refused it. William Wordsworth's character and gifts dignified the position but he was not required to write a single court poem. Tennyson was the ideal poet laureate. He both loved and honored Queen Victoria, and therefore his poems to her were not flattery. He held the post for 42 years.

Tennyson's successor, Alfred Austin, never attained great popularity. In 1913 Lord Asquith named Dr. Robert Bridges poet laureate. He was a scholar and an excellent but little-known poet. There was considerable disappointment, many preferring Rudyard Kipling, William

Watson, or Alfred Noyes. When Dr. Bridges died in 1930, John Masefield was chosen to succeed him. Cecil Day Lewis, who writes detective novels under the pen name Nicholas Blake, succeeded Masefield, who died in 1967. Outstanding poets laureate were Jonson, Dryden, Robert Southey, Wordsworth, and Tennyson.

POETRY (*pō'ĕt rē* or *pō'it rē*). No complete definition of poetry has ever been written. To some people rhyming lines make poetry. But, in fact, some of the great poetical works do not rhyme; for example, John Milton's *Paradise Lost*, William Shakespeare's plays, and the Psalms in the Bible. On the other hand, many rhymed verses, such as advertising jingles or nursery rhymes, are not generally called poetry. To learn what poetry is a person must read and study a great many poems of all kinds. However, it is possible to talk about the more common ways of choosing and arranging words in poetry.

Characteristics of Poetry

The language of poetry is different from everyday speech or writing. The difference often comes from the use of well-known words in an unusual order. For instance, in the first stanza of his poem "Stopping by Woods"[1] Robert Frost does not say, "I think I know who these woods belong to; but he will not see me stopping to watch the snow fall because he lives in the village." Frost writes:

> Whose woods these are I think I know.
> His House is in the village though;
> He will not see me stopping here
> To watch his woods fill up with snow.

The words are simple and well-known, but the poet has arranged them in such a way that the lines have a definite rhythm and end in rhyming words. Each line begins with a capital letter whether it begins a new sentence or not.

Rhyming words are those that sound alike, such as *know, though, snow*. Rhythm is the beat or the meter of the line. In poetry, the beats are the stressed words or syllables in the line. In the first line of the above stanza the

stressed words are: "Whose woods these are I think I know." Rhythm is the arrangement of stressed and unstressed words and syllables.

Usually a person would say, "I think I know whose woods these are." The rhythm remains the same even though the order has been changed. But *are* does not rhyme with *though* and *snow*. Poets often change the normal English word order so that lines will end with rhyming words. Or they may change the order so that the rhythm will be regular. Here, for example, are some lines from Walter de la Mare's "The Listeners"[1]:

> But no one descended to the Traveller;
> No head from the leaf-fringed sill
> Leaned over and looked into his grey eyes,
> Where he stood perplexed and still.

The poet could not say, "No head leaned over the leaf-fringed sill and looked into his grey eyes." The rhythm and the rhyme would be ruined. Changing the usual word order of a sentence is called *inversion*. It is common in poetry.

Look back at the phrase "fill up with snow" in the last line of the stanza from "Stopping by Woods." Boxes can be filled up, but can woods be filled up? This phrase gives a picture or an impression of the branches heavy with snow and the snow on the ground becoming deeper and deeper. It has taken many words to explain what Frost said in four short words. Using as few words as possible is called *compression* and is another trait of poetry.

One of the poems from *A Shropshire Lad* by A. E. Housman describes the early spring beauty of cherry trees full of white blooms, and gives his reaction to this beauty.

> Loveliest of trees, the cherry now
> Is hung with bloom along the bough,
> And stands about the woodland ride
> Wearing white for Eastertide.
>
> Now, of my threescore years and ten,
> Twenty will not come again,
> And take from seventy springs a score,
> It only leaves me fifty more.
>
> And since to look at things in bloom
> Fifty springs are little room,
> About the woodland I will go
> To see the cherry hung with snow.

---

[1]Courtesy Robert Frost.

[1]Reprinted by permission of The Literary Trustees of Walter de la Mare and The Society of Authors as their representative.

For rhyme the poet used *ride* instead of *road* and *tide* instead of *time* in the first stanza. In the second, he used *score,* which means 20 years, for compression, rhythm, and sound. And since he was writing about spring blooms, he used *fifty springs* instead of *fifty years.* Though he does not actually say it, Housman makes the reader think that the cherry trees "hung with bloom" or "hung with snow" are equally beautiful and can give the same pleasure. Here again simple, well-known words have been arranged through the poet's art to express an idea in poetical form.

As an experiment, here is the same idea expressed in prose:

At Eastertime the cherry trees covered with white blooms are the loveliest trees along the woodland road. I may live to be seventy years old, but I am already twenty. So I have only fifty more years to live. Fifty years is not enough time to enjoy things in bloom, so I'll go into the wood in the winter and see the snow-covered trees.

This prose statement is flat and dull. Not only has the rhyme and rhythm been lost, but the *poetry* has been destroyed. For in poetry the thought is so closely connected with the way the thought is expressed that the two cannot be separated. One can say in his own words what he thinks the poet is saying, but he must use the poet's words if he is to understand and appreciate the full meaning of the poem. This *fusion* of thought and form (the way the poem is written) is another quality of poetry.

The poet has at least two reasons for choosing words carefully and putting them together in a special way. He can express his ideas better and he can create a mood or tone that fits the subject-matter. By creating this tone, the poet can make the reader *feel* as well as *think.*

Compare the beginnings of these two poems. Here is the first stanza of one of the poems Tennyson wrote after the death of his good friend Arthur Hallam:

> Break, break, break,
>   On thy cold gray stones, O Sea!
> And I would that my tongue could utter
>   The thoughts that arise in me.

And here are the first four lines of the Fairy's song from Shakespeare's *A Midsummer Night's Dream:*

> Over hill, over dale,
>   Through bush, through brier,
> Over park, over pale,
>   Through flood, through fire.

Each "break" in the first line of Tennyson's poem is given equal stress. In the second line "o" sounds are repeated. In both ways Tennyson sets a slow pace that is fitting for a poem expressing sorrow. Shakespeare, on the other hand, used a quick, jumpy rhythm to show the dancing, light movements of a fairy.

The opening lines of Alfred Noyes's poem "The Highwayman"[1] tells a story of adventure and romance.

> The wind was a torrent of darkness among the
>   gusty trees,
> The moon was a ghostly galleon tossed upon
>   cloudy seas,
> The road was a ribbon of moonlight over the
>   purple moor,
> And the highwayman came riding—
>   Riding—riding—
> The highwayman came riding, up to the old
>   inn-door.

The words "torrent of darkness," "ghostly galleon," and "purple moor" suggest mystery. This stanza sets a scene where exciting things can happen. Read the lines aloud. The rhythm should suggest galloping hoof beats. According to the dictionary the word "moor" means a large tract of wasteland with low shrubs growing on it, but no trees. But moors are often pictured as empty, lonely places where strange things happen. Thus moor has come to suggest something more than its exact meaning. The use of a word to suggest special meaning is called *connotation.* Through its exact meaning and its connotation, the word acts in two ways. The meaning of the line or phrase in which it is used becomes richer and more complex.

In reading poetry the sounds, the rhythm, and the connotation of the poet's words are all important. But these are not the only uses that poets make of words.

Figures of Speech

In the last line of the first stanza of the poem by Housman the cherry trees are "Wearing

[1]Reprinted by permission of the publishers, J. B. Lippincott Company, from *Collected Poems, Volume I,* by Alfred Noyes. Copyright, 1906, by Alfred Noyes.

white for Eastertide." People wear things; trees do not. But poets sometime speak of nonhuman things as if they were human and give them human abilities and behavior. This is called *personification*.

Except for adjectives, comparison is probably the most often used method of describing something. To show his pleasure when he first read George Chapman's translation of Homer's great epic poems, John Keats used a comparison:

> Then felt I like some watcher of the skies
> When a new planet swims into his ken.

And William Wordsworth, describing the beauty of a young girl, wrote:

> Fair as a star, when only one
> Is shining in the sky.

These comparisons are *similes;* that is, comparisons using the words *like* or *as.*

Other comparisons are more direct. In the first line of "The Highwayman," Noyes wrote, "The moon was a ghostly galleon" and "The road was a ribbon of moonlight." The moon is not really a ship and a road is not a ribbon. The poet is making a comparison even though he does not use the words *like* or *as.* Such comparisons identify one object with another and are called *metaphors.*

Although simile and metaphor are technical terms, what they stand for are common in language. A person may say, for example, "He is a pig" instead of "He is greedy." Or he may say, "moves like lightning" instead of "moves swiftly." When he does, he is using similes and metaphors.

Kinds of Poetry

Poets have used different forms to write about almost every subject. In their handling of subject-matter, poets may be grave or gay, serious or humorous. Good poets always choose a form and meter suited to their subject and to the mood they wish to create.

Narrative poetry. A narrative poem is one that tells a story. The most famous narrative poems of all times are the *Iliad* and the *Odyssey,* the epics by the Greek poet Homer. An epic is a story of great heroes and their deeds told in a serious and formal style. Next to the

works by Homer, the best-known epics are the *Aeneid, The Divine Comedy, The Song of Roland,* and *Paradise Lost.* (See EPIC.)

Narrative poems range from very long works such as Sir Walter Scott's *The Lady of the Lake* and Henry W. Longfellow's *The Courtship of Miles Standish* to Robert Browning's "The Pied Piper of Hamelin," Robert Frost's "The Death of the Hired Man," and the ballads about Robin Hood. Today poets seldom write long narrative poems; but one well-known modern narrative poem is Stephen Vincent Benet's *John Brown's Body.*

Dramatic poetry. Shakespeare wrote the greatest dramatic poetry in the English language. Later poets such as John Dryden, Percy Bysshe Shelley, and Robert Browning wrote verse plays. In the 20th century poets, including T. S. Eliot, Christopher Fry, and W. H. Auden, have had successful verse plays produced.

Lyric poetry. Lyric poems express the poet's personal thoughts and feelings. They are usually shorter than narrative or dramatic poems. Lyrics may be songs, odes, elegies, or sonnets.

Lyric poems called songs are not necessarily written to be sung. If they are read aloud, however, their musical quality can be heard.

Odes were originally meant to be sung or chanted, like the choral odes in Greek drama. Odes usually are addressed to a person, thing, or quality; for example, Wordsworth's "Ode to Duty," Keats's "Ode on a Grecian Urn," and Shelley's "Ode to the West Wind." Odes are longer and more solemn than songs, and the stanza forms are more formal.

Elegies are poems written about death or in memory of someone who has died. Thomas Gray's "Elegy Written in a Country Churchyard" has death as its theme; Shelley's "Adonais" was written in memory of Keats; and Walt Whitman's "When Lilacs Last in the Dooryard Bloom'd" mourns Lincoln's death.

Sonnets may be written on any subject. They differ from other lyrics in that the form of each is the same, except for the rhyme scheme. It is always 14 lines long, and each line has five stressed words or syllables. (See SONNET.)

Blank Verse and Free Verse. Blank verse is unrhymed lines in regular meter with five stresses to a line. Shakespeare's plays and Milton's epics are written in blank verse. Robert Frost often used blank verse, as in the first four lines of "Birches"[1]:

> When I see birches bend to left and right
> Across the lines of straighter darker trees,
> I like to think some boy's been swinging them.
> But swinging doesn't bend them down to stay.

Free verse is poetry written without rhyme and with no regular rhythmic pattern. The following lines are from Whitman's elegy on Lincoln:

> In the swamp in secluded recesses,
> A shy and hidden bird is warbling a song.
>
> Solitary the thrush
> The hermit withdrawn to himself, avoiding
>   the settlements,
> Sings by himself a song.

Meter and Rhyme

Throughout this article words such as rhythm, meter, and rhyme scheme have been used. It is possible to read and understand poetry without being able to define these terms, but they are important in writing a poem.

To scan a line of poetry is to mark the rhythm or meter. In the line "Whose woods | these are | I think | I know," there are four pairs of stressed and unstressed words. Each pair is called a *foot*; the line is said to have four feet. Lines of poetry may have as few as one foot but may have as many as seven or eight.

The arrangement of stressed and unstressed words and syllables is called meter. There are four main kinds of meter.

iamb ‿′	anapest ‿‿′
trochee ′‿	dactyl ′‿‿

In the line scanned above the meter is iambic. Trochee is the reverse of iambus: "Earth re|ceives the | rain and | sunlight." Here is an example of anapest: "And the peak | of the hill | was all cov|ered with snow." Longfellow used dactylic meter in *Evangeline* "This is the | forest pri|meval. The | murmuring | pines and the |

hemlocks." Notice that the line ends with a trochaic foot.

Sometimes a poet will use different kinds of meter in one line. In the first three lines of "The Highwayman" there are six feet to a line. The first foot is iambic, the next three are anapestic, and the last two are iambic.

Knowledge of these technical terms can be useful, but the enjoyment and understanding of poetry is more important.

POINSETTIA (*poin sĕt'i ä*), one of the most popular plants for the Christmas season. It is grown for its great clusters of bright scarlet leaves at the ends of long stems. The small, inconspicuous flowers occur at the center of this mass of leaves. The brightly colored leaves are often referred to as the flowers. The foliage leaves are deeply lobed and bright, waxy green.

In the northern United States very large quantities of poinsettia are grown in greenhouses. In the southern portion, including Florida and southern California, the plant lives out-of-doors as a perennial. There it may become a shrub up

The bright red and green coloring of the poinsettia plant has made it a favorite Christmas decoration.

J. Horace McFarland Company

to 15 feet or more in height. Usually the large stems are cut back, often to the ground, every year or two. New shoots are then produced and later bloom profusely. In the greenhouse the plants are propagated from cuttings. If these are made as early as May, the plants grow large and tall by Christmas time. If propagated as late as August, or even September, the plants will bloom but are much shorter. The short plants are excellent for growing in pots.

POISON (*poi'z'n*) **GAS.** Poison gas is as near as the nearest automobile, for every gasoline engine makes a poison gas called carbon monoxide every time it runs. Also, this poison gas is made whenever a tightly closed stove burns wood or coal. The gas formed inside may leak from the stove into the room and not be noticed. Carbon monoxide can not be smelled or tasted, and it does not irritate the nose or lungs of a person who breathes it. It merely makes the person sleepy if the dose is small. A larger dose makes him unconscious, and a still larger dose kills him. If the coal, wood, or gasoline that made the carbon monoxide gas had had enough air or oxygen to burn completely, a harmless gas called carbon dioxide would have been formed. Manufactured city gas contains a high percentage of carbon monoxide, but natural gas does not. About the only protection against carbon monoxide is to keep it out of the room by proper chimney connections. Automobiles must not be run in closed garages.

Industrial Poison Gases

The makers of gasoline put a few drops of a very poisonous liquid in every gallon of gasoline to make engines run more smoothly and climb hills better. This material, which is called tetraethyl lead, can poison a person if enough of it gets on his skin or if he breathes enough of it.

Another useful poison gas is chlorine, which in its natural state is a heavy, greenish-yellow vapor. If this gas is cooled and compressed, it becomes a liquid and can be stored and shipped in steel cylinders. Chlorine is used to purify drinking water because it is poisonous to all kinds of germs and plant life in the water.

Sometimes one can smell the pungent odor of chlorine given off from water taken directly from the faucet. Chlorine gas has many other uses in industry and is made in great quantities.

Phosgene is another poison gas that is used in large quantities to produce dyes, medicines, and many other products. It is like chlorine in that it is a gas by nature but becomes a liquid when cooled and compressed. As a liquid it is shipped in steel containers as chlorine is. Phosgene is extremely poisonous when breathed. It smells like wet, moldy grass or like wet leaves soon after they fall. Not many persons are exposed to phosgene by living near factories where it is used. Some, however, may be exposed to phosgene generated when certain fire-fighting chemicals are sprayed onto any white hot fire. One of these chemicals is carbon tetrachloride. If it is sprayed onto a fire indoors, enough phosgene may be made to kill all the people in the room. Many firemen were killed by the gas before it was learned that phosgene was formed in this way.

In some cities the combination of different industrial gases released into the air makes up a kind of fog called smog. It makes people cough when they breathe it. If certain acid fumes and fine particles of metals are present in the smog, it can become poisonous. Once at least it was shown that smog had killed a large number of persons. Because of this danger, persons who live in industrial areas are studying smog and possible ways to prevent its accumulation.

For poison gas in mines, see COAL.

Military or War Gases

Two of the early war gases, chlorine and phosgene, have come to be important commercially. Several other war gases have also been put to other uses. Nitrogen mustard gas is a medicine. Chloropicrin, which causes vomiting, has proved effective in killing weevils in wheat and other grain in storage.

Two other war gases are used by police to overcome criminals who barricade themselves in houses and refuse to surrender. Tear gas in its original form is a sugarlike solid material. When it is heated it forms a vapor that attacks

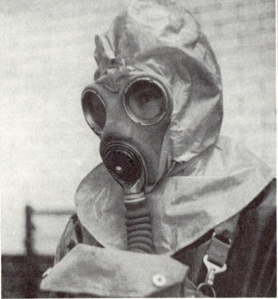

Courtesy (above left) Bituminous Coal Institute; photos, (above right)
Wide World, (left center) Herbert-Paul from Black Star, (below)
Ewing Galloway

Above left: The first thing workers must do when they enter a coal mine is to test for poison gas. Called a mine safety lamp, this lamp has a flame which burns blue when methane gas is present, yellow when all is well. Above right: A civil defense worker's rescue service equipment includes an all-purpose gas mask, a first-aid belt, a six-foot steel pry bar, and a radio unit. Left center: Gas mask with protective head and shoulder covering. The principal materials used in gas mask filters are charcoal and soda lime. Charcoal absorbs and holds most poisonous gases. Below: Smog over a factory and tenement district.

the eyes and causes temporary blindness. Tear gas is placed in grenades and paper projectiles and fired through the windows into the room where the criminal has taken refuge. The white cloud of tear gas soon blinds him so that he gives up. If the tear gas is not powerful enough, a sneeze gas can be used in the same way. It produces a much more powerful effect on the criminal. It makes him sneeze, gives him a terrible headache, and quickly makes him completely helpless so that the police have to carry him outside for fresh air. The police are protected by gas masks.

Modern war gases are extremely powerful and may act in several ways. A drop of liquid mustard gas on a person's skin, for instance, will cause a watery blister, as big as a hen's egg, that takes a long time to heal. The vapors of mustard gas attack the eyes, make them puff up, and blind a person for several days. If the vapor is breathed, blisters form inside the lungs and may kill the person.

An even more powerful liquid poison is called nerve gas. A very small amount in either the liquid or the vapor form causes temporary blindness and makes a person unable to stand or do any kind of work. A larger dose of nerve gas kills him quickly.

Protection

A gas mask purifies the air that passes through it by removing or neutralizing the poison gas. Some gases are made harmless by being breathed through a cloth soaked in water and baking soda. Other poisons require activated charcoal and other very fast-acting chemicals in the gas mask canister to destroy the poison gas during the short time the air is in the mask. Some war gases, such as mustard gas, require protective clothes to keep the liquid and vapors away from the body.

POISONOUS (*poi′z′n ŭs*) **PLANTS** cause sickness or death when touched or eaten. One of the best known in the United States is poison ivy. Touching it often causes a painful and irritating blistering of the skin. Some people are very sensitive to ivy poisoning. Poison sumac and poison oak affect some people in the same way. Poison oak is not an oak. It has been given this name because it often attaches itself to the bark of oak trees. It also grows as a bush from 3 to 15 feet tall. It is often found along the Pacific coast.

Farmers lose thousands of dollars a year because their animals eat poisonous plants. One of the most dangerous of these is the locoweed, found in the West. It is called *loco* from the Spanish word meaning "insane." Animals that eat locoweed lose all control of their movements and run around wildly. (See LOCOWEED.) Other poisonous plants that cause losses of cattle and sheep are death camass, certain lupines, larkspur, and some kinds of milkweed.

Some mushrooms are poisonous when eaten. People who do not know different kinds of mushrooms should not eat wild ones. (See MUSHROOM; NIGHTSHADE.)

POISONS (*poi′z′ns*) are substances that can kill or cause an injury to health. When taken in large amounts almost any substance, including salt or water, can be harmful. But usually poison means a chemical substance that is harmful in very small amounts.

Poisons enter the body in many ways. Usually it is swallowed. It may be breathed into the lungs or absorbed through the skin or the mucous membranes of the nose. It also may be injected into the skin. Some poisons act only if they enter the body in a certain way. For example, snake venom is not harmful if it is swallowed. But venom entering directly into the blood stream, because of a bite, may be deadly.

Many useful substances are also poisons. Chlorine, a poisonous gas used to purify water, may be present in small amounts in drinking water. Often drugs that are useful in small amounts may be poisonous in large doses.

There are three major kinds of poison. *Corrosive* poisons are acids and alkalis that destroy the body tissue. (See ACID; ALKALI.) *Irritant* poisons, such as arsenic, inflame the mucous membrane within the body. *Systemic* poisons, such as cyanide, affect the organ systems, such as the nervous system, heart, or kidneys.

Many poisons are gases. One of the deadliest

is carbon monoxide, a gas given off in car exhausts. (See CARBON ,DIOXIDE AND CARBON MONOXIDE; POISON GAS.)

Food poisoning is usually caused by bacteria. Modern sanitary conditions have reduced the danger of it.

Most poisonings are accidents. Often young children will swallow anything they find. Common household products that are poisonous are cosmetics, aspirin, sleeping pills, bleaches, lighter and cleaning fluid, insect killers, disinfectants, furniture polish and waxes.

Poisonous substances should be kept in locked medicine cabinets. Bottles should be closed tightly. Adults should never take a medicine without reading the label. They also should not keep medicines in unlabeled bottles.

Most poisons become dangerous only when people are careless and misuse them. Prevention of poison accidents is therefore of greatest importance. But once poisoning has taken place, quick and correct action may save a life.

Always call a doctor. If no help can be found, give a general antidote such as charcoal with water, milk of magnesia, large amounts of tea, milk, or egg whites mixed with milk. In a few minutes make the victim vomit.

If the poisoning is due to a gas, move the victim to fresh air immediately. Carry him—do not allow him to walk. Loosen tight clothing and give artificial respiration if necessary.

For poisons on skin or eyes, wash the skin or the eyes under continuous fresh water. Seconds count. Water is all that is needed. Never use chemicals or neutralizers.

For poisons due to the bite of snakes or scorpions, make the patient lie down. Apply tourniquets, using a belt or tie, or a piece of material. Place it on the arm or leg between the bite and the heart. Loosen the tourniquet every 15 minutes for one minute. Apply an ice pack to the bite.

ANTIDOTES FOR COMMON POISONS

CALL THE DOCTOR AT ONCE WHEN POISONING IS SUSPECTED. FIND OUT IF POSSIBLE WHAT THE PATIENT HAS TAKEN, SO THE DOCTOR WILL KNOW WHAT TO BRING WITH HIM. AT LEAST GIVE THE DOCTOR A BRIEF AND CALM DESCRIPTION OF HOW THE PATIENT ACTS. IF THE DOCTOR CANNOT BE REACHED, CALL THE LOCAL HOSPITAL OR POISON CONTROL CENTER.

Poison	Signs Which Suggest It	What to Do
Strong Acids	Burns in and pain about the mouth, abdominal pain, colic, nausea, vomiting, diarrhea, collapse.	Warm water drinks. Repeat every ten minutes. Milk or egg white, 1 to 2 ounces milk of magnesia.
	If breath smells like garlic.	AVOID ALL OILS.
Strong Alkalies	White coating, or burns in or about mouth, colic, nausea, vomiting, diarrhea, collapse.	Warm water drinks repeated frequently. Lemon juice, dilute vinegar, salt solution, 1 teaspoon in 1 glass, repeat in ten minutes.
Nerve Irritating Drugs	Excitement, rapid breathing, abdominal pains and cramps. Flushed face and body. May have nausea and vomiting.	Unless patient is having convulsions, produce vomiting. Use 1 teaspoon mustard in hot water or 1 tablespoon of ipecac. Repeat in 15 minutes.
Nerve Depressing Drugs	Drowsiness, slowed breathing, paralysis, unconsciousness, cold, clammy perspiration, face pale, convulsions, fainting.	If patient is conscious, produce vomiting. Artificial respiration if necessary. Apply dry heat. Black coffee. Keep patient awake and in motion if possible.
Suffocating Gases	Fainting, face pale, slow, shallow breathing, or no breathing.	Lay down in fresh air. Keep warm in blankets. Artificial respiration.

POLAND (*pō'lănd*), **EUROPE,** is a Communist country in east-central Europe. The boundaries of Poland have been changed many times. The last change took place in 1945. At the end of World War II, the Allied Powers (United States, Great Britain, and the Soviet Union) moved Poland's boundary westward to include territory formerly within Germany. On the other hand, almost the entire eastern half of Poland became part of the Soviet Union. As a result of the boundary moves Poland was reduced in size by one-fifth. Present-day Poland lies between the Baltic Sea on the north and Czechoslovakia on the south. On the east, the Bug River forms part of the boundary between Poland and the Soviet Union. On the west, the Oder and Neisse rivers separate the country from Germany. In the Polish language, the country is called *Polska*, which means "country of the plain." Because Poland is flat, it has been traditionally agricultural. Industry, however, has grown rapidly since World War II. The official name of the country is the Polish People's Republic.

Landscape

Most of Poland is a broad, flat lowland, with no great physical barriers to the movement of men. It therefore has been easy for people of other countries to invade Poland. The northern half of the country shows the effect of glacier movements during the Ice Age. The Baltic coastal plain is broken by moraines, which are ridges of earth and stone left by the glaciers. A heavy clay soil that covers much of northern Poland also was formed by glaciers. This soil is of low fertility, although often forested. In the northeast, lakes make up a large portion of the surface.

To the south, the land rises to a low platform. The glacial deposits become less extensive and then cease. Much of southern Poland is covered by loess, a soil that is composed of materials spread by the wind. The landscapes of the north and south are similar, but the loess makes the southern land more fertile.

The only mountainous portion of Poland is a narrow strip along the southern border. These mountains form the border between Poland and Czechoslovakia. In the southwest are the Sudetes, which reach an altitude of more than 5,000 feet, and are crossed by many passes. To the southeast, the Carpathian Mountains rise steeply from the plain to snow-capped peaks up to 8,000 feet high. A group of Carpathian peaks called the High Tatras are noted for their resemblance to the Swiss Alps. The two mountain ranges are separated by the Moravian Gap.

The Vistula is the longest and most important river of Poland. It flows for 664 miles from the Carpathians northward through central and northern Poland, and empties into the Baltic Sea. The broad, navigable river is used mainly to transport timber and coal. Other important rivers draining into the Baltic Sea are the Oder, the Bug, and the Warta.

Poland's climate ranges between the more moderate climates of western Europe and the colder climates of eastern Europe. Summers are cool, and winters range from moderately cold to very cold. The average January temperature of Warsaw is about 26 degrees Fahrenheit, and the average July temperature is about 65 degrees Fahrenheit. Annual rainfall varies from 20

Courtesy Centralna Agencja Fotografigzna

Although much of the port city of Szczecin was destroyed during World War II and later rebuilt, these fine old buildings remain on the Chrobry embankment.

inches in the lowlands to more than 50 inches in the southern mountains.

The country's forests are an important natural resource. Nearly one-fourth of Poland is covered by forests. Coniferous trees, such as pine and spruce, occupy more than 70 per cent of the total forest area. The remainder includes such deciduous trees as birch, beech, and elm. Animals that inhabit the forests and plains include the wildcat, moose, European bison, wild horse, wild goat, and lynx. They are, however, becoming scarce.

The People

Poland developed after the advances of Slavic peoples into Europe in the Middle Ages. At one time the Slavs occupied all of the area east of the Elbe and north of the Danube rivers. The Germans and Russians constantly invaded this area and absorbed many of the Slavs. One region, however, remained persistently Slavic.

PRODUCTS OF
POLAND

KEY TO SYMBOLS

- IRON & STEEL
- COAL
- IRON ORE
- MACHINERY
- LEAD
- SALT
- GLASS
- POTATOES

- SHIPPING
- ZINC ORE
- VINEYARDS
- OIL REFINING
- LIGNITE
- HOGS
- SUGAR BEETS
- DRUGS & CHEMICALS

- FORESTS
- CLOTHING MFG.
- LUMBERING

- RYE
- WHEAT
- TEXTILES

This is roughly the area of present-day Poland. The country was named by the Polanie, a tribal group of the central plain.

Before World War II, about one-third of the population of Poland was made up of minority groups such as Jews, Germans, Russians, and Czechoslovakians. After the war, the Allies agreed to deport the Germans in western Poland, which was formerly German. Poles who lived in the eastern territory annexed by the U.S.S.R. were then transferred to western Poland. Other minority groups were transferred to their own countries in a similar manner. Jewish groups accounted for about 3,000,000 of Poland's prewar population of 35,339,000. By the end of the war, Nazi extermination methods had reduced the Jewish population to fewer than 100,000. By 1960 the total population of

minority groups was only about 500,000.

There is no official religion in Poland. About 90 per cent of the population is Roman Catholic. Most of the remainder are Russian Orthodox, Protestant, and Jewish. Polish is the official language of the country. It is a western Slavic language that uses the Latin alphabet.

Poland has been the home of many scientists and statesmen. The founder of modern astronomy, Nicolaus Copernicus, was a Pole. Noted Polish statesmen include Tadeusz Kosciuszko, who aided George Washington in the American Revolution; musician Ignace Paderewski, the republic's first premier; and Joseph Pilsudski, one of the country's main leaders between World Wars I and II.

In music, Poland is especially famous for its dances. These include the polonaise, once a

Locator map of Poland.

FACTS ABOUT POLAND

CAPITAL: Warsaw. **NATIONAL ANTHEM:** *Jeszcze Polska Nie Zginela* ("Poland Is Not Yet Lost").

AREA: 120,359 square miles.

POPULATION (1960 census): 29,775,508; 25 persons per square mile; 49 per cent urban, 51 per cent rural.

MOUNTAIN RANGES: Carpathians, Karkonosze, Sudetes, Tatra.

HIGHEST MOUNTAIN PEAKS: Rysy (8,199 ft.), Mieguszowiecki Szczyt (7,999 ft.), Swinica (7,549 ft.).

LARGEST LAKES: Sniardwy, Mamry, Lebsko, Dabie, Goplo.

MOST IMPORTANT RIVERS: Vistula, Oder, Bug, Warta.

PLACES OF INTEREST: Warsaw (birthplaces of Chopin and Pulaski, and palaces of Polish kings); Cracow (resorts).

FORM OF GOVERNMENT: People's Republic.

CHIEF OF STATE: Chairman, Council of State.

HEAD OF GOVERNMENT: Chairman, Council of Ministers (premier).

LEGISLATURE: *Sejm* composed of 460 deputies, elected by the people on the basis of one for every 60,000 inhabitants; 4-year terms.

VOTING QUALIFICATIONS: Age 18.

POLITICAL DIVISIONS: 22 voivodeships (provinces); includes 5 independent cities.

CHIEF CITIES: Warsaw, Lodz, Cracow, Wroclaw, Poznan, Danzig (Gdansk).

CHIEF MANUFACTURED PRODUCTS: Food, textiles, basic metals, transportation equipment.

CHIEF AGRICULTURAL PRODUCTS: Potatoes, sugar beets, rye, wheat.

FLAG: Two horizontal bands; the top is white, the bottom red. (See FLAG.)

MONETARY UNIT: Zloty. Value: about 24 zlotys equal one U.S. dollar.

stately court dance, and the mazurka, which is a folk dance. The composer Frederic Chopin, a Pole, used these dance themes in his compositions.

How the People Make a Living

Before World War II, Poland was known chiefly as an agricultural country. After the war, the Communist government emphasized industrial programs. Border changes also stimulated industrial growth. When the German-Polish border was moved westward, it made most of the German part of the highly industrialized Silesia district a part of Poland. At the same time, the Soviet Union annexed about one-fifth of the country's agricultural land. By the 1960's only about 38 per cent of the people depended on agriculture for their living.

The country has an abundance of rich agricultural land, particularly in the central and southern regions. Altogether almost two-thirds of the land can be farmed. Grains are the most important crops. Rye and oats are grown in all parts of the country, and there also is much wheat and barley. Potatoes are raised on nearly one-fifth of the cultivated land and are well distributed throughout the country. Other crops include fodder plants, legumes, vegetables, and rapeseed. Sugar beets are the most important industrial crop; others include flax, hemp, hops, linseed, and chicory.

Farming in Poland is carried on very differently from farming in the United States. After World War II the large estates were broken up. The state took over most of them, and many were divided among the peasants who had worked on them. Many of the peasants, in turn, were made members of collective farms. They had to meet government goals and turn over most of what they produced to central collecting agencies. In late 1956 and 1957, when Communist control was relaxed in Poland, the trend quickly turned back to private ownership.

Under successive programs of economic development, beginning in 1950, Poland has made strenuous efforts to develop industry. Poland is fortunate in that it has many of the raw materials that it needs to supply industry. One of

Europe's major coal fields is located in Silesia, the leading industrial area of Poland. This district also has well-developed iron and steel industries that the Germans had built there when the region was part of Germany. Poland's mineral resources include lead, zinc, copper, cobalt, arsenic, barium, salt, and some nickel, iron ore, and manganese. Poland is one of the world's leading producers of zinc.

Outside of Silesia, manufacturing is concentrated in the larger cities. Under the planned economy, a major steel factory was built near Cracow, one of Poland's oldest cities. This plant, which began operation in 1954, is one of the largest integrated iron- and steelworks in Europe. Warsaw, the country's capital and largest city, also is an important industrial center. Before World War II, Warsaw produced many products needed by the people. Restoring the industrial capacity of this city became one of the most important postwar objectives. Among the traditional Warsaw industries are the processing of textiles, clothing, and food. Other industries, such as metal fabrication and ceramics, grew more important during the 1950's. Lodz, the second largest city of Poland, was one of the country's earliest manufacturing centers. Today it is a major center for the production of wool and cotton goods.

Polish trade since World War II has been increasingly with the Soviet Union and the Communist group of east European countries. Before 1940 Poland's exports consisted chiefly of metals, glass and ceramic ware, textiles, and wood products. In postwar Poland the chief exports are coal, lignite, ships, railroad cars, and foods, such as eggs, meat and meat products, and salt. Poland's major imports include petroleum, cotton, iron ore, and fertilizers.

Transportation and Communications

Poland depends mostly on its railroads for transportation. Railroads carry about 80 per cent of all freight and passengers. The rail network is densest in the former German and Austrian areas. East of the Vistula River the rail pattern thins out. All public transportation is state-owned.

The road network has expanded since World

Warsaw, the capital of Poland, is built on both banks of the Vistula River. Its tallest building, the Palace of Culture and Science, above left, was a gift from the U.S.S.R. in 1955.

War II, but maintenance is inadequate. Almost three-fourths of the roads are in need of repair. Only about 40 per cent of the 178,000 miles of highways are paved.

The country's inland waterways include 2,750 miles of navigable rivers and canals. The Oder and Vistula rivers connect inland ports with the Baltic Sea. The Oder, navigable for 400 miles, is an important route to the Silesian industrial region. The chief east-west water route follows the lower Bug River into a stretch of the Vistula River. The route continues westward through the Notec, Warta, and Oder rivers.

All communication services are owned and operated by the government. There are about 7,000 postal and telegraph offices. In 1966 the state operated 22 television stations and more than 20 radio stations.

Government

Poland has a Communist form of government. Its constitution, adopted in 1952, is modeled after that of the Soviet Union. Actual control of the country is held by the politburo of the United Workers' party. The first secretary of the party is the country's most powerful man. Officially heading the government is a 15-man Council of State. The council is elected by the *Sejm* (legislature). The 460 members of the *Sejm*, who serve four-year terms, are elected by all citizens 18 years of age or older. Local

governments are administered by people's councils.

Three major political parties exist: the Polish United Workers' party, the United Peasants' party, and the Democratic party. The Communist-dominated Polish United Workers' Party controls most of the seats in the *Sejm*.

Almost all Poles can read and write. Primary and secondary education is free and compulsory for children to the age of 18 or 19. Education is generally free also in universities and specialized schools. Higher education is supervised by the ministry of higher education. There are seven universities. The Roman Catholic university at Lublin is the only free, private university in the country. The National Library in Warsaw, established in 1928, is the largest in Poland.

According to the constitution, freedom of the press is guaranteed in Poland. Everything that is published, however, must be within the "interests of society." The Communist Polish United Workers' party and the goverment exercise varying degrees of press control.

Public welfare activities are supervised by the government, although some trade unions and private organizations also provide benefits. Social insurance covers all workers and employees. Old age, disability, and survivors pensions are provided as well as unemployment compensation and sickness and maternity benefits.

History

Polish history can be traced back to the 10th century A.D., when the Polanie conquered other Slavic tribes living in the valleys of the Vistula, Warta, and Oder rivers. In the last part of the 10th century the people of Poland were converted to Christianity. Under the first powerful ruler, Boleslaw I, Polish power in the early 11th century was extended from the Baltic Sea to the Carpathian Mountains and from the Elbe River to the Bug River. Poznan was the capital of the early empire. The capital was established at Cracow under Boleslaw III.

After several centuries of struggle King Wladyslaw I (1320–1333) united Poland. During the late 14th and early 15th centuries Poland became one of the greatest powers in Europe. Polish territory extended as far east as the Black Sea. In 1596, Warsaw, because of its more central location, replaced Cracow as the capital of the united Poland-Lithuania kingdom.

Toward the end of the 15th century and during the 200 years that followed, the Poles engaged in wars with the Turks, Swedes, Russians, and Tatars. The constant struggle through these years gradually weakened Poland. The religious troubles that came with the Reformation in the 16th century added to the country's problems. Poland emerged from the Reformation solidly Catholic, but it was torn by conflicts among the nobility.

By the middle of the 18th century Poland was without a strong central government and was helpless in the face of invaders. In 1772 the three powerful European powers of the period —Russia, Prussia, and Austria—each annexed a portion of Poland. This first partition of Poland gave the northern provinces to Prussia, the southern to Austria, and the eastern to Russia. The partition reduced Poland's size by almost one-third. A second partition in 1793 ceded more territory to Russia and Prussia, cutting Poland's size by another third. The Polish government during these partitions was controlled by the European powers.

In 1794 the Poles, under Tadeusz Kosciuszko, revolted. Thousands of people were killed, and part of Warsaw was destroyed, but the revolt failed. Another partition followed in 1795, and the name of Poland disappeared from the map for more than a century. In the 19th century the Poles made two major attempts to regain their independence. Each of these efforts—one in 1830 and one in 1863—was unsuccessful.

An independent Poland, the first in more than 120 years, grew out of World War I. Poland became a republic in 1918. The first premier of Poland under the new constitution was Ignace Paderewski. Joseph Pilsudski became chief of state and assumed dictatorial powers.

The new Poland ran into much trouble between World Wars I and II. One after another of the countries out of which Poland had been formed demanded that its territory be returned. War broke out between Russia and Poland over the eastern frontier, but the Poles, led by Pilsudski, defeated the Soviets in 1921.

In the 1930's, Germany once again became strong. The German dictator Adolf Hitler insisted that Danzig and the Polish Corridor should be part of Germany. These two places separated East Prussia and Germany and gave Poland its only Baltic outlet. The Poles refused to give up this territory, and on September 1, 1939, Hitler invaded Poland. The action touched off World War II. Shortly afterward the U.S.S.R. struck from the east, and by September 27 the poorly equipped Poles were forced to surrender.

Once again Poland was partitioned. This time the Soviets took a large part of the eastern area, and Germany took the western provinces including Danzig and the Corridor. The central portion was left as a Polish "government general" under German control.

In June 1941 Germany once again invaded Poland and overran all of the Polish territory. The Poles, particularly the Jews, suffered severely under Nazi rule. A majority of the Jews were killed. By the end of the war more than 6,000,000 Polish people had perished.

In the early part of 1945, the Soviet Army drove the Nazis out of Poland. At this time the Communists established control over Poland. In 1956, hungry workers in Poznan staged an uprising, demanding more freedom and food. As a result, Poland gained a partial break away from Soviet rule. In October 1956, a new premier, Wladyslaw Gomulka, was appointed. Although a Communist, he opposed Soviet domination and insisted that Poland be free to carry on its home affairs. In foreign affairs, and in the United Nations, Poland is allied with the Soviet Union. Through the early 1960's, Gomulka continued to lead the country as first secretary of the Polish United Workers' party.

POLAR (pō'lẽr) EXPLORATION (ĕks'plō rā'shŭn).

Among the most barren of all the world's regions are the icy areas around the North and South poles. With temperatures too cold for growing food, these lands offer little to attract settlers. Although there are some minerals and other resources, the cost of mining and transportation is too high. Since A.D. 1000 men have gone into the polar regions mainly to learn more about the earth, to find new trade routes, and for defense purposes, rather than to find new lands for settlement.

The history of polar expeditions is filled with heroic tales of both failure and success. Many explorers died because they did not know how to change their ways of living to meet polar conditions. They did not use the proper equipment, and they often developed diseases as a result of the lack of certain vitamins. The most successful early explorers were those who used the same kinds of food, clothing, housing, and dog sledges as the Eskimos used.

As men learned more about polar conditions and made better cold-weather equipment, polar exploration changed greatly. Ships changed from sail to steam or Diesel to the modern icebreaker. Instead of man-hauled sledges, dog teams or tractor-tread vehicles such as the "Weasel" and "Snow Cat" are used to cross polar lands. Helicopters and airplanes are used for covering long distances, for making land surveys from the air, and for dropping supplies. Exploring parties now can keep in contact with each other and with home bases by radio. As a result, modern expeditions can do much more work in less time and with less danger than could expeditions before the 20th century.

Arctic Exploration

The Arctic (north polar) Region is mainly an ice-covered ocean almost surrounded by land—the northern coasts of Europe, Asia, and North America and nearby islands. (See ARCTIC REGION.) Because the Arctic Region has such a long, cold winter and short, cool summer, trees will not grow there. However, there is some plant, animal, and ocean life which provides food for the fewer than 400,000 people who live there. Most of these people are descendants of migrants from north central Asia who settled in the Arctic before written records were kept. These settlers stayed alive in the Arctic by making full use of the land and ocean resources. Hunting and fishing supplied food; fur and skins were made into clothing; and skins, bones, stones, and even ice blocks were used to make houses. When food became scarce the settlers moved to a new location.

The earliest recorded European voyage into the Arctic Region was by the Greek navigator Pytheas from Massalia (Marseille). He sailed along the northwest coast of Europe about 325 B.C. and is believed to have reached Iceland. During the next thousand years there is no record of other Arctic explorers. Early in the 9th century A.D. long voyages in the North Atlantic Ocean were made by Irish monks, Basque whale hunters, and Norwegian sailors. They reached Greenland, Iceland, and Svalbard. Some of these voyagers settled in Iceland. The first real explorer of Greenland was Eric the Red, who sailed from Iceland in 982 and explored Greenland's west coast. He returned to Greenland in 986 with 14 ships and set up a colony, hoping to find good farm land. By the 15th century the colony had disappeared and all the viking settlers had died or mixed with the Eskimo people.

Since then few colonists have tried to make homes in the Arctic. Instead, they have gone to the far north for other reasons: to discover an ocean route to the Orient; to find products for trade; to learn more about the earth; and to set up defenses against air attack from across the North Pole.

During the 15th and 16th centuries, the leading sea-faring nations of western Europe— Portugal, France, England, and Holland— searched for a short and easy route to the Orient. They hoped to find a passage through the Arctic Ocean to the Pacific—either a Northeast Passage north of Asia or a Northwest Passage north of North America. By 1597 Willem Barents and J. H. van Linschoten had sailed northeast from Europe and reached the western shores of the Kara Sea. They explored the islands north of Eurasia, such as Svalbard and Novaya Zemlya. In the search for a Northwest Passage, explorers such as Martin Frobisher and John Davis reached the straits now named for them. In 1610 Henry Hudson sailed into Hudson Bay. Both to the northeast and northwest explorers had traveled as far as they could with the sailing ships and equipment of the early 17th century.

Since frozen seas blocked further progress in sailing the Arctic route to the Orient, in the 17th century men began to search Arctic Asia and North America for trade products. Furs were very valuable, and as fur traders pushed farther into new territory, the continents became better known.

Arctic trade routes were discovered much more rapidly in Asia than in North America. By 1600 Russian trade routes were opened up across Eurasia and along the rivers flowing to the Arctic Ocean. By 1649 a series of trading posts had been set up across Eurasia. On two expeditions from 1725 to 1729 and 1740 to 1741, Vitus Bering discovered Bering Sea and Strait and several islands in the northern Pacific. By 1775 Russian traders were exploring the Aleutians and the North American coast south to Vancouver Island. Charting of the Arctic shore of Siberia was completed by A. T. Middendorf

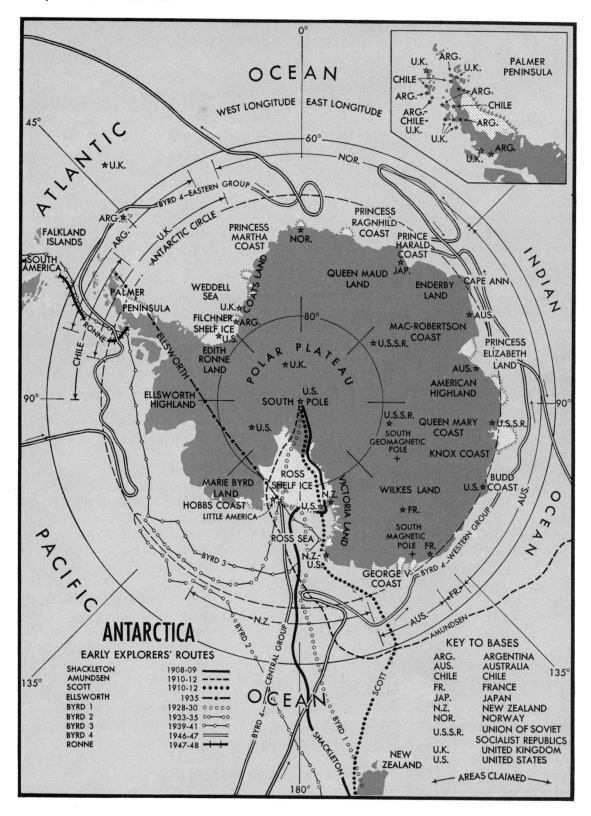

OCEAN

WEST LONGITUDE | EAST LONGITUDE

PALMER PENINSULA

U.K. ARG. U.K.
CHILE
ARG.
ARG.
CHILE
ARG.
CHILE-
U.K.
U.K.
U.K.
ARG.

0°

45°

ATLANTIC

NOR.

60°

BYRD 4—EASTERN GROUP

ANTARCTIC CIRCLE

U.K.

PRINCESS RAGNHILD COAST

PRINCE HARALD COAST

ARG.

FALKLAND ISLANDS

ARG.

SOUTH AMERICA

PRINCESS MARTHA COAST

NOR.

QUEEN MAUD LAND

JAP.

ENDERBY LAND

CAPE ANN

PALMER PENINSULA

WEDDELL SEA

U.K.

COATS LAND

80°

MAC-ROBERTSON COAST

U.S.S.R.

AUS.

PRINCESS ELIZABETH LAND

RONNE

CHILE

FILCHNER SHELF ICE

ARG.

U.S.

POLAR PLATEAU

U.K.

ELLSWORTH

EDITH RONNE LAND

AMERICAN HIGHLAND

AUS.

INDIAN

ELLSWORTH HIGHLAND

U.S.

SOUTH POLE

U.S.S.R.
SOUTH GEOMAGNETIC POLE

QUEEN MARY COAST

U.S.S.R.

90°

90°

KNOX COAST

MARIE BYRD LAND

ROSS SHELF ICE

VICTORIA LAND

N.Z.

WILKES LAND

BUDD COAST
U.S.

HOBBS COAST

LITTLE AMERICA

U.S.

FR.

BYRD 3

ROSS SEA

SOUTH MAGNETIC POLE

FR.

N.Z.
U.S.

BYRD 4—WESTERN GROUP

GEORGE V COAST

FR.

PACIFIC

N.Z.

AUS.

AMUNDSEN

135°

135°

BYRD 2

CENTRAL GROUP

ANTARCTICA

EARLY EXPLORERS' ROUTES

SHACKLETON	1908-09
AMUNDSEN	1910-12
SCOTT	1910-12
ELLSWORTH	1935
BYRD 1	1928-30
BYRD 2	1933-35
BYRD 3	1939-41
BYRD 4	1946-47
RONNE	1947-48

OCEAN

BYRD 4

SCOTT

SHACKLETON

BYRD 1

KEY TO BASES

ARG.	ARGENTINA
AUS.	AUSTRALIA
CHILE	CHILE
FR.	FRANCE
JAP.	JAPAN
N.Z.	NEW ZEALAND
NOR.	NORWAY
U.S.S.R.	UNION OF SOVIET SOCIALIST REPUBLICS
U.K.	UNITED KINGDOM
U.S.	UNITED STATES

NEW ZEALAND

← AREAS CLAIMED →

180°

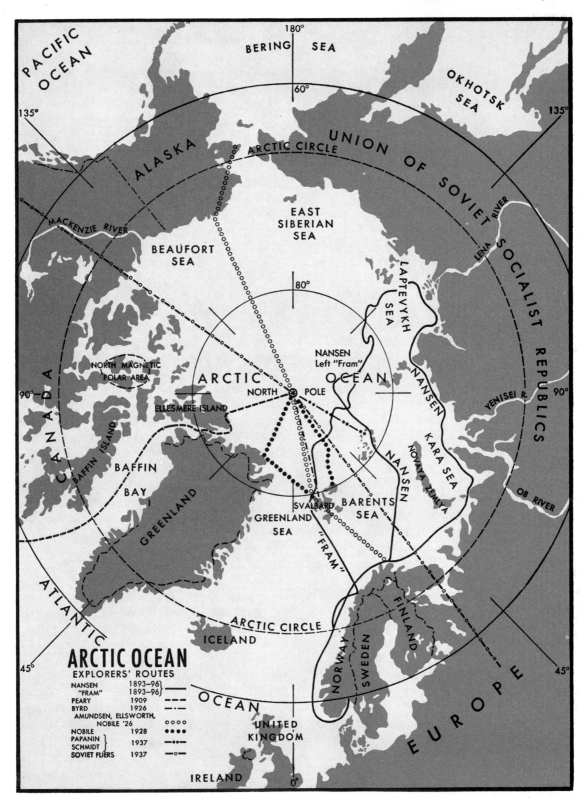

PACIFIC OCEAN

BERING SEA

OKHOTSK SEA

ALASKA

UNION OF SOVIET

ARCTIC CIRCLE

EAST SIBERIAN SEA

BEAUFORT SEA

MACKENZIE RIVER

LAPTEVYKH SEA

LENA RIVER

SOCIALIST REPUBLICS

NANSEN
Left "Fram"

NANSEN

NORTH MAGNETIC POLAR AREA

ARCTIC   OCEAN

CANADA

ELLESMERE ISLAND

NORTH POLE

NANSEN

KARA SEA

YENISEI R.

NOVAYA ZEMLYA

BAFFIN ISLAND

BAFFIN BAY

GREENLAND

SVALBARD

BARENTS SEA

OB RIVER

GREENLAND SEA

"FRAM"

ATLANTIC

FINLAND

ARCTIC CIRCLE

ICELAND

NORWAY

SWEDEN

EUROPE

ARCTIC OCEAN
EXPLORERS' ROUTES

NANSEN	1893–96	——
"FRAM"	1893–96	– – –
PEARY	1909	–·–·–
BYRD	1926	–··–··–
AMUNDSEN, ELLSWORTH, NOBILE '26		ooooo
NOBILE	1928	●●●●
PAPANIN	1937	
SCHMIDT	1937	–·–·–
SOVIET FLIERS	1937	–o–o–

OCEAN

UNITED KINGDOM

IRELAND

in 1843, and in 1878–1879 A. E. Nordenskiold made the first voyage through the Northeast Passage.

Arctic North America was not so easy to reach, and its exploration took place more slowly. Though some fur traders went inland from the Arctic Region as early as 1661, most explorations came after the Hudson's Bay Company was founded in 1670. During the next 150 years, forts and trading posts were set up to supply the traders and explorers who kept spreading farther north and west. One of the most noted explorers was Alexander Mackenzie, who followed the river now named for him to the Arctic Ocean in 1789. In 1793 he became the first white man to cross northern North America. (See MACKENZIE, SIR ALEXANDER.) Sir John Franklin led two expeditions across northern Canada from 1819 to 1821 and 1825 to 1826. During this time, the Arctic coast was being charted. Charting was completed in 1847 by John Rae.

With the Arctic coast line charted, Sir John Franklin set out in 1845 to find the Northwest Passage. His ships were frozen in the ice, food ran short, and all members of the expedition died. In an attempt to learn what had happened to the Franklin party, other expeditions searched northern Canada for many years. During the search they explored thousands of square miles of new country.

During this period the Northwest Passage was found. In 1851–1852 R. J. McClure, whose ship *Investigator* was frozen in the ice near Melville Island, walked over the frozen passage and returned home on the rescue ship *Resolute*. Not until 1906 did the first ship find a way through the Northwest Passage—the tiny *Gjoa* with Roald Amundsen in command. The *Gjoa* spent three years making the trip. The only ships that have made the trip in a single season are the icebreakers *St. Roch*, in 1944, and the *Labrador*, in 1954.

Most of the 19th- and 20-century expeditions were made to gain scientific knowledge, and much research and exploration were done. In 1882–1883, for the first International Polar Year, ten nations set up 12 observation stations around the North Pole. One of the United States parties, commanded by A. W. Greely, almost starved to death when relief ships failed to arrive on time. Many explorers mapped new areas of the north—Otto Sverdrup, Vilhjalmur Stefansson, D. B. MacMillan, and others.

Still no one had reached the North Pole. Since it is surrounded by an ice-covered ocean, many different ways to reach the pole were tried. In 1893 Fridtjof Nansen let his ship *Fram* be frozen in the ice, hoping the ocean currents would carry it over the pole. After drifting for two years without getting close, Nansen and his party tried to reach the pole on foot but failed. In 1897 S. A. Andree was lost trying to cross the pole in a balloon; four years later Umberto Cagni was forced back by lack of supplies.

Most determined of those who wanted the honor of first reaching the North Pole was Robert E. Peary. (See PEARY, ROBERT EDWIN.) Between 1891 and 1906 he made careful explorations to find the best route, studied methods and equipment, and made several attempts to push closer to the pole. In 1909 he tried again, this time with the help of supply parties which carried the provisions and built snow huts for shelter. At last on April 6, 1909, Peary reached the North Pole, with Matthew Henson and four Eskimos.

The airplane, radio, and other developments of the 20th century made careful scientific studies over a long period both possible and desirable. In 1926 Richard E. Byrd and Floyd Bennett were the first men to fly to the North Pole. They flew from Svalbard to the pole and back. (See BYRD, RICHARD EVELYN.) Two days after their flight, Roald Amundsen, Lincoln Ellsworth, and Umberto Nobile flew the dirigible *Norge* from the same base in Svalbard across the pole to Alaska. Nobile reached the North Pole in 1928 in the dirigible *Italia*, but on the return trip he crashed on the ice. Although most of his party was later rescued, Amundsen was lost while searching for them.

Since 1928 many flights have been made over the North Pole, and round-trip flights from land bases to the pole and back are common. Landings can be made on some parts of the ice. In 1937 the Soviet Union used planes to set four men on the ice at the North Pole, and they drifted across much of the Arctic Ocean. Research stations supplied by plane have been built by both United States and Russian parties on some of the large "ice islands" in the Arctic Ocean. Airplanes carrying passengers and goods now fly almost daily between the west coast of North America and Europe by way of Greenland.

The Arctic Region lies on the shortest air route between North America and Europe and is therefore important as the first line of defense for the United States and Canada. A chain of weather stations, radar stations, and air bases has been set up across the northern part of North America. (See Northwest Passage.)

In 1958 the U.S. Navy's atomic submarine *Nautilus* made the first voyage under the Arctic ice cap. It found the depth at the North Pole to be 13,410 feet. The polar ice was an average 12 feet thick, with some ridges 50 feet thick.

World-wide scientific studies which were first carried on during the International Polar Year in 1882–1883 were repeated in 1932–1933 and again during the International Geophysical Year in 1957–1958. (See Geophysical Year, International.) In addition, many research institutes work the year around on both short- and long-range studies on Arctic conditions.

Antarctic Exploration

Unlike the Arctic Region, the Antarctic Region is made up of a huge continent called Antarctica, a few offshore islands, and the surrounding ocean. (See Antarctic Region.) Most of Antarctica is a plateau averaging 6,000 feet in elevation, but there are peaks more than 15,000 feet high. Except for the highest peaks, almost everything is covered with a layer of ice and snow more than 7,000 feet thick in some places. The snow never melts, only mosses and lichens can grow, and there are no native people.

Antarctica is far away from where most of the world's people live. Until 1820 no one had ever seen Antarctica. Man did not set foot on it until 1893, and expeditions did not travel inland until the 20th century. Parts of Antarctica are still unexplored.

Map makers of the 15th and 16th centuries

The U.S.S. *Northwind* breaks a path through the ice in the Bay of Whales in Antarctica.

Courtesy Department of Defense

had drawn the continent of Antarctica on their maps even though they were not certain that there was such a land. However, after Bartholomeu Diaz and Fernando Magellan had sailed around Africa and South America, it was believed that there could not be such a land mass. Voyages toward the South Pole, including one by James Cook from 1772 to 1775, found only pack ice and a few small islands.

Nathaniel Palmer, captain of a United States sailing vessel, is thought to have been the first to sight the Antarctic mainland. In 1820 he discovered the mountainous peninsula, now called Palmer Peninsula. That same year British and Russian explorers sighted nearby islands: Edward Bransfield surveyed the South Shetland Islands north of Palmer Peninsula, but did not cross the Antarctic Circle, and a Russian expedition commanded by Fabian von Bellingshausen sighted Peter I and Alexander I islands.

Most of the ships in Antarctic waters were searching for whales and seals, and many recent land claims are based largely on the discoveries of these expeditions. In 1823 James Weddell discovered the sea now named for him. In 1830 John Biscoe sighted but did not reach the part of the Antarctic continent now called Enderby Land. In 1839 John Balleny discovered the Balleny Islands.

About this time interest in the Antarctic was so great in the United States, Great Britain, and France that each country sent a scientific expedition. Under Dumont d'Urville the French sighted the Adelie Coast in 1840. The same year Charles Wilkes led the United States expedition which sailed along the Adelie Coast, Enderby Land, Kemp Coast, and Wilkes Land. James Clark Ross, the British commander, sighted the continent at Cape Adare in 1841. He went ashore on a nearby island, claimed Victoria Land for the Queen of England, and named several mountains. He then crossed the Ross Sea along the huge Ross Shelf Ice, but was unable to land on the mainland.

For most of the rest of the 19th century Antarctic exploration was carried on by visitors who did what scientific work they could. C. A. Larsen from the Norwegian ship *Jason* made the first landing on the continent in 1893.

Not until 1897 did a ship, the *Belgica*, under the command of Adrien de Gerlache, spend the winter in Antarctic waters. Roald Amundsen was a member of the ship's party. The following year C. E. Borchgrevink led an expedition which spent the winter on the continent at Cape Adare.

In 1901 four Antarctic expeditions made scientific studies of the weather and the earth's magnetism. One of these expeditions was led by Robert F. Scott, who was the first Antarctic explorer to send out exploring parties from a land base. On this trip Scott discovered that the interior of the continent was a huge plateau. Ernest Shackleton, who had been with Scott, returned to Antarctica in 1908 as leader of his own party and worked out a route toward the South Pole.

Roald Amundsen, already famous for his Arctic explorations, led the first party to reach the South Pole on Dec. 14, 1911. With four companions on skis and 52 dogs to carry supplies, he set up in advance a series of supply bases. Scott started for the pole with four companions only four days after Amundsen, using man-hauled sledges. He did not reach the pole until January 18, 1912, and there found a tent set up by Amundsen. On the return trip all of Scott's party was lost.

After discovery of the South Pole, explorers explored other parts of the continent. Sir Douglas Mawson organized an Australian expedition which set up bases in Adelie Coast and Queen Mary Coast during 1911–1913; Mawson returned to the Antarctic from 1929 to 1931. Shackleton, who planned to cross the continent by way of the South Pole, discovered the Caird Coast, but his ship was crushed in the ice in 1915. His men camped for several months on a great block of ice. They finally were rescued after Shackleton sailed 750 miles to South Georgia in a 22-foot boat and returned with a rescue ship.

As in the Arctic Region, airplanes became important in Antarctic exploration. In 1928 Richard E. Byrd, who had been first to fly over the North Pole, reached the Ross Sea and set up a base called Little America. The base had weather-tight buildings, electric lights, and kerosene stoves. The expedition began mapping the continent from airplanes, with help from sledge parties exploring on the ground. On November 29, 1929, Byrd, Bernt Balchen, A. C. McKinley, and Harold June were the first men to fly over the South Pole.

Byrd's second expedition to Little America, from 1933 to 1935, continued the aerial and ground mapping, especially in Marie Byrd Land. Byrd himself spent a number of months alone in an advance base 123 miles south of Little America making scientific observations. Lincoln Ellsworth led expeditions to Antarctica in 1933–1934, 1935–1936, and 1938–1939. Byrd returned to Little America in 1939 but stayed only four months. The party stayed for another year.

In 1946–1947 Byrd led the United States Navy Operation "Highjump," the largest expedition to Antarctica that had ever been organized, with 13 ships, 19 planes, four helicopters, and 4,200 men. Its purpose was to train United States Navy men for polar work, map as much of the continent as possible, and test equipment under Antarctic conditions. In 1947–1948 Finn Ronne of the United States Navy was the leader of an expedition which discovered and charted the last unknown Antarctic coast and proved that Antarctica was a single continent.

Several nations have made land claims to Antarctic territory. Many of these claims overlap, and the countries have tried to support their claims by sending out expeditions or building bases on these lands. The United States has claimed no land and recognizes no claims by other countries. Chile, Argentina, and Great Britain have built bases in the South Shetland Islands and on Palmer Peninsula. From 1948 to 1951 French expeditions led by Andre Liotard were sent into Adelie Coast. A British-Scandinavian party under John Giaever explored wide areas in Queen Maud Land from 1949 to 1952. The Russian whaler *Slava* also did much exploring in Antarctic waters.

As part of the world-wide scientific study of the earth during the International Geophysical Year of 1957–1958, research teams from 11 nations set up 39 bases in many parts of Antarctica. From all bases scientific studies were made, exploring parties traveled farther into the interior, and mapping was continued.

The United States agreed to set up six stations for the International Geophysical Year Antarctic study, including one at the geographic South Pole. Before the research teams could begin work, however, the bases had to be built and supplied. In 1955–1956 Operation "Deepfreeze" was started. Under the over-all direction of Admiral Byrd, until his death in March 1957, and the operational command of Admiral George Dufek, 1,800 men built bases at Little America and Ross Island and stockpiled more than 4,000 tons of supplies. By early 1957 studies had begun at the six research stations.

On November 24, 1957, the British Commonwealth Transarctic expedition left Shackleton Base to cross Antarctica. The group of 12 men was led by Vivian Fuchs and joined by Sir Edmund Hillary. The group completed their journey of more than 2,000 miles on March 2, 1958, at Scott Base. The expedition was the first land crossing of Antarctica.

POLICE (*pō lēs'*) are the departments of government that enforce laws. In the world today there are two main types of police systems. One type serves democratic governments and the other serves governments of absolute power. Police of a democratic country enforce only the laws passed by the people through their representative form of government. Law-breakers are turned over to the courts for judgment and punishment. Police of a non-democratic government are more like a military force. They enforce laws made by the ruling monarch or ruling group of individuals. They often serve as both judge and executioner for those who break such laws.

Police Agencies in the United States

Usually the term police refers to law enforcement officers employed by a borough, town, city, county, state, or nation. A police force may be one man—such as a village constable or town marshal—or a force of many thousands as in New York City.

Police work includes many things. Above: An officer helps children cross streets. Below: When a crime is committed, officers investigate and collect evidence. Bottom: Police give first aid at an accident.

Courtesy (above, below) Oakland Police Department, (bottom) Chicago Police Department

The head of a police department most often has the title of chief of police, although it may be commissioner of police, superintendent, or director of public safety. The chief is appointed by the city or town council, commission, board of police commissioners, the mayor or city manager. In the past, appointments often have been political, but during the last 30 years more communities have selected the best qualified men through civil service examinations.

Town and city police are municipal agencies. Some heavily populated counties have county police forces which operate in the same way as municipal police. They are responsible for the areas in the county outside the limits of cities, towns, and villages. The county sheriff is elected to office and he employs a staff of deputies. The sheriff is also responsible for prisoners kept in the county jail.

State governments have police or traffic enforcement agencies, headed by a commissioner or superintendent who is usually appointed by the governor. State police have the authority to enforce law throughout the state.

Many federal agencies have law enforcement duties. For example, the Federal Bureau of Investigation is an agency within the Department of Justice, as is the Immigration and Border Patrol. The Secret Service, the Narcotics Bureau, and the Bureau of Internal Revenue are all within the Treasury Department. The Department of the Interior and the Department of Agriculture also enforce some laws. (See FEDERAL BUREAU OF INVESTIGATION; SECRET SERVICE, UNITED STATES.)

In the United States there is no one central department in charge of all police forces. The men who wrote the Constitution believed in individual freedom and local self-government. Because of this the United States has the most decentralized (independent) police system in the world. There are more than a dozen different types of agencies (totaling about 40,000) that enforce criminal law.

Police Systems in Other Countries

This decentralization is not true in other countries. England has less than 150 police agencies. Each of the larger cities may have a municipal police force of its own, but the policing of most towns, cities, and rural areas is done by county police, known as the county constabulary. The head of the department is the chief constable. The British government gives yearly subsidies (money) to the city and county police departments to help pay their costs. In return for this, the local forces must run their departments according to certain rules. In this way law enforcement is kept the same throughout the country. Inspectors of Constabularies are sent out by the Home Office to report on the service. If certain standards are not met, the subsidy may not be given. Famed Scotland Yard is the criminal investigation division of the Metropolitan Police in the London area. Local police forces may call in investigators from the "Yard" for help.

The Canadian police system is decentralized, but not as much as the United States system. The Royal Canadian Mounted Police is a national police force. The "Mounties" police the unsettled areas, the rural areas where there is no local police force, or even provinces and towns that pay for their services. (See CANADIAN MOUNTED POLICE, ROYAL.)

Each city in Canada may have its own municipal police department, or it may arrange for the Royal Canadian Mounted Police or the provincial (state) police to do the job. The provinces of Ontario and Quebec have their own police forces to enforce laws in rural areas or in towns where their services are asked for. Some departments of the national government also have certain law enforcement power.

Organization of police on the European continent is not like that of the United States, Canada, or Great Britain. Federal direction or control of the police is the rule. Many of the countries require that all citizens register and carry identification papers at all times.

Interpol (International Police Commission) acts as a co-operative clearing house of criminal information for European countries. Its services are also used by England and other countries.

France has both national and local police. The director of the *Sûreté Générale* directs federal police work. Paris has a municipal police

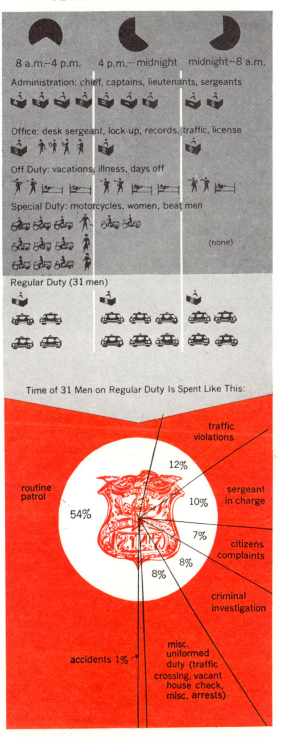

POLICE WORK IN A TYPICAL CITY
(Population 65,000)
72-Man Force Has These Duties:

8 a.m.–4 p.m. 4 p.m.–midnight midnight–8 a.m.

Administration: chief, captains, lieutenants, sergeants

Office: desk sergeant, lock-up, records, traffic, license

Off Duty: vacations, illness, days off

Special Duty: motorcycles, women, beat men
(none)

Regular Duty (31 men)

Time of 31 Men on Regular Duty Is Spent Like This:

traffic violations 12%
sergeant in charge 10%
citizens complaints 7%
criminal investigation 8%
misc. uniformed duty (traffic crossing, vacant house check, misc. arrests) 8%
accidents 1%
routine patrol 54%

force headed by a *prefect*.

Before the reign of dictator Adolf Hitler, Germany had a well-run state-controlled police system that had some control over municipal police forces. Hitler's *Gestapo* (Secret Police) was used to force the people to accept the dictator's laws. Since the end of World War II, the Western German Republic has been developing a democratic police system.

The U.S.S.R. has a national police force, the *MVD*. Trained like a secret army, it has great control over the people.

The Scandinavian countries have national-local police forces. The head of the national police and of the municipal police is called *politimester* in Norway and *polismestaren* in Sweden.

In Italy the national police are directed by the Director General of Public Security in the Ministry of the Interior. The *prefetto* is head of police forces in cities and districts.

South American countries have federal, state, or local police, or a combination of any of the three. In Brazil each of the states has an independent police department. Peru has both national and municipal police, while Guatemala and Honduras have national forces.

In Japan there is a National Police Agency. Tokyo has a Metropolitan Police Department. Korea has a national police force, as does Burma, Malaya, Laos, Indonesia, Finland, Iran, Israel, Lebanon, Liberia, and Libya. Taiwan (Republic of China) has a combination of national-provincial-metropolitan police.

Police Organization in the United States

Police departments are organized into several divisions, each having a special duty. The uniform division, backbone of the department, patrols the area, capturing those who break laws, and preventing crime. Traffic division officers enforce motor vehicle laws and find out who is responsible in traffic accidents. They also conduct a program of public education in traffic safety. The detective division makes the criminal investigations for the department. Through the use of special techniques and scientific aids detectives try to solve crimes. The communications division is in charge of the radio system

When anyone calls the police, a record is made of each call. If necessary, a police car is sent out. Above: The dispatcher radios the nearest police car. Maps above his head show where each car is located. Right: An officer may call the dispatcher from a call box. Below: An officer may receive the call in his car. On the seat is a walkie-talkie for use while he is away from his car.

Courtesy (above and below) Chicago Police Department, (right) Oakland Police Department

that sends patrol cars to trouble scenes and the street call-box system. It also operates the radio and teletype system which keeps the department in touch with all other police agencies in the state and nation.

The juvenile division or women's division handle all law enforcement for young people and children (minors) and problems in the community that may add to delinquency of minors.

These are the main units within a police force. Depending upon its size, there may be other divisions to handle special problems.

Police have no power to enforce law outside their own legal limits (city, town, village). Years ago a city police officer could not pass beyond the city limits to catch a criminal. Now, the "fresh pursuit" law gives a policeman the authority to pursue a fleeing criminal into the next county or state. Interstate "chase" agreements have been made that help all police forces to work together yet permits each to be independent.

Duties of Police

The duties of police in any country are to preserve the public peace and to protect persons and property. Violations of laws come to the police attention in one of these ways: citizens' complaints; reports of police officers; pick-up or on-view arrests by officers; complaints made direct to the city or county prosecutor, sheriff, judge; or by information from other police agencies.

A police officer in an average United States city works one of three shifts: the day shift, 8 A.M. to 4 P.M.; the night shift, 4 P.M. to midnight; and the midnight shift, from midnight to 8 A.M. He begins his tour of duty with roll call. During it, his sergeant or captain gives him the day's instructions, information on wanted criminals, and other information to help him while on duty.

If he is on foot patrol he will start his rounds, watching people, places of business, and motor vehicle traffic. He will give information to many people who stop to ask directions. If he is on patrol car duty, he will do much the same thing. The radio in the patrol car, however, will bring him orders to go to places where there is reported trouble. Such trouble may range from a bank robbery, to stopping a fight, to picking up a stray animal from the street.

While patrolling, the officer looks for anything that might cause harm to citizens or property, such as objects that do not belong on the street or sidewalk, broken street lights, etc. On his tour of duty he is a "trouble shooter" who must use good judgment in deciding what should be done and then doing it promptly.

History of Police

Police date back to the very earliest history of man. When primitive men formed clans and tribes for protection, rules of conduct were necessary. Since tribes were almost always at war, the leader or ruler usually depended upon his warriors to enforce the rules.

The Pharaohs of ancient Egypt used soldiers to carry out their orders. In early times the king, high priests, and elders used servants and soldiers to enforce their orders.

About the time of the birth of Christ, Caesar Augustus formed a special police force for the city of Rome. It was in use for about 350 years. Charlemagne started a new police force in A.D. 800.

From A.D. 700 to 800 people changed their ideas about law enforcement. It is not known who started the system of using police to protect the people, but it is believed to have been the Franks. The English police system and later the United States police system made uses of some of the ideas of the Franks.

In early England ten families in a community made up a *tithing*, and a head, or *tithing-man*, was chosen. Ten tithings became a *hundred*. The hundred elected a *reeve* as head man. Since these divisions could not be exact, a tithing often became a unit of 50 or 60 families, and a hundred expanded far beyond that. The reeve then became a *constable* and the tithing-man the *under-constable*. Several hundreds in a settled community became a shire (later to be known as county), and the head of the shire was the *shire-reeve* (later sheriff).

As the early kings of England gave vast es-

(Left to right) Monkemeyer, Fenno Jacobs from Black Star, Eric M. Sanford from Black Star, Philip D. Gendreau

Traffic policemen in (left to right) Nairobi, Kenya; Belgrade, Yugoslavia; Tokyo, Japan; and Singapore.

tates to noblemen, the noblemen selected the shire-reeves to rule under them. In areas not owned by noblemen, the king named the shire-reeve.

The tithing man was responsible for keeping *watch* and *ward*. The watch was a night guard and ward a day guard. The tithing man could call upon all able-bodied males over 16 for watch and ward duty.

As England's population increased, the reeves would get men in each town for night watch. The watch could stop and question all travelers and arrest any suspicious persons.

This system was used in England for centuries, with the watches and wards increased as needed. As early as 1800 the city of London had a night watch under municipal authorities and several groups of special officers under different heads. There was so much corruption and crime in London then that the people insisted upon reform. In 1829 the Metropolitan Police of London was organized under the direction of Sir Robert Peel. London police today are called "bobbies" after his nickname "Bobby." In 1840 England began organizing county police forces under a chief constable.

The colonists brought the English system to the United States. They had the night watch under constables, with all able-bodied men over 16 serving without pay. Most cities and towns used this system well into the 1800's. Later some cities paid the night watch.

The use of daytime police started in Boston in 1838 with a force of six men. In Boston and New York the old night watch and the day force continued with the mayor in charge of day forces and the constable in charge of night watchmen. An 1845 New York law and an 1856 Pennsylvania statute were the basis for modern police agencies in the United States.

These early policemen forces did not wear uniforms and many of them refused to wear badges. By 1855 some city police forces wore regulation caps or hats. Finally in 1856 New York City police adopted full police uniforms, but each ward of the city had its own style. Philadelphia police adopted a uniform in 1860.

The next step in the development of police systems in the United States was the appointment of city police boards or commissions in the 1850's and 1860's. This stopped politicians from controlling the police. Today some form of civil service system is used in almost every department.

Since 1900 more progress has been made in police organization and methods than in all other centuries combined. In 1904 the use of fingerprints for identification was adopted. Radio-equipped patrol cars, better training for police, more careful selection, promotion on merit, and use of scientific methods have made the United States police system one that is widely copied.

POLIOMYELITIS (*pō′lĭ ō mī′ĕ lī′tĭs*), or polio, is an infectious disease caused by a virus. Its full name is anterior poliomyelitis, also called infantile paralysis. When polio virus enters the body, it travels along nerves and in the blood to the spinal cord and brain. There it grows in cells in the gray matter of the cord. That is where it gets its name. *Polio* means gray, *myelos* refers to the spinal cord, and *itis* means inflammation. *Anterior* refers to the front part of the cord, where the motor nerve cells are located. *Anterior poliomyelitis*, therefore, means an inflammation of the gray matter of the front part of the spinal cord. When these nerve cells are swollen and infected, the muscles they control cannot operate. They are paralyzed. If the nerves recover, the muscles can move again. But if the nerve cells are killed by the virus, these muscles will always be paralyzed. (See NERVES AND NERVOUS SYSTEM.)

Polio occurs in epidemics, but some cases of it are always present. Although it most often attacks children, anybody can catch it. The fear of polio is far greater than the damage it does. The most common type causes a day or two of illness, headache, fever, sore throat, and upset stomach, but no paralysis. There are at least 100 of these cases to every 1 that is diagnosed as serious polio.

The polio virus spreads very easily. How it gets from one person to another is not completely known. The virus is believed to enter the body through the mouth and nose. It may be carried by anything that can get from an infected person to the nose or mouth of the new victim. Because of this, polio victims are kept away from others.

Polio can be divided into several kinds, depending on what part of the nervous system is infected. *Spinal* polio affects spinal nerves; *bulbar* polio affects a part of the brain; and a mixed bulbospinal type affects both brain and spinal nerves. Bulbar polio paralyzes the mus-

cles of respiration (breathing).

Once the infection is recognized, the patient should be hospitalized and separated from others. Complete rest may often limit the crippling effects of polio. In bulbar polio cases, breathing is performed mechanically by a Drinker respirator, or "iron lung," until the patient can breathe normally. Physical therapy helps to strengthen and retrain muscles weakened by polio.

Much progress has been made to find a polio vaccine. Dr. Jonas Salk and others developed a vaccine using killed polio virus. Vaccinations have shown that the number of paralytic cases can be reduced. Drs. A. B. Sabin and Hilary Kaprowski have used a "tamed" polio virus to give a very mild infection and bring about lasting immunity from paralytic polio.

POLITICAL (*pō lĭt′ĭ kăl*) **PARTIES.** In modern democracies, political parties are the organized groups through which people may express their beliefs and choice of government officials. When the United States Constitution was written in 1787, there was nothing in it about political parties. Yet parties soon appeared and became an important part of democratic government in the United States.

Even before the American Revolution (1775–1783), the people of the 13 English colonies had been divided by important issues. The American Revolution again divided the people into those who favored war against England and those who were Tories and favored obedience to the English Parliament.

After the war a new conflict arose within the United States. Some men wished to have a strong national government, while others wanted to leave most of the power in the hands of the state governments. The first group wrote the new constitution, and, in spite of great opposition, it was ratified by every state.

During the presidency of Washington (1789–1797) the two-party system began. The Federalist party of Washington, Alexander Hamilton, and John Adams controlled the government. It favored aid to commerce and a strong central government. (See FEDERALIST PARTY.) The Republican party of Thomas Jefferson and

James Madison took the opposite point of view on these issues. It had strong support among the southern planters and the farmers of the South and West.

In 1801 the Republicans came into power after the election of Jefferson as president. The Federalists were never again to win a presidential election, and soon after the War of 1812 this party almost disappeared. During the administration of Andrew Jackson (1829–1837), the Whig party was formed as a party opposed to Jackson and his policies. In general, the Whig party continued the policies of the Federalists. Its opponents, the followers of Jackson, took the name of Democrats. (See DEMOCRATIC PARTY; WHIG PARTY.)

The Whig party was not very successful. It won the presidency only twice, with the election of William Henry Harrison in 1840 and of Zachary Taylor in 1848. Following passage of the Kansas-Nebraska Act in 1854, the Republican party was formed. This party soon included many of the northern Whigs and became a major party, winning the presidency under Abraham Lincoln in 1860. (See KANSAS-NEBRASKA ACT; REPUBLICAN PARTY.)

The years from 1861 to 1933 can be called the "Republican era" of United States politics. During this time only two Democrats were elected president—Grover Cleveland and Woodrow Wilson. The election of Franklin D. Roosevelt in 1932 began a "Democratic era" that continued until the election of Dwight D. Eisenhower in 1952. The Democrats returned to power in 1960 with the election of John F. Kennedy. They remained in power with the election of Lyndon B. Johnson in 1964.

In some countries there is only one party, and voters have no choice between candidates or policies. The government is then known as a dictatorship, and there is little difference between the party and the government. One-party countries are found in eastern Europe, in the U.S.S.R., in China, and in parts of the Middle East, Asia and Latin America. (See COMMUNISM; FASCISM; NATIONAL SOCIALISM.)

In democracies there are either two parties or many parties. France, Italy, West Germany and Japan are examples of multi-party (many)

governments, with each country having at least four major and four minor parties. In multi-party democracies, the people themselves do not elect the leader of government, usually called the Prime Minister. The people elect the legislators, and in turn the legislature elects one of its members to be Prime Minister. The legislative body is made up of men from many different parties. A group of parties, called a *bloc*, agrees to support a certain man for Prime Minister, and he includes members of these parties in his cabinet.

The Two-Party System

Great Britain, Canada and the United States are examples of two-party democracy. Many reasons have been suggested why a country as large and with as many differences as the United States should have but two major parties. An important reason is that each party would like to elect the president. This makes even people who disagree with each other work together. In 1912 the Republican Party split between the "Old Guard" under President William H. Taft and the "Bull Moose" Progressives under former President Theodore Roosevelt. Both men between them had the majority of the votes, but the Democratic candidate, Woodrow Wilson, was elected because he received more votes than either alone. (See PROGRESSIVE PARTY.)

In other two-party countries such as Canada and Great Britain, the people elect the legislators and they elect the Prime Minister. Usually he is the leader of the largest party. (See CABINET; PARLIAMENT.)

An important result of the two-party system is that an election usually brings a clear victory to one party. This party has the majority needed to put its program into effect. In the United States sometimes, one party wins the presidency while the other party gains control of one or both houses of Congress. Then there must be a compromise. Another result of the two-party system is that both parties must appeal to every important interest in the country if they hope to win elections. It is for this reason that the party platforms or beliefs of the parties become somewhat alike, and party leaders fear to promise clear-cut programs.

Party Programs

When a party wins, its public duties continue. It must take over control of the executive (presidency and cabinet departments) and legislative (Congress) branches of the government, and either carry out its program or offer good reasons for changes. The minority party also plays its part as a critic of the majority party's policies and holds up to public view its own policies for comparison.

The programs of the major parties must try to meet the demands of every part of the population. High prices for their crops must be promised to farmers, good wages and security in their work to laborers, and economic policies that will help business to the manufacturing and trading interests. Since different conditions can change the needs of these interests, the party leaders must be able to choose new policies quickly and skillfully.

Political party leaders in the United States must also consider hundreds of racial, national, and religious groups, not to mention the great variety of reform groups. A politician in Boston, Massachusetts would be very unwise to displease the Irish; in Chicago, Illinois, the Polish; or in Milwaukee, Wisconsin, the people of German descent. In similar fashion, political parties must try to win support from Negroes, Jews, Catholics, and, indeed, every interest group whose vote is important.

Since both parties in the United States appeal to all important parts of the population, it is difficult to discover any Republican or Democratic ideas that are permanent. Certainly the differences within each party are greater than the differences between the parties. There are persons in both parties with nearly every shade of opinion on every major issue.

Many Western Europeans feel that the multiparty system allows a person to vote for the party which stands for exactly what the person believes. The voter in the United States must choose between only two parties which many times show little differences between them. But this mixture of different interests may be one reason the two-party system helps hold the country together. No single group or area feels that it is greatly threatened if a certain party wins. American history offers one example showing what can happen when one party is united on a controversial idea. Every major party before 1854 had both slavery and anti-slavery leaders. But the new Republican party, against slavery, won most of the anti-slavery voters. After that party's 1860 victory the South felt it could no longer work with the national government. (See CONFEDERATE STATES OF AMERICA; WAR BETWEEN THE STATES, THE.)

Party Organization

The two main parties in the United States have national organizations, headed by a national committee and by committees in the Senate and the House of Representatives. Each party, too, is organized in each of the 50 states under a state committee, and each party has a county committee in the country's more than 3,000 counties. There are also committees in nearly every one of the more than 120,000 precincts in the United States, and city organizations in almost every large city.

A national convention is held each presidential election year. This convention chooses the party's nominees for president and vice-president and adopts a platform. Beyond these duties it has little power.

Between conventions, the party is, in theory, run by a national chairman and a national committee. The national committee includes two representatives—one man and one woman—from each state as well as from the District of Columbia, and Puerto Rico.

The national committee meets at the call of the chairman, but such calls are not frequent. The national committee is little more than an advisory committee during the presidential campaign. After that it usually meets only to choose the city for the next national convention.

The chairman of the national committee is chosen by the committee at the national convention. Actually, the presidential nominee chooses the chairman and the national committee only accepts his choice. Once elected, the chairman's most important work is to plan and carry out the presidential campaign. He is also active during the congressional campaigns every two years. Between elections he may help to direct party plans, especially if his party is not in power.

Each party has meetings called caucuses in the Senate and in the House of Representatives. In caucus meetings each party plans its actions within the Senate or House. In the House there are other officials who plan action, including the speaker, the rules committee, the leader of the majority party in the House, and the party "whip"—the person who enforces party discipline and sees that the members of his party are present at important sessions. (See REPRESENTATIVES, HOUSE OF.)

State and Local Parties

Except for such individuals or groups as these, the national party is little more than a loose alliance of state and local parties. As a rule, these manage their own affairs. Once every four years they band together to try to win a presidential election. But the real power remains in the state and local parties.

There are several reasons for this lack of central power. The huge size of the country and its large population are partly responsible. The great majority of the people find national issues too distant from their own interests. Local issues, however, attract their interest, and it is these issues that are represented by the state and local parties. Also, the president and members of Congress are chosen by action of the states. As a result, even national elections are under the control of state and local parties.

Membership in United States parties is informal and easily gained. State law, more than party rules, defines membership of a party. Some states hold open primary elections. In these the ballots list all the parties and the voter chooses a party list of candidates in secret. In other states there is a closed party primary. There, by law, the voter must choose one party. In some states he must show that he voted for the same party's candidates in the last primary election. Though the voter declares himself a member of one party in the primary, he is of course free to vote for whomever he chooses in the regular election. (See ELECTION.)

The great majority of voters are party members. They are either active in party affairs or at least support the candidates of one party regularly. There are also a number of independent voters. The independent voter is important in a democratic government. To gain his support, the parties are likely to improve their party platforms and to offer more able candidates. On the other hand, the independent voter can not play any part in party affairs, including such important work as the choice of candidates and policies.

Third Parties in the United States

Although the platforms of the two major parties satisfy most of the voters, there still remains a dissatisfied minority. The groups that make up this minority can choose between two courses of action. They may form pressure groups in an effort to influence both parties, or they may form a third party and attempt to win control of local, state, or national offices.

The earliest third party, the Antimasonic party, offered a presidential candidate in the election of 1832.

Since then, many third parties, local and national, have appeared. Some of these, such as the American ("Know-Nothing") party and the Antimasonic party, did not last long. Other third parties, such as the Socialist party and the Prohibition party, have had long histories.

On two occasions (the Whigs and the Republicans) third parties have become major parties. In both cases they took the place of major parties which had lost much popular support.

This has also happened in other two-party democracies. For more than 100 years the two major parties of Britain were the Conservatives and the Liberals. In 1893 the Independent Labour Party was founded but remained a very minor party until 1910. By 1945 the Liberals had all but disappeared, and the two major parties are the Conservatives and the Labourites.

POLK (*pōk*), **JAMES KNOX** (1795–1849), was the 11th president of the United States. He came into office with a definite program and carried out much of it in one four-year term. Only Thomas Jefferson as president added as much territory to the Union. Yet few people would call Polk a great man. He was an example of what intelligence, honesty, and hard work can do.

Polk was born on November 2, 1795, in Mecklenburg County, North Carolina, the eldest of the ten children of Samuel and Jane (Knox) Polk. His ancestors came from Scotland and Ireland. His father was a farmer, and his mother the daughter of a captain in the American Revolution. She was a woman of intelligence and James learned many of his ways from her.

In 1806 Samuel Polk moved his family to Tennessee. Since James was a weak boy he was not of much help on the farm, therefore, he was able to continue his education. He attended schools in Tennessee, and in 1815 enrolled at the University of North Carolina. A good student, he won honors in mathematics and the classics.

Political Career

After graduation Polk returned to Tennessee

James Polk, U.S. President, 1845–1849.

Brown Brothers

Brown Brothers

Sarah Polk.

and began the study of law. In 1820 he was admitted to the bar. After three years of law practice he served two years in the Tennessee state legislature. By this time he was a friend and supporter of Andrew Jackson, one of the political leaders of the country.

On January 1, 1824, Polk married Sarah Childress, the daughter of a well-to-do farmer. She was very different from her husband. James Polk was cold and formal. Sarah was warm and charming.

When not quite 30 years of age, Polk was elected to the United States House of Representatives. There he opposed the program of President John Quincy Adams, and worked for the election of Andrew Jackson as president. When Jackson became president in 1829, Polk was a leader of his supporters in the House. Jackson was re-elected president in 1832. The major issue of that campaign was Jackson's opposition to the Bank of the United States. This was a private corporation in which the United States government owned one fifth of the stock. Jackson decided to destroy the bank, and asked Polk to lead the fight in Congress. (See JACKSON, ANDREW.)

In 1835 Polk was chosen Speaker of the House. Because he carried out the wishes of the president he was called a slave of Jackson, yet he handled a difficult job well. Although he wanted to stay in Congress he agreed to run for the governorship of Tennessee and try to defeat the opposing political party, the Whigs. He was elected governor in 1839, but was defeated in 1841 and 1843.

Elected President

As the presidential election year of 1844 approached, most Democrats felt that the former president, Martin Van Buren, was their best candidate. (See VAN BUREN, MARTIN.) The

Whigs were prepared to nominate the popular Henry Clay. (See CLAY, HENRY.) At this time Texas was an independent nation and many people in the United States felt that it should be joined (annexed) to the United States. Others were against annexation because it would bring more slave territory into the Union. Both Clay and Van Buren wanted to keep the Texas question out of the campaign. They each published a letter saying they did not want the annexation of Texas without the consent of Mexico.

The Democrats did not nominate Van Buren because of his stand on Texas and chose Polk who said, "Let Texas be re-annexed." Polk sometimes is called the first "dark horse" presidential candidate, meaning a person who comes from nowhere to win the race.

The Whigs believed that Polk would have no chance against their candidate, Henry Clay. The Democrats, however, were close to the feeling of the people. Their program called for the "re-occupation of Oregon and the re-annexation of Texas." At that time the Oregon country was in dispute between the United States and England. The Democrats believed all of Oregon belonged to the United States. As for Texas, Democrats said that it had been a part of the Louisiana Purchase of 1803 and was therefore a part of the United States.

Many people were expansionists in 1844. They dreamed of reaching the Pacific Ocean. Most of these people voted for Polk, who won the election. George M. Dallas was elected vice-president. Polk was not yet 50 years of age, the youngest president to that time.

As president, Polk set up four goals for his administration: (1) A reduction of the tariff (tax on imported goods). (2) An independent treasury. (3) Settlement of the Oregon boundary question. (4) The adding of California to the United States. During his four years in office he accomplished each of these goals.

The Walker Tariff (1846) lowered the tax on imported goods. It pleased the South which felt that a high tariff caused southerners to pay more for the things they bought. Under President Martin Van Buren an independent treasury system was started so that the federal government could keep its own funds. This system

was repealed in 1841, but under Polk another Independent Treasury Act was passed (1846).

The problem of the Oregon boundary was a difficult one. Oregon was the land west of the Rocky Mountains, running from 42° to 54° 40' north latitude. It was claimed by England and the United States. Since the two nations could not agree on a boundary line they decided that the territory should be open to settlement by the citizens of both countries. By the time Polk was inaugurated many people in the United States wanted all of Oregon and were shouting "54° 40' or fight."

At first Polk was willing to compromise with the British at the line of 49°. When the British refused, he demanded all of Oregon for the United States. Great Britain did not want to fight for a territory which was largely settled by people from the United States. They finally agreed to boundary at the 49th degree and in June 1846 a treaty was signed.

Mexican War

Polk wanted to get New Mexico and California for the United States. He hoped to get them peacefully from Mexico, but he was willing to fight for them if necessary.

Mexico had never recognized the independence of the Republic of Texas. She broke off relations with the United States when Texas was made a part of the Union. A dispute over the Texas boundary with Mexico developed. Polk supported the Texas claim but he made an effort to settle the quarrel peacefully. He sent a representative to Mexico to offer money for New Mexico, California, and the Rio Grande boundary. Mexico refused, so Polk ordered General Zachary Taylor's army to the Rio Grande. (See MEXICAN WAR.)

The President was getting ready to ask Congress to declare war when news arrived from General Taylor that Mexican troops had crossed the Rio Grande and attacked United States soldiers. Polk asked for troops and Congress declared war on May 11, 1846.

The Mexican War was not popular with everyone. Some people called it "Mr. Polk's war." However, it resulted in United States victory. By the Treaty of Guadalupe Hidalgo

(February 2, 1848) Mexico agreed to give the United States what is now the states of Arizona, New Mexico, California, Nevada, Utah, and parts of Colorado and Wyoming.

Polk had achieved his aims. At the end of his term in 1849 he retired to his Nashville home, "Polk Place." He had worked so hard as president that his health was damaged and he lived only a few months. He died on June 15, 1849, at the age of 53 years.

Polk's United States

The desire to expand was a strong force at the time of James K. Polk. Americans believed in their "manifest destiny"; that all the land westward to the Pacific Ocean was naturally theirs. No president followed the popular feeling better than Polk when he added Oregon and the territory from Mexico. During Polk's term of office one of the great movements of people in United States history began. The Mormons under their leader Brigham Young went to what is now Utah, and founded Salt Lake City. (See YOUNG, BRIGHAM.) Before Polk left office, gold was discovered in California. In 1849 the great gold rush brought many people to California. Iowa entered the Union in 1846 and Wisconsin in 1848.

More people also were coming to the United States. In Ireland failure of the potato crop caused a terrible famine and hundreds of thousands of Irish came to the United States looking for jobs. Immigration also increased from Sweden and Germany.

The growth of the country during the Polk administration raised a question that was to lead to the War between the States. Should slavery be permitted in the territories? During the Mexican War, Congressman David Wilmot of Pennsylvania proposed an amendment to a money bill, which declared that slavery should be prohibited in any territory acquired from Mexico. This was called the Wilmot Proviso. Southerners opposed it, but many Northerners favored it. The Senate defeated the Wilmot Proviso, but the debates led to formation of the Free Soil Party in the North. (See FREE-SOIL PARTY.)

During Polk's presidency Elias Howe patented the sewing machine (1846). The rotary printing press invented by Richard Hoe speeded up the printing of newspapers. Herman Melville published his first novels, and Henry Wadsworth Longfellow published "Evangeline." The U.S. Naval Academy was founded at Annapolis, Maryland, in 1845. The Smithsonian Institution was founded in Washington, D.C. (1846). In 1848 the first Woman's Right's Convention was held in Seneca Falls, New York.

POLO (*pō'lō*), **MARCO** (*c.* 1254–1324), a medieval oriental traveler, was born in Venice, Italy. He wrote a great travel book, *Marco Polo's Travels,* which shows that he was a careful observer. Yet he was only 17 years old when he started on his great journey to China.

Polo went with his father, Nicolo, and his uncle, Maffeo, who were returning to China on a second visit. During their first stay in Peiping, Kublai Khan, China's emperor, had asked a favor. He wanted some educated men to come to China and explain Christianity and teach the liberal arts. Therefore, Pope Gregory X sent two Dominican friars with them to the khan. The trip was so difficult that the Dominicans soon gave up and returned. The three Polos went on. Their way led down the Tigris River to Baghdad. They continued along the Tigris to its mouth, down the Persian Gulf to Hormuz, across Persia (where young

POLK'S LIFETIME

1787	U.S. Constitution.		**Polk's Term of**
1795	Polk born.		**Office (1845–1849)**
1812	War with England.		
1815	Polk starts college.		
1820	Missouri Compromise.	1845	Naval Academy at
1823	Monroe Doctrine.		Annapolis founded.
	Polk to legislature.		Independent Treasury.
1824	Polk married.		Walker Tariff.
1825	Erie Canal opened.		Irish potato famine.
	Polk to Congress.	1846	Settlement of Oregon
1832	Fight over Bank of U.S.		dispute.
1835	Polk Speaker of House.		Mexican War.
1836	Texas independent.		Iowa enters the Union.
1839	Polk governor of		Howe's sewing machine.
	Tennessee.		Smithsonian Institution.
1844	1st telegraph message.		Wilmot Proviso.
1845	Annexation of Texas.		Mormons move to Utah.
		1848	Treaty of Guadalupe
	PRESIDENT		Hidalgo ends war.
			Wisconsin enters Union.
1849	California Gold Rush.		1st Woman's Rights
	Polk dies.		Convention.
1850	Compromise of 1850.		Free Soil Party formed.

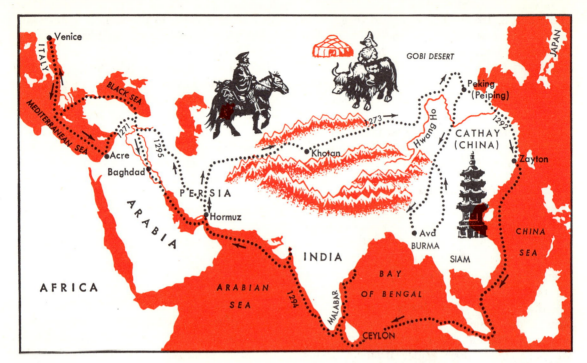

Marco Polo fell sick of a fever), into Afghanistan. There they stayed until Marco was well enough to continue on across the desert and into China. In 1275 they were met and escorted to Peiping and the court of Kublai Khan.

On that 3½ year journey across Asia young Marco Polo observed many things. Afterward he wrote about it so clearly that it is easy to trace the exact route the party followed. Generations of readers found it difficult to believe what he wrote so it was long thought of as a delightful story. But later travelers, such as Sir Henry Yule and Sven Hedin, have found what he described to be true.

Kublai Khan liked young Marco Polo and enrolled him among his attendants of honor. In 1277 Marco Polo was appointed commissioner to the imperial council and later governor of the city of Yangchow. These positions allowed him to travel to places as far apart as Siberia, Zanzibar, Madagascar, and Abyssinia.

In China Marco Polo found a civilization far ahead of that in Europe. The rulers governed well. There was religious tolerance, with Nestorian Christians, Mohammedans, Jews, Confucians, Buddhists, and Taoists living side by side in peace. He found a nation with a history many thousands of years old. (See CHINA; KUBLAI KHAN.)

In one of the large cities Polo found out that there were 300 baths for public use, with hot and cold water, and that common folks bathed daily. There were tree-shaded highways and grand palaces, paved roads, parks, and fine bridges. He saw people using paper money, still unknown in Europe. The Chinese were using coal, while in England it was not a common fuel until nearly 400 years later. Europe knew nothing of painting in oils until the 15th century, but the Chinese had used oil to mix their colors since the 7th century. Polo saw an oily paste made from petroleum for certain skin ailments, and even condensed milk, long before they were known in Europe. He also studied the birds and animals.

All that Polo saw and studied was reported to the khan. Because of his knowledge, Polo was also able to give the khan helpful advice. So the khan did not want him to leave.

What Marco Polo called "a lucky chance" allowed the Polos to return to Venice. The wife of Arghun, khan of Persia, had died and he had sent to the Peiping court for another woman of her tribe. A princess named Kukachin was chosen but her trip to Persia by land would be both dangerous and tiring. Marco Polo pointed out to the khan that travel by ship would be both easy and pleasant. So a ship was fitted out, and the Polos sailed with the princess.

They sailed south and west to Siam, then to Ceylon, India, and along the west coast of India to Hormuz. The marriage party went to Persia and the Polos continued northwest to the Black Sea. There they took a ship westward, through the Sea of Marmara, and to Venice. They arrived in the year 1295, all of them wealthy in gold and precious stones.

Marco Polo's adventures might not be known to us had it not been for an accident. In September 1298 the republics of Venice and Genoa went to war. Marco Polo was captured and placed in prison by the Genoans. He told his tale to a fellow prisoner, a scribe, who suggested the writing of the story. As a result, the first edition, one copy written in French, was done on parchment with a quill. It is now in the National Library in Paris, France.

POLO is a game played on horseback with a ball and stick. Its rules are similar to the rules for hockey. England, Argentina, and the United States are the chief polo centers of the world. In the late 19th century, polo was a recreational game among British cavalry units. The first U.S. polo game was played in 1883. When private persons play, only the wealthy are able to participate. Each player must have access to at least a half-dozen ponies. The better ones are valued at many thousands of dollars. Much care, patience, time, and expense are required in the training of polo horses. It takes several years to prepare horses for their first simple match.

During the 1930's polo, which had been a game that appealed only to high society, began to appeal to the general public. Low admission fees, the tours of English and Argentine teams, and regular matches at army camps created new interest in the United States. Indoor polo, played during the wintertime at armories, also brought the sport to the masses.

Because it is played on horseback, polo is one of the most difficult and fastest of sports. It demands the utmost physical endurance from both man and horse. A good player must have courage and co-ordination as well as horsemanship.

Since polo is a form of hockey on horseback the player must be able to ride expertly. At the same time he must be able to hit the bounding polo ball far and accurately with his long-shafted mallet.

The Polo Field

The game is played on a field 300 yards long

Long Island polo fields are the scene of many matches. Here is an exciting scrimmage between the Sands Point and Shelbourne teams at Westbury.

Acme

and 150 yards wide if boarded. A low board (about ten inches high) may enclose the playing area. If officials and players of both teams agree beforehand, the dimensions of the playing field may be made larger. The goals are placed at least 250 yards apart. The goal, eight yards in width, is marked by poles made of bamboo or other light wood. A player riding into the poles will not be hurt, for they break easily. A wooden ball, somewhat larger than a baseball, is used for the game.

Polo has no complicated rules. Each team, made up of four players, tries to hit the ball through the opponent's goal. Everything is fair except fouls or dangerous riding. The fraction of a point is scored against any team which commits a foul. Two mounted umpires referee the game.

The players are numbered 1, 2, 3, and 4. Numbers 1 and 2 play forward. Number 3 is halfback and Number 4 fullback. However these positions are not rigidly kept. If Number 4 sees the chance for a long ride down an open field he takes it. In the same way Numbers 1 and 2 may find themselves defending their own goal.

In the straight drive backward and forward, the usual shot in polo, the player rides parallel to and on the right side of the ball. For passing across the field to the left or for driving the ball backward, a good player will hit under his pony's neck. This shot demands excellent timing and a well-trained mount.

In the United States a game is divided into eight or six periods of $7\frac{1}{2}$ minutes each. In England there are seven periods, each of which is eight minutes long. The periods are called *chukkers*.

At the end of each chukker the players stop to change horses.

Handicaps

Except in open tournaments and international matches, all teams are handicapped. A good player has a handicap of from one to five goals. A player of international fame may have ten. Suppose the total handicaps of the players on one team amount to 15 and those of the other team to 20. The former will start the game with a score of five goals.

Polo is believed to be one of the oldest of games. Some think that both golf and hockey grew from it. It was played in the Orient from ancient times. In 1863 a British army officer introduced polo to India. From there it quickly spread to other parts of the world. In 1869 the tenth Hussars, a crack cavalry regiment, brought polo to England.

The first recorded match took place between two British regimental teams in 1871. In 1886 the first United States–British match was played in North America.

POMEGRANATE (*pŏm'grăn'ĭt*, *pŭm'grăn'ĭt*, *pŏm grăn'ĭt*, or *pŭm grăn'ĭt*). The pomegranate is a bushy tree, or shrub, that grows from 5 to 20 feet high. Its leaves are glossy, and at the ends of its slender twigs grow coral-red, waxlike flowers. The fruit is about the size of an orange. Its skin is like leather and colored a deep yellow with red. Inside the fruit are many small seeds. They are covered with a sweet, red, juicy pulp, which is often made into refreshing drinks. A kind of seedless pomegranate is prized as a fruit in India and Iran. The bark and roots of the pomegranate are used in tanning the finest kind of morocco leather. A medicine is sometimes made from the rind.

From very ancient times the pomegranate was grown in the warm countries of southern Asia, northern Africa, and southern Europe.

The leaves and fruit of the pomegranate.

J. Horace McFarland Company

Now it is common in South and Central America and in southern United States.

According to a legend of the ancient Greeks, the pomegranate was the fruit which Persephone, a daughter of Demeter, ate while in Hades. Because she swallowed six of the seeds she was forced to spend six months of each year in the underworld. (See CERES.) To the Greeks the pomegranate symbolized the powers of darkness. In China it symbolized fertility.

POMPANO (pŏm′pä nō). Because of their sweet firm flesh, many people consider pompanos the finest of food fish. They form one division of the horse-mackerel family and include nine American species.

The common pompano, which is about 18 inches long and weighs from 3 to 8 pounds, is found in the tropical waters of North and South America, mainly on the Atlantic coast. Its oval body narrows sharply at the tail and it has a blunt snout. Its back and sides are blue, and it is flecked with yellow underneath.

The round pompano is found all along the Atlantic coast as far north as Massachusetts, while the great pompano, which is sometimes three feet long, lives only in the warm waters from the West Indies to Florida.

The California pompano, or poppy fish, is really a barracuda. Pompanos spawn in the early spring, usually in the coastal rivers, and travel in large schools. They feed on shrimps and other shellfish and are caught in nets and seines.

POMPEII (pŏm pā′yē), **ITALY.** On August 24, A.D. 79, there was a great eruption of Mount Vesuvius, a volcano in southern Italy. The lava, stones, and ashes thrown up by the volcano completely buried two near-by towns. The town of Herculaneum, only two miles away, was deeply covered by a stream of mud which flowed down the slope of the mountain. Pompeii, farther along the coast, was buried by the rain of ashes and pebbles of light pumice stone.

Two letters were written about the eruption by an eyewitness, a young man named Pliny, who was staying near by at the time. Soon after it began, he went with his naturalist uncle to try to rescue people at Herculaneum. The elder Pliny was suffocated by the poisonous fumes, but his nephew lived to write the story of the disaster. He tells of the violent earthquake which threw down some of the buildings, of the dark clouds of smoke and the hot rain of steam and ashes, of persons fleeing from the

city and some perishing in the panic.

After the eruption the inhabitants of Pompeii dug tunnels and recovered some of their possessions; but the buildings themselves remained just as they were for more than 1,600 years. In 1763 men began to uncover the towns. The work of excavating at Pompeii is still going on, and nearly half the town is still buried. Herculaneum is also being dug out. These two cities are of special importance because they were never destroyed but were simply buried and preserved under volcanic debris until modern times.

History

Pompeii is on the shore of the beautiful Bay of Naples, at the mouth of the Sarno River. It was first settled in the 6th century B.C. by Italian people related to the Romans, and it was a busy trading center of the Sarno Valley. The population was mixed with Greeks who had settled all along the coast of southern Italy. Later the town was taken by the Samnites, an Italian tribe; and finally, with the rest of Italy, it was absorbed by Rome. In the 1st century B.C. it was a Roman town and its people were Roman citizens, even though many of them were Greeks or Samnites by birth.

The earliest houses, and some of the finest that are still standing, were built 200 years before the eruption. But the largest number were built, or at least repaired, in the 15 years prior to it. This was because a great earthquake in A.D. 63 had destroyed or damaged many of the temples and houses.

The Forum and Public Buildings

The main center of civic and community life was the forum. At one end stands the Temple of Jupiter, the chief Roman god. The temple is built on a high platform with great columns across the front. Along the sides are other temples, markets, and shops. At the other end of the forum is the basilica, a large hall with a platform on which the judge sat when he held court sessions. The main streets of Pompeii lead out from the forum in several directions toward the city gates.

The streets are narrow and are sometimes

The amphitheater in Pompeii held 20,000 spectators.

almost undamaged. The houses were usually only one- or two-storied, with rooms built around an open courtyard. The house from the outside is only a blank wall with a high entrance gate. Through the entrance door and front vestibule one enters the principal room, which was called the *atrium*. This is lighted from a large opening in the roof, at the four corners of which stand tall columns. The roof slopes inward toward the opening, to drain rain water into a shallow marble basin in the floor.

overshadowed by balconies. At the street corners the one-room shops displayed their wares on open counters to attract buyers. Narrow sidewalks kept the pedestrian from the puddles which must have covered the pavement during a rain. Steppingstones at the crossings are just far enough apart to leave tracks for the wheels of chariots and carts, which have worn deep ruts in the great paving stones. At many street corners there was a public fountain which supplied water for the poorer folk, for animals, or for thirsty passers-by.

There are two theaters, built much like modern ones except that the seats are stone benches arranged in a semicircle.

At the eastern edge of the town is the amphitheater, a building much like a modern football stadium, with stone benches encircling an oval space. This space was the arena, in which gladiators fought with one another or with wild beasts, usually lions or panthers.

The public baths were also recreational centers, somewhat like a public gymnasium with a swimming pool.

Pompeian Houses

Pompeii is most famous of all for its hundreds of houses which have been left standing

At the far end, opposite the entrance another high door leads out into the *peristyle*. This is an open courtyard enclosed by a one-story portico with a porch roof supported by columns. The life of the family revolved about the pleasant, sunny peristyle. Opening into it are the living rooms, the dining room, kitchen, and slaves' quarters. The courtyard was planted with grass and shrubbery, and often there was a marble fountain in the center. Along the flower-bordered paths were statues of bronze or marble on pedestals.

In the peristyle of many houses stands a shrine for the household gods. The walls of all the rooms are painted with decorative designs. Most commonly each wall of the room has panels of solid color—cream, red, or black—with a scene painted in the central panel as if it were a picture hanging on the wall.

Many of the pictures still hang on the walls but some of the best were taken to the museum in Naples. The same is true of the house furnishings, works of art, and children's toys. Thus, from Pompeii and Herculaneum, more has been learned about life in an ancient Roman town than is known about some much more recent periods in history.

POMPEY (*pŏm'pē*) (Gnaeus Pompeius Magnus) (106–48 b.c.). Pompey was a great military leader of ancient Rome. Like every young nobleman of that time, he grew up expecting to win election to political office. The highest of these was the consulship. A consul held office only for a year. Then the Senate usually made him commander of an army, or sent him to conquer new territory or to govern a country Rome had already conquered.

When Pompey was young, two of these military commanders, Marius and Sulla, were trying to control the government. So Rome often had civil war. Pompey decided to join Sulla's side. With an army of volunteers he won several battles against the Marians, and helped Sulla become dictator. For his great victories Sulla gave him the nickname of Magnus, "The Great."

The Roman Senate never trusted Pompey. He had risen by military success and not by election to office. However, he was the best general and most popular figure in Rome. For years he commanded the armies in all the major campaigns. He was elected consul in 70 b.c. after winning a war in Spain. Then for five years he was in the East, conquering new territory in Asia Minor and Palestine. When he returned in 62 b.c. everyone thought he would overthrow the government and make himself dictator as Sulla had done. Instead he disbanded his army and became a private citizen.

The Senate could easily have won Pompey to its side. The great orator Cicero tried to get them to support Pompey's plans. Instead they were against everything he wanted. (See Rome, Ancient.) Finally Pompey joined with Julius Caesar. Along with Crassus these two formed the First Triumvirate, meaning "The Three." They were very important in Roman politics for many years. (See Caesar, Gaius Julius.)

Pompey seemed to be the most powerful partner. But for the next ten years it was Caesar who held the important military command in Gaul. When the Gallic wars ended, everyone feared that Caesar would overthrow the government of Rome. The Senate was glad to turn to Pompey to defend the Republic.

When Caesar marched on Rome in 49 b.c. Pompey lost his nerve and retreated to Greece to gather a larger army. He finally met Caesar's forces in the Battle of Pharsalus, 48 b.c. Pompey was defeated and fled to Egypt. There he was murdered by men who hoped to gain the favor of the new dictator.

PONCE (*pôn'thā* or *pôn'sā* or *pŏns'*) **DE** (*thā* or *dē*) **LEON** (*lā ôn* or *lē'ŭn*), **JUAN** (*hwän*) (1460–1521), was a Spanish adventurer who discovered and tried to settle Florida.

He was born in Servas, Spain, the son of a nobleman. He sailed with Christopher Columbus on his second voyage to America in 1493. From 1502 to 1504 he took part in the Spanish conquest of the Caribbean islands.

In 1509 Ponce de Leon conquered Puerto Rico and was appointed the island's first Spanish governor. There he heard stories from the Indians about an island called Bimini on which there was a Fountain of Youth that could keep a man young forever. It became his ambition to find this wonderful island. The king of Spain gave him permission to colonize it.

Hostile Indians were the cause of Ponce de Leon's failure to found a Spanish colony in Florida.

In 1513 Ponce de Leon and three ships sailed north. They landed on a strange shore which he claimed for the Spanish. He named it Florida because he found it on Easter Sunday, called *Pascua Florida* in Spanish. He then sailed east still looking for Bimini. Leaving one of his ships to continue the search, he went back to Puerto Rico. From there he went to Spain in 1514. The king appointed him governor of "The Island of Florida" and gave him permission to colonize it. In 1521 he returned to Florida with 200 men and 50 horses and other animals. There were also monks and priests to convert the Indians to Christianity. Ponce de Leon landed near what is now Charlotte Harbor, but the natives were unfriendly. In a fight he was badly wounded by an Indian arrow and his men were forced back to the ships. Ponce de Leon died from his wounds a few days later in Cuba and was buried beneath the high altar of the Dominican Church of San Juan, Puerto Rico.

PONTIAC (*pŏn'tĭ ăk*) (1720?–1769) was an Indian chief who wanted to drive the British from North America.

He was chief of the Ottawa tribe, born in what is now Ohio. At that time, most of the tribes were friendly to the French and fought on their side during the wars between the French and the British. (See FRENCH AND INDIAN WAR.) When the French made peace with the British and gave up their lands in North America, the Indians continued to fight. British settlers who crossed the Appalachian Mountains wanted to farm the Indian lands. As a result, many tribes formed a confederation within which the Ottawa was the strongest. In the spring of 1763 there were surprise attacks on British forts in the area. Eight of the 12 forts were captured and the people killed.

Pontiac was in charge of the attack on Detroit, one of the largest forts. He and his warriors planned to enter the fort for peaceful purposes, with sawed-off guns hidden under their blankets. The plan failed when the commander heard of it. For five months the Indians surrounded the fort and kept anyone from getting out by land. Finally, in the summer of 1764,

British troops reached Detroit. Soon afterward many of the Indian tribes left the confederation and made peace with the British. The other tribes were defeated, and, in 1766, Pontiac made peace. Three years later he died. It is said that he was killed by another Indian.

PONY (*pō'nē*) **EXPRESS** (*ĕks prĕs'*) was the fastest way of getting a letter to the Pacific Coast of the United States during 1860 and 1861.

At that time there were not many people living in the western United States. California and Oregon had become states only a few years before. There were gold miners in Colorado and Nevada and a settlement of Mormons in Utah. These people liked to get mail from families and friends back East. In 1851 the government arranged to send mail to California and Oregon by sea. It took about a month for a letter to go from New York to California by ship, even when carried across the Isthmus of Panama by mules. Soon the government paid men to carry the mail in stagecoaches, a trip of 25 days. The people in the West wanted still faster mail delivery.

The idea of using fast horses or ponies to carry mail may have come from F. X. Aubrey who hauled goods down the Santa Fe Trail in freight wagons. On his trips from Missouri to Santa Fe, New Mexico, he left horses along the trail with traders and friendly Indians. He would return on horseback, changing a tired horse for a fresh one as he went along. His fastest trip over the 800 mile trail was made in $5\frac{1}{2}$ days.

The firm of Russell, Majors, and Waddell decided to set up a horseback mail to California. They were in the business of hauling goods all over the West in wagons. Along the trail they built 190 stations, or one about every 10 or 15 miles. Five hundred fast horses were bought and placed in corrals or pens at these stations. Some of the horses were so wild that they bucked every time a rider got on. They cost $150 each, at a time when most horses sold for $50.

The saddle used was very light. Over it was a leather covering called a *mochila*. The mail

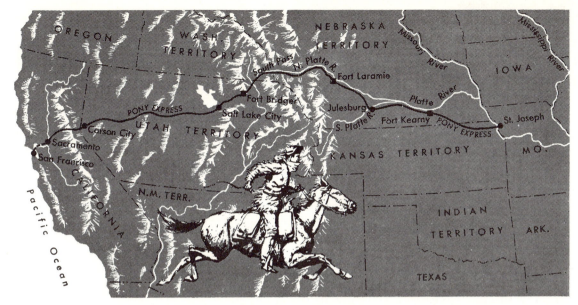

Route of the Pony Express.

was carried in pockets in the mochila. When a rider dashed up to a station, he took the mochila from his tired animal and threw it over the saddle of the waiting horse. Within seconds he was on his way again. Each rider carried a revolver and a knife. The weight of all equipment was 13 pounds. Riders could not weigh more than 125 pounds. About 15 pounds of letters were carried for $5 an ounce at first, later for $1 an ounce.

The Mail Leaves

The first pony, a white one, left St. Joseph, Missouri, on April 3, 1860. It carried mail that had come from the East by train. The rider was dressed in a red shirt, blue pants, and high-topped boots. Speeches were made, a band played, and the pony express was off. A ferry carried the horse and rider across the Missouri River. The rider changed his fancy clothes for others, and started across the prairies. Each rider rode as fast as he could for 10 or 15 miles until he came to the next station, where another horse was ready for him.

On April 13, 1860, the people of Sacramento, California, had been waiting for hours for the first mail to come by horseback from the East, 2,000 miles away. At last they saw the horse and rider followed by a cloud of dust. One of

these people was a reporter who wrote this story for his newspaper:

Amidst the firing and shouting, and waving hats and ladies' handkerchiefs, the pony was seen coming at a rattling pace down J Street. The little fellow stretched his neck well to the race and came at a fast pace down the street, which was wild with excitement. Out of this confusion emerged the Pony Express, trotting up to the door of the agency and depositing its mail ten days from St. Joseph to Sacramento. Hip, hip, hurrah for the Pony Express.

But there were often troubles along the way. Sometimes riders found that Indians had burned the stations or thieves had stolen the horses, but they kept on going. The mail had to go through. During an Indian uprising in Nevada, "Pony Bob" Haslam rode 380 miles in 36 hours. "Wild Bill" Cody once rode 320 miles when he found the stations burned and relief riders gone. A wagon train going west to find new homes once shot at the rider, Jay Keller. One of them said he thought Keller looked like an "Injun." Alex Carlyle's hat was shot off by an Indian, and after that he would never wear a hat again. One rider shot a rancher's dog that barked at him. The rancher threatened to shoot any pony express rider that passed that way again. After that the riders took the long way around that ranch. Cold weather and snow made life hard for these young men. Horses had to swim icy rivers. Snow was often so deep that a rider had to walk ahead of his horse to help break the trail. And yet, only one load of mail was ever lost.

The pony express lasted only 18 months. When the telegraph between the East and West was completed on October 24, 1861, there was no need for the fast pony mail. People could then send messages instantly across the nation. The little horses had run 616,000 miles back and forth over the 2,000-mile trail. This was 24 times the distance around the world. The pony express lost $400,000 for its owners, but people remember it as an exciting event when the nation was growing up, not as a failure.

POPE (*pōp*), **ALEXANDER** (1688–1744), was an English poet. He is probably quoted more than any other poet except Shakespeare. Two of Pope's sayings are: "To err is human; to forgive, divine"; "Fools rush in where angels fear to tread."

Pope was born in London. A hunchback, and always sickly, he looked different from other people. His religion also made him different, for he was a Roman Catholic when most Englishmen were Protestant. These differences may explain why he was often bitter and hard to get along with. He lived a quiet life, reading books and writing a great deal of poetry.

Pope received most of his education at home. When still a teen-ager, he began writing poetry.

Pope knew many different languages. His first really successful work was a translation of the writings of the Greek poet Homer. From this translation Pope earned enough money to buy a home on the Thames River. He lived there for the rest of his life, writing and entertaining many famous guests. Many leading writers were his very close friends.

Pope was a master of the rhyming couplet. This is two lines of poetry that rhyme together and contain one complete thought. Here is one of his best-known couplets:

> 'Tis education forms the common mind:
> Just as the twig is bent the tree's inclined.

Almost all of Pope's poetry was written in rhyming couplets.

Many of Pope's poems are very long and very serious. An example is the "Essay on Criticism," which tells what poetry should be like. But he could write funny things too. "The Rape of the Lock," which makes fun of fashionable people, is still enjoyed today.

POPLAR (*pŏp'lẽr*), tall, slender, fast-growing trees of the willow family. Thirty to 40 species are known. About half of them are native in Europe and western Asia, the others in North America. American species are called poplars, cottonwoods, or aspens. (See ASPEN.)

The leaves of many poplars have flattened stems that make them flutter in the slightest breeze. Poplar flowers are borne in spikes called catkins. The pollen-producing and the seed-producing flowers grow on different trees. The cottony seeds ripen quickly and are soon shed. Poplars, especially aspens, are often the first trees to grow again where fire has destroyed a forest. Young poplars provide needed shade for seedlings of other trees.

Poplars grow throughout North America

The cottonwood or poplar tree. Inset: Male (upper) and female (lower) flowers grow on separate trees.

Photos, Courtesy U.S. Forest Service

from Alaska to Mexico. Several species, mostly cottonwoods, are planted for shade or to protect prairies from heavy winds. Other kinds often planted include the white poplar, with leaves white-woolly underneath, the black poplar, and the Lombardy poplar. Poplars are not often planted in cities because their roots grow very long and sometimes damage sewers.

The buds of balsam poplars, found mostly in Canada, produce resin used in making cough medicine. Some poplars, especially the trembling aspen and the large-toothed aspen, are important wildlife plants. They are favorite foods of beaver. Deer, moose, and other mammals feed on the twigs, bark, and leaves. The buds provide winter food for grouse.

Poplar wood is light, soft, and weak. Its most general uses are for pulpwood, boxes and crates, excelsior, and matches. Some is used for fuel, and that of some species for lumber. Lumber commonly known as "yellow poplar" is wood of the tulip tree, of the Magnolia family.

Research has long been carried on with varieties and hybrids of poplars, trying to produce fast-growing trees that will resist disease. They would be used for reforesting cut-over pulpwood areas and for quick income from other forest lands.

POPPY (pŏp′ē) is the common name of many species of plants of the poppy family. All of them have milky or colored juice and usually showy flowers. Some poppies grow wild in almost every country in the north temperate zone. Several kinds are raised in gardens for their large, many-tinted flowers.

Oriental poppies, natives of the Mediterranean region, have the largest flowers, often six to eight inches across, white to red in color. Iceland poppies, from arctic regions, have small, fragrant flowers of different delicate colors. Alpine poppies are low-growing rock garden perennials with sweet-scented yellow or white flowers. The popular, many-colored Shirley poppies are cultivated forms of the corn, or Flanders poppy, a common wild flower of Europe and Asia. They are annuals.

The opium poppy, with gray-green leaves and white to purple flowers, is sometimes grown

J. Horace McFarland Company

The crimson Oriental poppy, largest of all poppies.

in gardens. It is widely cultivated in eastern countries for opium, made from the juice of its unripe seed pods. The ripe seeds are used in baking. Growing the plant is illegal in the United States. (See OPIUM.)

The plume poppy, native in eastern Asia, is a tall, bushy plant with bluish-gray leaves, topped by a showy cluster of white flowers. The California poppy, with satiny, creamy to bright orange flowers, grows wild in western United States. Cultivated varieties may have single or double flowers, some in shades of red.

Prickly poppies are natives of the warm, dry parts of the United States. They have white, yellow, or purplish poppylike flowers and thistlelike leaves. They become weeds in some places.

Poppies grow best in sunny places. Most kinds do well in ordinary garden soil. Seeds should be planted in the fall or in very early spring. Some poppies self-sow. Oriental poppies, true perennials, are grown from seed or from root-cuttings. Iceland and California poppies are perennials that bloom in their first season if the seeds are planted early.

POPULATION (*pŏp'ū lā'shŭn*) is the total number of people inhabiting an area. The United States makes such a count every ten years.

Some countries in the world count their populations more frequently; some less frequently. Some countries make only official estimates of the number of people that live within their borders. (See CENSUS.) The United Nations publishes an annual population estimate of all the countries of the world.

As a result, no one knows precisely how many people live in the world at any one time. In the mid-1960's a total of all the official counts and official estimates gave the world's population as about 3,250,000,000 people. The 1964 estimate made by the United Nations gave the world's total population as about 3,220,000,000. If all these people were distributed equally over the world there would be about 62 people living on each square mile of land (excluding Antarctica); that is, about nine families. These figures are easy to remember and they give a general idea of total population and average density. However, they do not tell the true story because people are not evenly distributed. In 1960 nearly eight million people lived in New York City. That is about the same number of people as lived in the state of Michigan.

Why Population Figures Change

There are many reasons why the same number of people do not live in all parts of the world. Some parts of the world are too dry to produce plants, including food crops, for human use; the Sahara Desert in Africa, for example. Other parts of the world are too cold; the Arctic regions, for example. Some parts of the world are too hard to reach. Some day people may learn how to find a living in these areas and will go to them to live. But as long as the favorable parts of the world provide food and clothing and shelter and all the other things people want, there will be parts of the world that have few or no people at all living in them.

Not all of the parts of the world that have favorable temperatures, rainfall, soils, minerals, and other things people use are equal in their populations. There are several reasons for this. Some parts of the world have these resources in greater abundance and in greater variety than others. Some of the world's resources are more conveniently located than others. The people living in some parts of the world have had the opportunity to make better use of their resources than people living in other parts.

The United States is a good example of a country that has a great variety and an abundance of resources. This has brought about a growth in population from 75,994,575 in 1900 to 179,323,175 in 1960. This was an increase in density from 28.0 to 49.6 persons for each square mile. By contrast, Australia, which has almost the same land area as the United States (excluding Alaska and Hawaii), in 1961 had about 10,500,000 persons, or 3.4 for each square mile. Almost half of Australia is desert where few people live. The Netherlands, with more than 850 persons for each square mile, and Japan, with more than 680, are two of the most heavily populated countries in the world.

The United States is also a good example of how people tend to live where conditions are more favorable than they are elsewhere. About 80 per cent of the people live in the eastern half of the country. Sixty-six per cent of the people live east of the Mississippi River. The greater density of population toward the east makes a difference in the distribution of cities. There are 130 cities in the United States with populations of 100,000 or more; 103 are in the eastern half of the country; 82 are east of the Mississippi River. Seventeen are on or near the West Coast; one is in Hawaii. Only nine large cities lie in the great area between the middle of the country and the West Coast. This is an area of broad, dry plains, of rolling foothills, and high, rugged mountains.

Population in an area rarely remains the same. Deaths and births take away and add people. Some people move out and some move in. Neither deaths and births nor emigrants and immigrants balance each other. As medical science learns more and teaches people more about health, the number of deaths from disease is decreased. Thus, if no one should go out of or come into an area, the population would tend to increase. There are a very few such areas because nearly all areas have people moving in and people moving out. People move into areas because they think opportunities are better in these areas than in the areas where they were. Sometimes discoveries of resources attract new settlers, or new inventions show people how they can use resources they have known about before. People move out of areas sometimes because populations increase to a point that there is not enough to support the people in the way they want to live. Sometimes people move out of areas in which the resources have been used up or they are not as abundant as they once were. Some people go to new areas because they enjoy developing new lands.

The reasons given for differences in populations or the movement of people are examples of the more important reasons. The United States is one of the "young" nations of the world. In its brief history are examples of all or nearly all the reasons why people live where they do, in the numbers that live there, and why the numbers differ from one place to another and one time to another.

POPULATION FIGURES OF THE UNITED STATES

POPULATION FIGURES FOR THE UNITED STATES, ITS OUTLYING TERRITORIES, POSSESSIONS AND STATES

United States and Its Possessions

	1960	1950
United States	179,323,175	150,697,361*
American Samoa	20,051	18,937
Guam	67,044	59,498
Panama Canal Zone	42,122	52,822
Puerto Rico	2,349,544	2,210,703
Virgin Islands	32,099	26,665

The States

	1960	1950
Alabama	3,266,740	3,061,743
Alaska	226,167	128,653
Arizona	1,302,161	749,587
Arkansas	1,786,272	1,909,511
California	15,717,204	10,586,223
Colorado	1,753,947	1,325,089
Connecticut	2,535,234	2,007,280
Delaware	446,292	318,085
District of Columbia	763,956	802,178
Florida	4,951,560	2,771,305
Georgia	3,943,116	3,444,578
Hawaii	632,772	499,794
Idaho	667,191	588,637
Illinois	10,081,158	8,712,176
Indiana	4,662,498	3,934,224
Iowa	2,757,537	2,621,073
Kansas	2,178,611	1,905,299
Kentucky	3,038,156	2,944,806
Louisiana	3,257,022	2,683,516
Maine	969,265	913,774
Maryland	3,100,689	2,343,001
Massachusetts	5,148,578	4,690,514
Michigan	7,823,194	6,371,766
Minnesota	3,413,864	2,982,483
Mississippi	2,178,141	2,178,914
Missouri	4,319,813	3,954,653
Montana	674,767	591,024
Nebraska	1,411,330	1,325,510
Nevada	285,278	160,083
New Hampshire	606,921	533,242
New Jersey	6,066,782	4,835,329

The States (Continued)

	1960	1950
New Mexico	951,023	681,187
New York	16,782,304	14,830,192
North Carolina	4,556,155	4,061,929
North Dakota	632,446	619,636
Ohio	9,706,397	7,946,627
Oklahoma	2,328,284	2,233,351
Oregon	1,768,687	1,521,341
Pennsylvania	11,319,366	10,498,012
Rhode Island	859,488	791,896
South Carolina	2,382,594	2,117,027
South Dakota	680,514	652,740
Tennessee	3,567,089	3,291,718
Texas	9,579,677	7,711,194
Utah	890,627	688,862
Vermont	389,881	377,747
Virginia	3,966,949	3,318,680
Washington	2,853,214	2,378,963
West Virginia	1,860,421	2,005,552
Wisconsin	3,951,777	3,434,575
Wyoming	330,066	290,529

Population of the United States: 1790 to 1960

Census year	Population	Increase over preceding census	
		Number	Per cent
1960	179,323,175	28,625,814	19.0
1950*	150,697,361	19,028,086	14.5
1940	131,669,275	8,894,229	7.2
1930	122,775,046	17,064,426	16.1
1920	105,710,620	13,728,354	14.9
1910	91,972,266	15,977,691	21.0
1900	75,994,575	13,046,861	20.7
1890	62,947,714	12,791,931	25.5
1880	50,155,783	10,337,334	26.0
1870	39,818,449	8,375,128	26.6
1860	31,443,321	8,251,445	35.6
1850	23,191,876	6,122,423	35.9
1840	17,069,453	4,203,433	32.7
1830	12,866,020	3,227,567	33.5
1820	9,638,453	2,398,572	33.1
1810	7,239,881	1,931,398	36.4
1800	5,308,483	1,379,269	35.1
1790	3,929,214	. . .	. . .

*Excludes Alaska and Hawaii, which became states in 1959.

POPULATION OF UNITED STATES PLACES OF 1,500 OR MORE, 1960 AND 1950

(c.) Indicates capital of state. * Town (township) population; includes places of 5,000 or more inhabitants not listed separately elsewhere. † Urban town (township).

Place	1960	1950	Place	1960	1950	Place	1960	1950	Place	1960	1950
ALABAMA:			ALA.—Cont.:			ARIZ.—Cont.:			ARK.—Cont.:		
Abbeville	2,524	2,162	Muscle Shoals	4,084	1,937	Sierra Vista	3,121		Van Buren	6,787	6,413
Adamsville	2,095		Northport	5,245	3,885	Somerton	1,613	1,825	Waldo	1,722	1,491
Alabaster	1,623		Oneonta	4,136	2,802	South Tucson	7,004	2,364	Waldron	1,619	1,292
Albertville	8,250	5,397	Opelika	15,678	12,295	Superior	4,875		Walnut Ridge	3,547	3,106
Alexander			Opp	5,535	5,240	Tempe	24,897	7,684	Warren	6,752	2,615
City	13,140	6,430	Oxford	3,603	1,697	Thatcher	1,581	1,284	West End	2,208	1,680
Aliceville	3,194	3,170	Ozark	9,534	5,238	Tolleson	3,886	3,042	West Helena	8,385	6,107
Andalusia	10,263	9,162	Parrish	1,608	757	Tucson	212,892	45,454	West Memphis	19,374	9,112
Anniston	33,657	31,066	Pell City	4,165	1,189	West Yuma	2,781	4,741	Wynne	4,922	4,142
Arab	2,989	1,592	Phenix City	27,630	23,305	Wickenburg	2,445	1,736			
Ashford	1,511	1,400	Piedmont	4,794	4,498	Willcox	2,441	1,266	CALIFORNIA:		
Ashland	1,610	1,593	Pleasant			Williams	3,559	2,152	Airport	3,689	
Athens	9,330	6,309	Grove	3,097	1,802	Winslow	8,862	6,518	Alameda	63,855	64,430
Atmore	8,173	5,720	Prattville	6,616	4,385	Yuma	23,974	9,145	Alamo	1,791	
Attalla	8,257	7,537	Prichard	47,371	19,014				Albany	14,804	17,590
Auburn	16,261	12,939	Rainbow City	1,625		ARKANSAS:			Alhambra	54,807	51,359
Bay Minette	5,197	3,732	Red Bay	1,954	1,805	Arkadelphia	8,069	6,819	Alisal	16,473	16,714
Bayou La			Roanoke	5,288	5,392	Ashdown	2,725	2,738	Altadena	40,568	
Batre	2,572		Russellville	6,628	6,012	Augusta	2,272	2,317	Alturas	2,819	2,819
Bessemer	33,054	28,445	Samson	1,932	2,204	Bald Knob	1,705	2,022	Alum Rock	18,942	
Birmingham	340,887	326,037	Saraland	4,595		Batesville	6,207	6,414	Anaheim	104,184	14,556
Boaz	4,654	3,078	Scottsboro	6,449	4,731	Beebe	1,697	1,192	Anderson	4,492	
Brent	1,879	1,110	Selma	28,385	22,840	Benton	10,399	6,277	Antioch	17,305	11,051
Brewton	6,309	5,146	Shawmut	1,898	3,266	Bentonville	3,649	2,942	Arcadia	41,005	23,066
Bridgeport	2,906	2,386	Sheffield	13,491	10,767	Berryville	1,999	1,753	Arcata	5,235	3,729
Brighton	2,884	1,689	Southwest			Blytheville	20,797	16,234	Arden-Arcade	73,352	
Brundidge	2,523	2,605	Lanett	2,189	1,631	Booneville	2,690	2,433	Arroyo Grande	3,291	1,723
Butler	1,765	659	Sylacauga	12,857	9,606	Brinkley	4,636	4,173	Artesia	9,993	
Calera	1,928	1,361	Talladega	17,742	13,134	Camden	15,823	11,372	Arvin	5,310	5,007
Carbon Hill	1,944	2,179	Tallassee	4,934	4,225	Carlisle	1,514	1,396	Atascadero	5,983	3,443
Carver Court.	1,818		Tarrant City	7,810	7,571	Clarendon	2,293	2,547	Atherton	7,717	3,630
Centre	2,392	1,672	Thomasville	3,182	2,425	Clarksville	3,919	4,343	Atwater	7,318	2,856
Centreville	1,981	1,160	Troy	10,234	8,555	Conway	9,791	8,610	Auburn	5,586	4,653
Chickasaw	10,002	4,920	Trussville	2,510	1,575	Corning	2,192	2,045	Avalon	1,536	1,506
Childersburg	4,884	4,023	Tuscaloosa	63,370	46,396	Cotton Plant	1,704	1,838	Avenal	3,147	3,982
Citronelle	1,918	1,350	Tuscumbia	8,994	6,734	Crossett	5,370	4,619	Azusa	20,497	11,042
Clanton	5,683	4,640	Tuskegee	1,750	6,712	Dardanelle	2,098	1,772	Bakersfield	56,848	34,784
Columbiana	2,264	1,761	Union Springs	3,704	3,232	De Queen	2,859	3,015	Baldwin Park	33,951	
Cordova	3,184	3,156	Uniontown	1,993	1,798	Dermott	3,665	3,601	Banning	10,250	7,034
Cullman	10,883	7,523	Vestavia Hills	1,029		De Witt	3,019	2,543	Barstow	11,644	6,135
Dadeville	2,840	2,354	Warrior	2,448	1,384	Dumas	3,540	2,512	Bayview-		
Daphne	1,527	1,041	West End			Earle	2,391	2,375	Rosewood	2,980	
Decatur	29,217	19,974	Anniston	5,485		El Dorado	25,292	23,076	Beaumont	4,288	3,152
Demopolis	7,377	5,004	Wetumpka	3,672	3,813	England	2,861	2,136	Bell	19,450	15,430
Dora	1,776	984	Winfield	2,907	2,108	Euclid Heights	2,030	2,090	Bellflower	45,909	
Dothan	31,440	21,584	York	2,932	1,774	Eudora	3,598	3,072	Bell Gardens	26,467	
East Brewton	2,511	2,173				Fayetteville	20,274	17,071	Belmont	15,996	5,567
Elba	4,321	2,936	ALASKA:			Fordyce	3,890	3,754	Belvedere	2,148	800
Enterprise	11,410	7,288	Anchorage	44,237	11,254	Forrest City	10,544	7,607	Benicia	6,070	7,284
Eufaula	8,357	6,900	College	1,755	424	Fort Smith	52,991	47,942	Ben Lomond	1,814	
Eutaw	2,784	2,348	Fairbanks	13,311	5,771	Greenwood	1,558	1,634	Berkeley	111,268	113,805
Evergreen	3,703	3,454	Graehl-Hamil-			Gurdon	2,166	2,390	Beverly Hills	30,817	29,032
Fairfax	3,107	2,717	ton Acres	2,162		Hamburg	2,904	2,655	Big Bear Lake	1,562	1,434
Fairfield	15,816	13,177	Juneau (c.)	6,797	5,956	Harrison	6,580	5,542	Bishop	2,875	2,891
Fairhope	4,858	3,354	Ketchikan	6,483	5,305	Heber Springs	2,265	2,109	Bly	1,554	
Fayette	4,227	3,707	Kodiak	2,628	1,710	Helena	11,500	11,236	Blythe	6,023	4,089
Florala	3,011	2,713	Mount			Hope	8,399	8,605	Bonnyville	4,686	
Florence	31,649	23,879	Edgecumbe	1,884	1,147	Hot Springs	28,337	29,307	Boyes Springs	2,462	
Foley	2,589	1,301	Nome	2,316	1,876	Hoxie	1,886	1,855	Brawley	12,703	11,922
Fort Payne	7,029	6,226	Petersburg	1,502	1,619	Hughes	1,960	1,686	Brea	8,487	3,208
Fultondale	2,001	1,304	Seward	1,891	2,114	Jacksonville	14,488	2,474	Brentwood	2,186	1,729
Gadsden	58,088	55,725	Sitka	3,237	1,985	Jonesboro	21,418	16,310	Buena Park	46,401	
Gardendale	4,712		Spenard	9,074	2,108	Lake Village	2,998	2,484	Burbank	90,155	78,577
Geneva	3,840	3,579				Leachville	1,507	1,230	Burlingame	24,036	19,886
Georgiana	2,093	1,596	ARIZONA:			Lepanto	1,585	1,683	Burton	4,635	2,381
Glencoe	2,592	1,466	Ajo	7,049	5,817	Little			Calexico	7,992	6,433
Goodwater	2,023	1,227	Avondale	6,151	2,505	Rock (c.)	107,813	102,213	Calipatria	2,548	1,428
Gordo	1,714	952	Benson	2,494	1,440	Lonoke	2,359	1,556	Calistoga	1,514	1,418
Graysville	2,870	879	Bisbee	9,914	3,801	McGehee	4,448	3,854	Camarillo	2,359	
Greensboro	3,081	2,217	Buckeye	2,286	1,932	Magnolia	10,651	6,918	Camarillo		
Greenville	6,894	6,781	Casa Grande	8,311	4,181	Malvern	9,566	8,072	Heights	1,704	
Greenwood	3,561	2,421	Central			Manila	1,753	1,729	Campbell	11,863	
Grove Hill	1,834	1,443	Heights	2,486		Marianna	5,134	4,530	Capistrano		
Guntersville	6,592	5,253	Chandler	9,531	3,799	Marked Tree	3,216	2,878	Beach	2,026	
Haleyville	3,740	3,331	Claypool	2,505		Marvell	1,690	1,121	Capitola	2,021	1,848
Hamilton	1,934	1,623	Clifton	4,191	3,466	Mena	4,388	4,445	Cardiff-by-the-		
Hartford	1,956	1,655	Coolidge	4,990	4,306	Monticello	4,412	4,501	Sea	3,149	
Hartselle	5,000	3,429	Cottonwood-			Morrilton	5,997	5,483	Carlsbad	9,253	
Headland	2,650	2,091	Clemenceau	1,879	1,626	Mountain			Carmel-by-the-		
Heflin	2,400	1,982	Douglas	11,925	9,442	Home	2,105	2,217	Sea	4,580	4,351
Hokes Bluff	1,619	1,158	El Mirage	1,723		Nashville	3,579	3,548	Carmichael	20,455	4,499
Homewood	20,289	12,866	Eloy	4,899	3,580	Newport	7,007	6,254	Carpinteria	4,998	2,864
Hueytown	5,997		Flagstaff	18,214	7,663	North Little			Carson	38,059	
Huntsville	72,365	16,437	Florence	2,143	1,776	Rock	58,032	44,097	Castro Valley	37,120	
Irondale	3,501	1,876	Gila Bend	1,813		Osceola	6,189	5,006	Castroville	2,838	1,865
Jackson	4,959	3,072	Gilbert	1,833	1,114	Ozark	1,965	1,757	Cathedral City	1,855	
Jacksonville	5,678	4,751	Glendale	15,696	8,179	Paragould	9,947	9,668	Central Valley	2,751	2,202
Jasper	10,799	8,589	Globe	6,217	6,419	Paris	3,007	3,731	Ceres	4,406	2,351
Lafayette	2,605	2,353	Goodyear	1,654	1,254	Piggott	2,776	2,558	Chester	1,553	1,197
Lanett	7,674	7,434	Hayden	1,760		Pine Bluff	44,037	37,162	Chico	14,757	12,272
Langdale	2,528	2,721	Holbrook	3,438	2,336	Pine Bluff			Chico-Vecino	4,688	3,967
Leeds	6,162	3,306	Kingman	4,525		Southeast	2,679		Chino	10,305	5,784
Linden	2,516	1,363	McNary	1,608	1,902	Pocahontas	3,665	3,840	Chowchilla	4,525	3,893
Lineville	1,612	1,548	Mammoth	1,913		Prescott	3,533	3,960	Chrisman	3,923	4,211
Lipscomb	2,811	2,550	Mesa	33,772	16,790	Rector	1,757	1,855	Chula Vista	42,034	15,927
Livingston	1,544	1,681	Miami	3,350	4,329	Rogers	5,700	4,962	Claremont	12,633	6,327
Luverne	2,238	2,221	Morenci	2,431	6,541	Russellville	8,921	8,166	Cloverdale	2,848	1,292
Marion	3,807	2,822	Nogales	7,286	6,153	Searcy	7,272	6,024	Clovis	5,546	2,766
Midfield	3,556		Page	2,960		Sheridan	1,938	1,893	Coachella	4,505	2,755
Mignon	2,271	3,053	Parker	1,642	1,201	Siloam Springs	3,953	3,270	Coalinga	5,965	5,539
Mobile	202,779	129,009	Peoria	2,593		Smackover	2,434	2,495	College Gar-		
Monroeville	3,632	2,772	Phoenix (c.)	439,170	106,818	Springdale	10,076	5,835	dens	4,132	
Montevallo	2,755	2,150	Plantsite	1,552		Stamps	2,591	2,552	Colton	18,666	14,465
Montgomery			Prescott	12,861	6,764	Star City	1,573	1,296	Colusa	3,518	3,031
(c.)	134,393	106,525	Safford	4,648	3,756	Stuttgart	9,661	7,276	Commerce	9,555	
Moulton	1,716	1,384	San Manuel	4,524		Texarkana	19,788	15,875	Compton	71,812	47,991
Mountain			Scottsdale	10,026		Trumann	4,511	3,744	Concord	36,208	6,953
Brook	12,680	8,359	Show Low	1,625		Tuckerman	1,539	1,253	Corcoran	4,976	3,150

Place	1960	1950
CALIF.—Cont.:		
Corning	3,006	2,537
Corona	13,336	10,223
Coronado	18,039	12,700
Corte Madera	5,962	1,933
Costa Mesa	37,550	...
Cotati	1,852	...
Covina	20,124	3,956
Crescent City	2,958	1,706
Crescent City Northwest	3,086	...
Crowley	3,950	...
Culver City	32,163	19,720
Cupertino	3,664	...
Cutler	2,191	1,768
Cutten	1,572	...
Cypress	1,753	...
Dairy Valley	3,508	...
Daly City	44,791	15,191
Danville	3,585	...
Davis	8,910	3,554
Delano	11,913	8,717
Del Mar	3,124	...
Del Monte Park	2,177	...
Del Paso Heights-Robla	11,495	...
Del Rey Oaks	1,831	...
Diablo	2,096	...
Dinuba	6,103	4,971
Dixon	2,970	1,714
Dos Palos	2,028	1,394
Downey	82,505	...
Duarte	13,962	...
Dunsmuir	2,873	2,256
Earlimart	2,897	2,162
East Los Angeles	104,270	...
East Modesto	2,084	...
East Porterville	3,538	...
East Whittier	19,884	...
Edgemont	1,628	...
El Cajon	37,618	5,600
El Centro	16,811	12,590
El Cerrito	25,437	18,011
Elk Grove	2,205	...
El Monte	4,186	2,502
El Monte	13,163	8,101
El Paso de Robles	6,677	4,835
El Rio	6,966	1,376
El Segundo	14,219	8,011
Elsinore	2,432	2,068
Emeryville	2,686	2,889
Empire	1,635	1,448
Encinitas	2,786	...
Enterprise	4,946	...
Escalon	1,763	...
Escondido	16,377	6,544
Eureka	28,137	23,058
Exeter	4,264	4,078
Fairfax	5,813	4,078
Fairfield	14,968	3,118
Fair Oaks	1,622	...
Fairview	3,586	...
Fallbrook	4,814	1,735
Farmersville	3,101	...
Fillmore	4,808	3,884
Firebaugh	2,070	821
Florence-Graham	38,164	...
Folsom	3,925	1,690
Fontana	14,659	...
Ford City	3,926	4,347
Fort Bragg	4,433	3,826
Fortuna	3,523	1,762
Fountain Valley	2,068	...
Fowler	1,892	1,857
Freedom	4,206	2,765
Fremont	43,790	...
Fresno	133,929	91,669
Fullerton	56,180	13,958
Galt	1,868	1,333
Gardena	35,943	14,405
Garden Grove	84,238	...
Gilroy	7,348	4,951
Glen Avon Heights	3,416	...
Glendale	119,442	95,702
Glendora	20,752	3,988
Gonzales	2,138	1,821
Grass Valley	4,876	5,283
Greenfield	1,680	1,309
Gridley	3,343	3,054
Grover City	5,210	...
Guadalupe	2,614	2,429
Gustine	2,300	1,984
Hagginwood	11,469	...
Half Moon Bay	1,957	...
Hanford	10,133	10,028
Hatton Fields	2,362	...
Hawthorne	33,035	16,316
Hayward	72,700	14,272
Healdsburg	4,816	3,258
Hemet	5,416	3,386
Hemet East	1,936	...
Hermosa Beach	16,115	11,826
Hillgrove	14,669	...
Hillsborough	7,554	3,552
Hollister	6,071	4,903
Holtville	3,080	2,472

Place	1960	1950
CALIF.—Cont.:		
Home Gardens	1,541	...
Hughson	1,898	1,816
Huntington Beach	11,492	5,237
Huntington Park	29,920	29,450
Imperial	2,658	1,759
Imperial Beach	17,773	...
Indio	9,745	5,300
Inglewood	63,390	46,185
Irwindale	1,518	...
Ivanhoe	1,616	1,172
Jackson	1,852	1,879
Kerman	1,970	1,563
Keyes	1,546	...
King City	2,937	2,347
Kingsburg	3,093	2,310
La Canada-Flintridge	18,338	...
Lafayette	7,114	...
Laguna Beach	9,288	6,661
La Habra	25,136	4,961
Lakeland Village	3,539	...
Lakeport	2,303	1,983
Lakewood	67,126	...
La Mesa	30,441	10,946
Lamont	6,177	3,571
Lancaster	26,012	3,594
La Puente	24,723	...
Larkspur	5,710	2,905
La Verne	6,516	4,198
Lawndale	21,740	...
Lemon Grove	19,348	...
Lemoore	2,561	2,153
Lennox	31,224	...
Lenwood	2,407	...
Leucadia	5,665	...
Lincoln	3,197	2,410
Linda	6,129	...
Lindsay	5,397	5,060
Live Oak	3,518	...
Live Oak	2,276	1,770
Livermore	16,058	4,364
Livingston	2,188	1,502
Lodi	22,229	13,798
Lomita	14,983	...
Lompoc	14,415	5,520
Long Beach	344,168	250,767
Los Alamitos	4,312	...
Los Altos	19,696	...
Los Altos Hills	3,412	...
Los Angeles	2,479,015	1,970,358
Los Banos	5,272	3,868
Los Gatos	9,036	4,907
Lynwood	31,614	25,823
McCloud	2,140	1,394
McFarland	3,686	...
Madera	14,430	10,497
Manhattan Beach	33,934	17,330
Manteca	8,242	3,804
Marina	3,310	...
Martinez	9,604	8,268
Martinez East	3,958	...
Marysville	9,553	7,826
Maywood	14,588	13,292
Meiners Oaks	3,513	2,446
Mendota	2,099	1,516
Menlo Park	26,957	13,587
Merced	20,068	15,278
Millbrae	15,873	8,972
Mill Valley	10,411	7,331
Milpitas	6,572	...
Mirada Hills	22,444	...
Mira Loma	3,982	1,555
Mirro Beach	1,907	...
Modesto	36,585	17,389
Mojave	1,845	2,055
Monrovia	27,079	20,186
Montalvo	2,028	...
Montclair	13,546	...
Montebello	32,097	21,735
Monterey	22,618	16,205
Monterey Park	37,821	20,395
Monte Sereno	1,506	...
Moorpark	2,902	1,146
Morada	2,156	...
Morgan Hill	3,151	1,627
Morro Bay	3,692	1,659
Mountain View	30,889	6,563
Mount Shasta	1,936	1,909
Mulberry	2,643	2,545
Napa	22,170	13,579
National City	32,771	21,199
Needles	4,590	4,051
Nevada City	2,353	2,505
Newark	9,884	...
Newhall	4,705	2,527
Newman	2,148	1,815
Newport Beach	26,564	12,120
Norco	4,964	1,584
Northcrest	1,945	...
North Highlands	21,271	...
North Sacramento	12,922	6,029
North Turlock	2,535	1,586
Norwalk	88,739	...
Novato	17,881	...
Nyeland Acres	1,619	...
Oakdale	4,980	4,064
Oakland	367,548	384,575

Place	1960	1950
CALIF.—Cont.:		
Oak View	2,448	1,648
Oceanside	24,971	12,881
Ojai	4,495	2,519
Olive Hurst	4,835	3,588
Ontario	46,617	22,872
Opal Cliffs	3,825	...
Orange	26,444	10,027
Orange Cove	2,885	2,395
Orinda	4,712	...
Orinda Village	5,568	...
Orland	2,534	2,067
Oroville	6,115	5,387
Oxnard	40,265	21,567
Pacheco	1,518	...
Pacifica	20,995	...
Pacific Grove	12,121	9,623
Palmdale	11,522	...
Palm Springs	13,468	7,660
Palo Alto	52,287	25,475
Palos Verdes Estates	9,564	1,963
Paradise	8,268	...
Paradise	5,616	4,426
Paramount	27,249	...
Pasadena	116,407	104,577
Patterson	2,246	1,343
Perris	2,950	1,807
Petaluma	14,035	10,315
Pico Rivera	49,150	...
Piedmont	11,117	10,132
Pinole	6,064	1,147
Pismo Beach	1,762	1,425
Pittsburg	19,062	12,763
Pittsburg East	1,977	...
Pittsburg West	5,188	...
Placentia	5,861	1,682
Placerville	4,439	3,749
Planada	1,704	...
Pleasant Hill	23,844	5,686
Pleasanton	4,203	2,244
Pomona	67,157	35,405
Port Chicago	1,746	...
Porterville	7,991	6,904
Port Hueneme	11,067	3,024
Portola	1,874	2,261
Poway	1,921	...
Quartz Hill	3,325	...
Quincy-East Quincy	2,723	...
Ramona	2,449	1,158
Rancho Cordova	7,429	...
Red Bluff	7,202	4,905
Redding	12,773	10,256
Redlands	26,289	18,429
Redondo Beach	46,986	25,226
Redwood City	46,290	25,544
Reedley	5,850	4,135
Rialto	18,567	3,156
Richmond	71,854	99,545
Ridgecrest	5,099	2,028
Rio Dell	3,222	1,862
Rio Linda	2,189	...
Rio Vista	2,616	1,831
Ripon	1,894	1,550
Riverbank	2,786	2,662
Riverside	84,332	46,764
Rohnerville	2,268	1,500
Rolling Hills	1,664	...
Rolling Hills Estates	3,941	...
Roseland	4,510	1,552
Rosemead	15,476	...
Roseville	13,421	8,723
Ross	2,551	2,179
Ryans Slough	3,634	1,727
Sacramento (c.)	191,667	137,572
St. Helena	2,722	2,297
Salinas	28,957	13,917
San Anselmo	11,584	9,188
San Bernardino	91,922	63,058
San Bruno	29,063	12,478
San Buenaventura	29,114	16,534
San Carlos	21,370	14,371
San Clemente	8,527	2,008
San Diego	573,224	334,387
San Fernando	16,093	12,992
San Francisco	740,316	775,357
San Gabriel	22,561	20,343
Sanger	8,072	6,400
San Jacinto	2,553	1,778
San Jose	204,196	95,280
San Leandro	65,962	27,542
San Lorenzo	23,773	...
San Luis Obispo	20,437	14,180
San Marino	13,658	11,230
San Mateo	69,870	41,782
San Pablo	19,687	14,476
San Rafael	20,460	13,848
Santa Ana	100,350	45,533
Santa Barbara	58,768	44,854
Santa Clara	58,880	11,702
Santa Cruz	25,596	21,970
Santa Fe Springs	16,342	...
Santa Maria	20,027	10,440
Santa Monica	83,249	71,595
Santa Paula	13,279	11,049
Santa Rosa	31,027	17,902
Santa Susana	2,310	...
Saranap	6,450	2,362

Place	1960	1950
CALIF.—Cont.:		
Saratoga	14,861	...
Saticoy	2,283	2,216
Sausalito	5,331	4,828
Seal Beach	6,994	3,553
Seaside	19,353	...
Sebastopol	2,694	2,601
Selma	6,934	5,964
Shafter	4,576	2,207
Shell Beach	1,820	...
Shore Acres	3,093	...
Sierra Madre	9,732	7,273
Signal Hill	4,627	4,040
Simi	2,107	...
Soledad	2,837	2,441
Sonoma	3,023	2,015
Sonora	2,725	2,448
South El Monte	4,850	...
South Gate	53,831	51,116
South Laguna	2,000	...
South Modesto	5,465	...
South Oroville	3,704	...
South Park	3,261	1,837
South Pasadena	19,706	16,935
South Sacramento-Fruitridge	16,443	...
South San Francisco	39,418	19,351
South San Gabriel	26,213	...
South Taft	1,910	2,918
South Turlock	1,577	1,492
South Yuba	3,200	...
Stanton	11,163	...
Stockton	86,321	70,853
Suisun City	2,470	946
Sunnymead	3,404	...
Sunnyvale	52,898	9,829
Susanville	5,598	5,338
Taft	3,822	3,707
Taft Heights	2,661	2,176
Tehachapi	3,161	1,685
Temple City	31,838	...
Thousand Oaks	2,934	1,243
Torrance	100,991	22,241
Tracy	11,289	8,410
Tulare	13,824	12,445
Turlock	9,116	6,235
Tustin	2,006	1,143
Twin Lakes	1,849	...
Ukiah	9,900	6,120
Union City	6,618	...
Upland	15,918	9,203
Vacaville	10,898	3,169
Vallejo	60,877	26,038
Visalia	15,791	11,749
Vista	14,795	1,705
Walnut Creek	9,903	2,420
Walnut Heights	5,080	...
Wasco	6,841	5,592
Waterford	1,780	1,777
Watsonville	13,293	11,572
Weaverville	1,736	...
Weed	3,223	2,739
West Covina	50,645	4,499
Westgate-Waverly-Park	2,191	...
West Hollywood	28,870	...
Westminster	25,750	...
West Modesto	1,897	2,038
Whittier	33,663	23,433
Willits	3,410	2,691
Willows	4,139	3,019
Winters	1,700	1,265
Woodlake	2,623	2,525
Woodland	13,524	9,386
Woodside	3,592	...
Yreka City	4,759	3,227
Yuba City	11,507	7,861
COLORADO:		
Akron	1,890	1,605
Alamosa	6,205	5,354
Arvada	19,242	...
Aurora	48,548	11,421
Boulder	37,718	19,999
Brighton	7,055	4,336
Broomfield Heights	4,535	...
Brush	3,621	2,431
Buena Vista	1,806	783
Burlington	2,090	2,247
Canon City	8,973	6,345
Center	1,600	2,024
Cherry Hills Village	1,931	750
Climax	1,609	...
Colorado Springs	70,194	45,472
Commerce Town	8,970	...
Cortez	6,764	2,680
Craig	3,984	3,080
Del Norte	1,856	2,048
Delta	3,832	4,097
Denver (c.)	493,887	415,786
Derby	10,124	2,840
Durango	10,530	7,459
Edgewater	4,314	2,580
Englewood	33,398	16,869
Florence	2,821	2,773

Place	1960	1950
COLO.—Cont.:		
Fort Collins	25,027	14,937
Fort Collins West	1,569	. . .
Fort Lupton	2,194	1,907
Fort Morgan	7,379	5,315
Fountain	1,602	713
Fruita	1,830	1,463
Glenwood Springs	3,637	2,412
Golden	7,118	5,238
Grand Junction	18,694	14,504
Greeley	26,314	20,354
Gunnison	3,477	2,770
Holyoke	1,555	1,558
Ivywild	11,065	2,849
Julesburg	1,840	1,951
Lafayette	2,612	2,090
La Junta	8,026	7,712
Lakewood	19,338	. . .
Lamar	7,369	6,829
Las Animas	3,402	3,223
Leadville	4,008	4,081
Limon	1,811	1,471
Lincoln Park	2,085	1,345
Littleton	13,670	3,378
Longmont	11,489	8,099
Louisville	2,073	1,978
Loveland	9,734	6,773
Manitou Springs	3,626	2,580
Meeker	1,655	1,658
Monte Vista	3,385	3,272
Montrose	5,044	4,964
Orchard Mesa	4,956	. . .
Pueblo	91,181	63,685
Rifle	2,135	1,525
Rocky Ford	4,929	4,087
Salida	4,560	4,553
Security	9,017	. . .
Sheridan	3,559	1,715
Springfield	1,791	2,041
Steamboat Springs	1,843	1,913
Sterling	10,751	7,534
Thornton	11,353	. . .
Trinidad	10,691	12,204
Walsenburg	5,071	5,596
Westminster	13,850	1,686
Wheat Ridge	21,619	. . .
Windsor	1,509	1,548
Wray	2,082	2,198
Yuma	1,919	1,908
CONNECTICUT:		
Ansonia	19,819	18,706
Avon*	5,273	3,171
Berlin*	11,250	7,470
Bethel	5,624	4,145
Bloomfield*	13,613	5,746
Branford	2,371	2,552
Bridgeport	156,748	158,709
Bristol	45,499	35,961
Cheshire	4,072	1,826
Clinton	2,693	. . .
Colchester	2,260	1,522
Collinsville	1,682	2,078
Conning Towers	3,457	. . .
Cromwell	2,889	1,541
Danbury	22,928	22,067
Danielson	4,642	4,554
Darien*	18,437	11,767
Deep River	2,166	2,034
Derby	12,132	10,259
East Hampton	1,574	1,481
East Hartford†	43,977	29,933
East Haven†	21,388	12,212
Enfield†	31,464	15,464
Fairfield†	46,183	30,489
Germantown	2,893	1,598
Glastonbury*	14,497	8,818
Greenwich†	53,793	40,835
Groton	10,111	7,036
Guilford	2,420	. . .
Hamden†	41,056	29,715
Hartford (c.)	162,178	177,397
Jewett City	3,608	3,702
Ledyard*	5,395	1,749
Litchfield*	6,264	4,964
Manchester†	42,102	34,116
Meriden	51,850	44,088
Middletown	33,250	29,711
Milford	41,662	. . .
Monroe*	6,402	2,892
Montville*	7,759	4,766
Moosup	2,760	2,909
Morningside Park	3,181	. . .
Mystic	2,536	2,266
Naugatuck	19,511	17,455
New Britain	82,201	73,726
New Canaan*	13,466	8,001
New Haven	152,048	164,443
Newington*	17,664	9,110
New London	34,182	30,551
New Milford	3,023	2,673
Newtown*	11,373	7,448
Niantic	2,788	1,746
North Branford*	6,771	2,017
North Grosvenordale	1,874	2,232
North Haven*	15,935	9,444
CONN.—Cont.:		
Norwalk	67,775	49,460
Norwich	38,506	23,429
Old Saybrook	1,671	. . .
Orange*	8,547	3,032
Pawcatuck	4,389	5,269
Plainfield	2,044	2,207
Plainville*	13,149	9,994
Plantsville	2,793	1,536
Portland	5,587	. . .
Putnam	6,952	8,181
Quaker Hill	1,671	1,260
Ridgefield	2,954	2,347
Rockville	9,478	8,016
Rocky Hill*	7,404	5,108
Seymour*	10,100	7,832
Shelton	18,190	12,694
Simsbury	2,745	1,771
Southbury*	5,186	3,828
South Coventry	3,568	1,617
Southington	9,952	5,955
South Windsor*	9,460	4,066
Stafford Springs	3,322	3,396
Stamford	92,713	74,293
Stonington	1,622	1,739
Storrs	6,054	. . .
Stratford†	45,012	33,428
Suffield*	6,779	4,895
Terryville	5,231	. . .
Thomaston	3,579	. . .
Torrington	30,045	27,820
Trumbull*	20,379	8,641
Unionville	2,246	2,197
Wallingford†	29,920	11,994
Warehouse Point	1,936	1,283
Waterbury	107,130	104,477
Watertown*	14,837	10,699
West Hartford†	62,382	44,402
West Haven†	43,002	32,010
West Mystic	3,268	2,362
Westport*	20,955	11,667
Wethersfield†	20,561	12,533
Willimantic	13,881	13,586
Wilton*	8,026	4,558
Windsor*	19,467	11,833
Windsor Locks*	11,411	5,221
Winsted	8,136	8,781
Wolcott*	8,889	3,553
Woodbridge*	5,182	2,822
Woodbury	3,910	. . .
DELAWARE:		
Bellefonte	1,536	1,472
Delaware City	1,658	1,363
Dover (c.)	7,250	6,223
Elsmere	7,319	5,314
Georgetown	1,765	1,923
Harrington	2,495	2,241
Laurel	2,709	2,700
Lewes	3,025	2,904
Middletown	2,191	1,755
Milford	5,795	5,179
Milton	1,617	1,321
Newark	11,404	6,731
New Castle	4,469	5,396
Rehoboth Beach	1,507	1,794
Seaford	4,430	3,087
Smyrna	3,241	2,346
Wilmington	95,827	110,356
DISTRICT OF COLUMBIA:		
Washington, D.C.	763,956	802,178
FLORIDA:		
Alachua	1,974	1,116
Apalachicola	3,099	3,222
Apopka	3,578	2,254
Arcadia	5,889	4,764
Atlantic Beach	3,125	1,604
Auburndale	5,595	3,763
Avon Park	6,073	4,612
Bartow	12,849	8,694
Bay Harbor Islands	3,249	296
Bayshore Gardens	2,297	. . .
Bee Ridge	2,043	. . .
Belleair	2,456	961
Belle Glade	11,273	7,219
Belle Isle	2,344	. . .
Bellglade Camp	1,658	1,497
Biscayne Park	2,911	2,009
Blountstown	2,375	2,118
Boca Raton	6,961	992
Bonifay	2,222	2,252
Boynton Beach	10,467	2,542
Bradenton	19,380	13,604
Bradenton South	3,400	. . .
Brandon	1,665	. . .
Brooksville	3,301	1,818
Brownsville	38,417	. . .
Bunnell	1,860	1,341
Cantonment	2,499	. . .
Carol City	21,749	. . .
Casselberry	2,463	407
FLA.—Cont.:		
Cedar Hammock	3,089	1,101
Century	2,046	1,350
Chattahoochee	9,699	8,473
Chipley	3,159	2,959
Chosen	1,858	1,873
Clearwater	34,653	15,581
Clermont	3,313	2,168
Clewiston	3,114	2,499
Cocoa	12,294	4,245
Cocoa Beach	3,475	246
Cocoa West	3,975	. . .
Combee Settlement	2,697	. . .
Coral Gables	34,793	19,837
Crescent City	1,629	1,393
Crestview	7,467	5,003
Cross City	1,857	1,522
Cutler Ridge	7,005	. . .
Dade City	4,759	3,806
Dania	7,065	4,540
Daytona Beach	37,395	30,187
Debary	2,362	. . .
Deerfield Beach	9,573	2,088
De Funiak Springs	5,282	3,077
De Land	10,775	8,652
Delray Beach	12,230	6,312
Dundee	1,554	1,152
Dunedin	8,444	3,202
Eau Gallie	12,300	1,554
Edgewater	2,051	837
Eloise	3,256	. . .
El Portal	2,079	1,371
Englewood	2,877	. . .
Ensley	1,836	. . .
Eustis	6,189	4,005
Fernandina Beach	7,276	554
Florida City	4,114	1,547
Fort Lauderdale	83,648	36,328
Fort Meade	4,014	2,803
Fort Myers	22,523	13,195
Fort Myers Beach	2,463	. . .
Fort Pierce	25,256	13,502
Fort Walton Beach	12,147	2,463
Frostproof	2,664	2,329
Fruitville	2,131	. . .
Gainesville	29,701	26,861
Gainesville East	2,393	. . .
Gainesville North	4,290	. . .
Gainesville West	2,725	. . .
Gibsonton	1,673	. . .
Gifford	3,509	1,459
Goulds	5,121	. . .
Graceville	2,307	1,638
Green Cove Springs	4,233	3,291
Groveland	1,747	1,028
Gulfport	9,730	3,702
Haines City	9,135	5,630
Hallandale	10,483	3,886
Havana	2,090	1,634
Hayden	5,471	. . .
Hialeah	66,972	19,676
High Springs	2,329	2,088
Holly Hill	4,182	3,232
Hollywood	35,237	14,351
Homestead	9,152	4,573
Immokalee	3,224	. . .
Indialantic	1,653	. . .
Indian Rocks Beach	1,940	. . .
Inverness	1,878	1,471
Jacksonville	201,030	204,517
Jacksonville Beach	12,049	6,430
Jasper	2,103	2,327
Kenneth City	2,114	. . .
Kensington Park	2,969	. . .
Key West	33,956	26,433
Kissimmee	6,845	4,310
Lacoochee	1,523	1,792
Lake Alfred	2,191	1,270
Lake City	9,465	7,571
Lake Holloway	3,172	. . .
Lakeland	41,350	30,851
Lake Park	3,589	489
Lake Wales	8,346	6,821
Lake Worth	20,758	11,777
Lantana	5,021	773
Largo	5,302	1,547
Leesburg	11,172	7,395
Leisure City	3,001	. . .
Lighthouse Point	2,453	. . .
Live Oak	6,544	4,064
Longwood	1,689	717
Lynn Haven	3,078	1,787
Macclenny	2,671	1,177
Madeira Beach	3,943	916
Madison	3,239	3,150
Maitland	3,570	889
Margate	2,646	. . .
Marianna	7,152	5,845
FLA.—Cont.:		
Melbourne	11,982	4,223
Memphis	2,647	. . .
Merritt Island	3,554	. . .
Miami	291,688	249,276
Miami Beach	63,145	46,282
Miami Shores	8,865	5,086
Miami Springs	11,229	5,108
Midway–Canaan	1,897	1,830
Milton	4,108	2,040
Miramar	5,485	. . .
Monticello	2,490	2,264
Mount Dora	3,756	3,028
Mulberry	2,922	2,024
Nokomis Laurel	2,253	. . .
Naples	4,655	1,465
Naranja	2,509	. . .
Neptune Beach	2,868	1,767
New Port Richey	3,520	1,512
New Smyrna Beach	8,781	5,775
Niceville	4,517	2,497
North Bay	2,006	198
North Miami	28,708	10,734
North Miami Beach	21,405	2,129
North Palm Beach	2,684	. . .
North Peninsula	3,476	. . .
Oakland Park	5,331	1,295
Ocala	13,598	11,741
Ocoee	2,628	1,370
Okeechobee	2,947	1,849
Oneco	1,530	. . .
Opalocka	9,810	5,271
Orange City	1,598	797
Orange Park	2,624	1,502
Orlando	88,135	52,367
Ormond Beach‡	8,658	3,418
Oviedo	1,926	1,601
Pahokee	4,709	4,472
Palatka	11,028	9,176
Palm Bay	2,808	. . .
Palm Beach	6,055	3,886
Palmetto	5,556	4,103
Palm Springs	2,503	. . .
Panama City	33,275	25,814
Parker	2,669	. . .
Pensacola	56,752	43,479
Perrine	6,424	2,859
Perry	8,030	2,797
Pinellas Park	10,848	2,924
Plantation	4,772	. . .
Plant City	15,711	9,230
Pompano Beach	15,992	5,682
Port Charlotte	3,197	. . .
Port Orange	1,801	1,201
Port Richey	1,931	376
Port St. Joe	4,217	2,752
Port Tampa	1,764	1,497
Princeton	1,719	. . .
Punta Gorda	3,157	1,915
Quincy	8,874	6,505
Richmond Heights	4,311	. . .
Riviera Beach	13,046	4,065
Rockledge	3,481	1,347
Rosedale	4,085	. . .
Ruskin	1,894	. . .
Safety Harbor	1,787	894
St. Augustine	14,734	13,555
St. Cloud	4,353	3,001
St. Petersburg	181,298	96,738
St. Petersburg Beach	6,268	722
Samoset	4,824	1,617
Sanford	19,175	11,935
Sarasota	34,083	18,896
Sebring	6,939	5,006
South Apopka	2,484	. . .
South Bay	1,631	1,050
South Daytona	1,954	692
South Miami	9,846	4,809
South Peninsula	3,741	. . .
Springfield	4,628	1,084
Starke	4,806	2,944
Stuart	4,791	2,912
Sunnyland	4,761	. . .
Surfside	3,157	1,852
Tallahassee (c.)	48,174	27,237
Tampa	274,970	124,681
Tarpon Springs	6,768	4,323
Tavares	2,724	1,763
Temple Terrace	3,812	433
Tice	4,377	1,133
Titusville	6,410	2,604
Trailer Estates	1,562	. . .
Treasure Island	3,506	75
Umatilla	1,717	1,312
Valparaiso	5,975	1,047
Venice	3,444	727
Vero Beach	8,849	4,746
Virginia Gardens	2,159	235

‡Ormond in 1950.

Place	1960	1950
FLA.—Cont.:		
Wahneta	1,796	...
Warrington	16,752	13,570
Watertown	2,109	1,473
Wauchula	3,411	2,872
West End	3,124	1,662
West Melbourne	2,266	...
West Miami	5,296	4,043
West Palm Beach	56,208	43,162
West Winter Haven	5,050	2,326
Westwood Lakes	22,517	...
Wildwood	2,170	2,019
Williston	1,582	1,323
Wilton Manor	8,257	883
Winston	3,323	1,870
Winter Garden	5,513	3,503
Winter Haven	16,277	8,605
Winter Park	17,162	8,250
Zephyrhills	2,887	1,826
GEORGIA:		
Acworth	2,359	1,466
Adel	4,321	2,776
Albany	55,890	31,155
Alma	3,515	2,588
Alto Park	2,526	1,195
Americus	13,472	11,389
Ashburn	3,291	2,918
Athens	31,355	28,180
Atlanta (c.)	487,455	331,314
Augusta	70,626	71,508
Austell	1,867	1,413
Avondale Estates	1,646	1,070
Bainbridge	12,714	7,562
Barnesville	4,919	4,185
Baxley	4,268	3,409
Blackshear	2,482	2,271
Blakely	3,580	3,234
Bloomfield Gardens	4,381	...
Bowdon	1,548	1,155
Bremen	3,132	2,299
Brunswick	21,703	17,954
Buena Vista	1,574	1,428
Buford	4,168	3,812
Cairo	7,427	5,577
Calhoun	3,587	3,231
Camilla	4,753	3,745
Canton	2,411	2,716
Carrollton	10,973	7,753
Cartersville	8,668	7,270
Cedartown	9,340	9,470
Celanese	1,500	1,945
Chamblee	6,635	3,445
Chickamauga	1,824	1,747
Clarkston	1,524	1,165
Claxton	2,672	1,923
Clayton	1,507	1,302
Cochran	4,714	3,357
College Park	23,469	14,535
Colquitt	1,556	1,664
Columbus	116,779	79,611
Commerce	3,551	3,351
Conyers	2,881	2,003
Cordele	10,609	9,462
Cornelia	2,936	2,424
Covington	8,167	5,192
Cumming	1,561	1,264
Cuthbert	4,300	4,025
Dahlonega	2,604	2,152
Dallas	2,065	1,817
Dalton	17,868	15,968
Darien	1,569	1,380
Dawson	5,062	4,411
Decatur	22,026	21,635
Dock Junction	5,417	4,160
Donalsonville	2,621	2,569
Doraville	4,437	472
Douglas	8,736	7,428
Douglasville	4,462	3,400
Dublin	13,814	10,232
East Dublin	1,677	...
East Griffin	1,715	1,539
Eastman	5,118	3,597
East Point	35,633	21,080
East Thomaston	2,237	3,082
Eatonton	3,612	2,749
Elberton	7,107	6,772
Elizabeth	1,620	1,067
Experiment	2,497	4,265
Fairburn	2,470	1,889
Fair Oaks	7,969	3,131
Fitzgerald	8,781	8,130
Folkston	1,810	1,515
Forest Park	14,201	2,653
Forsyth	3,697	3,125
Fort Oglethorpe	2,251	692
Fort Valley	8,310	6,820
Gainesville	16,523	11,936
Gainesville Cotton Mills	2,207	1,708
Garden City	5,451	1,557
Glennville	2,791	2,327
Gordon	1,793	1,761
Greensboro	2,773	2,688
Griffin	21,735	13,982
Hapeville	10,082	8,560
Hartwell	4,599	2,964
Hawkinsville	3,967	3,342

Place	1960	1950
GA.—Cont.:		
Hazlehurst	3,699	2,687
Hebardville	2,758	1,113
Hinesville	3,174	1,217
Hogansville	3,658	3,769
Homerville	2,634	1,787
Jackson	2,545	2,053
Jefferson	1,746	2,040
Jesup	7,304	4,605
Jonesboro	3,014	1,741
Kennesaw	1,507	564
Kingsland	1,536	1,169
La Fayette	5,588	4,884
La Grange	23,632	25,025
Lakeland	2,236	1,551
Lavonia	2,088	1,766
Lawrenceville	3,804	2,932
Lincoln Park	1,840	1,575
Lindale–Silver Creek	2,800	3,234
Lithonia	1,667	1,538
Louisville	2,413	2,231
Ludowici	1,578	1,332
Lyons	3,219	2,799
McCaysville	1,871	2,067
McDonough	2,224	1,635
McRae	2,738	1,904
Mableton	7,127	...
Macon	69,764	70,252
Madison	2,680	2,489
Manchester	4,115	4,036
Marietta	25,565	20,687
Marietta East	4,535	...
Metter	2,362	2,091
Midway–Hardwick	16,909	14,774
Milledgeville	11,117	8,835
Millen	3,633	3,449
Monroe	6,826	4,542
Montezuma	3,744	2,921
Monticello	1,931	1,918
Moultrie	15,764	11,639
Nashville	4,070	3,414
Newnan	12,169	8,218
Norcross	1,605	1,340
North Atlanta	12,661	5,930
North Canton	1,996	1,913
Ocilla	3,217	2,697
Pearson	1,615	1,402
Pelham	4,609	4,365
Perry	6,032	3,849
Phillipsburg	2,037	...
Porterdale	2,365	3,207
Port Wentworth	3,705	...
Quitman	5,071	4,769
Rockmart	3,938	3,821
Rome	32,226	29,615
Rossville	4,665	3,892
Roswell	2,983	2,123
Royston	2,333	2,039
St. Marys	3,272	1,348
St. Simons	3,199	...
Sandersville	5,425	4,480
Savannah	149,245	119,638
Shannon	1,629	1,676
Smyrna	10,157	2,005
Social Circle	1,780	1,685
Soperton	2,317	1,667
Sparta	1,921	1,954
Statesboro	8,356	6,097
Stone Mountain	1,976	1,899
Summerville	4,706	3,973
Swainsboro	5,943	4,300
Sylvania	3,469	2,939
Sylvester	3,610	2,623
Tallapoosa	2,744	2,826
Tennille	1,837	1,713
Thomaston	9,336	6,580
Thomasville	18,246	14,424
Thomson	4,522	3,489
Thunderbolt	1,925	1,238
Tifton	9,903	6,831
Toccoa	7,303	6,781
Trion	2,227	3,028
Union City	2,118	1,490
Union Point	1,615	1,724
Unionville	1,607	...
Valdosta	30,652	20,046
Vidalia	7,569	5,819
Vienna	2,099	2,202
Villa Rica	3,450	1,703
Wadley	1,898	1,624
Warner Robins	18,633	7,986
Warrenton	1,770	1,442
Washington	4,440	3,802
Waycross	20,944	18,899
Waynesboro	5,359	4,461
West Point	4,610	4,076
Winder	5,555	4,604
Wrens	1,628	1,380
Wrightsville	2,056	1,750
HAWAII:		
Aiea	11,826	3,714
Captain Cook	1,687	316
Ewa	3,257	3,429
Ewa Beach	2,459	...
Haleiwa	2,504	2,142
Hilo	25,966	27,198
Honolulu (c.)	294,194	248,034
Kahului	4,223	6,306
Kailua-Lanikai	25,622	7,740
Kaneohe	14,414	3,208

Place	1960	1950
HAWAII—Cont.:		
Kapaa	3,439	3,177
Kekaha	2,082	1,989
Lahaina	3,423	4,025
Laie	1,767	841
Lanai City	2,056	2,746
Lihue	3,908	3,870
Lualualei-Maili	5,045	1,528
Nanakuli	2,745	2,002
Paia	2,149	3,195
Papaikou	1,591	1,427
Puunene	3,054	...
Wahiawa	15,512	8,369
Waialua	2,689	2,602
Waianae-Makaha	6,844	1,000
Wailuku	6,969	7,424
Waimanalo	3,011	868
Whitmore	1,820	...
IDAHO:		
Alameda	10,660	4,694
American Falls	2,123	1,874
Ammon	1,882	447
Arco	1,562	961
Blackfoot	7,378	5,180
Boise City (c.)	34,481	34,393
Bonners Ferry	1,921	1,776
Buhl	3,059	2,870
Burley	7,508	5,924
Caldwell	12,230	10,487
Chubbuck	1,590	120
Coeur d'Alene	14,291	12,198
Collister	5,436	...
Emmett	3,769	3,067
Franklin	7,222	...
Garden City	1,681	764
Gooding	2,750	3,099
Grangeville	3,642	2,544
Idaho Falls	33,161	19,218
Jerome	4,761	4,523
Kellogg	5,061	4,913
Lewiston	12,691	12,985
Lewiston Orchards	9,680	...
Malad City	2,274	2,715
Meridian	2,081	1,810
Montpelier	3,146	2,682
Moscow	11,183	10,593
Mountain Home	5,984	1,887
Mountain View	4,898	3,084
Nampa	18,013	16,185
Orofino	2,471	1,656
Osburn	1,788	...
Payette	4,451	4,032
Pocatello	28,534	26,131
Post Falls	1,983	1,069
Preston	3,640	4,045
Priest River	1,749	1,592
Rexburg	4,767	4,253
Rigby	2,281	1,826
Rupert	4,153	3,098
St. Anthony	2,700	2,695
St. Maries	2,435	2,220
Salmon	2,944	2,648
Sandpoint	4,355	4,265
Shelley	2,612	1,856
Soda Springs	2,424	1,329
Twin Falls	20,126	17,600
Wallace	2,412	3,140
Weiser	4,208	3,961
Whitney	13,603	...
ILLINOIS:		
Abingdon	3,469	3,300
Addison	6,741	813
Albion	2,025	2,287
Aledo	3,080	2,919
Algonquin	2,014	1,223
Alorton	3,282	2,547
Alsip	3,770	1,228
Altamont	1,656	1,580
Alton	43,047	32,550
Alton North	1,505	...
Amboy	2,067	2,128
Anna	4,280	4,380
Antioch	2,268	1,307
Arcola	2,273	1,700
Arlington Heights	27,878	8,768
Arthur	2,120	1,573
Atlanta	1,568	1,331
Auburn	2,209	1,963
Aurora	63,715	50,576
Barrington	5,434	4,209
Barrington Hills	1,726	...
Bartlett	1,540	716
Bartonville	7,253	2,437
Batavia	7,496	5,838
Beardstown	6,294	6,080
Beckmeyer	1,056	1,045
Belleville	37,264	32,721
Bellevue	1,561	1,529
Bellwood	20,729	8,746
Belvidere	11,223	9,422
Bement	1,558	1,459
Benld	1,848	2,093
Bensenville	9,141	3,754
Benton	7,023	7,848
Berkeley	5,792	1,882
Berwyn	54,224	51,280

Place	1960	1950
ILL.—Cont.:		
Bethalto	3,235	2,115
Bloomington	36,271	34,163
Blue Island	19,618	17,622
Bourbonnais	3,336	1,598
Bradley	8,082	5,699
Braidwood	1,944	1,485
Breese	2,461	2,181
Bridgeport	2,260	2,358
Bridge View	7,334	1,393
Broadview	8,588	5,196
Brookfield	20,429	15,472
Brooklyn	1,922	2,568
Bunker Hill	1,524	1,238
Burnham	2,478	1,331
Bushnell	3,710	3,317
Byron	1,578	1,237
Cahokia	15,829	794
Cairo	9,348	12,123
Calumet City	25,000	15,799
Calumet Park	8,448	2,500
Cambridge	1,665	1,489
Canton	13,588	11,927
Carbondale	14,670	10,921
Carlinville	5,440	5,116
Carlyle	2,903	2,669
Carmi	6,152	5,574
Carpentersville	17,424	1,523
Carrier Mills	2,006	2,252
Carollton	2,558	2,437
Carterville	2,643	2,716
Carthage	3,325	3,214
Cary	2,530	943
Casey	2,890	2,734
Caseyville	2,455	1,209
Centralia	13,904	13,863
Central Park	2,676	2,489
Centreville	12,769	...
Champaign	49,583	39,563
Channel Lake	1,969	...
Charleston	10,505	9,164
Chenoa	1,523	1,452
Chester	4,460	5,389
Chicago	3,550,404	3,620,962
Chicago Heights	34,331	24,551
Chicago Ridge	5,748	888
Chillicothe	3,054	2,767
Christopher	2,854	3,545
Cicero	69,130	67,544
Clarendon Hills	5,885	2,437
Clinton	7,355	5,945
Coal City	2,852	2,220
Collinsville	14,217	11,862
Columbia	3,174	2,179
Cottage Hills	3,976	3,357
Country Club Hills	3,421	...
Crest Hill	5,887	...
Crete	3,463	2,298
Creve Coeur	6,684	5,499
Crystal Lake	8,314	4,832
Danville	41,856	37,864
Decatur	78,004	66,269
Deerfield	11,786	3,288
De Kalb	18,486	11,708
Depue	1,920	2,163
Des Plaines	34,886	14,994
Dewey Park	1,747	1,589
Dixmoor	3,076	1,327
Dixon	19,565	11,523
Dolton	18,746	5,558
Downers Grove	21,154	11,886
Dupo	2,937	2,239
Du Quoin	6,558	7,147
Dwight	3,086	2,843
East Alton	7,630	7,290
East Chicago Heights	3,270	1,548
East Dubuque	2,082	1,697
East Dundee	2,221	1,466
East Moline	16,732	13,913
East Peoria	12,310	8,698
East St. Louis	81,712	82,295
East Streator	1,517	...
Edwardsville	9,996	8,776
Effingham	8,172	6,892
Eldorado	3,573	4,500
Elgin	49,447	44,223
Elk Grove Village	6,608	...
Elmhurst	36,991	21,273
Elmwood	1,882	1,613
Elmwood Park	23,866	18,801
El Paso	1,964	1,818
Eureka	2,538	2,367
Evanston	79,283	73,641
Evergreen Park	24,178	10,531
Fairbury	2,937	2,433
Fairfield	6,362	5,576
Fairmont City	2,688	2,284
Farmer City	1,838	1,752
Farmington	2,831	2,651
Flora	5,331	5,255
Flossmoor	4,624	1,804
Forest Homes	2,025	...
Forest Park	14,452	14,969
Fox Lake	3,700	2,238
Fox River Grove	1,866	1,313
Franklin Park	18,322	8,899
Freeburg	1,908	1,661
Freeport	26,628	22,467

Place	1960	1950
ILL.—Cont.:		
Fulton	3,387	2,706
Gages Lake	3,395	...
Galena	4,410	4,648
Galesburg	37,243	31,425
Galva	3,060	2,886
Geneseo	5,169	4,325
Geneva	7,646	5,139
Genoa	2,330	1,690
Georgetown	3,544	3,294
Gibson City	3,453	3,029
Gillespie	3,569	4,105
Gilman	1,704	1,602
Girard	1,734	1,740
Glencoe	10,472	6,980
Glen Ellyn	15,972	9,524
Glenview	18,132	6,142
Grandview	2,214	1,349
Granite City	40,073	29,465
Grays Lake	3,762	1,970
Grayville	2,280	2,461
Green Rock	2,677	...
Greenville	4,569	4,069
Gurnee	1,831	1,097
Hamilton	2,228	1,776
Harrisburg	9,171	10,999
Hartford	2,355	1,909
Harvard	4,248	3,464
Harvey	29,071	20,683
Harwood Heights	5,688	655
Havana	4,363	4,379
Hazel Crest	6,205	2,129
Hegeler	1,640	...
Henry	2,278	1,966
Herrin	9,474	9,331
Hickory Hills	2,707	...
Highland	4,943	4,283
Highland Park	25,532	16,808
Highwood	4,499	3,813
Hillsboro	4,232	4,141
Hillside	7,794	2,131
Hinsdale	12,859	8,676
Hoffman Estates	8,296	...
Hometown	7,479	...
Homewood	13,371	5,887
Hoopeston	6,606	5,992
Island Lake	1,639	...
Itasca	3,564	1,274
Jacksonville	21,690	20,387
Jerome	1,666	689
Jerseyville	7,420	5,792
Johnston City	3,891	4,479
Joliet	66,780	51,601
Jonesboro	1,636	1,607
Justice	2,803	854
Kankakee	27,666	25,856
Kenilworth	2,959	2,789
Kewanee	16,324	16,821
Kincaid	1,544	1,793
Knoxville	2,560	2,209
Lacon	2,175	2,020
La Grange	15,285	12,002
La Grange Park	13,793	6,176
Lake Bluff	3,494	2,000
Lake Forest	10,687	7,819
Lake in the Hills	2,046	...
Lake Zurich	3,458	850
Lansing	18,098	8,682
La Salle	11,897	12,083
Lawrenceville	5,492	6,328
Lebanon	2,863	2,417
Leland Grove	1,731	...
Lemont	3,397	2,757
Lena	1,552	1,227
Leroy	2,088	1,820
Lewistown	2,603	2,630
Libertyville	8,560	5,425
Lincoln	16,890	14,362
Lincolnwood	11,744	3,072
Lisle	4,219	...
Litchfield	7,330	7,208
Lockport	7,560	4,955
Lombard	22,561	9,817
Long Lake	3,502	2,637
Loves Park	9,086	5,366
Lyons	9,936	6,120
McHenry	3,336	2,080
McLeansboro	2,951	3,008
Macomb	12,135	10,592
Madison	6,861	7,963
Manteno	2,225	1,789
Marengo	3,568	2,726
Marion	11,274	10,459
Marissa	1,722	1,652
Markham	11,704	2,753
Marquette Heights	2,517	...
Marseilles	4,347	4,514
Marshall	3,270	2,960
Mascoutah	3,625	3,009
Mason City	2,160	2,004
Matteson	3,225	1,211
Mattoon	19,088	17,547
Maywood	27,330	27,473
Melrose Park	22,291	13,366
Mendota	6,154	5,129
Merrionette Park	2,354	1,101
Metamora	1,808	1,368
Metropolis	7,339	6,093
Midlothian	6,605	3,216
Milan	3,065	1,737

Place	1960	1950
ILL.—Cont.:		
Milford	1,699	1,648
Millstadt	1,830	1,566
Minonk	2,001	1,955
Moline	42,705	37,397
Momence	2,949	2,644
Monmouth	10,372	10,193
Montgomery	2,122	773
Monticello	3,219	2,612
Morris	7,935	6,926
Morrison	4,159	3,531
Morton	5,325	3,693
Morton Grove	20,533	3,926
Mound City	1,669	2,167
Mounds	1,835	2,001
Mount Carmel	8,594	8,732
Mount Carroll	2,056	1,950
Mount Morris	3,075	2,709
Mount Olive	2,295	2,401
Mount Prospect	18,906	4,009
Mount Pulaski	1,689	1,526
Mount Sterling	2,262	2,246
Mount Vernon	15,566	15,600
Moweaqua	1,614	1,475
Mundelein	10,526	3,189
Murphysboro	8,673	9,241
Naperville	12,933	7,013
Nashville	2,606	2,432
New Athens	1,923	1,518
New Lenox	1,750	1,235
Newton	2,901	2,780
Niles	20,393	3,587
Nokomis	2,476	2,544
Normal	13,357	9,772
Norridge	14,087	3,428
North Aurora	2,088	921
Northbrook	11,635	3,348
North Chicago	22,938	8,628
North Chillicothe	2,259	1,741
Northfield	4,005	1,426
North Lake	12,318	4,361
North Pekin	2,025	1,758
North Quincy	2,256	2,985
North Riverside	7,989	3,230
Oak Forest	3,724	1,856
Oak Lawn	27,471	8,751
Oak Park	61,093	63,529
Oblong	1,817	1,639
O'Fallon	4,018	3,022
Oglesby	4,215	3,922
Olney	8,780	8,612
Olympia Fields	1,503	160
Oregon	3,732	3,205
Orland Park	2,592	788
Oswego	1,510	1,220
Ottawa	19,408	16,957
Palatine	11,504	4,079
Palestine	1,564	1,589
Palos Heights	3,775	...
Palos Hills	3,766	...
Palos Park	2,169	854
Pana	6,432	6,178
Paris	9,823	9,460
Park Forest	29,993	8,138
Park Ridge	32,659	16,602
Pawnee	1,517	974
Paxton	4,370	3,795
Pecatonica	1,659	1,438
Pekin	28,146	21,858
Peoria	103,162	111,856
Peoria Heights	7,064	5,425
Peotone	1,788	1,395
Peru	10,460	8,653
Petersburg	2,359	2,325
Phoenix	4,203	3,606
Pinckneyville	3,085	3,299
Pittsfield	4,089	3,564
Plainfield	2,183	1,764
Plano	3,343	2,154
Polo	2,551	2,242
Pontiac	8,435	7,562
Posen	4,517	1,795
Princeton	6,250	5,765
Prophetstown	1,802	1,691
Quincy	43,793	41,450
Rantoul	22,116	6,387
Red Bud	1,942	1,519
Riverdale	12,008	5,840
River Forest	12,695	10,823
River Grove	8,464	4,839
Riverside	9,750	9,153
Riverton	1,591	1,450
Roanoke	1,821	1,368
Robbins	7,511	4,766
Robinson	7,226	6,407
Rochelle	7,008	5,449
Rock Falls	10,261	7,983
Rockford	126,706	92,927
Rock Island	51,863	48,710
Rockton	1,833	1,432
Rolling Meadows	10,879	...
Romeoville	3,574	147
Roodhouse	2,352	2,368
Roselle	3,581	1,038
Rosewood Heights	4,572	1,836
Rosiclare	1,700	2,086
Round Lake Beach	5,011	1,892

Place	1960	1950
ILL.—Cont.:		
Round Lake Park	2,565	1,836
Roxana	2,090	1,911
Rushville	2,819	2,682
St. Charles	9,269	6,709
St. Elmo	1,503	1,716
Salem	6,165	6,159
Sandwich	3,842	3,027
Sauk	4,687	...
Savanna	4,950	5,058
Schiller Park	5,687	1,384
Seneca‡	1,719	1,435
Sesser	1,764	2,086
Shelbyville	4,821	4,462
Silvis	3,973	3,055
Skokie	59,364	14,832
South Beloit	3,781	3,221
South Chicago Heights	4,043	2,129
South Elgin	2,624	1,220
South Holland	10,412	3,247
South Jacksonville	2,340	1,165
South Roxana	2,010	...
South Streator	1,923	1,508
Sparta	3,452	3,576
Springfield (c.)	83,271	81,628
Spring Valley	5,371	4,916
Staunton	4,228	4,047
Steelville	1,569	1,353
Steger	6,432	4,358
Sterling	15,688	12,817
Stickney	6,239	3,317
Stockton	1,800	1,445
Stone Park	3,038	1,414
Streamwood	4,821	...
Streator	16,868	16,469
Sullivan	3,946	3,470
Summit	10,374	8,957
Swansea	3,018	1,816
Sycamore	6,961	5,912
Taylorville	8,801	9,188
Thornton	2,895	1,217
Tilton	2,598	1,638
Tinley Park	6,392	2,326
Tolono	1,539	1,065
Tremont	1,558	1,138
Trenton	1,866	1,432
Troy	1,778	1,260
Tuscola	3,875	2,960
Urbana	27,294	22,834
Valley View	1,741	...
Vandalia	5,537	5,471
Venetian Village	2,084	...
Venice	5,380	6,226
Vermilion Heights	1,568	...
Villa Grove	2,308	2,026
Villa Park	20,391	8,821
Virden	3,309	3,206
Virginia	1,669	1,572
Warrenville	3,134	1,891
Warsaw	1,938	2,002
Washington	5,919	4,285
Washington Park	6,601	5,840
Waterloo	3,739	2,821
Watseka	5,219	4,235
Wauconda	3,227	1,173
Waukegan	55,719	38,946
Westchester	18,092	4,308
West Chicago	6,854	3,973
West Dundee	2,530	1,948
Western Springs	10,838	6,364
West Frankfort	9,027	11,384
West Kankakee	3,197	2,784
Westmont	5,997	3,402
Westville	3,497	3,196
Wheaton	24,312	11,638
Wheeling	7,169	916
White Hall	3,012	3,082
Willow Springs	2,348	1,314
Wilmette	28,268	18,162
Wilmington	4,210	3,354
Winchester	1,657	1,591
Winfield	1,575	714
Winnetka	13,368	12,105
Winthrop Harbor	3,848	1,765
Wonder Lake	3,543	1,072
Wood Dale	3,071	1,857
Wood River	11,694	10,190
Woodstock	8,897	7,192
Worth	8,196	1,472
Wyoming	1,559	1,496
Yorkville	1,568	632
Zeigler	2,133	2,516
Zion	11,941	8,950
INDIANA:		
Albany	2,132	1,846
Alexandria	5,582	5,147
Anderson	49,061	46,820
Anderson East Side	3,778	...
Angola	4,746	5,081
Attica	4,341	3,862
Auburn	6,350	5,879
Aurora	4,119	4,780
Austin	3,838	2,906
Batesville	3,349	3,194

Place	1960	1950
IND.—Cont.:		
Bedford	13,024	12,562
Beech Grove	10,973	5,685
Berne	2,644	2,277
Bicknell	3,878	4,572
Bloomfield	2,224	2,086
Bloomington	31,357	28,163
Bluffton	6,238	6,076
Boonville	4,801	5,092
Bourbon	1,522	1,404
Brazil	8,853	8,434
Bremen	3,062	2,664
Broadview	1,865	1,630
Brookville	2,596	2,538
Brownsburg	4,478	1,578
Brownstown	2,158	1,998
Butler	2,176	1,914
Cambridge City	2,569	2,559
Cannelton	1,829	2,027
Cedar Lake	5,766	3,907
Centerville	2,378	1,386
Chandler	1,784	...
Charlestown	5,726	4,785
Chesterfield	2,588	1,086
Chesterton	4,335	3,175
Clarksville	8,088	5,905
Clinton	5,843	6,462
Columbia City	4,803	4,745
Columbus	20,778	18,370
Connersville	17,698	15,550
Corydon	2,701	1,944
Covington	2,759	2,235
Crawfordsville	14,231	12,851
Crestlawn	2,194	...
Crown Point	8,443	5,839
Culver	1,558	1,563
Daleville	1,548	...
Danville	3,287	2,802
Decatur	8,327	7,271
Delphi	2,517	2,530
Dunkirk	3,117	3,048
Dunlap	1,935	1,154
Dyer	3,993	1,556
East Chicago	57,669	54,263
East Columbus	1,912	...
East Gary	9,309	5,635
Eaton	1,529	1,598
Edgewood	2,119	796
Edinburg	3,664	3,283
Elkhart	40,274	35,646
Elwood	11,793	11,362
Evansville	141,543	128,636
Fairmont	3,080	2,646
Flora	1,742	1,657
Fort Branch	1,983	1,944
Fortville	2,209	1,786
Fort Wayne	161,776	133,607
Fowler	2,491	2,117
Frankfort	15,302	15,028
Franklin	9,453	7,316
French Lick	1,954	1,946
Garrett	4,364	4,291
Gary	178,320	133,911
Gas City	4,469	3,787
Goshen	13,718	13,003
Greencastle	8,506	6,888
Greendale	2,861	2,018
Greenfield	9,049	6,159
Greensburg	6,605	6,619
Greenwood	7,169	3,066
Griffith	9,483	4,470
Hagerstown	1,730	1,694
Hammond	111,698	87,594
Harrison Village	3,878	1,943
Hartford City	8,053	7,253
Highland	16,284	5,878
Hobart	18,680	10,244
Home Corner	2,636	3,950
Huntingburg	4,146	4,056
Huntington	16,185	15,079
Independence Hill	1,824	...
Indianapolis (c.)	476,258	427,173
Jasonville	2,436	2,937
Jasper	6,737	5,215
Jeffersonville	19,522	14,685
Jonesboro	2,260	1,973
Kendallville	6,765	6,119
Kentland	1,783	1,633
Knightstown	2,496	2,486
Knox	3,458	3,034
Kokomo	47,197	38,672
Lafayette	42,330	35,568
Lagrange	1,990	1,892
Lapel	1,772	1,389
La Porte	21,157	17,882
Lawrence	10,103	1,951
Lawrenceburg	5,004	4,806
Lebanon	9,523	7,631
Liberty	1,745	1,730
Ligonier	2,595	2,375
Linton	5,736	5,973
Logansport	21,106	21,031
Long Beach	2,007	1,103
Loogootee	2,858	2,424
Lowell	2,270	1,621
Madison	10,488	7,506
Marion	37,854	30,081
Martinsville	7,525	5,991
Meridian Hills	1,807	708
Michigan City	36,653	28,395

‡Crotty in 1950.

Place	1960	1950
IND.—Cont.:		
Middletown	2,033	1,731
Mishawaka	33,361	32,913
Mitchell	3,552	3,245
Monticello	4,035	3,467
Montpelier	1,954	1,826
Mooresville	3,856	2,264
Mount Vernon	5,970	6,150
Muncie	68,603	58,479
Munster	10,313	4,753
Nappanee	3,895	3,393
New Albany	37,812	29,346
New Castle	20,349	18,271
New Chicago	2,312	921
New Haven	3,396	2,336
New White-land	3,488	...
Noblesville	7,664	6,567
North Judson	1,942	1,705
North Manchester	4,377	3,977
North Vernon	4,062	3,488
Oakland City	3,016	3,539
Orleans	1,659	1,531
Paoli	2,754	2,575
Pendleton	2,472	2,082
Peru	14,453	13,308
Petersburg	2,939	3,035
Plainfield	5,460	2,585
Plymouth	7,558	6,704
Portage	11,822	...
Porter	2,189	1,458
Portland	6,999	7,064
Princeton	7,906	7,673
Redkey	1,746	1,639
Rensselaer	4,740	4,072
Richmond	44,149	39,539
Rising Sun	2,230	1,930
Rochester	4,883	4,673
Rockport	2,474	2,493
Rockville	2,756	2,467
Rushville	7,264	6,761
Salem	4,546	3,271
Schererville	2,875	1,457
Scottsburg	3,810	2,953
Sellersburg	2,679	1,664
Seymour	11,629	9,629
Shelbyville	14,317	11,734
Sheridan	2,165	1,965
South Bend	132,445	115,911
Speedway	9,624	5,498
Spencer	2,557	2,394
Sullivan	4,979	5,423
Syracuse	1,595	1,453
Tell City	6,609	5,735
Terre Haute	72,500	64,214
Tipton	5,604	5,633
Trail Creek	1,552	817
Union City	4,047	3,572
Union City Village	1,657	1,622
Upland	1,999	1,565
Valparaiso	15,227	12,028
Veedersburg	1,762	1,719
Vevay	1,503	1,309
Vincennes	18,046	18,831
Wabash	12,621	10,621
Walkerton	2,044	2,102
Warsaw	7,234	6,625
Washington	10,846	10,987
West Lafayette	12,680	11,873
West Terre Haute	3,006	3,357
Whiting	8,137	9,669
Winamac	2,375	2,166
Winchester	5,742	5,467
Winona Lake	1,928	1,366
Woodruff Place	1,501	1,557
Worthington	1,635	1,627
Zionsville	1,822	1,536
IOWA:		
Ackley	1,731	1,608
Adel	2,060	1,799
Albia	4,582	4,838
Algona	5,702	5,415
Ames	27,003	22,898
Anamosa	4,616	3,910
Ankeny	2,964	1,229
Atlantic	6,890	6,480
Audubon	2,928	2,808
Avoca	1,540	1,595
Bedford	1,807	2,000
Belle Plaine	2,923	3,056
Bellevue	2,181	1,932
Belmond	2,506	2,169
Bettendorf	11,534	5,132
Bloomfield	2,771	2,688
Boone	12,468	12,164
Britt	2,042	1,908
Burlington	32,430	30,613
Camanche	2,225	1,212
Carroll	7,682	6,231
Carter Lake	2,287	1,183
Cascade	1,601	1,299
Cedar Falls	21,195	14,334
Cedar Rapids	92,035	72,296
Centerville	6,629	7,625
Chariton	5,042	5,320
Charles City	9,964	10,309
Cherokee	7,724	7,705
Clarinda	5,901	5,086
Clarion	3,232	3,150
Clear Lake	6,158	4,977

Place	1960	1950
IOWA—Cont.:		
Clinton	33,589	30,379
Colfax	2,331	2,279
Coon Rapids	1,560	1,676
Coralville	2,357	977
Corning	2,041	2,104
Corydon	1,687	1,870
Council Bluffs	55,641	45,429
Cresco	3,809	3,638
Creston	7,667	8,317
Davenport	88,981	74,549
Decorah	6,435	6,060
Denison	4,930	4,554
Des Moines (c.)	208,982	177,965
De Witt	3,224	2,644
Dubuque	56,606	49,671
Dyersville	2,818	2,416
Eagle Grove	4,381	4,176
Eldora	3,225	3,107
Elkader	1,526	1,584
Emmetsburg	3,887	3,760
Estherville	7,927	6,719
Evansdale	5,738	3,571
Fairfield	8,054	7,299
Fayette	1,597	1,469
Forest City	2,930	2,766
Fort Dodge	28,399	25,115
Fort Madison	15,247	14,954
Garner	1,990	1,696
Glenwood	4,783	4,664
Greenfield	2,243	2,102
Grinnell	7,367	6,828
Grundy Center	2,403	2,135
Guthrie Center	2,071	2,042
Guttenberg	2,087	1,912
Hamburg	1,647	2,086
Hampton	4,501	4,432
Harlan	4,350	3,915
Hartley	1,738	1,611
Hawarden	2,544	2,625
Humboldt	4,031	3,219
Ida Grove	2,265	2,202
Independence	5,498	4,865
Indianola	7,062	5,145
Iowa City	33,443	27,212
Iowa Falls	5,565	4,900
Jefferson	4,570	4,326
Keokuk	16,316	16,144
Knoxville	7,817	7,625
Lake City	2,114	2,308
Lake Mills	1,758	1,560
Lamoni	2,173	2,196
La Porte City	1,953	1,770
Laurens	1,799	1,556
Le Claire	1,546	1,124
Le Mars	6,767	5,844
Leon	2,004	2,139
Logan	1,605	1,550
Madrid	2,286	1,829
Manchester	4,402	3,987
Manning	1,676	1,801
Manson	1,789	1,622
Mapleton	1,686	1,857
Maquoketa	5,909	4,307
Marengo	2,264	2,151
Marion	10,882	5,916
Marshalltown	22,521	19,821
Mason City	30,642	27,980
Missouri Valley	3,567	3,546
Monticello	3,190	2,888
Mount Ayr	1,738	1,793
Mount Pleasant	7,339	5,843
Mount Vernon	2,593	2,320
Muscatine	20,997	19,041
Nashua	1,737	1,609
Nevada	4,227	3,763
New Hampton	3,456	3,323
New London	1,694	1,510
Newton	15,381	11,723
Northwood	1,768	1,767
Oelwein	8,282	7,858
Ogden	1,525	1,486
Onawa	3,176	3,498
Orange City	2,707	2,166
Osage	3,753	3,436
Osceola	3,350	3,422
Oskaloosa	11,053	11,124
Ottumwa	33,871	33,631
Pella	5,198	4,427
Perry	6,442	6,174
Pocahontas	2,011	1,949
Postville	1,554	1,343
Red Oak	6,421	6,526
Reinbeck	1,621	1,460
Rock Rapids	2,780	2,640
Rock Valley	1,693	1,581
Rockwell City	2,313	2,333
Sac City	3,354	3,170
Sheldon	4,251	4,001
Shenandoah	6,567	6,938
Sibley	2,852	2,559
Sigourney	2,387	2,343
Sioux Center	2,275	1,860
Sioux City	89,159	83,991
Spencer	8,864	7,446
Spirit Lake	2,685	2,467
Storm Lake	7,728	6,954
Story City	1,773	1,545
Sumner	2,170	1,911
Tama	2,925	2,930
Tipton	2,862	2,633
Toledo	2,850	2,106
Traer	1,623	1,627
Urbandale	5,821	1,777

Place	1960	1950
IOWA—Cont.:		
Villisca	1,690	1,838
Vinton	4,781	4,307
Wapello	1,745	1,755
Washington	6,037	5,902
Waterloo	71,755	65,198
Waukon	3,639	3,158
Waverly	6,357	5,124
Webster City	8,520	7,611
West Burlington	2,560	1,614
West Des Moines	11,949	5,615
West Liberty	2,042	1,866
West Union	2,551	2,141
Wilton	1,750	1,446
Windsor Heights	4,715	1,414
Winterset	3,639	3,570
KANSAS:		
Abilene	6,746	5,775
Anthony	2,744	2,792
Arkansas City	14,262	12,903
Atchinson	12,529	12,792
Atwood	1,906	1,613
Augusta	6,434	4,483
Baldwin City	1,877	1,741
Baxter Springs	4,498	4,647
Belle Plaine	1,579	971
Belleville	2,940	2,858
Beloit	3,837	4,085
Bonner Springs	3,171	2,277
Burlington	2,113	2,304
Caldwell	1,788	2,000
Caney	2,682	2,876
Chanute	10,849	10,109
Cherryvale	2,783	2,952
Chetopa	1,538	1,671
Clay Center	4,613	4,528
Coffeyville	17,382	17,113
Colby	4,210	3,859
Columbus	3,395	3,490
Concordia	7,022	7,175
Council Grove	2,664	2,722
Derby	6,458	432
Dighton	1,526	1,246
Dodge City	13,520	11,262
El Dorado	12,523	11,037
Elkhart	1,780	1,132
Ellinwood	2,729	2,569
Ellis	2,218	2,649
Ellsworth	2,361	2,193
Emporia	18,190	15,669
Eudora	1,526	929
Eureka	4,055	3,958
Fairway	5,398	1,816
Fort Scott	9,410	10,335
Fredonia	3,233	3,257
Frontenac	1,713	1,569
Galena	3,827	4,029
Garden City	11,811	10,905
Gardner	1,619	676
Garnett	3,034	2,693
Girard	2,350	2,426
Goodland	4,459	4,690
Great Bend	16,670	12,665
Greensburg	1,988	1,723
Halstead	1,598	1,328
Harper	1,899	1,672
Hays	11,947	8,625
Haysville	5,836	...
Herington	3,702	3,775
Hiawatha	3,391	3,294
Hill City	2,421	1,432
Hillsboro	2,441	2,150
Hoisington	4,248	4,012
Holton	3,028	2,705
Horton	2,361	2,354
Hugoton	2,912	2,781
Humboldt	2,285	2,308
Hutchinson	37,574	33,575
Independence	11,222	11,335
Iola	6,885	7,094
Junction City	18,700	13,462
Kansas City	121,901	129,553
Kingman	3,582	3,200
Kinsley	2,263	2,479
Kiowa	1,674	1,561
La Crosse	1,767	1,769
Larned	5,001	4,447
Lawrence	32,858	23,351
Leavenworth	22,052	20,579
Leawood	7,466	1,167
Lenexa	2,487	803
Liberal	13,813	7,134
Lincoln Center	1,717	1,636
Lindsborg	2,609	2,383
Lyons	4,592	4,545
McPherson	9,996	8,689
Manhattan	22,993	19,056
Marion	2,169	2,050
Marysville	4,143	3,866
Meade	2,019	1,763
Medicine Lodge	3,072	2,288
Merriam	5,084	...
Minneapolis	2,024	1,801
Mission	4,626	...
Mission Hills	3,621	1,275
Mulvane	2,981	1,387
Neodesha	3,594	3,723
Ness City	1,653	1,612
Newton	14,877	11,590
Norton	3,345	3,060
Oakley	2,190	1,915

Place	1960	1950
KAN.—Cont.:		
Oberlin	2,337	2,019
Ogden	1,780	845
Olathe	10,987	5,593
Osage City	2,213	1,919
Osawatomie	4,622	4,347
Osborne	2,049	2,068
Oswego	2,027	1,997
Ottawa	10,673	10,081
Overland Park	21,110	...
Paola	4,784	3,972
Park City	2,687	...
Parsons	13,929	14,750
Phillipsburg	3,233	2,589
Pittsburg	18,678	19,341
Plainville	3,104	2,082
Prairie Village	25,356	...
Pratt	8,156	7,523
Roeland Park	8,949	...
Russell	6,113	6,483
Sabetha	2,318	2,173
St. Francis	1,594	1,892
St. John	1,753	1,735
St. Marys	1,509	1,201
Salina	43,202	26,176
Scott City	3,555	3,204
Sedan	1,677	1,640
Seneca	2,072	1,911
Shawnee	9,072	845
Smith Center	2,379	2,026
South Hutchinson	1,672	1,045
Stafford	1,862	2,005
Sterling	2,303	2,243
Stockton	2,073	1,867
Syracuse	1,888	2,075
Topeka (c.)	119,484	78,791
Ulysses	3,157	2,243
Valley Center	2,570	854
WaKeeney	2,808	2,446
Wamego	2,363	1,869
Washington	1,506	1,527
Wellington	8,809	7,747
Westwood	2,040	1,581
Wichita	254,698	168,279
Winfield	11,117	10,264
Yates Center	2,080	2,178
KENTUCKY:		
Albany	1,887	1,920
Ashland	31,283	31,131
Audubon Park	1,867	1,790
Barbourville	3,211	2,926
Bardstown	4,798	4,154
Beaver Dam	1,648	1,349
Beechwood Village	1,903	...
Bellevue	9,336	9,040
Benham	1,874	...
Benton	3,074	1,980
Berea	4,302	3,372
Bowling Green	28,338	18,347
Brandenburg	1,542	755
Burkesville	1,688	1,278
Cadiz	1,980	1,280
Calvert City	1,505	...
Campbellsville	6,966	3,477
Carlisle	1,601	1,524
Carrollton	3,218	3,226
Catlettsburg	3,874	4,750
Central City	3,694	4,110
Clinton	1,647	1,593
Columbia	2,255	2,167
Corbin	7,119	7,744
Covington	60,376	64,452
Cumberland	4,271	4,249
Cynthiana	5,641	4,847
Danville	9,010	8,686
Dawson Springs	3,002	2,374
Dayton	9,050	8,997
Earlington	2,786	2,753
East Somerset	3,645	...
Eddyville	1,858	1,840
Elizabethtown	9,641	5,807
Elsmere	4,607	3,483
Eminence	1,958	1,462
Erlanger	7,072	3,694
Falmouth	2,568	2,186
Flatwoods	3,741	...
Flemingsburg	2,067	1,502
Florence	5,837	1,325
Fort Thomas	14,896	10,870
Fort Wright	2,184	594
Frankfort (c.)	18,365	11,916
Franklin	5,319	4,343
Fulton	3,265	3,224
Georgetown	6,986	5,516
Glasgow	10,069	7,025
Grayson	1,692	1,383
Greensburg	2,334	1,032
Greenville	3,198	2,661
Harlan	4,177	4,786
Harrodsburg	6,061	5,262
Hartford	1,618	1,564
Hazard	5,958	6,985
Henderson	16,892	16,837
Hickman	1,537	2,037
Highland Heights	3,491	1,569
Hodgenville	1,985	1,695
Hopkinsville	19,465	12,526
Horse Cave	1,780	1,545
Irvine	2,955	3,259
Jackson	1,852	1,978
Jeffersontown	3,431	1,246

Place	1960	1950
KY.—Cont.:		
Jenkins	3,202	6,921
La Grange	2,168	1,558
Lakeside Park	2,214	988
Lancaster	3,021	2,402
Lawrenceburg	2,523	2,369
Lebanon	4,813	4,640
Lebanon Junction	1,527	1,243
Leitchfield	2,982	1,312
Lexington	62,810	55,534
Liberty	1,578	1,291
Livermore	1,506	1,441
London	4,035	3,426
Lone Oak	2,104	...
Louisa	2,071	2,015
Louisville	390,639	369,129
Ludlow	6,233	6,374
Lynch	3,810	...
Lynnview	1,711	...
Madisonville	13,110	11,132
Manchester	1,868	1,706
Marion	2,468	2,375
Mayfield	10,762	8,990
Maysville	8,484	8,632
Middlesborough	12,607	14,482
Middletown	2,764	...
Monticello	2,940	2,934
Morehead	4,170	3,102
Morganfield	3,741	3,257
Mount Sterling	5,370	5,294
Muldraugh	1,743	...
Murray	9,303	6,035
Newport	30,070	31,044
Nicholasville	4,275	3,406
Owensboro	42,471	33,651
Owensboro East	2,244	...
Paducah	34,479	32,828
Paintsville	4,025	4,309
Paris	7,791	6,912
Park Hills	4,076	2,577
Pikeville	4,754	5,154
Pineville	3,181	3,890
Pleasure Ridge Park	10,612	...
Prestonsburg	3,133	3,585
Princeton	5,618	5,388
Providence	3,771	3,905
Radcliff	3,384	...
Richmond	12,168	10,268
Russellville	5,861	4,529
St. Matthews	8,738	...
Scottsville	3,324	2,060
Shelbyville	4,525	4,403
Shepherdsville	1,525	953
Shively	15,155	2,401
Somerset	7,112	7,097
South Fort Mitchell	4,086	3,142
Southgate	2,070	1,903
Springfield	2,382	2,032
Stanford	2,019	1,861
Sturgis	2,209	2,222
Tompkinsville	2,091	1,859
Valley Station	10,553	...
Vanceburg	1,881	1,528
Versailles	4,060	2,760
Vine Grove	2,435	1,252
Walton	1,530	1,358
West Point	1,957	1,669
Wheelwright	1,518	2,037
Whitesburg	1,774	1,393
Williamsburg	3,478	3,348
Williamstown	1,611	1,466
Wilmore	2,773	2,337
Winchester	10,187	9,226
Woodlawn	1,688	...
LOUISIANA:		
Abbeville	10,414	9,338
Alexandria	40,279	34,913
Alexandria Southwest	2,782	...
Amite City	3,316	2,804
Anandale	2,827	...
Arcadia	2,547	2,241
Baker	4,823	762
Baldwin	1,548	1,138
Basile	1,932	1,572
Bastrop	15,193	12,769
Baton Rouge (c.)	152,419	125,629
Bayou Cane	3,173	2,212
Bernice	1,641	1,524
Berwick	3,880	2,619
Bogalusa	21,423	17,798
Bossier City	32,776	15,470
Breaux Bridge	3,303	2,492
Broussard	1,600	1,237
Bunkie	5,188	4,666
Buras-Triumph	4,908	1,799
Carencro	1,519	1,587
Church Point	3,606	2,897
Clinton	1,568	1,383
Colfax	1,934	1,651
Cottonport	1,581	1,534
Coushatta	1,663	1,788
Covington	6,754	5,113
Crowley	15,617	12,784
Cullen	2,194	...
Daigleville	5,906	4,809
Delcambre	1,857	1,463
Delhi	2,514	1,861

Place	1960	1950
LA.—Cont.:		
Denham Springs	5,991	2,053
De Quincy	3,928	3,837
De Ridder	7,188	5,799
Donaldsonville	6,082	4,150
Elton	1,595	1,434
Erath	2,019	1,514
Eunice	11,326	8,184
Farmerville	2,727	2,173
Ferriday	4,563	3,847
Franklin	8,673	6,144
Franklinton	3,141	2,342
Garyville	2,389	1,850
Golden Meadow	3,097	...
Gonzales	3,252	1,642
Goosport	16,778	8,318
Grambling	3,144	...
Gramercy	2,094	1,184
Grand Isle	2,074	...
Gretna	21,967	13,813
Gueydan	2,156	2,041
Hammond	10,563	8,010
Harahan	9,275	3,394
Haynesville	3,031	3,040
Hollywood	1,750	...
Homer	4,665	4,749
Houma	22,561	11,505
Independence	1,941	1,606
Iowa	1,857	...
Jackson	1,824	1,144
Jeanerette	5,568	4,692
Jefferson Heights	19,353	...
Jena	2,098	1,438
Jennings	11,887	9,663
Jonesboro	3,848	3,097
Jonesville	2,347	1,954
Kaplan	5,267	4,562
Kenner	17,037	5,535
Kentwood	2,607	2,417
Kinder	2,299	2,003
Lafayette	40,400	33,541
Lafayette Southwest	6,682	...
Lake Arthur	3,541	2,849
Lake Charles	63,392	41,272
Lake Providence	5,781	4,123
Laplace	3,541	2,352
Larose	2,796	1,286
Leesville	4,689	4,670
Lockport	2,221	1,388
Luling	2,122	...
Lutcher	3,274	2,198
Mamou	2,928	2,254
Mandeville	1,740	1,368
Mansfield	5,839	4,440
Mansura	1,579	1,439
Many	3,164	1,681
Maplewood	2,432	2,671
Marksville	4,257	3,635
Melville	1,939	1,901
Minden	12,785	9,787
Monroe	52,219	38,572
Morgan City	13,540	9,759
Natchitoches	13,924	9,914
New Iberia	29,062	16,467
New Orleans	627,525	570,445
New Roads	3,965	2,818
Norco	4,682	...
North Highlands	1,980	...
North Shreveport	7,701	...
Oakdale	6,618	5,598
Oak Grove	1,797	1,796
Oberlin	1,794	1,544
Opelousas	17,417	11,659
Patterson	2,923	1,938
Pineville	8,636	6,423
Plaquemine	7,689	5,747
Ponchatoula	4,727	4,090
Port Allen	5,026	3,097
Port Barre	1,876	1,066
Port Sulphur	2,868	...
Raceland	3,666	2,025
Rayne	8,634	6,485
Rayville	4,052	3,138
Reserve	5,297	4,465
Ruston	13,991	10,372
St. Francisville	1,661	936
St. Joseph	1,653	1,218
St. Martinville	6,468	4,614
Samtown	4,008	...
Seymourville	1,788	...
Shreveport	164,372	127,206
Simmesport	2,125	1,510
Slidell	6,356	3,464
Springhill	6,437	3,383
Sulphur	11,429	5,996
Tallulah	9,413	7,758
Thibodaux	13,403	7,730
Vidalia	4,313	1,641
Ville Platte	7,512	6,633
Vinton	2,987	2,597
Vivian	2,624	2,426
Welsh	3,332	2,416
Westlake	3,311	1,871
West Monroe	15,215	10,302
Westwego	9,815	8,328
White Castle	2,253	1,839
Winnfield	7,022	5,629
Winnsboro	4,437	3,655
Zachary	3,268	1,542

Place	1960	1950
MAINE:		
Auburn	24,449	23,134
Augusta (c.)	21,680	20,913
Bangor	38,912	31,558
Bar Harbor	2,444	2,572
Bath	10,717	10,644
Belfast	6,140	5,960
Berwick	1,557	1,326
Biddeford	19,255	20,836
Boothbay Harbor	2,252	1,810
Brewer	9,009	6,862
Bridgton	1,715	1,866
Brunswick	9,444	7,342
Bucksport	2,327	2,094
Calais	4,223	4,589
Camden	3,523	3,270
Cape Elizabeth	5,505	3,816
Caribou	8,305	4,500
Dexter	2,720	2,809
Dover-Foxcroft	2,481	2,566
East Millinocket	2,295	1,347
Eastport	2,537	3,123
Ellsworth	4,444	3,936
Fairfield	3,766	3,776
Falmouth*	5,976	4,342
Farmington	2,749	...
Fort Fairfield	3,082	2,521
Fort Kent	2,787	3,001
Freeport	1,801	1,622
Gardiner	6,897	6,649
Gorham	2,322	1,911
Greenville	1,893	1,651
Hallowell	3,169	3,404
Houlton	5,976	6,029
Kennebunk	2,804	...
Kittery	8,051	6,692
Lewiston	40,804	40,974
Limestone	1,772	...
Lincoln	3,616	2,548
Lisbon	1,542	...
Lisbon Falls	2,640	2,155
Livermore Falls	2,882	3,015
Machias	1,523	1,621
Madawaska	4,035	2,975
Madison	2,761	2,554
Mechanic Falls	1,992	1,867
Mexico	3,951	3,821
Millinocket	7,318	5,755
Milo	1,802	...
Newport	1,589	1,296
Norway	2,654	2,687
Oakland	1,880	1,605
Old Orchard Beach	4,431	4,593
Old Town	8,626	8,261
Orono	3,234	3,634
Pittsfield	3,232	3,012
Portland	72,566	77,634
Presque Isle	12,886	9,954
Randolph	1,585	1,599
Rockland	8,769	9,234
Rumford	7,233	7,888
Saco	10,515	10,324
Sanford	10,936	11,094
Scarborough*	6,418	4,600
Skowhegan	6,667	6,183
South Berwick	1,773	1,701
South Eliot	1,730	1,331
South Paris	2,063	2,067
South Portland	22,788	21,866
Springvale	2,379	2,745
Thomaston	2,342	2,398
Topsham	2,240	1,569
Van Buren	3,589	3,732
Waterville	18,695	18,287
Webster	4,747	...
Westbrook	13,820	12,284
Wilton	1,761	1,910
Winslow	3,640	2,916
Winthrop	2,260	1,885
Yarmouth	2,913	2,189
MARYLAND:		
Aberdeen	9,679	2,944
Annapolis (c.)	23,385	10,047
Arbutus-Halethrope Relay	22,402	...
Baltimore	939,024	949,708
Bel Air	4,300	2,578
Berlin	2,046	2,001
Berwyn Heights	2,376	674
Bethesda	56,527	...
Bladensburg	3,103	2,899
Brentwood	3,693	3,523
Brunswick	3,555	3,752
Cambridge	12,239	10,351
Capitol Heights	3,138	2,729
Carrollton	3,385	...
Catonsville	37,372	...
Centreville	1,863	1,804
Chestertown	3,602	3,143
Cheverly	5,223	3,318
Chevy Chase	2,405	1,971
Chevy Chase Section Four	2,243	...
Clinton	1,578	...
Cockeysville	2,582	...
College Park	18,482	11,170
Colmar Manor	1,772	1,732
Cresaptown	1,680	...

Place	1960	1950
MD.—Cont.:		
Crisfield	3,540	3,688
Cumberland	33,415	37,679
Denton	1,938	1,806
District Heights	7,524	1,735
Dundalk	82,428	...
Easton	6,337	4,836
Edgewood	1,670	...
Elkton	5,989	5,245
Essex	35,205	...
Fairmount Heights	2,308	2,097
Federalsburg	2,060	1,878
Forest Heights	3,524	1,125
Frederick	21,744	18,142
Frostburg	6,722	6,876
Gaithersburg	3,847	1,755
Glyndon-Reisterstown	4,216	2,077
Greenbelt	7,479	7,074
Hagerstown	36,660	36,260
Halfway	4,256	2,153
Hancock	2,004	963
Havre de Grace	8,510	7,809
Hillcrest Heights	15,295	...
Hyattsville	15,168	12,308
Kensington	2,175	1,611
Landover Hills	1,850	1,661
Langley Park	11,510	...
Lansdowne-Baltimore Highlands	13,134	...
Laurel	8,503	4,482
Lavale-Narrows Park	4,031	...
Lexington Park	7,039	...
Loch Raven	23,278	...
Lonaconing	2,077	2,289
Middle River	10,825	...
Morningside	1,708	1,520
Mount Rainier	9,855	10,989
Mount Savage	1,639	2,094
North East	1,628	1,517
Oakland	1,977	1,640
Odenton	1,914	1,059
Orchard Beach	1,691	1,203
Overlea	10,795	...
Owings-Mills	3,810	...
Parkville-Carney	27,236	...
Pikesville	18,737	...
Pocomoke City	3,329	3,191
Riverdale	4,389	5,530
Riviera Beach	4,902	1,849
Rockville	26,090	6,934
Salisbury	16,302	15,141
Seat Pleasant	5,365	2,255
Severna Park-Round Bay	3,728	1,095
Silver Spring	66,348	...
Snow Hill	2,311	2,091
Sparrows Point-Fort Howard-Edgemere	11,775	...
Stoneleigh-Rodgers Forge	15,645	...
Suitland-Silver Hill	10,300	...
Takoma Park	16,799	13,341
Taneytown	1,519	1,420
Thurmont	1,998	1,676
Timonium-Lutherville	12,265	...
Towson	19,090	...
University Park	3,098	2,205
Westernport	3,559	3,431
Westminster	6,123	6,140
Wheaton	54,635	...
Williamsport	1,853	1,890
Woodland Beach	1,855	...
Woodlawn-Rockdale-Millford Mills	19,254	...
MASSACHUSETTS:		
Abington*	10,607	7,152
Acton*	7,238	3,510
Acushnet*	5,755	4,401
Adams	11,949	...
Agawam*	15,718	10,166
Amesbury	9,625	9,711
Amherst	10,306	7,900
Andover*	15,878	12,437
Arlington†	49,953	44,353
Ashland*	7,779	3,500
Athol	10,161	9,708
Attleboro	27,118	23,809
Auburn*	14,047	8,840
Ayer	3,323	3,107
Baldwinsville	1,631	1,407
Bedford*	10,969	5,234
Belchertown*	5,186	4,487
Bellingham*	6,774	4,100
Belmont†	28,715	27,381
Beverly	36,108	28,884
Blackstone*	5,130	4,968
Boston (c.)	697,197	801,444

Place	1960	1950
MASS.—Cont.:		
Braintree†	31,069	23,161
Bridgewater	4,296	3,445
Brockton	72,813	62,860
Brookline†	54,044	57,589
Burlington*	12,852	3,250
Buzzards Bay	2,170	1,459
Cambridge	107,716	120,740
Canton*	12,771	7,465
Chelmsford*	15,130	9,407
Chelsea	33,749	38,912
Chicopee	61,553	49,211
Clinton†	12,848	12,287
Cohasset	2,748	2,009
Concord	3,188	2,299
Dalton*	6,436	4,772
Danvers†	21,926	15,720
Dartmouth*	14,607	11,115
Dedham†	23,869	18,487
Dracut*	13,674	8,666
East Bridgewater*	6,139	4,412
East Douglas	1,695	1,846
East Falmouth	1,655	1,405
Easthampton*	12,326	10,694
East Longmeadow*	10,294	4,881
Easton*	9,078	6,244
Everett	43,544	45,982
Fairhaven*	14,339	12,764
Fall River	99,942	111,963
Falmouth	3,308	2,713
Fisherville	1,663	...
Fitchburg	43,021	42,691
Foxborough	3,169	2,774
Framingham†	44,526	28,086
Franklin	6,391	5,348
Gardner	19,038	19,581
Georgetown	2,005	1,578
Gloucester	25,789	25,167
Great Barrington	2,943	3,913
Greenfield	14,389	15,075
Hamilton*	5,488	2,764
Hanover*	5,923	3,389
Haverhill	46,346	47,280
Hingham*	15,378	10,665
Holbrook*	10,104	4,004
Holden	1,704	...
Holliston	2,447	1,908
Holyoke	52,689	54,661
Hopedale	2,904	2,797
Hopkinton	2,754	1,829
Hudson	7,897	...
Hull†	7,055	3,379
Hyannis	5,139	4,235
Ipswich	4,617	4,952
Lawrence	70,933	80,536
Lee	3,078	2,847
Leicester	1,750	...
Lenox	1,713	1,604
Leominster	27,929	24,075
Lexington†	27,691	17,335
Lincoln*	5,613	2,427
Littleton Common	2,277	1,017
Longmeadow*	10,565	6,508
Lowell	92,107	97,249
Ludlow*	13,805	8,660
Lunenburg*	6,334	3,906
Lynn	94,478	99,738
Lynnfield*	8,398	3,927
Malden	57,676	59,804
Mansfield	4,674	4,808
Marblehead†	18,521	13,765
Marborough	18,819	15,756
Marshfield*	6,748	3,267
Mattapoisett	1,640	...
Maynard†	7,695	6,978
Medfield	2,424	1,696
Medford	64,971	66,113
Medway	1,602	1,276
Melrose	29,619	26,988
Merino Village	3,099	3,118
Methuen†	28,114	24,447
Middleborough	6,003	5,889
Milford	13,722	14,396
Millbury*	9,623	8,347
Millis-Clicquet	2,588	1,419
Milton†	26,375	22,395
Monson	2,413	2,436
Nahant†	3,960	2,679
Nantucket	2,804	2,901
Natick†	28,831	19,838
Needham†	25,793	16,313
New Bedford	102,477	109,189
Newburyport	14,004	14,111
Newton	92,384	81,994
North Adams	19,905	21,567
Northampton	30,058	29,063
North Andover*	10,908	8,485
North Attleborough*	14,777	12,146
Northborough	2,516	1,442
Northbridge	2,128	...
North Brookfield	2,615	2,599
North Plymouth	3,467	...
North Reading†	8,331	4,402
North Scituate	3,421	...
North Uxbridge	1,882	...
Norton	1,501	...
Norwell*	5,207	2,515
Norwood†	24,898	16,636
MASS.—Cont.:		
Onset	1,714	1,674
Orange	3,689	4,048
Oxford	6,985	3,238
Palmer	3,888	3,440
Peabody	32,202	22,645
Pinehurst	1,991	2,905
Pittsfield	57,879	53,348
Plymouth	6,488	10,540
Provincetown	3,346	3,745
Quincy	87,409	83,835
Randolph†	18,900	9,982
Reading†	19,259	14,006
Revere	40,080	36,763
Rockland*	13,119	8,960
Rockport	3,511	2,911
Rutland	1,744	1,629
Salem	39,211	41,880
Saugus†	20,666	17,162
Scituate	3,229	1,457
Seekonk*	8,399	6,104
Sharon	5,888	2,815
Shelburne Falls	2,097	2,364
Shirley	1,762	...
Shore Acres-Sand Hill	1,778	1,026
Shrewsbury*	16,622	10,594
Silver Lake	4,654	2,024
Somerset†	12,196	8,566
Somerville	94,697	102,351
Southbridge	15,889	16,748
South Hadley*	14,956	10,145
South Lancaster	1,891	1,462
Southwick*	5,139	2,855
South Yarmouth	2,029	1,185
Spencer	5,593	5,259
Springfield	174,463	162,399
Stoneham†	17,821	13,229
Stoughton*	16,328	11,146
Sudbury*	7,447	2,596
Swampscott†	13,294	11,580
Swansea*	9,916	6,121
Taunton	41,132	40,109
Three Rivers	3,082	2,359
Turners Falls	4,917	5,179
Upton-West Upton	1,991	1,765
Uxbridge	3,377	...
Vineyard Haven	1,701	1,864
Wakefield†	24,295	19,633
Walpole*	14,068	9,109
Waltham	55,413	47,187
Ware	6,650	6,217
Wareham-Wareham Center	1,739	1,460
Warren	1,616	1,550
Watertown†	39,092	37,329
Wayland*	10,444	4,407
Webster	12,072	12,160
Wellesley†	26,071	20,549
Westborough	4,011	3,443
West Boylston*	5,526	2,570
West Bridgewater*	5,061	4,059
West Concord	1,556	1,285
Westfield	26,302	20,962
Westford*	6,261	4,262
West Medway	1,818	1,625
Weston*	8,261	5,026
Westport*	6,641	4,989
West Springfield*	24,924	20,438
Westwood*	10,354	5,837
Weymouth†	48,177	32,690
Whitinsville	5,102	5,662
Whitman†	10,485	8,413
Wilbraham*	7,387	4,003
Williamstown	5,428	5,015
Wilmington	2,250	1,331
Winchendon	3,839	4,019
Winchester†	19,376	15,509
Winthrop†	20,303	19,496
Woburn	31,214	20,492
Worcester	186,587	203,486
Wrentham	1,790	1,119
MICHIGAN:		
Adrian	20,347	18,393
Albion	12,749	10,406
Algonac	3,190	2,639
Allegan	4,822	4,801
Allen Park	37,494	12,329
Alma	8,978	8,341
Alpena	14,682	13,135
Anchor Bay Gardens	1,830	1,127
Ann Arbor	67,340	48,251
Austin Lake	3,520	2,032
Bad Axe	2,998	2,973
Bangor	2,109	1,694
Battle Creek	44,169	48,666
Bay City	53,604	52,523
Bayport Park Lakeside	1,569	1,209
Beechwood	2,323	1,567
Belding	4,887	4,436
Belleville	1,921	1,722
Benton Harbor	19,136	18,769
Benton Heights	6,112	6,160
Berkley	23,275	17,931
Berrien Springs	1,953	1,761
Bessemer	3,304	3,509
MICH.—Cont.:		
Beverly Hills	8,633	...
Big Rapids	8,686	6,736
Birmingham	25,525	15,467
Blissfield	2,653	2,365
Bloomfield Hills	2,378	1,468
Boyne City	2,797	3,028
Brighton	2,282	1,861
Bronson	2,267	2,106
Brownlee Park	3,307	...
Buchanan	5,341	5,224
Cadillac	10,112	10,425
Caro	3,534	3,464
Cass City	1,945	1,762
Cassopolis	2,027	1,527
Cedar Springs	1,768	1,378
Center Line	10,164	7,659
Charlevoix	2,751	2,695
Charlotte	7,657	6,606
Cheboygan	5,859	5,687
Chelsea	3,355	2,580
Chesaning	2,770	2,264
Clare	2,442	2,440
Clawson	14,795	5,196
Clio	2,212	1,963
Coldwater	8,880	8,594
Constantine	1,710	1,514
Coopersville	1,584	1,371
Corunna	2,764	2,358
Croswell	1,817	1,775
Crystal Falls	2,203	2,316
Davison	3,761	1,745
Dearborn	112,007	94,994
Decatur	1,827	1,664
Detroit	1,670,144	1,849,568
Detroit Beach	1,571	...
Dexter	1,702	1,307
Dowagiac	7,208	6,542
Dundee	2,377	1,975
Durand	3,312	3,194
East Detroit	45,756	21,461
East Grand Rapids	10,924	6,403
East Jordan	1,919	1,779
East Lansing	30,198	20,325
Eastlawn	17,652	4,127
East Tawas	2,462	2,040
Eaton Rapids	4,052	3,509
Ecorse	17,328	17,948
Escanaba	15,391	15,170
Essexville	4,590	3,167
Euclid Center	2,343	...
Evart	1,775	1,578
Fair Plain	7,998	4,134
Farmington	6,881	2,325
Fenton	6,142	4,226
Ferndale	31,347	29,675
Ferrysburg	2,590	1,454
Flat Rock	4,696	1,931
Flint	196,940	163,143
Flushing	3,761	2,226
Fowlerville	1,674	1,466
Frankenmuth	1,728	1,208
Frankfort	1,690	1,605
Franklin	2,262	...
Fraser	7,027	1,379
Fremont	3,384	3,056
Garden City	38,017	9,012
Gaylord	2,568	2,271
Gibraltar	2,196	...
Gladstone	5,267	4,831
Gladwin	2,226	1,878
Grand Blanc	1,565	998
Grand Haven	11,066	9,536
Grand Ledge	5,165	4,506
Grand Rapids	177,313	176,515
Grandville	7,975	2,022
Grayling	2,015	2,066
Greenville	7,440	6,668
Grosse Pointe	6,631	6,283
Grosse Pointe Farms	12,172	9,410
Grosse Pointe Park	15,457	13,075
Grosse Pointe Shores	2,301	1,032
Grosse Pointe Woods	18,580	10,381
Hamtramck	34,137	43,355
Hancock	5,022	5,223
Harbor Beach	2,282	2,349
Harper Woods	19,995	9,148
Hart	1,990	2,172
Hartford	2,305	1,838
Hastings	6,375	6,096
Hazel Park	25,631	17,770
Highland Park	38,063	46,393
Hillsdale	7,629	7,297
Holland	24,777	15,858
Holly	3,269	2,663
Holt	4,818	...
Homer	1,629	1,301
Houghton	3,393	3,829
Howell	4,861	4,353
Hudson	2,546	2,773
Hudsonville	2,649	1,101
Huntington Woods	8,746	4,949
Imlay City	1,968	1,654
Inkster	39,097	16,728
Ionia	6,754	6,412
Iron Mountain	9,299	9,679
Iron River	3,754	4,048
Ironwood	10,265	11,466
MICH.—Cont.:		
Ishpeming	8,857	8,962
Ithaca	2,611	2,377
Jackson	50,720	51,088
Jonesville	1,896	1,594
Kalamazoo	82,089	57,704
Keego Harbor	2,761	...
Kingsford	5,084	5,038
Lake Odessa	1,806	1,596
Lake Orion	2,698	2,385
Lake Orion Heights	1,918	1,075
Lakeview	10,384	...
Lakewood	1,815	...
L'Anse	2,397	2,376
Lansing (c.)	107,807	92,129
Lapeer	6,160	6,143
Lathrup Village	3,556	...
Laurium	3,058	3,211
Leslie	1,807	1,543
Level Park-Oak Park	3,017	1,364
Lincoln Park	53,933	29,310
Livonia	66,702	17,534
Lowell	2,545	2,191
Ludington	9,421	9,506
Madison Heights	33,343	...
Manchester	1,568	1,388
Manistee	8,324	8,642
Manistique	4,875	5,086
Manitou Beach-Devils Lake	1,544	1,273
Marine City	4,404	4,270
Marlette	1,640	1,489
Marquette	19,824	17,202
Marshall	6,736	5,777
Marysville	4,065	2,534
Mason	4,522	3,514
Melvindale	13,089	9,483
Menominee	11,289	11,151
Michigan Center	4,611	3,012
Midland	27,779	14,285
Milan	3,616	2,768
Milford	4,323	1,924
Monroe	22,968	21,467
Montague	2,366	1,530
Morenci	2,053	1,983
Mount Clemens	21,016	17,027
Mount Morris	3,484	2,890
Mount Pleasant	14,875	11,393
Munising	4,228	4,339
Muskegon	46,485	48,429
Muskegon Heights	19,552	18,828
Nashville	1,525	1,374
Negaunee	6,126	6,472
New Baltimore	3,159	2,043
Newberry	2,612	2,802
New Buffalo	2,128	1,565
Niles	13,842	13,145
North Muskegon	3,855	2,424
Northville	3,967	3,240
Norway	3,171	3,258
Novi	6,390	...
Oak Park	36,632	5,267
Ontonagon	2,358	2,307
Otsego	4,142	3,990
Ovid	1,505	1,410
Owosso	17,006	15,948
Oxford	2,357	2,305
Parchment	1,565	1,179
Patterson Gardens	1,747	1,548
Paw Paw	2,970	2,382
Paw Paw Lake	3,518	1,625
Petoskey	6,138	6,468
Plainwell	3,125	2,767
Pleasant Ridge	3,807	3,594
Plymouth	8,766	6,637
Pontiac	82,233	73,681
Port Huron	36,084	35,725
Portland	3,330	2,807
Quincy	1,602	1,527
Reed City	2,184	2,241
Richmond	2,667	2,025
River Rouge	18,147	20,549
Riverview	7,237	1,432
Rochester	5,431	4,279
Rockford	2,074	1,937
Rockwood	2,026	1,044
Rogers City	4,722	3,873
Romeo	3,327	2,985
Romulus	1,798	...
Roosevelt Park	2,578	1,254
Roseville	50,195	15,816
Royal Oak	80,612	46,898
Saginaw	98,265	92,918
St. Charles	1,959	1,469
St. Clair	4,538	4,098
St. Clair Shores	76,657	19,823
St. Ignace	3,334	2,946
St. Johns	5,629	4,954
St. Joseph	11,755	10,223
St. Louis	3,808	3,347
Saline	2,334	1,533
Sandusky	2,066	1,819
Sault Ste. Marie	18,722	17,912
Sebewaing	2,026	1,911
Shelby	1,603	1,500
Southfield	31,501	...

Place	1960	1950
MICH.—Cont.:		
Southgate	29,404	. . .
South Haven	6,149	5,629
South Lyon	1,753	1,312
South Monroe	2,919	2,275
Sparlingville	1,877	1,393
Sparta	2,749	2,327
Springfield	4,605	. . .
Springfield Place	5,136	. . .
Spring Lake	2,063	1,824
Stambaugh	1,876	1,969
Sturgis	8,915	7,786
Sunrise Heights	1,569	1,094
Swartz Creek	3,006	. . .
Sylvan Lake	2,004	1,165
Tawas City	1,810	1,441
Tecumseh	7,045	4,020
Temperance	2,215	1,062
Three Oaks	1,763	1,572
Three Rivers	7,092	6,785
Traverse City	18,432	16,974
Trenton	18,439	6,222
Troy	19,382	. . .
Union City	1,669	1,564
Vassar	2,680	2,530
Verona Park	1,884	1,342
Vicksburg	2,224	2,171
Wakefield	3,231	3,344
Walled Lake	3,550	. . .
Warren	89,246	727
Watervliet	1,818	1,327
Wayland	2,019	1,591
Wayne	16,034	9,409
West Branch	2,025	2,098
Whitehall	2,590	1,819
White-Lake-Seven Harbors	2,748	1,385
Williamston	2,214	2,051
Wixom	1,531	. . .
Wolf Lake	2,525	1,591
Wolverine Lake	2,404	. . .
Woodland Beach	1,944	. . .
Wyandotte	43,519	36,846
Wyoming	45,829	. . .
Yale	1,621	1,641
Ypsilanti	20,957	18,302
Zeeland	3,702	3,075
MINNESOTA:		
Ada	2,064	2,121
Aitkin	1,829	2,079
Albert Lea	17,108	13,545
Alexandria	6,713	6,319
Anoka	10,562	7,396
Appleton	2,172	2,256
Arden Hills	3,930	. . .
Arlington	1,601	1,313
Aurora	2,799	1,371
Austin	27,908	23,100
Babbitt	2,587	. . .
Barnesville	1,632	1,593
Baudette	1,597	929
Bayport	3,205	2,502
Belle Plaine	1,931	1,708
Bemidji	9,958	10,001
Benson	3,678	3,398
Biwabik	1,836	1,245
Blaine	7,570	. . .
Blooming Prairie	1,778	1,442
Bloomington	50,498	. . .
Blue Earth	4,200	3,843
Brainerd	12,898	12,637
Breckenridge	4,335	3,623
Brooklyn Center	24,356	4,284
Brooklyn Park	10,197	. . .
Buffalo	2,322	1,914
Buhl	1,526	1,462
Caledonia	2,563	2,243
Cambridge	2,728	1,790
Canby	2,146	2,173
Cannon Falls	2,055	1,831
Cass Lake	1,586	1,936
Chaska	2,501	2,008
Chatfield	1,841	1,605
Chisholm	7,144	6,861
Circle Pines	2,789	. . .
Cloquet	9,013	7,685
Cold Spring	1,760	1,488
Columbia Heights	17,533	8,175
Coon Rapids	14,931	. . .
Crookston	8,546	7,352
Crosby	2,629	2,777
Crystal	24,283	5,713
Dawson	1,766	1,834
Deephaven	3,286	1,823
Delano	1,612	1,386
Detroit Lakes	5,633	5,787
Dilworth	2,102	1,429
Duluth	106,884	104,511
East Grand Forks	6,998	5,049
Edina	28,501	9,744
Elbow Lake	1,521	1,398
Elk River	1,763	1,399
Ely	5,438	5,474
Eveleth	5,721	5,872
Excelsior	2,020	1,763
Fairmont	9,745	8,193
Falcon Heights	5,927	3,884
Faribault	16,926	16,028

Place	1960	1950
MINN.—Cont.:		
Farmington	2,300	1,916
Fergus Falls	13,733	12,917
Forest Lake	2,347	1,766
Fosston	1,704	1,614
Fridley	15,173	3,796
Gaylord	1,631	1,229
Gilbert	2,591	2,247
Glencoe	3,216	2,801
Glenwood	2,631	2,666
Golden Hill	2,190	. . .
Golden Valley	14,559	5,551
Grand Rapids	7,265	6,019
Granite Falls	2,728	2,511
Hallock	1,527	1,552
Hastings	8,965	6,560
Hibbing	17,731	16,276
Hopkins	11,370	7,595
Hoyt Lakes	3,186	. . .
Hutchinson	6,207	4,690
International Falls	6,778	6,269
Jackson	3,370	3,313
Kasson	1,732	1,353
Keewatin	1,651	1,807
Kenyon	1,624	1,651
La Crescent	2,624	1,229
Lake City	3,494	3,457
Lake Crystal	1,652	1,430
Lakefield	1,789	1,651
Lauderdale	1,676	1,033
Le Center	1,597	1,314
Le Sueur	3,310	2,713
Lino Lakes	2,329	. . .
Litchfield	5,078	4,608
Little Canada	3,512	. . .
Little Falls	7,551	6,717
Long Prairie	2,414	2,443
Luverne	4,249	3,650
Madelia	2,190	1,790
Madison	2,380	2,303
Mahtomedi	2,127	1,375
Mankato	23,797	18,809
Maple Grove	2,213	. . .
Maplewood	18,519	. . .
Marshall	6,681	5,923
Melrose	2,135	2,106
Mendota Heights	5,028	. . .
Milaca	1,821	1,917
Minneapolis	482,872	521,718
Minnetonka	25,037	. . .
Montevideo	5,693	5,459
Montgomery	2,118	1,913
Moorhead	22,934	14,870
Moose Lake	1,514	1,603
Mora	2,329	2,018
Morningside	1,981	1,699
Morris	4,199	3,811
Mound	5,440	2,061
Mounds View	6,416	. . .
Mountain Iron	1,808	1,377
Mountain Lake	1,943	1,733
Nashwauk	1,712	2,029
New Brighton	6,448	2,218
New Hope	3,552	. . .
Newport	2,349	1,672
New Prague	2,533	1,915
New Ulm	11,114	9,348
Northfield	8,707	7,487
North Mankato	5,927	4,788
North St. Paul	8,520	4,248
Olivia	2,355	2,012
Orono	5,643	. . .
Ortonville	2,674	2,577
Osseo	2,104	1,167
Owatonna	13,409	10,191
Park Rapids	3,047	3,027
Paynesville	1,754	1,503
Pelican Rapids	1,693	1,676
Perham	2,019	1,926
Pine City	1,972	1,937
Pipestone	5,324	5,269
Plainview	1,833	1,524
Plymouth	9,576	. . .
Princeton	2,353	2,108
Proctor	2,963	2,693
Red Lake Falls	1,520	1,733
Red Wing	10,528	10,645
Redwood Falls	4,285	3,813
Richfield	42,523	17,502
Robbinsdale	16,381	11,289
Rochester	40,663	29,885
Roseau	2,146	2,231
Roseville	23,997	6,437
St. Anthony	5,084	1,406
St. Charles	1,882	1,548
St. Cloud	33,815	28,410
St. James	4,174	3,861
St. Louis Park	43,310	22,644
St. Paul (c.)	313,411	311,349
St. Paul Park	3,267	2,438
St. Peter	8,484	7,754
Sandstone	1,552	1,097
Sauk Centre	3,573	3,140
Sauk Rapids	4,038	3,410
Shakopee	5,201	3,185
Shoreview	7,157	. . .
Shorewood	3,197	. . .
Silver Bay	3,723	. . .
Slayton	2,487	1,887
Sleepy Eye	3,492	3,278
South International Falls	2,479	1,840
South St. Paul	22,032	15,909
Springfield	2,701	2,574

Place	1960	1950
MINN.—Cont.:		
Spring Lake Park	3,260	. . .
Spring Valley	2,628	2,467
Staples	2,706	2,782
Stewartville	1,670	1,193
Stillwater	8,310	7,674
Thief River Falls	7,151	6,926
Tracy	2,862	3,020
Two Harbors	4,695	4,400
Vadnais Heights	2,459	. . .
Virginia	14,034	12,486
Wabasha	2,500	2,468
Waconia	2,048	1,569
Wadena	4,381	3,958
Waite Park	2,016	1,639
Warren	2,007	1,779
Waseca	5,898	4,927
Waterville	1,623	1,627
Wayzata	3,219	1,791
Wells	2,897	2,475
West St. Paul	13,101	7,955
Wheaton	2,102	1,948
White Bear Lake	12,849	3,646
Willmar	10,417	9,410
Windom	3,691	3,165
Winnebago	2,088	2,127
Winona	24,895	25,031
Worthington	9,015	7,923
Zumbrota	1,830	1,686
MISSISSIPPI:		
Aberdeen	6,450	5,290
Amory	6,474	4,990
Baldwyn	2,023	1,567
Batesville	3,284	2,463
Bay St. Louis	5,073	4,621
Bay Springs	1,544	1,302
Belzoni	4,142	4,071
Biloxi	44,053	37,425
Booneville	3,480	3,295
Brandon	2,139	1,827
Brookhaven	9,885	7,801
Bruce	1,698	1,719
Calhoun City	1,714	1,319
Canton	9,707	7,048
Carthage	2,442	1,925
Charleston	2,528	2,629
Clarksdale	21,105	16,539
Cleveland	10,172	6,747
Clinton	3,438	2,255
Collins	1,537	1,293
Columbia	7,117	6,124
Columbus	24,771	17,172
Corinth	11,453	9,785
Crystal Springs	4,496	3,676
D'Iberville	3,005	1,429
Drew	2,143	1,681
Durant	2,617	2,311
East Side	4,318	1,215
Ellisville	4,592	3,579
Fayette	1,626	1,498
Forest	3,917	2,874
Fulton	1,706	1,343
Greenville	41,502	29,936
Greenville North	2,516	. . .
Greenwood	20,436	18,061
Grenada	7,914	7,388
Gulfport	30,204	22,659
Handsboro	1,577	. . .
Hattiesburg	34,989	29,474
Hazlehurst	3,400	3,397
Hernando	1,898	1,206
Hollandale	2,646	2,346
Holly Springs	5,621	3,276
Houston	2,577	1,664
Indianola	6,714	4,369
Itta Bena	1,914	1,725
Iuka	2,010	1,527
Jackson (c.)	144,422	98,271
Kosciusko	6,800	6,753
Kreole	1,870	1,106
Laurel	27,889	25,038
Leland	6,295	4,736
Lexington	2,839	3,198
Long Beach	4,770	2,703
Louisville	5,066	5,282
Lucedale	1,977	1,631
Lumberton	2,108	1,803
McComb	12,020	10,401
McComb South	1,865	. . .
Macon	2,432	2,241
Magee	2,039	1,738
Magnolia	2,083	1,984
Marks	2,572	2,209
Mendenhall	1,946	1,539
Meridian	49,374	41,893
Mississippi City	4,169	. . .
Moorhead	1,754	1,749
Morton	2,260	1,664
Moss Point	6,631	3,782
Natchez	23,791	22,740
New Albany	5,151	3,680
Newton	3,178	2,912
Ocean Springs	5,025	3,058
Okolona	2,622	2,167
Oxford	5,283	3,956
Pascagoula	17,155	10,805
Pass Christian	3,881	3,383
Pearl	5,081	. . .
Petal	4,007	2,148

Place	1960	1950
MISS.—Cont.:		
Philadelphia	5,017	4,472
Picayune	7,834	6,707
Pontotoc	2,108	1,596
Poplarville	2,136	1,852
Port Gibson	2,861	2,920
Purvis	1,614	1,270
Quitman	2,030	1,817
Ripley	2,668	2,383
Rolling Fork	1,619	1,229
Rosedale	2,339	2,197
Ruleville	1,902	1,521
Sardis	2,098	1,913
Senatobia	3,259	2,108
Shaw	2,062	1,892
Shelby	2,384	2,148
Starkville	9,041	7,107
Summit	1,663	1,558
Tupelo	17,221	11,527
Tylertown	1,532	1,331
Union	1,726	1,559
University	3,597	. . .
Vicksburg	29,143	27,948
Water Valley	3,206	3,213
Waynesboro	3,892	3,442
West Gulfport	3,323	. . .
West Point	8,550	6,432
Wiggins	1,591	1,436
Winona	4,282	3,441
Woodville	1,856	1,609
Yazoo City	11,236	9,746
MISSOURI:		
Albany	1,662	1,850
Aurora	4,683	4,153
Ava	1,581	1,611
Ballwin	5,710	. . .
Bellefontaine Neighbors	13,650	. . .
Bel-Nor	2,388	1,290
Bel-Ridge	4,395	1,116
Belton	4,897	1,233
Berkeley	18,676	5,268
Bernie	1,578	1,308
Bethany	2,771	2,714
Blue Springs	2,555	1,068
Bolivar	3,512	3,482
Bonne Terre	3,219	3,533
Boonville	7,090	6,686
Bowling Green	2,650	2,396
Branson	1,887	1,314
Breckenridge Hills	6,299	4,063
Brentwood	12,250	7,504
Bridgeton	7,820	202
Brookfield	5,694	5,810
Butler	3,791	3,333
California	2,788	2,627
Calverton Park	1,714	514
Cameron	3,674	3,570
Campbell	1,964	1,931
Canton	2,562	2,490
Cape Girardeau	24,947	21,578
Carrollton	4,554	4,380
Carthage	11,264	11,188
Caruthersville	8,643	8,614
Centralia	3,200	2,460
Chaffee	2,862	3,134
Charleston	5,911	5,501
Chillicothe	9,236	8,694
Clayton	15,245	16,035
Clinton	6,925	6,075
Columbia	36,650	31,974
Country Club Hills	1,763	1,731
Crestwood	11,106	1,645
Creve Coeur	5,122	2,040
Crystal City	3,678	3,499
Cuba	1,672	1,301
Dellwood	4,720	. . .
Desloge	2,308	1,957
De Soto	5,804	5,357
Des Peres	4,362	1,172
Dexter	5,519	4,624
East Prairie	3,449	3,033
Eldon	3,158	2,766
Eldorado Springs	2,864	2,618
Ellisville	2,732	628
Elvins	1,818	1,977
Excelsior Springs	6,473	5,888
Farmington	5,618	4,490
Fayette	3,294	3,144
Ferguson	22,149	11,573
Festus	7,021	5,199
Flat River	4,515	5,308
Florissant	38,166	3,737
Fredericktown	3,484	3,696
Frontenac	3,089	1,099
Fulton	11,131	10,052
Gallatin	1,658	1,634
Gladstone	14,502	. . .
Glendale	7,048	4,930
Granby	1,808	1,670
Grandview	6,027	1,556
Hamilton	1,701	1,728
Hanley Hills	3,308	2,219
Hannibal	20,028	20,444
Harrisonville	3,510	2,530
Hayti	3,737	3,302
Hazelwood	6,045	336
Herculaneum	1,767	1,603
Hermann	2,536	2,523
Higginsville	4,003	3,428

Place	1960	1950
MO.—Cont.:		
Hillsdale	2,788	2,902
Holden	1,951	1,765
Houston	1,660	1,277
Huntsville	1,526	1,520
Independence	62,328	36,963
Jackson	4,875	3,707
Jefferson City (c.)	28,228	25,099
Jennings	19,965	15,282
Joplin	38,958	38,711
Kahoka	2,160	1,847
Kansas City	475,539	456,622
Kennett	9,098	8,685
Kinloch	6,501	5,957
Kirksville	13,123	11,110
Kirkwood	29,421	18,640
Knob Noster	2,292	585
Ladue	9,466	5,386
Lamar	3,608	3,233
Lebanon	8,220	6,808
Lees Summit	8,267	2,554
Lexington	4,845	5,074
Liberty	8,909	4,709
Louisiana	4,286	4,389
Macon	4,547	4,152
Malden	5,007	3,396
Manchester	2,021	...
Maplewood	12,552	13,416
Marceline	2,872	3,172
Marshall	9,572	8,850
Marshfield	2,221	1,925
Maryville	7,807	6,834
Memphis	2,106	2,035
Mexico	12,889	11,623
Milan	1,670	1,972
Moberly	13,170	13,115
Moline Acres	3,132	99
Monett	5,359	4,771
Monroe City	2,337	2,093
Montgomery City	1,918	1,679
Mountain Grove	3,176	3,106
Mount Vernon	2,381	2,057
Neosho	7,452	5,790
Nevada	8,416	8,009
New Madrid	2,867	2,726
Normandy	4,452	2,306
North Kansas City	5,657	3,886
Northwoods	4,701	1,602
Oakland	1,552	1,041
Odessa	2,034	1,969
O'Fallon	3,770	789
Olivette	8,257	1,761
Overland	22,763	11,566
Owensville	2,379	1,946
Ozark	1,536	1,087
Pacific	2,795	1,985
Pagedale	5,106	3,866
Palmyra	2,933	2,295
Perryville	5,117	4,591
Piedmont	1,555	1,548
Pine Lawn	5,943	6,425
Plattsburg	1,663	1,655
Pleasant Hill	2,689	2,200
Poplar Bluff	15,926	15,064
Portageville	2,505	2,662
Potosi	2,805	2,359
Raytown	17,083	...
Republic	1,519	965
Rich Hill	1,699	1,820
Richland	1,662	1,133
Richmond	4,604	4,299
Richmond Heights	15,622	15,045
Riverview	3,706	...
Rock Hill	6,523	3,847
Rolla	11,132	9,354
St. Ann	12,155	4,557
St. Charles	21,189	14,314
St. Clair	2,711	1,779
Ste. Genevieve	4,443	3,992
St. James	2,384	1,996
St. John	7,342	2,499
St. Joseph	79,673	78,588
St. Louis	750,026	856,796
Salem	3,870	3,611
Salisbury	1,787	1,676
Savannah	2,455	2,332
Scott City	1,963	1,834
Sedalia	23,874	20,354
Shelbina	2,067	2,113
Shrewsbury	4,730	3,382
Sikeston	13,765	11,640
Slater	2,767	2,836
Springfield	95,865	66,731
Steele	2,301	2,360
Sugar Creek	2,663	1,858
Sullivan	4,098	3,019
Sunset Hills	3,525	...
Tarkio	2,160	2,221
Thayer	1,713	1,639
Tipton	1,639	1,234
Trenton	6,262	6,157
Troy	1,779	1,738
Union	3,937	2,917
Unionville	1,896	2,050
University City	51,249	39,892
Valley Park	3,452	2,956
Vandalia	3,055	2,624
Versailles	2,047	1,929
Vinita Park	2,204	1,801
Warrensburg	9,689	6,857

Place	1960	1950
MO.—Cont.:		
Warrenton	1,869	1,584
Warson Woods	1,746	529
Washington	7,961	6,850
Waynesville	2,377	1,010
Webb City	6,740	6,919
Webster Groves	28,990	23,390
Wellston	7,979	9,396
Wellsville	1,523	1,519
Wentzville	2,742	1,227
West Plains	5,836	4,918
Willow Springs	1,913	1,914
Windsor	2,714	2,429
Woodson Terrace	6,048	616
MONTANA:		
Anaconda	12,054	11,254
Baker	2,365	1,772
Big Timber	1,660	1,679
Billings	52,851	31,834
Bozeman	13,361	11,325
Browning	2,011	1,691
Butte	27,877	33,251
Centerville-Dublin Gulch	3,398	1,825
Chinook	2,326	2,307
Choteau	1,966	1,618
Columbia Falls	2,132	1,232
Conrad	2,665	1,865
Cut Bank	4,539	3,721
Deer Lodge	4,681	3,779
Dillon	3,690	3,268
Floral Park	4,079	...
Forsyth	2,032	1,906
Fort Benton	1,887	1,522
Glasgow	6,398	3,821
Glendive	7,058	5,254
Great Falls	55,357	39,214
Hamilton	2,475	2,678
Hardin	2,789	2,306
Harlowton	1,734	1,733
Havre	10,740	8,086
Helena (c.)	20,227	17,581
Kalispell	10,151	9,737
Laurel	4,601	3,663
Lewistown	7,408	6,573
Libby	2,828	2,401
Livingston	8,229	7,683
Malta	2,239	2,095
Miles City	9,665	9,243
Missoula	27,090	22,485
Missoula Southwest	3,817	...
Orchard Homes	2,019	1,545
Plentywood	2,121	1,862
Polson	2,314	2,280
Poplar	1,565	1,169
Red Lodge	2,278	2,730
Roundup	2,842	2,856
Scobey	1,726	1,628
Shelby	4,017	3,058
Sidney	4,564	3,987
Silver Bow Park	4,798	...
Townsend	1,528	1,316
Whitefish	2,965	3,268
White Sulphur Springs	1,519	1,025
Wolf Point	3,585	2,557
NEBRASKA:		
Ainsworth	1,982	2,150
Albion	1,982	2,132
Alliance	7,845	7,891
Ashland	1,989	1,713
Auburn	3,229	3,422
Aurora	2,576	2,455
Bayard	1,519	1,869
Beatrice	12,132	11,813
Bellevue	8,831	3,858
Blair	4,931	3,815
Bridgeport	1,645	1,631
Broken Bow	3,482	3,396
Central City	2,406	2,394
Chadron	5,079	4,687
Columbus	12,476	8,884
Cozad	3,184	2,910
Crawford	1,588	1,824
Crete	3,546	3,692
David City	2,304	2,321
Fairbury	5,572	6,395
Falls City	5,598	6,203
Fremont	19,698	14,762
Geneva	2,352	2,031
Gering	4,585	3,842
Gordon	2,223	2,058
Gothenburg	3,050	2,977
Grand Island	25,742	22,682
Hartington	1,648	1,660
Hastings	21,412	20,211
Hebron	1,920	2,000
Holdrege	5,226	4,381
Kearney	14,210	12,115
Kimball	4,384	2,048
Lexington	5,572	5,068
Lincoln (c.)	128,521	98,884
McCook	8,301	7,678
Madison	1,513	1,663
Minden	2,383	2,120
Mitchell	1,920	2,101
Nebraska City	7,252	6,872
Neligh	1,776	1,822

Place	1960	1950
NEB.—Cont.:		
Norfolk	13,640	11,335
North Platte	17,184	15,433
Ogallala	4,250	3,456
Omaha	301,598	251,117
O'Neill	3,181	3,027
Ord	2,413	2,239
Papillion	2,235	1,034
Pell-Lincoln Hwy.	1,709	...
Plattsmouth	6,244	4,874
Ralston	2,977	1,300
Red Cloud	1,525	1,744
St. Paul	1,714	1,676
Schuyler	3,096	2,883
Scottsbluff	13,377	12,858
Seward	4,208	3,154
Sidney	8,004	4,912
South Sioux City	7,200	5,557
Superior	2,935	3,227
Tecumseh	1,887	1,930
Tekamah	1,788	1,914
Valentine	2,875	2,700
Wahoo	3,610	3,128
Wayne	4,217	3,595
West Point	2,921	2,658
Wymore	1,975	2,258
York	6,173	6,178
NEVADA:		
Babbitt	2,159	2,464
Boulder City	4,059	...
Carson City (c.)	5,163	3,082
East Ely	1,796	...
Elko	6,298	5,393
Ely	4,018	3,558
Fallon	2,734	2,400
Hawthorne	2,838	...
Henderson	12,525	...
Las Vegas	64,405	24,624
Lovelock	1,948	1,604
McGill	2,195	2,297
North Las Vegas	18,422	3,875
Reno	51,470	32,497
Sparks	16,618	8,203
Tonopah	1,679	1,375
Winnemucca	3,453	2,847
Yerington	1,764	1,157
NEW HAMPSHIRE:		
Berlin	17,821	16,615
Claremont	13,563	12,811
Colebrook	1,550	1,265
Concord (c.)	28,991	27,988
Dover	19,131	15,874
Durham	4,688	4,172
Exeter	5,896	4,977
Farmington	2,241	2,285
Franklin	6,742	6,552
Goffstown	7,230	5,638
Gorham	1,945	1,739
Groveton	2,004	1,918
Hampton	3,281	1,614
Hanover	5,649	4,999
Hillsborough	1,645	1,670
Hudson	3,651	2,382
Jaffrey	1,648	...
Keene	17,562	15,638
Laconia	15,288	14,745
Lancaster	2,392	2,296
Lebanon	9,299	...
Littleton	3,355	3,819
Manchester	88,282	82,732
Milford	3,916	3,269
Nashua	39,096	34,669
Newmarket	2,745	2,172
Newport	3,222	3,062
Peterborough	1,931	1,506
Plymouth	2,244	2,107
Portsmouth	25,833	18,830
Rochester	15,927	13,776
Salem Depot	2,523	1,637
Somersworth	8,529	6,927
Suncook	2,318	...
West Derry	4,468	...
Wolfeboro	1,557	1,271
Woodsville	1,596	1,542
NEW JERSEY:		
Absecon	4,320	2,355
Allendale	4,092	2,409
Alpha	2,406	2,117
Asbury Park	17,366	17,094
Atlantic City	59,544	61,657
Atlantic Highlands	4,119	3,083
Audubon	10,440	9,531
Audubon Park	1,713	1,859
Avon-by-the Sea	1,707	1,650
Barrington	7,943	2,651
Basking Ridge	2,483	1,899
Bayonne	74,215	77,203
Beachwood	2,765	1,251
Belleville	35,005	32,019
Bellmawr	11,853	5,213
Belmar	5,190	4,636
Belvidere	2,636	2,406
Bergenfield	27,203	17,647
Berkeley Heights*	8,721	3,466

Place	1960	1950
N.J.—Cont.:		
Berlin	3,578	2,339
Bernardsville	5,515	3,956
Beverly	3,400	3,084
Blansingburg	1,702	...
Bloomfield	51,867	49,307
Bloomingdale	5,293	3,251
Bogota	7,965	7,662
Boonton	7,981	7,163
Bordentown	4,974	5,497
Bordentown*	5,936	2,033
Bound Brook	10,263	8,347
Bradley Beach	4,204	3,911
Brick*	16,299	4,319
Bridgeton	20,966	18,378
Bridgewater*	15,789	8,234
Brielle	2,619	1,328
Brigantine	4,201	1,267
Brooklawn	2,504	2,262
Budd Lake	1,520	1,032
Buena	3,243	2,640
Burlington	12,687	12,051
Burlington*	6,291	3,441
Butler	5,414	4,050
Caldwell	6,942	6,270
Camden	117,159	124,555
Cape May	4,477	3,607
Cape May Court House	1,749	1,093
Carlstadt	6,042	5,591
Carteret	20,502	13,030
Cedar Grove†	14,603	8,022
Chatham	9,517	7,391
Chatham*	5,931	2,825
Cinnaminson*	8,302	3,144
Clark†	12,195	4,352
Clayton	4,711	3,023
Clementon	3,766	3,191
Cliffside Park	17,642	17,116
Clifton	82,084	64,511
Closter	7,767	3,376
Collingswood	17,370	15,800
Cranford†	26,424	18,602
Cresskill	7,290	3,534
Deal	1,889	1,064
Delaware†	31,522	10,358
Delran*	5,327	2,447
Demarest	4,231	1,786
Denville*	10,632	6,055
Deptford*	17,878	7,304
Dover	13,034	11,174
Dumont	18,882	13,013
Dunellen	6,840	6,291
East Brunswick*	19,965	5,699
East Newark	1,872	2,173
East Orange	77,259	79,340
East Paterson	19,344	15,386
East Rutherford	7,769	7,438
Eatontown	10,334	3,044
Edgewater	4,113	3,952
Edison†‡	44,799	16,348
Egg Harbor*	5,593	4,991
Egg Harbor City	4,416	3,838
Elizabeth	107,689	112,817
Elmer	1,505	1,460
Emerson	6,849	1,744
Englewood	26,057	23,145
Englewood Cliffs	2,913	966
Essex Fells	2,174	1,617
Ewing†	26,628	16,840
Fair Haven	5,678	3,560
Fair Lawn	36,421	23,885
Fairview	9,399	8,661
Fanwood	7,963	3,228
Flemington	3,232	3,058
Florence	4,215	...
Florham Park	7,222	2,385
Fort Lee	21,815	11,648
Franklin	3,624	3,864
Franklin* (Gloucester Co.)	7,451	5,056
Franklin* (Somerset Co.)	19,858	9,601
Franklin Lakes	3,316	2,021
Freehold	9,140	7,550
Galloway*	5,634	4,140
Garfield	29,253	27,550
Garwood	5,426	4,622
Gibbsboro	2,141	906
Gibbstown	2,820	2,546
Gilford Park	1,560	...
Glassboro	10,253	5,867
Glen Ridge	8,322	7,620
Glen Rock	12,896	7,145
Gloucester*	17,591	7,952
Gloucester City	15,511	14,357
Guttenberg	5,118	5,566
Hackensack	30,521	29,219
Hackettstown	5,276	3,894
Haddon†	17,099	12,379
Haddonfield	13,201	10,495
Haddon Heights	9,260	7,287
Haledon	6,161	6,204
Hamburg	1,532	1,305
Hamilton†	65,035	41,156
Hamilton*	6,017	3,774
Hammonton	9,854	8,411
Hanover*	9,329	3,756

‡Raritan in 1950.

Place	1960	1950
N.J.—Cont.:		
Harrington Park	3,581	1,634
Harrison	11,743	13,490
Hasbrouck Heights	13,046	9,181
Haworth	3,215	1,612
Hawthorne	17,735	14,816
High Bridge	2,148	1,854
Highland Park	11,049	9,721
Highlands	3,536	2,959
Hightstown	4,317	3,712
Hillcrest	1,922	...
Hillsborough*	7,584	3,875
Hillsdale	8,734	4,127
Hillside†	22,304	21,007
Hoboken	48,441	50,676
Hohokus	3,988	2,254
Hopatcong	3,391	1,173
Hopewell	1,928	1,869
Hopewell*	7,818	4,731
Howell*	11,153	6,696
Huntington	1,879	...
Irvington	59,379	59,201
Jackson*	5,939	3,513
Jamesburg	2,853	2,307
Jefferson*	6,884	2,744
Jersey City	276,101	299,017
Keansburg	6,854	5,559
Kearny	37,472	39,952
Kenilworth	8,379	4,922
Keyport	6,440	5,888
Kinnelon	4,431	1,350
Lakehurst	2,780	1,518
Lake Mohawk	4,647	1,873
Lakewood	13,004	9,970
Lambertville	4,269	4,477
Laurel Springs	2,028	1,540
Lawnside	2,155	1,566
Lawrence*	13,665	8,499
Leonia	8,384	7,378
Levittown†‡	11,861	852
Lincoln Park	6,048	3,376
Linden	39,931	30,644
Lindenwold	7,335	3,479
Linwood	3,847	1,925
Little Falls†	9,730	6,405
Little Ferry	6,175	4,955
Little Silver	5,202	2,595
Livingston†	23,124	9,932
Lodi	23,502	15,392
Long Branch	26,228	23,090
Lower Penns Neck*	10,417	7,376
Lyndhurst†	21,867	19,980
Madison	15,122	10,417
Madison*	22,772	7,366
Magnolia	4,199	1,883
Mahwah*	7,376	4,880
Manasquan	4,022	3,178
Mantua*	7,991	3,548
Manville	10,995	8,597
Maple Shade†	12,947	6,560
Maplewood†	23,977	25,201
Margate City	9,474	4,715
Marlboro*	8,038	6,359
Matawan	5,097	3,739
Matawan*	7,359	3,888
Maywood	11,460	8,667
Medford Lakes	2,876	461
Mendham	2,371	1,724
Merchantville	4,075	4,183
Metuchen	14,041	9,879
Middlesex	10,520	5,943
Middletown†	39,675	16,203
Midland Park	7,543	5,164
Millburn†	18,799	14,560
Milltown	5,435	3,786
Millville	19,096	16,041
Monroe*	5,831	4,082
Montclair	43,129	43,927
Montvale	3,699	1,856
Montville*	6,772	4,159
Moonachie	3,052	1,775
Moorestown*	12,497	9,123
Morris*	12,092	7,432
Morris Plains	4,703	2,707
Morristown	17,712	17,124
Mountain Lakes	4,037	2,806
Mountainside	6,325	2,046
Mount Ephraim	5,447	4,449
Mount Holly†	13,271	8,206
Mount Laurel*	5,249	2,817
National Park	3,380	2,419
Neptune†	21,487	13,613
Neptune City	4,013	3,073
Netcong	2,765	2,284
Newark	405,220	438,776
New Brunswick	40,139	38,811
New Egypt	1,737	1,294
New Hanover†	28,528	18,168
New Milford	18,810	6,006
New Providence	10,243	3,380
New Shrewsbury	7,313	...
Newton	6,563	5,781
North Arlington	17,477	15,970
North Bergen	42,387	41,560
North Brunswick*	10,099	6,450
North Caldwell	4,163	1,781

Place	1960	1950
N.J.—Cont.:		
Northfield	5,849	3,498
North Haledon	6,026	3,550
North Plainfield	16,993	12,766
North Princeton	4,506	1,721
Northvale	2,892	1,455
North Wildwood	3,598	3,158
Norwood	2,852	1,792
Nutley	29,513	26,992
Oakhurst	4,374	2,388
Oakland	9,446	1,817
Oaklyn	4,778	4,889
Ocean City	7,618	6,040
Oceanport	4,937	7,588
Old Tappan	2,330	828
Oradell	7,487	3,665
Orange	35,789	38,037
Palisades Park	11,943	9,635
Palmyra	7,036	5,802
Paramus	23,238	6,268
Park Ridge	6,389	3,189
Parsippany-Troy Hills†	25,557	15,290
Passaic	53,963	57,702
Passaic*	5,537	3,429
Paterson	143,663	139,336
Paulsboro	8,121	7,842
Peapack-Gladstone	1,804	1,450
Pemberton*	13,726	4,751
Pennington	2,063	1,682
Pennsauken†	33,771	22,767
Penns Grove	6,176	6,669
Pequannock*	10,553	5,254
Perth Amboy	38,007	41,330
Phillipsburg	18,502	18,919
Pine Hill	3,939	2,546
Piscataway*	19,890	10,180
Pitman	8,644	6,960
Plainfield	45,330	42,366
Pleasantville	15,172	11,938
Point Pleasant	10,182	4,009
Point Pleasant Beach	3,873	2,000
Pompton Lakes	9,445	4,654
Port Norris	1,789	1,735
Princeton	11,890	12,230
Prospect Park	5,201	5,242
Rahway	27,699	21,290
Ramsey	9,527	4,670
Randolph*	7,295	4,293
Raritan†	15,334	2,763
Raritan	6,137	5,131
Readington*	6,147	4,080
Red Bank	12,482	12,743
Ridgefield	10,788	8,312
Ridgefield Park	12,701	11,993
Ridgewood	25,391	17,481
Ringwood	4,182	1,752
Riverdale	2,596	1,352
River Edge	13,264	9,204
Riverside†	8,474	7,199
Riverton	3,324	2,761
River Vale*	5,616	1,699
Rochelle Park†	6,119	4,483
Rockaway	5,413	3,812
Rockaway*	10,356	4,418
Roebling	3,272	...
Roseland	2,804	2,019
Roselle	21,032	17,681
Roselle Park	12,546	11,537
Roxbury*	9,983	5,707
Rumson	6,405	4,044
Runnemede	8,396	4,217
Rutherford	20,473	17,411
Saddle Brook†	13,834	7,955
Saddle River	1,776	1,003
Salem	8,941	9,050
Sayreville	22,553	10,338
Scotch Plains†	18,491	9,069
Seabrook Farms	1,798	2,284
Sea Girt	1,798	1,178
Secaucus	12,154	9,750
Shrewsbury	3,222	1,613
Somerdale	4,839	1,417
Somers Point	4,504	2,480
Somerville	12,458	11,571
South Amboy	8,422	8,422
South Belmar	1,537	1,294
South Bound Brook	3,626	2,905
South Brunswick*	10,278	4,001
South Orange	16,175	15,230
South Plainfield	17,879	8,008
South River	13,397	11,308
South Toms River	1,603	492
Spotswood	5,788	2,325
Springfield†	14,467	7,214
Spring Lake	2,922	2,008
Spring Lake Heights	3,309	1,798
Stanhope	1,814	1,351
Stratford	4,308	1,356
Summit	23,677	17,929
Sussex	1,656	1,541
Swedesboro	2,449	2,459
Teaneck†	42,085	33,772
Tenafly	14,264	9,651
Toms River	6,062	2,517

Place	1960	1950
N.J.—Cont.:		
Totowa	10,897	6,045
Trenton (c.)	114,167	128,009
Tuckerton	1,536	1,332
Union†	51,499	38,004
Union Beach	5,862	3,636
Union City	52,180	55,537
Upper Penns Neck*	7,595	6,717
Upper Saddle River	3,570	706
Ventnor City	8,688	8,158
Verona	13,782	10,921
Villas	2,085	...
Vineland	37,685	8,155
Waldwick	10,495	3,963
Wallington	9,261	8,910
Wanamassa	3,928	2,512
Wanaque	7,126	4,222
Warren*	5,386	3,316
Washington	5,723	4,802
Washington*	6,654	1,208
Watchung	3,312	1,818
Wayne†	29,353	11,822
Weehawken†	13,504	14,830
Wenonah	2,100	1,511
West Belmar	2,511	2,058
West Caldwell	8,314	4,666
West Deptford*	11,152	5,446
Westfield	31,447	21,243
West Long Branch	5,337	2,739
West Milford*	8,157	3,650
West New York	35,547	37,683
West Orange	39,895	28,605
West Paterson	7,602	3,931
Westville	4,951	4,731
Westwood	9,046	6,766
Wharton	5,006	3,853
Wildwood	4,690	5,475
Wildwood Crest	3,011	1,772
Williamstown	2,722	2,632
Winslow*	0,142	5,102
Woodbine	2,823	2,417
Woodbridge†	78,846	35,758
Woodbury	12,453	10,931
Woodbury Heights	1,723	1,373
Woodcliff Lake	2,742	1,420
Wood-Lynne	3,128	2,776
Wood-Ridge	7,964	6,283
Woodstown	2,942	2,345
Wrightstown	4,846	1,199
Wyckoff†	11,205	5,590
NEW MEXICO:		
Alamogordo	21,723	6,783
Albuquerque	201,189	96,815
Artesia	12,000	8,244
Aztec	4,137	885
Bayard	2,327	2,119
Belen	5,031	4,495
Bernalillo	2,574	1,922
Carlsbad	25,541	17,975
Carrizozo	1,546	1,389
Clayton	3,314	3,515
Clovis	23,713	17,318
Deming	6,764	5,672
Espanola	1,976	1,446
Eunice	3,531	2,352
Farmington	23,786	3,637
Fort Sumner	1,809	1,982
Gallup	14,089	9,133
Grants	10,274	2,251
Hobbs	26,275	13,875
Hurley	1,851	...
Jal	3,051	2,047
Las Cruces	29,367	12,325
Las Vegas city	7,790	7,494
Las Vegas town	6,028	6,269
Lordsburg	3,436	3,525
Los Alamos	12,584	9,934
Loving	1,646	1,487
Lovington	9,660	3,134
Milan	2,658	...
Mountainair	1,605	1,418
Portales	9,695	8,112
Ranchos de Taos	1,668	1,386
Raton	8,146	8,241
Roswell	39,593	25,738
Ruidoso	1,557	806
Santa Fe (c.)	34,676	27,998
Santa Rita	1,772	2,135
Santa Rosa	2,220	2,199
Silver City	6,972	7,022
Socorro	5,271	4,334
Springer	1,564	1,558
State College-Mesilla Park	4,387	...
Taos	2,163	1,815
Truth or Consequences	4,269	4,563
Tucumcari	8,143	8,419
Tularosa	3,200	1,642
Zuni Pueblo	3,585	2,563
NEW YORK:		
Adams	1,914	1,762
Addison	2,185	1,920
Akron	2,841	2,481

Place	1960	1950
N.Y.—Cont.:		
Albany (c.)	129,726	134,995
Albion	5,182	4,850
Alden	2,042	1,252
Alexandria Bay	1,583	1,688
Alfred	2,807	2,053
Allegany	2,064	1,738
Amenia*	7,546	7,481
Amityville	8,318	6,164
Amsterdam	28,772	32,240
Amsterdam*	5,400	4,698
Angola	2,499	1,936
Arcade	1,930	1,818
Ardsley	3,991	1,744
Arlington	8,317	5,374
Athens	1,754	1,545
Attica	2,758	2,676
Auburn	35,249	36,722
Ausable Forks	2,026	1,643
Avon	2,772	2,412
Babylon	11,062	6,015
Bainbridge	1,712	1,505
Baldwin	30,204	...
Baldwinsville	5,985	4,495
Ballston Spa	4,991	4,937
Balmville	1,538	...
Batavia	18,210	17,799
Bath	6,166	5,416
Bayville	3,962	1,981
Beacon	13,922	14,012
Bellmore	12,784	...
Bellport	2,461	1,449
Bethlehem*	18,936	13,065
Bethpage-Old Bethpage	20,515	...
Binghamton	75,941	80,674
Blasdell	3,909	3,127
Boonville	2,403	2,329
Boston*	5,106	2,302
Brentwood	15,387	2,803
Brewster	1,714	1,810
Briarcliff Manor	5,105	2,494
Brighton*	27,849	18,036
Brightwaters	3,193	2,336
Brockport	5,256	4,748
Bronxville	6,744	6,778
Brunswick*	9,004	5,967
Buchanan	2,019	1,820
Buffalo	532,759	580,132
Caledonia	1,917	1,683
Cambridge	1,748	1,692
Camden	2,694	2,407
Camillus*	18,328	6,735
Canajoharie	2,681	2,761
Canandaigua	9,370	8,332
Canastota	4,896	4,458
Canisteo	2,731	2,625
Canton	5,046	4,379
Carmel*	9,113	5,458
Carthage	4,216	4,420
Castleton-on-Hudson	1,752	1,751
Catskill	5,825	5,392
Cayuga Heights	2,788	1,131
Cazenovia	2,584	1,946
Cedarhurst	6,954	6,051
Celoron	1,507	1,555
Centereach	8,524	...
Center Moriches	2,521	1,761
Centerport	3,628	...
Champlain	1,549	1,505
Chatham	2,426	2,304
Cheektowaga-Northwest	52,362	...
Cheektowaga-Southwest	12,766	...
Chenango*	9,858	5,747
Chili*	11,237	5,283
Chittenango	3,180	1,307
Clayton	1,996	1,981
Clifton Springs	1,953	1,838
Clinton	1,855	1,630
Clyde	2,693	2,492
Cobleskill	3,471	3,208
Cohoes	20,129	21,727
Cold Spring	2,083	1,788
Cold Spring Harbor	1,705	...
Collins*	6,984	6,862
Colonie	6,992	2,068
Commach	9,613	...
Cooperstown	2,553	2,727
Copiague	14,081	...
Corinth	3,193	3,161
Corning	17,085	17,684
Corning*	6,732	4,275
Cornwall	2,785	2,211
Cornwall Southwest	2,824	...
Cortland	19,181	18,152
Cortlandville*	5,660	4,058
Coxsackie	2,849	2,722
Croton-on-Hudson	6,812	4,837
Cuba	1,949	1,783
Dannemora	4,835	4,122
Dansville	5,460	5,253
Deer Park	16,726	...
Delhi	2,307	2,223
Depew	13,580	7,217
Deposit	2,025	2,016
Dobbs Ferry	9,260	6,268

‡Willingboro in 1950.

Place	1960	1950
N.Y.—Cont.:		
Dolgeville	3,058	3,204
Dover*	8,776	7,460
Dryden*	7,353	5,006
Dunkirk	18,205	18,007
East Aurora	6,791	5,962
East Greenbush*	9,107	6,338
East Hampton	1,772	1,737
East Hills	7,184	2,547
East Massapequa	14,779	...
East Meadow	46,036	...
East Middletown	1,752	1,485
East Neck	3,789	...
East Northport	8,381	3,842
East Rochester	8,152	7,022
East Rockaway	10,721	7,970
East Syracuse	4,708	4,766
East Williston	2,940	1,734
Eden	2,366	1,394
Eggertsville	44,807	...
Ellenville	5,003	4,225
Elma*	7,468	4,020
Elmira	46,517	49,716
Elmira Heights	5,157	5,009
Elmira Southeast	6,698	...
Elmont	30,138	...
Elmsford	3,795	3,147
Endicott	18,775	20,050
Fairport	5,507	5,267
Fairview	8,626	1,721
Falconer	3,343	3,292
Fallsburgh*	6,748	6,321
Farmingdale	6,128	4,492
Farmingville	2,134	...
Fayetteville	4,311	2,624
Fenton*	5,920	4,168
Fernwood	2,108	...
Fishkill*	7,083	3,863
Floral Park	17,499	14,582
Florida	1,550	1,376
Flower Hill	4,594	1,948
Fort Edward	3,737	3,797
Fort Plain	2,809	2,935
Frankfort	3,872	3,844
Franklin Square	32,483	...
Franklinville	2,124	2,092
Fredonia	8,477	7,095
Freeport	34,419	24,680
Frewsburg	1,623	1,383
Fulton	14,261	13,922
Garden City	23,948	14,486
Garden City Park-Herricks	15,364	...
Gates*	13,755	7,925
Geneseo	3,284	2,838
Geneva	17,286	17,144
Glen Cove	23,817	15,130
Glens Falls	18,580	19,610
Gloversville	21,741	23,634
Goshen	3,906	3,311
Gouverneur	4,946	4,916
Gowanda	3,352	3,289
Grand Island*	9,607	3,090
Granville	2,715	2,826
Great Neck	10,171	7,759
Great Neck Estates	3,262	2,464
Great Neck Plaza	4,948	4,246
Greece*	48,670	25,508
Greene	2,051	1,628
Green Island	3,533	4,016
Greenlawn	5,422	1,000
Greenport	2,608	3,028
Greenwich	2,263	2,212
Groton	2,123	2,150
Halesite	2,857	...
Hamburg	9,145	6,938
Hamburg-Lake Shore	11,527	...
Hamilton	3,348	3,507
Hancock	1,830	1,560
Harris Hill	3,944	...
Harrison*	19,201	13,577
Hastings-on-Hudson	8,979	7,565
Haverstraw	5,771	5,818
Hempstead	34,641	29,135
Henrietta Northeast	6,403	...
Herkimer	9,396	9,400
Hewlett Harbor	1,610	411
Hicksville	50,405	...
Highland	2,931	3,035
Highland Falls	4,469	3,930
Holbrook	3,441	...
Holley	1,788	1,551
Homer	3,622	3,244
Honeoye Falls	2,143	1,460
Hoosick Falls	4,023	4,297
Hornell	13,907	15,049
Horseheads	7,207	3,606
Hudson	11,075	11,629
Hudson Falls	7,752	7,236
Huntington	11,255	9,324
Huntington Station	23,438	9,924
Hyde Park	1,979	1,059
N.Y.—Cont.:		
Ilion	10,199	9,363
Inwood	10,362	...
Irondequoit*	55,337	34,417
Irvington	5,494	3,657
Island Park	3,846	2,031
Ithaca	28,799	29,257
Jamestown	41,818	43,354
Jericho	10,795	...
Johnson City	19,118	19,249
Johnstown	10,390	10,923
Johnstown*	5,120	4,153
Keeseville	2,213	1,977
Kenmore	21,261	20,066
Kings Park	4,949	10,960
Kings Point	5,410	2,445
Kingston	29,260	28,817
Lackawanna	29,564	27,658
La Grange*	6,079	2,280
Lake Carmel	2,735	1,055
Lake Erie Beach	2,117	...
Lake Placid	2,998	2,999
Lake Ronkonkoma	4,841	...
Lake Success	2,954	1,264
Lakewood	3,933	3,013
Lancaster	12,254	8,665
Larchmont	6,789	6,330
Lawrence	5,907	4,681
Le Roy	4,662	4,721
Levittown	65,276	...
Lewiston	3,320	1,626
Liberty	4,704	4,658
Lincoln Park	2,707	1,527
Lindenhurst	20,905	8,644
Little Falls	8,935	9,541
Liverpool	3,487	2,933
Livingston Manor	2,080	...
Lloyd Harbor	2,521	945
Lockport	26,443	25,133
Lockport*	6,492	3,945
Locust Grove	11,558	...
Long Beach	26,473	15,586
Lowville	3,616	3,671
Lynbrook	19,881	17,314
Lyons	4,673	4,217
Malone	8,737	9,501
Malverne	9,968	8,086
Mamaroneck	17,673	15,016
Manchester*	6,242	5,755
Manlius	1,997	1,742
Manorhaven	3,566	1,819
Marcellus	1,697	1,382
Marcy*	7,024	5,210
Marlboro	1,733	1,709
Massapequa	32,900	...
Massapequa Park	19,904	2,334
Massena	15,478	13,137
Mastic Beach	3,035	1,079
Mastic Shirley	3,397	...
Mayville	1,619	1,492
Mechanicville	6,831	7,385
Medina	6,681	6,179
Melrose Park	2,058	1,803
Menands	2,314	2,453
Merrick	18,789	...
Middleport	1,882	1,641
Middletown	23,475	22,586
Millbrook	1,717	1,568
Mineola	20,519	14,831
Minoa	1,838	1,008
Mohawk	3,533	3,196
Monroe	3,323	1,753
Monticello	5,222	4,223
Montour Falls	1,533	1,457
Moravia	1,575	1,480
Mount Kisco	6,805	5,907
Mount Morris	3,250	3,450
Mount Vernon	76,010	71,899
Munsey Park	2,847	2,048
Nesconset	1,964	...
Newark	12,868	10,295
Newburgh	30,979	31,956
Newfane*	8,523	5,801
New Hartford	2,468	1,947
New Hyde Park	10,808	7,349
New Paltz	3,041	2,285
New Rochelle	76,812	59,725
New Scotland*	5,818	3,956
New Windsor	4,041	2,754
New York City	7,781,984	7,891,957
New York Mills	3,788	3,366
Niagara*	7,503	4,729
Niagara Falls	102,394	90,872
Niskayuna*	14,032	9,442
North Bellmore	19,639	...
North Castle*	6,797	3,855
North Collins	1,574	1,325
North Greenbush*	8,161	4,913
North Merrick	12,976	...
North New Hyde Park	17,929	...
North Pelham	5,326	5,046
Northport	5,972	3,859
North Syracuse	7,412	3,356
North Tarrytown	8,818	8,740
North Tonawanda	34,757	24,731
N.Y.—Cont.:		
North Valley Stream	17,239	...
Norwich	9,175	8,816
Norwood	2,200	1,995
Nyack	6,062	5,889
Oakfield	2,070	1,781
Oceanside	30,448	...
Ogdensburg	16,122	16,166
Old Westbury	2,064	1,160
Olean	21,868	22,884
Oneida	11,677	11,325
Oneonta	13,412	13,564
Onondaga*	13,429	9,351
Orchard Park	3,278	2,054
Oriskany	1,580	1,346
Ossining	18,662	16,098
Oswego	22,155	22,647
Owego	5,417	5,350
Oxford	1,871	1,811
Painted Post	2,570	2,405
Palmyra	3,476	3,034
Parma*	6,277	4,049
Patchogue	8,838	7,361
Pawling	1,734	1,430
Peekskill	18,737	17,731
Pelham	1,964	1,843
Pelham Manor	6,114	5,306
Penfield*	12,601	4,847
Penn Yan	5,770	5,481
Perry	4,629	4,533
Phelps	1,887	1,650
Philmont	1,750	1,792
Phoenix	2,408	1,917
Piermont	1,906	1,897
Pittsford	1,749	1,668
Plainedge	21,973	...
Plainview	27,710	...
Plattsburgh	20,172	17,738
Plattsburgh*	13,390	3,713
Pleasantville	5,877	4,861
Port Chester	24,960	23,970
Port Dickinson	2,295	2,199
Port Ewen	2,622	1,885
Port Henry	1,767	1,831
Port Jefferson	2,336	3,296
Port Jervis	9,268	9,372
Port Washington	15,657	...
Potsdam	7,765	7,491
Poughkeepsie	38,330	41,023
Pulaski	2,256	2,033
Ravena	2,410	2,006
Red Hook	1,719	1,225
Rensselaer	10,506	10,856
Rhinebeck	2,093	1,923
Richfield Springs	1,630	1,534
Riverhead	5,830	4,892
Rochdale	1,800	1,219
Rochester	318,611	332,488
Rockville Centre	26,355	22,362
Rocky Point	2,261	...
Rome	51,646	41,682
Ronkonkoma	4,220	1,334
Roosevelt	12,883	...
Roslyn	2,681	1,612
Rotterdam	16,871	...
Rouses Point	2,160	2,001
Rye	14,225	11,721
Sag Harbor	2,346	2,373
St. James	3,524	1,390
St. Johnsville	2,196	2,210
Salamanca	8,480	8,861
Sands Point	2,161	860
San Romeo	11,996	...
Saranac Lake	6,421	6,913
Saratoga Springs	16,630	15,473
Saugerties	4,286	3,907
Sauquoit	1,715	1,227
Scarsdale	17,968	13,156
Schaghticoke*	5,269	4,019
Schenectady	81,682	91,785
Scotia	7,625	7,812
Scottsville	1,863	1,025
Sea Cliff	5,669	4,868
Seaford	14,718	...
Selden	1,604	1,743
Seneca Falls	7,439	6,634
Sherburne	1,647	1,604
Sherrill	2,922	2,236
Shrub Oak	1,874	...
Sidney	5,157	4,815
Silver Creek	3,310	3,068
Skaneateles	2,921	2,331
Sloan	5,803	4,698
Sloatsburg	2,565	2,018
Smithtown Branch	1,986	1,424
Sodus	1,645	1,588
Solvay	8,732	7,868
Sound Beach	1,625	...
Southampton	4,582	4,042
South Farmingdale	16,318	...
South Glens Falls	4,129	3,645
South Huntington	7,084	1,274
South Nyack	3,113	3,102
South Westbury	11,977	...
Spencerport	2,461	1,595
Spring Valley	6,538	4,500
N.Y.—Cont.:		
Springville	3,852	3,322
Stewart Manor	2,422	1,879
Stony Brook	3,548	...
Stony Point	3,330	1,438
Suffern	5,094	4,010
Syracuse	216,038	220,583
Tarrytown	11,109	8,851
Thomaston	2,767	2,045
Ticonderoga	3,568	3,517
Tonawanda	21,561	14,561
Tonawanda†	83,771	...
Troy	67,492	72,311
Trumansburg	1,768	1,479
Tuckahoe	6,423	5,991
Tupper Lake	5,200	5,441
Ulster*	8,448	4,411
Unadilla	1,586	1,317
Uniondale	20,041	...
Upper Nyack	1,833	1,195
Utica	100,410	101,531
Valley Stream	38,629	26,854
Vernon Valley	5,998	...
Verona*	5,305	4,017
Vestal*	16,806	8,902
Victory Heights	2,528	1,857
Walden	4,851	4,559
Walton	3,855	3,947
Wantagh	34,172	...
Wappingers Falls	4,447	3,490
Warrensburg	2,240	2,358
Warsaw	3,653	3,713
Warwick	3,218	2,674
Waterford	2,915	2,968
Waterloo	5,098	4,438
Watertown	33,306	34,350
Waterville	1,901	1,634
Watervliet	13,917	15,197
Watkins Glen	2,813	3,052
Waverly	5,950	6,037
Wayland	2,003	1,834
Webster	3,060	1,773
Weedsport	1,731	1,588
Wellsville	5,967	6,402
Westbury	14,757	7,112
West Carthage	2,167	2,000
West Elmira	5,763	3,833
Westfield	3,878	3,663
West Glens Falls	2,725	1,665
West Haverstraw	5,020	3,099
West Hempstead-Lakeview	24,783	...
West Seneca	23,138	...
Wheatfield*	8,008	4,720
Whitehall	4,016	4,457
White Plains	50,485	43,466
Whitesboro	4,784	3,902
Williamson	1,690	1,520
Williamsville	6,316	4,649
Williston Park	8,255	7,505
Wilson*	5,319	3,696
Winona Lakes	1,655	...
Wolcott	1,641	1,516
Woodmere	14,011	...
Yonkers	190,634	152,798
Yorktown	3,576	...
Yorktown Heights	2,478	...
Yorkville	3,749	3,528
Youngstown	1,848	932
NORTH CAROLINA:		
Aberdeen	1,531	1,603
Ahoskie	4,583	3,579
Albemarle	12,261	11,798
Archdale	1,520	1,218
Asheboro	9,449	7,701
Asheboro South	1,515	...
Asheville	60,192	53,000
Ayden	3,108	2,282
Badin	1,905	2,126
Balfours	3,805	1,936
Barker Heights	2,184	1,569
Beaufort	2,922	3,212
Belhaven	2,386	2,528
Belmont	5,007	5,330
Belmont-South Rosemary	2,043	3,173
Benson	2,355	2,102
Bessemer City	4,017	3,961
Bethel	1,578	1,402
Boger City	1,728	...
Bonnie Doone	4,481	...
Boone	3,686	2,973
Brevard	4,857	3,908
Burgaw	1,750	1,613
Burlington	33,199	24,560
Canton	5,068	4,906
Carrboro	1,997	1,795
Cary	3,356	1,446
Chadbourn	2,323	2,103
Chapel Hill	12,573	9,177
Charlotte	201,564	134,042
Cherryville	3,607	3,492
China Grove	1,500	1,491
Clayton	3,302	2,229
Clinton	7,461	4,414
Concord	17,799	16,486
Concord North	2,199	...

Place	1960	1950
N.C.—Cont.:		
Conover	2,281	1,164
Cooleemee	1,609	1,925
Cramerton	3,123	3,211
Dallas	3,270	2,454
Davidson	2,573	2,423
Draper	3,382	3,629
Dunn	7,566	6,316
Durham	78,302	71,311
East Fayetteville	2,797	...
East Gastonia	3,326	3,733
East Marion	2,442	2,901
East Rockingham	3,211	...
East Spencer	2,171	2,444
East Wilmington	5,520	1,623
Edenton	4,458	4,468
Elizabeth City	14,062	12,685
Elizabethtown	1,625	1,611
Elkin	2,868	2,842
Enfield	2,978	2,361
Erwin	3,183	3,344
Fairmont	2,286	2,319
Farmville	3,997	2,942
Fayetteville	47,106	34,715
Fayetteville North	3,071	...
Flat Rock	1,808	...
Forest City	6,556	4,971
Franklin	2,173	1,975
Franklinton	1,513	1,414
Fremont	1,609	1,395
Fuquay Springs	3,389	1,992
Garner	3,451	1,180
Gastonia	37,276	23,069
Gibsonville	1,784	1,866
Glen Raven	2,418	...
Goldsboro	28,873	21,454
Graham	7,723	5,026
Granite Falls	2,644	2,286
Greensboro	119,574	74,389
Greenville	22,860	16,724
Grifton	1,816	510
Hamlet	4,460	5,061
Havelock	2,433	...
Hazelwood	1,925	1,769
Henderson	12,740	10,996
Hendersonville	5,911	6,103
Hertford	2,068	2,096
Hickory	19,328	14,755
Hickory East	3,274	...
Hickory North	1,541	...
High Point	62,063	39,973
Hudson	1,536	922
Jacksonville	13,491	3,960
Jonesville	1,895	1,768
Kannapolis	34,647	28,448
Kernersville	2,942	2,396
Kings Mountain	8,008	7,206
Kinston	24,819	18,336
La Grange	2,133	1,852
Landis	1,763	1,827
Landis Northeast	1,517	...
Laurinburg	8,242	7,134
Leaksville	6,427	4,045
Lenoir	10,257	7,888
Lexington	16,093	13,571
Lincolnton	5,699	5,423
Longhurst	1,546	1,539
Longview	2,997	2,291
Louisburg	2,862	2,545
Lowell	2,784	2,313
Lumberton	15,305	9,186
Madison	1,912	1,789
Maiden	2,039	1,952
Marion	3,345	2,740
Mars Hill	1,574	1,404
Maxton	1,755	1,974
Mayodan	2,366	2,246
Mebane	2,364	2,068
Midway Park	4,164	3,703
Mocksville	2,379	1,909
Monroe	10,882	10,140
Mooresville	6,918	7,121
Morehead City	5,583	5,144
Morganton	9,186	8,311
Mount Airy	7,055	7,192
Mount Holly	4,037	2,241
Mount Olive	4,673	3,732
Murfreesboro	2,643	2,140
Murphy	2,235	2,433
New Bern	15,717	15,812
Newton	6,658	6,039
North Belmont	8,328	3,948
North Henderson	1,995	1,873
North Wilkesboro	4,197	4,379
Norwood	1,844	1,735
Owens	5,207	...
Oxford	6,978	6,685
Pineville	1,514	1,373
Plymouth	4,666	4,486
Raeford	3,058	2,030
Raleigh (c.)	93,931	65,679
Randleman	2,232	2,066
Red Springs	2,767	2,245
Reidsville	14,267	11,708
Rex	1,515	...
Richmond Hill	2,943	2,303
Roanoke Rapids	13,320	8,156

Place	1960	1950
N.C.—Cont.:		
Robersonville	1,684	1,414
Rockingham	5,512	3,356
Rocky Mount	32,147	27,697
Roxboro	5,147	4,321
Rural Hall	1,503	...
Rutherfordton	3,392	3,146
St. Pauls	2,249	2,251
Salisbury	21,297	20,102
Sanford	12,253	10,013
Scotland Neck	2,974	2,730
Selma	3,102	2,639
Shelby	17,698	15,508
Siler City	4,455	2,501
Smithfield	6,117	5,574
South Belmont	2,286	...
Southern Pines	5,198	4,272
South Fayetteville	3,411	3,428
South Gastonia	3,762	6,465
South Henderson	2,017	...
Southport	2,034	1,748
South Salisbury	3,065	...
South Wilmington	2,238	...
Spencer	2,904	3,242
Spindale	4,082	3,891
Spray	4,565	...
Spring Lake	4,110	...
Spruce Pine	2,504	2,280
Stanley	1,980	1,644
Statesville	19,844	16,901
Swannanoa	2,189	...
Sylva	1,564	1,382
Tabor City	2,338	2,033
Tarboro	8,411	8,120
Thomasville	15,190	11,154
Toast	2,023	1,401
Troy	2,346	2,213
Tryon	2,223	1,985
Valdese	2,941	2,730
Wadesboro	3,744	3,408
Wake Forest	2,664	3,704
Wallace	2,285	1,622
Warsaw	2,221	1,598
Washington	9,939	9,698
Waynesville	6,159	5,295
Weldon	2,165	2,295
Wendell	1,620	1,253
West Concord	5,510	...
West Marion	2,335	1,233
Whiteville	4,683	4,238
Wilkesboro	1,568	1,370
Williamston	6,924	4,975
Wilmington	44,013	45,043
Wilson	28,753	23,010
Windsor	1,813	1,781
Winston-Salem	111,135	87,811
Yadkinville	1,644	820
Zebulon	1,534	1,378
NORTH DAKOTA:		
Bismarck (c.)	27,670	18,640
Bottineau	2,613	2,268
Bowman	1,730	1,382
Cando	1,566	1,530
Carrington	2,438	2,101
Crosby	1,759	1,689
Devils Lake	6,299	6,427
Dickinson	9,971	7,469
Ellendale	1,800	1,759
Enderlin	1,596	1,504
Fargo	46,662	38,256
Garrison	1,794	1,890
Grafton	5,885	4,901
Grand Forks	34,451	26,836
Harvey	2,365	2,337
Hettinger	1,769	1,762
Jamestown	15,163	10,697
Kenmare	1,696	1,712
Langdon	2,151	1,838
Larimore	1,714	1,374
Linton	1,826	1,675
Lisbon	2,093	2,031
Mandan	10,525	7,298
Mayville	2,168	1,790
Minot	30,604	22,032
New Rockford	2,177	2,185
New Town	1,586	...
Oakes	1,650	1,774
Park River	1,813	1,692
Rugby	2,972	2,907
South West Fargo	3,328	1,032
Stanley	1,795	1,486
Tioga	2,087	456
Valley City	7,809	6,851
Wahpeton	5,876	5,125
Watford City	1,865	1,371
Williston	11,866	7,378
OHIO:		
Ada	3,918	3,640
Akron	290,351	274,605
Alliance	28,362	26,161
Amberley	2,951	885
Amherst	6,750	3,542
Arcanum	1,678	1,530
Archbold	2,348	1,486
Ashland	17,419	14,287
Ashtabula	24,559	23,696
Ashville	1,639	1,303
Athens	16,470	11,660
Aurora	4,049	571

Place	1960	1950
OHIO—Cont.:		
Avon	6,002	2,773
Avon Lake	9,403	4,342
Baltimore	2,116	1,843
Barberton	33,805	27,820
Barnesville	4,425	4,665
Batavia	1,729	1,445
Bay	14,489	6,917
Beachwood	6,089	1,073
Bedford	15,223	9,105
Bedford Heights	5,275	...
Bellaire	11,502	12,573
Bellefontaine	11,424	10,232
Bellevue	8,286	6,906
Bellville	1,621	1,355
Belpre	5,418	2,451
Berea	16,592	12,051
Bethel	2,019	1,932
Bexley	14,319	12,378
Blanchester	2,944	2,109
Blue Ash	8,341	...
Bluffton	2,591	2,432
Bowling Green	13,574	12,005
Bradford	2,148	2,055
Brecksville	5,435	2,664
Brewster	2,025	1,618
Bridgeport	3,824	4,309
Brilliant	2,174	2,066
Broadview Heights	6,209	2,279
Brooklyn	10,733	6,317
Brook Park	12,856	2,606
Brookville	3,184	1,908
Brunswick	11,725	...
Bryan	7,361	6,365
Buckey Lake	2,129	1,401
Bucyrus	12,276	10,327
Byesville	2,447	2,236
Cadiz	3,259	3,020
Calcutta	2,221	...
Caldwell	1,999	1,767
Cambridge	14,562	14,739
Campbell	13,406	12,882
Canal Fulton	1,555	1,258
Canal Winchester	1,976	1,194
Canfield	3,252	1,465
Canton	113,631	116,912
Cardington	1,613	1,465
Carey	3,722	3,260
Carrollton	2,786	2,658
Cedarville	1,702	1,292
Celina	7,659	5,703
Centerville	3,490	827
Chagrin Falls	3,458	3,085
Chardon	3,154	2,478
Cheviot	10,701	9,944
Chillicothe	24,957	20,133
Cincinnati	502,550	503,998
Circleville	11,059	8,723
Cleveland	876,050	914,808
Cleveland Heights	61,813	59,141
Cleves	2,076	1,981
Clyde	4,826	4,083
Coal Grove	2,961	2,492
Coldwater	2,766	2,217
Columbiana	4,164	3,369
Columbus (c.)	471,316	375,901
Columbus Grove	2,104	1,936
Conneaut	10,557	10,230
Cortland	1,957	1,259
Coshocton	13,106	11,675
Covington	2,473	2,172
Crestline	5,521	4,614
Creston	1,522	1,300
Crooksville	2,958	2,960
Crystal Lakes	1,569	1,115
Cuyahoga Falls	47,922	29,195
Dayton	262,332	243,872
Deer Park	8,423	7,241
Defiance	14,553	11,265
Delaware	13,282	11,804
Delphos	6,961	6,220
Delta	2,376	2,120
Dennison	4,158	4,432
Deshler	1,824	1,623
Dover	11,300	9,852
Doylestown	1,873	1,358
East Ashtabula	4,179	2,390
East Canton	1,521	1,001
East Cleveland	37,991	40,047
Eastlake	12,467	7,486
East Liverpool	22,306	24,217
East Palestine	5,232	5,195
Eaton	5,034	4,242
Eaton Estates	1,733	...
Edgerton	1,566	1,246
Elmwood Place	3,813	4,113
Elyria	43,782	30,307
Englewood	1,515	678
Euclid	62,998	41,396
Fairborn	19,453	7,847
Fairfax	2,430	...
Fairfield	9,734	...
Fairport	4,267	4,519
Fairview Park	14,624	9,311
Findlay	30,344	23,845
Fostoria	15,732	14,351
Franklin	7,917	5,388
Fredericktown	1,531	1,467
Fremont	17,573	16,537
Gahanna	2,717	596
Galion	12,650	9,952

Place	1960	1950
OHIO—Cont.:		
Gallipolis	8,775	7,871
Garfield Heights	38,455	21,662
Garrettsville	1,662	1,504
Gates Mills	1,588	1,056
Geneva	5,677	4,718
Genoa	1,957	1,723
Georgetown	2,674	2,200
Germantown	3,399	2,479
Gibsonburg	2,540	2,281
Girard	12,997	10,113
Glendale	2,823	2,402
Glouster	2,255	2,327
Golf Manor	4,648	3,603
Grafton	1,683	1,194
Grandview Heights	8,270	7,659
Granville	2,868	2,653
Greenfield	5,422	4,862
Greenhills	5,407	3,005
Greenville	10,585	8,859
Grove City	8,107	2,339
Groveport	2,043	1,165
Hamilton	72,354	57,951
Harrison	3,878	1,943
Heath	2,426	...
Hicksville	3,116	2,629
Highland Heights	2,929	762
Hilliard	5,633	610
Hillsboro	5,474	5,126
Hubbard	7,137	4,560
Hudson	2,438	1,538
Huron	5,197	2,515
Independence	6,868	3,105
Indian Hill	4,526	2,090
Ironton	15,745	16,333
Jackson	6,980	6,504
Jamestown	1,730	1,345
Jefferson‡	2,116	1,844
Jefferson§	2,774	1,647
Johnstown	2,881	1,220
Kent	17,830	12,418
Kenton	8,747	8,475
Kettering	54,462	...
Lakemore	2,765	2,463
Lakeville	4,181	3,432
Lakewood	66,154	68,071
Lancaster	29,916	24,180
Lebanon	5,993	4,618
Leetonia	2,543	2,565
Leipsic	1,802	1,706
Lima	51,037	50,246
Lincoln Hts.‖	8,004	...
Lincoln Hts.¶	7,798	5,531
Lisbon	3,579	3,293
Liverpool North	1,575	...
Lockland	5,292	5,736
Lodi	2,213	1,523
Logan	6,417	5,972
London	6,379	5,222
Lorain	68,932	51,202
Loudonville	2,611	2,523
Louisville	5,116	3,801
Loveland	5,008	2,149
Lowellville	2,055	2,227
Lyndhurst	16,805	7,359
McArthur	1,529	1,466
McConnelsville	2,257	1,941
McDonald	2,727	1,858
Madeira	6,744	2,689
Magnolia	1,596	901
Manchester	2,172	2,281
Mansfield	47,325	43,564
Mansfield Southeast	2,961	...
Maple Heights	31,667	15,586
Mariemont	4,120	3,514
Marietta	16,847	16,006
Marion	37,079	33,817
Martins Ferry	11,919	13,220
Marysville	4,952	4,256
Mason	4,727	1,196
Massillon	31,236	29,594
Masury	2,512	2,151
Maumee	12,063	5,548
Mayfield ♀	2,747	1,926
Mayfield ♁	1,977	805
Mayfield Heights	13,478	5,807
Mechanicsburg	1,810	1,920
Medina	8,235	5,097
Mentor	4,354	2,383
Mentor-on-the-Lake	3,290	1,413
Miamisburg	9,893	6,329
Middleburg Heights	7,282	2,299
Middleport	3,373	3,446
Middletown	42,115	33,695
Milford	4,131	2,448
Millersburg	3,101	2,398
Minerva	3,833	3,280
Mingo Junction	4,987	4,464
Minster	2,193	1,728
Mogadore	3,851	1,818
Montgomery	3,075	579
Montpelier	4,131	3,867
Moraine	2,262	...
Moreland Hills	2,188	1,040
Mount Gilead	2,788	2,351
Mount Healthy	6,553	5,533
Mount Vernon	13,284	12,185
Munroe Falls	1,828	933

‡Ashtabula Co. §Madison Co. ‖Richland Co.
¶Hamilton Co. ♀Butler Co. ♁Cuyahoga Co.

Place	1960	1950
OHIO—Cont.:		
Napoleon	6,739	5,335
Navarre	1,698	1,763
Nelsonville	4,834	4,845
Newark	41,790	34,275
New Boston	3,984	4,754
New Bremen	1,972	1,546
Newburgh Heights	3,512	3,689
New Carlisle	4,107	1,640
Newcomerstown	4,273	4,514
New Concord	2,127	1,797
New Lexington	4,514	4,233
New London	2,392	2,023
New Miami	2,360	1,860
New Paris	1,679	1,046
New Philadelphia	14,241	12,948
New Richmond	2,834	1,960
Newton Falls	5,038	4,451
Newtown	1,750	1,462
Niles	19,545	16,773
North Baltimore	3,011	2,771
North Canton	7,727	4,032
North College Hill	12,035	7,921
North Kingsville	1,854	1,271
North Olmsted	16,290	6,604
North Ridgeville	8,057	...
North Royalton	9,290	3,939
North Zanesville	2,201	1,544
Norwalk	12,900	9,775
Norwood	34,580	35,001
Oak Harbor	2,903	2,370
Oak Hill	1,748	1,615
Oakwood city	10,493	9,691
Oakwood village	3,283	...
Oberlin	8,198	7,062
Obetz	1,984	1,049
Olmsted Falls	2,144	1,137
Oneida-Rolling-Mill Park	6,504	...
Ontario	3,049	...
Orange	2,006	897
Oregon	13,319	...
Orrville	6,511	5,153
Ottawa	3,245	2,962
Ottawa Hills	3,870	2,333
Oxford	7,828	6,944
Painesville	16,116	14,432
Parkview	2,018	661
Parma	82,845	28,897
Parma Heights	18,100	3,901
Paulding	2,936	2,352
Peebles	1,601	1,498
Pepper Pike	3,217	874
Perrysburg	5,519	4,006
Piqua	19,219	17,447
Plain City	2,146	1,715
Plymouth	1,822	1,510
Poland	2,766	1,652
Pomeroy	3,345	3,656
Port Clinton	6,870	5,541
Portsmouth	33,637	36,798
Powhatan Point	2,147	2,135
Ravenna	10,918	9,857
Reading	12,832	7,836
Reynoldsburg	7,793	724
Richmond Heights	5,068	891
Richwood	2,137	1,866
Ripley	2,174	1,792
Rittman	5,410	3,810
Rocky River	18,097	11,237
Rosedale	8,204	...
Roseville	1,749	1,808
Rossford	4,406	3,963
Sabina	2,313	1,696
St. Bernard	6,778	7,066
St. Clairsville	3,865	3,040
St. Marys	7,737	6,208
Salem	13,854	12,754
Salineville	1,898	2,018
Sandusky	31,989	29,375
Sandusky South	4,724	...
Sebring	4,439	4,045
Seven Hills	5,708	1,350
Shadyside	5,028	4,433
Shaker Heights	36,460	28,222
Sharonville	3,890	1,318
Sharon West	3,365	...
Sheffield	1,664	1,147
Sheffield Lake	6,884	2,381
Shelby	9,106	7,971
Shreve	1,617	1,287
Sidney	14,663	11,491
Silver Lake	2,655	1,040
Silverton	6,682	4,827
Solon	6,333	2,570
South Amherst	1,657	1,020
South Charleston	1,505	1,452
South Euclid	27,569	15,432
South Lebanon	2,720	1,291
South Point	1,663	804
South Zanesville	1,557	1,477

Place	1960	1950
OHIO—Cont.:		
Spencerville	2,061	1,826
Springdale	3,556	...
Springfield	82,723	78,508
Steubenville	32,495	38,872
Story Prairie	1,720	...
Stow	12,194	...
Strasburg	1,687	1,366
Strongsville	8,504	3,504
Struthers	15,631	11,941
Swanton	2,306	1,740
Sylvania	5,187	2,433
Tallmadge	10,246	5,821
Terrace Park	2,023	1,265
Tiffin	21,478	18,952
Tiltonsville	2,454	2,202
Tipp City	4,267	3,304
Toledo	318,003	303,616
Toronto	7,780	7,253
Trenton	3,064	987
Trotwood	4,992	1,066
Troy	13,685	10,661
Twinsburg	4,098	...
Uhrichsville	6,201	6,614
Union City	1,657	1,622
Uniontown	1,668	...
University Heights	16,641	11,566
Upper Arlington	28,486	9,024
Upper Sandusky	4,941	4,397
Urbana	10,461	9,335
Utica	1,854	1,510
Vandalia	6,342	927
Van Wert	11,323	10,364
Vermilion	4,785	2,214
Versailles	2,159	1,812
Wadsworth	10,635	7,966
Walbridge	2,142	1,152
Walton Hills	1,776	...
Wapakoneta	6,756	5,797
Warren	59,648	49,856
Warrensville Heights	10,609	4,126
Washington	12,388	10,560
Waterville	1,856	1,110
Wauseon	4,311	3,494
Waverly	3,830	1,679
Wellington	3,599	2,992
Wellston	5,728	5,691
Wellsville	7,117	7,854
West Alexandria	1,524	1,183
West Carrollton	4,749	2,876
Westerville	7,011	4,112
Westlake	12,906	4,912
West Liberty	1,522	1,397
West Milton‡	2,972	2,101
West Portsmouth	3,100	2,613
West Union	1,762	1,508
Wheelersburg	2,682	1,013
Whitehall	20,818	4,877
Wickliffe	15,760	5,002
Willard	5,457	4,744
Williamsburg	1,956	1,490
Willoughby	15,058	5,602
Willoughby Hills	4,241	...
Willowick	18,749	3,677
Wilmington	8,915	7,387
Windham	3,777	3,968
Wintersville	3,597	1,950
Withamsville	2,811	...
Woodlawn	3,007	1,335
Woodsfield	2,956	2,410
Woodville	1,700	1,358
Wooster	17,046	14,005
Worthington	9,239	2,141
Wyoming	7,736	5,582
Xenia	20,445	12,877
Yellow Springs	4,167	2,896
Yorkville	1,801	1,854
Youngstown	166,689	168,330
Zanesville	39,077	40,517
OKLAHOMA:		
Ada	14,347	15,995
Altus	21,225	9,735
Alva	6,258	6,505
Anadarko	6,299	6,184
Antlers	2,085	2,506
Ardmore	20,184	17,890
Arkoma	1,862	1,691
Atoka	2,877	2,653
Barnsdall	1,663	1,708
Bartlesville	27,893	19,228
Beaver	2,087	1,495
Bethany	12,342	5,705
Bixby	1,711	1,517
Blackwell	9,588	9,199
Boise City	1,978	1,902
Bristow	4,795	5,400
Broken Arrow	5,928	3,262
Broken Bow	2,087	1,838
Buffalo	1,618	1,544
Burns Flat	2,280	...
Carnegie	1,500	1,719
Chandler	2,524	2,724
Checotah	2,614	2,638
Chelsea	1,541	1,437
Cherokee	2,410	2,635
Chickasha	14,866	15,842
Claremore	6,639	5,494

Place	1960	1950
OKLA.—Cont.:		
Cleveland	2,519	2,464
Clinton	9,617	7,555
Coalgate	1,689	1,984
Collinsville	2,526	2,011
Comanche	2,082	2,083
Commerce	2,378	2,442
Coweta	1,858	1,601
Cushing	8,619	8,414
Davis	2,203	1,928
Del City	12,934	2,504
Dewey	3,994	2,513
Drumright	4,190	5,028
Duncan	20,009	15,325
Durant	10,467	10,541
Edmond	8,577	6,086
Elk City	8,196	7,962
El Reno	11,015	10,991
Enid	38,859	36,017
Eufaula	2,382	2,540
Fairfax	2,076	2,017
Fairview	2,213	2,411
Frederick	5,879	5,467
Granfield	1,606	1,232
Guthrie	9,502	10,113
Guymon	5,768	4,718
Hartshorne	1,903	2,330
Haskell	1,887	1,676
Healdton	2,898	2,578
Heavener	1,891	2,103
Henryetta	6,551	7,987
Hobart	5,132	5,380
Holdenville	5,712	6,192
Hollis	3,006	3,089
Hominy	2,866	2,702
Hooker	1,684	1,842
Hugo	6,287	5,984
Idabel	4,967	4,671
Jenks	1,734	1,037
Kingfisher	3,249	3,345
Konawa	1,555	2,707
Laverne	1,937	1,269
Lawton	61,697	34,757
Lindsay	4,258	3,021
McAlester	17,419	17,878
Madill	3,084	2,791
Mangum	3,950	4,271
Marietta	1,933	1,875
Marlow	4,027	3,399
Maysville	1,530	1,294
Miami	12,869	11,801
Midway	2,292	...
Midwest City	36,058	10,166
Moore	1,783	942
Muskogee	38,059	37,289
New Cordell§	3,589	2,920
Newkirk	2,092	2,201
Nichols Hills	4,897	2,606
Norman	33,412	27,006
Nowata	4,163	3,965
Okemah	2,836	3,454
Oklahoma City (c.)	324,253	243,504
Okmulgee	15,951	18,317
Owasso	2,032	431
Pauls Valley	6,856	6,896
Pawhuska	5,414	5,331
Pawnee	2,303	2,861
Perry	5,210	5,137
Picher	2,553	3,951
Ponca City	24,411	20,180
Poteau	4,428	4,776
Prague	1,545	1,546
Prattville	2,530	...
Pryor Creek	6,476	4,486
Purcell	3,729	3,546
Sallisaw	3,351	2,885
Sand Springs	7,754	6,994
Sapulpa	14,282	13,031
Sayre	2,913	3,362
Seminole	11,464	11,863
Shattuck	1,625	1,692
Shawnee	24,326	22,948
Skiatook	2,503	1,734
Snyder	1,663	1,646
Stigler	1,923	2,125
Stillwater	23,965	20,238
Stilwell	1,916	1,813
Stroud	2,456	2,450
Sulphur	4,737	4,389
Tahlequah	5,840	4,750
Tecumseh	2,630	2,275
The Village	12,118	...
Tishomingo	2,381	2,325
Tonkawa	3,415	3,643
Tulsa	261,685	182,740
Vinita	6,027	5,518
Wagoner	4,469	4,395
Walters	2,825	2,743
Warr Acres	7,135	2,378
Watonga	3,252	3,249
Waurika	1,933	2,327
Waynoka	1,794	2,018
Weatherford	4,499	3,529
Wetumka	1,798	2,025
Wewoka	5,954	6,747
Wilburton	1,772	1,939
Wilson	1,647	1,832
Woodward	7,747	5,915
Wynnewood	2,509	2,423
Yukon	3,076	1,990
OREGON:		
Albany	12,926	10,115
Altamont	10,811	9,419
Ashland	9,119	7,739

Place	1960	1950
ORE.—Cont.:		
Astoria	11,239	12,331
Baker	9,986	9,471
Bandon	1,653	1,251
Barnes	5,076	...
Beaverton	5,937	2,512
Bend	11,936	11,409
Brookings	2,637	...
Bunker Hill	1,655	1,409
Burns	3,523	3,093
Canby	2,168	1,671
Central Point	2,289	1,667
Coos Bay	7,084	6,223
Coquille	4,730	3,523
Corvallis	20,669	16,207
Cottage Grove	3,895	3,536
Dallas	5,072	4,793
Dalles‖	10,493	7,676
Empire	3,781	2,261
Enterprise	1,932	1,718
Eugene	50,977	35,879
Florence	1,642	1,026
Forest Grove	5,628	4,343
Four Corners	4,743	1,284
Fruitdale	2,158	1,711
Gladstone	3,854	2,434
Gold Beach	1,765	677
Grants Pass	10,118	8,116
Gresham	3,944	3,049
Hayesville	4,568	2,697
Heppner	1,661	1,648
Hermiston	4,402	3,804
Hillsboro	8,232	5,142
Hood River	3,657	3,701
Independence	1,930	1,987
John Day	1,520	1,597
Junction City	1,614	1,475
Keizer	5,288	...
Klamath Falls	16,949	15,875
La Grande	9,014	8,635
Lakeview	3,260	2,831
Lebanon	5,858	5,873
McMinnville	7,656	6,635
Madras	1,515	1,258
Medford	24,425	17,305
Milton-Freewater	4,110	...
Milwaukie	9,099	5,253
Molalla	1,501	1,497
Monmouth	2,229	1,956
Myrtle Creek	2,231	1,781
Myrtle Point	2,886	2,033
Newberg	4,204	3,946
Newport	5,344	3,241
North Bend	7,512	6,099
Nyssa	2,611	2,525
Oakridge	1,973	1,562
Ontario	5,101	4,465
Oregon City	7,996	7,682
Oswego	8,906	3,316
Pendleton	14,434	11,774
Pilot Rock	1,695	847
Portland	372,676	373,628
Prineville	3,263	3,233
Redmond	3,340	2,956
Reedsport	2,998	2,288
Roseburg	11,467	8,390
St. Helens	5,022	4,711
Salem (c.)	49,142	43,140
Salem Heights	10,770	2,351
Seaside	3,877	3,886
Sheridan	1,763	1,922
Silverton	3,081	3,146
South Medford	2,306	1,226
Springfield	19,616	10,807
Stayton	2,108	1,507
Sutherlin	2,452	2,230
Sweet Home	3,353	3,603
Tillamook	4,244	3,685
Toledo	3,053	2,323
Warrenton	1,717	1,896
West Linn	3,933	2,945
Winston	2,395	...
Woodburn	3,120	2,395
PENNSYLVANIA:		
Abington†	55,831	28,988
Adams*	5,946	6,128
Akron	2,167	1,028
Albion	1,630	1,729
Aldan	4,324	3,430
Aliquippa	26,369	26,132
Allegheny* (Blair Co.)	5,056	3,836
Allegheny* (Westmoreland Co.)	5,363	4,627
Allentown	108,347	106,756
Altoona	69,407	77,177
Ambler	6,765	4,565
Ambridge	13,865	16,429
Annville†	4,264	3,699
Antrim*	5,729	4,684
Apollo	2,694	3,015
Archbald	5,471	6,304
Arlington Heights-Pocono Park	1,569	...
Arnold	9,437	10,263
Ashland	5,237	6,192
Ashley	4,258	5,243
Aspinwall	3,727	4,084
Aston†	10,595	5,576
Athens	4,515	4,430
Atlas	1,574	3,090

‡Milton in 1950. §Cordell in 1950. ‖The Dalles in 1950.

Place	1960	1950
PA.—Cont.:		
Avalon	6,859	6,463
Avoca	3,562	4,040
Baden	6,109	3,732
Baldwin	24,489	...
Baldwin†	3,004	10,743
Bangor	5,766	6,050
Barnesboro	3,035	3,442
Bath	1,736	1,824
Beaver	6,160	6,360
Beaverdale-Lloydell	1,862	2,560
Beaver Falls	16,240	17,375
Bedford	3,696	3,521
Bellefonte	6,088	5,651
Belle Vernon	1,784	2,271
Belleville	1,539	1,304
Bellevue	11,412	11,604
Bellwood	2,330	2,559
Ben Avon	2,553	2,465
Bensalem*	23,478	11,365
Bentleyville	3,160	3,295
Benzinger*	5,934	3,802
Berlin	1,600	1,507
Berwick	13,353	14,010
Bethel	23,650	11,324
Bethlehem	75,408	66,340
Bethlehem*	6,439	3,940
Big Beaver	2,381	...
Birdsboro	3,025	3,158
Blairsville	4,930	5,000
Blakely	6,374	6,828
Blawnox	2,085	2,165
Bloomsburg	10,655	10,633
Blossburg	1,956	1,954
Borough†	2,917	2,750
Boswell	1,508	1,679
Boyertown	4,067	4,074
Brackenridge	5,697	6,178
Braddock	12,337	16,488
Braddock Hills	2,414	1,965
Bradford	15,061	17,354
Bradford*	5,314	4,535
Brentwood	13,706	12,535
Bridgeport	5,306	5,827
Bridgeville	7,112	5,650
Brighton*	6,260	2,474
Bristol	12,364	12,710
Bristol†	59,298	12,184
Brockway	2,563	2,650
Brookhaven	5,280	1,042
Brookville	4,620	4,274
Brownsville	6,055	7,643
Burgettstown	2,383	2,379
Burnham	2,755	2,954
Butler	20,975	23,482
California	5,978	2,831
Caln*	6,685	5,779
Cambria*	5,594	5,846
Cambridge Springs	2,031	2,246
Camp Hill	8,559	5,934
Canonsburg	11,877	12,072
Canton	2,102	2,118
Carbondale	13,595	16,296
Carlisle	16,623	16,812
Carnegie	11,887	12,105
Carroll*	6,205	4,531
Carrolltown	1,525	1,452
Castle Shannon	11,836	5,459
Catasauqua	5,062	4,923
Catawissa	1,824	2,000
Cecil*	8,563	7,743
Center*	7,113	3,995
Centerville	5,088	245
Central City	1,604	1,935
Chambersburg	17,670	17,212
Charleroi	8,148	9,872
Chatwood	3,621	1,572
Cheltenham†	35,990	22,854
Chester	63,658	66,039
Chester†	3,602	3,547
Cheswick	2,734	1,534
Chippewa*	6,051	2,987
Churchill	3,428	1,733
Clairton	18,389	19,652
Clarion	4,958	4,409
Clarks Summit	3,693	2,940
Clearfield	9,270	9,357
Cleona	1,988	1,483
Clifton Heights	8,005	7,549
Clymer	2,251	2,500
Coaldale	3,949	5,318
Coatesville	12,971	13,826
Collegeville	2,254	1,900
Collier*	8,021	8,039
Collingdale	10,268	8,443
Columbia	12,075	11,993
Colwyn	3,074	2,143
Conemaugh*	8,084	8,281
Conewango*	6,377	5,680
Connellsville	12,814	13,293
Conshohocken	10,259	10,922
Conway	1,926	1,570
Coopersburg	1,800	1,462
Coplay	3,701	2,994
Coraopolis	9,643	10,498
Cornwall	1,934	1,760
Corry	7,744	7,911
Coudersport	2,889	3,210
Crafton	8,418	8,066
Cranberry*	6,682	5,224
Cresson	2,659	2,569
Cressona	1,854	1,758
Cumberland*	6,662	7,801
Cumru*	7,250	5,242
PA.—Cont.:		
Curwensville	3,231	3,332
Dale	2,807	3,310
Dallas	2,586	1,674
Dallastown	3,615	3,304
Danville	6,889	6,994
Darby	14,059	13,154
Darby†	12,598	3,454
Denver	1,875	1,658
Derry	3,426	3,752
Dickson City	7,738	8,948
Donora	11,131	12,186
Dormont	13,098	13,405
Dover*	6,399	3,864
Downingtown	5,598	4,948
Doylestown	5,917	5,262
Dravosburg	3,458	3,786
Du Bois	10,667	11,497
Dunbar	1,536	1,363
Dunbar*	7,656	8,409
Duncannon	1,800	1,852
Dunmore	18,917	20,305
Dupont	3,669	4,107
Duquesne	15,019	17,620
Duryea	5,626	6,655
East Conemaugh	3,334	4,101
East Deer†	2,865	3,185
East Faxon	3,641	...
East Greenville	1,931	1,945
East Huntingdon*	6,574	5,984
East Lampeter*	7,399	5,166
East Lansdowne	3,224	3,527
East McKeesport	3,470	3,171
East Norriton*	7,773	2,987
Easton	31,955	35,632
East Pennsboro*	8,977	5,582
East Petersburg	2,053	1,268
East Pittsburgh	4,122	5,259
East Stroudsburg	7,674	7,274
Easttown*	6,907	3,811
East Uniontown	2,424	2,138
East Vincent*	5,453	4,576
East Washington	2,483	2,304
East Weissport	2,057	1,814
East Whiteland*	5,078	1,740
Ebensburg	4,111	4,086
Economy	5,925	...
Eddystone	3,006	3,014
Edgewood (Allegheny Co.)	5,124	5,292
Edgewood (Northumberland Co.)	3,399	...
Edgeworth	2,030	1,466
Edinboro	1,703	1,567
Edwardsville	5,711	6,686
Elizabeth	2,597	2,615
Elizabeth*	14,159	9,978
Elizabethtown	6,780	5,083
Elkland	2,189	2,326
Ellwood City	12,413	12,945
Emmaus	10,262	7,780
Emporium	3,397	3,646
Emsworth	3,341	3,128
Ephrata	7,688	7,027
Erie	138,440	130,803
Etna	5,519	6,750
Evans City‡	1,825	1,637
Everett	2,279	2,297
Exeter	4,747	5,130
Exeter*	8,488	5,278
Export	1,518	1,690
Fairchance	2,120	2,091
Fairhope-Arnold City	2,803	...
Fallowfield*	5,350	4,214
Fairview*	6,530	5,514
Fairview-Ferndale	4,067	...
Falls†	29,082	3,540
Farrell	13,793	13,644
Faxon	1,841	...
Ferndale	2,717	2,619
Fleetwood	2,647	2,338
Flemington	1,608	1,446
Florin	1,518	1,319
Folcroft	7,013	1,909
Ford City	5,440	5,352
Forest City	2,651	3,122
Forest Hills	8,796	6,301
Forty Fort	6,431	6,173
Foster*	5,603	4,890
Fountain Hill	5,428	5,456
Fox Chapel	3,302	1,721
Frackville	5,654	6,541
Franklin*	8,517	4,937
Franklin	9,586	10,006
Freedom	2,895	3,000
Freeland	5,068	5,909
Freemansburg	1,652	1,739
Freeport	2,439	2,685
Frisco	1,578	...
Galeton	1,646	1,646
Gallitzin	2,783	3,102
PA.—Cont.:		
Garden View	2,418	2,024
Geistown	3,186	2,148
Georges*	7,140	8,581
German*	8,442	12,040
Gettysburg	7,960	7,046
Gilberton	1,712	2,641
Girard	2,451	2,141
Girardville	2,958	3,864
Glassport	8,418	8,707
Glen Lyon	4,173	3,921
Glenolden	7,249	6,450
Glen Rock	1,546	1,477
Greencastle	2,988	2,661
Greene*	6,953	5,229
Greensburg	17,383	16,923
Green Tree	5,226	2,818
Greenville	8,765	9,210
Grove City	8,368	7,411
Guilford*	7,388	5,057
Hallstead	1,580	1,445
Hamburg	3,747	3,805
Hampden*	6,558	2,095
Hampton*	10,641	6,104
Hanover	15,538	14,048
Hanover*	12,781	15,051
Harborcreek*	10,569	7,475
Harmony†	5,106	4,501
Harrisburg (c.)	79,697	89,544
Harrison†	15,710	15,116
Hastings	1,751	1,846
Hatboro	7,315	4,788
Hatfield	1,941	1,624
Hatfield*	5,759	3,101
Haverford†	54,019	39,641
Hazle*	7,478	9,279
Hazleton	32,056	35,491
Heidelberg	2,118	2,250
Hellertown	6,716	5,435
Hempfield†	29,704	22,463
Herminie	1,571	2,072
Hershey	6,851	...
Highfield	2,471	...
Highland Park	1,534	1,212
Highspire	2,999	2,799
Hillcrest	3,541	...
Hiller	1,746	1,326
Hilltown*	5,549	3,688
Hollidaysburg	6,475	6,483
Homeacre	3,508	...
Homer City	2,471	2,372
Homestead	7,502	10,046
Honesdale	5,569	5,662
Hopewell*	13,359	6,044
Hopwood	1,615	1,099
Horsham*	8,933	3,663
Houston	1,865	1,957
Hughestown	1,615	1,888
Hughesville	2,218	2,095
Hummelstown	4,474	3,789
Huntingdon	7,234	7,330
Imperial	1,592	1,895
Indiana	13,005	11,743
Indiana*	5,751	4,196
Industry	2,338	...
Ingram	4,730	4,236
Irwin	4,270	4,228
Jeannette	16,565	16,172
Jefferson	8,280	...
Jenkintown	5,017	5,130
Jermyn	2,568	2,535
Jersey Shore	5,613	5,595
Jim Thorpe§	5,945	6,091
Johnsonburg	4,966	4,567
Johnstown	53,949	63,232
Kane	5,380	5,706
Kenhorst	2,815	2,551
Kennedy*	5,806	3,142
Kennett Square	4,355	3,699
Kingston	20,261	21,096
Kingston*	5,450	4,482
Kittanning	6,793	7,731
Kulpmont	4,288	5,199
Kutztown	3,312	3,110
Lake City‖	1,722	1,369
Lancaster	61,055	63,774
Lancaster†	10,020	6,859
Landisville	1,690	...
Langhorne Manor	1,506	781
Lansdale	12,612	9,762
Lansdowne	12,601	12,169
Lansford	5,958	7,487
Larksville	4,390	6,360
Latrobe	11,932	11,811
Laureldale	4,051	3,585
Lawrence Park†	4,403	4,154
Lebanon	30,045	28,156
Leechburg	3,545	4,042
Leetsdale	2,153	2,411
Lehighton	6,318	6,565
Leith	1,622	2,018
Lemoyne	4,662	4,605
Lewisburg	5,523	5,268
Lewistown	12,640	13,894
Liberty	3,624	1,900
Ligonier	2,276	2,160
Ligonier*	5,566	4,690
Lilly	1,642	1,898
Limerick*	5,110	3,290
Lincoln	1,686	...
Linntown	1,628	1,131
Lititz	5,987	5,568
Littlestown	2,756	2,635
Lock Haven	11,748	11,381
PA.—Cont.:		
Logan*	10,123	9,060
Lower Allen*	11,614	5,115
Lower Burrell	11,952	...
Lower Chichester†	4,460	2,938
Lower Makefield*	8,604	3,211
Lower Merion†	59,420	48,745
Lower Moreland*	5,731	2,245
Lower Paxton*	17,618	6,546
Lower Providence*	9,955	5,887
Lower Saucon*	5,536	4,506
Lower Southampton†	12,619	3,562
Lucerne	1,524	1,073
Luzerne	5,118	6,176
Lykens	2,527	2,735
Lyndora	3,232	...
Lynnwood	2,230	...
McAdoo	3,560	4,260
McCandless*	14,582	6,488
McChesneytown-Loyalhanna	3,138	...
McDonald	3,141	3,543
McKeesport	45,489	51,502
McKees Rocks	13,185	16,241
McSherrystown	2,839	2,510
Mahanoy City	8,536	10,934
Malvern	2,268	1,764
Manchester*	5,519	3,397
Manheim	4,790	4,246
Manheim*	14,855	9,289
Manor* (Armstrong Co.)	5,013	4,798
Manor* (Lancaster Co.)	6,939	4,461
Mansfield	2,678	2,657
Marcus Hook	3,299	3,843
Marietta	2,385	2,442
Marple†	19,722	4,779
Mars	1,522	1,385
Marshallton	2,316	3,390
Martinsburg	1,772	1,562
Marysville	2,580	2,158
Masontown	4,730	4,550
Matamoras	2,087	1,761
Mayfield	1,996	2,373
Meadowlands	1,967	1,059
Meadville	16,671	18,972
Mechanicsburg	8,123	6,786
Mechanicsville	1,758	1,294
Media	5,803	5,726
Mercer	2,800	2,397
Mercersburg	1,759	1,613
Meridian	1,649	1,317
Meyersdale	2,901	3,137
Middletown	11,182	9,184
Middletown† (Bucks Co.)	26,894	4,987
Middletown* (Delaware Co.)	11,256	6,038
Midland	6,425	6,491
Midway	1,568	1,271
Mifflinburg	2,476	2,259
Millcreek†	28,441	17,037
Millersburg	2,984	2,861
Millersville	3,883	2,551
Mill Hall	1,891	1,677
Millvale	6,624	7,287
Milroy	1,666	1,443
Milton	7,972	8,578
Minersville	6,606	7,783
Mohnton	2,223	2,004
Monaca	8,394	7,415
Monessen	18,424	17,896
Monongahela	8,388	8,922
Monroeville	22,446	...
Montgomery	2,150	2,166
Montoursville	5,211	3,293
Montrose	2,363	2,075
Moon*	10,642	7,096
Moosic	4,243	3,965
Morrisville	7,790	6,787
Morton	2,207	1,352
Mount Carmel	10,760	14,222
Mount Holly Springs	1,840	1,701
Mount Joy	3,292	3,006
Mount Lebanon†	35,361	26,604
Mount Oliver	5,980	6,646
Mount Penn	3,574	3,635
Mount Pleasant	6,107	5,883
Mount Union	4,091	4,690
Mount Wolf	1,514	1,164
Muhlenberg*	10,955	7,001
Muncy	2,830	2,756
Munhall	17,312	16,437
Myerstown	3,268	3,050
Nanticoke	15,601	20,160
Nanty-Glo	4,608	5,425
Narberth	5,109	5,407
Nazareth	6,209	5,830
Nescopeck	1,934	1,907
Nesquehoning	2,714	...
Nether Providence†	10,380	6,173
New Bethlehem	1,599	1,604
New Brighton	8,397	9,535
New Castle	44,790	48,834

‡Evansburg in 1950. §Merger of East Mauch Chunk and Mauch Chunk. ‖North Girard in 1950.

Place	1960	1950
PA.—Cont.:		
New Castle Northwest	2,007	...
New Cumberland	9,257	6,204
New Eagle	2,670	2,316
New Holland	3,425	2,602
New Kensington	23,485	25,146
New Philadelphia	1,702	2,200
Newport	1,861	1,893
New Salem-Buffington	1,834	2,131
Newtown	2,323	2,095
Newtown*	9,270	3,518
Newville	1,656	1,788
New Wilmington	2,203	1,948
Noblestown-Sturgeon	1,709	1,375
Norristown	38,925	38,126
Northampton	8,866	9,332
Northampton*	6,006	2,248
North Apollo	1,741	1,502
North Belle Vernon	3,148	3,147
North Braddock	13,204	14,724
North Catasauqua	2,805	2,629
North Charleroi	2,259	2,554
North East	4,217	4,247
North Huntingdon*	21,853	11,536
North Middleton*	5,079	3,208
North Sewickley	5,379	3,555
Northumberland	4,156	4,207
North Vandergrift	1,827	1,878
North Versailles†	13,583	9,821
North Wales	3,673	2,998
North Whitehall*	5,061	4,337
North York	2,290	2,445
Norwood	6,729	5,246
Oakdale	1,695	1,572
Oakland	2,303	1,909
Oakmont	7,504	7,264
Oakwood	3,303	2,267
O'Hara*	8,681	5,768
Oil City	17,692	19,581
Old Forge	8,928	9,749
Oliver	3,015	2,180
Olyphant	5,864	7,047
Orwigsburg	2,131	2,309
Osceola	1,777	1,992
Oxford	3,376	3,091
Palmer Heights	2,597	...
Palmerton	5,942	6,646
Palmyra	6,999	5,910
Parkesburg	2,759	2,611
Parkside	2,426	1,637
Parkville	4,516	3,299
Patton	2,880	3,148
Paxtang	1,916	1,857
Pen Argyl	3,693	3,878
Penbrook	3,671	3,691
Penn*	10,702	7,461
Penndel	2,158	1,100
Penn Hills†	51,512	25,280
Pennsburg	1,698	1,625
Perkasie	4,650	4,358
Perryopolis	1,799	...
Peters*	7,126	3,004
Philadelphia	2,002,512	2,071,605
Philipsburg	3,872	3,988
Phoenixville	13,797	12,932
Pine Grove	2,267	2,237
Pitcairn	5,383	5,857
Pittsburgh	604,332	676,806
Pittston	12,407	15,012
Plains*	10,995	12,541
Pleasant Hills	8,573	3,808
Plum	10,241	...
Plymouth	10,401	13,021
Plymouth*	11,430	5,118
Plymptonville	1,822	1,352
Point Marion	1,853	2,197
Polk	3,574	4,004
Portage	3,933	4,371
Port Allegany	2,742	2,519
Port Carbon	2,775	3,024
Port Vue	6,635	4,756
Pottstown	26,144	22,589
Pottsville	21,659	23,640
Pricedale-Sandfield	1,548	2,357
Prospect Park	6,596	5,834
Punxsutawney	8,805	8,969
Quakertown	6,305	5,673
Quincy*	5,084	4,647
Radnor†	21,697	14,709
Rankin	5,164	6,941
Reading	98,177	109,320
Red Lion	5,594	5,119
Renovo	3,316	3,751
Republic	1,921	...
Reserve†	4,230	3,533
Reynoldsville	3,158	3,569
PA.—Cont.:		
Richland* (Allegheny Co.)	6,453	3,527
Richland* (Cambria Co.)	9,234	4,930
Ridgway	6,387	6,244
Ridley†	35,738	17,212
Ridley Park	7,387	4,921
Riverside	1,580	524
Roaring Spring	2,937	2,771
Robesonia	1,579	1,590
Robinson*	7,935	4,769
Rochester	5,952	7,197
Rockledge	2,587	2,261
Rocky Grove	3,168	3,111
Roseto	1,630	1,676
Ross†	25,952	15,744
Royersford	3,969	3,862
Russelton	1,613	1,670
St. Clair	5,159	5,856
St. Marys	8,065	7,846
Salem*	5,143	5,072
Salisbury*	7,294	4,583
Sandy	2,070	1,866
Sayre	7,917	7,735
Schuylkill Haven	6,470	6,597
Scott†	19,094	8,686
Scottdale	6,244	6,249
Scranton	111,443	125,536
Selinsgrove	3,948	3,514
Sellersville	2,497	2,373
Sewickley	6,157	5,836
Shaler†	24,939	16,430
Shamokin	13,674	16,879
Sharon	25,267	26,454
Sharon Hill	7,123	5,464
Sharpsburg	6,096	7,296
Sharpsville	6,061	5,414
Sheffield	1,971	2,087
Shenandoah	11,073	15,704
Shenandoah Heights	1,721	1,798
Shenango*	7,516	5,540
Shickshinny	1,843	2,156
Shillington	5,639	5,059
Shippensburg	6,138	5,722
Sinking Spring	2,244	1,982
Slatington	4,316	4,343
Slippery Rock	2,563	2,294
Smethport	1,725	1,797
Smith*	6,362	6,619
Snowden*	7,384	4,540
Somerset	6,347	5,936
Somerset*	6,808	5,976
Souderton	5,381	4,521
South Coatesville	2,032	1,996
South Connellsville	2,434	2,610
South Fayette*	10,728	9,979
South Fork	2,053	2,616
South Greensburg	3,058	2,980
South Huntingdon*	6,073	5,901
South Lebanon*	6,584	4,488
South Middleton*	5,424	4,204
Southmont	2,857	2,278
South Pottstown	1,850	1,504
South Uniontown	3,603	3,425
Southwest Greensburg	3,264	3,144
South Whitehall*	10,932	5,604
South Williamsport	6,972	6,364
Spangler	2,658	3,013
Spring* (Berks Co.)	8,934	4,867
Spring* (Centre Co.)	5,018	4,600
Spring City	3,162	3,258
Springdale	5,602	4,939
Springettsbury*	14,232	5,537
Springfield† (Delaware Co.)	26,733	10,917
Springfield† (Montgomery Co.)	20,652	11,403
Spring Garden†	11,387	8,338
Spring Grove	1,675	1,238
State College	22,409	17,227
Steelton	11,266	12,574
Stowe†	11,730	12,210
Stowe	2,765	2,524
Strabana	3,036	2,861
Stroudsburg	6,070	6,361
Sugar Notch	1,524	2,002
Summit Hill	4,386	4,924
Sunbury	13,687	15,570
Susquehanna*	17,474	11,081
Susquehanna Depot	2,591	2,646
Swarthmore	5,753	4,825
Swatara*	14,795	9,350
Swissvale	15,089	16,488
Swoyersville	6,751	7,795
Tamaqua	10,173	11,508
Tarentum	8,232	9,540
PA.—Cont.:		
Taylor	6,148	7,176
Telford	2,763	2,042
Temple	1,633	1,460
Throop	4,732	5,861
Titusville	8,356	8,923
Topton	1,684	1,572
Towanda	4,293	4,069
Tower City	1,968	2,054
Trafford	4,330	3,965
Trainer	2,358	2,001
Tredyffrin*	16,004	7,836
Tremont	1,893	2,102
Trevorton	2,597	2,545
Tullytown	2,452	648
Tunkhannock	2,297	2,170
Turtle Creek	10,607	12,363
Tyrone	7,792	8,214
Union*	5,611	3,924
Union City	3,819	3,911
Uniontown	17,942	20,471
United	2,044	...
Unity*	15,519	12,392
Upland	4,343	4,081
Upper Chichester*	9,682	6,997
Upper Darby†	93,158	84,951
Upper Dublin*	10,184	6,637
Upper Merion*	17,096	6,404
Upper Moreland†	21,032	8,936
Upper Providence* (Delaware Co.)	6,059	3,598
Upper Providence*‡	5,607	4,486
Upper St. Clair*	8,287	3,629
Upper Saucon*	5,926	4,240
Upper Southampton*	7,941	2,027
Upper Yoder*	5,474	3,872
Valley View	1,540	1,618
Vandergrift	8,742	9,524
Verona	4,032	4,325
Versailles	2,297	2,484
Walnutport	1,609	1,427
Warminster†	15,994	7,127
Warren	14,505	14,849
Washington	23,545	26,280
Washington*	6,889	4,674
Washington North	2,077	...
Washington West	3,951	...
Watsontown	2,431	2,327
Waynesboro	10,427	10,334
Waynesburg	5,188	5,514
Weatherly	2,591	2,622
Wellsboro	4,369	4,215
Wesleyville	3,534	3,411
West Brownsville	1,907	1,610
West Chester	15,705	15,168
West Conshohocken	2,254	2,482
West Fairview	1,718	1,896
West Grove	1,607	1,521
West Hazleton	6,278	6,988
West Hempfield*	5,318	3,578
West Homestead	4,155	3,257
West Lampeter*	5,520	4,119
West Lawn	2,059	2,144
West Lebanon	2,301	2,048
West Manchester*	9,505	5,438
West Mayfield	2,201	1,768
West Mead*	5,117	4,818
West Mifflin	27,289	17,985
Westmont	6,573	4,410
West Newton	3,982	3,619
West Norriton†	8,342	4,879
West Pittston	6,998	7,230
West Reading	4,938	5,072
West View	8,079	7,581
West Wyoming	3,166	2,863
West York	5,526	5,756
Wheatland	1,813	1,402
Whitaker	2,130	2,149
White*	6,884	5,340
Whitehall	16,075	7,342
Whitehall*	14,528	11,269
White Haven	1,778	1,461
Whitemarsh*	12,286	5,977
White Oak	9,047	6,159
Whitpain*	7,331	3,063
Wilder	1,787	...
Wilkes-Barre	63,551	76,826
Wilkes-Barre†	4,319	5,267
Wilkins†	8,272	4,261
Wilkinsburg	30,066	31,418
Williamsburg	1,792	1,792
Williamsport	41,967	45,047
Williamstown	2,097	2,332
Willistown*	6,492	2,709
Wilmerding	4,349	5,325
Wilson	8,465	8,159
Windber	6,994	8,010
Wind Gap	1,930	1,577
Winton	5,456	6,280
Wormleysburg	1,794	1,511
Wrightsville	2,345	2,104
Wyoming	4,127	4,511
PA.—Cont.:		
Wyomissing	5,044	4,187
Wyomissing Hills	1,644	646
Yardley	2,271	1,916
Yeadon	11,610	11,068
York	54,504	59,953
York*	8,506	4,502
Youngsville	2,211	1,944
Youngwood	2,813	2,720
Zelienople	3,284	2,981
RHODE ISLAND:		
Barrington†	13,826	8,246
Bristol†	14,570	12,320
Central Falls	19,858	23,550
Coventry*	15,432	9,869
Cranston	66,766	55,060
Cumberland*	18,792	12,842
East Greenwich*	6,100	4,923
East Providence	41,955	35,871
Jamestown	1,843	1,757
Johnston*	17,160	12,725
Kingston	2,616	2,156
Lincoln*	13,551	11,270
Narragansett	1,741	...
Newport	47,049	37,564
Newport East	2,643	...
North Providence†	18,220	13,927
North Smithfield*	7,632	5,726
Pascoag	2,983	...
Pawtucket	81,001	81,436
Portsmouth*	8,251	6,578
Providence (c.)	207,498	248,674
Scituate*	5,210	3,905
Smithfield*	9,442	6,690
Tiverton*	9,461	5,659
Wakefield-Peacedale	5,569	5,224
Warren*	8,750	8,513
Warwick	68,504	43,028
Westerly	9,698	8,415
West Warwick†	21,414	19,096
Wickford	2,934	2,437
Woonsocket	47,080	50,211
SOUTH CAROLINA:		
Abbeville	5,436	5,395
Aiken	11,243	7,083
Aiken South	2,980	...
Aiken West	2,602	...
Allendale	3,114	2,474
Anderson	41,316	19,770
Andrews	2,995	2,702
Arcadia	2,458	2,554
Arkwright	1,656	1,266
Bamberg	3,081	2,954
Barnwell	4,568	2,005
Batesburg	3,806	3,169
Beaufort	6,298	5,081
Belton	5,106	3,371
Bendale	1,544	...
Bennettsville	6,963	5,140
Bishopville	3,586	3,076
Blacksburg	2,174	2,056
Blackville	1,901	1,294
Calhoun Falls	2,525	2,396
Camden	6,842	6,986
Cayce	8,517	3,294
Charleston	65,925	70,174
Cheraw	5,171	4,836
Chester	6,906	6,893
Chesterfield	1,532	1,530
City View	2,475	...
Clemson	1,587	1,204
Clinton	7,937	7,168
Clover	3,500	3,276
Columbia (c.)	97,433	86,914
Conway	8,563	6,073
Cowpens	2,038	1,879
Darlington	6,710	6,619
Denmark	3,221	2,814
Dillon	6,173	5,171
Easley	8,283	6,316
East Gaffney	4,779	4,289
Edgefield	2,876	2,518
Estill	1,865	1,659
Fairfax	1,814	1,567
Florence	24,722	22,513
Forest Acres	3,842	3,240
Fort Mill	3,315	3,204
Fountain Inn	2,385	1,325
Gaffney	10,435	8,123
Georgetown	12,261	6,004
Gloverville	1,551	...
Great Falls	3,030	3,533
Greenville	66,188	58,161
Greenwood	16,644	13,806
Greer	8,967	5,050
Hampton	2,486	2,007
Hartsville	6,392	5,658
Honea Path	3,453	2,840
Industrial-Aragon Mills	1,656	1,868
Inman	1,714	1,514
Inman Mills	1,769	1,776
Jackson	1,746	...
Joanna	1,831	...
Johnston	2,119	1,426

‡Montgomery Co.

Place	1960	1950
S.C.—Cont.:		
Kershaw	1,567	1,376
Kingstree	3,847	3,621
Lake City	6,059	5,112
Lancaster	7,999	7,159
Lancaster Mills	3,274	...
Landrum	1,930	1,333
Latta	1,901	1,602
Laurens	9,598	8,658
Leesville	1,619	1,453
Liberty	2,657	2,291
Loris	1,702	1,614
McColl	2,479	2,688
McCormick	1,998	1,744
Madison	1,904	...
Manning	3,917	2,775
Marion	7,174	6,834
Monarch Mills	1,990	2,158
Moncks Corner	2,030	1,818
Mount Pleasant	5,116	1,857
Mullins	6,229	4,916
Myrtle Beach	7,834	3,345
Newberry	8,208	7,546
New Ellenton	2,309	...
North Augusta	10,348	3,659
North Hartsville	1,899	1,743
Orangeburg	13,852	15,322
Pageland	2,020	1,925
Pendleton	2,358	1,432
Pickens	2,198	1,961
Piedmont	2,108	2,673
Pinehurst-Sheppard Park	1,708	1,419
Rock Hill	29,404	24,502
St. George	1,833	1,938
St. Matthews	2,433	2,351
Saluda	2,089	1,594
Saxon	3,917	3,088
Seneca	5,227	3,649
Shannontown	7,064	5,828
Simpsonville	2,282	1,529
South Greenwood	2,520	3,712
Spartanburg	44,352	36,795
Springdale	2,981	...
Summerton	1,504	1,419
Summerville	3,633	3,312
Sumter	23,062	20,185
Timmonsville	2,178	2,001
Travelers Rest	1,973	...
Union	10,191	9,730
Victor Mills	2,018	2,654
Walhalla	3,431	3,104
Walterboro	5,417	4,616
Ware Shoals	2,671	3,032
West Columbia	6,410	1,543
West Hartsville	2,427	2,287
Westminster	2,413	2,219
Whitmire	2,663	3,006
Whitney	2,502	1,611
Williamston	3,721	2,782
Williston	2,722	896
Windy Hill	2,201	1,710
Winnsboro	3,479	3,267
Winnsboro Mills	2,411	2,936
Woodruff	3,679	3,831
York	4,758	4,181
SOUTH DAKOTA:		
Aberdeen	23,073	21,051
Belle Fourche	4,087	3,540
Beresford	1,794	1,686
Brookings	10,558	7,764
Canton	2,511	2,530
Chamberlain	2,598	1,912
Custer	2,105	2,017
Deadwood	3,045	3,288
Dell Rapids	1,863	1,650
Edgemont	1,772	1,158
Eureka	1,555	1,576
Flandreau	2,129	2,193
Fort Pierre	2,649	951
Gettysburg	1,950	1,555
Hot Springs	4,943	5,030
Huron	14,180	12,788
Lead	6,211	6,422
Lemmon	2,412	2,760
Madison	5,420	5,153
Milbank	3,500	2,982
Miller	2,081	1,916
Mitchell	12,555	12,123
Mobridge	4,391	3,753
Parkston	1,514	1,354
Pierre (c.)	10,088	5,715
Rapid City	42,399	25,310
Redfield	2,952	2,655
Sioux Falls	65,466	52,696
Sisseton	3,218	2,871
Spearfish	3,682	2,755
Sturgis	4,639	3,471
Vermillion	6,102	5,337
Wagner	1,586	1,528
Watertown	14,077	12,699
Webster	2,409	2,503
Winner	3,705	3,252
Yankton	9,279	7,709
TENNESSEE:		
Alamo	1,665	1,501
Alcoa	6,395	6,355

Place	1960	1950
TENN.—Cont.:		
Athens	12,103	8,618
Banner Hill	2,132	2,873
Belle Meade	3,082	2,831
Bemis	3,127	3,248
Berry Hill	1,551	1,248
Bolivar	3,338	2,429
Bristol	17,582	16,771
Brownsville	5,424	4,711
Camden	2,774	2,029
Carthage	2,021	1,604
Centerville	1,678	1,532
Chattanooga	130,009	131,041
Clarksville	22,021	16,246
Cleveland	16,196	12,605
Clinton	4,943	3,712
Collierville	2,020	1,153
Colonial Heights	2,312	...
Columbia	17,624	10,911
Cookeville	7,805	6,924
Covington	5,298	4,379
Cowan	1,979	1,835
Crossville	4,668	2,291
Daisy	1,508	1,336
Dayton	3,500	3,191
Decherd	1,704	1,435
Dickson	5,028	3,348
Donelson	17,195	1,765
Dresden	1,510	1,509
Dupontonia	1,896	...
Dyer	1,909	1,864
Dyersburg	12,499	10,885
Eagleton Village	5,068	...
East Ridge	19,570	9,645
Elizabethton	10,896	10,754
Englewood	1,574	1,545
Erwin	3,210	3,387
Etowah	3,223	3,261
Fayetteville	6,804	5,447
Forest Hills	2,101	...
Fountain City	10,365	...
Franklin	6,977	5,475
Gallatin	7,901	5,107
Gatlinburg	1,764	1,301
Goodlettsville	3,163	...
Greeneville	11,759	8,721
Greenfield	1,779	1,706
Halls	1,890	1,808
Harriman	5,931	6,389
Hartsville	1,712	1,130
Henderson	2,691	2,532
Hohenwald	2,194	1,703
Humboldt	8,482	7,426
Huntingdon	2,119	2,043
Inglewood	26,527	...
Jackson	34,376	30,207
Jamestown	1,727	2,115
Jefferson City	4,550	3,633
Jellico	2,210	1,556
Johnson City	31,187	27,864
Johnson City Southeast	2,435	...
Kingsport	26,314	19,571
Kingston	2,010	1,627
Knoxville	111,827	124,769
Lafayette	1,590	1,195
LaFollette	6,204	5,797
Lake City	1,914	1,827
Lawrenceburg	8,042	5,442
Lebanon	10,512	7,913
Lenoir City	4,979	5,159
Lewisburg	6,338	5,164
Lexington	3,943	3,566
Livingston	2,817	2,082
Long Island	1,925	2,147
Lookout Mountain	1,817	1,675
Loudon	3,812	3,567
Lynn Gardens	5,261	...
McKenzie	3,780	3,774
McMinnville	9,013	7,577
Madison	13,583	...
Madisonville	1,812	1,487
Manchester	3,930	2,341
Martin	4,750	4,082
Maryville	10,348	7,742
Memphis	497,524	396,000
Milan	5,208	4,938
Millington	6,059	4,696
Monterey	2,069	2,043
Morrison City	2,426	...
Morristown	21,267	13,019
Mount Pleasant	2,921	2,931
Murfreesboro	18,991	13,052
Nashville (c.)	170,874	174,307
Newbern	1,695	1,734
Newport	6,448	3,892
New Providence	4,451	1,825
Oak Hill	4,490	...
Oak Ridge	27,169	...
Oneida	2,480	1,304
Paris	9,325	8,826
Parsons	1,859	1,640
Plainfield	2,127	...
Portland	2,424	1,660
Providence	3,830	...
Pulaski	6,616	5,762
Red Bank–White Oak	10,777	...
Ripley	3,782	3,318
Rockwood	5,345	4,272
Rogersville	3,121	2,545

Place	1960	1950
TENN.—Cont.:		
Savannah	4,315	1,698
Selmer	1,897	1,759
Sevierville	2,890	1,620
Shelbyville	10,466	9,456
Signal Mountain	3,413	1,786
Smithville	2,348	1,558
Smyrna	3,612	1,544
Soddy	2,206	2,157
Somerville	1,820	1,760
South Cleveland	1,512	...
South Fulton	2,512	2,119
South Harriman	2,884	2,761
South Pittsburg	4,130	2,573
Sparta	4,510	4,299
Spring City	1,800	1,725
Springfield	9,221	6,506
Sweetwater	4,145	4,199
Tiftona	3,520	...
Tiptonville	2,068	1,953
Tracy City	1,577	1,414
Trenton	4,225	3,868
Tullahoma	12,242	7,562
Union City	8,837	7,665
Waverly	2,891	1,892
West View Park	4,722	...
Whitehaven	13,894	1,311
Whitwell	1,857	...
Winchester	4,760	3,974
Woodbine–Radnor–Glencliff	14,485	...
Woodbury	1,562	1,000
Woodmont–Green Hills–Glendale	23,161	...
TEXAS:		
Abernathy	2,491	1,692
Abilene	90,368	45,570
Alamo	4,121	3,017
Alamo Heights	7,552	8,000
Albany	2,174	2,241
Alice	20,861	16,449
Alice Southwest	1,813	...
Alpine	4,740	5,261
Alvarado	1,907	1,656
Alvin	5,643	3,701
Amarillo	137,969	74,246
Anahuac	1,985	1,284
Andrews	11,135	3,294
Angleton	7,312	3,399
Anson	2,890	2,708
Aransas Pass	6,956	5,396
Archer City	1,974	1,901
Arlington	44,775	7,692
Asherton	1,890	2,425
Athens	7,086	5,194
Atlanta	4,076	3,782
Austin (c.)	186,545	132,459
Azle	2,969	...
Bacliff	1,707	...
Baird	1,633	1,821
Balch Springs	6,821	...
Ballinger	5,043	5,302
Barrett	2,364	...
Bartlett	1,540	1,727
Bastrop	3,001	3,176
Bay City	11,656	9,427
Baytown	28,159	22,983
Beaumont	119,175	94,014
Bedford	2,706	...
Beeville	13,811	9,348
Bellaire	19,872	10,173
Bellmead	5,127	...
Bellville	2,218	2,112
Belton	8,163	6,246
Benavides	2,459	3,016
Benbrook	3,254	617
Beverly Hills	1,728	701
Big Lake	2,668	2,152
Big Spring	31,230	17,286
Bishop	3,722	2,731
Bloomington	1,756	...
Boerne	2,169	1,802
Bonham	7,357	7,049
Borger	20,911	18,059
Bowie	4,566	4,544
Brackettville	1,662	1,858
Brady	5,338	5,944
Breckenridge	6,273	6,610
Brenham	7,740	6,941
Bridge City	4,677	...
Bridgeport	3,218	2,049
Brownfield	10,286	6,161
Brownsville	48,040	36,066
Brownwood	16,974	20,181
Bryan	27,542	18,102
Bunker Hill Village	2,216	...
Burkburnett	7,621	4,555
Burleson	2,345	791
Burnet	2,214	2,394
Caldwell	2,204	2,109
Calvert	2,073	2,548
Cameron	5,640	5,052
Canadian	2,239	2,700
Canyon	5,864	4,364
Carrizo Springs	5,699	4,316
Carrollton	4,242	1,610

Place	1960	1950
TEX.—Cont.:		
Carthage	5,262	4,750
Castle Hills	2,622	...
Castroville	1,508	985
Cedar Hill	1,848	732
Center	4,510	4,323
Childress	6,399	7,619
Cisco	4,499	5,230
Clarendon	2,172	2,577
Clarksville	3,851	4,353
Cleburne	15,381	12,905
Cleveland	5,838	5,183
Clifton	2,335	1,837
Clute City	4,501	...
Cockrell Hill	3,104	2,207
Coleman	6,371	6,530
College Station	11,396	7,925
Colorado City	6,457	6,774
Columbus	3,656	2,878
Comanche	3,415	3,840
Commerce	5,789	5,889
Conroe	9,192	7,298
Cooper	2,213	2,350
Copperas Cove	4,567	1,052
Corpus Christi	167,690	108,287
Corsicana	20,344	19,211
Cotulla	3,960	4,418
Cove City	1,749	...
Crane	3,796	2,154
Crockett	5,356	5,932
Crosbyton	2,088	1,879
Crowell	1,703	1,912
Crystal City	9,101	7,198
Cuero	7,338	7,498
Daingerfield	3,133	1,668
Daisetta	1,500	1,764
Dalhart	5,160	5,918
Dallas	679,684	434,462
Dayton	3,367	1,820
Decatur	3,563	2,922
Deer Park	4,865	736
De Kalb	2,042	1,928
De Leon	2,022	2,241
Del Rio	18,612	14,211
Denison	22,748	17,504
Denton	26,844	21,372
Denver City	4,302	1,855
De Soto	1,969	298
Devine	2,522	1,672
Diboll	2,506	2,391
Dickinson	4,715	2,704
Dilley	2,118	1,809
Dimmitt	2,935	1,461
Donna	7,522	7,171
Donnybrook Place	2,537	...
Dublin	2,443	2,761
Dumas	8,477	6,127
Duncanville	3,774	841
Eagle Lake	3,565	2,787
Eagle Pass	12,094	7,276
Eastland	3,292	3,626
Edcouch	2,814	2,925
Edinburg	18,706	12,383
Edna	5,038	3,855
El Campo	7,700	6,237
El Campo South	1,884	...
Eldorado	1,815	1,663
Electra	4,759	4,970
Elgin	3,511	3,168
El Paso	276,687	130,485
Elsa	3,847	3,179
Ennis	9,347	7,815
Euless	2,062	...
Fabens	3,134	3,089
Fairfield	1,781	1,742
Falfurrias	6,515	6,712
Farmers Branch	13,441	915
Farmersville	2,021	1,955
Ferris	1,807	1,735
Floresville	2,126	1,949
Floydada	3,769	3,210
Forest Hill	3,221	1,519
Forney	1,544	1,425
Fort Stockton	6,373	4,444
Fort Worth	356,268	278,778
Fredericksburg	4,629	3,854
Freeport	11,619	6,012
Freer	2,724	2,280
Friona	2,048	1,202
Fritch	1,846	...
Gainesville	13,083	11,246
Galena Park	10,852	7,186
Galveston	67,175	66,568
Ganado	1,626	1,258
Garland	38,501	10,571
Gatesville	4,626	3,856
Georgetown	5,218	4,951
George West	1,878	1,533
Giddings	2,821	2,532
Gilmer	4,312	4,096
Gladewater	5,742	5,305
Goliad	1,782	1,584
Gonzales	5,829	5,659
Graham	8,505	6,742
Granbury	2,227	1,683
Grand Prairie	30,386	14,594
Grand Saline	2,006	1,810
Grapevine	2,821	1,824
Greenville	19,087	14,727
Gregory	1,970	...
Griffing Park	2,267	2,096
Groesbeck	2,498	2,182
Groves	17,304	...

Place	1960	1950
TEX.—Cont.:		
Hale Center	2,196	1,626
Hallettsville	2,808	2,000
Haltom City	23,133	5,760
Hamilton	3,106	3,077
Hamlin	3,791	3,569
Harlingen	41,207	23,229
Haskell	4,016	3,836
Hearne	5,072	4,872
Hebbronville	3,987	4,302
Hempstead	1,505	1,395
Henderson	9,666	6,833
Henrietta	3,062	2,813
Hereford	7,652	5,207
Highland Park	10,411	11,405
Highlands	4,336	2,723
Highway Village	1,927	...
Hillsboro	7,402	8,363
Hitchcock	5,216	...
Hondo	4,992	4,188
Honey Grove	2,071	2,340
Hooks	2,048	2,319
Houston	938,219	596,163
Hubbard	1,628	1,768
Hughes Springs	1,813	1,445
Humble	1,711	1,388
Hunters Creek Village	2,478	...
Huntsville	11,999	9,820
Hurst	10,165	...
Ingleside	3,022	...
Iowa Park	3,295	2,110
Irving	45,985	2,621
Jacinto City	9,547	6,856
Jacksboro	3,816	2,951
Jacksonville	9,590	8,607
Jasper	4,889	4,403
Jefferson	3,082	3,164
Jourdanton	1,504	1,481
Junction	2,441	2,471
Karnes City	2,693	2,588
Katy	1,569	849
Kaufman	3,087	2,714
Keene	1,532	...
Kenedy	4,301	4,234
Kennedale	1,521	1,046
Kermit	10,465	6,912
Kerryville	8,901	7,691
Kilgore	10,092	9,638
Killeen	23,377	7,045
Kingsville	25,297	16,898
Kirbyville	1,660	1,150
Kleburg	3,572	...
Knox City	1,805	1,489
Kountze	1,768	1,651
Lacy-Lakeview	2,272	...
La Feria	3,047	2,952
La Grange	3,623	2,738
Lake Jackson	9,651	2,897
Lakeview	3,849	3,091
Lakewood	1,882	...
Lake Worth Village	3,833	2,351
La Marque	13,969	...
Lamesa	12,438	10,704
Lampasas	5,061	4,869
Lancaster	7,501	2,632
La Porte	4,512	4,429
Laredo	60,678	51,910
League City	2,622	1,341
Legion	1,691	...
Levelland	10,153	8,264
Lewisville	3,956	1,516
Liberty	6,127	4,163
Linden	1,832	1,744
Littlefield	7,236	6,540
Livingston	3,398	2,865
Llano	2,656	2,954
Lockhart	6,084	5,573
Lockney	2,141	1,692
Lone Star	1,513	...
Longview	40,050	24,502
Lubbock	128,691	71,747
Lufkin	17,641	15,135
Luling	4,412	4,297
Lyford	1,554	1,473
McAllen	32,728	20,067
McCamey	3,375	3,121
McGregor	4,642	2,669
McKinney	13,763	10,560
McNair	1,880	1,313
Madisonville	2,324	2,393
Malakoff	1,657	1,286
Marble Falls	2,161	2,044
Marfa	2,799	3,603
Marlin	6,918	7,099
Marshall	23,846	22,327
Mart	2,197	2,269
Mason	1,910	2,456
Mathis	6,075	4,050
Memphis	3,332	3,810
Menard	1,914	2,685
Mercedes	10,943	10,081
Merkel	2,312	2,338
Mesquite	27,526	1,696
Mexia	6,121	6,627
Midland	62,625	21,713
Midlothian	1,521	1,177
Mineola	3,810	3,626
Mineral Wells	11,053	7,801
Mission	14,081	10,765
Monahans	8,567	6,311
Morton	2,731	2,274

Place	1960	1950
TEX.—Cont.:		
Mount Pleasant	8,027	6,342
Muleshoe	3,871	2,477
Munday	1,978	2,280
Nacogdoches	12,674	12,327
Naples	1,692	1,346
Navasota	4,937	5,188
Nederland	12,036	3,805
New Boston	2,773	2,688
New Braunfels	15,631	12,210
Nixon	1,751	1,875
Nocona	3,127	3,022
North Richland Hills	8,662	...
Odem	2,088	1,680
Odessa	80,338	29,495
Olmos Park	2,457	2,841
Olney	3,872	3,765
Olton	1,917	1,201
Orange	25,605	21,174
Overton	1,950	2,001
Ozona	3,361	2,885
Paducah	2,392	2,952
Palacios	3,676	2,799
Palestine	13,974	12,503
Pampa	24,664	16,583
Panhandle	1,958	1,406
Paris	20,977	21,643
Pasadena	58,737	22,483
Pear Ridge	3,470	2,029
Pearsall	4,957	4,481
Pecos	12,728	8,054
Perryton	7,903	4,417
Pharr	14,106	8,690
Phillips	3,605	4,105
Philrich	2,067	...
Pinehurst	1,703	...
Piney Point Village	1,790	...
Pittsburg	3,796	3,142
Plainview	18,735	14,044
Plano	3,695	2,126
Pleasanton	3,467	2,913
Port Arthur	66,676	57,530
Port Isabel	3,575	2,372
Portland	2,538	1,292
Port Lavaca	8,864	5,599
Port Neches	8,696	5,448
Post	4,663	3,141
Poteet	2,811	2,487
Prairie View	2,326	...
Premont	3,049	2,619
Quanah	4,564	4,589
Ralls	2,229	1,779
Ranger	3,313	3,989
Raymondville	9,385	9,136
Refugio	4,944	4,666
Richardson	16,810	1,289
Richland Hills	7,804	...
Richmond	3,668	2,030
Rio Grande City	5,835	3,992
River Oaks	8,444	7,097
Robinson	2,111	...
Robstown	10,266	7,278
Rockdale	4,481	2,321
Rockport	2,989	2,266
Rockwall	2,166	1,501
Rosebud	1,644	1,730
Rosenberg	9,698	6,210
Rotan	2,788	3,163
Round Rock	1,878	1,438
Rusk	4,900	6,598
Sabinal	1,747	1,974
San Angelo	58,815	52,093
San Antonio	587,718	408,442
San Augustine	2,584	2,510
San Benito	16,422	13,271
Sanderson	2,189	2,047
San Diego	4,351	4,397
San Juan	4,371	3,413
San Marcos	12,713	9,980
San Pedro	7,634	8,127
San Saba	2,728	3,400
Sansom Park Village	4,175	1,611
Santa Rosa	1,572	400
Schertz	2,281	...
Schulenburg	2,207	2,005
Seagoville	3,745	1,927
Seagraves	2,307	2,101
Sealy	2,328	1,942
Seguin	14,299	9,733
Seminole	5,737	3,479
Seymour	3,789	3,779
Shamrock	3,113	3,322
Sherman	24,988	20,150
Shiner	1,945	1,778
Silsbee	6,277	3,179
Sinton	6,008	4,254
Slaton	6,568	5,036
Smithville	2,933	3,379
Snyder	13,850	12,010
Sonora	2,619	2,633
Sour Lake	1,602	1,630
South Houston	7,523	4,126
Spearman	3,555	1,852
Spring Valley	3,004	...
Spur	2,170	2,183
Stamford	5,259	5,819
Stanton	2,228	1,603
Stephenville	7,359	7,155
Stinnett	2,695	1,170
Sugar Land	2,802	...
Sulphur Springs	9,160	8,991

Place	1960	1950
TEX.—Cont.:		
Sunray	1,967	1,530
Sunrise	1,708	1,616
Sweeny	3,087	1,393
Sweetwater	13,914	13,619
Taft	3,463	2,978
Taft Southwest	1,927	...
Tahoka	3,012	2,848
Taylor	9,434	9,071
Teague	2,728	2,925
Temple	30,419	25,467
Terrell	13,803	11,544
Terrell Hills	5,572	2,708
Texarkana	30,218	24,753
Texas City	32,065	16,620
Three Rivers	1,932	2,026
Tomball	1,713	1,065
Trinity	1,787	2,054
Troup	1,667	1,539
Tulia	4,410	3,222
Tyler	51,230	38,968
University Park	23,202	24,275
Uvalde	10,293	8,674
Van Alstyne	1,608	1,649
Van Horn	1,953	1,161
Vernon	12,141	12,651
Victoria	33,047	16,126
Vidor	4,938	2,136
Waco	97,808	84,706
Waxahachie	12,749	11,204
Weatherford	9,759	8,093
Weimar	2,006	1,663
Wellington	3,137	3,676
Weslaco	15,649	7,514
West	2,352	2,130
West Columbia	2,947	2,100
West Orange	4,848	...
West University Place	14,628	17,074
Westworth	3,321	529
Wharton	5,734	4,450
Wharton West	1,609	...
Whitesboro	2,485	1,854
White Settlement	11,513	10,827
Wichita Falls	101,724	68,042
Wills Point	2,281	2,030
Wilmer	1,785	465
Wink	1,863	1,521
Winnsboro	2,675	2,512
Winters	3,266	2,676
Woodsboro	2,081	1,836
Woodville	1,920	1,863
Wylie	1,804	1,295
Yoakum	5,761	5,231
Yorktown	2,527	2,596
Zapata	2,031	1,409
UTAH:		
American Fork	6,373	5,126
Beaver	1,548	1,685
Bingham Canyon	1,516	2,569
Blanding	1,805	1,177
Bountiful	17,039	6,004
Brigham City	11,728	6,790
Cedar City	7,543	6,106
Centerville	2,361	1,262
Clearfield	8,833	4,723
Delta	1,576	1,703
Dragerton	2,959	3,453
Ephraim	1,801	1,987
Farmington	1,951	1,468
Fillmore	1,602	1,890
Grantsville	2,166	1,537
Heber	2,936	2,936
Helper	2,459	2,850
Hyrum	1,728	1,704
Kanab	1,645	1,287
Kaysville	3,608	1,898
Kearns	17,172	...
Layton	9,027	3,456
Lehi	4,377	3,627
Logan	18,731	16,832
Magna	6,442	3,502
Manti	1,739	2,051
Mapleton	1,516	1,175
Midvale	5,802	3,996
Moab	4,682	1,274
Monticello	1,845	1,172
Mount Pleasant	1,572	2,030
Murray	16,806	9,006
Nephi	2,566	2,990
North Ogden	2,621	1,105
North Salt Lake	1,655	255
Ogden	70,197	57,112
Orem	18,394	8,351
Payson	4,237	3,998
Pleasant Grove	4,772	3,195
Price	6,802	6,010
Provo	36,047	28,937
Richfield	4,412	4,212
Riverdale	1,848	871
Riverton	1,993	1,666
Roosevelt	1,812	1,628
Roy	9,239	3,723
St. George	5,130	4,562
Salina	1,618	1,789
Salt Lake City (c.)	189,454	182,121
Sandy City	3,322	2,095
Smithfield	2,512	2,383
South Ogden	7,405	3,763

Place	1960	1950
UTAH—Cont.:		
South Salt Lake	9,520	7,704
Spanish Fork City	6,472	5,230
Springville	7,913	6,475
Sunnyside	1,740	1,881
Sunset	4,235	993
Tooele	9,133	7,269
Tremonton	2,115	1,662
Vernal	3,655	2,845
Washington Terrace	6,441	...
West Jordan	3,009	2,107
VERMONT:		
Barre	10,387	10,922
Bellows Falls	3,831	3,881
Bennington	8,023	8,002
Brandon	1,675	1,673
Brattleboro	9,315	9,606
Burlington	35,531	33,155
Essex Junction	5,340	2,741
Hardwick	1,521	1,696
Ludlow	1,658	1,678
Middlebury	3,688	3,614
Montpelier (c.)	8,782	8,599
Morrisville	2,047	1,995
Newport	5,019	5,217
Northfield	2,159	2,262
Poultney	1,810	1,685
Proctor	1,978	1,813
Randolph	2,122	2,223
Richford	1,663	1,916
Rutland	18,325	17,659
St. Albans	8,806	8,552
St. Johnsbury	6,809	7,370
Shelburne Road Section	2,037	...
Springfield	6,600	4,940
Swanton	2,390	2,275
Vergennes	1,921	1,736
Waterbury	2,984	3,153
West Rutland	1,991	2,172
White River Junction	2,546	2,365
Williston Road Section	3,259	...
Windsor	3,256	3,467
Winooski	7,420	6,734
VIRGINIA:		
Abingdon	4,758	4,709
Alexandria	91,023	61,787
Altavista	3,299	3,332
Appalachia	2,456	2,915
Arlington County	163,401	57,040
Ashland	2,773	2,610
Bassetts	3,148	3,421
Bedford	5,921	4,061
Berryville	1,645	1,401
Big Stone Gap	4,688	5,173
Blacksburg	7,070	3,358
Blackstone	3,659	3,536
Bluefield	4,235	4,212
Bridgewater	1,815	1,537
Bristol	17,144	15,954
Buena Vista	6,300	5,214
Cape Charles	2,041	2,427
Charlottesville	29,427	25,969
Chase City	3,207	2,519
Chatham	1,822	1,456
Chincoteague	2,131	2,724
Christiansburg	3,653	2,967
Clarksville	1,530	1,035
Clifton Forge	5,268	5,795
Coeburn	2,471	760
Collinsville	3,586	...
Colonial Beach	1,769	1,464
Colonial Heights	9,587	6,077
Covington	11,062	5,860
Crewe	2,012	2,030
Culpeper	2,412	2,527
Danville	46,577	35,066
Elkton	1,506	1,361
Emporia	5,535	5,664
Ettrick	2,998	3,030
Exmore	1,566	1,362
Fairfax	13,585	1,946
Falls Church	10,192	7,535
Farmville	4,293	4,375
Franklin	7,264	4,670
Fredericksburg	13,639	12,158
Front Royal	7,949	8,115
Galax	5,254	5,248
Gate City	2,142	2,126
Glenwood	1,857	1,913
Grundy	2,287	1,947
Hampton	89,258	5,966
Harrisonburg	11,916	10,810
Herndon	1,960	1,461
Hopewell	17,895	10,219
Jericho	2,300	...
Lawrenceville	1,941	2,239
Lebanon	2,085	672
Leesburg	2,869	1,703
Lenox	1,520	...
Lexington	7,537	5,976
Lloyd Place	2,282	...
Luray	3,014	2,731
Lynchburg	54,790	47,727
Manassas	3,555	1,804
Manassas Park	5,342	...
Marion	8,385	6,982

Place	1960	1950	Place	1960	1950
VA.—Cont.:			**WASH.—Cont.:**		
Martinsville	18,798	17,251	Monroe	1,901	1,556
Narrows	2,508	2,520	Montesano	2,486	2,328
Newport News	113,662	42,358	Moses Lake	11,299	2,679
Norfolk	304,869	213,513	Mountlake Terrace	9,122	...
North Virginia Beach	2,587	1,593	Mount Vernon	7,921	5,230
Norton	5,013	4,315	Navy Yard City	3,341	3,030
Oceana	2,448	...	Newport	1,513	1,385
Onancock	1,759	1,353	Normandy Park	3,224	...
Orange	2,955	2,571	Oak Harbor	3,942	1,193
Pearisburg	2,268	2,005	Okanogan	2,001	2,013
Pennington Gap	1,799	2,090	Olympia (c.)	18,273	15,819
Petersburg	36,750	35,054	Omak	4,068	3,791
Pleasant Hill	2,636	...	Opportunity	12,465	...
Poquoson	4,278	...	Orting	1,520	1,299
Portsmouth	114,773	80,039	Othello	2,669	526
Pulaski	10,469	9,202	Pacific	1,577	755
Radford	9,371	9,026	Pasco	14,522	10,228
Richlands	4,963	4,648	Pasco West	2,894	...
Richmond (c.)	219,958	230,310	Pinehurst	3,989	...
Roanoke	97,110	91,921	Pomeroy	1,677	1,775
Salem	16,058	6,823	Port Angeles	12,653	11,233
Saltville	2,344	2,678	Port Orchard	2,778	2,320
Seatack	3,120	...	Port Townsend	5,074	6,888
Shenandoah	1,839	1,903	Poulsbo	1,505	1,014
South Boston	5,974	6,057	Prosser	2,763	2,636
South Hill	2,569	2,153	Pullman	12,957	12,022
South Norfolk	22,035	10,434	Puyallup	12,063	10,010
Springfield	10,783	...	Quincy	3,269	804
Staunton	22,232	19,927	Raymond	3,301	4,110
Strasburg	2,428	2,022	Renton	18,453	16,039
Suffolk	12,609	12,339	Richland	23,548	...
Tazewell	3,000	1,347	Ritzville	2,173	2,145
Triangle	2,948	...	Rocky Point-Marine Drive	2,733	...
Victoria	1,737	1,607	Seattle	557,087	467,591
Vienna	11,440	2,029	Sedro-Woolley	3,705	3,299
Vinton	3,432	3,629	Selah	2,824	2,489
Virginia Beach	8,091	5,390	Shelton	5,651	5,045
Warrenton	3,522	1,797	Shoultes	3,159	1,973
Waverly	1,601	1,502	Snohomish	3,894	3,094
Waynesboro	15,694	12,357	Soap Lake	1,591	2,091
West Point	1,678	1,919	South Bend	1,671	1,857
Williamsburg	6,832	6,735	South Broad-way	3,661	3,229
Winchester	15,110	13,841	Spokane	181,608	161,721
Wise	2,614	1,574	Steilacoom	1,569	1,233
Woodstock	2,083	1,816	Sumner	3,156	2,816
Wytheville	5,634	5,513	Sunnyside	6,208	4,194
			Tacoma	147,979	143,673
WASHINGTON:			Toppenish	5,667	5,265
Aberdeen	18,741	19,653	Tukwila	1,804	800
Anacortes	8,414	6,919	Tumwater	3,885	2,725
Arlington	2,025	1,635	Union Gap	2,100	1,766
Auburn	11,933	6,497	Vancouver	32,464	41,664
Bellevue	12,809	...	Walla Walla	24,536	22,102
Bellingham	34,688	34,112	Walla Walla East	1,557	...
Beverly Park South	1,950	...	Wapato	3,137	3,185
Blaine	1,735	1,693	Washougal	2,672	1,577
Bothell	2,237	1,019	Wenatchee	16,726	13,072
Bremerton	28,922	27,678	West Clarkston-Highland	2,851	1,920
Buckley	3,538	2,705	West Wenatchee	2,518	...
Burlington	2,968	2,350	White Salmon	1,590	1,353
Camas	5,666	4,725	Yakima	43,284	38,486
Cashmere	1,891	1,768			
Centralia	8,586	8,657	**WEST VIRGINIA:**		
Central Park	1,622	...	Amherstdale-Robinette	1,716	2,387
Chehalis	5,199	5,639	Ansted	1,511	1,543
Chelan	2,402	2,157	Barboursville	2,331	1,943
Cheney	3,173	2,797	Beckley	18,642	19,397
Chewelah	1,525	1,683	Belington	1,528	1,699
Clarkston	6,209	5,617	Benwood	2,850	3,485
Cle Elum	1,816	2,206	Bethlehem	2,308	1,146
Clyde Hill	1,871	...	Bluefield	19,256	21,506
Colfax	2,860	3,057	Boomer-Harewood	1,657	2,096
College Place	4,031	3,174	Bridgeport	4,199	2,414
Columbia Heights	2,227	...	Buckhannon	6,386	6,016
Colville	3,806	3,033	Cameron	1,652	1,736
Dayton	2,913	2,979	Cedar Grove	1,569	1,738
Des Moines	1,987	...	Charleston (c.)	85,796	73,501
East Wenatchee Bench	2,327	...	Charles Town	3,329	3,035
Edmonds	8,016	2,057	Chesapeake	2,699	2,566
Ellensburg	8,625	8,430	Chester	3,787	3,758
Elma	1,811	1,543	Clarksburg	28,112	32,014
Enetai	2,539	...	Clendenin	1,510	1,475
Enumclaw	3,269	2,789	Crab Orchard	1,953	1,544
Ephrata	6,548	4,589	Despard	1,763	1,976
Everett	40,304	33,849	Dunbar	11,006	8,032
Fairview	2,758	3,309	East View	1,704	1,642
Fircrest	3,565	1,459	Elkins	8,307	9,121
Fruitvale	3,345	3,654	Fairmont	27,477	29,346
Garrett	1,641	...	Fayetteville	1,848	1,952
Goldendale	2,536	1,907	Follansbee	4,052	4,435
Grandview	3,366	2,503	Glendale	1,905	1,467
Green Acres	2,074	1,287	Glen Jean-Hilltop	1,665	...
Hoquiam	10,762	11,123	Glenville	1,828	1,789
Houghton	2,426	1,005	Grafton	5,791	7,365
Issaquah	1,870	955	Henlawson	1,670	1,750
Kelso	8,379	7,345	Hinton	5,197	5,780
Kennewick	14,244	10,106	Holden-Beebe	1,900	2,229
Kent	9,017	3,278	Huntington	83,627	86,353
Kirkland	6,025	4,713	Hurricane	1,970	1,463
Lacey	6,630	...	Kenova	4,577	4,320
Lake Stevens	1,538	2,586	Keyser	6,192	6,347
Longview	23,349	20,339			
Lynden	2,542	2,161			
Lynnwood	7,207	...			
Marysville	3,117	2,259			
Medical Lake	4,765	4,488			
Medina	2,285	...			
Millwood	1,776	1,240			
Milton	2,218	1,374			

Courtesy Turkish Tourist and Information Office in New York

Place	1960	1950	Place	1960	1950
W.VA.—Cont.:			**W.VA.—Cont.:**		
Kingwood	2,530	2,186	Stonewood	2,202	2,066
Lewisburg	2,259	2,192	Summersville	2,008	1,628
Logan	4,185	5,079	Terra Alta	1,504	1,649
McMechen	2,999	3,518	Verdunville	2,260	...
Mabscott	1,591	1,665	Vienna	9,381	6,020
Madison	2,215	2,025	War	3,006	3,992
Mannington	2,996	3,241	Weirton	28,201	24,005
Marlinton	1,586	1,645	Welch	5,313	6,603
Marmet	2,500	2,515	Wellsburg	5,514	5,787
Martinsburg	15,179	15,621	Weston	8,754	8,945
Milton	1,714	1,552	Westover	4,749	4,318
Montgomery	3,000	3,484	Wheeling	53,400	58,891
Morgantown	22,487	25,525	White Sulphur Springs	2,676	2,643
Moundsville	15,163	14,772	Williamson	6,746	8,624
Mount Gay	3,386	...	Williamstown	2,632	2,001
Mount Hope	2,000	2,588			
Mullens	3,544	3,470	**WISCONSIN:**		
New Cumberland	2,076	2,119	Algoma	3,855	3,384
Newell	1,842	2,101	Altoona	2,114	1,713
New Martinsville	5,607	4,084	Amery	1,769	1,625
Nitro	6,894	3,314	Antigo	9,691	9,902
Nutter Fort	2,440	2,285	Appleton	48,411	34,010
Oak Hill	4,711	4,518	Arcadia	2,084	1,949
Paden City	3,137	2,588	Ashland	10,132	10,640
Parkersburg	44,797	29,684	Baraboo	7,660	7,264
Parsons	1,798	2,009	Barron	2,338	2,355
Pennsboro	1,660	1,753	Barton	1,569	1,039
Petersburg	2,079	1,898	Bayside	3,181	...
Philippi	2,228	2,531	Beaver Dam	13,118	11,867
Piedmont	2,307	2,665	Beloit	32,846	29,590
Point Pleasant	5,785	4,596	Berlin	4,838	4,693
Princeton	8,393	8,279	Black River Falls	3,195	2,824
Ranson	1,974	1,436	Bloomer	2,834	2,556
Ravenswood	3,410	1,175	Boscobel	2,608	2,347
Richwood	4,110	5,321	Brillion	1,783	1,390
Ripley	2,756	1,813	Brodhead	2,444	2,016
Romney	2,203	2,059	Brookfield	19,812	...
Ronceverte	1,882	2,301	Brown Deer	11,280	...
St. Albans	15,103	9,870	Burlington	5,856	4,780
St. Marys	2,443	2,196	Butler	2,274	1,047
Salem	2,366	2,578	Cedarburg	5,191	2,810
Shinnston	2,724	2,793	Chetek	1,729	1,585
Sistersville	2,331	2,313	Chilton	2,578	2,367
Smithers	1,696	2,208	Chippewa Falls	11,708	11,088
South Charleston	19,180	16,686	Clintonville	4,778	4,657
Spencer	2,660	2,587	Columbus	3,467	3,250
Sprague	3,073	2,626	Cornell	1,685	1,944
			Crandon	1,679	1,922

The world's population is not evenly distributed over the continents. Polar, desert, tropical, and mountainous regions have light population densities. Some parts of the world do not have the resources needed to support large populations, and some locations are inconvenient. Many acres of farm area usually can support only a few people, but thousands of people gather in city areas because of better employment opportunities.

Howard Oberlin

Ernest Day, Idaho Historical Society

Place	1960	1950	Place	1960	1950	Place	1960	1950	Place	1960	1950
WIS.—Cont.:			WIS.—Cont.:			WIS.—Cont.:			WIS.—Cont.:		
Cuba City	1,673	1,333	Lancaster	3,703	3,266	Phillips	1,524	1,775	Union Grove	1,970	1,358
Cudahy	17,975	12,182	Little Chute	5,099	4,152	Platteville	6,957	5,751	Viroqua	3,926	3,795
Cumberland	1,860	1,872	Lodi	1,620	1,416	Plymouth	5,128	4,543	Washburn	1,896	2,070
Darlington	2,349	2,174	Madison (c.)	126,706	96,056	Portage	7,822	7,334	Waterford	1,500	1,100
Delafield	2,334	...	Manitowoc	32,275	27,598	Port Edwards	1,849	1,336	Waterloo	1,947	1,667
Delavan	4,846	4,007	Maple Bluff	1,565	1,361	Port			Watertown	13,943	12,417
Delavan Lake	1,884	...	Marinette	13,329	14,178	Washington	5,984	4,755	Waukesha	30,004	21,233
De Pere	10,045	8,146	Marshfield	14,153	12,394	Prairie du			Waunakee	1,611	1,042
Dodgeville	2,911	2,532	Mauston	3,531	3,171	Chien	5,649	5,392	Waupaca	3,984	3,921
Durand	2,039	1,961	Mayville	3,607	3,010	Prairie du Sac	1,676	1,402	Waupun	7,935	6,725
Eau Claire	37,987	36,058	Medford	3,260	2,799	Prescott	1,536	1,005	Wausau	31,943	30,414
Edgerton	4,000	3,507	Menasha	14,647	12,385	Princeton	1,509	1,371	Wauwatosa	56,923	33,324
Elkhorn	3,586	2,935	Menomonee			Pulaski	1,540	1,210	West Allis	68,157	42,959
Ellsworth	1,701	1,475	Falls	18,276	2,469	Racine	89,144	71,193	West Bend	9,969	6,849
Elm Grove	4,994	...	Menomonie	8,624	8,245	Randolph	1,507	1,350	West		
Elroy	1,505	1,654	Mequon	8,543	...	Reedsburg	4,371	4,072	Milwaukee	5,043	5,429
Evansville	2,858	2,531	Merrill	9,451	8,951	Rhinelander	8,790	8,774	West Salem	1,707	1,376
Fennimore	1,747	1,696	Middleton	4,410	2,110	Rice Lake	7,303	6,898	Whitefish Bay	18,390	14,665
Fond du Lac	32,719	29,936	Milton	1,671	1,549	Richland			Whitewater	6,380	5,101
Fort Atkinson	7,908	6,280	Milwaukee	741,324	637,392	Center	4,746	4,608	Wisconsin Dells	2,105	1,957
Fox Point	7,315	2,585	Mineral Point	2,385	2,284	Ripon	6,163	5,619	Wisconsin		
Franklin	10,006	...	Mondovi	2,320	2,285	River Falls	4,857	3,877	Rapids	15,042	13,496
Glendale	9,537	...	Monona	8,178	2,544	Rothschild	2,550	1,425	WYOMING:		
Grafton	3,748	1,489	Monroe	8,050	7,037	St. Francis	10,065	...	Buffalo	2,907	2,674
Green Bay	62,888	52,735	Mosinee	2,067	1,453	Sauk City	2,095	1,755	Casper	38,930	23,673
Greendale	6,843	2,752	Mount Horeb	1,991	1,716	Schofield	3,038	1,948	Cheyenne (c.)	43,505	31,935
Greenfield	17,636	...	Mukwonago	1,877	1,207	Seymour	2,045	1,760	Cody	4,838	3,872
Hales Corners	5,549	...	Neenah	18,057	12,437	Shawano	6,103	5,894	Douglas	2,822	2,544
Hartford	5,627	4,549	Neillsville	2,728	2,663	Sheboygan	45,747	42,365	Evanston	4,901	3,863
Hartland	2,088	1,190	Nekoosa	2,515	2,352	Sheboygan			Gillette	3,580	2,191
Hayward	1,540	1,577	New Berlin	15,788	...	Falls	4,061	3,599	Glenrock	1,584	1,110
Herrington	2,405	...	New Holstein	2,401	1,831	Shorewood	15,990	16,199	Green River	3,497	3,187
Horicon	2,996	2,664	New London	5,288	4,922	Shorewood			Greybull	2,286	2,262
Howard	3,485	...	New Richmond	3,316	2,886	Hills	2,320	1,594	Kemmerer	2,028	1,667
Hudson	4,325	3,435	Niagara	2,098	2,022	South			Lander	4,182	3,349
Hurley	2,763	3,034	North Fond du			Milwaukee	20,307	12,855	Laramie	17,520	15,581
Janesville	35,164	24,899	Lac	2,549	2,291	Southwest			Lovell	2,451	2,508
Jefferson	4,548	3,625	Oak Creek	9,372	...	Wausau	4,105	2,677	Lusk	1,890	2,089
Juneau	1,718	1,444	Oconomowoc	6,682	5,345	Sparta	6,080	5,893	Mountain View	1,721	...
Kaukauna	10,096	8,337	Oconto	4,805	5,055	Spooner	2,398	2,597	Newcastle	4,345	3,395
Kenosha	67,899	54,368	Oconto Falls	2,331	2,050	Stanley	2,014	2,014	Powell	4,740	3,804
Kewaskum	1,572	1,183	Okauchee	1,879	1,673	Stevens Point	17,837	16,564	Rawlins	8,968	7,415
Kewaunee	2,772	2,583	Omro	1,991	1,470	Stoughton	5,555	4,833	Riverton	6,845	4,142
Kiel	2,524	2,129	Onalaska	3,161	2,561	Sturgeon Bay	7,353	7,054	Rock Springs	10,371	10,857
Kimberly	5,322	3,179	Oregon	1,701	1,341	Sun Prairie	4,008	2,263	Sheridan	11,651	11,500
Kohler	1,524	1,716	Oshkosh	45,110	41,084	Superior	33,563	35,325	Thermopolis	3,955	2,870
La Crosse	47,575	47,535	Park Falls	2,919	2,924	Thiensville	2,507	897	Torrington	4,188	3,247
Ladysmith	3,584	3,924	Perrygo Place	4,475	3,315	Tomah	5,321	4,760	Wheatland	2,350	2,286
Lake Geneva	4,929	4,300	Peshtigo	2,504	2,279	Tomahawk	3,348	3,534	Worland	5,806	4,202
Lake Mills	2,951	2,516	Pewaukee	2,484	1,792	Two Rivers	12,393	10,243			

POPULATION FIGURES OF CANADA

Population Figures of Canada by Provinces and Territories

Province or Territory	1966	1961	Province or Territory	1966	1961
Alberta	1,463,203	1,331,944	Ontario	6,960,870	6,236,092
British Columbia	1,873,674	1,629,082	Prince Edward Island	108,535	104,629
Manitoba	963,066	921,686	Quebec	5,780,845	5,259,211
New Brunswick	616,788	597,936	Saskatchewan	955,344	925,181
Newfoundland	493,396	457,853	Yukon Territory	14,382	14,628
Northwest Territories	28,738	22,998			
Nova Scotia	756,039	737,007	Total	20,014,880	18,238,247

POPULATION OF CANADIAN INCORPORATED PLACES OF 1,500 OR MORE,
1966 and 1961

*Indicates that city, town, or village was incorporated after June 1, 1961.

Place	1966	1961	Place	1966	1961	Place	1966	1961	Place	1966	1961
ALBERTA:			B.C.—Cont.:			N.B.—Cont.:			N.S.—Cont.:		
Athabasca	1,551	1,487	Kinnaird	2,869	2,123	Campbellton	10,175	9,873	Bridgewater	4,755	4,496
Barrhead	2,592	2,286	Ladysmith	3,410	2,173	Caraquet	3,047	*	Dartmouth	58,745	46,966
Blairmore	1,779	1,980	Lake Cowichan	2,353	2,149	Chatham	8,136	7,109	Digby	2,305	2,308
Bonnyville	2,237	1,736	Langley	2,800	2,365	Dalhousie	6,107	5,856	Dominion	2,960	2,999
Brooks	3,354	2,827	Merritt	4,500	3,039	Dieppe	3,847	4,032	Glace Bay	23,516	24,186
Calgary	330,575	249,641	Mission City	3,412	3,251	Edmundston	12,517	12,791	Halifax	86,792	92,511
Camrose	8,362	6,939	Nanaimo	15,188	14,135	Fredericton	22,460	19,683	Inverness	2,022	2,109
Cardston	2,721	2,801	Nelson	9,504	7,074	Grand Falls	4,158	3,983	Kentville	5,176	4,612
Claresholm	2,569	2,143	New West-			Lancaster	15,836	13,849	Liverpool	3,607	3,712
Coaldale	2,541	2,592	minster	38,013	33,654	Marysville	3,572	3,233	Louisbourg	1,617	1,417
Coleman	1,507	1,713	North			Milltown	1,952	1,892	Lunenburg	3,154	3,056
Didsbury	1,586	1,254	Kamloops	11,319	6,456	Moncton	45,847	43,840	Middleton	1,765	1,921
Drayton			North			Newcastle	5,911	5,236	New Glasgow	10,489	9,782
Valley	3,352	3,854	Vancouver	26,851	23,656	Oromocto	14,112	12,120	New Water-		
Drumheller	3,574	2,931	Oliver	1,563	1,774	Sackville	3,186	3,038	ford	9,725	10,592
Edmonton	376,925	281,027	Penticton	15,330	13,859	St. Andrews	1,719	1,531	North Sydney	8,752	8,657
Edson	3,788	3,198	Port Alberni	13,755	11,560	Saint John	51,567	55,153	Parrsboro	1,835	1,834
Fairview	1,884	1,506	Port			St. Leonard	1,635	1,666	Pictou	4,254	4,534
Fort Macleod	2,709	2,490	Coquitlam	11,121	8,111	St. Stephen	3,285	3,380	Port Hawkes-		
Fort			Port Moody	7,021	4,789	Shediac	2,134	2,159	burg	1,866	1,346
McMurray	2,614	1,186	Prince George	24,471	13,877	Shippegan	1,741	1,631	Shelburne	2,654	2,408
Fort Sas-			Prince Rupert	14,677	11,987	Sussex	3,607	3,457	Springhill	5,380	5,836
katchewan	4,152	2,972	Princeton	2,151	2,163	Tracadie	2,018	*	Stellarton	5,191	5,327
Grand Centre	1,731	1,493	Quesnel	5,725	4,673	Woodstock	4,442	4,305	Sydney	32,767	33,617
Grande Prairie	11,417	8,352	Revelstoke	4,791	3,624				Sydney Mines	9,171	9,122
Hanna	2,633	2,645	Rossland	4,264	4,354	NEWFOUND-			Trenton	3,229	3,140
High Prairie	2,241	1,756	Salmon Arm	1,854	1,506	LAND:			Truro	13,007	12,421
High River	2,239	2,276	Sidney	3,165	1,558	Badger	1,192	*	Westville	4,147	4,159
Hinton	4,307	3,529	Smithers	3,135	2,487	Baie Verte	2,144	958	Windsor	3,765	3,823
Innisfail	2,531	2,270	Trail	11,600	11,850	Bay Roberts	3,455	1,328	Wolfville	2,533	2,413
Lacombe	3,035	3,029	Vancouver	410,375	384,522	Bishop's Falls	4,127	*	Yarmouth	8,319	8,636
Leduc	2,856	2,356	Vanderhoof	1,507	1,460	Bonavista	4,192	*			
Lethbridge	37,186	35,454	Vernon	11,423	10,250	Botwood	4,277	3,680	ONTARIO:		
Medicine Hat	25,574	24,484	Victoria	57,453	54,941	Burgeo	1,682	1,454	Acton	4,416	4,144
Olds	2,999	2,433	Warfield	2,255	2,212	Carbonear	4,584	4,234	Ajax	9,412	7,758
Peace River	4,087	2,543	White Rock	7,787	6,453	Channel-Port			Alexandria	2,864	2,597
Pincher Creek	2,882	2,961	Williams Lake	3,167	2,120	aux Basques	5,692	4,141	Alliston	3,149	2,884
Ponoka	4,421	3,938				Clarenville	1,813	1,541	Almonte	3,556	3,267
Raymond	1,950	2,362	MANITOBA:			Corner Brook	27,116	25,185	Amherstburg	4,641	4,452
Redcliff	2,141	2,221	Altona	2,129	2,026	Deer Lake	4,289	3,998	Arnprior	5,693	5,474
Red Deer	26,171	19,612	Beausejour	2,214	1,770	Dunville	1,622	*	Aurora	10,425	8,791
Rimbey	1,502	1,266	Brandon	29,981	28,166	Fortune	1,703	1,360	Aylmer	4,501	4,705
Rocky Moun-			Brooklands	4,181	4,369	Gander	7,183	5,725	Bancroft	2,152	2,615
tain House	2,446	2,360	Carman	1,922	1,930	Grand Bank	3,143	2,703	Barrie	24,016	21,169
St. Albert	9,736	4,059	Dauphin	8,655	7,374	Grand Falls	7,451	*	Beamsville	3,886	2,537
St. Paul	3,543	2,823	East Kildonan	28,796	27,305	Happy Valley	4,215	*	Belle River	2,280	1,854
Slave Lake	1,716	468	Flin Flon	10,201	11,104	Harbour Grace	2,811	2,650	Belleville	32,785	30,655
Stettler	3,988	3,639	Gimli	2,262	1,841	Lewisporte	2,892	2,702	Blenheim	3,356	3,151
Taber	4,584	3,951	Killarney	1,836	1,729	Marystown	1,894	1,691	Blind River	3,617	4,093
Valleyview	1,827	1,077	Minnedosa	2,305	2,211	Mount Pearl	4,428	2,785	Bolton	2,344	2,104
Vegreville	3,598	2,908	Morden	3,097	2,793	Placentia	1,847	1,610	Bowmanville	8,513	7,397
Vermilion	2,685	2,449	Neepawa	3,229	3,197	St. Alban's	1,715	*	Bracebridge	3,045	2,927
Vulcan	1,505	1,310	Portage la			St. Anthony	2,269	1,820	Bradford	2,529	2,342
Wainwright	3,867	3,351	Prairie	13,012	12,388	St. George's	2,046	*	Brampton	36,264	18,467
Westlock	2,685	1,838	Rivers	1,685	1,574	St. John's	79,884	63,633	Brantford	59,854	55,201
Wetaskiwin	6,008	5,300	Roblin	1,617	1,368	St. Lawrence	2,130	2,095	Bridgeport	2,111	1,672
Whitecourt	2,279	1,054	Russell	1,511	1,263	Springdale	2,773	*	Brighton	2,766	2,403
			St. Boniface	43,214	37,600	Stephenville	5,910	6,043	Brockville	19,266	17,744
BRITISH			St. James	35,685	33,977	Stephenville			Burlington	65,941	47,008
COLUMBIA:			St. Vital	29,528	*	Crossing	2,433	2,209	Caledonia	2,725	2,198
Alberni	4,783	4,616	Selkirk	9,157	8,576	Upper Island			Campbellford	3,445	3,478
Castlegar	3,440	2,253	Souris	1,829	1,537	Cove	1,790	*	Capreol	3,092	3,003
Chilliwack	8,681	8,259	Steinbach	4,648	3,739	Wabana	7,884	8,026	Cardinal	1,947	1,944
Comox	2,671	1,756	Stonewall	1,577	1,420	Windsor	6,692	5,505	Carleton Place	4,819	4,796
Courtenay	4,913	3,485	Swan River	3,470	3,163				Chatham	32,424	29,826
Cranbrook	7,549	5,549	The Pas	5,031	4,671	NORTHWEST			Chelmsford	2,752	2,559
Creston	2,920	2,460	Transcona	19,761	14,248	TERRI-			Chesley	1,686	1,697
Dawson Creek	12,392	10,946	Tuxedo	2,480	1,627	TORIES:			Chippawa	3,877	3,256
Duncan	4,299	3,726	Virden	2,933	2,708	Fort Smith	2,120	*	Clinton	3,280	3,491
Fernie	2,715	2,661	West Kildonan	22,240	20,007	Hay River	2,002	*	Cobalt	2,211	2,209
Fort St. John	6,749	3,619	Winkler	2,570	2,529	Yellowknife	3,741	*	Cobourg	11,524	10,646
Golden	2,590	1,776	Winnipeg	257,005	265,429				Cochrane	4,775	4,521
Grand Forks	2,556	2,347				NOVA			Collingwood	8,471	8,385
Hope	2,948	2,751	NEW BRUNS-			SCOTIA:			Coniston	2,692	2,692
Kamloops	10,759	10,076	WICK:			Amherst	10,551	10,788	Copper Cliff	3,505	3,600
Kelowna	17,006	13,188	Bathurst	15,256	5,494	Antigonish	4,856	4,344	Cornwall	45,766	43,639
Kimberley	5,901	6,013							Crystal Beach	1,857	1,886

Place	1966	1961
ONT.—Cont.:		
Deep River	5,573	5,377
Delhi	3,503	3,427
Deseronto	1,836	1,797
Dresden	2,372	2,346
Dryden	6,732	5,728
Dundas	15,501	12,912
Dunnville	5,402	5,181
Durham	2,410	2,180
Eastview	24,269	24,555
Elmira	4,047	3,337
Elora	1,644	1,486
Englehart	1,790	1,786
Espanola	5,567	5,353
Essex	3,742	3,428
Exeter	3,226	3,047
Fergus	4,376	3,831
Fonthill	2,790	2,324
Forest	2,151	2,188
Forest Hill	23,135	20,489
Fort Erie	9,793	9,027
Fort Frances	9,524	9,481
Fort William	48,208	45,214
Frankford	1,823	1,642
Galt	33,491	27,830
Gananoque	5,237	5,096
Georgetown	11,832	10,298
Geraldton	3,658	3,375
Goderich	6,710	6,411
Gravenhurst	3,257	3,077
Grimsby	6,634	5,148
Guelph	51,377	39,838
Hagersville	2,169	2,075
Haileybury	3,117	2,638
Hamilton	298,121	273,991
Hanover	4,665	4,401
Harriston	1,748	1,631
Harrow	1,941	1,787
Hawkesbury	9,188	8,661
Hearst	2,882	2,373
Hespeler	5,381	4,519
Huntsville	3,342	3,189
Ingersoll	7,249	6,874
Iroquois Falls	1,834	1,681
Kapuskasing	12,617	6,870
Keewatin	2,089	2,197
Kemptville	2,182	1,959
Kenora	11,295	10,904
Kincardine	2,823	2,841
Kingston	59,004	53,526
Kingsville	3,545	3,041
Kitchener	93,255	74,485
Lakefield	2,242	2,167
Leamington	9,554	9,030
Leaside	21,250	18,579
Levack	3,025	3,178
Lindsay	12,090	11,399
Listowel	4,526	4,002
Lively	3,169	1,527
London	194,416	3,211
Long Branch	12,980	11,039
Markham	7,769	4,294
Mattawa	3,143	3,314
Meaford	3,866	3,834
Midland	10,129	8,656
Milton	6,601	5,629
Mimico	19,431	18,212
Mitchell	2,371	2,247
Morrisburg	1,938	1,820
Mount Forest	2,859	2,623
Napanee	4,603	4,500
Newcastle	1,684	1,272
New Hamburg	2,438	2,181
New Liskeard	5,259	4,896
Newmarket	9,758	8,932
New Toronto	13,234	13,384
Niagara	3,113	2,712
Niagara Falls	56,891	22,351
North Bay	23,635	23,781
Norwich	1,692	1,703
Oakville	52,793	10,366
Orangeville	5,588	4,593
Orillia	15,295	15,345
Oshawa	78,082	62,415
Ottawa	290,741	268,206
Owen Sound	17,769	17,421
Palmerston	1,631	1,554
Paris	6,271	5,820
Parry Sound	5,901	6,004
Pembroke	16,262	16,791
Penetanguishene	5,349	5,340
Perth	5,559	5,360
Petawawa	5,574	4,509
Peterborough	56,177	47,185
Petrolia	3,929	3,708
Pickering	1,991	1,755
Picton	5,027	4,862
Point Edward	2,903	2,744
Port Arthur	48,340	45,276
Port Colborne	17,986	14,886
Port Credit	8,475	7,203
Port Dover	3,220	3,064
Port Elgin	2,058	1,632
Port Hope	8,656	8,091
Port Perry	2,651	2,262
Prescott	5,176	5,366
Preston	13,380	11,577
Renfrew	9,502	8,935
Richmond Hill	19,773	16,446
Ridgetown	2,678	2,603
Rockcliffe Park	2,246	2,084
Rockland	3,513	3,037
St. Catharines	97,101	84,472

Place	1966	1961
ONT—Cont.:		
St. Clair Beach	1,746	1,460
St. Mary's	4,750	4,482
St. Thomas	22,983	22,469
Sarnia	54,552	50,976
Sault Ste. Marie	74,594	43,088
Seaforth	2,241	2,255
Simcoe	9,929	8,754
Sioux Lookout	2,667	2,453
Smiths Falls	9,876	9,603
Southampton	1,759	1,818
Stayner	1,772	1,671
Stittsville	1,651	1,508
Stoney Creek	7,243	6,043
Stouffville	3,883	3,188
Stratford	23,068	20,467
Strathroy	5,786	5,150
Streetsville	5,884	5,056
Sturgeon Falls	6,430	6,288
Sudbury	84,888	80,120
Sutton	1,594	1,470
Swansea	9,703	9,628
Tecumseh	4,922	4,476
Thessalon	1,688	1,725
Thorold	8,843	8,633
Tilbury	3,304	3,030
Tillsonburg	6,526	6,600
Timmins	29,303	27,551
Toronto	664,584	672,407
Trenton	13,746	13,183
Tweed	1,747	1,791
Uxbridge	2,621	2,316
Vankleek Hill	1,662	1,735
Walkerton	4,380	3,851
Wallaceburg	10,696	7,881
Waterdown	1,935	1,844
Waterford	2,379	2,221
Waterloo	29,889	21,366
Welland	39,960	36,079
Weston	11,047	9,715
Wheatley	1,547	1,362
Whitby	17,273	14,685
Wiarton	2,034	2,138
Windsor	192,544	114,367
Wingham	2,974	2,922
Woodbridge	2,473	2,315
Woodstock	24,027	20,486
PRINCE EDWARD ISLAND:		
Charlottetown	18,427	18,318
Parkdale	2,071	1,735
Sherwood	2,407	1,580
Summerside	10,042	8,611
QUEBEC:		
Acton Vale	4,489	3,957
Alma	22,195	13,309
Amos	6,838	6,080
Amqui	3,854	3,659
Anjou	22,477	9,511
Arthabaska	3,907	2,977
Arvida	15,342	14,460
Asbestos	10,534	11,083
Aylmer	7,231	6,286
Bagotville	5,876	5,629
Baie-Comeau	12,236	7,956
Baie-d'Urfe	4,061	3,549
Baie-St-Paul	4,702	4,674
Beaconsfield	15,702	10,064
Beauceville	1,905	1,645
Beauceville-Est	2,222	1,920
Beauharnois	8,810	8,704
Beauport	11,742	9,192
Beaupre	2,926	2,587
Becancour	8,336	320
Bedford	2,926	2,855
Belair	3,408	*
Beloeil	10,152	6,283
Bernierville	2,477	2,706
Berthierville	3,943	3,708
Black Lake	4,186	4,180
Bois-des-Filion	3,219	2,499
Boucherville	15,338	7,403
Bourlamaque	4,122	3,344
Bromptonville	2,826	2,726
Brossard	11,884	3,778
Brownsburg	3,596	3,617
Buckingham	7,227	7,421
Cabano	2,528	2,695
Candiac	3,178	1,050
Cap-Chat	2,026	2,035
Cap-de-la-Madeleine	29,433	26,925
Carignan	2,975	*
Causapscal	3,210	3,463
Chambly	10,798	3,737
Chandler	3,608	3,406
Chapais	2,459	2,363
Charlemagne	3,569	3,068
Charlesbourg	24,926	14,308
Charny	4,762	4,189
Chateauguay	12,460	7,570
Chateauguay-Centre	14,096	7,591
Chibougamau	8,902	4,765
Chicoutimi	32,526	31,657
Chicoutimi-Nord	12,814	11,229
Chute-aux-Outardes	1,921	1,336
Clermont	3,175	3,114

Place	1966	1961
QUE.—Cont.:		
Coaticook	6,984	6,906
Contrecoeur	2,301	2,007
Cookshire	1,599	1,412
Cote-St-Luc	20,546	13,266
Courville	5,724	4,670
Cowansville	10,692	7,050
Crabtree	1,509	1,313
Danville	2,578	2,562
Delson	2,601	2,075
Desbiens	1,979	1,970
Deschenes	1,791	2,090
Deux-Montagnes	8,069	7,274
Disraeli	3,111	3,079
Dolbeau	6,630	6,052
Dollard-des-Ormeaux	12,297	1,248
Donnacona	4,815	4,812
Dorion	6,033	4,996
Dorval	20,905	18,592
Drummondville	29,216	27,909
Drummondville-Ouest	2,682	2,057
Drummondville-Sud	8,725	*
Duberger	8,489	4,707
East Angus	4,909	4,756
Farnham	6,752	6,354
Ferme-Neuve	1,944	1,971
Forestville	1,572	1,529
Fort-Coulonge	1,846	1,823
Gagnon	3,999	1,900
Gaspe	2,938	2,603
Gatineau	17,727	13,022
Giffard	12,585	10,129
Granby	34,349	31,463
Grand'Mere	16,407	15,806
Greenfield Park	12,288	7,807
Grenville	1,501	1,330
Hampstead	6,158	4,557
Hauterive	11,366	5,980
Hudson	1,642	1,671
Hudson Heights	1,543	1,540
Hull	60,176	56,929
Huntingdon	3,167	3,134
Iberville	8,400	7,588
Ile-Perrot	3,578	3,106
Jacques-Cartier	52,527	40,807
Joliette	19,188	18,008
Jonquiere	29,663	28,588
Kenogami	11,534	11,816
Lac-Etchemin	2,492	2,297
Lachine	43,155	38,630
Lachute	10,215	7,560
Lac-Megantic	6,958	7,015
Lafleche	13,433	10,984
Lafontaine	2,346	1,556
La Guadeloupe	1,877	1,728
La Malbaie	4,307	2,580
L'Annonciation	2,040	1,042
La Pocatiere	3,470	3,086
La Prairie	8,122	7,328
La Providence	4,712	4,251
LaSalle	48,322	30,904
La Sarre	4,798	3,944
L'Assomption	4,662	4,448
La Tuque	13,554	13,023
Laurentides	1,653	1,698
Lauzon	12,877	11,533
Laval	196,088	124,741
LeMoyne	8,888	8,057
Lennoxville	3,977	3,699
L'Epiphanie	2,664	2,663
Lery	2,130	1,957
Les Saules	6,242	4,098
Levis	15,627	15,112
Longueuil	25,593	24,131
Loretteville	9,465	6,522
Lorraine	1,627	197
Louiseville	4,236	4,138
Luceville	1,564	1,419
Macamic	1,770	1,614
Magog	13,797	13,139
Malartic	6,606	6,998
Maniwaki	6,404	6,349
Maple Grove	1,600	1,412
Marieville	4,368	3,802
Masson	2,249	1,933
Matagami	2,244	*
Matane	11,109	9,190
McMasterville	2,456	2,075
Melocheville	1,667	1,666
Mistassini	3,884	3,461
Mont-Joli	6,366	6,178
Mont-Laurier	6,140	5,859
Montmagny	12,241	6,850
Montmorency	5,541	5,985
Montreal	1,222,255	1,191,062
Montreal-Est	5,779	5,884
Montreal-Nord	67,806	48,433
Montreal-Ouest	6,612	6,446
Mont-Royal	21,845	21,182
Mont-St-Hilaire	4,807	2,911
Murdochville	3,028	2,951
Napierville	2,010	1,812

Place	1966	1961
QUE.—Cont.:		
Nazareth	1,965	*
Neufchatel	6,618	*
Nicolet	4,707	4,441
Noranda	11,521	11,447
Normandin	2,174	1,838
Notre-Dame-de-Lorette	5,691	3,961
Notre-Dame-des-Laurentides	4,446	*
Notre-Dame-du-Lac	1,545	1,695
Orsainville	7,068	4,236
Outremont	30,881	30,753
Pierrefonds	27,924	12,171
Pierreville	1,529	1,559
Pincourt	5,656	2,685
Plessisville	7,238	6,570
Pointe-aux-Trembles	29,888	21,926
Pointe-Claire	26,784	22,709
Pointe-Gatineau	11,053	8,854
Pont-Rouge	3,229	2,988
Port-Alfred	9,551	9,066
Port-Cartier	3,537	3,458
Price	2,939	3,094
Princeville	3,589	3,174
Quebec	166,984	171,979
Rawdon	2,539	2,388
Repentigny	14,976	9,139
Richelieu	1,663	1,612
Richmond	4,014	4,072
Rigaud	1,959	1,990
Rimouski	20,330	17,739
Rimouski-Est	2,043	1,581
Riviere-du-Loup	11,637	10,835
Riviere-du-Moulin	4,542	4,386
Roberval	8,552	7,739
Rock Island	1,596	1,608
Rosemere	6,429	6,158
Rouyn	18,581	18,716
Roxboro	7,930	6,298
Ste-Agathe-des-Monts	6,010	5,725
St-Ambroise	1,559	1,576
Ste-Anne-de-Beaupre	1,523	1,878
Ste-Anne-de-Bellevue	5,334	4,044
St-Antoine-des-Laurentides	4,401	3,005
St-Basile-Sud	1,843	1,709
St-Boniface-de-Shawinigan	2,670	917
St-Bruno-de-Montarville	10,712	6,760
St-Cesaire	2,240	2,097
St-David-de-l'Auberiviere	2,962	*
St-Emile	2,104	1,806
St-Eustache	7,319	5,463
St-Felicien	5,104	5,133
Ste-Foy	48,298	29,716
St-Gabriel-de-Brandon	3,464	3,425
Ste-Genevieve	2,596	2,397
St-Georges	6,680	4,082
St-Georges	1,992	1,775
St-Georges-Ouest	5,538	4,755
St-Hubert	17,215	14,380
St-Hyacinthe	23,781	20,439
St-Jacques	2,000	2,038
St-Jean	27,784	26,988
St-Jean-Chrysostome	1,633	*
St-Jean-de-Boischatel	1,648	1,576
St-Jean-Eudes	2,721	2,873
St-Jerome	2,089	1,962
St-Jerome	26,511	24,546
St-Joseph	4,879	3,799
St-Joseph-de-Beauce	2,805	2,484
St-Joseph-de-Sorel	3,725	3,588
St-Jovite	3,083	2,692
St-Lambert	16,003	14,531
St-Laurent	59,479	49,805
St-Leonard	25,328	4,893
St-Luc	3,581	*
St-Marc-des-Carrieres	2,681	2,622
Ste-Marie	4,192	3,662
St-Michel	71,446	55,978
St-Nicolas	1,635	*
St-Pamphile	3,516	*
St-Pascal	2,216	2,144
Ste-Philomene	3,234	*
St-Pie	1,652	1,434
St-Pierre	7,066	6,795
St-Raymond	4,318	3,931
St-Remi	2,221	2,276
St-Romuald-d'Etchemin	7,375	*
Ste-Rosalie	1,618	1,255
St-Sauveur-des-Monts	1,908	1,702
Ste-Thecle	1,881	2,009
Ste-Therese	15,628	11,771

Place	1966	1961	Place	1966	1961	Place	1966	1961	Place	1966	1961
QUE.—Cont.:			QUE.—Cont.:			SASK.—Cont.:			SASK.—Cont.:		
St-Tite	3,113	3,250	Trois-Rivieres	57,540	53,477	Battleford	1,766	1,627	Moosomin	2,141	1,781
Sayabec	2,228	2,314	Trois-Rivieres-Ouest	6,345	*	Biggar	2,755	2,702	Nipawin	3,963	3,836
Schefferville	3,086	3,178	Val-d'Or	12,147	10,983	Canora	2,734	2,117	North Battleford	12,262	11,230
Senneterre	3,567	3,246	Valleyfield	29,111	27,297	Creighton	1,710	1,729	Oxbow	1,569	1,359
Sept-Iles	18,950	14,196	Vanier	9,362	8,733	Esterhazy	3,190	1,114	Prince Albert	26,269	24,168
Shawinigan	30,777	32,169	Varennes	2,382	2,240	Estevan	9,062	7,728	Regina	131,127	112,141
Shawinigan-Sud	12,250	12,683	Vaudreuil	3,105	897	Eston	1,548	1,695	Rosetown	2,658	2,250
Shawville	1,652	1,534	Vercheres	1,918	1,768	Fort Qu'Appelle	1,600	1,521	Saskatoon	115,892	95,526
Sherbrooke	75,690	66,554	Verdun	76,832	78,317	Gravelbourg	1,626	1,499	Shaunavon	2,318	2,154
Sillery	14,737	14,109	Victoriaville	21,320	18,720	Hudson Bay	1,957	1,601	Swift Current	14,485	12,186
Sorel	19,021	17,147	Ville-Marie	1,962	1,710	Humboldt	3,979	3,245	Tisdale	2,914	2,402
Sutton	1,877	1,755	Villeneuve	2,829	1,934	Indian Head	1,891	1,802	Unity	2,154	1,902
Temiscaming	2,799	2,517	Warwick	2,577	2,487	Kamsack	2,982	2,968	Weyburn	9,000	9,101
Templeton	3,267	2,965	Waterloo	4,765	4,543	Kindersley	3,534	2,990	Wilkie	1,603	1,612
Terrebonne	7,480	6,207	Westmount	24,107	25,012	Lloydminster	7,071	5,667	Wynyard	1,956	1,686
Thetford Mines	21,614	21,618	Windsor	6,496	6,589	Maple Creek	2,359	2,291	Yorkton	12,645	9,995
Thurso	3,332	3,310	SASKATCHEWAN			Meadow Lake	3,375	2,803	YUKON TERRITORY:		
Tracy	10,918	8,171				Melfort	4,386	4,039	Whitehorse	4,771	5,031
Trois-Pistoles	4,710	4,349	Assiniboia	2,872	2,491	Melville	5,690	5,191			
						Moose Jaw	33,417	33,206			

POPULIST (*pŏp′ū list*) **PARTY** was a U.S. political party during the 1890's. Its official name was the People's Party of the United States of America. It was formed at a convention in Cincinnati, Ohio, in 1891, by farmers from the South and Northwest who wanted to improve their living conditions.

The 1890's were difficult years for farmers. They received low prices for their crops but paid high prices for farm equipment and high freight rates for shipping crops to market. Many farmers blamed the bankers, manufacturers, merchants, and railroad owners for their troubles. They believed that these people controlled both the Democratic and the Republican parties, so the farmers decided to organize their own party.

The most important issue for the Populists was "free silver." They believed that the government should buy more silver and put more money in circulation. They thought that this would make it easier for farmers to pay their debts. Many farmers had borrowed money to pay for land, but could not repay the loans.

The Populists also demanded government reforms. They wanted the people to vote for senators instead of having the state legislatures elect them. They wanted an income tax and the right of initiative and referendum. (See INITIATIVE, REFERENDUM, AND RECALL.) These reforms were eventually adopted, some by the state governments, some by the federal government. The Populists also wanted government ownership of railroads and of telegraph and telephone companies.

In 1892 the Populists nominated General James B. Weaver of Iowa for president. Weaver was defeated, although the party elected a number of congressmen. Weaver received more than a million votes and had 22 votes in the electoral college. His greatest support came from the states of Kansas, Nebraska, Nevada, Idaho, and Colorado. The Populists were never able to win the support of the city workers.

The party received strong support in the 1894 congressional elections and hoped to elect a president in 1896. Their plans were upset when the Democrats nominated William Jennings Bryan. He supported the Populist position on the "free silver" issue. The Populists had no choice but to support Bryan, who lost to Republican William McKinley. (See BRYAN, WILLIAM JENNINGS.)

The strength of the Populist party declined after 1896. The Democrats had taken over many Populist issues and many members of the party supported Democratic candidates. The Populists never elected a president, but they did make the major parties aware of the discontent of the farming populace of the United States. Many of their proposals were finally adopted by both the Democrats and Republicans and became laws.

PORCELAIN (*pōr′sĕ lĭn* or *pōrs′lĭn*) or **CHINA** is a hard, white, ceramic ware that is clear enough to let light through. It also is nonabsorbent, sonorous enough to ring sharply when tapped with a fingernail, and vitrified (fired at such high heat that its ingredients melt to a glasslike substance). The name porcelain comes from a shell called *porcellana* that has a white, translucent interior. Italian artists once used the shell to hold paints.

The name china was given to porcelain by Europeans because the first porcelain seen in the Western world came from the country of China.

The Chinese knew of the basic ingredients of porcelain, a white clay called *kaolin* and a feldspar called *petuntse*. The first Oriental porcelain was made as early as A.D. 500. As the arts of shaping, baking or firing, and glazing were refined, the emperors valued porcelain so highly that they kept the secret of its manufacture in China for many centuries.

One reason that the Chinese were able to keep their secret for a long time was that their porcelain was made in villages located at a distance from the cities. The few European travelers visited only the large trading centers. In certain isolated villages, the local residents worked together to make and improve their porcelain wares. They helped each other from the preparation of the clay to its final firing. Since the production of a whole village was fired in the same ovens, or kilns, the entire population would turn out to help. A firing usually lasted several days. Each generation of clay workers prepared the clays and other ingredients for the next generation, because aged materials made the finest porcelain.

By the 15th century at the latest, porcelain objects of the Ming dynasty found their way into Western countries when the Saracens brought wares from China across the Asiatic plains on the backs of camels. During the 16th century, Portuguese explorers brought porcelain across the seas by ships. This hard, glistening pottery that Europeans did not know how to make was highly valued. The blue porcelains that the Chinese potters made were particularly prized by the Westerners.

The art of making porcelain spread from China to Korea in the 10th century, and then to Japan in the 17th century.

In the 17th century the East India Company began to import the delicate porcelain wares. Before the introduction of Chinese porcelain, European potters made only coarse earthenware. All over Europe potters and even alchemists, the early chemists, searched for the formula of the white porcelain. In 1580, under the patronage of the Medicis, Florentine craftsmen started producing what they thought was true porcelain, but what actually was only a variety of glass. Many European potters manufactured this Florentine type of ware.

The first European to succeed in producing a real porcelain was Johann Boettger of Meissen, Germany, who finally discovered its formula in 1709. From then on, factories spread over Europe. In England, the making of china started in 1745. The town of Sevres, France, began making its famous porcelains in 1769, and the Italian Capo di Monte ware dates from about the same period.

Experimentation resulted in three kinds of porcelain. The first, sometimes called true porcelain, was the hard-paste variety made by the Chinese. It is still the kind most often made today. The second kind of ware was that originated by the Florentines, and, although really a glass, is called soft-paste porcelain. It is very

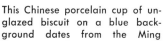
This Chinese porcelain cup of unglazed biscuit on a blue background dates from the Ming dynasty.

Courtesy (left) Percival David Foundation of Chinese Art, (right) Mr. and Mrs. Sigmund J. Katy; photo, (center) Staatliche Porzellan-manufaktur Nymphenburg

This German porcelain bust of Graf Sigismund Von Haimhausen by F. A. Bustelli, and this English porcelain bowl, with a view of Chelsea waterfront, were made about 1760.

rare today. The third, developed by the English and similar to the hard-paste porcelain, is bone china. For this the ashes of animal bones are added to the clay to make firing at lower temperatures possible.

The inventor of the first successful bone china, Josiah Spode, discovered its formula in 1805. English bone china, including Spode, is still manufactured and admired today. Bone china is difficult to produce because it has a tendency to warp during the firing process, so the cost of producing perfect pieces makes it quite expensive. Some of England's fine potteries, as Wedgwood and Royal Doulton, also produce some less expensive wares as well as bone china.

For hard-paste porcelain, potters mix kaolin, feldspar, and other substances to the consistency of thick cream. Then they form this mixture into shape by throwing, pressing, or casting. After the wares are shaped and dried, they are fired in a kiln at intense heat. After the first trip to the kiln the pieces are called bisque, or biscuit, and are a flat white color. They are then coated with glaze—which is dipped, painted, or sprayed on—and returned to the kiln to be refired. This second baking is called the glaze, or glost, firing. It melts the glaze into the paste of the bodies, forming a surface so hard that even steel cannot scratch it. After a piece has cooled

A china dinner plate of contemporary American design.

Courtesy of Lenox, Inc.

from the glost firing, any further decoration desired is painted on over the glaze. The ware is then fired for a final time, but at a much lower temperature.

Western countries today produce better porcelain wares than the Far Eastern countries do. Many years of study of the Oriental processes, continued research, and more rapid industrialization have helped Germany, England, and the United States excel in the production of fine porcelains. Porcelain, in addition to its use in table china, has been found valuable as a material for bathroom fixtures, scientific laboratory ware, and electronics equipment. Certain new kinds of porcelain are used in the engines of jet planes and in the making of guided missiles. Hardness, strength, and resistance to corrosives are qualities that make porcelain useful in modern technology. (See POTTERY.)

PORCUPINE (*pôr′kū pĭn*) is a large, stout rodent with a small head and short legs. The North American species has a thick, muscular tail. Except on the undersides and parts of the face, the porcupine is covered with barbed quills. A single porcupine may have as many as 30,000 quills. Normally the quills lie down on the body and are nearly hidden by the long guard hairs.

The North American porcupines grow to about 36 inches in length and average about 15 to 20 pounds. They live in the heavily forested areas of Canada and the United States. Often they make their homes in hollow trees. These animals are active mainly at night. They spend summer nights searching for land and water plants to eat. During the fall and winter their food is mainly the inner bark of trees, such as pine, hemlock, and aspen.

The animal is good natured and generally harmless, but if it is alarmed it whirls its backside toward the danger, stands its quills on end, and swings its tail quickly and forcefully against anything that touches it. The loosely attached quills stick into an attacker on touch, but the porcupine cannot actually throw its quills.

Porcupines of the New World belong to the Erethizontidae family of animals while those of the Old World belong to the Hystricidae family.

Courtesy San Diego Zoo

With a slap of its tail, the Arizona porcupine, about 36 inches long, can drive its quills into an enemy's skin.

The porcupines of South and Central America have shorter quills than the North American variety and have prehensile tails (adapted to seize or grasp). The porcupines of Europe, Africa, and India live in burrows and have quills that are thick and sometimes more than one foot long.

PORT-AU-PRINCE (*pōrt'ō prins'*), **HAITI,** is the capital, largest city, and chief port of the country of Haiti in the West Indies. It is on a bay in the Gulf of La Gonave, a large inlet of the Caribbean Sea. The city's climate is warm and humid, with an average temperature of 81 degrees Fahrenheit.

The old section of Port-au-Prince is built along the bay. The new section overlooks the old from the surrounding hills. Champ-de-Mars, a large, square park in the center of the city, is the center of Port-au-Prince's social and civic life. Clustered near it are the government buildings, including the National Palace, theaters, hotels, restaurants, and some of the city's fine old homes. Near the water front is one of the most picturesque sites of the city, the Iron Market (Marche Fer), where merchants display their wares. The University of Haiti is located in the city.

Port-au-Prince's location on the edge of the fertile Cul-de-Sac Plain makes it an important food-processing center. The industries include textiles and leather goods factories, sugar, rice,

and flour mills, rum distilleries, breweries, and tobacco and vegetable oil plants.

Port-au-Prince was founded in 1749. It served as the capital of the former French colony of Saint-Domingue. In 1751 and again in 1770 the city was destroyed by earthquakes. Hurricanes, fires, and civil wars have also caused great damage at various times.

The majority of the people of Port-au-Prince are Negroes. In 1950 the population of the city was 134,117. By 1959 it was estimated to have decreased to 112,296.

PORTER (*pōr'tēr*), **DAVID DIXON** (*dĭk's'n*) (1813–1891), was a U.S. Naval officer and one of the leaders of the Union Navy during the Civil War. He was born in Chester, Pennsylvania, the son of a U.S. Navy officer who had won fame during the War of 1812. David sailed West Indian waters on his first voyage in 1823–1824 with his father. In 1826 his father quit the U.S. Navy after a disagreement with superiors and took a position with the Mexican Navy. David went with him and served in the Mexican Navy until he was captured by the Spanish. After his release in 1829 he became a midshipman in the U.S. Navy.

During the Mexican War he commanded a paddle-wheel steamer. By the time of the Civil War he was a high-ranking officer. He was with Commander David G. Farragut, his foster brother, when Farragut and General Ulysses S. Grant tried to win control of the Mississippi from the Confederacy. (See FARRAGUT, DAVID GLASGOW; WAR BETWEEN THE STATES.) In 1862 Porter's ships bombarded two forts that guarded the Mississippi River while Farragut moved his ships past the forts and seized New Orleans. The following year Porter worked with Grant in seizing the important Confederate fortress at Vicksburg, Mississippi.

In 1864 Porter was put in charge of the ships that were blockading the Atlantic Coast in order to keep European supplies from reaching the Confederates. Within a year these ships helped the Union Army capture Wilmington and Fort Fisher, both in North Carolina. This victory helped bring the war to an end.

After the war Porter became superintendent

of the Naval Academy at Annapolis, Maryland. He improved the curriculum and introduced the first athletics to the academy. In 1866 Porter became vice-admiral, and in 1870 he succeeded Farragut as admiral. From 1877 until his death in 1891 he served as chairman of the Naval Board of Inspection.

PORTLAND (*pōrt'lănd*), MAINE,

is a seaport in the southwestern part of the state. It has grown steadily since its founding in 1716 and is now Maine's largest city. Portland is built on a hilly peninsula that extends into Casco Bay, a broad inlet of the Atlantic Ocean. It has an excellent deepwater harbor.

Among the chief industries of Portland are the manufacture of paper, shoes, chemicals, textiles, marine supplies, and wood products; food processing; and fishing. Portland's fishing fleets bring in large catches of cod, haddock, tuna, and lobster, a sea food for which Maine is well known. The city's busy port facilities also handle tons of wood pulp, paper, lumber, petroleum, grain, coal, clay, and sulfur.

The first settlement on the site of Portland was made in 1633. In 1676 it was destroyed by Indians, later rebuilt, and again destroyed. The first permanent settlement, called Falmouth, was made in 1716. In 1775, during the American Revolution, the settlement was bombarded by a British fleet. On July 4, 1786, it was named Portland and was incorporated as a town. Portland was the state capital from 1820 to 1831. In the following year Portland was chartered as a city. A great fire destroyed nearly one-third of the city in 1866.

Since 1923 Portland has had a council-manager form of government. Its population in 1960 was 72,566.

PORTLAND, OREGON,

is the largest city in the state and one of the country's chief Pacific Coast ports. The city is built on the banks of the Willamette River, about ten miles south of where it flows into the Columbia River. The mountains of the Cascade Range lie to the east of the city, those of the Coast Range to the west. Snow-capped Mount Hood, 45 miles east of Portland, can be seen on the horizon. Portland's water supply comes from Bull Run Reservoir in the Cascade Range.

The city's chief products are lumber and wood products, including shingles, doors, window and door frames, and sashes. The city has furniture factories, textile and paper mills, metal and chemical industries, and fruit, vegetable, and salmon canneries. Most of Portland's factories use electric power from nearby Bonneville Dam. During World War II shipbuilding developed into one of the city's main industries.

Among the many products shipped from Portland's busy water front are lumber, wool, paper, grain, flour, livestock, and canned and frozen foods. Incoming ships bring cargoes of copra, burlap, coffee, sugar, and iron and steel.

Portland's beauty and climate make it a pleasant tourist center. Winds blowing from the Pacific Ocean keep the summers mild and the

Portland, often referred to as "The City of Roses," is in northwest Oregon on the Willamette River, 50 miles from snow-capped Mt. Hood.

Ray Atkeson

winters cool. The average yearly temperature is about 55 degrees Fahrenheit. About 40 inches of rain falls annually, mostly during the winter.

The city has more than 100 parks, including the International Rose Test Gardens and the sunken gardens of Peninsula Park. The Civic Auditorium houses the Oregon Historical Society and the Portland Symphony Orchestra. Among the several colleges are the University of Portland and Portland State, Reed, and Lewis and Clark colleges. Portland stages its famous Rose Festival and flower parade each June.

The city was founded in 1845 and was named for Portland, Maine. It was an important supply center during the gold rushes in California (1850) and Alaska (1897–1900). It was incorporated as a city in 1851.

Portland is governed by a mayor and a board of five commissioners. The population of Portland in 1960 was 372,676.

PORT OF SPAIN, TRINIDAD AND TOBAGO,

is the capital, largest city, and chief port of the two-island country. It is located on the island of Trinidad.

Port of Spain is a beautiful city with attractive buildings, squares, and several parks. Woodford Square, in the business section, is the principal square. Near it is the Red House, the main government building. In the center of the city are Queen's Park Savannah, Government House, and the Royal Botanical Gardens.

Commerce and industry in the country are centered in Port of Spain. Manufacturing includes brewing, food processing, and the production of plastic, textile, and paper goods. Tourism is also an important industry.

Port of Spain is a major transportation center. Good roads link the city with other parts of the island, and air routes and shipping lines connect it with foreign cities. Its position on the world's shipping routes makes it one of the major trade centers of the Caribbean area.

In 1560 Port of Spain was founded on the site of an old Indian village, Conquerabia. In 1783 the city became capital of Trinidad. In 1962 it was made capital of Trinidad and Tobago when that country became independent. The city's population was 91,200 in 1965.

PORTUGAL (*pōr'tū gäl*), **EUROPE,** is a small country, roughly rectangular in shape, that covers the southwestern strip of the Iberian Peninsula. It also includes the Azores and the Madeira islands in the Atlantic Ocean. Mainland Portugal is bordered on the east and north by Spain; and on the west and south by the Atlantic Ocean. Portugal has seven overseas provinces: Angola, Portuguese Guinea, and Mozambique in Africa; Cape Verde Islands and the two islands of Sao Tome (St. Thomas) and Principe (Prince's) in the Atlantic Ocean off the west coast of Africa; Macao in Asia; and Portuguese Timor in Oceania. A former overseas province, Portuguese India, was made up of three small areas in India. The Indian government, however, seized control of all three in 1961.

Physical Features

The Tagus (Tejo) River flows in a general east-west direction across Portugal, dividing the country approximately in half. The part north of the Tagus is generally hilly, and the part south is generally level. Along the Atlantic Ocean, in both the north and the south, lie sandy coasts. In the north, Serra da Estrela, the highest mountain range in Portugal, rises 6,532 feet above sea level. The country's main rivers, in addition to the Tagus, are the Douro, Guadiana, and Minho. All of them rise in Spain.

The climate of Portugal is generally mild. In the mountainous region of the north, ocean winds bring much rain and dampness. Moving southward, however, the climate becomes more and more dry. In the northeast the winters are severe and the summers are hot. In the south the summers are also hot, but the winters are mild.

Portugal has some fine forests. On the slopes of the mountains are pine forests, and groves of olive trees cover much of the lower, hilly areas. Vineyards are cultivated chiefly in the river valleys. In the south are cork oak, cypress, orange, lemon, olive, and fig trees. Only grasses grow in the driest sections of the south.

Portugal's mineral resources include coal, copper, iron ore, sulfur, tin, and wolframite, the

PRODUCTS OF PORTUGAL

KEY TO SYMBOLS

CATTLE

CORK

FISHING

FRUIT AND NUTS (ALMONDS)

GENERAL FARMING

FISH CANNING

WINE

CITRUS FRUITS

SHEEP

OLIVES

TEXTILES

RESIN TURPENTINE PITCH

SHIPPING

VINEYARDS

FORESTS

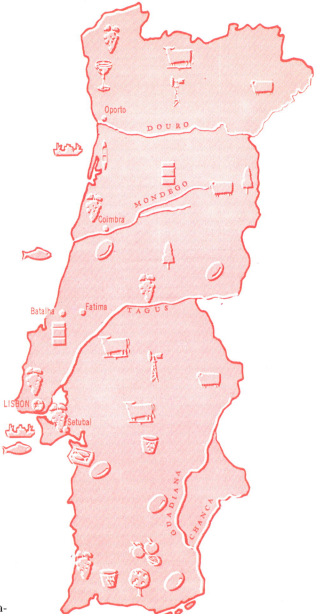

source of tungsten. The mining of these minerals has not been greatly developed. Some mineral products are exported.

The People

The Portuguese people are a result of the intermingling of various races and cultures—Iberians, Romans, Goths, Arabs, Berbers, Lusitanians, Germans, Phoenicians, and Jews. The population is now homogeneous, but the physical make-up and some of the customs of the people reflect the influence of these groups. Portuguese is the language of the country, and more than 90 per cent of the people are Roman Catholics.

Most of the Portuguese people live in rural areas. The area north of the Tagus River is far more heavily populated than the area south. Although many Portuguese emigrate each year (mainly to Brazil), overpopulation is a serious problem in such areas as Minho Province. The chief port, largest city, and capital of Portugal is Lisbon. It is situated on a fine sheltered harbor near the mouth of the Tagus River. (See

LISBON.) The second largest city, Oporto (Port), is also an important port.

How the People Make a Living

Portugal is a land of peasant farmers and fishermen. About 40 per cent of the people are farmers, but much of the land is unsuited to agriculture. Soil erosion is a problem, and the farming methods used are out of date. As a result, poverty is widespread. In many areas of the north, where the soil is fertile and the climate suitable, the land is too rugged to farm. In the south the land is flatter, but there is not enough rainfall to support crops. In the more heavily populated north, the people are crowded onto small farms. In the south the land is divided into huge estates that are cultivated largely by tenant farmers. The best agricultural regions are along the Tagus River.

The main crops of Portugal are wheat, corn, rye, oats, barley, rice, beans, potatoes, citrus fruits, olives, grapes, and cork. The grains are grown on the more level lands. Fruit and olive trees grow in the drier regions of the south.

The cork harvested from the cork oak trees is

FACTS ABOUT PORTUGAL

CAPITAL: Lisbon.

AREA: 35,553 square miles.

POPULATION: 9,415,000 (1967 estimate).

CHIEF LANGUAGE: Portuguese.

CHIEF RELIGION: Roman Catholic.

CHIEF MOUNTAIN RANGE: Serra da Estrela.

CHIEF MOUNTAIN PEAKS (height in feet); Estrela (6,532); Montemuro (4,534); Gerez (4,944).

MOST IMPORTANT RIVERS: Douro, Tagus (Tejo), Guadiana, Minho.

PLACES OF INTEREST: Fatima, religious architecture at Alcobaca and Batalha; Tower of Belem.

FORM OF GOVERNMENT: Unitary corporative republic.

HEAD OF GOVERNMENT: Premier.

CHIEF OF STATE: President.

LEGISLATURE: National Assembly (advised by Corporative Chamber).

POLITICAL DIVISIONS: 22 districts.

CHIEF CITIES: (1967 estimates) Lisbon (824,000); Oporto (322,800).

LEADING INDUSTRIES: Agriculture, fishing.

CHIEF PRODUCTS: *Agricultural,* cork, corn, grapes, oats, potatoes, rice, rye, wheat, livestock; *Manufactured,* processed foods, leather goods, ships, textiles, tobacco; *Mined,* coal, copper, iron ore, sulfur, tin, wolframite.

CURRENCY: Escudo; 28.70 escudos equal one U.S. dollar.

NATIONAL ANTHEM: A Portuguesa ("The Portuguese").

a valuable crop. Portugal is the world's largest producer of cork. The country is famous for its wines. There are many vineyards in the Oporto area. Port wines come from this region and are named for the city of Oporto. Madeira produces the famous Madeira wines. Livestock raising is an important part of agriculture in Portugal. The farmers and shepherds raise herds of cattle, sheep, goats, and pigs. Mules, horses, and oxen do much of the work on the farms.

Fishing villages line the coasts of Portugal. Sardines are the most important catch, but tuna, herring, and cod are also important sea products. The Portuguese diet is made up chiefly of fish, vegetables, and fruit. Few can afford to buy meat.

Lisbon and Oporto are the manufacturing centers of Portugal. Most of the factories are concerned with food processing and the preparation of products for export. The country's chief exports are cork and cork products, canned fish, cotton fabrics, and wines. In addition to these products, the factories turn out textiles, olive oil, leather goods, fertilizers, cement, soap, and various consumer goods. Products of the pine forests—resin and turpentine—are important.

Government

Portugal is governed under the constitution of 1933, which states that the country is a corporative republic. Under this system of government, various economic and social groups—such as agriculture, credit and insurance, fishing and canning, transport and tourism—are organized into corporations that have a voice in the government. Corporation representatives make up the Corporative Chamber, a body that advises the National Assembly, the lawmaking body.

The National Assembly has 130 members who are elected by the people. The president of Portugal is chosen for a term of seven years by an electoral college, which is made up of members of the National Assembly and the Corporative Chamber and of representatives from the municipalities and overseas provinces. Although the president appoints the premier, the premier is the more powerful.

Photos, Roger Coster from Rapho-Gullimette

Above: Parliament's palace is in the capital city of Lisbon.

Right: A Portuguese man carves a wooden spoon.

Education

In recent years the Portuguese government has done much to improve the country's schools. More than 60 per cent of the people are now able to read and write. The government also supports an adult education program.

The University of Coimbra, Portugal's oldest university, was founded in 1290, and the University of Lisbon and the University of Oporto were founded in 1911.

History

The history of Portugal was the same as that of Spain until the 12th century. Many centuries before that time, a group of people called the Iberians occupied the area that is now Spain and Portugal. The Celts, a group of people from the more northerly parts of Europe, swept down into the Iberian Peninsula probably in the 7th and 6th centuries B.C. The Romans invaded the peninsula in the 2nd and 1st centuries B.C. The Lusitanians, a tribe living in what is now Portugal, fiercely resisted the Roman invasion, but they were defeated, and in the 1st century B.C. the area became the Roman province of Lusitania. The Iberian Peninsula remained under Roman control until the 5th century A.D. when the barbaric Visigoths overran the area.

In A.D. 711 the Moors of northern Africa invaded the Iberian Peninsula and defeated the Visigoths. For several centuries, the Moors occupied the territory south of the Douro River. Christian kingdoms controlled the area north of the river. In the 12th century this northern region became known as Portugal and was controlled by the Spanish kingdom of Leon. Alphonso Henriques governed as the count of Portugal. He succeeded in freeing Portugal from the rule of Leon in 1143. He also pushed south to Lisbon and captured the city from the Moors. By the time Alphonso died in 1185, he had doubled Portugal's territory. His descendants further extended the boundaries so that by the end of the 14th century they included all of modern-day Portugal.

The reign of John I (1385–1433) of the House of Aviz marked the beginning of Portugal's period of greatness. He married Philippa of Lancaster, from England, and made an alliance with her country that has lasted to modern times. John's son Prince Henry the Navigator explored the coast of Africa. (See HENRY THE NAVIGATOR.) The Azores and Madeira island groups became colonies of Portugal. Gradually Portuguese navigators worked down the west coast of Africa, and in 1488 Bartholomeu Diaz rounded the Cape of Good Hope and opened the way to India. In 1498 Vasco da Gama reached India and founded Portuguese India. (See GAMA, VASCO DA.) In 1500 another Portuguese navigator, Pedro Alvares Cabral, sailing for India, landed on the Brazilian coast and claimed it for Portugal. One of his ships discovered Madagascar a year later.

Throughout this period of exploration, Portugal discovered and took possession of its overseas provinces. By the middle of the 16th century Portugal controlled trade with the Orient and was one of the most powerful nations of Europe. In 1580 Philip II of Spain captured the Portuguese throne. Spanish kings controlled Portugal until 1640 when finally they were driven out. At that time John IV of the House of Braganza took the throne of Portugal.

During the period of Spanish rule, Portugal lost much of its overseas territory. After the country regained its freedom, however, a new period of prosperity began, largely because of the wealth of the colony of Brazil.

Top: The main events in the history of Portugal are shown in the colorful mosaic sidewalks of Liberty Avenue in the Portuguese capital city of Lisbon. Bottom: The Palace of Pena, now a tourist attraction, was once the residence of the royal family of Portugal.

(Top) Pix, (bottom) Burton Holmes from Ewing Galloway

In 1755 a disastrous earthquake nearly destroyed Lisbon. During this time Joseph I was king of Portugal, but the country was actually controlled by a dictator—the Marquis of Pombal. Throughout the 19th century the rulers of the House of Braganza continued to rule Portugal. In 1910 a revolution brought an end to the monarchy and Portugal became a republic. A period of chaos followed, and in 1926 General Antonio Oscar de Fragoso Carmona took over the government. He appointed Antonio de Oliveira Salazar to be minister of finance. In 1932 Salazar became the country's premier and its dictator. In 1958 Rear Admiral Americo Deus Rodriguez Tomas was elected president, but Salazar continued to rule.

In January 1961 Henrique Galvao, leading a band of rebels, seized the *Santa Maria*, a Portuguese ocean liner cruising in the Caribbean Sea. The rebels hoped the seizure would help to

bring about the downfall of the Salazar government. Their attempt, however, failed.

In 1968 Salazar fell gravely ill. Marcello Caetano took his place as premier.

PORTUGUESE (*pŏr'tu gēz*) **GUINEA** (*gĭn'ē*), **AFRICA,** is a small country on the great bulge of the western part of the continent. It has an area of 13,948 square miles and is wedged between Senegal, on the north, and Guinea, on the east and south. The Atlantic Ocean forms its western border. Portugal governs the region as an overseas province. It is headed by a governor appointed by the Portuguese government.

The coast line is deeply indented by the mouths of rivers. Some of these are navigable for 100 miles into the interior. About 60 small islands and islets are found along the coast. Most of the province is fairly low. The highest elevations are only about 600 feet above sea level, near the southeastern boundary.

The province has an unhealthy climate. The temperature and the humidity are high most of the year. The average temperature for May, the hottest month, is 85 degrees Fahrenheit. For January, the coolest month, it is 77 degrees. During the wet season about 75 inches of rain falls, mainly between May and November. The rest of the year there is very little rain. During the dry season the *harmattan* winds blow almost every day, making the climate very uncomfortable. They are hot, dry, and sand-filled winds which blow out from the Sahara Desert across the central part of western Africa.

Most of Portuguese Guinea has dense tropical vegetation. Mangrove forests and palm trees cover the coastal area. East of this is a belt of dense tropical forests with ebony, ironwood, and mahogany. The interior is savanna grassland, and baobab and acacia trees are common.

The chief industry is the production of palm oil. Some copper ore, bauxite, iron ore, lead ore, and lumber are also produced. The principal occupation is agriculture, with rice as the main crop. Most of the rice is grown for home use, but a small amount is exported. Bananas and oil palms are grown near the coast. Farther inland, peanuts and millet are the most important crops. Peanuts, oil seeds, and palm kernels

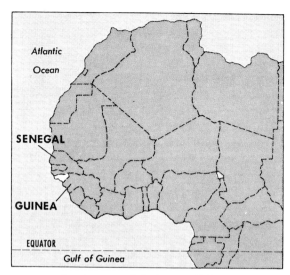

Locator map of Portuguese Guinea.

are the chief exports of Portuguese Guinea. Palm oil and hides are also exported.

Most of the country's people belong to the Fulani and Mandingo groups, which are Muslim. The rest of the people follow the traditional religious beliefs of their tribal groups. There are both tribal and Christian mission schools. A small group of Europeans lives in the territory, mostly in the port towns.

Bissau is the capital and the port for most of the exports. It is on an island near the mouth of the Geba River. The population of the Bissau district is 55,958 (1960 census). Other ports are Bolama and Cacheu.

Transportation is very poor. There are no railroads. Although there are more than 1,800 miles of roads, many of them cannot be used during the rainy season. Waterways are the most important means of transportation. About 1,000 miles of the rivers are navigable.

The first European to visit the region is thought to have been Nuno Tristao, a Portuguese sailor. He sailed down the African coast in 1446. Several Portuguese trading stations were started on the coast. Later it became an important center for the Portuguese slave trade. Gold and ivory were exported from the trading stations. Portugal governed Guinea with the Cape Verde Islands until 1879, when Portuguese Guinea became a separate colony. The province became an overseas province in 1951.

The population of Portuguese Guinea is estimated at 528,000 (1967).

PORTUGUESE OVERSEAS PROVINCES are seven territories controlled by Portugal but located apart from the country proper. These provinces have a total land area of 805,325 square miles, of which about 99 per cent is on the African continent. Their total population is about 14,449,500 (1967 estimate). Each province is headed by a governor or governor-general who is appointed by the Portuguese government.

The three mainland African provinces of Angola, Mozambique, and Portuguese Guinea include more than 80 per cent of the Portuguese overseas population. The province of Cape Verde is composed of a cluster of islands lying off the western coast of Africa in the Atlantic Ocean. The province of Sao Tome and Principe is composed of two islands lying near the African coast in the Gulf of Guinea. (See ANGOLA; CAPE VERDE ISLANDS; MOZAMBIQUE; PORTU-GUESE GUINEA.)

Two of the Portuguese provinces are in Asia. Macao, the smallest and most densely settled (more than 28,200 persons per square mile) of all the overseas provinces, is on the coast of southern China. It consists of a peninsula and two small islands (Taipa and Coloani) near the mouth of the Canton River. Almost all of the people of the province live on the peninsula in the city of Macao.

The province of Portuguese Timor, in Southeast Asia, consists of the eastern part of the island of Timor, a small territory called Oe-Cusse on the island's northwestern coast, and several nearby islands. The rest of Timor is part of the Republic of Indonesia. (See TIMOR.)

For 450 years Portugal controlled the territories of Goa, Diu, and Damao on the west coast of India. Together they were known as Portuguese India. In December 1961, however, Indian troops moved into the territories and the land was annexed to India.

POSTAL (*pōs′t'l*) **SYSTEM** (*sĭs′tĕm* or *sĭs′tĭm*). No department of the United States government touches the daily lives of so many people as the Post Office. No other agency gives so much service for so little money. It is hard to realize how recent this institution is in world history. There were, to be sure, in the ancient empires of Persia and Rome, systems of forwarding dispatches along the well-built roads. But they were strictly official dispatches, concerned with government business; private individuals had to find their own messengers.

During most of the Middle Ages there was even less organization. Merchant guilds and associations, such as the Hanseatic League and certain universities, maintained a limited messenger service for the use of their members as early as the 13th century. There was also a state post in France in 1464, but little is known about its history.

It was in the 16th century that governments began to maintain regular postal services. Their interest was threefold: (1) to enable them to inspect suspicious and especially foreign correspondence; (2) to produce revenue; (3) to provide service for the public. The last, which was probably the least important in the beginning, has become the chief and practically the only purpose of the postal service today.

In England the government maintained a postal system under Henry VIII, which was considerably enlarged under Elizabeth I and James I. Elizabeth in 1591 prohibited the sending of letters abroad by any but the authorized messengers. James I made a similar prohibition to inland mail in 1609, thus introducing what is recognized as a necessary feature of a good postal system—government monopoly. Mails were dispatched by riders on horseback and, 100 years later, by coaches.

In 1653 a local Paris postal service was established by the French king. A rate of one sou was charged, and stamps were used. In imitation of this an enterprising London merchant in 1680 established a penny post for the city and suburbs, with hundreds of receiving offices, hourly collections, 10 to 12 deliveries a day in business centers, and 4 to 8 in the greater part of London. The government took it over as soon at it began to show a profit and continued the service till 1801. The English postal rates outside London, payable on delivery, were so

Courtesy Public Roads Administration

Mail service by pony express was replaced by the telegraph line shown here under construction.

high that poor people could scarcely afford to receive letters. The story is told that Sir Rowland Hill, to whose efforts people owe the modern postal system, was once at a post office when a poor girl came for her mail. The postmaster handed her a letter with 15 pence postage due. She looked at it, remarked that it was from her brother, but handed it back, saying she could not pay the postage. Sir Rowland paid it for her. The incident made such an impression on him that he did not cease his efforts till the whole system was changed in 1840. Stamps were introduced, and rates made uniform for all distances within the country, varying only according to the weight of the piece, the basic rate being fixed at one penny for one-half ounce. The weight limit was raised to one ounce in 1871 and to four ounces in 1897. The rate was raised to one and one-half pence during World War I. All other countries modeled their postal systems on that of Great Britain. The International Postal Union was formed in 1874 to which nearly all nations now belong.

In the earliest colonial times in North America letters had to be sent by special messengers or by the hands of obliging travelers. A little later stations were established and riders dispatched whenever enough letters had accumulated to pay expenses. From 1707 to 1775 the British Post Office operated American branches. The postmaster general of America then received a salary of £200 a year, plus whatever he liked to charge for newspapers. Benjamin Franklin was the first postmaster general under the Con-

tinental Congress. Rates were high, from 6 cents for 30 miles up to 25 cents for 450 miles or more, for a single sheet. No envelopes were used; the letters were folded so as to show the number of sheets. There were no stamps, but the postmaster wrote the amount of postage due on the outside of the letter. If prepaid, he wrote "paid"; if not, it was sent collect. Members of Congress and heads of government departments had the franking privilege; that is, they could use the mails free.

In 1776 there were 28 post offices in the United States; in 1795, 453; in 1901, 76,945, the highest number ever reached, for the rural free delivery routes later reduced the number. During George Washington's first term as president efforts were made to speed up the mails to 100 miles in 24 hours. The journey of 90 miles from New York City to Philadelphia, Pennsylvania, was then taking 30 hours. Before long, steamboats were carrying the mails. Beginning in 1834, railroads were also used for this purpose, traveling at a speed of 25 miles an hour through the eastern part of the country. Railway Mail Service was introduced in 1864. Stamps were introduced in 1847.

During the winning of the West the postal service offered its most romantic adventure. At first the mail went by overland stage from St. Joseph, Missouri, to San Francisco, California, taking many weeks for the trip. But in 1860 a "fast mail service" by pony express was inaugurated. It covered the distance from St. Joseph, Missouri, to Sacramento, California, in eight days. This was a private enterprise, carrying the mails under contract. There were 80 riders, all young men under 20, including William Cody ("Buffalo Bill") who was then only 14 years old. They rode an average of 75 to 100 miles a day, two minutes being allowed for changing horses at one of the 190 stations, which were about 10 to 15 miles apart. It was an important institution for over a year. But late in 1861 the telegraph line went through to California, and the pony express disappeared.

The growth of the Post Office Department furnishes an excellent measure for the growth of the country. The registry system was introduced in 1855; free delivery for towns of 50,000 or over in 1863 (later extended to towns of 10,000 or over); village delivery in 1912; money order system in 1864; special delivery in 1885; rural free delivery in 1896; postal savings banks in 1911; enlarged parcel post system (with C.O.D. service) in 1913; air mail in 1918. Day and night transcontinental air mail service was established in 1924; special handling service in 1925; air transportation of mail to foreign countries in 1928; and highway post offices in 1941. V-mail service was inaugurated on June 15, 1942. Letters were photographed on film of small size (microfilm), sent overseas, and reproduced there. The system grew to a worldwide network of stations, which, until it was discontinued in November 1945, had microfilmed more than 1,250,000,000 letters. V-mail released valuable cargo space on planes and vessels during World War II, and permitted the rapid movement of regular mail.

International Postal Service

The entrance of the United States into World War II resulted in a disruption of U.S. air mail service to foreign countries. After the close of hostilities, however, the service was restored, with routes to many countries either in operation or authorized. Regular flying routes were restored between the United States, Europe, Central and South America.

On April 29, 1947, the U.S. Post Office Department inaugurated "air letter" service to all foreign countries. Designed for the purpose of world-wide mailing for ten cents, the air letter sheet is the postwar sequel to the V-mail. Unlike V-mail, however, air letter sheets are not photographed but are designed to average a minimum of 150 to the pound.

Experiments in the use of helicopters to transmit mail in the Los Angeles and Chicago areas were conducted in 1946. In the same year, demonstration flights were made with Flying Mail Cars in which mail was sorted en route. There has been a constant expansion in the list of mailable articles. Magazines were first accepted in 1799, illustrated advertising matter in 1845; books in 1851 (limit four pounds); engravings, photographs, stationery, seeds, and cuttings in 1861. Postal cards (which originated in Austria in 1869) were authorized in the United States in 1873. The four principal classes of mail are: (1) written communications; (2) periodicals; (3) miscellaneous printed matter; (4) merchandise or parcel post.

Printed matter, in the form of circulars, may be sent out as "permit mail." That is, permission may be obtained to mail any number of similar circulars without stamping each envelope. The charge is made according to the weight of the entire lot. Business firms sometimes use mail meters, which will stamp impressions on any envelope for the amount of postage required.

Courtesy
U.S. Post Office Department

The U.S. Post Office Department strives to speed the ever-growing quantity of mail. The sorting machine, left, can sort about 36,000 letters in an hour. The canceling machine, right, cancels letters, invalidating the stamps for re-use, faster than the eye can follow.

The machine is set at the post office to stamp no more than the equivalent of the money paid.

In the enlargement of the fourth class by the Parcel Post Act of 1912, the 4 pound limit was discarded and packages up to 50 pounds in weight were permitted to be sent anywhere in the United States, containing almost anything so long as it was not of a nature to injure the contents of mail bags or the employees. The size of parcel post packages is now limited to 100 inches in girth and length combined and 70 pounds in weight. The post office undertakes to collect C.O.D., to insure, to deliver by special delivery, or to give "special handling" which entitles the packages to the same speed in transmission as first-class mail. Millions of letters badly addressed are deciphered and delivered, or else returned to senders, yearly. When all efforts to find either addressee or sender are in vain, the misdirected or unmailable article is sent to the dead letter office where it is opened. If the name of the sender is found inside, it is returned. Careless addresses send 15,000,000 letters to the dead letter office each year.

In order to keep up with the vast and ever-increasing volume of mail, people are constantly working out new mechanical and administrative devices. Many labor-saving machines are used in the big post offices. Fast express trains pick up and deliver mail bags without stopping. Underground pneumatic tubes are used for local transmission of letters; there are about 27 miles of double lines in New York City and Brooklyn, New York. Each mail car on the railroads is now a post office, where the clerks sort out the mail for the next stop. Then it can go directly to the substation where it belongs or to the other train to which it is to be transferred. The same is done on the transatlantic steamships. Air-mail service has made it possible to get a letter from New York City to Mexico City, Mexico, in less than 18 hours.

In 1943 a "zone number" was added to the addresses of people living in the larger cities. In 1963 a ZIP code (zone improvement plan) was adopted. The five digit ZIP number corresponds with the addressee's area, state, and city zones, and makes it easier and quicker for the post office to sort and deliver mail.

Postal Notes

Postal notes were used first in 1945. These notes may be purchased at all first and second class post offices in the United States in amounts from one cent to 10 dollars, inclusive. A fee of five cents is charged for each postal note. A postal note may be cashed at any post office in the United States if presented within two calendar months from the date of issue. The payee is required to sign the postal note before it is paid, and payment will be made only upon proper identification.

In the United States it requires an organization with more than 500,000 men and women, working night and day, using every means of transportation, to provide regular delivery of mail.

POSTER (*pōs'tẽr*). A poster is a message "posted" for people to see. It calls attention to a product, or an event, or a service. The use of posters for this purpose is not new. Posters or wall-paintings have been found in the ruins of Egypt. The Romans posted signs to advertise events in the Coliseum. In the 15th century printing made it easier to make many copies of a notice or advertisement. Some were passed out in the streets as "handbills" and some were pasted up (posted) on walls or fences. With the invention of lithography in 1796 colored pictures were added to the type and the modern poster was born. (See ADVERTISING.)

Today outdoor advertising billboards are the most familiar kind of poster. A study of them will show that they follow the rules for good posters. People passing by do not usually stop to read a poster. Its message must be presented so it can be read in a glance. Thus a good poster has few colors, few words, and a simple design.

The poster should be designed or arranged around a center of interest. The main lines should direct the eye to this spot, and here is the place for the most important word or picture on the poster. This is often the brightest color area in a poster, too.

The lettering of a good poster is simple and easy to read. People will not stop to figure out what small, fancy lettering says. Most of the lettering should be in one spot. Extra words may draw attention away from the really important message.

Colors in posters are usually bold and bright. Contrasting light and dark colors can be seen for greater distances. A few large areas of color are better than many little spots that may make the poster look cluttered and confused. If there is an illustration it must be clear and simple. Some of the details are usually left out to simplify the design.

In poster work it is better to draw an object so its silhouette can be recognized even though the illustration is drawn in detail. This will help people know what the poster is about when they are still too far away to see details. The silhouette of a hand with the fingers spread out is easier to recognize as a hand at a much greater distance than the outline of a fist or the thin strange shape of the side of a hand. The profile of a man's head is instantly known, while the outline of a front view could be mistaken for many other things.

An original idea or unusual treatment in a poster helps attract attention. A short phrase or slogan will stick in people's minds after they turn away from the poster itself. This keeps them thinking about the poster's message longer.

How to Make a Poster

Posters are often used to advertise school events.

In making a poster, first decide on the message, illustration, and colors. Plan on rough paper how these will fit together in a design that will best show the main idea. Think of a clever illustration, a bold phrase, striking colors, and materials that everyone will look at and remember.

In planning a poster keep in mind that it does not have to be simply paint on paper. You may find uses for materials such as cloth, matches, cork, wood, metal, sponge, rubber, leaves, and twigs.

One way to work out a poster is with cut paper. There are many interesting papers which give the appearance of metal, wood, or cloth. Newspaper and photographs can also be used in cut paper posters. If you are using paint, get show card or *tempera* colors rather than water colors because they are easy to handle and give a flat surface. Crayons are not too good for getting large areas colored evenly.

If a number of posters are needed, one way to make them quickly is to use *stencils*. Stencils are made of thin sheets of metal, paper, or other material with a design cut into them. The stencil is then laid upon a surface—the poster paper or wood or whatever is to be decorated. When a fairly stiff brush dipped in show card color or oil paint is tapped over the open places in the stencil, the pattern is transferred to the surface beneath. Poster painters often use this method for lettering because it saves time.

Heavy paper coated with paraffin, or a thin

SUGGESTIONS FOR SCHOOL POSTERS ANNOUNCING A PLAY OR OTHER SCHOOL EVENTS

HOLD STENCIL TIGHTLY WHEN YOU APPLY THE PAINT

cardboard, is the best material to have for stencil-making. The beauty of a stenciled design or picture is in the bold strokes which they permit. Trace on thin paper whatever design is planned. When you have corrected the design until it suits you, transfer this design to the stencil paper. Remember that the spaces you trace for cutting out must be broken here and there. Otherwise your whole design will fall out of the paper when you cut it. After the design is transferred to the stencil paper, cut out the sections which you wish to appear in color on the finished paper.

If you want two colors on the finished poster, two stencils must be cut, each with only its own color areas cut out.

Place the stencil on the poster board in the exact position you want the design to be. Hold the stencil firmly in place. Dip a brush with short, stiff bristles into the paint, being careful not to get too much paint on it. Tap the brush gently over the stencil. Don't move it back and forth over the stencil as you would paint a wall.

When you finish coloring, lift the stencil carefully. Wipe it dry before you make the next poster. Do not print the second color on your poster until the first is dry. It is best to print the first color on all the posters before going on to the second color.

POTASSIUM (*pō tăs′ĭ ŭm*). Potassium is a metal, light in weight, soft, and with a low melting point. It will float on water and melt in hot water. But it is very dangerous to put potassium in water. Because it is an active metal it combines quickly with the oxygen in water and sets free the hydrogen. This causes enough heat to set fire to the hydrogen which burns with a violet flame.

If a piece of potassium is cut the new surface has a shiny look. This changes quickly because the metal combines with the oxygen of the air to form a dull covering. The metal therefore must be protected from air and moisture. It is stored in bottles filled with gasoline. Its chemical symbol is K from the word *kalium,* its atomic number is 19, its atomic weight 39.102, and its valence is +1. (See CHEMISTRY.) Potassium is a member of the alkali metals group. (See PERIODIC TABLE OF THE ELEMENTS.)

It was the first of the elements to be discovered by the use of an electric current. Sir Humphry Davy made the discovery on October 6, 1807. Davy described the newly discovered substance in these words: "small globules having a high metallic luster, and being precisely similar in visible character to quicksilver, appeared, some of which burned with explosions and bright flames as soon as they formed, and others remained and were merely tarnished and finally covered by a white film which formed on their surface."

Because it is such an active metal potassium can not exist free in nature. But it forms some of the most stable compounds known. It forms part of the micas and feldspars of igneous rocks and clays. Potassium can be separated from the other elements in its compounds by electrolysis; however, the pure metal is little used in industry.

Compounds of potassium are used in the manufacture of soap, glass, matches, fireworks, drugs, and photographic preparations. Its cyanide is one of the deadliest poisons known to science. Potassium is necessary to plant life and is one of the three elements used in manufactured fertilizers. It will dissolve many metals. It is used in the cyanide process for extracting gold from ores that do not have much gold in them. Potassium is very sensitive to light and for this reason is used in the photoelectric cell.

The largest supplies of potash salts, as potassium compounds are called, are found in the famous Stassfurt deposits of Germany. These salts are water soluble sulfates and chlorides which are easily used. Similar beds have been discovered in the southwestern United States and developed on a large scale. Previous to World War I the United States had no sizable sources of domestic supply and was dependent upon Germany. In the period between World Wars I and II, United States deposits were developed so that the country was no longer short of this important raw material.

POTATO ($p\bar{o}$ $t\bar{a}'t\bar{o}$) is a plant native of the highlands of Ecuador and Peru, where it grows wild today. It was introduced into Spain probably early in the 16th century by the Spaniards returning from Peru. It is generally believed that Spaniards brought the potato to North America. But the best evidence is that it was first brought to New Hampshire from Ireland in 1719.

The potato plant belongs to the nightshade family, which also includes the tomato and tobacco. The potato itself is a thickened underground stem. It is a storehouse for the starch manufactured by the leaves of the plant. The "eyes" of the potato are really undeveloped buds.

During the 17th century the popularity of the potato increased greatly. By 1846 the people of Ireland were dependent upon the potato crop for a large part of their food. When the potato blight destroyed the crop that year, thousands of people died of famine. At the present time the potato crop is one of the most important in the world. The U.S.S.R., Germany, Poland, France, the United States, and Czechoslovakia stand at the head of the principal producers. In the United States, the states nearest the Canadian border and east of the Mississippi produce abundant crops. Idaho, Colorado, California, and Atlantic seaboard states from New Jersey south also produce large supplies. Florida is one of the principal regions supplying new potatoes in early summer.

The potato of today is very different from its South American ancestor. The change was brought about through breeding and methods of cultivation. A potato breeder is constantly working to get certain qualities. He desires high yield per acre, resistance to disease, good keeping qualities, shallow eyes that are few in number, vigorous plants, and good color and flavor of flesh. Some of these can be obtained by providing good soil conditions and proper fertilizers. One of the first principles in breeding potatoes is to decide what qualities are desirable. Then select for seed only those plants which show these qualities. The crop must be watched carefully and any plant which shows some valuable new trait should be marked.

From this a new strain may be selected. The main method of breeding is to cross plants which show different valuable traits in order to produce seeds that may have the best traits of both parents. This method requires precise knowledge and rigorous testing of the new varieties.

The potato is not commonly grown from seed, but from pieces of the tuber which have the buds, or eyes. These buds grow into new plants. Tubers selected for growing the new crop are called seed potatoes. Of course, they are not true seeds. If seed potatoes are infected by disease, they should be carefully disinfected before planting. Some diseases can not be destroyed in this way. Seed potatoes with such diseases should not be planted. After disinfection and drying, the seed tubers should be cut into pieces that have one or two eyes each. The average potato will make four such pieces. These pieces should be planted 3 to 5 inches deep, depending on the soil, and 12 inches apart, in rows that are 2 or more feet apart. The exact distance depends upon the richness of the soil and the tools to be used in cultivation.

The plant grows best in cool climates, in a light sandy or clay loam. The soil should be loosened to a depth of about seven inches and well broken. Growth will be better if thoroughly decayed animal manure and commercial fertilizers are added to the soil before planting, if the soil is not rich in the beginning.

Mechanical planters are largely used in the United States, mainly because of the high cost of labor. The machines used are generally of two types. The picker type is operated by one man. There is also the platform type, which has an automatic feeding device. The latter is operated by two men.

The plant, which bears white or purplish flowers, grows to a height of from one to three feet. The crop may be harvested when the tops have withered. All the potatoes should be dug, even the little ones. They may then be stored for the winter in well-ventilated dirt cellars or in earth pits, if the soil is well drained, or else in frost-proof storage houses above ground.

Potatoes have a large number of enemies, both plant and animal. Among the insects the Colorado beetle and the flea beetle and leaf hoppers do the most damage. Spraying with Bordeaux mixture will help to control them. Among the plant enemies are a number of parasitic fungi and bacteria which cause scurf, blight, wilt, rot, and scab. The best method of fighting these pests is to select resistant tubers for breeding and to disinfect the seed tubers

single blossom

flower cluster

underground stems and tubers of the potato plant

The compound leaves of the potato plant manufacture the starch that is stored in the potatoes.

Sebago

White Rose

Irish Cobbler

Bliss Triumph

Kennebec

Red Pontiac

Chippewa

Katahdin

Cherokee

Russet Burbank

carefully before planting. The fungus enemies live in the soil throughout the winter. Others may winter on diseased tubers. Late blight of potato, a fungus, often destroys large acreages. It may be partially controlled through sprays. Several virus diseases are also very serious. In general these can be kept in check only by planting tubers free from the disease or by using varieties which are resistant to them. One of the principal problems being investigated at present is the breeding of new varieties of potatoes resistant to various diseases.

The chief uses of potatoes are as a food, for the manufacture of potato starch, and for the distilling of alcohol. In some European countries potatoes are dried and stored, much as one stores grain. They are also ground to make potato flour.

POTATO BUG (*bŭg*). Until the United States was settled beyond the Rocky Mountains the potato bug, or Colorado potato beetle, lived mainly on sandburs or buffalo burs. As soon as the new settlers planted potatoes, this beetle attacked them and thrived on them. Slowly it began to move eastward, spoiling the potato crops as it went. In 1859 it was found near Omaha, Nebraska. Ten years later Ohio farmers were beginning to complain, and by 1870, potato bugs were destroying crops in Ontario, Canada. In 1872 they reached New York, and a few years later were common along the north Atlantic Coast. The spread southward took a little longer.

The potato bug belongs to the family Chrysomelidae. A full-grown bug is about one-half inch long. Its general color is yellow, but its head is black and there are two rows of black spots on each side of its body. Each of its wings is edged with black along the inner side, and the wing covers are marked with five black stripes.

Potato bugs damage plants by eating the leaves and by boring into the stalk. The female, which spends the winter underground or beneath some temporary shelter, deposits her eggs in batches of from 5 to 70 on the underside of young plant leaves. In the course of 6 weeks, a single female deposits from 200 to

Above: Larva and eggs of a potato bug, enlarged. Below: A full-grown bug is about one-half inch long.

1,800 eggs. The shiny orange larvae hatch out in about seven days and feed on young potato leaves for two or three weeks.

Then they enter the earth to spend their pupal stage. This period lasts a little less than two weeks. Each year there are usually three generations of potato bugs in the South and two in the North.

The best way to rid potato plants of the pests is to spray them with a combination of Paris green and Bordeaux mixture.

Powdered arsenate of lead, sprinkled on plants wet with dew, is another remedy. Birds, snakes, toads, and other bugs prey on potato bugs and help kill them.

POTOMAC (*pō tō′măk*) **RIVER, UNITED STATES.** One of the largest and most beautiful rivers in the eastern United States is the Potomac River. It rises in the Allegheny Mountains of West Virginia and flows about 287 miles southeast into Chesapeake Bay. The lower Potomac Valley below Washington, D.C., has been "drowned" by rise of sea level. Now it is a long narrow bay, several miles wide at its mouth, through which large ships can sail up as far as Washington.

The Potomac River is rich in historical interest. Before European settlers came, it was a much-used waterway of the Indians, and its broad wooded valley was an Indian hunting ground. In 1608 Captain John Smith entered Chesapeake Bay and sailed up this river, which he called "Patowmack" after an Indian tribe living nearby. During the War Between the States, several battles were fought along the Potomac Valley. Many historic spots are located on the banks of the Potomac River, including Mount Vernon; Arlington National Cemetery; Harpers Ferry, West Virginia; and

Cumberland, Maryland, eastern end of the National Road of pioneer days.

POTTERY (pŏt'ēr ē), in a broad sense, is any object made of clay and hardened by heat. In a narrower sense, it includes only the coarser stoneware and earthenware, and not commercial bricks and tiles or fine porcelain or china. (See PORCELAIN OR CHINA.)

Making pottery is an old art. Yet pottery is made today much as it was in the time of the oldest known civilization. Modern machine methods of making pottery differ from ancient methods only in their greater speed. No one knows when or where it was first discovered that clay, mixed with water, could be molded and turned into a hard, stonelike substance by baking or firing. Nor does anyone know when it was discovered that this pottery could be given a glasslike finish by glazing with a mixture of silica (sand), other minerals, and water before firing it again. Yet these two processes are the underlying principles of all pottery making.

Pottery can be divided into three general classes: stoneware, the cheapest and coarsest grade; earthenware, a medium grade which is most commonly used; and porcelain or china, the finest and most expensive grade.

Pottery ware may also be classified according to its use, the type of clay, the glaze, and how waterproof or nonporous the body becomes in firing.

The Chimu Indians of Peru made colorful little pottery ornaments like these many years ago.

Photos, James Sawders

Stoneware crocks and jars usually are made from a single clay. In firing, the clay acquires a tan color and becomes nonporous in the kiln heat. Stoneware may be glazed by soda fumes made by throwing salt onto the kiln fires after the ware has become nonporous. However, modern stoneware is coated with a mixture that fuses to a glaze at the heat which renders the clay body nonporous.

While stoneware is generally for useful purposes, much stoneware is made in the form of vases and jars for garden decorations. These stoneware vases are often decorated with mineral colors mixed in the glaze.

Earthenware pottery is made from a mixture of clay and minerals. The body of the ware is fired until it is nearly waterproof. The clay mixtures forming the body of the ware must be very fine and carefully prepared. At the present time the earthenware for table use made by modern machine methods may be quite thin and has a glasslike finish, but is not translucent. Often it is decorated under the glaze or over the glaze in the same way as porcelain or china. Earthenware dishes are widely used and quite inexpensive. These same earthenware pottery bodies are used in the production of artware vases.

Porcelain (sometimes called china because it originated in the country of China) is somewhat similar to earthen tableware; however, the clay and mineral mixtures are designed so that the body will become translucent in firing. Porcelain tableware is fired at a high heat. Also, after being glazed it is fired at an even higher heat in order to vitrify the body, or give it a glasslike finish. The glaze on porcelain is hard and is resistant to wear.

Porcelains used in spark plugs and electric insulators are especially compounded so that when they are fired to complete vitrification they will not let an electric current pass through them. The body and glaze are fired as carefully as are those used in the finest art porcelains.

Often items of pottery such as vases, bowls, and figurines are called "ceramics." While this artware is correctly termed ceramics, it is important to remember that pottery is only one branch of the ceramic industry.

The following pictures show step by step the procedures used in making ceramic objects in a pottery workshop.

PLATE 1 POTTERY (1) The variety of color and texture of the pottery shown here is caused by using different materials in the glaze combined with various intricate firing processes. (2) The shaping of a bowl starts by placing a lump of clay on the fast-spinning potter's wheel. The potter presses with one hand on the outside. At the same time, he uses the other hand to shape the top. (3) The finishing touches of the shaping of the bowl are made while the clay is still soft and can be molded. The potter's wheel is turned slowly and the potter delicately shapes the upper rim of the bowl.

Photos, Dalzell Hatfield Galleries

1

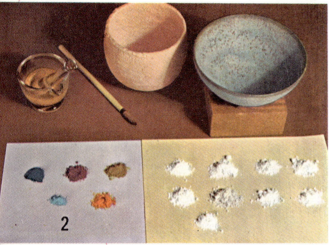

2

PLATE 2 POTTERY (1) After the bowl is shaped on the potter's wheel, it is allowed to dry until it is practically "leather-hard." Then it is put upside down on the potter's wheel and carefully centered. The wheel is set in motion. The base of the bowl is shaped by cutting off any excess clay with turning tools, as shown here. After the turning, all pieces are carefully cleaned and allowed to dry completely. They are then fired for the first time (bisque). (2) Fourteen different chemicals and minerals went into the making of the glaze for the Pompeian green bowl to the right. The separate chemicals and minerals are shown in the foreground. The prepared glaze is seen in the mortar to the left. Before the green bowl went through the glaze fire, it looked pink and rough like the bowl in the middle. The pink bowl has gone through the first firing. This changed its clay chemically, gave strength to the clay, and made it impervious to treatment with water. (3) The glazing process is started with the careful weighing of all glaze materials. The materials are then thoroughly mixed and prepared with water to which some gum has been added as an adhesive.

Photos, Dalzell Hatfield Galleries

3

PLATE 3 POTTERY (1) The potter applies the prepared glaze with a brush. Several coats are applied to each piece. After glazing, the pieces are allowed to dry completely before being fired for the second time (glaze fire). (2) The glaze kiln is ready for firing. The pieces have been carefully set on stilts to prevent their sticking to the kiln shelves. Care is taken in placing the pieces to avoid their touching each other.

Photos, Dalzell Hatfield Galleries

PLATE 4 POTTERY The completed objects. (1) The glaze kiln is opened after the firing. The pieces show their final color and texture which was developed during the glaze fire. (2) The color of the glaze of the bottle-shaped vase comes from the use of iron oxide. This bottle, in addition to its regular glaze fire, has undergone a second firing which produced the vase's particular shade of color. (3) Two semirough textured bowls. (4) The bowl on the left, with its rough and craterlike texture, is a green lavastone bowl. The two smaller bowls have been glaze fired a second time.

Photos, Dalzell Hatfield Galleries

The ceramic industry produces everything from common brick to fine porcelain, everything made of glass, and all porcelain enameled ware. The enamel on the kitchen range, sink, and refrigerator is of the same sort of glass mixture as that used for glazes on pottery. Even false teeth and grinding wheels used for shaping metal parts or grinding glass surfaces are made of ceramic materials.

Refractory or heat-resistant brick used on the inside of furnaces in the iron and steel manufacturing industry is another member of the ceramic family, to which pottery belongs. Ceramic substances are also used as coatings for jet-engine parts. Metal parts that are coated with ceramics can better withstand the intense heat of the airplane engines and, thus, last much longer.

The English word, "ceramic," comes from the ancient Greek adjective, *keramos*, which referred to ware made by firing clay articles. Both words are related to the old Sanskrit root meaning "to fire." Since the Greeks in early times used *keramos* to mean "fired stuff," it can be seen that it was the process rather than the materials that they had in mind.

Therefore, the ceramic industry can be defined as the industry concerned with the manufacture of products by the action of heat on earthy materials.

Steps in Pottery Making

Clays differ greatly in their color and in the way they react to the heat of firing. The first step in making any clay into pottery is to clean it of all small stones and pebbles. Bits of iron, which would make yellowish-brown stains in white pottery, are usually removed by a set of magnets. The clean clay is ground very fine and mixed with water. Substances, such as flint, fine sand, feldspar, and other minerals, are often mixed with the clay. Often oxide of cobalt is added as a bleach. The soupy mixture of clay and water is strained through very fine meshed screens. Then it is squeezed and pressed until it is about as thick as putty.

The next step in pottery making is to fashion the clay into the desired shapes. The most primitive method for fashioning articles of clay is the *coil method*. In this method, which is still in use today, the clay is molded entirely by hand. The potter rolls the clay out into a thin rope. Then, after making a base, he starts at the bottom of the bowl or pot and builds the clay rope into a vessel.

An improvement over the coil method known even in ancient times is the *potter's wheel*. The potter's wheel is simply a flat revolving disk. The wheel may be turned by hand, by a pedal, or by electricity or steam.

The potter, or thrower, takes a lump of clay just large enough to make the vessel he desires and throws it onto the revolving wheel. Then he hollows out the center of the lump with his thumbs and draws and pulls at its sides with his wet hands. When he has made the shape he wishes, he smooths the inside with a wet sponge. The outside he polishes with a piece of leather. Handles are molded separately and fastened on while the clay is still wet. The finished article is cut off the wheel with a piece of wire and put aside to dry. It may be polished once more on a lathe before it is fired. Some art pottery is still made on a potter's wheel. However, where pottery or dishes are made in large amounts, a method called *jiggering* is

One of Mexico's most famous products is pottery. Here a finished bowl is being dipped into whitewash. The bowl will then be set in the sun to dry.

Evelyn Hofer from Pix

Photos, (1) *Herbert Lanks from Black Star*, (2) *Pix*, (3) *Horace Bristol from Black Star*, (4) *Ries from Black Star*

(1) A Guatemalan woman works on a clay water jar. (2) An Iranian craftsman shapes a vase as his potter's wheel spins. (3) A Japanese woman applies slip by hand in a primitive pottery shop. (4) A potter in Bavaria molds a plate on a potter's wheel. He smooths the edges and makes them uniform by using the cutting machine in front of him.

Photos, left: Ewing Galloway; right: Pix

Left: A skillful Czechoslovakian artist applies decoration to vases. Right: Natives in Cameroon, West Africa, make earthenware vessels, figures, and statuettes.

used. A jigger machine is something like a potter's wheel, and flat pieces such as plates and saucers are made on it. A round, flat piece of clay shaped like a pancake is pressed down on a plaster mold shaped like the top side of the dish, for the plate is made upside down. This mold is then put on the turning wheel. A tool shaped like the bottom side of the plate is then scraped around the flat piece of clay on the mold. This forms the bottom shape of the plate.

Another method used for very delicate ware is *casting*. A mold is made of plaster of Paris, fashioned in sections so that it can be taken apart easily. This mold is filled with liquid clay called *slip*. The porous plaster of Paris absorbs the water in the clay, and a thin shell of firm clay is formed on the inside of the mold. The liquid clay in the middle of the mold is poured out. As soon as the clay lining has hardened, the mold is taken apart.

After the vessels have been shaped, they are dried thoroughly in a drying room. Then they are packed into *saggers*, large vessels of fire clay shaped like washtubs. The saggers are stacked in a kiln, the door of the kiln is blocked with firebricks, and the fires are lighted. The temperature in the kiln is raised to as much as 3,000 degrees Fahrenheit. It is kept at that tempera-ture from one to three days. In the intense heat the particles of clay are fused together. The pottery is left in the kiln until it cools. Then it is unpacked. In this shape it is called *bisque ware*.

The next step is to put a fine, glasslike glaze on the rough, porous bisque ware. The glaze is made of much the same materials as glass—flint, feldspar, and litharge (lead oxide). These materials are ground very fine. Then they are mixed with water to form a liquid. The glaze is poured into large vats. Skilled workmen dip each article into it, being careful that the article is covered with an even coating of glaze. The glaze may also be applied by spraying, brushing, or pouring it on the article. Then the articles are put in glaze kilns. The temperature in the kilns is raised very slowly and then lowered again carefully. The glaze melts in the kilns and changes to a thin coating of glass.

Coarse pottery is sometimes glazed by throwing common salt into the saggers when the first firing has been completed. The heat changes the salt to a vapor that settles on the articles and forms a transparent glaze. Beautiful effects are gained by using various minerals that produce different colors.

Often the same mineral will produce different

colors depending upon various firing conditions. For example, copper oxide can be blue, green, red, or purple when it is fired at different temperatures, on different bisques, and under different conditions.

Some pottery is so beautiful in its shape and coloring that it needs no further decoration. Usually, however, designs are painted on it. These designs may be applied by hand or transferred in color from engraved plates to wet tissue paper, which is placed on the clay. The clay absorbs the colors and the paper is soaked off with water. This process is called *decalcomania*. The decorations may be put on before glazing, on the unfired glaze, or on the glaze after firing. In the last case the articles must be fired a third time. Since colors change greatly in the firing process, they must be chosen very carefully.

Many people have discovered the fascination of creating their own ceramic pieces and pottery making as a hobby is being enjoyed more and more every year. Nearly everywhere in the United States, schools have been founded where people learn all the basic steps necessary for making bowls, dishes, vases, and figurines.

Pottery of Other Peoples

The pottery of the Pueblo Indians in North America is perhaps the most famous primitive pottery. Among ancient peoples the Greeks were probably the most skilled pottery makers. Their ware often was decorated with delicate designs in black on a red background. The Egyptians and Assyrians had already made fine pottery before the Greeks developed the art. The Romans, who followed the Greeks, did some excellent work. After the fall of the Roman Empire, for many years the finest pottery in Europe was that made by the Moors in Spain. Later the Italians developed majolica, a heavily enameled ware, and faience.

Other famous European wares are the blue delftware of Holland, the fine work of Bernard Palissy in France, and the various types of English pottery, such as Staffordshire, Wedgwood, and Leeds pottery. In the United States pottery making began shortly after the American Revolution. Today the greatest pottery centers are

in Ohio, New Jersey, New York, Pennsylvania, and West Virginia. California has recently become a center for artware. Some of the most beautiful wares produced in the United States are Rookwood and Lenox wares.

POULTRY (*pōl'trē*). Charles Darwin, the great naturalist, said that the chicken that struts about the back yard is descended from a little, red partridgelike fowl which runs wild in the jungles of India and the Malay Peninsula. If chickens were first domesticated in the East, it must have happened very long ago. They have since spread all over the world. There are over a hundred breeds and strains. Generally speaking, these breeds may be divided into two classes: the heavy ones, raised primarily for their meat, and the lightweight, egg-laying breeds. The heavy, meaty chickens have come directly from Asia. They include the Cochins, weighing up to 16 pounds, the Brahmas, and the Lang-

Many thousands of eggs are hatched each year in incubators. Inset: The eggs are placed on trays in an incubator. Below: The chicks hatch 21 days later.

Courtesy Hays Bros. Hatchery

Courtesy (1, 2, 3) Poultry Tribune; A. O. Schilling, photographer; Photos, (4, 5, 6) L. P. Graham

(1) Silver Spangled Hamburg cockerel, (2) Blue Andalusian hen, (3) Light Brahma hen, (4) Black-tailed Japanese Bantam cock, (5) Silver Sebright Bantam hen, (6) Buff Cochin Bantam hen.

shans. From these have been bred a number of strains somewhat lighter in weight, but exceptionally good layers. These are known as general-purpose fowl, as they are good for both laying and meat. The most popular of these are the Plymouth (Barred) Rocks, the Rhode Island Reds, the Wyandottes, and the Orpingtons.

The lightweight egg-laying breeds come from the Mediterranean countries. Of these the White Leghorns are the most common. They are special favorites on the large commercial poultry farms. The Black Minorcas and the Mottled Anconas also belong to this type. These varieties lay an egg whose shell is chalky white. The heavier breeds produce eggs of various shades of brown. The people of New England, especially in and around Boston, prefer brown eggs. In that region the poultry farms are almost entirely stocked with Rhode Island Reds or Barred Rocks. White eggs bring higher prices in New York.

At the beginning of the 19th century the average farm kept from a few dozen to perhaps a hundred chickens in the barn yard; chickens of all sizes and colors, mixed with turkeys and ducks and geese. The farmer himself considered them as a side line. The care of them fell to the housewife or to the children, the profits from the sale of eggs being theirs as pin money. The hens laid in the hay loft, under the barn, or even out in the bushes. Sometimes the eggs, no longer fresh, were not found till days later.

Influence of the Incubator

The small farm flock is still very common. The incubator, however, has made poultry raising one of the chief agricultural industries. The ancient Egyptians hatched eggs in big stone or brick vaults, heated with rotting manure. This method was not possible in the changeable climates of northern Europe and the United States. So up to a few years ago the farmer who wanted to increase his flock had to wait until one or more of his hens was ready to brood. A broody hen is one which stops laying, and sits on a nest. As one hen usually can hatch out not more than a dozen eggs at a time, the farmer who could raise 200 to 300 chickens a year was doing well.

The modern incubator is either heated by electricity, or the warmth is supplied through hot water or steam pipes. It may hatch out hundreds of thousands of eggs at one time. Thus commercial hatcheries have been started. Some of them are operated by corporations, hatching out several millions of chicks in a season. When a chick is hatched it has enough food stored inside it to supply it with nourishment for three days. Therefore, it can be shipped in a cardboard box by mail or express for distances up to 1,000 miles.

The large majority of farmers, therefore, do not bother with broody hens. Usually they sell them to the butcher. It is cheaper to buy day-old chicks at from 10 to 40 cents apiece and brood them in larger numbers. Even ducks can be obtained in this way. However, they must be incubated separately, as a duck egg requires 28 days of incubation. A hen egg is hatched in 21. Most hatcheries buy hatching eggs from farmers and then sell their chicks outright. In some communities where there are many poultry farms there are hatcheries which do what is called *custom hatching*. The farmers bring their eggs there on certain days and place them in the incubator on trays which they rent. They return in 21 days to get their chicks.

Raising Chicks as a Business

When the chicks are hatched they are placed under the brooder. This consists of a stove with a metal "umbrella" over it, which throws the heat downward to the floor. Thus from 300 to 400 chicks can be brooded around one stove. There are poultry farms where from 10 to 20 stoves are kept going at once.

Great skill is required in the care of the baby chicks, especially during the first two months. There are diseases so deadly that they may kill over half the flock. Disease can spread quickly under the crowded conditions that result from this large-scale hatching and brooding method. When the chicks are from six to eight weeks of age they no longer need heat. Then they are encouraged to roost instead of nestling under the stove canopy. At about this time the cockerels are sold to the butcher. Usually they number just about half of the flock. Very few farmers now keep roosters with their flocks, unless they sell hatching eggs to the hatcheries or hatch from their own eggs. There are many poultry farms on which the crow of a rooster is never heard.

When a pullet is five or six months old it begins to lay. Then the modern poultry farmer puts her into the laying house. However, during the summertime she is put on pasture. For scientists have found that the hen can and will make thrifty use of the food value in green forage. Moreover, the hen which gets access to sunlight is healthier, for sunlight is a fine source of the important vitamin D.

The barn yard fowl of many shapes and colors is largely a thing of the past. This is partly because of the educational campaigns of the state agricultural colleges. Also, the hatcheries sell only purebred stock. At one time the hen that laid 200 eggs in one year was a prize bird. Now from 300 to 350 eggs may be laid by the prize layers, and the best breeders get rid of or sell to the butcher the birds that lay less than 200. Many state agricultural colleges hold yearly egg-laying contests. These are followed with the greatest interest by the whole poultry world, through the weekly reports of the agricultural papers. The owner of the winning hen reaps a handsome reward, since her eggs may command as much as ten dollars apiece when sold for hatching purposes.

Farmers have modern methods in poultry

Courtesy (1, 3, 8, 9) U. S. Department of Agriculture, (2, 5, 6, 7) Poultry Tribune; A. O. Schilling, photographer; Photos (4, 10, 11, 12) L. P. Graham

The popular lightweight egg-laying breeds of chickens are included on this page: (1) Plymouth (Barred) Rock cockerel; (2) White Plymouth Rock pullet; (3) White Plymouth Rock cockerel; (4) White Orpington pullet; (5) Single Comb White Leghorn hen; (6) Single Comb White Leghorn cock; (7) New Hampshire cock; (8) Rhode Island Red pullet; (9) Rhode Island Red cockerel; (10) Partridge Cochin hen; (11) White Wyandotte hen; (12) White Wyandotte cockerel.

raising because the market demands highest quality eggs. Nearly everywhere the poultry farmers form co-operative associations, through which the eggs are marketed. The co-operative association sells the eggs in bulk. It also grades them, candling them to see that they are fresh. This is done by holding the egg before a hole in a box within which is a strong light. At one end of the egg is an air bubble, or space. In a fresh egg, this should be about the size of a dime. If it is larger, the egg is not so fresh. The air bubble shows in the light, and experts can tell by its size just how old the egg is. Blood clots also can be detected.

Years ago egg prices were very high in the fall and winter, and very low in the spring. This was because the chickens moulted in the fall and stopped laying, and, owing to the short hours of daylight during the winter, never laid heavily again till spring. The egg dealers therefore bought large quantities of eggs in spring, and put them into storage to be sold in winter. Now there are very few farmers who do not light their hen houses to give the hen 12 to 15 hours of light during the months of short daylight. This makes the hens eat more, and therefore lay more. If, however, the hens lay heavily during the winter they lay less in the spring. The modern brooder stove enables farmers to brood chicks in February and March. Then they have their pullets laying in August and September, when the old hens begin moulting.

The Department of Agriculture in Washington has for several years been reporting an annual increase of from 10 to 15 per cent in the hen population of the country. There are two important egg producing centers in the United States. One is in California, around Petaluma, the other in New Jersey, around Vineland. The larger number of the nation's eggs, however, are laid on the general farms in the Middle West and the Northwest, more especially in the corn belt, where grain is cheap. There the cold storage men buy their supplies in the spring, shipping them East for sale in the fall and winter. Drying and powdering has also been developed, especially in the Midwest, as a means of conveniently storing and shipping eggs. In World War II almost all eggs shipped from the United States to England and other far places were converted to a dry powder, with a dozen powdered eggs weighing only about a third of a pound in that form.

The name bantam was originally used for a particular breed of chicken. It was distinguished by its small size, by feathered legs and feet, and by brilliant coloring. These chickens were raised in Bantam—a district of Java for which they were named—and in Japan. Now the name is applied to very small chickens and ducks of many breeds. Bantams, though small, are good for food. The hens lay well in winter, the eggs, however, being small.

Ducks, Geese, Turkeys

Duck farming is a very minor industry, compared with chicken farming. Long Island is an important center for duck farming. However, there is only a small margin of profit in raising ducks. For this reason one farm must keep from five to ten thousand layers. There are two main breeds of ducks: the Indian Runner, small but a prolific layer, and the heavier Pekin duck, also a good layer, but raised mainly for meat.

Geese are still largely a product of the barnyard, for they need a great deal of free range to thrive. The turkey industry, on the other hand, has become a sizeable one in recent years. Turkeys are pastured in large flocks in some areas of the Midwest, being fed grain and supplementing that with green feed and insects. Some farmers keep a flock of turkeys mainly for their value in controlling grasshoppers. New England was once the important turkey raising region. A disease known as black-head, which killed off the young poults, proved so discouraging that farmers gave up raising them. Among domestic turkeys the best known market birds are the large bronze turkeys, the white Holland birds, and the smaller Bourbon Reds.
(See TURKEY.)

POWER (pou'ĕr). Man must work in order to live. To grow food, the soil must be plowed and seeded; the crops must be harvested, transported, and processed. Material for clothing has to be grown or made, woven into cloth, sewed into clothes, and transported. Steel for buildings and bridges has to be made, cut, drilled, and riveted. Coal for heating homes and driving engines has to be mined and carried to homes and factories. Almost everything used in living has been made by work.

To help do this work man has invented many kinds of machines. Some machines are run by hand, but most need a large amount of power to do work. This needed power is furnished today by engines, motors, and turbines. These may be water, steam, gas, gasoline, Diesel, electric, jet rocket, or atomic. Each is a source of power.

At the dawn of history, man's only power was his own muscles. To move a tree or a rock took many men a long time. Sometimes one group of men would enslave another group and force them to work. Large slaveholding nations, such as ancient Egypt, developed in this way. Egyptian slaves spent their lives dragging stones to build the pyramids for the Pharaohs.

Over thousands of years, men learned to use the power of animals to do work. Oxen and horses pulled wagons, plowed fields, and did heavy work such as grinding grain or pumping water out of mines. Other kinds of power were found in nature. One of the first was the power in rivers, which could float logs downstream. Later men made rafts to carry cargo.

Men also learned to use the power of wind to sail boats. The power of the wind saved men from rowing. Wind also was used to turn windmills for power to grind grain and pump water. Such windmills can still be seen in the Netherlands. Smaller ones are used on some farms in the United States for pumping water.

Windmills can also be used to generate electricity. Engineers have experimented with windmills of modern design, placed high on mountains, to generate electricity. But men have found other sources of power far more helpful than wind. By burning fuels such as coal and oil man has made heat engines.

The first known use of the heat from fire to power an engine occurred about 2,000 years ago. A Greek philosopher named Hero made the first steam engine. However, it was too small to do any work.

In 1705 Thomas Newcomen, an Englishman, invented a practical steam engine. It was used for pumping water out of coal mines. However, it used too much fuel. At that time metal parts could not be made to fit closely together, and there were too many leaks where steam could escape. Later in the 18th century James Watt made an improved engine in which the parts fitted better. He made valves that worked automatically, so that no one had to stand by and operate the valves which made the piston move up and down. (See STEAM ENGINE.)

In order to sell his steam engines, Watt had to measure their power or rate of doing work. These engines were first used to replace the horses that were used as power in pumping water out of coal mines. He compared the rate at which the engine did the work with the rate at which horses could do the same amount of work. Thus his engines had a certain amount of *horsepower*. In order to measure this, he first had a horse lift a certain weight. A horse pulling a rope attached to a pulley could lift about 550 pounds a distance of one foot in one second. If a steam engine could do the same amount of work in the same time it was then said to have one horsepower. If an engine could lift twice as much weight in one second, it was said to have two horsepower. Power has been measured by horsepower ever since.

In 1803 Robert Fulton used Watt's steam engine to drive a boat. In the 1820's George Stephenson built a steam railroad in England. (See RAILROAD; STEPHENSON FAMILY.)

The steam engine was an *external-combustion engine*, which means that the burning took place in a furnace outside the boiler. This is what made the steam engine so heavy.

The gasoline engine, which was developed by Nicholas Otto of Germany in 1878, was the first step toward solving the problem of weight. This was called an *internal-combustion engine* because it burned the gasoline inside the cylinder. Since it did not need a separate furnace, it was much lighter than a steam engine of the same horsepower.

The Diesel engine works much like the gasoline engine, but it uses a cheaper oil for fuel and also is heavier. It can therefore best be used in boats, trains, and trucks where weight is not important. Modern jet aircraft and rockets also make use of the power of burning fuel. They work on a principle of science known as *action and reaction*. (See AIRPLANE; JET PROPULSION.)

Another type of engine, based on the old windmill principle, is the turbine. A turbine engine is simply a bladed, spinning wheel, pushed by air, water, steam, or burning gas. (For descriptions of these kinds of engines, see INTERNAL-COMBUSTION ENGINE; TURBINE.)

The most recent source of power that man has discovered is atomic energy. Atomic power is developed in a device called an *atomic pile* (*reactor*). The heat of the reactor produces steam which operates a steam turbine to generate electric current. (See ATOMIC ENERGY.)

The advantage of atomic power is that a tiny amount of fuel produces great heat. One pound of ordinary uranium can make as much heat in an atomic pile as ten tons of coal.

Another possible source of power is sunlight. Engines that run by this power are called *solar engines*. A simple kind of solar engine is a large mirror that focuses light like a lens. The focused light may heat water in a pipe and produce steam. Scientists are also experimenting with ways of making electricity directly from sunlight. Power from solar batteries will operate portable radios and even an entire city telephone system.

The growth of power since the 18th century has been so rapid throughout the world that it has completely changed man's way of living. (See INDUSTRIAL REVOLUTION.) During the 100 years from 1850 to 1950 power and machinery increased at such a rate that in 1950 one worker in the United States could produce six times as much goods in one hour as a worker could in 1850. In 1850 79% of the power used for doing work came from horses, 15% from men, and 6% from engines. In 1950 only 3% came from horses, 3% from men, and 94% from engines and machines.

The 20th century is the age of power and has been called the beginning of the Atomic Age. New uses of power are making ever greater changes in man's way of life. Each new source of power will add to these changes.

PRAGUE (*präg* or *prāg*) (PRAHA [*prä′há*]), **CZECHOSLOVAKIA,** is the largest city of the country. It has enjoyed great power and suffered much oppression. At one time it was the capital of the ancient kingdom of Bohemia. Later it was the chief city of the German protectorate of Bohemia and Moravia. Today it is the capital of Czechoslovakia. (See CZECHOSLOVAKIA.)

Prague is in a rich agricultural area among the foothills of the mountains in central Bohemia. The city is built on both sides of the Moldau (Vltava) River. The climate of the area is mild. The Czech people made Prague their capital in about the 10th century and protected it with two castles which are still standing. During the Middle Ages, the energetic rulers of the Czech kingdom of Bohemia spread the cultural influence of the city far beyond the country's frontiers. The city grew rapidly in wealth and population. It finally outgrew its old boundaries, and spread out on both sides of the river. Prague has many exquisite buildings of Gothic and Baroque style. In Old Prague, on the right bank of the river, may still be seen the ancient market place with its picturesque town halls and the Gothic Tyn Church. The Tyn Church was the center of the Hussite movement. This movement was a protest against the Catholic church and against the great landowners of Bohemia. It was named after its first leader and martyr, John Huss (1370?–1415), a professor at the University of Prague. Although the Hussite movement was defeated, it laid the foundations for the Reformation.

The Moldau River is spanned by the ancient Charles Bridge, built of stone and adorned with numerous statues of saints and kings. The government buildings are grouped around the fortress, Hradcany Castle, ancient home of the Bohemian kings and the residence of Czechoslovakia's president today. In the center of this area is the Cathedral of St. Vitus, begun in the 10th century.

Prague is a center of finance, industry, and culture, as well as the country's transportation hub. Many of Prague's industries are highly specialized. Heavy and precision engineering

Camera Press-Pix from Publix

Many Medieval and Baroque buildings with their towers and spires give Prague the distinctive appearance of an Old World city. The former kings of Bohemia once lived in a castle built on Hradcany Hill overlooking the city.

have become especially important. Among the city's chief products are automobiles, airplanes, other transportation goods, and heavy industrial equipment, including boilers, cranes, and turbines. The food processing, chemical, and clothing industries are also important.

The Charles University, founded in 1348, is famous throughout central and eastern Europe. It was closed by the Nazis, with all other schools of higher education, during the German occupation of Czechoslovakia in World War II.

Modern History

Bohemia came under the rule of the Austrian House of Hapsburg in the 16th century and was part of the Austro-Hungarian Empire from 1867 to 1918. By the Versailles Treaty (1919) it became part of the republic of Czechoslovakia, with Prague as the capital. Following many centuries of oppression by Austria, an independent Czechoslovakia began to make great technical and cultural advancements.

This rich and democratic country, however,

The charming city of Prague spreads out along both banks of the Moldau River. Spanning the river is the Charles Bridge, built of stone in the 14th century. Numerous statues of saints and kings decorate the bridge.

Pix

formed a political and geographic obstacle to Nazi German expansion in eastern Europe. On March 15, 1939, Nazi troops marched into Prague and the country became a protectorate of Germany, but resistance to German rule became so strong that in 1941 Reinhard Heydrich, second in command of the Nazi secret police, was sent to Prague. Toward the end of the war the citizens of Prague rose against their oppressors. About 5,000 Prague citizens died before the U.S.S.R. Army finally took the city from the Germans.

Today Prague is the capital of Czechoslovakia once again. In 1948, however, the government of Czechoslovakia was taken over by the Communists. Since that time, the country has been a satellite nation of the U.S.S.R.

The population of this city is 998,493 (1961).

PRAIRIE (*prār'ē*) **DOG** is a small rodent related to the marmot. They are called "dogs" only because their danger signal sounds like the yappy bark of a tiny dog. Prairie dogs are fat little animals about 16 inches long, with tiny ears, shining black eyes, and short tails. Their bodies are covered with dull brown fur.

Although prairie dogs are found only in North

The prairie dog, about 16 inches long, is a burrowing rodent of the squirrel family.

John H. Gerard

America, there are a number of different species that live all through the West from Mexico to southern Canada. Their homes are on the plains, often in dry, desert-like places. They always live together in villages of from 40 to more than 1,000 inhabitants. In some regions, their villages are even larger. In Arizona more than 7,000 holes were found in one square mile.

Prairie dogs dig deep burrows and build a crater around the entrance to keep out the rain. From the entrance the hole runs almost straight down to a depth of about 14 feet. Then it turns into a horizontal passage along which are built nests and storerooms for winter food.

Prairie dogs take to their burrows only when danger threatens or when they want a nap. The rest of the time they are busy hunting roots and grass, or acting as sentries for the colony. If an enemy comes near, one of the sentries gives a shrill warning bark. At the sound, all the prairie dogs roaming outside their burrows freeze in their tracks. If the sentry does not bark again, they go on with their business, but if the signal is repeated, each prairie dog hurries to its burrow for safety.

Rattlesnakes and burrowing owls are sometimes found in empty holes of prairie dogs, but they do not live together. Actually, the rattlers eat the young prairie dogs and the prairie dogs pull the owls to pieces. Since prairie dogs are destructive to crops, the government has made efforts to get rid of them.

PRAXITELES (*prăk sĭt''l ēz*) was the greatest Greek sculptor of the 4th century B.C. He was the first to represent gods as graceful people, suggesting their perfect beauty rather than their power. His easy poses and delicate modeling of marble surfaces influenced later Greek sculptors.

The only existing statue known to be his work was found in 1877. It is a marble figure of Hermes and the infant Dionysus. Hermes is a strong, graceful young man. He stands in an easy, lounging position. In one arm, resting on a tree trunk, he holds Dionysus. The other arm has been broken, but it once held a bunch of grapes, for which the child is reaching.

Many of Praxiteles' works are mentioned

Courtesy, the Vatican Museum and Galleries

A copy of Praxiteles' Aphrodite shows the graceful style of his statues of Greek gods and goddesses.

with admiration by ancient writers, but copies of only a few have been found. The most famous is the Aphrodite he made for Cnidus, a Roman copy of which is in the Vatican. Another is the "Capitoline Faun," about which Nathaniel Hawthorne wrote in his *The Marble Faun*. A third is the Apollo Sauroctonus, a statue of a boy leaning against a tree, about to kill a lizard with an arrow.

PREHISTORIC (*prē'is tôr'ĭk*) **ANIMALS** are creatures that lived in the geologic past. They swam in the seas and roamed the Earth long before history was recorded. Their existence is known through fossil remains found in rocks. Sometimes the remains are whole skeletons. Most often they are merely fragments, such as a piece of shell or bone. Even the tiniest bits, however, enable scientists to supply much information about ancient life. They have reconstructed animals so that a great deal is known of how they looked and how they lived.

Excellent examples of these reconstructions are on display in museums. (See FOSSIL; GEOLOGY.)

The first animals appeared in Precambrian times, more than 2 billion years ago. They were primitive, wormlike creatures. During the millions of years that followed, many other, more advanced, animals evolved. They included huge mollusks, armored fish, giant amphibians and reptiles, and lastly, mammals, including man. (See EVOLUTION; MAN.)

PREPOSITION (*prĕp'ŭ zĭsh'ŭn*), in grammar, is one of the parts of speech. It is small but plays an important part in the expression of ideas. *Preposition* means "that which is set before." Thus, prepositions stand before or introduce phrases which modify (describe or limit) other words in the sentence.

A thousand years ago English had only a few prepositions. Relationships between words were then more often shown by endings attached to the words themselves. As these endings gradually were lost from the language, the use of prepositions increased. In English today one still says "The man's hat," in which an ending to the word *man* is added to show that the hat is his. But one can also say, "The hat of the man," and express the same relationship by means of a prepositional phrase. In the phrase "of the man" *of* is the preposition, *the* is an article, and *man* is the noun introduced by the preposition.

Prepositions are used only to introduce prepositional phrases. These phrases are used like adjectives and adverbs. That is, they are used to modify nouns and verbs. Generally the prepositional phrase follows the word it modifies. Here are some examples of prepositional phrases used as adjectives:

The top *of the table* was clean.

Books *by Rudyard Kipling* are popular.

Here are some examples of prepositional phrases used as adverbs:

The boy fell *off the roof.*

Some coins were found *under the carpet.* Adverbial prepositional phrases are sometimes used at the beginning of sentences to provide a pleasing change in the usual word order. For example: "*From the window* I watched the sunset." "*Below the waterfalls* was a calm pool."

In the examples given so far all the prepositions have been single words. There are also compound prepositions made up of two or three words which have the effect of a single preposition. Some of these compounds are in spite of, because of, on account of, in place of, instead of, according to. You may say, "I stayed home *because of* the crowds," "*On account of* my brother's illness I could not attend the party."

A number of prepositions are used with exact meanings. Here are some pairs of prepositions which sometimes cause confusion:

In, into: In signifies the place where something is; *into* signifies motion toward a place. We say, "The children are *in* their rooms," when we mean that they are already there. But we say, "The children went *into their rooms*," to show the motion toward a place.

Between, among: Between is used in referring to two persons or things; *among* is used for more than two. We say, "I could not choose *between* the two books." "This secret was shared *among* their many friends."

With, from: One parts *with* an object, but parts *from* a person. For example, "I could not bear to part *with* my mother's watch." "How can a mother part *from* her children?"

With, to: We agree *with* a person, but we agree *to* a suggestion. Thus, "I agree completely *with* your ideas." "They agreed *to* the conditions he demanded."

From, than: Than is sometimes incorrectly used after *different* in making a comparison. The accepted phrase is *different from. Than* is not a preposition but a conjunction. We should say, "This chair is different *from* that." "He played a different part *from* that of former years."

One form to avoid is *repeating* the preposition. For example: "The hunter could not remember the name of the store *from* which he had bought the gun *from*."

PRESBYTERIANS (*prĕz' bŭ tĭr' ē ŭnz*) are the members of the Presbyterian family of Protestant churches. Presbyterian actually refers to the form of church government. The form of the Presbyterian church is "representative government" in which the people elect representatives to rule for them. Because the men who were chosen as representatives were usually the older and more experienced men, they were called "elders." The Greek word for elder is "presbuteros." Since the "u" is like the English "y," the church governed by elders is known as Presbyterian.

At the time that Martin Luther was beginning religious reforms in Germany, John Calvin was doing the same work in Switzerland. Calvin's *Institutes* set forth not only his religious beliefs but also a plan of church organization under the leadership of presbyters or elders. His ideas were widely adopted all over Europe, but his influence was most felt in France, Scotland, Holland, and Switzerland.

The church in France grew so powerful that its members (the French Huguenots) were persecuted and left the country in large numbers. Many of them migrated to Holland where the church was already established. Some of the original features of Presbyterianism were changed, and the new organization became known as the Dutch Reformed Church.

Introduced by John Knox into Scotland, Presbyterianism became the recognized state church of that country. Although it was never strongly established in England, a council named by the British Parliament and known as the Westminster Assembly worked out in 1643 the *Westminster Confession*, the *Larger and Shorter Catechisms*, the *Form of Government*, and the *Directory for Worship*. Despite the separation of the original group into several sects, these four books remain the official standards of the church.

By the 17th century the Huguenots had brought Presbyterianism to North America. Encouraged by the addition of immigrants from Scotland and Ireland, the church was formally organized at Philadelphia in 1706. Presbyterians took a leading part in the struggle for independence. Their interest in education led them to establish many schools and colleges. Of these Princeton University is best known.

Many divisions have occurred within the church. At the present time there are ten different groups in the United States. The largest, called the United Presbyterian Church in the U.S.A., has more than 3,200,000 members in more than 9,000 churches.

Presbyterians observe only two sacraments: baptism and the Lord's Supper, or communion. Their services consist of Scripture reading, prayer, singing, and preaching. The pastors are teaching elders who preach and look after the spiritual welfare of the congregation. The ruling elders have the supervision of all the spiritual life of the church. The Board of Deacons aids the poor and unfortunate. All financial affairs are in the care of a Board of Trustees. Like the ruling elders and the deacons they are elected from and by the congregation.

The organization of the three largest divisions in the United States follows this plan. The presbytery is the governing agency through which the individual churches of a district are united, supervised, and controlled. Each local church sends as its representatives its pastor and one ruling elder. The lines which limit a presbytery are county or city boundaries.

The synod is composed of delegates from the various presbyteries. Except in small or lightly populated states, the synod follows state lines so there are 33 synods in the United States.

The national governing body, which meets once a year, is known as the General Assembly. It is the body which has supreme authority. It is made up of commissioners, ministers, and elders elected by the presbyteries. The Assembly surveys and reviews the plans, progress, and finances of the three boards and the commission which carry on the work of the church: Board of National Missions, Board of Christian Education, Board of Pensions, and Commission on Ecumenical Mission and Relations.

PRESCOTT (*prĕs′kŭt*), **WILLIAM HICKLING** (*hik′ling*) (1796–1859), was one of the first important U.S. historians to be recognized throughout the world for his work. He is remembered chiefly for his books on Spanish history.

Born in Salem, Massachusetts, the son of a lawyer, Prescott was graduated from Harvard in 1814. While in college he had become blind in one eye through an accident. A number of

years were spent in travel and, by means of a secretary, in intensive study. In 1829 he began to write the *History of the Reign of Ferdinand and Isabella the Catholic.* After eight laborious years the book appeared and was instantly popular. Prescott had breathed life and interest into facts hitherto dry and dull. The account of early Spanish activity in America was continued in his next book, the *History of the Conquest of Mexico.* This was followed, four years later, by the *History of the Conquest of Peru.* Five years later two volumes of the *History of the Reign of Philip the Second* were published. The historian died before completing this fourth history.

Prescott was a careful worker and spared neither money nor time on his histories. His accounts of Spanish America were written, however, before present-day archaeological discoveries. They are not strictly accurate in the light of modern knowledge.

PRESIDENT (*prĕz′ŭd ŭnt*) is the head of a club or business organization and in many countries is the head of government. In some countries, such as Italy, the U.S.S.R., or West Germany, the president has little power. He is the man who represents the state at official and ceremonial affairs and signs important official papers. In countries where the president is head of the government in name only, the real power lies with a prime minister or a premier.

The word *president* came to America in colonial days. In the English colonial system, the president was the officer who presided over the provincial council. The same term was given to the presiding officer in the Continental Congresses, 1774–1781, and in the Congress created by the Articles of Confederation, 1781–1789. In the confederation the president had few powers.

Under the United States Constitution the president has become the most powerful elected official in the world. He is the real head of the country. More than any other individual, he is responsible for deciding what the country's domestic and foreign policy shall be. He proposes new laws for Congress to pass and vetoes those he does not like. He is the commander in chief of all the armed forces. He sees that the laws of Congress are faithfully carried out. He appoints thousands of executive and judicial officials, including the justices of the Supreme Court. Since the president, with his vice-president, is the only national officer elected on a nationwide basis, he is the spokesman for the whole country. (See CONSTITUTION OF THE UNITED STATES.)

The Constitution sets forth only a few rules about who can become president. To be eligible for election as president, a person must be a natural-born citizen, at least 35 years old, and for 14 years a resident within the United States. No person can become president who has been convicted of a major crime.

The president's term of office is four years. At first, the Constitution did not limit the number of times a president might be re-elected. Both George Washington and Thomas Jefferson refused to be candidates for third terms. This two-term tradition lasted for more than a century. It was broken when Franklin D. Roosevelt was elected to third and fourth terms. The Constitution was amended in 1951 to hold future presidents to a limit of two elected terms. This Twenty-second Amendment also provides that if a person has served more than two years of a predecessor's term, he cannot be elected more than once.

The Constitution does not provide that the president shall be chosen by popular vote but by the votes of electors. The electors are chosen by the voters within each state. In almost every election, however, the popular vote has decided presidential elections. This has come about because the electors in the various states usually promise in advance to vote for the candidate nominated by their political party. (See ELECTORAL COLLEGE.)

If the president dies, resigns, or is removed from office, the vice-president becomes president. The Twenty-fifth Amendment (1967) provides that if the president is unable to perform his duties, the vice-president shall become "acting president" until the president recovers. The amendment also provides that, when the office of vice-president becomes vacant, the president, with the approval of Congress, shall nominate

a vice-president. (See VICE-PRESIDENT.)

The Constitution gives Congress the job of deciding on the line of succession after the vice-president. If both the offices of president and vice-president are vacant at the same time, the 1947 Presidential Succession Act provides that the speaker of the House of Representatives and then the acting president of the Senate shall be next in line for the presidency. Following them, succession falls to cabinet members in this order: secretary of state, secretary of the treasury, secretary of defense, attorney general, postmaster general, secretary of the interior, secretary of agriculture, secretary of commerce, and secretary of labor. The 1947 succession law has not been amended to include the cabinet posts created since then. In actual fact, no official beyond the vice-president has ever succeeded to the presidency.

The voters cast their ballots for presidential electors in November every fourth year. The electors then meet at their state capitals in mid-December to cast the electoral votes officially. The president takes the oath of office at noon on the following January 20 at inaugural ceremonies in Washington, D.C. When a president dies, however, the vice-president takes the oath immediately and privately. Following his inauguration, the president takes up residence in the White House. The Constitution gives Congress the power to set the president's salary; but no president's salary may be raised or lowered during his term of office. The president receives $200,000 yearly, subject to taxes. An additional $50,000 expense account is tax-free. Upon leaving office, he is entitled to an allowance of $25,000 a year, clerical help, office space, and free mailing privileges. Widows of former presidents are entitled to a pension of $10,000 yearly.

Limits on Presidential Powers

There are certain constitutional and political checks on the president's authority. Although he may recommend legislation to Congress, either house may refuse to pass it. Congress can also refuse to appropriate the money needed to carry out a presidential program. If the president dislikes a measure passed by Congress, he may veto it. Congress, however, can override a veto if both houses pass the bill again by at least a two-thirds majority. (See VETO.)

The Senate has some control over the president in other ways. The president has the power to make appointments, but the Senate can reject them. The president has the power to make treaties, but they do not go into effect until they are approved by at least two-thirds of the Senate.

The House of Representatives has the power to impeach the president for treason, bribery, or other serious offenses. He may then be removed from office by a two-thirds vote of the Senate sitting as a court, with the House prosecuting the charges. Only once has a chief executive been put on trial—in the case of the impeachment of President Andrew Johnson in 1868, when only one vote was lacking to find him guilty. (See IMPEACHMENT; JOHNSON, ANDREW.)

The voters also have a check on the president. When he runs for re-election, the people have a chance to express their approval or disapproval of his policies.

Growth of Presidential Powers

Events of recent years have placed more power in the hands of the president. When Franklin D. Roosevelt took office in 1933, the country was in the worst depression crisis in its history. Congress acted swiftly to give him great powers to deal with the emergency. He was given powers to create new government agencies and to spend huge sums of money. (See ROOSEVELT, FRANKLIN DELANO.)

Presidential authority always increases in wartime, and World War II was no exception. After the United States declared war in December 1941, the president became the commander in chief of the greatest army, navy, and air force the world had ever known. He was also chief of a great home-front effort to raise the money, to forge the weapons, and to unite the home front for total war.

Even before the end of the war in 1945, the president of the United States had become a leader of the countries and peoples fighting the Axis powers. He played a leading part in forming the United Nations. After victory, when the world was divided by the cold war, the United States became the leader of the free world resisting Communist expansion. Because of this new role, the president has been one of the leaders in shaping the economic, military, and political policies of the nations working for a peaceful world.

The office of president has grown as the United States has grown; but, at the same time, enough controls have been retained to keep the president from becoming a dictator. The depression in the 1930's led many countries to turn to dictatorships to solve their problems. Other democracies fell because of the strain of fighting World War II, and still others were unable to handle the many great problems of the 1950's and 1960's. The power and influence of the United States presidency have grown in the 20th century and have enabled the United States government to act quickly and decisively in time of emergency without endangering democratic freedom.

PRIBILOF (*prĭb'ŭ lôf*) **ISLANDS, BERING SEA,** are four small islands off the southwest coast of Alaska. They have a total area of about 62 square miles. To these tiny islands in the Bering Sea, 85 percent of all the fur seals in the world come each spring to breed and rear their young.

The islands are named Saint Paul, Saint George, Otter, and Walrus. They are volcanic islands, covered with a thin, rocky soil and very little vegetation. Only grasses, small willow trees, and a few shrubs are found. The cool, moist climate is ideal for developing good, thick pelts on fur-bearing animals. The islands were discovered in 1786 by Gerasim Pribilof, a Russian navigator. When the United States bought Alaska in 1867, it also received the Pribilof Islands.

Seal hunters reduced the millions of fur seals to less than 200,000, and people feared that all the seals might be killed. In 1911 the North Pacific Sealing Convention reached an agreement signed by the United States, Great Britain, Russia, and Japan to limit the number killed. The seal herd has grown until now there are more than four million. The islands are inhabited by a few government agents and about 600 Aleuts who work for the sealing ships during the hunting season. In winter they trap foxes. Otter and Walrus Islands have no permanent inhabitants.

PRICE (*prīs*) is what a person pays to get something that he needs or wants. It is usually an amount of money but can also be goods of equal worth.

Many prices are given special names. The price of labor is called *wages* or *salaries*. The price for the use of a house is called *rent*. The number of francs a dollar will buy is called the *rate of exchange*. The price of money is called *interest*.

A single issue of a daily newspaper will show the prices paid for many kinds of things. Advertisements show prices such as $1.79 or 98 cents. Shoppers then know how much they will have to pay for each item. The financial page has long columns of figures showing the prices of stocks and bonds. The "help wanted" ads show how much is offered for various kinds of labor, the "for rent" ads how much it costs to rent various kinds of houses.

Every time anyone anywhere buys or sells anything for money, a price has been set. Many people have a part in the price-making of one article. First of all, there are the producers of raw materials, for example, the farmer who is buying feed or machinery and selling milk, corn, or cattle. Then there are the dairies, corn flakes manufacturers, or meat packers who process raw materials; next, the wholesalers, the grocers, and the bankers. There are the factory owners hiring thousands of workers and the housewives shopping in the stores. All of these people help to make prices.

Through changes in prices grocers know what goods and how much of each to place on the shelves. Prices explain in part why some people have higher incomes than others. (An income is the price of the service a person sells.) Motion picture stars make a great deal of money because millions of people pay to see them perform. The larger the crowds, the higher the income of the movie star. The incomes and profits of business firms also depend for the most part on their producing something which the public is willing to pay for.

Prices help guide businessmen in deciding what, when, where, and how much to produce. Prices also show them which customers to sell to, what laborers to hire, and how much to pay them. When prices rise on the things they sell, they buy more raw materials, hire more workers, raise wages, build new factories and equipment, and expand production. Business booms. When prices fall, workers are laid off, there is less money in the pay envelope, less is made, less is shipped, less is sold. If prices fall and these things happen to a large number of firms and industries at the same time, people begin to speak of a *slump* or a *depression*.

When prices go up the prices of the things a person consumes usually rise faster than the person's income. It is then said that the *cost of living* has gone up. The high cost of living is part of a bigger problem known as *inflation*. Every big war has brought with it different amounts of inflation. So many and so great are the evils of great inflation that nations become weak and governments fall if price inflation is not kept under control. That is why many nations have price controls during periods of war and national emergency.

There are also many special price problems. The farm problem is one of farm prices going down while the prices of the things farmers buy remain high. Wheat prices at the farm may be low and bread prices high. Then in the United States Congress is asked for laws to put the prices of the things the farmers sell on a *parity* with the prices of the things they buy.

Labor unions feel their wages are too low. The railroads feel that passenger and freight rates are too low. The telephone companies want to raise the price of telephone calls, and utilities to get more for gas and electricity. A manufacturing concern may feel that the prices at which producers abroad can make things for home consumers are too low. They, therefore, get the government to keep out the cheaper foreign product. It does this by putting high tax (a tariff) on foreign goods. (See TARIFF.) This, of course, lets producers in the home country get higher prices for the things made there. Sometimes producers get together with others in the same business in their own and in other countries to raise the price of their product. They set a monopoly price. However, most prices are determined by rival buyers and sellers in competitive markets.

PRIESTLEY (*prēst'lē*), **JOSEPH** (1733–1804), was a pioneer of experimental chemistry who discovered several gases. He was also a minister, a fine scholar, a writer of political pamphlets, and an inventor.

Born in England, at Fieldhead, Yorkshire, Priestley was educated privately. At the Nonconformist Academy of Daventry, he learned a number of ancient and modern languages. In 1755 he began preaching and spent the next few years teaching and acting as a minister. While in charge of Mill Hill Chapel, Leeds, he wrote a *History of Electricity*. He also invented the pneumatic trough which made it possible to collect and experiment with gases. At the same time he wrote pamphlets supporting the cause of the American Colonies.

In 1772, Priestley became librarian and companion to Lord Shelburne who gave him free time for his scientific experiments. Two years later he discovered oxygen. Although he knew what this gas was like and that it was needed for breathing and burning, he did not know what the gas was. Antoine Lavoisier, to whom Priestley described his experiment, called it oxygen and gave the discovery its true importance. (See LAVOISIER, ANTOINE LAURENT; OXYGEN.)

Among other gases, Priestley discovered sulfur dioxide and hydrochloric acid gas. In 1780 he left Shelburne and became a minister at Birmingham. For his defense of the French Revolution, the French made him a citizen. He became unpopular for his support of the United States and France, however, and in 1791 his chapel, his house, and all his notes were destroyed by an angry mob. Three years later he emigrated to the United States and spent the last ten years of his life at Northumberland, Pennsylvania.

PRIMROSE (*prĭm'rōz'*) is any plant of the genus *Primula*, a group of low-growing, perennial plants of the primrose family. About 450 species are known, mostly natives of central Asia, but some of Europe and North America.

Primroses, including species called cowslip and oxlip, have been grown in Europe for centuries. The dried leaves are sometimes used in medicines. Through the years new species, hybrids, and varieties have been grown. Their many-colored, five-parted flowers have made them springtime favorites in gardens in many countries. The flowers, white, cream, yellow, orange, pink, red, violet, and blue, many with centers of different tint grow singly or in clusters. Several species, raised in greenhouses, are sold as potted plants. The leaves of a few, such as the one called poison primrose, irritate the skin of some persons. Primroses are grown from seed. Large plants may be divided.

A few plants are called primroses although they are not of the same family. They include yellow-flowered Arabian-primroses; cape-primroses, relatives of African violets, and evening-primroses. The evening primroses are cultivated forms of native North American plants.

The primrose is a favorite spring flower.

J. Horace McFarland Company

PRINCE (*prĭns*) **EDWARD** (*ĕd'wĕrd*) **ISLAND** (*ī'lănd*), **CANADA,** a Canadian province, is just off the east coast of Canada in the southern part of the Gulf of St. Lawrence. It is the smallest of the ten Canadian provinces in both size and population. The island is crescent shaped, 140 miles long, and from 4 to 40 miles wide. Its area of 2,184 square miles makes it just one-tenth the size of the next smallest province, Nova Scotia, and about the size of Delaware, second smallest state of the United States. Northumberland Strait separates Prince Edward Island from Nova Scotia and New Brunswick on the mainland of Canada.

Land and Climate

The 1,100-mile coastline of Prince Edward Island is broken by many bays and inlets. In two places bays and rivers almost cut through the island. The north coast has sandy beaches that rise gently from the water to a range of low sand dunes. The southern coastline is more rugged. There many low cliffs of red sandstone face the Northumberland Strait. The lowland surface of the island is broken by hills, although none of them rises as high as 500 feet. The underlying rock is mainly red sandstone. The soil is deep reddish in color, almost free of stones, fertile, and easily cultivated.

The climate of Prince Edward Island is mild. The warming waters around it keep the winters from being too cold and the summers from being too hot. Furthermore the island is out of the path of the cold winter winds. Average temperatures on a January day rise to about 26 degrees Fahrenheit and fall to an average low of 10 degrees at night. In July these averages are 73 degrees for the day and 58 degrees for the night. There are about 40 inches of rain a year. Heavy dews are common during the summer and autumn months.

The People and Their Work

Although its total population is small, Prince Edward Island is the most thickly settled part of Canada. There is an average of 49.7 people to each square mile. About one-third of the people live on farms, and nearly three-quarters are rural dwellers. Over 95 percent are Ca-

nadian born and descendants of early settlers. About 82 percent of the people are British in origin, and 16 percent are French. In 1961 there were 348 Micmac Indians living on one reserve.

Prince Edward Island has been called the "Garden of the Gulf." This is because almost the whole province is under cultivation. An ideal climate, a long growing season, and a rich red soil combine to produce very high crop yields. The leading farm product is seed potatoes, and about three-quarters of the acreage is used for certified seed potatoes. Table potatoes are of high quality and are easily sold. Other agricultural products which are exported include butter and cheese, bacon, beef, poultry, turnips, and fruits, especially strawberries and blueberries. Prince Edward Island bacon is as famous as its seed potatoes. Pigs also are exported for breeding purposes. Poultry raising is very important. It is estimated that 45 percent of all chicken canned in Canada is prepared on the island.

At one time the breeding and raising of silver and platinum foxes were important to the

FACTS ABOUT PRINCE EDWARD ISLAND

TOTAL AREA: 2,184 square miles; 0.1 percent of all of Canada.
POPULATION: 108,535 (1966); 37 percent urban, 63 percent rural.
CAPITAL: Charlottetown.
RIVERS: Hillsborough, North.
BAYS: Cascumpeque, Malpeque, Cardigan, Hillsborough, Egmont, Bedeque.
NATIONAL PARKS: Prince Edward Island (4,480 acres), Fort Amherst Historic Park (222 acres).
NATIONAL BACKGROUNDS: British 82 percent; French 16 percent.
UNIVERSITIES AND COLLEGES: Prince of Wales College and St. Dunstan's University, both at Charlottetown.
CHIEF CITIES: Charlottetown, Summerside, Montague, Souris.
VOTING AGE FOR PROVINCIAL ELECTIONS: 21.
PROVINCIAL HOLIDAYS: Boxing Day (December 26).
CHIEF DATES:
    1534—Discovered by Jacques Cartier.
    1719—First French colony founded.
    1745—Taken by the British.
    1748—Restored to the French.
    1763—Ceded to Britain as part of Nova Scotia.
    1769—Separated from Nova Scotia as independent colony.
    1798—Named Prince Edward Island.
    1851—Granted self-government.
    1873—Became province of Canada.

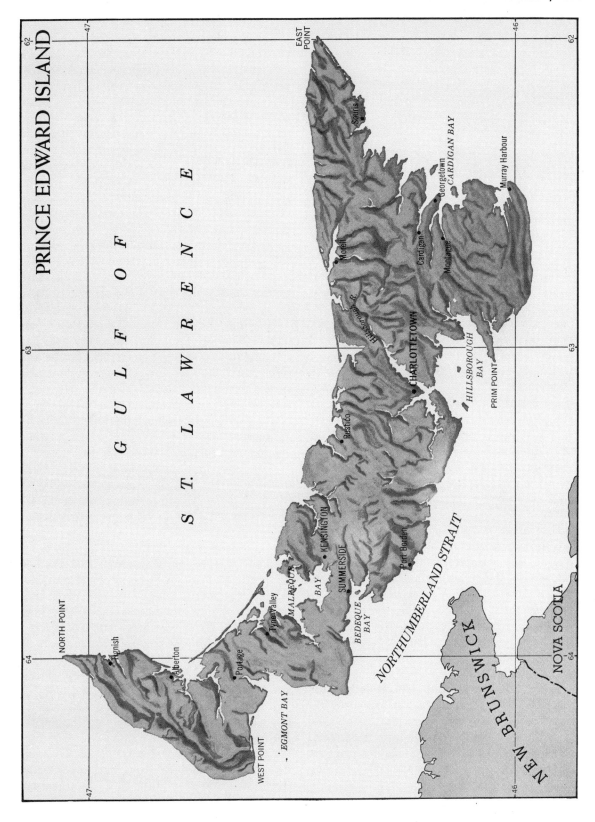

PRINCE EDWARD ISLAND

GULF OF

ST. LAWRENCE

EAST POINT

Souris

CARDIGAN BAY

Georgetown

Murray Harbour

Morell

Cardigan

Montague

Hillsborough R.

CHARLOTTETOWN

HILLSBOROUGH BAY

PRIM POINT

Rustico

KENSINGTON

Port Borden

SUMMERSIDE

MALPEQUE BAY

NORTHUMBERLAND STRAIT

Tyne Valley

BEDEQUE BAY

NORTH POINT

Tignish

Alberton

Portage

EGMONT BAY

WEST POINT

NEW BRUNSWICK

NOVA SCOTIA

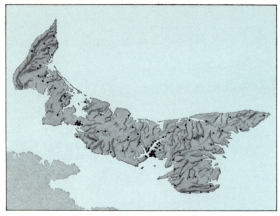

Where the people live on Prince Edward Island. Each dot equals 1,000 persons.

island. Fox farming as an industry was first started on Prince Edward Island by Charles Dalton and Robert Oulton. But as fur styles changed, fox farms have almost disappeared from the island.

The fisheries are next in importance as a source of wealth and income to the province. Lobsters are by far the most valuable product of the fisheries. Cod, herring, and mackerel are caught on nearby fishing banks in the Gulf of St. Lawrence. Oysters, clams, and smelts are taken from inshore waters. The oysters from Malpeque Bay are famous for their flavor and quality. By gathering Irish moss, which is really a seaweed, fishermen add to their income.

The forests of the island once were important in the lumbering industry of the New World. But when it became known that the soil was so well suited for agriculture, most of the trees were removed, often by burning. Today only about one-third of the whole province is forested. These forests are mostly in the form of woodlots, found at the back of farms. Trees cut are mainly exported for use as pit props in mines and for pulp.

There is no heavy industry on Prince Edward Island. The processing of food from the farms and fisheries is almost the only manufacturing. Blankets are made from the wool of native sheep. About half the manufacturing industry is centered in the capital city of Charlottetown.

Transportation

The island is connected with the mainland at two points. From Port Borden the powerful ice breaking ferry *Abegweit* carries trains, trucks, and automobiles as well as passengers to Cape Tormentine, New Brunswick. When traffic is too heavy a smaller steamer also runs on the same route. Two boats carry trucks, automobiles, and passengers from Wood Island to Caribou Island, Nova Scotia, during spring, summer, and fall months. Steamers call at such ports as Charlottetown, Summerside, Georgetown, and Souris to carry away heavy cargoes of farm produce. Some of them bring in fertilizer for island farms. A regular summer and autumn steamer service connects Charlottetown with St. John's, Newfoundland. Farm produce makes up most of the cargoes of these boats too.

Maritime Central Airways, with headquarters in Charlottetown, flies regularly between the province and other parts of Canada and the United States. This airways system also carries perishable goods to markets. Strawberries are sometimes flown from Charlottetown to points as far away as Boston, Massachusetts.

Transportation services within the province are by the Canadian National Railways and a bus system. Modern trucking services carry many goods to various parts of the province. Many of the roads are paved so that motor vehicles can move easily from place to place.

Cities

Charlottetown, on Hillsborough Bay along the southeast coast, is the capital and only city in the province. Its harbor is closed to shipping for only a few weeks in early spring. Many of the streets are lined with shade trees, and there are interesting public squares and attractive public buildings. There are no slums. These features give the city a quiet and restful atmosphere. The population is 18,427 (1966).

Summerside (1966 population, 10,042) is the second community in size. It is located at the head of Bedeque Bay and has a good harbor. Summerside was the center of the province's silver fox industry, and the Canadian Fox Breeders Association still has its headquarters

PRINCE EDWARD ISLAND

LEADING INDUSTRIES AND PRODUCTS

AGRICULTURE: Potatoes, livestock, dairy products.
CONSTRUCTION: Buildings, engineering projects.
MANUFACTURING: Food and beverages.
FISHERIES: Lobster, smelt, oyster.

KEY TO SYMBOLS

FURS

POTATOES

SHEEP

POULTRY

SHIPPING

GENERAL FARMING

LOBSTERS

FISHING

CATTLE

FRUIT

DAIRYING

OYSTERS

FISH CANNING

VEGETABLES

HOGS

Souris

Georgetown

Montague

Murray Harbour

MORELL R.

MONTAGUE R.

HILLSBOROUGH R.

CHARLOTTETOWN

Port Borden

DUNK RIVER

Summerside

MALPEQUE BAY

Tignish

NEWFOUNDLAND

GULF OF ST. LAWRENCE

NEW BRUNSWICK

NOVA SCOTIA

ATLANTIC OCEAN

MAINE

Photos, Courtesy National Film Board

Left: Prince Edward Island pioneered the fox-farming industry. Above: Potatoes are an important crop on the island.

there. Just outside the town is a large Royal Canadian Air Force Training School.

Recreation

Prince Edward Island is well known as a holiday resort. The sandy beaches, mild climate, and warm waters of the Gulf of St. Lawrence are ideal for swimming. The many easy-to-reach streams are well stocked with fish. At Charlottetown there is a race track for harness racing.

The province has several historic sites. The best known of these is "Green Gables," made famous by Lucy Maud Montgomery, who wrote about it in her books, *Anne of Green Gables, Anne of the Island,* and *Anne of Avonlea.* A large part of the north shore has been made into a National Park. Another place of interest is the Confederation Chamber in the Legislative Building at Charlottetown.

Government

Like all other Canadian provinces Prince Edward Island is governed according to the terms of the British North America Act. The Legislative Assembly has 30 members elected for not more than five years. Half of them are Assemblymen who are chosen on the basis of universal adult suffrage. The other half, called

Councillors, are elected by property holders.

Under the terms of Confederation the province has four representatives in the Senate of Canada. At present four members are elected to the House of Commons at Ottawa.

Education

The school system is administered by a Minister of Education who is a member of the provincial government. Since the province is largely rural, most of the schools are of one or two rooms. Charlottetown and Summerside, however, have some large and modern buildings. The cost of building and maintaining schools is paid by the local community, but the provincial government helps to pay teachers' salaries. Rural and village schools give eight grades of elementary work and two grades of high school. In Charlottetown and Summerside, pupils study to the end of senior high school.

Prince of Wales College and St. Dunstan's University, both at Charlottetown, are the two centers of higher learning. Prince of Wales College offers a two-year college course and has the teacher training school of the province. It is run by the provincial government. St. Dunstan's University gives degrees in arts, science, and commerce. It is directed by the

Roman Catholic church. Charlottetown also has a Provincial Vocational School and a Dominion Agricultural Experimental Station.

The province has a good library service. It was started in 1933 by the Carnegie Corporation of New York, but is now run by the provincial government. Library headquarters are at Prince of Wales College, and there are 24 branches throughout the province.

History

Micmac Indians were the first people to live on Prince Edward Island. Their name for it was *Abegweit*, which means the "Home Cradled on the Waves." The first European to see the island was Jacques Cartier, who discovered it in 1534. Years later Samuel de Champlain named it Ile St. Jean. The French held claim to it, but did not settle there until after 1713, when Acadia was ceded to England.

The whole of what was called New France, including Ile St. Jean, became a British possession after the French and Indian War in 1763. The island was then made a part of Nova Scotia, but in 1769 it became a separate colony. In 1798 it was named after Prince Edward, the Duke of Kent, who was the father of Queen Victoria.

For over 100 years two political problems faced the people of the island. In 1767 all the

Paul's Photos

Prince Edward Island is level and low and well adapted to farming. It is often called the "Garden of the Gulf."

land of the colony was given to landlords in Britain. Tenants on estates had to work for these landlords, not for themselves. The second problem was that of gaining democratic self-government. This was won in 1851. The problem of absentee landlords was settled in 1867 when the Dominion of Canada was formed.

The first step toward Confederation was taken in 1864. Then delegates from all the British North American colonies met at Charlottetown to consider a plan of union. This meeting led to the Confederation of four Canadian colonies in 1867. This is why Charlottetown is called the "Cradle of Confederation." Prince Edward Island decided not to join at that time because its people did not like the terms of union. Soon, however, better terms

Inshore fishing: Taking oysters off the ocean bottom with long-handled tongs.

Courtesy Canadian Consulate General of Chicago, National Film Board photo

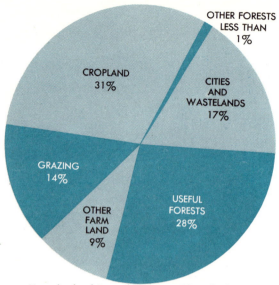

How the land is used in Prince Edward Island.

were offered and on July 1, 1873, Prince Edward Island became a part of the Canadian Dominion.

Famous People

Probably the best-known native of Prince Edward Island is Lucy Maud Montgomery, author of the famous "Anne" books. Sir Joseph Pope, born at Charlottetown, was the son of one of the "Fathers of Confederation." For many years he played a leading part in Ca-

How the people of Prince Edward Island make a living.

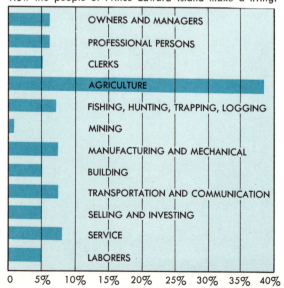

nadian public life. Cyrus MacMillan was well known as a professor of English literature at McGill University in Montreal; in his later years he was a member of the Canadian Cabinet. Sir William MacDonald, who gave large sums of money to McGill University, was born in Charlottetown.

The population of Prince Edward Island is 108,535 (1966).

PRINTING (*prĭnt'ĭng*) is reproduction by impression. Few knew how to read in the 5th century when the first printing was done by the Chinese and Japanese. At that time and for hundreds of years afterward books were so scarce and so hard to make that few people could read, or had books from which to learn.

The first printers used blocks of wood as the printing forms. Pictures were carved into their faces. The blocks were then inked and printed on the rude presses of the day. Later, words were added to the pictures, but these too had to be carefully carved into the wood. The printers of that time were really artists and woodcarvers rather than printers as they are known now. Each page of a book had to be cut painstakingly by hand from a block of wood or metal. Thus, the printing of a book of any size was a long and expensive process.

As a result few books were produced. These were owned by the few wealthy people who could pay the printer for the many hours spent in cutting each letter of the book into the wooden blocks. A method of shortening the long labor of hand carving each page was needed but it was nearly a thousand years before any real change was made in the method used to reproduce the written word. Many men throughout Europe were at work on the problem. Johann Gutenberg, a German printer living in Mainz, is generally believed to be the man who first solved the problem. Gutenberg hit upon the idea of using movable metal type. The first book printed by this method was the so-called Gutenberg Bible, published in 1456. (See BIBLE; GUTENBERG, JOHANN.)

Gutenberg's type was cast in a mold, each letter separately. When taken out of the mold, the type could be easily assembled, or "set" in words, lines, and pages. Once set and printed, the pages were broken up, and the letters reset and used again to print other pages. This system is still in use today, though later inventors have greatly speeded up the ways in which the type is cast and set. In modern print shops the type is usually set by machines of several different kinds, operated in much the same fashion as a typewriter. The basic method is still that invented by Gutenberg. (See TYPESETTING MACHINE.)

Gutenberg's method was adopted throughout Europe. In Germany, printing spread from Mainz along the Rhine River to other towns. In Italy, Aldus Manutius was one of the famous early printers. In England, William Caxton printed some of the most famous of English books. Printers cut their own molds for the type so that their printing was like different kinds of handwriting. One could easily tell by looking at the book the name of the printer who had made it. After that day many hundreds of *type faces* were cut. Each is different but in many cases it is so similar to other faces that only an expert typographer can detect the difference.

Printing came to the Americas with the Spaniards, who built the first press in North America at Mexico City in 1539. Just 100 years later a press was set up in Cambridge, Massachusetts.

This was the forerunner of the many colonial presses which later spread the fiery speeches of the patriots urging independence from England. Among the most famous of the early American printers was Benjamin Franklin. He achieved fame as a statesman, author, and inventor but signed his will simply "B. Franklin, printer."

The first printing press was a crude wooden affair called the screw press. The wooden blocks or forms were inked and laid on the bed of the press and covered with the sheet of paper to be printed. The platen, a flat wooden surface, was then screwed down onto the paper, pressing it firmly against the inked form underneath. A blanket of cloth or some other soft material was generally placed between the platen and the sheet so that the impression would not be too heavy and the form would not punch through the paper. After each sheet was printed, the platen had to be raised, the form re-inked, and another sheet placed in position for printing. The printing was almost as slow and laborious a task as the cutting of the wooden blocks which composed the form.

As the movable type of Gutenberg came into general use books were more in demand. The screw press proved too slow to keep pace with the needs of the printers, and various improvements were invented to speed up the press. In

Left: The cylinder (at right) grips a sheet of paper. As the cylinder turns, the paper is carried around it. At the same time the bed of the press (at left) which contains the type moves to and fro, and the paper is printed. Right: After it is printed the paper looks like this. Thirty-two pages are printed at the same time on one sheet.

Photos, Courtesy Patricia Lapp

about 1620 Willem Blaeu devised a means of rolling the bed of the press in and out under the platen. The Earl of Stanhope built the first cast iron press in England in 1800. A few years later the screw was done away with, and a lever used to raise and lower the heavy platen.

In England about 1815 a revolving impression cylinder took the place of the old platen and the cylinder press resulted. In the cylinder press the sheet of paper to be printed is not laid directly on the form in the bed of the press but is fed into a set of "grippers" on the impression cylinder. As their name indicates, the grippers hold the sheet in position against the outside of the cylinder. As the cylinder rolls over, the paper is pressed against the inked form. When the sheet has gone over the form and is completely printed, it is released by the grippers, and a fresh sheet is fed into position. This press was far faster than the old hand presses which it replaced. In addition it was larger and could print many more pages at a time. The cylinder press was rapidly improved, and new cylinder combinations brought forth the "perfecting" press. This was a cylinder press with two beds and two impression cylinders. The perfecting press prints both sides of the paper as a sheet goes through it.

Another development during the latter part of the 19th century was the two-color press, which prints two colors on one side of the sheet at each impression. It opened the way for economical color printing. This press was followed during recent years by the huge multicolor presses. These presses print the bright-colored pictures and advertisements in newspapers and magazines. They print as many as five colors at each impression, at high speed and with the perfect accuracy (called "register") which today's printing demands.

Make-ready of the Press

When a "form," or group of type pages, is ready to be printed, the pages are locked in a large steel frame called a chase. The chase holds them in position on the bed of the press. The pages are printed in numbers which can be divided by 4, usually 16 or 32 at a time. They must be very carefully placed in the chase so that when the sheet is printed and folded, the pages will follow each other in the correct order.

The illustration shows a layout, or imposition, for a 32 page sheet. You can make a similar one by folding an oblong sheet of paper in half four times. Start with a long edge toward you and make the first fold from right to left. After each fold turn the last fold toward you and again fold from right to left. This makes a 32 page section of a book. Hold this folded section with the long fold to your left. Now if you slit the lower right hand corner, number the pages from 1 to 32 and open the sheet, you will have the sheet layout in the illustration. There are many other layouts that may be used. This depends upon the number of pages in the form, and the kind of folding machine which is to fold the printed sheet. Before starting the press, the printer must check his form and fold the sheet just as you did to be

This shows how the pages will be placed on the printed sheet. The printing in this case yields one set of 32 pages, after the sheet is printed on both sides.

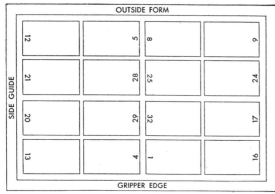

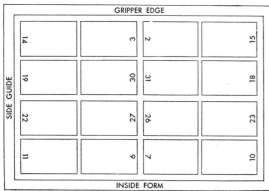

TWO 16's, SHEETWISE, PRESS-SHEET LAYOUT

sure it will read correctly.

Once the pages are correctly imposed, or placed in the chase, the pressman must see that they register properly. That is, he must adjust the pages in the form so that they have correct margins between them, and so that pages on opposite sides of the sheet are exactly back to back. Register is extremely important in printing books which have colored illustrations. Forms containing pages which print in color must be printed with a separate form for each color. The forms must be in precisely the correct position or the colored picture will be blurred and fuzzy,—"out of register" as the pressmen call it.

After the form is in register the pressman runs one or two sheets to see how the sheet is printing. On these first sheets some parts of the form print very dark with lots of ink and heavy impression. Others are much too light and do not take enough ink. Before the form is ready to run, it must be evened out so that all parts of the sheet print alike.

The illustrations must take enough ink to bring out all the details of the pictures but not so much that they are flooded with ink. In order to do this the pressman must make adjustments, either under the pages in the bed of the press, or on the impression cylinder. The pages that print too lightly may be "underlaid" by laying a sheet of paper under the page. This makes it a little higher so that it will press harder against the impression cylinder and leave more ink on the sheet. In the case of pages that print too dark, some of the packing on the impression cylinder is cut out where those pages print. The pages are not squeezed so hard, and less ink is transferred to the printed sheet.

In many cases, where thousands of copies of the form are needed, the individual pages of type and illustrations are molded and cast and plated. Plates of a metal harder than type are used to save the type from the wear of a long press run (see ELECTROTYPING). When this is done, it is sometimes possible to build underlays and overlays into the plates before they are placed on the press. The metal plate is softened with heat, and the underlays and overlays are forced into the face and the back of the plates under extreme pressure. The resulting plate is not perfectly smooth because of the make-ready that has been added to it. However, it will print a smooth even impression with very little further work when it reaches the press.

The pressman must care for countless other little details before the press is ready. The delicate mechanical feeding devices which place the sheets in position must be carefully adjusted. Similarly the corresponding device which takes the sheet from the grippers and places it in the delivery tray must be adjusted also. Inking rollers must be placed and the ink supply adjusted in the "fountain." Thus it is easily understandable that the make-ready of a complicated form may require hours and even days of preparation. This all takes place before the pressman can push the button which starts the run.

Once running, the printed sheet must be carefully watched to see that impression and color do not vary and that each sheet is of the fine quality demanded by modern books. The pressman's task is a painstakingly careful one. The modern printer must serve a long apprenticeship before he is qualified to handle the complicated presses of today.

The Rotary Press

The cylinder press was a great improvement over the older printing machines. Even so it was unable to produce enough work at the constantly higher speeds demanded by the growing printing industry of the 19th century. To fill the need for faster presses, Richard Hoe of New York patented the first rotary press in 1846. The paper in the cylinder press was fed in sheets but the rotary press unwound its paper from a roll. The rotary press printed both sides of this continuous roll as it ran through the printing cylinders. Richard Hoe also eliminated the heavy flat bed which was used in the cylinder machines. He placed the forms to be printed on revolving cylinders, each of which had its own impression cylinder. Today the forms used on rotary presses are all plates made from pages of type and illustrations. These plates are curved to fit the cylinder upon which they are fastened.

Finally, the rotary press delivers its sheets all folded, for a folder is usually attached to the front of the press. To keep the printed sheet from smearing when it is folded, many rotary presses now use either gas or electric heaters to dry the ink. They would burn the paper but for the high speed at which it passes through the heat. All these improvements made for far greater speed and cheaper printing which could be sold to ever-increasing numbers of readers at low cost. The development of the rotary press was an important factor in the growth of large newspapers. It greatly increased the rapidity with which they can place the news before their readers.

As in the case of the cylinder press, later improvements added much to Hoe's original press. Now huge banks of presses, printing as many as 144 pages at each impression are common in every large printing factory. The rotary press also prints in colors, as many as four to each side of the sheet. This is done in such fine register and tone that it can now handle all but the very finest of book printings.

Other Printing Processes

So far mention has been made of only the most common kind of printing, relief printing. Actually there are four basic printing methods. In the relief printing discussed, the printing is done from raised surfaces. These are inked and transfer their image to the sheet as impression is applied.

In the second method the printing is done from a flat surface upon which the characters to be printed are outlined in ink. This method is called planographic printing since the form is a flat plane. (See LITHOGRAPHY.)

The third method that is commonly used is intaglio or gravure printing. This method is the opposite of relief printing. The image to be printed is cut or etched into a metal sheet or cylinder which is inked and wiped clean. The ink remains in the tiny wells etched into the hard surface of the metal. When the sheet touches the metal under the pressure of the impression cylinder, the ink is pulled out of the wells, and an exact reproduction is made on the sheet. The most common use of the gravure process is in the picture sections of newspapers. There the gravure process is combined with the rotary press to produce great quantities of these "rotogravure" sections at great speed and low cost.

Screen stencil printing is a modern form of a very old printing process. Usually bolting silk is stretched over a wooden frame. The design to be printed is on the silk. The stencil is placed on the surface to be printed, and ink is forced through the open areas of the stencil. Other fabrics may be used instead of the silk. Silk screen printing is economical for short runs and is often used for posters and show cards.

PRISON (*prĭz″n*). Prisons are usually thought of as places where men and women are locked up for breaking the law. Centuries ago, however, nobles and men of importance were at times captured and imprisoned for revenge or until they were ransomed. Nations at war have established prisons in which to keep prisoners of war. During World War II camps or prisons were established in which nations locked up enemy aliens. The United States, for example, imprisoned persons who were living in the country but were not United States citizens and who were suspected of disloyalty.

It was not until the 19th century that prisons began to be used for the punishment or correction of law violators. Prisons before that time were places where those accused of breaking the law were held until trial. After the prisoners were tried, the sentence of the court was immediately carried out. They were not sentenced to serve a term in prison. Those who had been declared guilty were put to death, whipped, or given other forms of bodily punishment, or fined.

Gradually men began to see that this cruel treatment did not prevent crime. The result was that imprisonment began to be used as a substitute for the death penalty and bodily punishment. In England and in some of the European countries, places called workhouses or houses of correction were established after about 1550. Those places were used to im-

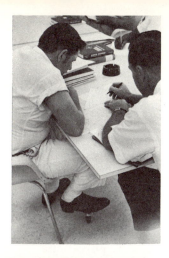

Courtesy (left) the Washington Department of Institutions, (top left and above) U.S. Bureau of Prisons, photo, Dehnel, (right and top right) U.S. Bureau of Prisons, photo, Harr—Hedrich-Blessing

Modern prison programs try to improve the inmate's employment prospects, training him for a job such as baking, left, and printing, above. A teacher reviews a test with an inmate, top left. The control room, top right, with surveillance equipment, and the chapel, right, are at the Marion, Illinois, federal penitentiary.

prison beggars, vagabonds, family deserters, debtors, and those guilty of minor offenses. The workhouses were then right at hand for use as prisons for keeping more serious offenders. These workhouses were not sufficiently safe to house long-term prisoners, and thus prisons began to be built which furnished greater security.

Most of these prisons were unfit places to keep human beings. They were frequently dirty, badly lighted, and cold. Food was bad and the treatment was harsh. Prisoners were thrown together, whether they were young or old, first offenders or hardened criminals. There was no work or training program; the inmates sat in idleness.

In the late 18th century such conditions aroused the interest of men like the Englishman John Howard. He traveled throughout Europe to discover the best methods of caring for prisoners and urged the British government to reform its prisons. In Belgium, Hippolyte Vilain built a model workhouse. He declared that

prisoners should be separated according to the extent of their criminal activity, and that they should be given a chance to work and learn a trade. Conditions in prisons began to improve.

In the United States the Quakers in Pennsylvania did much to better conditions in prisons. Their activity brought about changes in the Walnut Street Jail in Philadelphia. Arrangements were made, in 1790, for separation of first offenders from hardened criminals, for work and trade training, and for wages to be paid to the prisoners. Many of the ideas carried out in the building and management of the Walnut Street Jail, and of the Auburn Prison in New York, were adopted in the prisons which were built later throughout the country.

In the United States there are four main divisions in the prison system. There are first the jails and lockups in almost every village and city. Next come the county jails, found in practically every county in the various states. Each state has its own system of prisons and reformatories. The fourth group consists of the penal institutions which the federal government maintains for those who have violated federal laws.

Jails in villages and cities are used mainly for keeping accused persons awaiting trial, or for those sentenced to serve short terms for violation of local laws, or for minor crimes, called misdemeanors. County jails in general are used for the same purpose as those of the towns and cities, although, of course, they serve a larger area. Usually those sentenced to long terms for serious offenses, called felonies, are transferred to state prisons. The United States government has its own system of institutions for those who have violated federal law. Because this system has a large number of institutions, it is possible to provide places for the treatment of different types of offenders. Thus there are institutions for hardened offenders, for habitual offenders, for younger men, and for women.

Today more and more people are coming to believe that it is the task of the prison to help bring about the reformation of the inmate. It is estimated that 95 per cent of those in prison are released sooner or later. If nothing has been done in prison to help them, many of them are more dangerous to life and property after release than they were before. The prison must help the prisoner change his ways of thinking and his attitudes, and equip him for useful work.

In the more progressive prisons, the entire program aims at bringing about reformation. By a process which is called classification, prisoners are separated according to sex, age, the extent to which they have engaged in crime, their needs, and their abilities. Each institution has a staff of experts. Attention is first given to the prisoner's health, because often a man's physical condition, or physical defect, may have led him into crime. There are chaplains to help the prisoner with his religious problems; psychologists and psychiatrists to take care of mental difficulties; counselors to help with personal problems and foster new attitudes; academic schools to make up for lack of education; vocational schools to fit him for the job for which he is qualified. In addition there are recreational activities to keep him sound in mind and body. Experts realize that to carry on this program prisons should not be large; they should not have more than 1,000 prisoners.

Separate institutions are beginning to be built for the criminally insane, for offenders who are feeble-minded, for alcoholics, for drug addicts, for habitual criminals, and for first offenders. There are separate institutions for men who must be carefully guarded and for men who may be allowed much liberty. To take care of the latter, prisons are being built without walls or watchtowers, and many states have forestry camps and agricultural camps for them.

PRIVET (*prĭv′ ŭt*) is one of several shrubs of the genus *Ligustrum*. It is a member of the olive family, Oleaceae. There are about 50 species of privets, none of which are native to the United States. They are widely grown for ornament because of their handsome foliage and fragrant white flowers. The small, tubular flowers, which grow in dense clusters, are followed by small black, blue, or greenish globular fruits that often hang on during the winter. Privets are popular also because they are relatively free of insect and fungus enemies and because several varieties do well under city conditions.

Privet bushes make an ideal hedge because their foliage and stems grow thick and dense. Frequent trimming and cropping gives them a neat, ornamental appearance.

Richard Keane

The common European priv-
et has leaves 1¾ to 2½
inches long; its berries are
bluish black, above. The
small, white flowers occur
in dense clusters, left.

John H. Gerard

Several species are grown for hedges. The best known of them is the common European privet, *Ligustrum vulgare*, which is native to Europe and northern Africa. It sometimes reaches a height of 15 feet. When the branches of the privet are trimmed often and fairly closely, dense hedges result. Most species of privet have small leaves that stay on late in the fall or through the winter in parts of the United States where the weather is mild. They are hardy as far north as Chicago, Illinois. Privets widely grown in the South and West include the wax, or glossy, privet, the Japanese privet, and the California privet.

PROBABILITY (*präb′ ŭ bĭl′ ŭt ē*) is a measure of the likelihood that an event will happen. If an event cannot happen, its probability is zero. If it is certain to happen, its probability is one. All other degrees of probability are expressed in proper fractions. (See FRACTION.)

The determination of a mathematical probability usually begins with a listing of all probabilities, which is called a sample space. For a coin toss, there are two events, both equally likely to happen, and the sample space is simply: {heads, tails}, or {H, T}. The probability of tossing a head is the ratio of the number of heads on the coin, which is 1, to the total number of sides on the coin, which is 2. The probability of a head, therefore, is $\frac{1}{2}$; the probability of a tail is also $\frac{1}{2}$.

The sum of all probabilities for a sample space must add up to 1. If the probability that an event will take place is $\frac{4}{7}$, then the probability that it will not take place is $\frac{3}{7}$, because $\frac{4}{7} + \frac{3}{7} = 1$. An event and its opposite completely "fill" a sample space.

An example that illustrates facts about probabilities is the random removal of one ball from a bag of 12 balls that are all the same except for color. If 4 balls are red, 5 balls are white, and 3 balls are green, the sample space could be described this way:

{R1, R2, R3, R4, W1, W2, W3, W4, W5, G1, G2, G3}.

Each ball is equally likely to be chosen, so there are 12 events, each with $\frac{1}{12}$ probability. The probability of drawing a red ball on the first draw is $\frac{4}{12}$ (or expressed as a simpler fraction: $\frac{1}{3}$); for a white ball the probability is $\frac{5}{12}$; for a green ball the probability is $\frac{3}{12}$ (or $\frac{1}{4}$).

Another example might be that of a man dining in a Chinese restaurant who liked egg roll and shrimp equally well for an appetizer, and egg foo young, chicken chow mein, and beef chop suey equally well for a main course. The probability of his choice for the two courses can be worked out. The probability of his choice of egg roll and chicken chow mein, for example, can be found by using a sample space set up as a tree diagram:

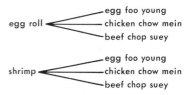

The diagram shows that there are 2 × 3, or 6, combinations of the two courses. Only one of these is egg roll and chicken chow mein. The probability for this combination is, thus, $\frac{1}{6}$.

If the appetizer is considered by itself, egg roll has a probability of $\frac{1}{2}$ that it will be chosen. For the main course, chicken chow mein has a probability of $\frac{1}{3}$. Another way to find the probability that both events will take place is to multiply the two probabilities. $\frac{1}{2} \times \frac{1}{3}$, or $\frac{1}{6}$, which agrees with the previous method. Multiplication of probabilities can be used whenever the two events are independent, that is, when the choice for one event has no effect on the choice for the other.

The same ideas apply to finding probabilities of more than two events. Suppose a dime, nickel, and penny are tossed. Each has the same sample space: {H, T}, with $\frac{1}{2}$ as the probability for each event. The probability for the combination of H on the dime, T on the nickel, and T on the penny, or HTT, is the product of the separate probabilities: $\frac{1}{2} \times \frac{1}{2} \times \frac{1}{2} = \frac{1}{8}$. The probability of THT in that order is also $\frac{1}{8}$, as is the probability of TTH. The probability of tossing one head and two tails, if it makes no difference which is the head, can be found by adding the probabilities of the three ways of its happening: $\frac{1}{8} + \frac{1}{8} + \frac{1}{8} = \frac{3}{8}$.

A combined sample space showing all three coins at once is:

Dime	Nickel	Penny	Results
		H	HHH
	H	T	HHT
H			
	T	H	HTH
		T	HTT*
		H	THH
	H	T	THT*
T			
	T	H	TTH*
		T	TTT

*The probability of HTT or THT or TTH is $\frac{3}{8}$.

A useful device for solving problems of this nature is Pascal's triangle. Each number in the triangular array is the sum of the two numbers just above it. The fourth row of the array — 1, 3, 3, 1 — corresponds to the problem of the three coins. As shown in the sample space above, there are eight possible ways in which the coins can land: 1 way with no heads, 3 ways with one head, 3 ways with two heads, and 1 way with three heads.

```
                    1
                 1     1
              1     2     1
           1     3     3     1
        1     4     6     4     1
     1     5    10    10     5     1
   1    6    15    20    15     6    1
 1    7    21    35    35    21    7    1
1   8   28   56   70   56   28   8   1
1  9  36  84  126 126  84  36  9  1
1 10 45 120 210 252 210 120 45 10 1
```

Pascal's Triangle

A further use of Pascal's triangle is shown in an example of a true-false test with ten questions. The answer for one question does not affect the choice in the next. The sample space for each question is {T, F} with each event having a probability of $\frac{1}{2}$. On a test of ten questions, the probability of getting a perfect score without even looking at the questions is $\frac{1}{2} \times \frac{1}{2} \times \frac{1}{2} \times \frac{1}{2} \times \frac{1}{2} \times \frac{1}{2} \times \frac{1}{2} \times \frac{1}{2} \times \frac{1}{2} \times \frac{1}{2} = \frac{1}{1024}$. The probabilities for other scores can be found from the bottom row of Pascal's triangle: 1, 10, 45, 120, 210, 252, 210, 120, 45, 10, 1. The probability of guessing 9 correctly is $\frac{10}{1024}$, or $\frac{5}{512}$; for 6 correct, $\frac{210}{1024}$, or $\frac{105}{512}$; for 2 correct, $\frac{45}{1024}$; for 1 correct, $\frac{10}{1024}$, or $\frac{5}{512}$; and for none correct, $\frac{1}{1024}$. The most probable outcome is that half of the answers will be correct. The probability for this is $\frac{252}{1024}$, or $\frac{63}{256}$, which is less than $\frac{1}{4}$.

In insurance, baseball averages, weather prediction, and so forth, probabilities cannot be determined from such simple sample spaces. They are based instead on a study of collected information and the estimation of probabilities from past occurrences. Estimations are made by finding the ratio of the frequency of some event to the total number of events. For very large numbers of cases, the exact and estimated kinds of probability nearly agree. (See STATISTICS.)

Although in tossing three coins the mathematical probability, for example, of three heads turning up is $\frac{1}{8}$, there is no guarantee that 9 out of every 72 tosses of three coins will be three heads. Many more tosses are required to display this probability. After 8,000 tosses of three coins, however, there is a good chance that three heads will turn up about 1,000 times; more likely, between 995 and 1,009 times.

Odds has a slightly different meaning from *probability*. Odds are found by taking the ratio of the number of favorable events to the number of unfavorable events in a sample space. If three coins are tossed, the odds in favor of getting two heads are 3 to 5; the odds against two heads are 5 to 3.

PROBATION (*prō bā' shŭn*) **AND PAROLE** (*pŭ-rōl'*) are methods for rehabilitating persons who have broken the law. Under both methods, the lawbreaker lives in the community rather than being locked up.

After the court finds a person guilty, the judge may send him to prison if he is an adult or to a training school if he is a juvenile. (See JUVENILE DELINQUENCY; PRISON.) The judge may, however, follow another course of action. Instead of sending the offender away, he may put him on probation for a specified period of time. The word *probation* comes from a Latin word meaning to prove or test. A person who is on probation is allowed to remain in the community while he proves to the court that he is able to stay out of trouble. A person on probation, called a probationer, may live at home and continue going to work or to school. He must report regularly to a probation officer, who supervises his activities and helps him with his problems.

Not every offender is given a chance for probation. Before deciding on the sentence, the judge may ask a probation officer to investigate the offender's character and background. The judge wants to know what kind of person the offender is, if he has committed previous crimes, where he lives, and how he spends his time. The seriousness of the crime is also taken into consideration. If the judge considers it likely that the offender will not break the law again, he releases him on probation. If, however, the probationer does not follow the rules laid down by the court, or if he commits another crime, he will be brought back to court. The judge can then send him to an institution as he might have done in the first place.

If an offender is sent to an institution, he may be released on parole after he has served part of his sentence. The word *parole* comes from a French expression meaning word of honor. The parolee gives his word that he will live by certain rules and will not break the law again. As in probation, many factors are taken into consideration before a person is released on parole. The parolee, too, must report to an officer who is expected to give him expert guidance and help him adjust to living in society. If the parolee violates the conditions of his parole, he is brought back to the institution and must stay until he completes his sentence, or until the parole board gives him another chance for parole.

History

In the early 19th century in England, some enlightened judges were worried about the effects of imprisonment on young lawbreakers and those who had committed no previous crimes. In such cases the offender was sometimes given a suspended sentence and placed under the supervision of his parents or other responsible adults. In 1841 in Boston, Massachusetts, a shoemaker named John Augustus asked the court to put a young man on probation. Instead of being sent to jail, the man was allowed to live with Augustus, who got him a job and helped him so much that the judge hardly recognized him when he was brought back to court. During the rest of his life, Augustus helped more than 2,000 people who were placed on probation to him. In 1878, as a result of the work of Augustus and his followers, the state of Massachusetts passed the first U.S. probation law. Parole laws were also enacted in many states during the last decades of the 19th century. The idea of parole had originated in Great Britain earlier in the century and had spread to the United States.

Purpose and Results

Today there are more than 17,000 U.S. probation and parole officers serving federal, state, and county courts and prisons. Many more are needed in order to serve all courts and institutions adequately.

Probation and parole officers must be qualified

to help people overcome the problems that got them into trouble. In the United States, the National Council on Crime and Delinquency recommends special professional training as a qualification for probation and parole work. The council also suggests that each officer should have fewer than 25 persons to supervise and no more than five reports to prepare for the parole board or judge. Actually, however, the caseload carried by most probation and parole workers is several times greater than this suggested number. Furthermore, few U.S. probation and parole officers are trained professional social workers. In many European countries, these positions must be filled by volunteer workers from social welfare agencies.

Probation and parole are important techniques for the rehabilitation of lawbreakers. Their cost to the community is a great deal less than the cost of imprisonment. In addition, many criminologists feel that they are a more successful means of reforming lawbreakers. The experience of imprisonment often does the offender more harm than good. Sociologists have shown that inexperienced lawbreakers learn new methods of crime while in prison. On the other hand, studies indicate that a large percentage of offenders can be placed on probation without getting into trouble again. Probation avoids the shame of imprisonment, keeps the family together, prevents loss of employment, and provides someone to turn to for guidance. Parole offers the offender an opportunity for quicker rehabilitation and allows him to be a useful citizen while serving the remainder of his sentence.

PROGRESSIVE PARTY (*prŭ grĕs′ĭv pärt′ē*) was a United States political organization begun during William Howard Taft's administration (1909–1913). At that time Republican Senator Robert M. La Follette of Wisconsin and Representative George W. Norris of Nebraska led a group of liberal Republican congressmen in a break with their party. These liberal Republicans, known as insurgents, felt that Taft was not continuing the popular policies of Theodore Roosevelt. They opposed the high Payne-Aldrich Tariff of 1909 and joined the Democrats in voting to reduce the powers of Joseph G. Cannon, Republican speaker of the House of Representatives.

Early in 1912 Theodore Roosevelt declared himself against Taft. At the Republican convention that year Taft won the nomination, and the insurgents followed Roosevelt out of the convention. They set up the Progressive party, adopting the bull moose as its symbol. Roosevelt became the "Bull Moose" presidential candidate, with Hiram W. Johnson, governor of California, for the vice-presidency. Their platform urged more effective control of trusts, suffrage for women, an end to child labor, and other reforms —many of which later became law. The election of 1912 was won by Woodrow Wilson, the Democratic nominee, and Roosevelt ran second.

In 1916, however, Roosevelt refused the Progressive nomination. His desertion of the party weakened it considerably. La Follette ran unsuccessfully for the presidency in 1924. The following year he died, and the Progressives were without a leader.

La Follette's sons continued the Progressive party in Wisconsin. In 1938 an attempt was made to start the party on a national scale again. In the Wisconsin elections that year, however, the opposing parties pooled their strength and defeated the Progressive candidates. Through the years of World War II the Wisconsin Progressives lost strength, and at a statewide conference in 1946 they voted to return to the Republican party. (See WISCONSIN, UNITED STATES.)

More recently another party named the Progressive party was created. In 1947 Henry A. Wallace, former secretary of commerce, announced that he was leaving the Democratic party, which he accused of a warlike policy toward the U.S.S.R. Wallace was nominated for the presidency at a Progressive party convention in 1948. Senator Glen Taylor of Idaho was chosen as his running mate. The Progressives opposed both the Republicans and the Democrats and sought the support of labor and minority elements. They were widely accused of being "pro-Communist." In the 1948 election Wallace and Taylor received only slightly more than 1,000,000 votes. In 1952 the party's candidates fared even worse, and thereafter the party had no candidates.

In Greek mythology, Prometheus, a friend to mankind, was chained to a rock after angering Zeus, ruler of the universe. A vulture tortured Prometheus every day for thousands of years until Hercules set him free.

PROMETHEUS (*prŭ mē′ thōōs* or *prŭ mē′ thē ŭs*) was in Greek legend a Titan who stole fire from the gods for the benefit of men on Earth. He was the friend and helper of man, eager to give mankind secrets of the gods. Prometheus was older than the gods, the son of Iapetus the Titan. In the war between Saturn and Zeus, Prometheus took the side of Zeus, and, according to one story, was entrusted with the creation of man. While his brother Epimetheus made the animals, Prometheus fashioned images in the likeness of the gods and gave these images life. Then he ascended to heaven. Lighting his torch at the chariot of the sun he presented fire to his new men. Zeus took away this gift when he quarreled with men, but Prometheus stole fire from heaven and brought it back to mankind.

Because of his love for man Prometheus aroused the anger of Zeus. He was chained to a rock in the Caucasus Mountains. Every day for thousands of years a vulture came and devoured his liver, which immediately grew again. Zeus offered to release him if he would reveal a secret which threatened the rule of the gods, but Prometheus refused to be freed in this way. He bore his torture unflinchingly for he knew that in the 13th generation a son of Zeus would release him. And so it came to pass, for Hercules killed the vulture and set Prometheus free. The story of Prometheus was told by many great poets, among them Aeschylus and Percy Bysshe Shelley.

PRONOUN (*prō′ noun*) is a part of speech that substitutes for a noun. Through the use of pronouns one can refer to himself, to other persons, and to things without being required to repeat their names constantly. In a language without pronouns one should have to say, "John brought John's books into John's house and placed the books in the books' shelves." Instead of this awkward kind of expression one can say conveniently in English, "John brought *his* books into *his* house, and placed *them* on *their* shelves." In this sentence the words *his, them,* and *their* are pronouns. *His* stands in place of the possessive noun "John's"; *them* and *their* stand in the place of "books."

It can be seen from these examples that a pronoun is a word which is used in the place of a noun.

Pronouns can show many relationships in the English sentence. One kind of relationship is called Person. Pronouns of the First Person are used by a speaker referring to himself or by speakers referring to themselves. *I* and *we* are pronouns of the First Person. The Second Person refers to a person or persons spoken to. The pronoun *you* is used to address one person or several persons. Pronouns of the Third Person refer to persons and things in addition to the speaker and those to whom he is speaking. The pronouns *he, she, it,* and *they* are pronouns of the Third Person.

A second relationship is called Case. Pronouns of the Nominative Case are used as the subjects of sentences and following all forms of the verb "to be." Pronouns of the Possessive Case are used to show possession, as in *his* books, *her* doll, *your* friends, *my* room, and *their* plans. Pronouns of the Objective Case are used as the objects of verbs (John hit *him*), as the objects of prepositions (play with *me*), and as indirect objects (Mary gave *me* candy).

The third relationship expressed by pronouns is called Number. Pronouns which refer to one person or thing are in the Singular Number: *I, me, you, he, she, it.* Pronouns which refer to more than one person or thing are in the Plural Number: *we, us, you, they.*

First Person	*Singular*	*Plural*
Nominative	I	we
Possessive	my *or* mine	our *or* ours
Objective	me	us

Second Person		
Nominative	you	you
Possessive	your *or* yours	your *or* yours
Objective	you	you

Third Person	*Singular*			*Plural*
	Masculine	Feminine	Neuter	
Nominative	he	she	it	they
Possessive	his	her *or* hers	its	their *or* theirs
Objective	him	her	it	them

The pronouns of the table above are called personal pronouns. Compound personal pronouns are formed by adding the words *self* or *selves* to the pronoun form, as in *myself, yourself, yourselves, themselves.* The forms *hisself* and *theirselves* are not acceptable in modern English.

A second class of pronouns is called relative pronouns. These are *who* (referring to person); *which* (referring to things); *that* (referring to both persons and things) and *what,* which is used with the meaning of "that which," as in: "He knew *what* he wanted"; "*What* you are saying is hard to understand." *Who* and *which* have forms to show number and case as follows:

	Singular and Plural	*Singular and Plural*
Nominative	who	which
Possessive	whose	whose
Objective	whom	which

The word "relative" is used to describe these pronouns because they refer or relate to some noun or pronoun, called the antecedent, which has been used earlier in the sentence.

The case form of the relative pronoun *who* is determined by its use in the clause which it introduces. We say, "The man *who* came in is Mr. Smith." *Who* is the subject of the clause, "who came in" and is therefore in the nominative case. In the sentence "There is Mr. Smith, for *whom* I have been looking," *whom* is the object of the preposition *for* and is therefore used in the objective case.

Compound relative pronouns are made by adding the endings *ever* or *soever* to the relatives *who, which,* and *what.* Examples: "Give *whoever* comes this ticket." "The pictures are placed on *whichever* wall is the more convenient." In formal English writing the compound *whoever* takes the form *whomever* when it is the object of a verb or the object of a preposition. Example: "We will invite *whomever* you may wish."

Pronouns which are used in asking questions

are called interrogative pronouns. These are *who, which,* and *what.* Examples: "*Who* is coming?" "*Which* suit shall I wear?" "*What* is the date?" In formal writing *whom* is used in questions when it is the object of a verb or of a preposition. Examples: "*Whom* are you inviting?" "By *whom* was this book written?"

Pronouns which are used to point out certain persons and things are called demonstrative pronouns. These are *this, that, these,* and *those.* *This* and *these* refer to persons or objects close at hand; *that* and *those* refer to persons or objects farther away. Thus one says, "Take *this* pencil and *these* books," when the objects are directly before him. One says, "Take *that* pencil and *those* books," when the objects are not immediately before him. The demonstrative pronouns must agree in number with the nouns that they modify. It is correct to say, "I like *this kind* of pie; I prefer *those kinds* of cakes."

Words such as *one, each, any, anybody, none, some,* and *someone* are called indefinite pronouns because they do not refer to a particular person or thing. These words are usually singular in number. They are followed by verbs and pronouns in the singular number. Examples: "*One* must always do *his* best." "*Each* is taken aside separately." "*Everyone* should have *his* (or *her*) own pencil."

PROPAGANDA (*prŏp'ä găn'dä*) is a message that is intended to make people think or act in a certain way. People use propaganda to try to make others think or act in the way they wish them to think or act. The word "propaganda" comes from the Latin word *propagare*, which means "to diffuse" or "to spread." Propaganda messages are spread not only by books, radio, television, and posters; they are also spread by word of mouth. One person hears something and tells another, who in turn tells someone else. This is how rumor, a very important way of spreading propaganda, begins.

The purpose of propaganda is to persuade. For example, a boy wanting to play baseball on a hot summer day may try to persuade his mother to let him do so. But she thinks he may become overtired and overheated. The boy, trying to change his mother's mind, will offer

reasons why he should be permitted to play. He may tell her that the neighbor lady has let her boy play baseball, or he may argue that the weather is really not so warm, and that it will be healthful to play. What this boy tells his mother is a form of propaganda. He wants her to do as he wishes.

Uses of Propaganda

Propaganda is used in several ways. It may be written in newspapers, books, or plays; it may be heard in speeches or seen in movies; it may be expressed in paintings, posters, leaflets, and photographs. The most common uses of propaganda are in warfare, politics, religion, selling, and advertising.

Propaganda can tell the truth, and it can also spread falsehoods. Sometimes the propagandist intends to deceive. This is often true in times of war. A government, in order to prevent the loss of spirit or morale among its people, may claim victories in battles that never have taken place.

The Germans spread this type of propaganda during World War II (1939–1945). Although the defeat of the German armies was certain toward the end of the war, the German government broadcast and published reports that its armies had been victorious.

In politics every campaign speech or rally, every campaign button and poster is an act of propaganda. The voters are being persuaded. The candidate tries to make them vote the way he wants them to vote. Even in a school classroom when class officers are chosen, propaganda is put to use. The students paint posters and give speeches, to persuade other students to vote for a certain candidate.

Religious propaganda also tries to make people think and act in a certain way. A missionary journeying to another land uses propaganda to persuade the natives of the area to believe as the missionary does. Churches also use propaganda to gain support for projects such as slum-clearance and child-care organizations.

One of the most common forms of propaganda is advertising. Advertisements in newspapers and magazines tell the reader to buy a certain kind of automobile, or a certain kind of toothpaste, or any other particular item. The same kind of propaganda may be heard on the radio and seen on television. Each manufacturer wants the public to believe that his product is the best, or the cheapest, or the most useful. In this way the manufacturer urges people to buy his product.

International Propaganda

International propaganda is used during wartime and during times of peace. All through the ages people have tried, by threats or

promises, to persuade their enemies and friends. Modern propaganda has made use of many new ways to send propaganda. One way, used especially in wartime, is to drop leaflets from airplanes. Sometimes propaganda from one nation to another is in the form of economic aid to friendly countries which have been victims of disasters such as war, floods, or earthquakes. Or aid may be given in the form of food and clothing. This type of propaganda is used to develop a friendly feeling between nations.

Propaganda is widely used on all levels of international relations. At international meetings diplomats often use propaganda to make their arguments stronger and more convincing to their audiences. The "Cold War" is an example of international propaganda directed at both friends and enemies. Each of the major groups of powers makes use of persuasive propaganda to win friends. (See INTERNATIONAL RELATIONS.)

Much of international propaganda can be called *psychological warfare*. In this type of warfare persons are not harmed bodily, but their minds, thoughts, and beliefs come under attack.

Propaganda Techniques

After World War I (1914–1918) persons all over the world began to give more attention to propaganda. They became more and more convinced that it could be very useful if properly handled. Therefore people began to study the best ways by which messages might be sent to other people. The likes and dislikes, fears, superstitions, and customs of many peoples were studied in order to find out how they might be most easily influenced. Out of this study came some of the methods most used in the different types of propaganda today.

The political orator often uses what are known as *"glittering generalities."* These are beautiful phrases, rich in flowery expression, but with little meaning. Examples of this device would include phrases such as "patriotic duty," "moral right," or "the Christian way." *Name calling* is another technique of propaganda. Politicians, diplomats, or political parties use this technique to insult or ridicule the opponent and provoke him to fight back. The *"sentimental approach"* is another type. A salesman using this approach will implore a customer to buy so that he, the salesman, may pay his way through college.

In advertising, the *testimonial* technique of expert opinion or expert advice is often used. The advertiser mentions "persons who should know" (scientists, executives, actresses, etc.), who endorse the product to convince the reader or listener that he should follow the good example. In politics, religion, and even in psychological warfare the *band wagon* technique is often used. The audience is urged to join the majority and to follow the leader. A form of this method is often used in advertising. Persons are urged to buy something but are told that the supply is limited and that they must act now (buy) if they want to have what so many others before them have already bought.

Another device is *card stacking*. Only certain facts or falsehoods are selected and emphasized to put over an idea. *Slogans* and *catch-phrases* are widely used today. A *whispering campaign* starts rumors. Often these are introduced by "they say." *Transfer* is the method used to carry the good reputation of one thing to another in order to make it more acceptable.

Government Controls on Propaganda

Some governments want to make sure that their people do not read or listen to messages coming to them from other countries. They use propaganda on their own people to tell them what to believe, whom to like, or what to hate. This type of propaganda is also known as *ideological guidance*. People so propagandized are not free. They can listen only to certain radio programs and read only the books, magazines, and newspapers which have been approved by their government. Much of what they read and hear is propaganda planted by their leaders.

The United States government, like the governments of all democracies, does not control domestic propaganda. It does use psychological warfare especially in times of war, and it sends propaganda to other parts of the world. The United States Information Agency is the government's major propaganda agency. Its purpose is to tell people in other parts of the world about the United States and the way its people live. The "Voice of America" is an important part of this organization. It broadcasts many hours a day, in many languages, to many countries.

Propaganda is not a modern invention, but has been used for thousands of years. The oldest examples are the writings of the Old Testament. In these the prophets tried to persuade others to follow their religious beliefs. In ancient Rome propaganda was used to tell of the

greatness of the state. Another example of historical propaganda is found in the Middle Ages when stories and rumors were spread to gain support for the crusades.

Today propaganda is widely used and is applied in a scientific manner. In order to avoid harmful effects it is necessary for persons to recognize the devices used in propaganda. One must be able to tell the difference between harmful propaganda and propaganda which is for the benefit of the reader or listener. Some propaganda is meant to deceive. Dictatorships of all kinds spread this type. But propaganda used to raise money for a worthwhile cause may be beneficial with no falsehood involved.

PROPHET (prŏf'ĕt).
According to the Old Testament of the Bible, a prophet was one who not only foretold the future but was also one who was inspired by God to tell the people how God wanted them to live.

The prophets thought of themselves as religious leaders who should warn the people of the punishment they would earn if they were wicked. All of the prophets spoke of God's holiness. They taught the people to live good and simple lives. Many of the prophets also wrote down what they had to say.

Two groups of prophets were recorded in the Old Testament: the *Former Prophets* and the *Latter Prophets*. The Former Prophets lived between the 13th century B.C. and 586 B.C. (the fall of Jerusalem). According to Jewish belief, Moses was the first prophet. Christians look on him as the lawgiver. They think of Samuel as the first prophet. Samuel was a priest and also a state adviser. Important early prophets included Elijah and Elisha, who warned the people against worshiping false idols.

The greatest age of prophecy lasted 500 years beginning about 750 B.C. This was the time of the Latter Prophets—3 major and 12 minor. The major prophets were Isaiah, Jeremiah, and Ezekiel.

The minor prophets were those who left very short records of their sayings. They included Amos, Hosea, Micah, Zephaniah, Nahum, Haggai, Zechariah, Malachi, Obadiah, Joel, and Jonah.

The minor prophets promised the people the evil times would become good times if God's laws were obeyed. Some predicted the destruction of the city of Nineveh because the people were leading evil lives. Later prophets rebuilt the temple which had been destroyed when the Jews were exiled in Babylon in the 6th century.

John the Baptist was the last of the prophets of the Old Testament.

(See also articles on individual prophets.)

PROTECTIVE (prō tĕk'tĭv) COLORATION (kŭl'ĕr ā'shŭn).
The coloring of most animals either matches or blends with that of their surroundings. Leaf-eating caterpillars and tree frogs are usually green. Desert animals such as camels, desert spiders, and desert snakes are generally sandy colored. The polar bear of the frozen north is white. This blending of colors is called *protective coloration*, for such coloring helps to conceal an animal from its enemies.

For ground dwellers in the woods of the Temperate Zone, brown is a good protective color. It blends with the dry leaves and the earth. Brown is especially effective when it is not a solid shade, but darker here and lighter there, like the ground itself. Often in the spring a person may be startled by a mother grouse rushing out from her nest. Even after locating a grouse's nest it is almost impossible to see the mother upon it. When her tail is spread fanwise against the trunk of a rough-barked tree and her brownish body is resting on a nest of dead leaves, she practically fades from sight.

Forest animals that lie hidden among bushes and in trees are often spotted or mottled. Their marking resembles the light and dark effect of sunlight through leaves. This type of marking is often seen in the cat family. Familiar examples are the bobcat, the European wildcat, and the leopard. Another camouflaged cat is the tiger. It wears stripes, the best disguise for animals who live among tall grasses and shrubs.

Fish and other water dwellers and birds that spend much time on the wing are generally colored darker above and lighter below. If an enemy is above a fish or bird it can not spot its prey easily against the darkish background of deep water or earth. If an enemy is below, it

PLATE 1 PROTECTIVE COLORATION Above left: The harmless bumblebee moth (above) and the true bumble-bee look almost identical. The enemies of the moth do not attack.it for fear of a sting. Above right: A stick caterpillar has the shape and the color of a tree twig. Below: On the grasslands below Mount Kilimanjaro in eastern Africa, these giraffes blend into their surroundings. Their spotted coloring adapts them to many kinds of landscapes.

(Above left and above right) Hess from Three Lions, (below) Commander Gatti Expeditions

Photos, Hess from Three Lions

PLATE 2 PROTECTIVE COLORATION Top: A fawn blends into the forest background of brown autumn leaves. Above left: At first glance, the leaf fish looks like a leaf. Right: Tree hoppers that live on raspberry, currant, and apple twigs are not noticed by other animals and by farmers because they look like thorns. They are pests, however, and can kill the plants.

can not find its victim easily against the illuminated surface of water or sky.

In areas where the land is bare for part of the year and covered with snow for the rest, many animals have a change of clothes. The arctic fox, the variable hare, the stoat, and the ptarmigan all wear brownish coats in summer and white ones in winter.

Some animals can change their color the moment they change their background. Chameleons can do this. They become green, gold, brown, or blackish as they move from one background to another. Flounders too have a considerable color range. They conceal themselves by imitating the changing colors of the sea floor.

Other Forms of Protection

Another type of animal coloration at first sight seems to be the opposite of protective. This is *warning coloration*. The animals that wear warning colors are poisonous, have painful stings, or taste bad. If an enemy has once had an unpleasant experience with one of them he will not forget it. In the future he will avoid the brilliant creature that harmed him. Among the familar animals with warning colors are the bees and wasps in their costumes of yellow and black. Poisonous amphibians and reptiles wear showy clothes.

Some animals have concealed markings that are seen only in flight. The white tail feathers of the junco or the white "powder puff" of the cottontail rabbit are examples of this. Such *flash colors* may be very showy and brightly colored and may be combined with an otherwise concealing coloration.

Some animals such as the stick insects and leaf butterflies are camouflaged by matching the form as well as the color of their surroundings. Some animals are protected by looking so much like a poisonous or bad-tasting creature that they are left alone. This is called *mimicry*. The viceroy butterfly, which seems to taste good to birds, looks almost exactly like the monarch butterfly, which does not.

These various methods of protection described appear that way to human beings. It must be remembered that animal eyesight differs from human. An object that a person may find hard to see may be seen very clearly by certain animals. Besides, many animals depend upon smell and hearing rather than upon sight in finding their prey.

PROTEIN (*prō′tē in* or *prō′tēn*). Protein is a substance found in all living cells. The word protein comes from a Greek word meaning "first," because proteins are thought to be the most important part of living matter. Each kind of cell has its own protein. The proteins are made up of combinations of substances called *amino acids*. There are more than 21 different amino acids. Each amino acid group contains the chemical element nitrogen, in addition to carbon, hydrogen, and oxygen. Some of the amino acids also carry the element sulfur.

The different amino acids can combine in different ways to form different proteins. This might be compared with the weaving of different types of threads in several patterns to form particular fabrics. Each protein is different in some way from every other protein, yet they all contain nitrogen. There is an average of about 16 per cent nitrogen in each of the common food proteins. Scientists report that there are thousands of different proteins. Several proteins are often combined to make what seems to be one substance. For example, meat is known to be made up of at least 12 to 15 different proteins.

Many foods are important because of the proteins they contain: milk, eggs, lean meats, fish, peas, beans, peanuts, and certain grains. In addition, woolens, silks, furs, and leather are protein materials.

There is plenty of nitrogen in the air, but all animals and most plants need to have it changed before they can use it. Certain groups of bacteria living in the soil change nitrogen in the air into forms that plants can absorb and use. The plants use these nitrogen-containing substances in forming plant proteins. The plant proteins are eaten by animals and are the basic source of nitrogen for animals. The plant proteins are broken down to amino acids in the digestive tract of the animal. The animal body then combines the amino acids in

Dr. H. Fernandez-Moran, Department of Biophysics, University of Chicago

A view of a protein from cabbage leaves is shown above magnified 570,000 times.

many ways, making animal proteins. (See NITROGEN.)

Man needs certain amino acids which his body can not make for itself. He must get them from the protein in the food he eats. These are called the *essential amino acids,* which means that the body can not get along without them. Not only certain kinds of amino acids, but definite amounts of them, are necessary so that the body tissues can use what they need. Foods from animal sources, such as eggs, milk, meats, and cheese, give the body the essential amino acids if enough of these foods are eaten. Plant proteins, such as those in peas, beans, and cereals, do not contain all the essential amino acids. However, the plant proteins are valuable in the diet when combined with some of the animal proteins.

Man cannot store amino acids, so the different kinds needed to form protein have to be taken into the body at the same time. Bread and milk have to be eaten at the same meal, so the amino acids they provide can be used together to form new body tissue. Moderate amounts of different kinds of protein foods should be eaten at each meal. In this way a person is certain to get enough of the essential amino acids to meet the body's protein needs. (See FOOD; NUTRITION.)

PROTESTANT (prŏt′ĕs tănt or prŏt′ĭs tănt) **EPISCOPAL** (ē pĭs′kō päl) **CHURCH** is a religious body in the United States that is a branch of the Church of England. It was established during England's golden age of discovery and exploration in the New World.

On their first Sunday in the New World the colonists of England's settlement at Jamestown, Virginia, attended services conducted by their chaplain, the Reverend Robert Hunt. The church was made of an old sail attached to several trees to protect the worshipers from sun and rain. The settlers sat on rough logs. Their chaplain preached from a pulpit made by nailing a plank to two trees. By the time of the Revolution the church was established in the colonies to the north, east, and south.

The Protestant Episcopal church believes in apostolic succession; that is, that an apostle sets apart the man who is to succeed him, and he in turn sets apart another to take his place. When the break with England came, the church in America realized that their bishops must be men who were set apart in this way. The Reverend Samuel Seabury of Connecticut was elected first bishop in America. He was consecrated in Aberdeen, Scotland. Three years later William White of Philadelphia, Pennsylvania, and Samuel Provoost of New York City were consecrated in the chapel of Lambeth Palace in London. Through these three churchmen and patriots the apostolic succession was secured for the church in America.

With the spreading frontiers the church grew slowly in many directions. It has extended its work far beyond North America into the Orient, India, and Liberia.

The governing body of the church is the General Convention, which meets every three years. The convention is composed of the House of Bishops and the House of Deputies. The deputies are clergy and laymen elected by the various dioceses (districts) throughout the church.

Between sessions of the General Convention the church's work is carried on by a National Council which does work in six departments: Missions, Social Service, Religious Education, Finance, Publicity, and Field. Ninety-six dioceses and missionary districts cover the United States and its possessions. Also, there are 13 foreign missionary districts. Elected bishops have authority over the dioceses, each of which is composed of a number of parishes, local churches, and missions.

The teaching of the church is set forth in the official worship book, the *Book of Common Prayer*. The faith is briefly summed up in the Apostles' Creed and stated more fully in the Nicene Creed.

The church maintains the historic episcopate, with the threefold ministry, bishops, priests, and deacons.

PROTEUS (*prō′tūs* or *prō′tē ŭs*), the "old man of the sea," was said to have been the son of Poseidon and Amphitrite, the god and goddess of the sea. Proteus had the gift of prophecy and the power of changing his shape at will.

When the bees of Aristaeus died (as a penalty because he caused the death of Eurydice), Aristaeus' mother, Cyrene, a sea nymph, told him to ask Proteus what to do. She led him to the old man's cave. There Aristaeus lay hidden until Proteus ascended from the sea with his herd of sea calves. The beekeeper bound him while he slept and Proteus, finding himself captured, turned himself first into a fire, then a flood, then a beast, then into many other horrible forms. But he could not escape from the chains. So he finally resumed his own shape

and asked Aristaeus what he wanted. Aristaeus told him about his bees and Proteus instructed him to sacrifice four bulls and four cows and to pay funeral honors to Eurydice. Aristaeus did so and on the ninth day he found a new swarm of bees in one of the carcasses.

Proteus always refused to foretell future events unless he was captured and could not escape. Using a method similar to that employed by Aristaeus, the Greek heroes Menelaus and Odysseus forced the old man to explain how they could pacify the angry gods. A later story tells that Proteus was a king of Egypt and that to his court Hermes conducted the real Helen, while Paris, who had stolen the Greek princess, went on to Troy with only a phantom.

PROTOPLASM (*prō′tō plăz′m*) is a form of matter. The chemist can combine elements to make many different materials. However, there is one substance he has not yet been able to make. That substance is protoplasm, the living part of all plants and animals. All organisms—plant or animal—are composed of cells. There may be many millions of cells, as in the human being, or there may be one, as in the Protozoa. In Protozoa, man, whale, and dandelion, the walls of the cells enclose the same life substance—protoplasm. In each cell the protoplasm consists chiefly of two parts: the more solid, central part, called the *nucleus,* and the softer, more liquid part, the *cytoplasm.*

Scientists have found that each type of living thing has its own kind of protoplasm, and that the different types of cells within an organism each have special forms of protoplasm. Chemists have found that although protoplasm varies, 99 per cent of its bulk is made of carbon, hydrogen, oxygen, and nitrogen, with traces of many other elements. Just what makes protoplasm alive is still unknown, but it is known that everything that can be done only by living things is carried out by protoplasm.

When food is taken into a living body it is first digested—that is, it is turned into liquid form. Then the digested food must be taken into and made a part of the protoplasm, a process known as assimilation. Exactly what takes place during assimilation is not known. It is known that assimilation results in replacing worn-out protoplasm and making more protoplasm. In doing this protoplasm builds up dead matter into living material and changes foreign material into substances like itself. When food is assimilated the cell grows larger and may divide into two cells. Each of those two may divide, and so the process goes on. This process is known as growth. Protoplasm also stores and releases all the energy that plants and animals have. All protoplasm and bodies built from protoplasm have periods of action and of rest.

Protoplasm is sensitive to stimuli or shocks from the outside. A strong light or heat will kill it. Chemicals attract or repel it. Electric currents cause it to behave in various ways.

The knowledge of protoplasmic activities was one of modern science's greatest discoveries. The explanation of protoplasm and its activities remains a challenge to science.

PROTOZOA (*prō′tō zō′ä*). In a teaspoonful of pond water there may be a million or more animals, each so tiny that it can be seen only through a microscope. These, the simplest animals known, since they consist of a single cell, have the group name of Protozoa. All of them live in water or in moist places. They are of great interest to scientists because the single cells of which they are made carry on all the various tasks necessary to keep a plant or animal alive. They can hunt and eat food, digest it and make it into living matter. They can breathe and burn the food they eat and throw off waste. They can also reproduce themselves. They reproduce either by dividing themselves into halves, each of which becomes a complete, separate animal, or by growing little swellings, called *buds*, which break off and form separate, new animals.

Because there are more than 15,000 different types of Protozoa known, the group is divided into subgroups or classes. The simplest forms, such as the Amoeba and its relatives, have pseudopods or "false feet" that flow out in various directions and contract back into the body. They make up the class Rhizopoda (from the Greek for "root feet"). This class is further subdivided into orders. One order is called the Foraminifera, or hole borers. The one-celled animals in this order have tiny shells of chalk with little holes through which the soft living protoplasm protrudes. They are common in warm and temperate seas. When they die their shells fall to the bottom, and in the course of centuries chalk deposits form from accumulations of their skeletons. A piece of natural chalk, examined under the microscope, will show some of these minute skeletons. Another order of rhizopods, called the Radiolaria, make minute glassy shells of exquisite beauty out of quartz. Accumulations of their skeletons form flint deposits.

The more complicated Protozoa are grouped mainly in the class Infusoria. These animals have little hairs extending from their cells. These they use somewhat as oars in pushing their way through water. In some forms there

These are four types of protozoa drawn many times their natural size. From left to right they are: amoeba, paramecium, euglena (one of the flagellates), and radiolaria.

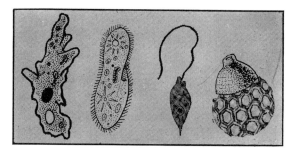

are only one or two large hairs called *flagellae* (singular, *flagella*). These are called Flagellata. Other forms of Infusoria, however, have numerous hairlike threads, called *cilia*, extending from their cells. They are called Ciliata. The most advanced forms of Protozoa belong to this group. It includes the slipper animalcules (Paramecium) with a free-swimming, slipper-shaped body; the bell animalcules (Vorticella), with a bell-shaped body anchored by a stalk; and the trumpet animalcules (Stentor).

The Rhizopoda and Infusoria are the two chief classes of Protozoa. A third class is the Sporozoa, which are parasites in man and other animals and form spores in certain stages of their life cycles. Some of these cause diseases such as malaria and sleeping sickness in man. However, not all the scientists who work with Protozoa divide them into these three classes. Instead some use slightly different schemes.

The scientists who specialize in the study of one-celled animals are called protozoologists; the fascinating work they do is called the science of protozoology. (See BIOLOGY.)

PROVIDENCE (prŏv′ ĭ dĕns), RHODE ISLAND,

capital of the state, has grown where the Providence River joins Narragansett Bay. From one of the earliest settlements in New England, it has grown into the most important industrial and commercial city in the state.

The city's leading industry is textile manufacturing. Although worsted cloth is still a major product, woolens and cottons are not as important as they once were. The city is a world leader in making jewelry and silverware. Other industries include metal goods, especially precision instruments, and rubber goods.

Trade is a leading activity. However, since it is near the major ports of Boston, Massachusetts, and New York City, Providence is only a secondary port. It imports oil, coal, and lumber, and exports textiles and metal goods.

Providence was founded in 1636 by Roger Williams who had left the Massachusetts Bay Colony when he was ordered to give up his religious beliefs. In 1644 he was given a royal charter for the colony. In 1647 four settlements were incorporated as the Providence Planta-

tions, later the state of Rhode Island. (See RHODE ISLAND; WILLIAMS, ROGER.)

Providence started as a farming center but when the first wharf was built in 1680 the village was soon in the trading and shipping business. Molasses was imported from the West Indies. It was used to make rum, then an important export. Trade was cut off during the American Revolution when the British at the mouth of the bay held Newport.

After the Revolution textile mills and jewelry factories were built, and industry became more important than trade. Industrial products tend to be small, lightweight, and expensive, due more to the skill of the workmen than to the materials in them.

The population increased to almost 12,000 by 1820 and 50 years later the city had grown to 69,000. Growth was steady until about 1920 when the cotton textiles mills started moving out of New England. Since then the population has grown more slowly but the city continues as a leading industrial and commercial center.

Since its early days Providence has been the cultural and governmental center of the state. It has always been at least the part-time capital, but not until 1900 was it made the only capital of the state. The capitol building has collections of historical documents, relics, and paintings.

Brown University, chartered in 1764 as Rhode Island College and moved to Providence in 1770, is an old and well-known educational center. Providence College, Rhode Island College, and Bryant College are some of the other schools in Providence. Most of the educational centers have excellent libraries, museums, art exhibits, and historical buildings.

The city government has a mayor and council. It operates under a charter written in 1832. The population of Providence in 1960 was 207,-498.

PRUNE (pro͞on). Prunes are the dried fruit of

certain kinds of plum trees. The plums used to make prunes are quite solid and rich in sugar, so that they will dry without becoming sour or shriveling too much. The plums to be used for prunes are often allowed to become so ripe that they fall from the trees. They are then put through one of several drying processes. In places with little rain they are often dried in the sun from six to ten days. In places where there is more rain they are dried by artificial heat. In Europe they may be partly cooked before being dried in the sun. The prunes are graded or sorted by size for shipping in bags or cartons. Some small types of prunes have 130 prunes to the pound, while larger ones have only 30 or 40.

More prunes are grown and prepared in the Santa Clara Valley in California than in any other place of the same size in the world. In Oregon and Washington many large Italian prunes are produced. Prunes are also grown in France, Germany, Hungary, Spain, South Africa, and Australia.

PRUSSIA (*prŭsh'ä*). The term Prussia is used to describe a former German territory on the south shore of the Baltic Sea to the east and west of the Vistula River. The term Prussia also refers to a much larger kingdom and state that grew around the original territory.

Prussia first became important in history when the military order of Teutonic Knights conquered the heathen Prussians living near the mouth of the Vistula River, added new lands, and set up a powerful state. Prussia was divided into West Prussia and East Prussia. In wars in the 15th century, however, the Teutonic Knights lost all their lands except East Prussia to Poland. In 1660 Prussia under Frederick William, the Great Elector of Brandenburg, broke away from Poland. Frederick William slowly brought together many of his lands beyond the original territory of Prussia. In 1701 Frederick William's son was given the royal title of Frederick I, King of Prussia. While this title was supposed to apply only to East Prussia, which was known as the Kingdom of Prussia between 1701 and 1871, the term "kingdom of Prussia" was also used to describe all the lands of the house of Hohenzollern.

The kingdom of Prussia was greatly enlarged in the 18th century by Frederick the Great through the addition of Silesia and West Prussia. In the Napoleonic Wars the kingdom lost much territory. However, in 1815, by the Peace of Vienna, Prussia gained much new territory for helping to defeat Napoleon. It became even stronger by forming the *Zollverein*, or customs union, which brought all the German states except Austria under the leadership of Prussia.

In 1862 King William I appointed Otto von Bismarck prime minister of Prussia. (See BISMARCK, OTTO EDUARD LEOPOLD; WILLIAM [EMPERORS OF GERMANY].) Bismarck was determined to unite Germany under a Prussian king. After the war with France in 1870–1871 ended in victory for Prussia, the German Empire was proclaimed in 1871 with William I of Prussia as emperor. (See FRANCO-PRUSSIAN WAR.) Prussia was by far the largest and most powerful state in the German Empire. The *Junkers*, a powerful landowning and military aristocracy group of East Prussia, controlled Prussia and, therefore, much of the German Empire.

With the overthrow of the German Empire in 1918, a small part of West Prussia became part of Poland. By the constitution of 1919, Prussia was made a democratic parliamentary republic and one of the parts of the federal Weimar Republic. During Adolf Hitler's rise to power in the 1930's, Prussia was the center of growth of the military might of the Third Reich. In 1945, at the end of World War II, Prussia east of the Oder and Neisse rivers was placed under Polish rule, and the northeastern part of East Prussia passed to the Soviet Union. The rest of the old state of Prussia was divided into or became parts of a number of new German states in both East and West Germany. In 1947 the Allied Control Council formally dissolved the Prussian state by law. (See GERMANY.)

PSYCHIATRY (*sī kī'ä trĭ*) **AND PSYCHOANALYSIS** (*sī'kō ä năl'ĭ sĭs*). Psychiatry is the branch of medicine which deals with the mind and the emotions of people. A psychiatrist is a physician who treats mental or emotional illnesses rather than physical illnesses. As with physical illnesses, mental illnesses may be minor or very serious. They may also be what is called chronic, and so take a long time to cure, just as tuberculosis takes a long time to cure.

A person sometimes has thoughts and feelings that are disturbing to him. They do not seem to make sense. He knows of no reason for having them, or, if he does know of a reason, knowing it does not make him comfortable enough so that he can go about his daily activities happily. When this happens he may try to forget these thoughts and feelings. He may even succeed in forgetting, but still he will not go about his daily activities in a satisfactory way. What has happened is that he has only hidden these thoughts and feelings from his *conscious* thinking. Actually, they remain in what is called the *unconscious* part of his mind, and they continue to affect his everyday behavior. He may not be able to get along with people, or do his work, or enjoy his free time. When these ideas and feelings become so disturbing that he is not able to do his daily activities as well as he ought, he is not in good health. It can then be said that he is in need of psychiatric help.

One of the most important forms of treatment the psychiatrist uses is called *psychotherapy*. In psychotherapy the patient talks about what he remembers of his past, what he is doing at present, the thoughts he has, and how he feels about things. Because of his special training, the psychiatrist can learn from the patient's talk what the patient is upset about and what has caused the upset. Then he can help the patient to get at the source of the problem.

The goal of psychotherapy is not only to make the patient happier but to make it possible for him to use his actual ability to live a full life. For example, a student may be unable to study because he spends most of his time either worrying over his ideas and feelings or trying to forget them. If he can be freed of these worries he will be able to concentrate on his studying, which means that it will come to him more easily than it did before. Such a student needs psychotherapy to change in this way because what he is worrying about is often not the real problem. The real problem and its cause may be forgotten and thus unconscious. It usually takes the professional help of a psychiatrist for a person to recall his real problem

and to understand it.

In the treatment of a person of this type, the psychiatrist helps him to remember what he has forgotten and then encourages him to see that he need not worry about it. When the matter itself is recalled, it will sometimes appear as nothing worth worrying about. If it does appear as something worth worrying about, the psychiatrist helps the person to understand its real nature. When such a problem is truly understood it loses its terror and therefore can be more easily solved. The person no longer tries to hide it in the dark background of his mind, and he is free to put all of his effort into his daily life.

The psychiatrist also treats those who are in danger of becoming mentally ill. The illness might develop in the future because of the great strain such a person is under as a result of fighting the feelings and ideas that bother him. This means that already he is not living to the fullest of his ability. Moreover, he can get rid of his worries only by hiding them in the unconscious part of his mind—which, as has been explained, does not really help. Again, if he is helped to see the way in which he misunderstands his experiences and feelings, or is helped to recall and understand those things that he has forgotten, he will be under less strain and thus avoid mental illness.

The psychiatrist also treats those who have become mentally ill. Before the latter part of the 19th century, mental illness was believed to be incurable. But as psychiatrists learn more about mental illness they are able to cure more and more people. These cures are brought about by different methods. Some patients are put in a living situation that for a time lessens the strain upon them; some can be helped by the use of certain drugs, some by a type of treatment called *shock therapy,* and some by psychotherapy.

Psychosomatic medicine is another area of interest for the psychiatrist. Many physical illnesses are brought about partly because of emotional strain. Such illnesses are called *psychosomatic.* Among the diseases in which emotional strain plays a part are asthma, hay fever, some skin diseases, ulcers of the stomach and other parts of the intestinal tract, and high blood pressure. For such diseases, psychiatrists work closely with doctors who specialize in the diseases. The treatment thus combines other forms of medical help with psychotherapy.

Child Psychiatry

Many psychiatrists believe that most of the emotional and mental difficulties that adults have are caused by problems that develop in childhood. They believe that much unhappiness in later life could be avoided if children with even minor difficulties had psychotherapy. Child psychiatry is therefore an important part of psychiatry. Children can be treated at any age at which the need becomes clear. They have been successfully treated by psychotherapy at the age of two or three years. But the very young child can not be treated directly by the psychiatrist. The psychiatrist can only advise the parents on how the child should be handled.

Psychoanalysis

Psychoanalysis is a special type of psychotherapy. It was begun in the early part of the 20th century by Sigmund Freud. It has been further developed by many others. It was chiefly through this approach to emotional and mental disturbances that it was learned that forgotten feelings and thoughts often affect a person's behavior and present feelings. Thus, psychoanalysis has influenced all types of psychotherapy.

The psychiatrist uses psychoanalysis to help the person recall the experiences, ideas, and feelings he had in childhood and that are now forgotten and imprisoned in the unconscious. That which is forgotten is gradually revealed in three major ways. First of all, dreams give a clue. Dreams express the feelings a person has about problems and experiences imprisoned in his unconscious mind. For this reason, if a person learns to understand his dreams he has a good clue to his unconscious wishes and to his so-called forgotten experiences. Second, the person's present feelings and behavior may be understandable when they are seen as being partly the result of his feelings about events

of the past; thus his behavior offers a clue. Third, many clues are brought to light by *free association*. In free association the patient says whatever comes to his mind, whether to him it makes sense or not, and whether he is ashamed of it or not. As a result of uncovering, refeeling, and rethinking the past through these three means, the patient gains a clearer understanding of why he behaves the way he does. With this understanding he finds a change in his feelings about his present experiences. He no longer looks at present events in a strange way because of the influence of past events. The patient who is being psychoanalyzed must see the psychiatrist three to six times a week for at least a year and often for much longer.

PSYCHOLOGY (*sī kŏl'ō jĭ*). Psychology is the study of how people and animals behave. Psychologists are interested in how and why people do such things as learn, think, remember, feel, see, hear, and talk. They study how animals react to simple problems and how people react to simple and hard problems. They also study the differences between people, and how people get along with each other.

Fields of Psychology

Child psychology is the study of how children grow and learn to do harder things. It also shows how very different children are from each other and how adults and children differ.

There are many interesting ways in which animals and human beings are alike. The field of *comparative psychology* studies many animals, such as ants, rats, monkeys, dogs, and even earthworms. These animals are compared with people. Comparative psychologists also study the different races of people.

Social psychology is the study of ways people do things together. Boys and girls in groups at home, at school, and at play do not do the same things. They are studied by social psychologists. Other groups, such as are found in crowds, are studied by social psychologists.

Abnormal psychology is the study of people who have become unable to behave as other people do. Psychologists study the causes of these difficulties to find ways in which these persons can be helped, just as a doctor studies how to cure a disease. Clinical psychologists who work in mental hospitals and child guidance clinics have made a particular study of this field of psychology.

Physiological psychology is concerned with behavior changes which result from changes within the body. For example, such drugs as alcohol change people's behavior. When a person's brain is damaged, he often is unable to behave normally. Animals are used for many of the studies in this field.

There are a number of ways in which psychology is applied. In business and industry there are many special problems which psychologists help solve. They work out ways to select workers for jobs. Sometimes they experiment with different conditions such as lighting, heating, and ventilation. They study how people feel about their work and the company for which they work. These psychologists must know a great deal about *industrial* and *business psychology*.

Educational psychology is another applied field. This is the study of school learning and individual differences among students. Educational psychologists experiment with different methods of teaching. They also work with children who learn less easily than others. Helping boys and girls to select a vocation may be one of their tasks.

Methods of Psychology

One of the first tasks of a psychologist is to describe behavior. It is often helpful to learn the many ways in which people are alike. For example, people usually want to be active for part of the time; they usually want people to admire them; they are angry sometimes, love somebody, and are afraid of something. They learn to crawl, stand up, walk, and jump, although not everybody can do these things at the same age. Psychologists use a method called *systematic observation* for discovering facts of this kind. By keeping careful records, writing down just what babies were able to do from day to day, and then comparing these records, psychologists found that nearly all children learn to do these things in the same

order.

Sometimes it is not possible to observe behavior. Then the psychologist may have to ask people who have known the person to describe his behavior. This is called the *anecdotal method*. A teacher might tell the psychologist what she remembered about a children's quarrel. The teacher could tell only what she had noticed, and she might have forgotten some of what happened. So the anecdotal method is used only when it is the only way information can be collected. It is most often used when a case study is being made of one person.

A man may be interested in finding out what kind of work he can best learn to do. The psychologist who makes a case study gathers all the facts about the person's early life, his school work, hobbies, home background, and other details. Most of these facts are obtained in a talk between the man and the psychologist. This is called an *interview*. Some tests may be given to see how well the man can do certain tasks. Then the psychologist interprets the records of the tests and the interview materials. The man will then have more information to help him decide on an occupation.

The reason tests were first made was to find out how people differ. Some people hear better than others. Some learn music easily, while others are better at building things. These differences are measured by tests. The *testing method* has given much information about the many abilities, attitudes, interests, and achievements of people.

When it is of interest or value to know how large groups of people behave, or the effect of one person on many others, or the opinions of people about what is happening in the world, *public opinion polls* may be made. Many persons are interviewed, and the results are combined. This method is one of the ways of studying opinions or attitudes.

Very often the *experimental method* is used. One group of people may be taught lessons from books, while another group learns from radio talks. Then the amount each group learned is compared. Of course the psychologist must carefully control the two groups to see that they are alike in as many ways as possible before the two methods are used. He will see that the groups are about the same age and are about equal in ability to learn. He will control how long they study, what is told them about the purpose of the experiment, and other conditions which might affect the results.

Doctors who treat people who are mentally sick sometimes use a method called *psychoanalysis*. The physician talks with the patient, who tells everything he can remember about himself, his thoughts, his feelings, and his wishes. Often after a year or two, in which he sees the doctor almost every day, the patient discovers feelings and wishes which he did not know he had. He may remember things of which he was unconscious before, and thus find the reason why he was ill or unhappy. Children sometimes go to a psychoanalyst, and he helps them also.

In the *clinical method* a physician, a psychologist, and a social worker all study a person. They get all the facts they can about his early life by interviewing him and many of the people who are interested in him. They study his health and his abilities, his family background, and all that they can learn about what might influence his behavior. Then they prepare a long written report, a case study, giving all the material each has collected. They meet together and decide what is best to help the person solve his difficulties.

Psychological methods are different depending on what question is being answered. The scientist collects his information and then decides what the results mean. Then other scientists can repeat the study to see if the results are the same.

Psychologists at Work

Some psychologists work in schools where they help teachers plan the work for very bright children or children who learn more slowly than others. Sometimes a boy or girl who has difficulty with only one subject, such as reading or arithmetic, may get help from the psychologist.

Other psychologists work in clinics and hospitals where the clinical method is used to study people. Sometimes clinical psychologists help treat patients; sometimes they give special tests when the physician wishes information about the mental ability of the patient.

A great many psychologists work for the government. They make tests which are given when men apply for such jobs as postman, truck driver, fireman, policeman, or clerk. They may give tests for drivers' licenses. They also make and give tests for the armed services, so that military men may be put to work in suitable jobs during military service.

PTOLEMY (*tŏl′ĕ mē*) (CLAUDIUS [*klạ′dĭ ŭs*] PTOLEMAEUS [*tŏl′ĕ mē ŭs*]). Columbus believed he could sail west to India because of maps made by a scholar named Ptolemy. These maps had been made hundreds of years before Christopher Columbus' time; yet they helped him discover the New World. This was only one of several achievements in which Ptolemy's beliefs and discoveries played a part.

Although his works have lived, almost noth-

From the top of a temple near Alexandria, Egypt, Ptolemy studied the stars and developed his theory of the Earth as the center of the universe.

ing is known of Ptolemy's life. He was probably born in the Grecian-Egyptian city of Ptolemais Hermii and died when about 78. He was at the height of his fame between A.D. 127 and 151. His observatory was on top of a temple near the Egyptian city of Alexandria.

Ptolemy realized that the sciences of mathematics, geography, and astronomy are closely related. He used his mathematical knowledge to prove that the earth was round. He also studied the revolving movements of the heavenly bodies. The *geocentric* theory that the earth is the center of the universe was developed by him. This theory was generally accepted until replaced by the Copernican system. (See COPERNICUS, NICOLAUS.)

Ptolemy was the first man of ancient times to study geography scientifically. His maps of Asia and Africa and his notes on latitude and longitude were collected in his *Guide to Geography*. Although these maps were incorrect they led Columbus to believe he could reach India by sailing west across the Atlantic.

His greatest work was *The Mathematical Collection*, or *Almagest* (The Greatest). In this he developed and explained plane and spherical trigonometry. Many ideas in it were not developed further for 1,400 years.

PTOLEMY [Kings of Egypt]. When Alexander the Great died in 323 B.C. his generals divided his empire among themselves. One of these generals, a Macedonian named Ptolemy, became satrap or governor of Egypt. In 306 B.C., when all the generals took the title of king, he became king of Egypt. Thus he founded the long line of Ptolemies who ruled Egypt from 323 to 30 B.C.

PTOLEMY I (367?–283 B.C.), the founder of the line, was a genial soldier who attracted to his standard the best of the paid soldiers of Macedon and Greece. For many years after he became ruler of Egypt, he was involved in wars. He fought against the other generals and the regent who was appointed by Alexander to rule over his empire. In 315 Ptolemy entered into an alliance against Antigonus, the general who had taken Asia for his province. First one side occupied Palestine and Cyprus, then the other.

Antigonus was finally defeated and slain in 301. Ptolemy occupied Palestine for the fourth time and thereafter was free to develop his kingdom in peace.

Ptolemy won the respect of the Egyptians. He built canals and roads, and developed the commercial importance of the country. He also started the great library at Alexandria. He himself was a writer and composed an honest and scholarly history of Alexander's campaigns. Ptolemy I, who is known as Ptolemy Soter, a title meaning "savior," gave up his throne in 285 and was succeeded by a younger son.

PTOLEMY II (309–246 B.C.), surnamed Philadelphus, was not a soldier like his father, but a brilliant king. He increased the library and appointed Callimachus its keeper. He was the patron of poets, including Theocritus, and of scientists. He started a zoo at Alexandria. At his command the canal from the Red Sea to the Nile was opened and the Pharos, the famous lighthouse, was built. In accordance with Egyptian custom Ptolemy II married his sister, Arsinoe and revived the splendor of the court of the Pharaohs.

PTOLEMY III (282?–221 B.C.), surnamed Euergetes, was the son of Ptolemy II. He made the kingdom of the Ptolemies the most powerful on the Mediterranean. He marched to Babylonia and Thrace and joined Cyrenaica (Libya) to Egypt by his marriage with Berenice, daughter of its ruler. He adopted and patronized the Egyptian religion.

The rest of the Ptolemies were weak and luxury-loving kings who brought Egypt into touch with Rome. Ptolemy V (210–181 B.C.), surnamed Epiphanes, was allied with Rome against Antiochus the Great of Syria. Ptolemy XII (reigned 80–51 B.C.) left the kingdom to his eldest son, Ptolemy XIII, who married his sister, Cleopatra. The young king was killed in the Alexandrine War of Julius Caesar (48–47). A still younger brother, Ptolemy XIV, was associated as ruler with Cleopatra until he died in 44, probably through her contrivance. Ptolemy XV was, according to Cleopatra, her son by Julius Caesar. He ruled with his mother from 45 to 30, when she took her life. In that year he was put to death by Octavian, who then made Egypt a Roman province. (See AUGUSTUS; CLEOPATRA.)

PUBLIC (*pŭb′lĭk*) **HEALTH.** Public health is the science of preventing illness and improving the health of communities. The public health physician works with groups of persons. The private or family physician usually works with individual persons. The public health doctor is more concerned with the prevention of diseases than is the family doctor. The work of the public health doctor includes public or community arrangements for treating groups of persons. He also works with individuals who are already sick when this benefits or affects the public. He may work with persons who have been with the sick person.

When a person gets sick with a stomach ache, cold, or sore throat, a private physician is usually called. He finds out what caused the illness and how sick the person is. He then decides what is needed to help him get better. He may order medicine, rest in bed, an operation, or a combination of these. However, if a person, his neighbor across the street, a friend who visited him from the other side of town, and others all get sick at about the same time with the same thing, the public health physician becomes concerned with the problem. He, together with public health nurses, sanitary inspectors, and many trained assistants, finds out what caused the illness. It may come from food that has spoiled and contains harmful germs, or from germs or other harmful substances that have got into milk or water. It may come from some child or adult who is spreading a disease directly to other persons. The public health doctor does what is necessary to stop the spread of the disease and sees that those who are ill get treated. He tries to stop the disease from starting again at a later date.

Many years ago widespread diseases were common. They are common today in countries or areas where public health services are not well developed and effective. Sore throats, severe stomach disorders, colds, influenza, and many more serious illnesses such as smallpox, dysentery, and plague sometimes spread like wildfire to thousands and even millions of persons, killing large numbers of them. Such widespread diseases are called epidemics. Such epidemics showed the need for public health services and public health departments. However, until the discovery of the germs and viruses that caused many of these diseases, the health departments were not very successful. After these discoveries, they were often able to find out how many of these diseases spread. They learned that diseases may spread directly from one person to another or by way of flies, rats, lice, unclean water or food, and other means.

A good health department can prevent the spread of most epidemic diseases that formerly killed and crippled thousands. In fact, many of these diseases can be stopped before they get a start.

Examples of Public Health Services

Almost any disease or disorder that affects large numbers of persons can be studied by public health experts. Programs may be planned to cure or prevent most of these diseases.

For example, accurate figures on the number and location of all old and new cases of tuberculosis throughout the city or county may be kept. Thus, whenever new cases occur, the health department can find out from whom the disease was caught. The patients can then be treated so that they no longer spread tuberculosis to others. The public health department may also X-ray the chests of all children in certain grades of school. Any case of tuberculosis can be found before it is so far advanced that it spreads to other children in the schoolroom.

Many health departments also have special laboratories that make tests to see exactly what type of disease a person has and whether or not the disease is in a catching stage. Some of the laboratories also make vaccines to help prevent certain diseases.

This same type of public health program may be applied to illnesses or disorders that are not catching. If many persons working in a factory develop the same sort of sickness, a public health investigation may find that they are

Public health doctors are concerned with the prevention and spread of disease. Their work includes treatment of groups of persons. Together with public health nurses and other personnel, they work for the public good.

breathing in dangerous dust or vapors. The health department can correct this by making the necessary laws to control the working conditions. Inspections can be made to enforce the laws. Public health methods control catching diseases such as typhoid fever, diphtheria, and smallpox. They can also help with sicknesses that are not catching, such as those caused by accidents, cancer, and mental disease.

The health department also makes sure that water and milk supplies are safe and clean and that sewage systems are satisfactory and will not spread disease. They help the family and the personal physician with the care given to mothers and to newly born babies. Where necessary they see that the babies are vaccinated and protected from childhood diseases.

Health departments and boards of health were first developed in an effort to prevent serious epidemics. It was found that they were so helpful in preventing many other diseases that laws were passed establishing health departments. Now many cities and counties and all states in the United States have tax-supported health departments.

National Health Services

In addition to these city, county, and state health departments, many public health services are carried out by federal or nation-wide health "departments." The United States Department of Health, Education, and Welfare helps state and local health departments with many of their problems and programs. It also helps when states do not have enough money to carry out needed public health services on their own.

In the United States, which has so many different states, the problems of clean and safe food, milk, water, drugs, and air often cross state boundaries. The federal health services help with these interstate health problems. They also help other countries to control major health problems and communicable diseases. They also make sure that persons from other countries with contagious diseases do not enter the United States (quarantine service).

Voluntary Public Health Agencies

Not all public health services are official (tax-supported) agencies. Many very valuable services come from unofficial agencies financed by public contributions. These are called voluntary agencies. They include organizations such as the National Foundation for Infantile Paralysis (sponsoring the March of Dimes), the National Society for Crippled Children and Adults (which sells Easter seals), the National Tuberculosis Association (which sells Christmas seals), and others.

These agencies can often carry out public health activities on a volunteer basis that official agencies can not do or do not have enough money to do thoroughly.

Official and voluntary public health agencies, working with each other and with the co-operation and help of private physicians, nurses, hospitals, research scientists, and others, have achieved remarkable results. They have made the United States one of the healthiest nations in the world. As a result of this team work the average person born today can expect to have a life span 15 years longer than that of his grandfather.

PUCCINI (*poot chē′nē* or *poo chē′nē*), **GIACO-MO** (*jä′kō mō*) (1858–1924), was the greatest Italian opera composer of his time. *La Boheme, Madame Butterfly,* and *Tosca* remain popular throughout the years. His operas are performed more often than those of any other composer, except perhaps Richard Wagner or Giuseppe Verdi.

Puccini was born at Lucca, Italy, into a family of distinguished musicians. He studied music at Milan Conservatory under Amilcare Ponchi-

Giacomo Puccini.

elli. Soon after he left there he wrote *Le Villi,* his first opera. Nine years later Puccini produced *Manon Lescaut.* This was based on the story Jules Massenet used in his *Manon.* Then followed *La Boheme,* the most popular of Puccini's operas. *La Boheme* is full of the romantic gaiety and tragic sadness of Latin Quarter life in Paris. *Madame Butterfly,* another outstanding success, is the story of an unhappy romance between an oriental girl and an American. *Tosca* is based on a bloodcurdling drama by Victorien Sardou. *The Girl of the Golden West,* based upon a play by David Belasco, had its world premier at the Metropolitan Opera in New York City on December 10, 1910.

Puccini composed ten operas, a few pieces of church music, and two minuets for strings. He had a feeling for the theater which no other composer has ever equalled. With a few vivid strokes Puccini was able to translate a dramatic situation into music. His librettos have added much to the popularity of his operas. They tell for the most part believable yet dramatic tales. In all his work the Italian love for color and feeling is present.

PUERTO RICO (*pwer′tä rē′kō*), **WEST IN-DIES,** is the smallest of the Greater Antilles, which include the large islands of the West Indies. Puerto Rico is at the eastern end of this group. The island was formerly called Porto Rico, and long ago the Indian inhabitants called it Boriquen.

Puerto Rico is bounded on the north and east by the Atlantic Ocean, on the south by the Caribbean Sea, and on the west by the Mona Passage, a sea channel separating it from the island of Hispaniola.

Many hill clusters rise little by little from the plain around the coast toward the interior of the island. These hills are linked together into eight mountain chains, the largest running east and west the whole length of Puerto Rico. Its highest peak reaches about 4,400 feet.

The abundant rain that falls on Puerto Rico is collected by four rivers and 1,300 smaller streams, creeks, and ravines, some of which contain water only during the rainy season. Most of these are in the north.

The south of the island must be irrigated for agriculture. The soil in both the north and south is very rich.

The tropical and sunny climate is modified by northeast trade winds—the same winds as those that took Columbus to the island. The average annual temperature is 76 degrees Fahrenheit, and the temperature seldom varies more than 7 degrees from this figure. This means that the climate is uniform and healthful. But high winds, called hurricanes, always accompanied by the heaviest of rains, blow across the country each year at irregular intervals. Many people and animals drown in the swollen rivers at these times.

To make room for pastures and cultivated fields, the old forests have been almost entirely destroyed. There are very few wild animals, and they are small ones—toads, lizards (among them the interesting iguana), a few harmless snakes, and some birds such as gulls, coots, herons, pelicans, frigate birds, tree ducks, hawks, parrots, and wild pigeons. Few birds survive the hurricanes. The ferretlike mongoose is the only four-footed wild animal.

Puerto Rico was discovered by Columbus in 1493. He named it San Juan Bautista. In 1508 Juan Ponce de Leon was commissioned to settle the island for the king of Spain. Ponce de Leon founded the village of Caparra near the south shore of San Juan Bay, which he had named "rich harbor" (Puerto Rico) because it had many natural advantages as a port. The name came to be applied to the island as a whole.

As Puerto Rico was the nearest to Spain in sailing time of all the West Indian islands, it had great military value. The Spaniards built huge forts and sea walls around the capital city, San Juan. By the 17th century they had converted it into a stronghold of the Spanish Empire in the New World. Little attention was paid to de-

(1) Netting is stretched over the plants to protect them from the sun on this Puerto Rico tobacco farm. (2) The mule is carrying a load of bananas to town. (3) These low-cost modern homes at Mayaguez were built by the government to relieve the housing shortage.

Photos, (1, 3) Ewing Galloway, (2) Lotte Jay-Pix

veloping the island's resources, but the Spanish people were educated like the European Spaniards, and their language and customs were carefully preserved. The Spanish Crown paid the expenses of the local government and the military establishment until the first quarter of the 19th century, when revenue from the island's trade made it self-supporting.

Having lost the war with the United States in 1898, Spain ceded Puerto Rico, which became a United States possession. In 1917 Puerto Ricans were made United States citizens. Their government continued to be headed by a governor from the United States until 1946, when a Puerto Rican was appointed governor by the President. In 1948 Puerto Ricans elected their first governor, Luis Munoz Marin, who governed the island through 1964. His successor was Roberto Sanchez Vilella, governor from 1965 to 1968. Both men were from the Popular Democratic Party.

Since 1952 Puerto Rico has officially been a self-governing commonwealth voluntarily associated with the United States. In 1967 this relationship was endorsed by voters in a plebiscite on the island's future that gave Puerto Ricans a choice between commonwealth status, statehood (supported by a strong minority), and independence. Luis A. Ferre became governor in 1969. His party, the New Progressive, was committed to eventual statehood for Puerto Rico.

Puerto Rico is one of the most thickly populated areas of the Earth. Its inhabitants are crowded into only 3,421 square miles. Three-quarters of the people are of Spanish descent. The remaining quarter are mixtures of white and Negro.

In 1941 the Puerto Rican government began to give thousands of tenants small parcels of land, up to nearly three acres each, which they might hold for life. The government has in recent years encouraged the investment of United States capital in the island for the purpose of opening factories of all kinds. It has purchased sugar mills, railroad and city transportation companies, electric power companies, water and sewage services, and is exploiting them for the public benefit. Sanitation, public education, and other government services have been improved.

San Juan, the largest city, is the seat of the island government. Various federal agencies have offices in the city. Many commercial and industrial United States firms have their Caribbean area headquarters there. The commercial airport is an important intercontinental link. The University of Puerto Rico, included within the area of Greater San Juan, has contributed, through its Institute of Tropical Medicine, to the advancement of knowledge of tropical diseases. (See San Juan.)

Puerto Rico's main products are sugar, tobacco, coffee, and embroidery work. Sugar is the island's chief export.

Up to the present the population has grown beyond the island's natural means to support it. But laborers are now earning better wages, and living conditions are improving. Those responsible for the people's welfare believe that better living conditions will help to control population growth. The population was 2,349,544 in 1960 but was estimated at 2,749,000 in 1968.

PUFFIN (*pŭf'ŭn*) **AND MURRE** (*mēr*) are two birds of the auk family, Alcidae. Puffins have compressed, triangular bills. Murres, also called guillemots, have either slender or thick bills.

The tufted puffin is about 15 inches high. It resembles a parrot; in fact, sailors call it the "sea parrot." It is marked in the breeding season so that its face resembles that of a clown. There is a white facial mask set off by a huge red, blue, and yellow beak abruptly curved to a point, red eyelids, and two waving feather horns of rich straw color. The feet and legs are of vermilion hue. The back and wings are a glossy blue-black. The bird seems to be masquerading, but its actions are anything but clownish. It is most dignified and sedate.

Tufted puffins, auks, and murres belong to the same family. Tufted puffins are Arctic diving sea birds which frequent shores of Siberia, Alaska, and Canada. They are exceedingly hardy, spending their winters upon the ocean and returning to shore only when a storm of unusual severity arises. With the coming of spring and the nesting season, the tufted puffins land on some friendly cliff. Then it is that both males and females flaunt the gay and ridiculous beaks and plumage. Later, the great red beak falls

The tufted puffin is a diving sea bird about 15 inches high. During the nesting season both male and female birds have white faces and large red beaks.

away, the white facial mask disappears, and the entire head becomes a dull black. The natives of the North Pacific value the puffin for its plumage and also eat its flesh.

The common puffin, about 13 inches long, is very similar, but has no tuft or crest. It is very squat, with short legs. Its cousins, the murres, about 17 inches long, are found in the North Atlantic. Their legs are short and they sit upright with the rear flat on the ground. They have long necks and beaks. The head, neck, and back are blackish brown, and the underparts pure white.

PULASKI (*pū lăs′kē* or *pū lăs′kĭ*), **CASIMIR** (*kăz′ĭ mĭr*), Count (1748-1779). Count Casimir Pulaski of Poland found he was unable to free his own people from foreign oppression. So he gave his life in fighting for the liberty of the American colonists during the Revolutionary War. Pulaski's birthplace is what became known as the Ukraine. When he was only 22 years old he led the army that successfully re-sisted the Russians in Lithuania. In 1772, his army was defeated. Upon being falsely accused of plotting against King Stanislas Poniatowski, he was forced to leave his country. During his exile, he met Benjamin Franklin in Paris. Pulaski became so interested in the American struggle for independence, that he sailed for America to help the Colonists. His first battle, at Brandywine, proved his ability as an officer. Congress made him a brigadier general in command of cavalry.

Pulaski was a brave soldier and a skilled general. However, some of his men objected to following the command of a foreigner who spoke very broken English. He was given permission, therefore, to form his own command of men who were themselves foreigners and soldiers of fortune. The Pulaski Legion soon became famed for its valor in battle. When the British were attacking Charleston, South Carolina, Pulaski held it for five days, despite the willingness of the townspeople to surrender. When the Americans tried to take Savannah, Georgia, the Royalist stronghold, Pulaski commanded the whole field of attack. During the losing battle he was fatally wounded in the thigh. A few days later he died on board an American battleship. A statue was erected in Savannah, in 1824 in recognition of Pulaski's brave and generous service to the United States.

PULITZER (*pū′lĭt sẽr*), **JOSEPH** (1847–1911). The name of Joseph Pulitzer is famous in the history of United States journalism. He was born at Budapest, Hungary. His father was a Jewish grain merchant, and his mother a German Roman Catholic. The youth was bitterly disappointed when an eye defect kept him out of the Hungarian army and the French Foreign Legion. So eager was he to fight, that in 1864 he made the long trip to the United States and joined the Union army.

After his discharge he went to St. Louis, Missouri, where he soon became a prominent figure among the German settlers. In 1869 he was a member of the Missouri legislature. He helped to nominate Horace Greeley for president. Then he entered the newspaper business, publishing a daily paper in the German language. Later he purchased the St. Louis *Dispatch,* which he combined with the *Post,* making the present-day St. Louis *Post-Dispatch.* Its strong editorials, demanding changes in the tariff and honest city government, gained a reputation for the newspaper. In 1883 Pulitzer was able to buy the New York *World.* Under his fearless direction the newspaper quickly prospered.

When William R. Hearst purchased the New York *Journal* in 1895 Pulitzer was faced with a strong rival. He met the competition by reducing the price of the *World* from 2 cents to 1. The *Evening World* was established in 1887. It was not a financial success the first year, but Pulitzer's sound management soon made it prosperous. Meantime he became blind, but kept in close touch with the *World.* Editorials in Pulitzer's three newspapers were largely free of party politics. They showed sympathy for labor, and were noted for their honesty.

In his will Joseph Pulitzer made provisions for the "Pulitzer Awards." These are annual prizes for the best work in literature, drama, music, and journalism in the United States. He also provided funds for three European scholarships for the study of political, social, and moral conditions.

Pulitzer established a fund for a gold medal to be awarded annually for the most disinterested and worthy public service given by any United States newspaper. He left money with which to establish the School of Journalism of Columbia University, New York City.

PUMA (*pū'mä*). The puma belongs to the cat family. It is also known as the mountain lion, the cougar, and, in America, the panther. Pumas once lived from British Columbia, in Canada, over all the United States, and south through Mexico, Central, and South America.

Today the puma is found in the United States in southern Florida and the wilder areas of the western part of the country. It also lives in British Columbia. Pumas are also found in the mountains of Central America and in most of South America except the Amazon River Basin.

Pumas vary greatly in size and weight, depending on their age, sex, and where they live. They may be from six to eight feet long, in-

cluding the two-foot tail. They weigh from 80 to 225 pounds. In color the puma's coat varies from red to yellowish brown and gray. Some live to be 17 years of age although their average life span is about half of this. Every two or three years the female puma has a litter from one to six kittens. Its den may be in a cave on a mountain side, in thick brush, or under a fallen tree.

Like other cats, pumas eat meat, including deer, squirrels, rabbits, and even mice. Their habit of killing domestic stock such as sheep and cattle have made them unwelcome in stock-raising areas. As a result, they are scarce in many places. They are usually hunted with dogs that run them until they take to a tree.

Pumas are a natural check on deer. If allowed to multiply too quickly, the deer would soon exhaust all available food. In the United States, national parks and forests are refuges for pumas.

PUMP (*pŭmp*). Historians say that water was raised by mechanical means many centuries before the Christian Era. An early method used consisted of a bucket on the end of a rope. The addition of a "sweep," or windlass, improved upon this method.

The ancient Egyptians lifted water by means of buckets fastened around the rim of a wheel. As the wheel was turned each bucket in turn was scooped full of water. At the top of the revolution the water was emptied into a trough or storage basin. Another primitive system was that of pots attached to an endless chain or rope. The Greeks used these same methods in their wells as early as the 15th century B.C. Many remains of early Roman pumps have been dug up. The Egyptians and the Romans are credited with using the principle of the screw in water-lifting machines. (See IRRIGATION.) It is interesting to note that the first general use made of the steam engine was to drive pumping machinery. It is probable that about the 3rd century B.C. a pump was devised which drew water up from a well by means of atmospheric pressure.

Of the many varieties of pumps probably the most commonly seen are *suction* and *force*

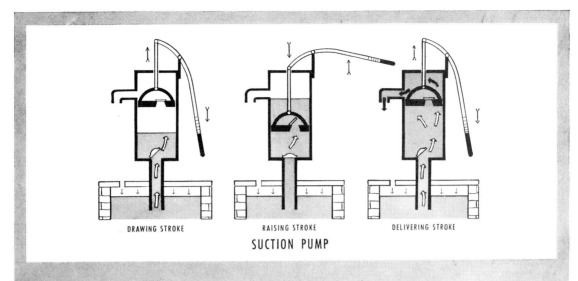

DRAWING STROKE   RAISING STROKE   DELIVERING STROKE

SUCTION PUMP

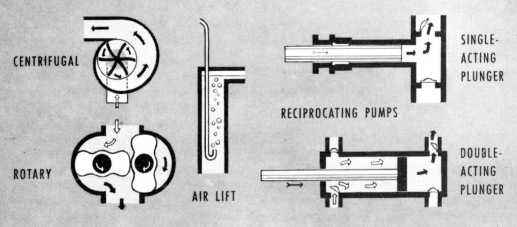

CENTRIFUGAL

ROTARY

AIR LIFT

RECIPROCATING PUMPS

SINGLE-ACTING PLUNGER

DOUBLE-ACTING PLUNGER

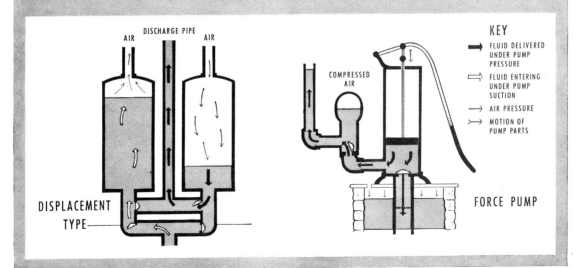

AIR   DISCHARGE PIPE   AIR

COMPRESSED AIR

DISPLACEMENT TYPE

FORCE PUMP

KEY

➡ FLUID DELIVERED UNDER PUMP PRESSURE

⇨ FLUID ENTERING UNDER PUMP SUCTION

→ AIR PRESSURE

↣ MOTION OF PUMP PARTS

pumps. Atmospheric pressure aids the suction pump. Air has weight, and it exerts pressure. (See AIR; BAROMETER.) When one drinks an ice cream soda through a straw, the liquid comes up the straw. By suction, the air in the straw has been removed. The pressure of the atmosphere, pushing down on the liquid in the glass, causes the liquid to rise and take the place of the removed air. Atmospheric pressure at sea level will push mercury up a closed tube from which the air has been exhausted to a height of about 30 *inches* and water to about 33 *feet*.

The suction pump simply removes the air from a pipe whose lower end is under water. Then, as in the case of the soda in the straw, the pressure of the atmosphere pushes water up the pipe. To make the physical work of removing the air in the pipe easier, the ordinary hand pump employs the principle of the first class of lever. (See MACHINE.) The force pump is really a suction pump with an added device. This device enables it to raise a liquid to a greater height than can be reached by atmospheric pressure.

Other types of pumps have various features which make them useful in performing certain classes of pumping work. The *centrifugal* pump in its simplest form consists of an "impeller" fitted with vanes and rotating in a closed casing. The liquid to be pumped is supplied to the center of the impeller. Through rotating in the impeller its pressure is increased by centrifugal force. Then the liquid is delivered at the outside boundary with an increased pressure and high velocity. A *reciprocating* pump may be either single or double acting. In a single acting reciprocating pump, liquid is drawn into the pump through a suction valve on one stroke. It is forced out through the delivery valve on the return stroke. By fitting suction and delivery valves on both sides of the plunger, the pump is made double acting.

There are two main types of *rotary* pumps. In one, a drum mounted eccentrically (off center) in its casing carries one or more sliding diaphragms which make contact with the interior of the casing. In the other type, two rotating drums are used. These are mounted on parallel axes and coupled together by two equal gear wheels mounted on the shafts outside the casing. These pumps are well adapted for working over a wide range of speeds with comparatively low heads and with widely varying discharges. Their advantage over the reciprocating pump lies in their practically continuous discharge. Also, their efficiency does not fall off so quickly with discharge variations as it does in centrifugal pumps.

In a *jet pump* a high-pressure liquid supply is conducted to a small nozzle. From the nozzle it issues into a suction chamber as a jet having a high velocity and a relatively low pressure. The suction chamber surrounding the jet is connected to the suction reservoir. If the pressure at the jet is sufficiently low, liquid is lifted into this chamber. It is forced, by the impact of the high velocity jet, into a discharge pipe whose suction gradually increases in the direction of flow. The efficiency of such a pump is low.

A *gas pump*, known as the Humphrey Gas Pump, raises liquid by the direct action of the pressure accompanying the explosion and expansion of a gas-air mixture. The mixture is fired by an electric spark.

The *air-lift pump* consists of an open-ended vertical lift pipe, the lower end of which is submerged in the liquid to be raised. The upper end delivers the liquid into a discharge tank at the height desired. Compressed air is supplied through an air pipe to the lower end of the lift pipe. Rising in the form of small bubbles through the liquid in the lift pipe, it forms a mixture of lower specific gravity than the liquid itself. The pressure of the liquid surrounding the pipe then raises the lighter mixture above the supply level and out of the top of the lift pipe. The possible lift depends upon the amount of air supplied and upon the depth of submersion of the bottom of the lift pipe. For best results the depth of submersion should be about one and one half times the height of the lift.

A displacement type of compressed air pump is much used in mines and excavating work. It consists of two reservoirs connected by suitable valves so that air may be pumped from one to the other. As the air is taken from one it fills with liquid. When it is full the air is pumped back to it, driving the contained liquid out the discharge pipe. The action is alternated between the two tanks, and this creates a very efficient pump.

Pumps may be worked by hand, animals, wind or water power, gas or steam engines, electric motors, or compressed air. (See HYDRAULIC MACHINERY.)

PUMPKIN (*pŭmp'kĭn*). To many children in the United States, Halloween without a jack-o' lantern made from a hollow pumpkin would hardly seem like Halloween. Like the squash the pumpkin is a member of the gourd family. It grows on a coarse, running vine which is sometimes 20 feet long. Its yellow, bell-like flowers grow among the large prickly leaves. They develop into globe-shaped fruit which matures in the late summer or fall. When ripe these fruits may be two feet in diameter, although smaller ones are less coarse and of better flavor. They are usually bright orange. Some species, however, are dark green, or green striped with orange. Inside the thick, fleshy rind are many flat white seeds enclosed in a stringy pulp. Pumpkins serve as a vegetable and for making pies. They are also used as food for cattle and pigs. They are often planted among rows of corn and grow with little attention. The Indians planted their pumpkins in just this way long before white men came to America.

PUNCTUATION (*pŭngk'tū ā'shŭn*). In the days when books were written by hand by patient monks and clerks, very little punctuation was used. There were few readers. Those who did read books had plenty of leisure to decipher the meaning without the use of punctuation marks. With the invention of printing in the 15th century the number of books and the number of readers greatly increased. As people read more rapidly, they felt the need for some kind of marks to separate sentences and to show the divisions of thought within sentences. To answer this need printers invented signals to help the reader. In the years that followed the modern type of punctuation gradually developed.

Strictly speaking there are no rules of punctuation. The marks people use are determined by the general practice of printers. However, most of these marks are used with such common agreement that they may be called rules. Since the purpose of punctuation is to make meaning clear to the reader, modern punctuation may be grouped into three classes: separate-thought punctuation; clear-meaning punctuation; and special-signal punctuation.

Separate-Thought Punctuation

The purpose of this class of punctuation is to indicate the close of a complete thought. What is called "sentence-sense" is the ability to recognize each unit of complete thought and to separate this complete thought from all others by means of end punctuation. The marks of separate-thought punctuation are: period, question mark, exclamation mark, and semicolon.

A *period* is used at the close of a statement (declarative sentence) or a command (imperative sentence).

Examples: The tree grew to a great height.
Take that dog away.

The *question mark* is used at the close of a question (interrogative sentence).

Examples: Will he come?
Why do you do that?

An *exclamation mark* is used at the close of an exclamation (exclamatory sentence) or after an interjection (a word or words expressing surprise, pain, fear, etc.).

Examples: How fine they look!
Look, it's snowing!
Hurrah! Ouch! My goodness!

The *semicolon* is used as separate-thought punctuation when it stands between the independent clauses of a compound sentence when a conjunction is omitted.

Examples: The huge airplane taxied slowly to the landing stage; crowds of people pressed forward to see it.
The room quieted as the teacher entered; pupils bent to their work; soon there was not a sound to be heard.

The semicolon is also used before the conjunctive adverbs *therefore, hence, so, accord-*

ingly, and *nevertheless;* also before *namely, thus,* and *that is,* when these introduce examples or illustrations in a sentence.

> Examples: The command was given to take cover; accordingly, the men concealed themselves behind trees, stumps, and rocks.
>
> The pupils were assigned three units of study; namely, flies, beetles, and butterflies.

Clear-Meaning Punctuation

The purpose of clear-meaning punctuation is to guide the reader along the lines of thought intended by the writer and to set off words and phrases which interrupt or introduce the principal thought of the sentence. The marks used for clear-meaning punctuation are the comma and occasionally the semicolon.

Since the *comma* is used in many ways, these uses are numbered and illustrated as follows:

1. To set off independent clauses in a compound sentence when they are connected by the conjunctions *and, but, or, nor.* The comma is placed before the conjunction.

> Examples: Tom ran to the door, but no one followed him.
>
> You may choose the book you want, or you may leave the choice to me.

When the conjunction *and* merely adds a second thought to the first, the comma is frequently omitted.

> Example: Dark clouds rolled up and the rain began to fall.

2. To set off the members of a series. When a conjunction is used between the last two items of the series a comma may be placed before the conjunction.

> Example: Jane quickly put on her hat, coat, and mittens.

3. To set off an adverbial clause which comes before the main clause.

> Example: When the train arrived, no one came forward to meet him.

4. To separate the items in a date or an address.

> Example: The traveler reached Kansas City, Missouri, on March 25, 1944.

5. To set off a word or phrase in **apposition** (an explanatory word or phrase standing beside another word or phrase and of equal rank with it).

> Examples: Frank Thompson, my best friend, was elected president of the class.
>
> The hostess presented the winner with the first prize, a silver cup.

6. To set off a name or title used in direct address.

> Examples: Come, friends, take these chairs.
>
> I hope, John, you have learned your lesson.

7. To set off a direct quotation from the words which introduce it.

> Examples: Mary shouted, "Bring more wood."
>
> "If you like," said Father, "I shall take you all to the zoo."

8. To set off phrases of the absolute construction.

> Example: The day being fine, we started for the mountains.

9. To set off parenthetical expressions.

> Examples: He is not, despite what you say, a traitor.
>
> I thought, indeed, that he would return.

10. To set off nonrestrictive adjective clauses (the nonrestrictive clause is one which supplies additional information about the word which it modifies).

> Examples: The Tower of London, which in former years was a prison, is now a museum.
>
> The man surrendered his ticket to the conductor, who examined it thoroughly.

Occasionally, very long clauses containing commas are set off from each other by the use of a *semicolon.* The purpose of the semicolon here is to make easier the meaning which might be confused by a long series of commas.

> Example: Unquestionably the new laws, which are called into being by the public interest, convenience, and necessity, are just; though there will be many who will protest, and perhaps even defy, them.

Special-Signal Punctuation

The marks of punctuation in this group are

employed to signal to the reader that the words which follow or are enclosed by the marks bear a particular relationship to the sentence as a whole. They are like signal flags to guide the reader to the correct meaning. The marks are: colon, dash, parentheses, quotation marks, and hyphen.

The *colon* has two distinct uses.

1. After a formal salutation in a letter.

>   Examples: Gentlemen: Dear Sir: Dear Mr. Stevens:

2. To set off particularly a list, a long or formal quotation, or a formal explanation.

>   Examples: Henry's studies include the following courses: English, mathematics, French, history, and philosophy.
>
>   The old woman made this her constant motto: "Never put off until tomorrow what you can do today."
>
>   A long life of mingled happiness and sorrow had brought him to this conclusion: no man may safely judge the motives of another.

The *dash* is used:

1. To show a sudden change in thought.

>   Example: I have made a profound study of— but this will bore you.

2. To set off an expression which is thrust into the sentence (a parenthetical expression).

>   Example: Very few people—it is pitiful how few—knew that he still lived.

Parentheses are used to enclose words, phrases, and clauses that are inserted into a sentence by way of comment or explanation.

>   Examples: The great General (Washington) retired to the woods at Valley Forge to pray.
>
>   Frank gave the conductor five cents (his last coin) and rode hopefully toward a new job.

Quotation marks are used to show the exact words said by a speaker and to separate these words from other words in the sentence. The following statements indicate the ways in which quotations are commonly marked.

1. A direct quotation is enclosed in double quotation marks.

>   Example: "Why are you carrying that hammer?" Paul enquired.
>
>   John answered, "I have to repair my boat."

2. A quotation within a quotation is enclosed in single quotation marks.

>   Example: Jean said, "I promised to recite the poem 'The Wanderer' for the program Friday."

3. Slang words, or words used in an unusual sense, are sometimes set off by quotation marks.

>   Examples: Henry was the sort of fellow known as a "good guy."
>
>   Give me a ride in that "coffee-grinder" of yours.

The *hyphen* is used between the parts of compound words; for example, strong-minded, ninety-six, clear-spoken. It is also used at the end of a line of writing or print when a word must be divided.

Capital Letters

The following types of words regularly begin with a capital letter:

The first word in a sentence.

All proper nouns. Boston, Mississippi, Joan, The Times.

Adjectives made from proper nouns. American, French, Lutheran.

Names and titles for God. Lord, Saviour, Heavenly Father.

Titles of honor or respect. Doctor, Mayor, General.

The first word of a direct quotation. Tom said, "Give me one."

The first word of every line of poetry.

Names of the months and days of the week. January, Monday.

The first word of the title of a book or an article. It is also correct to capitalize each important word of a title, excepting articles, prepositions, and conjunctions.

The following types of words are sometimes capitalized and sometimes not, as indicated:

The names indicating directions are not begun with capitals unless they are used as names of sections of the country.

>   Examples: He comes from the North but has lived for some years in the East.

Turn east on Main Street and continue to the south end of the Square.

When the names of things are personified, that is, addressed as persons, they are begun with capital letters.

Examples: "Oh, tell me where is Fancy bred?"
And now comes Winter dressed in ice and snow.

Words such as street, avenue, city, school, university, and the like are capitalized only when they form part of a name.

Examples: Wisconsin River, Lincoln School, Third Street.
I cross the street and go down the avenue on my way to school.

Words such as mother, father, aunt, uncle, begin with a capital letter when they are used as part of a name or as a title.

Examples: Old Mother Hubbard went to the cupboard.
Please stop in and see Father.
My mother took my brother and sister to the movies.

Abbreviations

Words which are shortened forms of titles begin with a capital letter and end with a period; for example, Dr., Mr., Mrs., Rev. (Reverend), Lieut. (Lieutenant), Pfc. (Private First-Class). Other abbreviations begin with a small letter and end with a period; for example, oz. (ounce), doz. (dozen), ft. (foot), yd. (yard), in. (inch), tsp. (teaspoon).

Contractions

Contractions are shortened forms of words or are two words put together in shortened form. An apostrophe is used to mark the point of contraction.

Examples: I'll, he'll, can't, shouldn't, isn't, etc.

PUPIN (*pū pēn'*), **MICHAEL IDVORSKY** (1858–1935), United States scientist and inventor, was born in what is now Yugoslavia on October 4, 1858. Even as a boy herding sheep in the Serbian hills he was curious about the world around him. During the long nights he studied the stars and wondered about their twinkle.

When Pupin came to the United States at the age of 15 years he had five cents, spoke no English, and knew no one. For two years he did odd jobs. He spent many evenings in Cooper Union, a free educational institution in New York City. When 17 years old, he found work in a cracker factory. He used the boiler room as his laboratory, and slept in the factory attic with a German worker who taught him Greek and Latin.

His brilliant work in the entrance examinations for Columbia University won him a four-year scholarship. After graduation he was awarded a fellowship in science, studied at Cambridge University in England, and received a doctor's degree at Berlin in 1889. He returned to Columbia as instructor in the newly organized department of electrical engineering.

Pupin greatly improved X-ray photography and solar astronomy. He worked out an apparatus for electrical tuning and rectification. His induction coil made long-distance telephone calls possible. He was responsible for several of the ideas that were used later in radio inventions. Electro-scientists in the United States learned much from him. His autobiography, *From Immigrant to Inventor,* was published in 1923.

PURE FOOD AND DRUG ACTS are laws in the United States that require manufacturers and producers to meet high standards. They help to make sure of the wholesomeness of food, and the pureness of drugs and cosmetics sold to the public. The first federal law was passed in 1906. Since then most states have passed similar laws.

The senses of smell and taste are not enough to test the wholesomeness of food. Food packagers and canners may use chemicals that easily pass any test by only taste or smell. At times the quality of foods may not be what the manufacturers say it is. (See ADULTERATION.) To discover the strength, quality, and purity of drugs, drug compounds, and cosmetics, chemical tests must be made.

The United States Constitution says that the federal government may regulate commerce between states (interstate) and foreign commerce. When food, drugs, or cosmetics, are shipped from one state to another they are in interstate commerce. Therefore, federal food and drug laws apply to such shipments and forbid commerce in any items that are adulterated or misbranded. This applies to manufactured foods and products, or to natural foods. Government agents may open, examine, test, and stop shipments of these items. The post office helps by seizing impure shipments that are made by mail.

Law officers ask a federal court for an order called a *libel*. This gives them the right (the authority) to seize suspected goods. After a hearing in court, the goods may be condemned (declared unsafe) and destroyed. The manufacturer or shipper may be fined or sent to prison.

PURITANS (*pū′rĭ tänz*). A Puritan is a person who wishes to make clean or purify everything around him. In England, during the reign of Queen Elizabeth I, a group of Protestants became known as Puritans. They did not wish to keep the forms and rules of the Church of England, the government church.

This group of dissenters could be divided into three smaller groups. The first wanted to change (purify) the form of worship within the Church. They did not like the use of vestments (the clothes worn by priests) or the Book of Common Prayer. They were known as Puritans. The second group wanted the Church of England to be under a *presbyter,* an elected elder. They followed the teachings of John Calvin, and later started the Presbyterian Church in England and Scotland. The third group, known as Separatists, believed that a church established by the government was wrong. They wanted to separate or break with the Church of England.

Puritan ideas were religious, but they were related to what was happening to the country as well. As the large feudal estates disappeared, the middle or merchant class grew in numbers in England. These merchants were against the trade regulations set up by the landowners. The Puritans wanted greater

Peter A. Juley & Son

Augustus Saint-Gaudens' statue "The Puritan" shows clearly the simple clothing worn by the Puritans.

freedom in their business. Instead of producing just enough to meet the demands, they wanted to produce more goods to make profits.

To make themselves known in the country, the Puritans dressed severely in simple clothes of dark colors. They wore their hair cut close to their heads. For this they were named "Round Heads." These farmers, merchants, and professional men sometimes became fanatics who looked down upon those around because of their own "pure and sinless" way of life.

Massachusetts and Virginia

Puritan merchants sent fishing expeditions into the waters near Plymouth, Massachusetts. There a group of Separatists, the Pilgrims, had started a colony. (See MAYFLOWER; PLYMOUTH.) In 1629 King Charles I gave the Puritans permission to settle in the New England area. With their charter they came to America and set up the Massachusetts Bay Colony at what is now Boston.

There the most radical forms of Puritanism were practiced. Although there was freedom of action, the Puritan made himself a judge of his fellowmen. No Roman Catholic priest was allowed to live in the colony. The Puritans persecuted those not accepting their religion just as the Church of England had done to them.

Women who cut their hair like men were fined. Women were also fined if they did not spin as much wool or flax daily as the selectmen of the church required. On Sunday persons were forbidden to run or even walk "except reverently" to and from church. They thought of the Indians as less than human and treated them in that way.

One of the most unusual results of the Puritan's beliefs took place when the people accepted the idea that supernatural evil spirits lived in the human body. In New England from 1647 to 1692 there was hysteria and terror as adults and children accused innocent neighbors of tormenting them. After more than 30 so-called witches had been put to death and hundreds more were accused, New England stopped the Salem trials and the prisoners were released. (See MATHER, COTTON.)

Another 118 Puritans went to Virginia, but religious persecution forced them to leave. Some returned to England. Others settled in Maryland where there was freedom of worship.

Puritans in England

Puritan migrations to America slowed up as the middle class in England took over more power in Parliament. The Puritans were against the king and the church. During the reigns of James I (1603–1625) and Charles I (1625–1649), the Puritans were treated unfairly. Puritans in Parliament led the fight against Charles I and forced him to agree to the Petition of Right in 1628. By the Petition the king could get money only by calling Parliament into session. In 1629 Charles I dissolved Parliament when it protested against the taxes he had levied. For 11 years Charles ruled

alone, but in 1640 he needed money. Political disorder and rebellion of the Scots caused Charles to call what became known as the Long Parliament. Parliament, led by Puritans, made 19 demands on the king. It called for reform of the Church of England, persecution of the Roman Catholics, and control of the army. (See CHARLES I [KING OF ENGLAND]; JAMES [KINGS OF ENGLAND].)

When the king refused, Civil War between the Puritans (Round Heads) and the supporters of the king (Cavaliers) began (1642). The Puritans won. The king was later tried, convicted, and beheaded as a traitor. Oliver Cromwell, the Puritan leader, became lord protector of England in 1653 and ruled until his death in 1658. (See CROMWELL, OLIVER.) His son Richard then took power, but he was a weak ruler. The followers of the king were able to restore the throne to Charles II (1660). (See CHARLES II [KING OF ENGLAND].) The most important result of the revolution in England was the growth of the democratic feeling among the people.

After the revolution of 1688, there was more religious freedom in England and in the colonies, although the dissenters and Puritans had to help support the Church of England. In the colonies, the Puritans continued to be powerful in New England. Puritan churches became known by the name Congregationalist. (See CONGREGATIONALISM.)

In modern times, the word "puritan" has come to mean a person who wants to purify the habits of others. Many so-called "puritan" laws do not allow baseball games and work on Sunday. These are called Blue Laws. (See BLUE LAW.)

PUSAN (*poō sän*), **KOREA,** is the largest port and second-largest city in the Republic of Korea. It is on the southeast coast and has an excellent deep harbor. Mok-to Island to the south shelters the harbor from storms. Pusan is the nearest Korean port to Japan. Before World War II it was the chief port for Japanese commerce in both Korea and Manchuria.

The city is built along the shoreline for a distance of more than five miles. The docks line the harbor for nearly two miles. Part of the city is on the island of Mok-to. The downtown area has many tall buildings. However, the buildings and houses away from the center of the city are small and crowded. The buildings in most of the city are made of wood or rough brick.

The city has two universities; the main one is Pusan University. Pusan is the leading industrial center of the Republic of Korea. Manufactured products include cast iron, aluminum, petroleum products, and rubber goods (chiefly bicycle tires).

The Japanese first invaded the Pusan area in 1592 and made the city a trading center for Japanese goods. Korea was annexed to Japan in 1910, and Pusan grew quickly into a modern city. Until the end of World War II, many Japanese lived there. Now the population is almost entirely Korean. During the Korean War (1950–1953), Pusan was the principal port for men and supplies of the United Nations forces. Pusan's population is 1,049,000.

PUSHKIN (*push'kin*), **ALEXANDER** (1799–1837), was Russia's greatest poet. He also is considered the first great author of modern Russia. Many of his novels, stories, and plays were patterned after the works of the English writers Lord Byron and William Shakespeare.

Pushkin was born in Moscow on June 6, 1799, the great-grandson of a Negro general who had served Peter the Great. While in school, Pushkin showed signs of becoming a good poet. He left school in 1817 and joined the ministry of foreign affairs. About this time he began his first important writing, a long poem called *Russlan and Ludmila*. It was not completed until 1820. This same year Pushkin was exiled to southern Russia for writing *An Ode to Liberty* and other revolutionary verses. He was inspired by the natural beauty of the Caucasus and the Crimea and wrote such poems as *The Captive of the Caucasus, The Robber Brothers,* and *The Fountain of Bakhchisarai.*

In 1825 Pushkin set out to write a tragedy in the style of Shakespeare. The result was his play *Boris Godunov*, which was not published until 1831. This play was like Shakespeare's *Macbeth*. The Russian composer Modest Mussorgsky based an opera on it.

Pushkin's most popular work was a novel in verse, *Eugene Onegin,* completed in 1832. He used Byron's style of writing in this novel. Another Russian composer, Peter Tschaikovsky, used it in composing an opera. He also wrote a second opera based on a work by Pushkin, a tale called *The Queen of Spades.*

PUZZLE (*pŭz'l*). The earliest mention of puzzles can be found in the Bible. Here are many references to mysterious dreams, contests in riddles, and meanings hidden in certain letter arrangements.

Greek mythology often mentions the Sphinx. This was a monster having the head of a woman, the body of a lion, the wings of a bird, and the tail of a serpent. She asked the Thebans a riddle and killed all who were unable to guess the answer. Her riddle was: "What is that animal which in the morning goes forth on four feet, at noon on two, and in the evening on three; and is weakest when it has most feet?" The answer is "Man." When her riddle was finally correctly guessed by Oedipus, she threw herself from her rock and died.

The Orientals were great admirers of mysterious problems. These were popular with the people of ancient India, China, and Arabia. Later they are found also in Rome. Puzzles were not so popular during the early Christian Era, but were revived in the Middle Ages. Then it was fashionable to publish the results of the alchemists' searches in puzzling language. Several forms of puzzles were developed then and were passed on to modern times.

In ancient Greece cryptography had great popularity. This is the art of writing messages that could be read only by persons knowing a certain secret. The message was written in *cipher.* Persons reading it had to have the *key.* The earliest form of cryptogram used a strip of parchment wound around a staff in spiral form with the edges meeting. The message was written along the line formed by the joining of the spiral of parchment. It was then unwound and sent to another person. He could read it only after rewinding it in a spiral on a like staff.

The palindrome is an interesting form of old puzzle. This is made up of a statement which reads the same either forward or backward. Many examples of this type of puzzle are found among the writings of the ancient Greeks and Romans. An example of a palindrome is "MADAM I'M ADAM," which might have been Adam's first speech to Eve, had he spoken English.

It is said that Napoleon is responsible for this palindrome, "ABLE WAS I ERE I SAW ELBA."

PYGMALION (*pĭg mā'lĭ ŏn*). According to a Greek legend, there once lived a king of Cyprus, whose name was Pygmalion. He found so much fault with women that he said he would never marry. Pygmalion was a sculptor and made an ivory statue of a woman so beautiful and perfect that it seemed to be alive. He admired his own work and fell in love with the statue. Sometimes he could not believe the statue was only ivory. He gave it presents of bright shells, colored stones, flowers, and beads, which would have pleased a real woman. He clothed the statue in dresses and jewels, and called it his wife.

The island of Cyprus was considered sacred to the goddess Aphrodite (Venus). One day, after a ceremony in her honor, Pygmalion asked Aphrodite for a wife who was like the ivory statue. He returned home and went to his statue which, to his joy and amazement, the goddess had brought to life. Pygmalion and the maiden were married. (In modern literature, the name Galatea was given to the statue.)

PYLE (*pīl*), **HOWARD** (*hou'ĕrd*) (1853–1911). Picturesque events in the lives of the early settlers of New Amsterdam and New England were a favorite subject of the United States artist and author Howard Pyle. He was born at Wilmington, Delaware. He obtained his training in etching and painting in Philadelphia, Pennsylvania, and New York City schools. He rapidly made a reputation as a magazine illustrator.

After establishing a name for himself by the vigor, simplicity, and directness of his painting, etching, and pen-and-ink work, he began to write fiction. His stories for children showed that his literary skill was hardly less than his artistic ability. Among the books he both illustrated and wrote were *The Merry Adventures of Robin Hood, The Book of Pirates, Otto of the Silver Hand*, and *Jack Ballister's Fortunes*.

After 1879 he returned to live in Wilmington, where he founded an art school. He also painted murals, two of which are "The Battle of Nashville" in the capitol at St. Paul, Minnesota, and "The Landing of Carteret," in the courthouse at Newark, New Jersey. He was elected to the National Academy of Design in 1907.

PYRAMID (*pĭr'ă mĭd*). Although the pyramids of Egypt were the oldest of the ancient "Seven Wonders of the World," they alone have survived. To the traveler, approaching Cairo from Alexandria, they first become visible from a distance of about 20 miles, clear-cut against the turquoise blue sky. From Cairo it is a drive of eight miles toward the west on a well-paved and well-shaded causeway to the edge of the Libyan Desert. There stand the three famous structures, the Pyramids of Giza.

A pyramid has been very simply defined as a solid, or almost solid, structure with a square base and with triangular sides which meet in an apex. Genuine pyramids, with a few insignificant exceptions, are found only in Egypt. The so-called pyramids of Mexico and of Central and South America have flat tops. There are still a great many of these strange buildings standing in Egypt. The western desert rim is fairly strewn with their ruins for 70 miles south of Cairo. They are the tombs of the ancient Egyptian kings, who believed that their future lives depended upon the perfect preservation of their bodies. The dead were therefore embalmed, and the mummies were hidden below the level of the ground in the interior of these great masses of stone. Even the inner passageways were blocked and concealed from possible robbers. Rulers of later periods tried to pull them down to use their stones for building but found it cheaper to cut new stones.

No one knows exactly how old the pyramids are. A thousand years before Christ they were already old and mysterious, just as they are today. The Great Pyramid at Giza has been

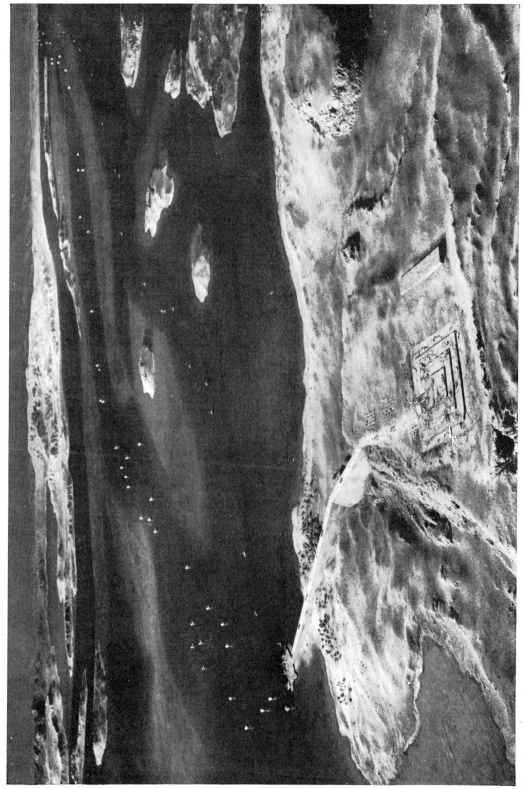

Here is a story in photographs showing how the great pyramids of Giza are thought to have been built about 5,000 years ago in the valley of the Nile. The models photographed on this and the next seven pages were built for *Britannica Junior Encyclopædia* by Norman Bel Geddes in 1945. Above is the site chosen by the Egyptian King Cheops (Khufu) for his tomb, which was the first of the three pyramids. Preparations for the building lasted ten years.

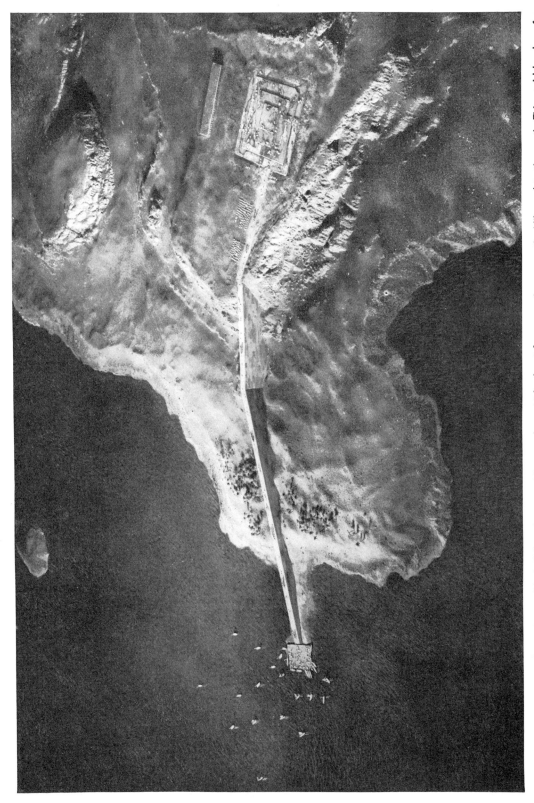

The blocks of limestone and granite used in building the pyramids were brought by boat from quarries across the Nile and to the south. This could be done for only three months each spring when the Nile was flooded. It took 20 years and some 500,000 trips to bring all the stone needed. Boats unloaded at a landing space connected to the site by a stone road. The blocks, weighing about two tons each, were then pulled up the road on sledges by gangs of men.

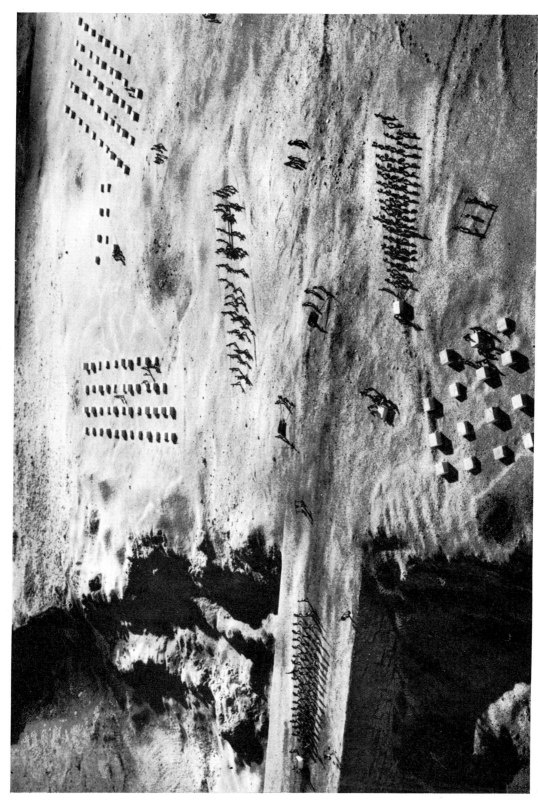

Stone blocks pulled up the road were laid out in neat rows and then pulled to the site by other gangs of men. The pyramid is formed of about 2,300,000 such blocks. Rough buildings were built on the site to house the 100,000 workmen who helped build the pyramid.

As the pyramid rose, a huge ramp made of earth with mud-brick walls might have been built to get materials up to the higher levels. At the beginning, the ramp might have been only five feet high, but slowly it became higher and longer. Gangs of about 40 men pulled blocks up the ramp while others returned to get more from the rows at the bottom. They moved 500 stones a day. In the foreground is the small ramp up to the entrance passage, later sealed up.

Each layer of the pyramid was made of two-ton blocks of limestone set side by side. Mortar was used more to slide the stones into place than to cement them together. The layers were begun at the far side with the men working back to the top of the ramp. Blocks in the center were rough. Those forming the steps down the sides were cut more carefully. In the center is the beginning of the king's chamber set in great slabs of dark granite.

When completed, the Great Pyramid measured 755 feet at the base and was 482 feet high. The final surface was made of very smooth white limestone with almost invisible joints. This fine stone finish was stolen thousands of years later by Arabs for mosques and houses in Cairo. At the base of the east side of the pyramid is the pyramid temple. The small pyramids and the long flat tombs were built for the king's mother and others of noble blood. Above, the royal party, on the roof of the temple, watches a religious procession. Guards are lined up on each side and a large crowd looks on at the right.

The pyramids of Giza, from left to right, in the order in which they were built, are those of Cheops, Chephren, and Menkeure. Each one has its pyramid temple and long stone road. Beyond the second pyramid is the Great Sphinx.

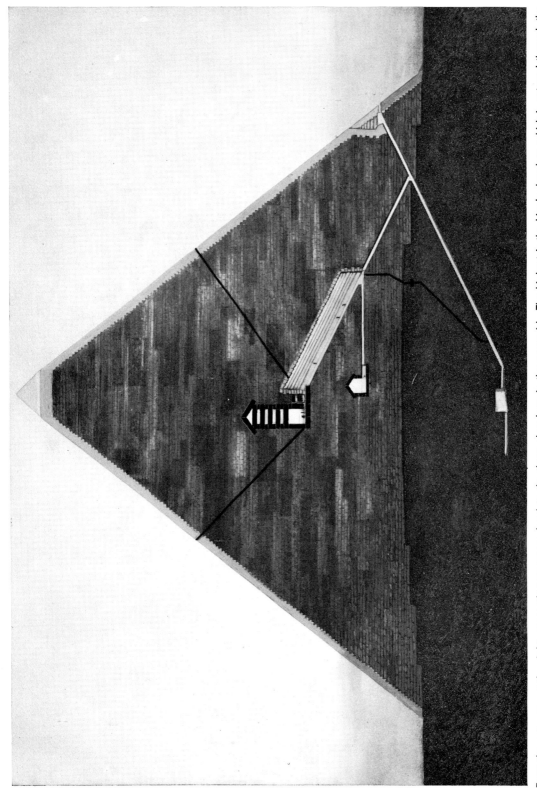

From the entrance at the right, connecting passages lead to the three chambers in the pyramid. The highest is the king's chamber, which is entered through the Great Passage, a tall sloping space. Below is the queen's chamber. The third chamber is underground. The crooked tunnel leading to it may have been a secret passage. Of the two air vents leading upward from the king's chamber, the one at the right points to the North Star.

attributed to King Cheops, about 2575 B.C. The oldest true pyramid, that at Medum, was probably built by King Snefru of the 3rd dynasty about 2600 B.C. Egyptian kings continued to build pyramids until about 1700 B.C.

An Outstanding Engineering Feat

The building of these tremendous structures was a marvelous engineering feat. According to Herodotus, the largest, the Great Pyramid at Giza, built by Cheops (Khufu), an Egyptian king, employed 100,000 men for 20 years. Each block of stone is 7 feet high, and some are 18 feet long. Many were quarried across the Nile. Ten years were spent in preparing the site, in excavating the underground chamber, and in constructing stone-paved causeways, several of which can be traced today. The perpendicular height of the pyramid was originally 482 feet but is now 451 feet since the outer casing disappeared long ago. The length of each side is 755 feet. So accurate was the work that the average variation in the length of the four sides is only six-tenths of an inch. The whole area occupied is about 13 acres. Originally the surface was smooth and polished from top to bottom, and the joints were invisible. Some blocks inside, 40 feet long, are so closely fitted together that they would, as has been said, "pinch a hair at any point." (See Frontispiece of this volume.)

The second of the three pyramids is 471 feet high. It was built by Chephren (or Khafra), successor to Cheops, about 2550 B.C. Part of the original casing remains at the top. Its burial chambers were excavated in the bedrock underneath, and the masonry seems solid. Remains of barracks for 4,000 workmen still exist. The third and smallest pyramid, 215 feet high, was built by Menkeure (or Mycerinus), successor of Chephren, about 2525 B.C.

The burial chambers of the pyramids were richly furnished as if prepared for the living. As protection in case the grave should be robbed, as often happened, pictures of all the activities of an industrious people were sculptured or painted on the walls. Numerous likenesses of the dead were scattered about to take the place of the body if it should be stolen, so that the "double," or soul, should not be home-less. Much of the art that remains is very beautiful and the workmanship is superb. One burial chamber of the third dynasty is completely lined with green-blue tile. Another is lined with alabaster, exquisitely carved and decorated. Long religious inscriptions are found, for a temple was usually attached to each pyramid. There the worship of the deceased pharaoh was conducted by priests who were regularly paid. Unfortunately most of the tombs in Egypt were robbed centuries ago, but the magnificent tomb of King Tutenkhamon, discovered by Lord Carnarvon and Howard Carter at Luxor in 1922, was found intact. Though not a pyramid tomb, the contents and arrangements give an excellent idea of the earlier tombs.

PYRAMUS (*pĭr'ä mŭs*) **AND THISBE** (*thĭz'bē*). In ancient Babylon there lived two neighboring families. One of them had a son named Pyramus and the other a daughter named Thisbe. The young people were in love but their parents forbade their seeing each other. The lovers, however, found a crack in the wall between the two houses and used to talk and pass messages through it.

One day at dawn Pyramus and Thisbe came to the wall. They arranged to meet each other at nightfall by the tomb of Ninus outside the city. Thisbe arrived first and sat by the tomb waiting for her lover. Suddenly a lion appeared, its jaws dripping with blood. Thisbe fled dropping her veil in terror. The lion chewed the veil and left it torn and bloody. When Pyramus arrived he found the veil and saw the tracks of the lion in the sand. Thinking that Thisbe had been killed and overwhelmed with grief, he drew his sword and plunged it into his body. A little later Thisbe came out of her hiding place. Still trembling with fear she walked toward the tomb. There she found Pyramus lying dead. She caught his lifeless body in her arms, and, drawing out the sword, drove it into her own heart. It was the Latin poet, Ovid, who told this tale of the unfortunate lovers.

PYRENEES (*pĭr'ĕ nēz*) **MOUNTAINS, EUROPE.** The Pyrenees form a natural barrier between France and Spain. The mountains are about

240 miles long, rising rapidly from the Mediterranean Sea on the east and declining sharply toward the Bay of Biscay and the Atlantic Ocean on the west. Streams from melting snow on their lofty peaks make the high valleys suitable for agriculture and sheep raising. These mountain torrents which often form high waterfalls are a noted feature of the Pyrenees. They are used for the generation of electricity, which is conveyed to cities such as Barcelona for use in industry.

The boundary line between France and Spain runs along the central ridge of the mountains. This is a political division, however. The Pyrenees are also divided into two parts in a natural way.

The eastern half lacks the heavy rainfall and snow of the western half and is characterized by bare granite peaks. The Catalans live there. (See CATALONIA.) The western half enjoys heavy rainfall; the slopes are wooded and the valleys fertile and green. This is the country of the Basques. (See BASQUE.)

As the Basques and Catalans do not intermingle, the eastern and western sections of the Pyrenees differ as widely in the character of the people as in the climate and formation of the mountains.

There are only a few passes through the Pyrenees, the easiest being at the eastern and western ends where the chief railroads run. The highest point, Pico de Aneto in the central Pyrenees, has an altitude of 11,168 feet. Because they can not communicate easily with the outside world, the remote villages have not changed much with the passage of time. This isolation also explains the continued independence of Andorra, a tiny republic deep in the mountains, about 65 miles from the Mediterranean Sea. (See ANDORRA.)

PYROMETER (*pī rŏm'ĕ tēr*). People working in industry and science often need instruments for measuring extremely high temperatures. Ordinary thermometers can not be used to measure heat such as is given off by blast furnaces or by an electric arc. Instruments used to measure these great heats are called pyrometers, meaning fire measurers.

The simplest instrument of this kind is a special mercury thermometer. Instead of glass it is made of quartz tubing. The space above the mercury is filled with nitrogen or carbon dioxide, under pressure. Such thermometers register temperatures up to 450 degrees Centigrade.

For still higher temperatures two types of thermoelectric pyrometers are used. The *resistance* thermometer makes use of the fact that the electrical resistance of a metal changes with the temperature. These changes in resistance of the circuit are converted to read directly in degrees, either Centigrade or Fahrenheit. Platinum is the metal most used in the resistance thermometer. It registers temperature from 300 degrees below zero Fahrenheit to 3,000 degrees above.

The second type of thermoelectric pyrometer is the *thermocouple* type. Two wires of different metals, usually platinum and a platinum alloy, are joined. The free ends are connected to a sensitive measuring instrument. When the connection is heated, an electric current will flow. The force of this current is shown on the register in terms of heat. Radiant heat from the sun may be measured by the thermocouple.

Thermoelectric pyrometers give the temperature to a fraction of a degree and may be recorded at a distance from the source of heat.

PYRRHUS (*pĭr'ŭs*) (318–272 B.C.). When Hannibal was once asked whom he considered the three greatest generals of history, he replied: "Alexander, Pyrrhus, and I myself."

Pyrrhus was king of Epirus in Greece, and was distantly connected with Alexander the Great. In his youth he went as a hostage to the court of Ptolemy at Alexandria where he learned the arts of war and civilization. In 281 when he was about 37 years old the people of Tarentum in Italy sent to him for help against the Romans. He landed in Italy with an army and a number of elephants and met the Romans in battle at Heraclea (280 B.C.).

Pyrrhus won a complete victory, but at a fearful cost. From this came the expression "Pyrrhic Victory," meaning a victory too expensive to be worth while.

Pyrrhus was then joined by the Greek cities of Italy and the Samnites and Lucanians. He offered peace but the Romans boldly refused to accept it. In 279 he defeated them again at Asculum, but again suffered such losses that he could not march on Rome. He crossed to Sicily and spent three years driving out the Carthaginians. By this time the Tarentines had lost confidence in him and refused to supply him with money. At Beneventum in 275 he was defeated by the Romans and returned to Greece. He attacked Sparta in 273 but was thrown back. The next year he was killed in a night skirmish in the streets of Argos. He impressed Greeks and Romans alike by his chivalry and courtesy to enemies.

PYTHAGORAS (pĭ thăg'ō răs) AND PYTHAGO-REANS (pĭ thăg'ō rē'ănz or pĭ thăg'ō rē'ănz).

(582–507? B.C.). The famous "47th problem in Euclid"—that the square of the hypotenuse of a right-angled triangle equals the sum of the squares of the other two sides—was discovered by Pythagoras. He was a Greek philosopher and mathematician, founder of the Pythagorean school of philosophy. Pythagoras was born on the island of Samos. When he was about 50 years old he settled at Crotona in Italy and founded a religious brotherhood of philosophers. He is said to have traveled from Persia to Gaul in search of wisdom and to have been admitted to the religious mysteries of Egypt.

The first Pythagoreans were attacked by hostile mobs and many were killed in their meeting places. Pythagoras may have died with them or retired to Metapontum. Later Pythagoreans developed from his teachings a religious philosophy that later was the source of much medieval magic. They believed in the power of numbers. Two expressed a line, three a surface, four a solid; six stood for the soul, seven for health and light, eight for love.

They had a theory of the solar system which was nearly correct. The earth, they said, is a sphere revolving round a central fire, and as the spheres revolve they make music. Music to them best expressed the universe, since harmony depends on a law of numbers. Pythagoras knew, for example, the simple arithmetical relations between notes in fourths, fifths, and octaves. Knowing many simple astronomical ratios made it seem plausible to look upon numbers as the ruling principle of the universe. The Pythagoreans accepted the theory of atoms and believed in reincarnation of the soul.

PYTHON (pī'thŏn).

A legend of the Greek god Apollo says he avenged his mother, Leto, by killing the dragon Python because it had persecuted her. The name of that legendary dragon has been given to a monstrous snake, which inhabits the tropical regions of Asia, Africa, and Australia, and lives to a considerable age. The python is the largest of the nonpoisonous snakes called boas. Boas kill their victims by crushing them in their coils and then swallowing them whole. The common python is often 20 feet long. The python of India may reach a length of 30 feet, but a fully grown Australian python is only about 6 feet long. The python prefers marshy regions by shallow ponds. Its brown, yellow, and black body, with diamond-shaped markings, lies hidden among jungle shadows or along the branches of trees. Great elastic muscles lining the entire body give this serpent enormous strength. It can devour an animal as large as a goat by stretching its mouth to a huge size. The female lays about a dozen tough-shelled eggs.

The Indian python can be 30 feet long. Most pythons like to be in trees or to lie quietly in water.

New York Zoological Society

The powerful serpents called pythons are not poisonous. They kill their prey, mainly birds and small mammals, by coiling around and crushing them. The ball, or royal, python, above, is about 4 feet long. It inhabits West Africa. The reticulated, or regal, python, below, of the Malay Peninsula may grow 30 feet long.

Courtesy (below) Field Museum of Natural History; photo, (above) New York Zoological Society

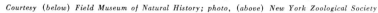

(1) The mountain quail. (2) The bobwhite (10 inches long). (3) The scaled quail. (4) Mearn's quail. (5) The tufted California quail. (These birds are drawn to scale of the bobwhite.)

QUAIL (*kwāl*). American quails belong to the order Gallinae. Most of the 70 species live in the tropics, only seven being found in the United States. Six of these dwell in the western states:

The Bobwhite

The one quail in the eastern half of North America is the "bobwhite," so named because of its call. It is known also as a partridge. It helps farmers by feeding on insect pests and enormous amounts of weed seeds.

When America was first settled, the bobwhite was found from Maine to the Gulf of Mexico. It furnished many a meal for the pioneer's table.

The bobwhite is still hunted and is highly prized as food. The hunter must be keen of eye if he is not aided by dogs, for the bird blends into the thicket or grass perfectly. When a covey, or flock, suddenly rises with a dull roar of beating wings, to fly low and swiftly in many directions, the amazed sportsman may stand helpless.

The bobwhite is about ten inches long and plump of body. It is fully feathered and of rich reddish brown or chestnut color. Paler stripes extend back over the eyes and neck. The neck and throat show dark stripes, and the breast is mottled.

The quails are ground-dwelling birds. They are about the build of the common chicken, and use their wings only for short flights. They nest on the ground. They teach their young early in life the secret of hiding. A passer-by may almost step on one, and it will not budge. They are a cheerful, industrious and good-natured type, and only in the mating season will the cocks show fight.

Nests are built in any sheltered or hidden nook, and there are a dozen or more pure-white eggs. The young are hatched out in 24 days, and almost immediately take care of themselves.

Other species of quail in North America are

the hooded quail, the mountain quail, the scaled quail, Gambel's quail, Mearns's quail, and the California quail. The last is found along the Pacific Coast and in Colorado.

The general tone of the plumage of the California quail is a deep ashy brown. Its chest is slate blue with a patch of chestnut below. Its most distinctive mark is a gracefully curving plume on the top of its head. Its call is made up of three notes, instead of the two of the bob-white. It sounds something like *ka-ka-kao*. It builds ground nests and has from 12 to 16 eggs, creamy in color with splotches of brown or old gold.

QUARANTINE (*kwŏr'än tēn*). A quarantine is a period of time during which people or animals, or even ships or planes, are kept away from others. Quarantines are ordered by government health officers when there is danger that a contagious disease may be spread from the infected person or animal to others.

The length of time required for quarantine depends upon the disease. The word comes from the Latin *quadraginta*, which means 40 days. In older times there were many epidemics of serious diseases. Ships coming from areas where these diseases were known were held 40 days as a safe quarantine period.

Contagious diseases have become far less common because of vaccinations. (See IM-MUNITY AND RESISTANCE TO DISEASE.) But there is still need for quarantine in cases of poliomyelitis, typhoid fever, or diphtheria.

Present-day regulations are meant to keep contagious diseases from entering a country. When a boat or airplane arrives, the passengers must show proof of their vaccinations and injections. If a passenger has one of the contagious diseases being guarded against, he will be quarantined in a hospital.

Quarantine regulations are most needed to prevent the spread of some virus infections for which there is no good preventive vaccine. In 1957 Asian influenza caused illness in many parts of the world. It was necessary to remove from incoming ships people suspected of having influenza. They were quarantined in hospitals until they were well.

QUARRYING (*kwŏr'ē ing*). When men wish to dig minerals out of the earth they usually have to burrow into it like moles. Sometimes, however, they can treat a mountain as if it were a giant cheese and slice off rock in chunks. Or, they may break it up with explosives and scoop it out with a power shovel, working entirely from the surface. But when a surface operation is worked for the rock itself, rather than some mineral contained in the rock, it is usually called quarrying. Building stones such as granite, sandstone, limestone, marble, and slate are usually quarried.

All these stones, with their many varieties, are found in most parts of the globe. Consequently, convenience of working is usually the deciding factor in choosing the location of a quarry. A hillside or mountainside is preferred because the material can be drawn out along a level roadway. It is usually easier to keep the quarry free from water. Sometimes a vein of slate will be followed at a slant down into the earth. Then the quarry becomes like a coal mine. Galleries are dug to right and left and the material is hauled out on cars. There are such slate quarries in Wales and France which have been worked for several centuries.

Quarrying Methods

Granite is the most difficult stone to quarry because it is very hard and does not split easily. It must, therefore, be cut out into rectangular blocks. This is usually done by drilling rows of holes, some from the top and some from the side of a block. The block is then split loose by various methods. The most ancient of these and the one used by the Egyptians was to plug the holes tight with dry wood which was then swelled with water. Usually weak charges of blasting powder are used or the rock is split by the plug-and-feather method. In this method two semicircular pieces of steel, called feathers, are placed in each hole and between them is driven a steel "plug," or wedge.

Limestones, sandstones, and slate are more easily quarried than granite because they are stratified or lie in layers. Usually all that is necessary is to split them off by drilling. There are even some sandstones which can simply be

Courtesy (1) Indiana Limestone Institute; photos, (2, 3) Korth for Lime & Stone Co.

(1) Removing limestone for building purposes from a quarry ledge. Blocks are in layers and can easily be split off by drilling. (2) A close-up of a dynamite drill. Rows of holes are made and charged with explosives. (3) The blasting has loosened large chunks from the solid hillside of limestone. They are loaded by derrick into transport cars and carried to factories for processing.

pried out in blocks with crowbars and wedges. When broken stone is desired, as in road building or for manufacturing cement, high explosives, such as dynamite, are used to break up the rock.

Of all quarry products, marble is the most valuable and demands the greatest skill from the workmen. It is in the marble quarries of Vermont, Georgia, and Italy that quarrying machinery was most highly developed. First in order among these machines, which are now used for other rocks as well as for marble, comes the exploring machinery. Formerly the value of a quarry site had to be judged largely by outward appearances. Now a coring machine is used which drills a hole sometimes hundreds of feet deep and draws out a stone cylinder two or three inches in diameter. From this cylinder the depth and quality of the deposit may be determined.

Next among quarrying machinery comes the channeling machine which does the up-and-down cutting that separates the blocks vertically. A power-operated chisel mounted on a car cuts a groove, or channel. It runs on carefully laid tracks on top of the rock. As it moves back and forth it chisels a groove about one inch wide into the rock to the desired depth of the blocks of rock to be removed. A stream of water passes along the groove to remove the dust. After the floor of the quarry has been covered with parallel grooves in one direction, other grooves are cut at right angles to the first set. This divides the floor into cubes, or oblong blocks. These blocks are then loosened horizontally by drilling and wedging at the bottom and hoisted out with derricks.

After the stone is removed from the quarry it may be necessary to cut it up into smaller blocks. This is done by drilling, by sawing, or by the plug-and-feather method. These smaller blocks are often polished and finished off at the quarry.

Vermont leads the states in the production of marble and granite and is second only to Pennsylvania in its output of slate. Indiana leads in the production of limestone, its Bedford limestone being especially famous. The bulk and weight of quarry products make transportation very expensive. For this reason all but the rarer and more valuable quarry products are used near the point of production. This leads to the opening of quarries near every city provided stone suitable for use is available, and makes quarrying a widespread industry.

QUARTZ (*kwarts*) is a colorless, transparent, common mineral. It is one of the most widely distributed minerals. Quartz is one form of silica, or SiO_2, a compound of silicon and oxygen. These elements together make up almost three-quarters of the weight of the Earth's crust. Most people see silica in one form or another every day. (See MINERAL.)

Natural silica occurs in many different forms, depending on how completely it is crystallized and what impurities it contains. Silica can be crystalline, cryptocrystalline (hidden crystalline), or amorphous (noncrystalline). Quartz, which is crystalline silica, shows distinct outlines of individual crystals that usually can be seen by the naked eye. (See CRYSTAL.)

In quartz each silicon atom is surrounded by four oxygen atoms at the corners of a tetrahedron, or three-sided pyramid. Each oxygen atom is, in turn, linked to two different silicon

Quartz crystals are almost identical, whether formed by nature or by man. Their shape is determined by the atomic pattern of four oxygen atoms joined to one silicon atom; this pattern repeats throughout the crystal.

Photo, B. M. Shaub

atoms in neighboring pyramids. The pyramids are stacked together to form three-dimensional frameworks. The different ways in which this stacking occurs produce the different forms of crystalline silica, such as quartz, tridymite, and cristobalite.

Quartz is by far the commonest form of crystalline silica. It is found often in large, clear, colorless six-sided crystals with pyramid-like ends, sometimes called rock crystal. Although pure quartz is colorless, impurities can make it red, yellow, brown, green, blue, lavender, black, or milky white. Amethyst is quartz with impurities that make it purple or bluish violet. Citrine is a yellow, transparent variety of quartz. When cut and polished, it resembles topaz. Smoky quartz is a dark, semitransparent variety that is known as cairngorm. (See GEM.)

Some of the most common rocks, such as granite, contain large amounts of quartz. Because quartz is hard enough to cut glass and because it resists attack by acids, quartz tends to remain while other minerals in rocks weather away. This accounts for the fact that frequently sand consists mainly of quartz that comes from the erosion of old rocks. Sandstone consists of grains of quartz sand cemented together. This natural cement may be more silica or a number of other minerals. In the rock quartzite the grains of quartz are cemented into a hard compact mass by new quartz crystals that grew between or replaced the original grains. (See GRANITE; SAND; SANDSTONE.)

Quartz sand is important in making cement for building and in glassmaking. It is also used as an abrasive in sandpaper. Thin slices cut from clear and nearly perfect quartz crystals are used in radio broadcasting equipment to keep it working on its proper frequency. Quartz crystals are used also as lenses in optical equipment. Most of the high-quality quartz crystals needed for these purposes are found in Brazil. They are expensive. Now useful quartz crystals are grown artificially to help meet the demand. (See ABRASIVE; CEMENT; GLASS.)

Pure quartz melts at 2,930 degrees Fahrenheit, or 1,610 degrees Celsius (centigrade). It fuses into a glass that is more transparent than ordinary window glass. It is extremely heat re-sistant, as well as resistant to attack by chemicals. A dish made from it may be heated red hot and plunged into ice water without being harmed in any way. This property makes it a useful material for laboratory utensils.

QUEBEC (*kwē bĕk'*), **CANADA,** is the country's largest province. It includes 594,860 square miles of land and water, which is almost one-sixth of the total area of Canada. It is in eastern Canada, bounded on the east by New-foundland, the Gulf of St. Lawrence, and New

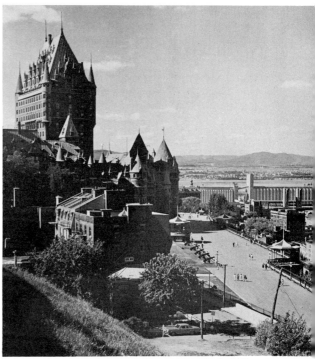

J. Allan Cash from Rapho-Guillumette
The medieval-style Chateau Frontenac, a noted resort hotel, overlooks Quebec City and the St. Lawrence River.

Brunswick; to the south is the United States; to the west are Ontario and Hudson Bay; and to the north are Hudson Strait and Ungava Bay.

In the south, Quebec covers both sides of the St. Lawrence River and includes many great industrial cities as well as Montreal, the largest city in Canada. On the north the province has great areas of cold, unsettled lands. It has both French and English traditions, both city and rural life, and great extremes in climate.

Thus it may be said that Quebec includes

most things that are "Canadian."

The story of Quebec can be read in its name, emblems, and mottoes. The word Quebec is an Algonquin Indian word which probably means strait or sudden narrowing in a river. Near the city of Quebec, the St. Lawrence River has such a narrow spot, and the city gave its name to the entire province.

On the provincial coat of arms, which was adopted in 1863, are the lilies of France, the lion of England, and the maple leaves of Canada. The coat of arms pictures the long struggle between the French and the English before the land became Canada. The motto of Quebec, which is "Je me souviens" ("I remember"), was adopted in 1830. It expresses the French

---

FACTS ABOUT QUEBEC

TOTAL AREA: 594,860 square miles (including 71,000 square miles of fresh water); 15.4 percent of all of Canada.
POPULATION: 5,780,845 (1966); 78 percent urban, 22 percent rural.
CAPITAL: Quebec.
MOUNTAINS: Mount Jacques Cartier (4,160 feet, highest of Appalachians), Roundtop Mountain (3,175 feet, highest of Notre Dame Mountains).
LAKES: Mistassini (840 square miles), Minto (485 square miles), Clearwater (535 square miles), Bienville (392 square miles), St. John (414 square miles).
RIVERS: St. Lawrence, Saguenay, Ottawa, Koksoak, Eastmain.
BAYS: Hudson, James, Ungava, Chaleur.
WATERFALLS: Shawinigan, Montmorency, Heming, Chat.
HISTORIC PARKS: Fort Chambly (2.5 acres), Fort Lennox (210 acres), Sir Wilfrid Laurier's Birthplace (1 acre).
NATIONAL BACKGROUNDS: French 83 percent, British 12 percent.
UNIVERSITIES AND COLLEGES: McGill University, Montreal; University of Bishop's College, Lennoxville; University of Montreal; Laval University, Quebec; Sir George Williams College, Montreal.
CHIEF CITIES: Montreal, Quebec, Verdun, Sherbrooke, Three Rivers, Hull, Chicoutimi.
VOTING AGE FOR PROVINCIAL ELECTIONS: 21.
PROVINCIAL HOLIDAYS: The Festival of the Epiphany, Ash Wednesday, Ascension Day, St. John the Baptist's Day, All Saints' Day, Conception Day.
FLORAL EMBLEM: Maple leaf (unofficial).
CHIEF DATES:
  1534—Discovered by Jacques Cartier.
  1608—City of Quebec founded by Champlain.
  1642—Montreal founded.
  1759—Wolfe defeated Montcalm.
  1763—Ceded to the British by the French.
  1774—Became province under Quebec Act.
  1867—Became province of Canada.

Canadians' love of tradition. The flag that was adopted in 1948 is a white cross and lilies on a blue field. It is the most recent reminder of the French origins of many of the people.

Land

The valley of the St. Lawrence runs from the city of Quebec to the western side of the province. It is the fertile, thickly populated plain that makes up a part of the rich St. Lawrence Lowlands running through Ontario. South of the St. Lawrence River are the Notre Dame Mountains, the northern section of the Appalachians. In the northeast of the Gaspe Peninsula are the Shickshock Mountains. Almost all of the province is part of the great Canadian Shield. In the southeast of the shield are the Laurentian Mountains, a plateau of low mountains.

In addition to the great St. Lawrence River, Quebec has the Saguenay, Ottawa, Richelieu, and many other valuable rivers. (See ST. LAWRENCE RIVER.) The Ottawa River drains about 56,000 square miles of land and flows nearly 700 miles into the St. Lawrence. From the Richelieu River boats can travel all the way south to New York City in the United States.

There are about 100,000 square miles of forest land in Quebec, about 80 per cent of which is owned by the government. Another 71,000 square miles of rivers and lakes give Quebec variety and beauty in its scenery.

Climate

Because of the differences in latitude, Quebec has great differences in climate. In the St. Lawrence Valley the summers are warm and the winters cold, with much snow. The plateau north of the city of Quebec has more than 120 inches of snowfall a year. This is one reason why skiing is so popular in this part of the province.

At Port Harrison on Hudson Bay the average high daytime temperature in January is only −10 degrees Fahrenheit, while the average low at night is −26 degrees. But at Sherbrooke in the St. Lawrence Valley the temperature on a January day is about 24 degrees and

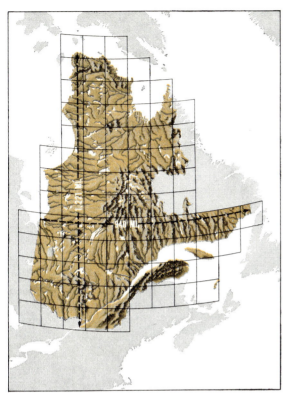

The size of Quebec. Each square marks an area 100 miles long and 100 miles wide.

many of the ways of their ancestors, living in Canada has made a new type of people—the French Canadians. In general, however, the French Canadians are true to their background. They are independent, warm-hearted, and lively.

The Roman Catholic faith is very important to the French Canadians. This can be seen by the role that the church plays in their way of life. After 1763 the parish priest in each town or village took a leading role in the life of his flock.

In the same way, Catholic Action and other youth and adult groups are important in the lives of French Canadians today.

Religious holidays are of great importance to the people. June 24, feast of St. John the Baptist, patron of French Canadians, is a great day. At dusk on June 23, crowds gather around the fires of the saint (*feux de la St. Jean*), gigantic bonfires that are blessed before being kindled. Speeches, folk songs, and dances carry the rejoicings far into the summer night. June 24 is celebrated by colorful parades with floats and bands. For such holiday occasions, decorations are mainly the provincial flag, the tricolor of France, and the pope's white and yellow flag.

Most city people in Quebec can speak Eng-

at night about 4 degrees.

In July at Port Harrison the average daytime high is 55 degrees Fahrenheit and the low at night is 39 degrees. But at Sherbrooke in July the average high temperature goes to 78 degrees with a low average of 58 degrees at night. Rainfall varies greatly too. In the south the yearly average rainfall is about 40 inches; in the north it is 15 inches.

The People

In 1763 Quebec had a population of 65,000. There are about 85 times that number today. Until the 20th century most of the people in Quebec were farmers, but now about two-thirds of them live in cities. The great majority of the people of Quebec are of French descent. English and other national groups make up only 17 per cent of the population. About 20,000 Indians, descendants of the first owners of the land, live on federal reserves.

Although the French in Canada have kept

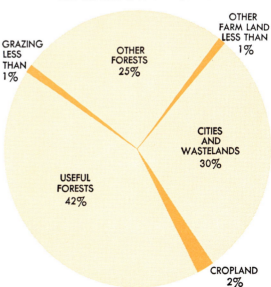

How the land is used in Quebec.

GRAZING LESS THAN 1%

OTHER FORESTS 25%

OTHER FARM LAND LESS THAN 1%

CITIES AND WASTELANDS 30%

USEFUL FORESTS 42%

CROPLAND 2%

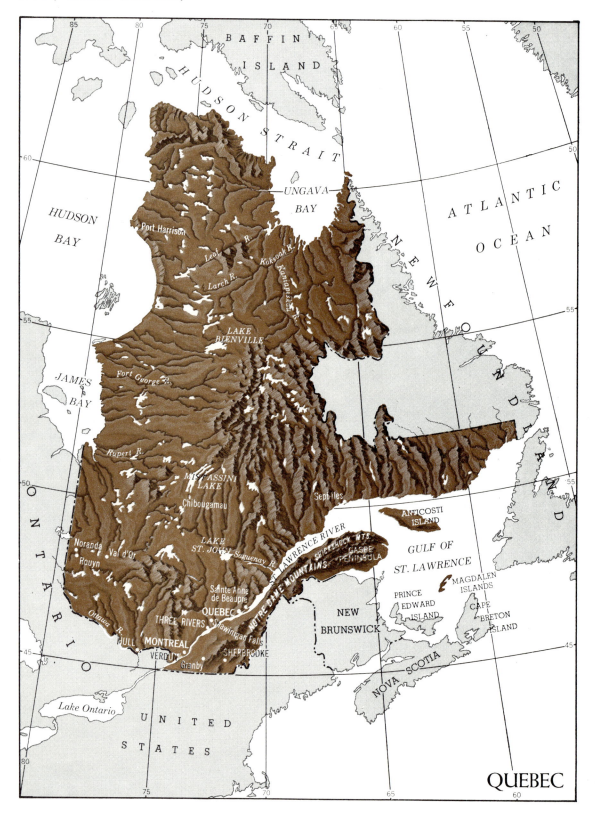

QUEBEC

lish, but French is the common language of the people. This French is something like the language of the Norman farmer in France, with a number of English words added. There is as much difference between the French spoken in Canada and the French spoken in France as there is between the English spoken in the United States and the English spoken in England.

How the People Make a Living

In the value of its manufactures Quebec is second only to Ontario. Together the two provinces produce about 80 per cent of Canada's manufactures. Quebec leads all provinces in the manufacture of tobacco and tobacco products, textiles, clothing, leather products, paper products, and petroleum and coal products. It is also the leader in the great pulp and paper industry. The value of its pulp and paper products equals about half of Canada's total. Quebec alone makes the paper for two out of every five pages of newspapers printed in the United States.

Quebec's mineral production increased greatly after World War II, contributing to growth in manufacturing. This increase was partly a result of the discovery of iron ore deposits west of Ungava Bay and along the Labrador boundary. Large quantities of gold and copper are mined in the Noranda-Rouyn district. Also great progress has been made in mining these metals in the Chibougamau (which means "land of promise") district between Lake St. John and James Bay.

Quebec mines produce about one-half of the world's annual supply of asbestos. It is Canada's only producer of molybdenite and titanium ore. It ranks second in the production of copper, gold, and zinc.

Quebec is the richest province in water-power resources and development. Its turbine plants develop more than one-third of all of Canada's horsepower. Canada itself ranks second in the world in water-power development. The Beauharnois development on the St. Lawrence River and the Aluminium Company of Canada's plant on the Saguenay are the largest water-power developments in Canada. Most

How the people of Quebec make a living.

of the water power of the St. Maurice River has been developed. On this river, about 240 miles above Three Rivers, the Gouin Dam has helped to make a great reservoir.

In income from the sale of farm products, Quebec is the third-ranking province. But Quebec is slightly ahead of Ontario as the leading producer of milk products. The Department of Agriculture of Quebec performs many different services for farmers. In addition, many agricultural societies and co-operative associations help and encourage farmers to improve the methods of production and distribution of their products.

In 1900 Alphonse Desjardins founded La Caisse Populaire, a co-operative savings bank for people with only small sums of money. His system was modeled after one that had been used in Switzerland, Germany, and Italy since 1875. The *caisses populaires* grew rapidly and spread to Ontario and even New England, where they inspired credit unions. In 1949 the Catholic School Commission of Montreal opened *caisses populaires* for children. Among about 130,000 pupils, almost 100,000 belong to the savings banks. During the first seven years the pupils deposited $5,500,000. The actual credit amounted to $2,070,000. This idea encourages saving and teaches young persons

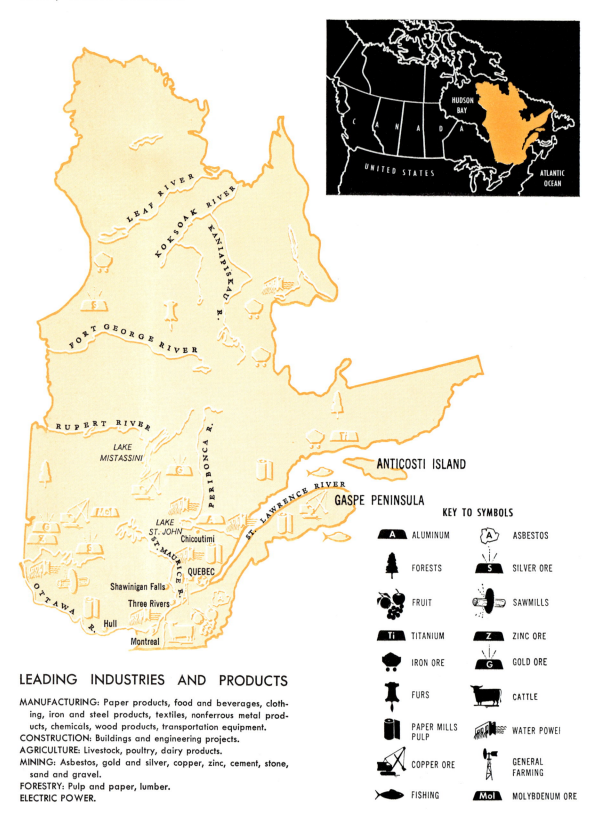

ANTICOSTI ISLAND

GASPE PENINSULA

KEY TO SYMBOLS

A	ALUMINUM	**A**	ASBESTOS
	FORESTS	**S**	SILVER ORE
	FRUIT		SAWMILLS
Ti	TITANIUM	**Z**	ZINC ORE
	IRON ORE	**G**	GOLD ORE
	FURS		CATTLE
	PAPER MILLS PULP		WATER POWER
	COPPER ORE		GENERAL FARMING
	FISHING	**Mol**	MOLYBDENUM ORE

LEADING INDUSTRIES AND PRODUCTS

MANUFACTURING: Paper products, food and beverages, clothing, iron and steel products, textiles, nonferrous metal products, chemicals, wood products, transportation equipment.

CONSTRUCTION: Buildings and engineering projects.

AGRICULTURE: Livestock, poultry, dairy products.

MINING: Asbestos, gold and silver, copper, zinc, cement, stone, sand and gravel.

FORESTRY: Pulp and paper, lumber.

ELECTRIC POWER.

how to use money wisely.

Transportation

The people of Quebec have the choice of many ways of travel: rivers and canals, highways, railroads, and air lines. Private cars, busses, trucks, and trailers travel the 43,000 miles of highway that cross the province. The principal roads are kept open by snowplow during even the worst winter snowstorm. One of the world's great seaways is formed by the St. Lawrence River, most of which is in Quebec. (See ST. LAWRENCE RIVER.)

Other rivers and canals are closed to navigation during the winter months. But while ferries are shorebound, the ice is often so thick that cars and trucks may cross safely.

Air traffic is on the increase. More than 4,000 passengers a month use Air Canada Airlines in Quebec alone. Between Montreal and Quebec city there are five flights daily. Distant places such as Val d'Or, Noranda-Rouyn, Sept

Where the people live in Quebec. Each dot equals 1,000 persons, except within metropolitan areas shown by circles.

Canadian Government Travel Bureau

The Gaspe country, with Perce Rock and Bonaventure Island in the background.

Iles, and Saguenay are reached in two or three hours by plane from Quebec city. Transportation by truck is very important to the province. Trucks carry products and materials from the distant and out-of-the-way places in the province to the consumers and manufacturers.

Cities

With well over 1,000,000 inhabitants, Montreal is second in population only to Paris among the French cities of the world. (See MONTREAL.) Quebec city, the provincial capital, gave its name to the entire province. (See QUEBEC, QUEBEC.) A few miles downstream, past the Montmorency Falls, is Ste. Anne de Beaupre. There is the shrine that is visited by many Canadian and United States pilgrims. These pilgrimages date back to 1568. Hull, opposite Ottawa, Ontario, is a thriving industrial city, independent of Ottawa. Sherbrooke, called "Queen of the Eastern Townships," is an industrial and intellectual center.

Three Rivers (Trois Rivieres) is known for its pulp and paper industry, its school of papermaking, and its textile and power plants. The first industrial plant in North America was built there in 1738. Granby is an industrial

© *Photographic Surveys*

Quebec mines produce about one-half of the world's supply of asbestos.

The province's largest universities are Montreal, Laval, and McGill. The University of Montreal has about 14,000 students. The language usually used for instruction there is French, as it is also at Laval University.

Montreal and Quebec city have their own health departments. Sixty-seven health units have the task of taking health information to the rural areas. Visiting nurses enter homes, advise parents, report on sanitary conditions, and, if necessary, help the family doctor.

city on the south shore of the St. Maurice River. (For populations, see the article POPULATION.)

Education and Public Health

The provincial Department of Education controls the Quebec school system. Unlike the other provinces, Quebec has traditionally had two separate systems of public education—one Roman Catholic and French-speaking, the other Protestant and English-speaking. Although the school system was reorganized in 1964, the split between Catholic and Protestant schools remains. School attendance is compulsory to age 15.

In addition to the system of public schools, there is also a widespread system of private education. The *colleges classiques,* or classical colleges, are private institutions operated mainly by Roman Catholic clergy. In an eight-year course of instruction, these schools provide an education roughly equivalent to secondary and undergraduate education in public schools. Classes are conducted in French. Most graduates of the classical colleges go on to universities for professional training.

The province also supports a number of specialized institutions including schools of agriculture, technical institutes, centers for the study of fine arts, and the St. Jean Military College.

Recreation

Many parishes have recreation centers, each offering activities to suit the different tastes of the parishioners. Les Compagnons de St. Laurent, an amateur theatrical company founded by Father Emile Legault of Holy Cross in 1937, twice won the Bessborough Trophy in Canada-wide dramatic festivals. When the original members of this company went on to win fame as professionals, Father Legault formed another company. Made up largely of students from the University of Montreal, this group produces only religious plays.

In 1955 the Theatre du Nouveau Monde of Montreal was invited to the Paris Drama Festival. It was the first time a Canadian group had received this honor. The Montreal Repertory Theatre has had to expand in order to meet the demands of its audiences. Montreal also supports a symphony orchestra, which offers regular programs. The city also has a Junior Symphony Orchestra. In 1955 the International Congress of Musical Youth (Jeunesse Musicales) was held in Montreal and attended by young persons from 18 nations.

Quebec has an ideal climate for winter sports, and skating, skiing, and hockey are the most popular. The great enthusiasm among the followers of the Montreal Canadiens hockey team, as well as the great number of Canadians on hockey teams in Canada and the United States, justifies the saying that hockey is the national sport of the French Canadian.

Ideal spots for fishing and hunting make these sports favorites also.

Government

The provincial Parliament is made up of the 24 life members of the Legislative Council and 92 elected members of the Legislative Assembly. From these are chosen the 20 or so ministers of the Executive Council. In a few districts there are enough English Canadians to elect English-Canadian candidates.

History

The history of Quebec is largely the history of New France and the French Canadians. The institutions, language, and culture of the people of Quebec today show how the French Canadians have held on to their way of life.

In the 15th century Portuguese, Venetian, Genoese, and Spanish sailors braved the unknown Atlantic Ocean in search of a western route to the riches of the East. It is not known what part of Canada was first touched by Europeans. The earliest records about the newfound lands north of the 45th parallel were made by Jacques Cartier. Cartier was sent out by the king of France first in 1534. (See CARTIER, JACQUES.) It was not until 1603, however, that Samuel de Champlain crossed the ocean with orders to establish a colony and Christianize the Indians. On his fourth trip, in 1608, he built a fort at the foot of Cape Diamond. This was the first dwelling of what is today Quebec city. But for years traders, missionaries, and explorers were the only people at this outpost.

Life in the New World was not very comfortable. The log houses had oiled skins or parchment for windows, and only a little light could filter through. The fire on the hearth served for cooking and heating. Water came from the river or a nearby spring in the summer, and from frozen snow in the winter. For recreation there was only a trip on the river, or a walk in the woods with a loaded musket in case of an Indian attack. Once a year a boat from the homeland brought in people, supplies, and news from the outside world. In spite of the terrible hardships of such a life, Louis Hebert came to Quebec in 1617 with his wife, brother-in-law, and three children. They were the first to settle, till the soil, and bring up a family in Canada.

Among the heroes of this story of New France were the brown- or black-robed priests who were missionaries, explorers, and interpreters; the *coureurs de bois* who went in search of furs and adventure; the explorers who traced each discovery on their maps; and the soldiers who had to learn the ways of Indian warfare. Every advance of these men brought a new fort, mission, trading post, or settlement.

In 1634 a fort was set up where two rivers flowed into the St. Lawrence, and named Les Trois Rivieres (the Three Rivers). Though it was discovered that the St. Maurice emptied into the St. Lawrence with three mouths, the name remained. In 1642 Paul de Chomedey,

On Quebec's rivers millions of logs are floated to sawmills and electric power is generated.

Courtesy Canadian Consulate General of Chicago, photo by George Hunter

Sieur de Maisonneuve, founded Ville Marie (now Montreal). He also built a fort (now Sorel) on the south shore of the St. Lawrence, midway between the present Montreal and Three Rivers. In 1668 Pierre Boucher founded a parish, Boucherville, also on the south shore.

Slowly but surely the French brought Christianity and civilization to the wilds of this land. Forts grew into settlements; missions became parishes; forests gave way to fields and pastures. In the town of Quebec, the Ursuline nuns taught the French and Indian girls; the Jesuit fathers instructed the boys in their classical college, opened in 1635. In 1639 was opened the first hospital in North America, the Hotel Dieu.

In Montreal the same work was carried on with the same spirit. During the winter of 1660 the Iroquois tried to wipe out the white men and their settlements. To Montreal came the news that as soon as the ice thawed on the river hundreds of Iroquois would destroy Montreal and from there go on to Three Rivers and Quebec.

The commander of the fort at Montreal was Adam Dollard. He was a young officer in his early 20's who had come from France only a few years before. With a group of only 16 men he set out to battle for the new land. At Long

The business section of Montreal, Quebec's largest city.

National Film Board

Sault, they found a tumble-down fort and were joined by 40 friendly Hurons. There they surprised the Iroquois and held them off for eight days. But at last the Hurons deserted and the Iroquois burst into the fort to find the defenders dead or dying. Nevertheless, young Dollard's defeat saved Montreal. The Iroquois were too weakened to go on with their attack.

A trio of great men helped New France to take a big step forward. Bishop Francois Xavier de Laval-Montmorency guided the spiritual and intellectual life of the 2,500 Canadians and many more widely scattered Indians. Jean Talon, an able government administrator, started the people toward business prosperity. Louis Frontenac, who became governor in 1672, was able to control the Indians. If his plans of settlement had been followed, France might have held on to its possessions in the New World. (See CANADIAN HISTORY; FRONTENAC, COUNT LOUIS DE BUADE DE.)

Meanwhile the struggle over new possessions between France and England grew more and more serious. In 1713 the Treaty of Utrecht gave Newfoundland, Hudson Bay, and Acadia to England. But the rivalry between the countries was not settled until the French and Indian War, which began in 1754. In this war the French were at first successful. But victory finally went to the British in 1759 when James Wolfe defeated the Marquis de Montcalm on the Plains of Abraham.

At Ste. Foy in the following spring the French general Francois Gaston de Levis won some measure of revenge, but the British brought in reserves and forced Levis to retreat to Montreal. There the British surrounded his small forces, and in September 1760 the Marquis de Vaudreuil signed the papers of surrender. By the Treaty of Paris in 1763 France was forced to give all of Canada to England. (See FRENCH AND INDIAN WAR.)

The war left about 65,000 French Canadians to be ruled by England, the enemy of their mother country. Under such conditions the people turned to their priests for leadership. The British, however, did not prove to be hard conquerors. The first three governors were sympathetic to the French Canadians. More-

A lumber company doctor helping an Indian woman and child at his office in the Gatineau River district.

over, the Quebec Act of 1774 officially recognized the French-Canadian culture and Roman Catholic religion. Throughout Canada's history this act has provided the legal basis for the almost separate development of French Canada.

Disagreements between Canadians of French descent and those of British descent, however, began soon after large numbers of British settlers moved in. These new settlers were farmer-soldiers and Loyalists who had left New England during the American Revolution. The Constitution of 1791 tried to recognize these differences by dividing Canada into two parts: Lower Canada (now Quebec) and Upper Canada (now Ontario). Both the French and the British became more and more unhappy under these conditions. The leader of the French opposition was Louis Joseph Papineau. The anger of the people finally burst into open rebellion in 1837. The rebellion was put down, and Papineau was exiled.

The incident led to the Act of Union in 1840.

Although this act gave better legislation to the country, it was unjust to the French Canadians. At this time Louis Lafontaine came to the aid of his fellow citizens. He joined with Robert Baldwin of Upper Canada to form the United Reform party. (See BALDWIN, ROBERT.) After the union in 1840 these men went to Parliament and insisted on the conditions of Lord Durham's report. (See CANADIAN HISTORY.)

It took a long struggle to win these demands. Twenty-seven years later the British North America Act divided Canada into the provinces of Quebec, Ontario, Nova Scotia, and New Brunswick. Each province had its own Parliament as well as representation in Ottawa. This gave the French Canadians, pioneers and civilizers of the land, a fair amount of control over their own affairs.

As a result of these events, French Canadians have kept their individual character. This can be seen by any visitor in Quebec. There are French Catholic public schools, bilingual (two-language) federal checks, and spoken French on the Canadian Broadcasting Corporation radio and television stations. Conflicting interests between English- and French-speaking Canadians have been a major problem in modern Canada. Some French Canadians would like to form their own separate, independent state.

Each year a blessing is given the fishing fleet by the parish priest.

Courtesy Canadian Consulate General of Chicago, Canadian Pacific Railway photo

At Lake Beauport, Quebec, is one of the many ski resorts that help make the province a popular recreation area.

Many other French Canadians are important in the history of Quebec and Canada. Marguerite Bourgeoys (1620–1700) founded the first Canadian teaching community. St. Isaac Jogues (1607–1646) and St. Jean de Brebeuf (1593–1649) were Jesuit missionaries who went deep into the forests to bring Christianity to the Indians. Daniel Greysolon, Sieur Dulhut (1636–1710), is remembered for his explorations and trading in unknown Indian territory; Duluth, Minnesota, is named after him.

Louis Jolliet (1645–1700), a noted discoverer, crossed Lake Michigan with Father Jacques Marquette (1637–1675) and discovered the Mississippi. (See JOLLIET, LOUIS; MARQUETTE, JACQUES.) Rene Robert Cavelier, Sieur de La Salle (1643–1687), completed Jolliet's discovery by sailing down the long river to the Gulf of Mexico. He planted a cross at the river mouth and named the surrounding country Louisiane in honor of the French king. (See LA SALLE, RENE ROBERT CAVELIER, SIEUR DE.) Antoine de la Mothe Cadillac (1660?–1720), a soldier of fortune, set up a post for fur trading at the narrow strait (called *detroit* in French) between Lake Erie and Lake St. Clair.

Pierre Le Moyne, Sieur d'Iberville (1661–1706), is the best known of 11 famous brothers. He journeyed to the icy waters of Hudson Bay, to barren Newfoundland, and to the warm shores of the Gulf of Mexico. One of his brothers, Jean Le Moyne, Sieur de Bienville, founded New Orleans. (See BIENVILLE, JEAN BAPTISTE LE MOYNE, SIEUR DE.) Pierre de Varennes, Sieur de la Verendrye (1685–1749), made several journeys to find the west coast. His sons were the first white men to view the Canadian Rockies.

Sir Wilfrid Laurier (1841–1919), politician and brilliant orator, was the first French-Canadian prime minister of Canada. (See LAURIER, SIR WILFRID.) Henri Bourassa (1868–1952), journalist and politician, fought for the rights of the French Canadians and the political independence of Canada. (See BOURASSA, HENRI.) Louis Stephen St. Laurent (1882–   ), prime minister from 1948 to 1957, was French Canadian on his father's side. (See ST. LAURENT, LOUIS STEPHEN.) Another French Canadian, Pierre Trudeau, became prime minister in 1968.

QUEBEC, QUEBEC, is a Canadian city on the north bank of the St. Lawrence River, 400 miles from the Atlantic Ocean. Along the river is a narrow plain, which rises sharply to a height of 333 feet on the north. This height of land is named Cape Diamond, and on it, like a crown, stands the Citadel.

The river widens opposite the city to form the harbor of Quebec, with room for many ships. Just below the harbor is the fertile Island of Orleans. Three miles above the city, where the river is narrower, stands the Quebec Bridge. Seven miles below Quebec, where the Montmorency River enters the St. Lawrence, are the Montmorency Falls. These falls, while narrower than Niagara, are over 100 feet higher.

On the plain along the river is the old part of the city, called the Lower Town. There the streets are winding and narrow and the houses old and quaint. The shop signs and street names are almost all in French. This part of the city looks like a town in France. Near the river are the industries: paper manufactures, shipbuilding, and shipping. Grain elevators handle millions of bushels of grain annually, out is the wall that surrounds the old city and runs up the steep slope of Cape Diamond.

The Citadel, first built by the French, was rebuilt by the British about 1830. It now serves as headquarters of the Royal 22nd Regiment as well as a summer residence for the governor general of Canada. Next to the Citadel is the Chateau Frontenac, a 17-story hotel.

To the west of the Citadel lie the Plains of Abraham, made famous by the battle of that name fought in 1759. There, under General James Wolfe, the British defeated the French to gain control in the New World. (See MONTCALM AND WOLFE.)

The population of the metropolitan area is 413,397 (1966). That of the city is 166,984.

Photographic Survey Corporation Ltd.

The Citadel, on Cape Diamond, is the highest point in Quebec city. The Plains of Abraham are to the left.

and the port ships millions of feet of lumber. Other manufacturing plants include shoe factories and iron foundries.

The Upper Town has grown up the steep slopes and is as modern as Lower Town is old. There are wide streets, beautiful residences, and the stone legislative buildings of the provincial Parliament. The Bois de Coulonge, residence of the lieutenant governor, is a palatial mansion overlooking the St. Lawrence River.

Among the many old buildings in the city are the Ursuline Convent; the Hotel Dieu, oldest hospital in America; and two churches, Notre Dame des Victoires and the Basilica, built in 1647. Laval University, the oldest French university in America, was founded in 1852.

Only about 11,000 of the people of Quebec speak English as their native tongue. Many, however, speak both French and English.

History

Quebec was founded by the French under Samuel de Champlain in 1608. (See CHAMPLAIN, SAMUEL DE.) It grew like a seacoast settlement of the 17th century in France. Today the history of the city can be seen in its buildings and monuments. The structure that stands

QUEBRACHO (*kä brä′chō*) **AND QUEBRACHO COLORADO.** This small, often poorly formed South American tree is closely related to the sumacs. Its brick-red heartwood contains 20 to 30 per cent of soluble tannin. The name "quebracho" is derived from the Portuguese and means "axe-breaker." It is so named because of the heavy, hard, and flinty nature of the wood. Throughout its range, which embraces an area of approximately 300,000 square miles, the trees occur singly or in small groves along water courses in the jungles of northern Argentina, Uruguay, Paraguay, southeastern Bolivia, and southern Brazil.

In modern practice the trees are felled and cut into bolts 4 feet to 12 feet in length. Bark and nearly tannin-free, worthless sapwood are removed. Then the heartwood bolts are hauled or dragged by oxen to the nearest railhead for shipment to either Buenos Aires, Argentina, or Montevideo, Uruguay, for processing. At the extraction plants the wood is reduced to chips or shavings and placed in large copper extractors.

Then hot water or steam is admitted to the charged tanks and the soluble parts of wood are quickly leached out. The extract is immediately cooled and filtered in the absence of air to prevent chemical change. It is then pumped into evaporators where surplus water is removed. The concentrate is poured into suitable containers for shipment. Upon cooling, it solidifies. The chips which are left are used for fuel to produce steam employed in the process.

Annual production of quebracho tannin extract varies between 150,000 to 200,000 tons, the bulk of which is consumed in the United States and Europe. Hides tanned with quebracho extract are very dark. In practice quebracho tannin is usually blended with other tanning materials to produce leathers of lighter shades. Quebracho Colorado (red quebracho) should be distinguished from quebracho blanco or the white quebracho of Brazil. This latter species is a large tree of the dogbane family. White quebracho is also a source of tannin but of more importance as a source of timber.

QUICKSAND (*kwick'sand*). A treacherous deposit of fine sand so filled with water that it flows easily is called quicksand. The smooth rounded grains of the sand are lubricated by the surrounding water and slide past each other easily. Such material flows like a thick fluid, and cows or other animals that tread on quick-sand may be swallowed without a trace. Buried layers of quicksand may yield, either slowly or suddenly, and engulf buildings, roadways, or other structures placed on them. In 1875 at Pueblo, Colorado, a whole train including the engine sank into a bed of quicksand and was never recovered, although the sand was probed to a depth of 50 feet.

Beds of quicksand were generally formed where rivers deposited fine sand over underlying clay. Water can not escape because of the clay beneath and thus keeps the quicksand saturated. Similar conditions may occur along certain seashores near the mouths of large rivers.

When engineers have to build foundations of buildings or other structures in quicksand, they may freeze the sand by brine sent through pipes driven in the deposit. Another method is to sink a caisson. This is a steel chamber filled with compressed air which holds out the water and sand while workmen construct a foundation or tunnel lining of concrete or other material strong enough to resist the quicksand. Large

A pocket of quicksand may be formed over a bed of clay or rock that does not allow the water to drain away. The deposit is a mixture with water that flows like a thick liquid. The sand on the top may be dry. Since the man is lighter than the mixture of sand and water he will not sink any further if he remains still.

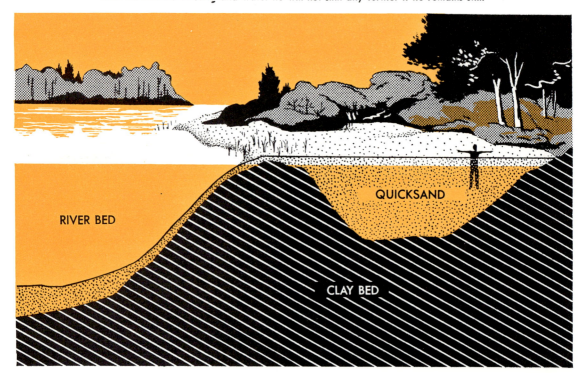

RIVER BED

QUICKSAND

CLAY BED

foundations have to be carried down to the firm material below the quicksand. (See CAISSON.)

QUINCE (*kwĭns*). For more than 2,000 years the quince has been cultivated in Asia Minor. Its cultivation has always been limited, however, and few varieties have been developed. The quince is a small, many-branched tree, or shrub. It is a member of the rose family. Its rose or white flowers are large and look like those of the pear. Its firm yellow fruits are shaped like very large pears or apples. Quinces are seldom eaten raw, except in warm countries where exposure to the hot sun makes them less sour.

Quinces are highly valued in making preserves, jellies, and marmalades because they give flavor and acidity when mixed with other fruits. Quince seeds were once used in medicine. Although the fruit of the Japanese quince can not be eaten, it is grown for the beauty of its flowers. These are white, brilliant rose, or deep red. They bloom in early spring and summer.

Some quince fruits have a very pleasant odor and are placed among clothing to give fragrance. Quince trees grow quickly on light soil, but they live longer on heavy soil. The best United States orchards, which are located in western New York, are planted on well-drained land.

QUININE (*kwĭ′nīn, kwĭ nēn′,* or *kwĭn′ēn*). From the bark of the cinchona tree, a native of Latin America, comes the drug quinine used in the cure of malaria. (See MALARIA.) According to legend the healing properties of the bark were first discovered by an Indian of Loja, Peru. He told his discovery to the Jesuit priests near by about 1600. The Indians called the bark *quina-quina*, which means "bark with healing powers." Quinine, one of the drugs obtained from the powdered bark, was introduced into modern medicine in 1816.

The quinine crystals are silky, needlelike, and bitter. From the crystals the bitter quinine tonics are made which are used in the treatment of malaria. They reduce fever, prevent the destruction of the red corpuscles, and check the growth of the malaria germs. In malarial districts small doses of quinine are taken daily as a preventive of the disease. Quinine is also used as a nerve stimulant and a general tonic. It is often found in cold tablets, where it is of little value. Quinidine, a quinine derivative, is used in treatment of various heart irregularities.

Quinine, taken to excess, affects the hearing, causes dizziness, congestion of the brain, and coma. It is dangerous to use unless it has been prescribed by a reliable physician. Some people can not take even a small dose without harmful effects which may range from a temporary rash

J. Horace McFarland Company

Left: The Japanese quince is grown for the beauty of its flowers, which may be white, rose, or deep red. Above: The fruit is used for preserves, but can not be eaten raw.

to convulsions.

In 1852 the Dutch took seeds of cinchona trees to Java in the East Indies where they began to raise them. Their plantation method of growing yielded a bark superior in quinine content to that of the wild South American trees. In time Java became the largest producer in the world. It supplies more than 90 per cent of the amount used yearly. India, Ceylon, and South America furnish the rest.

At the time of World War II the Japanese captured the Dutch East Indies, now called Indonesia, and cut off the world's supply of Java quinine. Search for the wild trees and accumulation of the bark in South America was then stimulated once more. The quantities so obtained were small compared with those commercially produced on plantations. Large plantings of trees were made in Puerto Rico. The United States had stored some quantities of it, and people in the United States were asked to turn in any supplies of the drug which they had. It was then given to the government for the use of the armed forces where it was especially needed for troops in malaria areas, such as the South Pacific.

In the meantime research was increased on two drugs, Atabrine and Plasmochin. These had been used to some extent as substitutes for quinine but without much success. The contents of Atabrine (Quinacrine), a German product, were not stable. Plasmochin, which was more poisonous and less effective than quinine, was of little use.

Out of United States research during World War II came Chloroquine. Although related to quinine, Chloroquine is now considered more valuable. It is not only more effective than quinine, but is less harmful. Next in order of usefulness comes Atabrine, which keeps down the fever and chills of malaria and holds the infection in check. However, Atabrine turns the skin yellow. Quinine itself, from a practical standpoint, is about third in usefulness, because it is harder to get than the manufactured drugs. Totaquine is a mixed, cheap extract of the bark. It is used only when purer products are not available, as during World War II. The sources of quinine held by the Japanese during World War II are now considered to be much less important than before the new synthetic drugs were available.

QUITO ($k\bar{e}'t\bar{o}$), **ECUADOR,** the capital city of Ecuador, is in the Andean highlands more than 9,300 feet above sea level. Nearby are about 30 volcanoes, some of which are among the largest in the world. At night, clouds over the volcanoes take on a red color which is the reflection of red-hot lava boiling in the volcanoes' cones. Earthquakes sometimes cause serious damage to homes and other buildings.

Although it is only a few miles south of the Equator, Quito has an average yearly temperature of 54 degrees Fahrenheit. The temperature is kept comfortable by the high altitude. Moreover, temperatures change little from month to month, because Quito is so near the Equator.

Quito was an important Indian city when it was conquered by the Spanish in 1534. Today it is still a center for surrounding Indian communities. The population of Quito increased rapidly from about 142,000 in 1940 to 210,000 in 1950 and 400,650 in 1965. The city is smaller than Guayaquil, the chief commercial city of Ecuador, which is on the Pacific coast 300 miles away. But Quito is a center of the woolen and cotton industries. Leather goods and forest products are also made there. Skilled Indian workers make beautiful objects out of wood, ivory, gold, and silver. Quito also prides itself as a cultural center. Its churches have many art treasures, and its art school is the oldest in the Western Hemisphere.

The streets of Quito are laid out in a crisscross pattern of squares, like those of most Spanish colonial cities. Some of the streets run far up the slopes of Mount Pichincha, a volcano on the west. Climbing these slopes causes a person who is not used to the thin air to become quickly out of breath.

Facing the main square (the Plaza Independencia) are the cathedral, the government palace, and the City Hall. Other important institutions in Quito are the university, 11 monasteries, an astronomical observatory, and a national museum of fine arts.

PRINTED IN THE U.S.A. BY THE PLIMPTON PRESS

THE SECRET ROOM

A Secret Room's beyond this door
For younger readers to explore.
The things inside it, as you'll see,
Are not arranged from A to Z.
They're just a lot of stuff you may
Have fun with on a rainy day.
Where? When? How? or Why?
Well, give The Secret Room a try.

Stories and poems, pictures too,
Are in The Secret Room on view.
So turn the pages, keep on turning:
Some for laughing, some for learning,
Some for this mood, some for that,
And others just for looking at.
To find out more—
Open the Door.

You Will Find
a Secret Room to Explore
in Every Volume of Britannica Junior
Except in Volume One

Poem overleaf by Clifton Fadiman

Now you're in
THE SECRET ROOM
and here is what you'll find

Some of the biggest fishes in the world and some

of the most dangerous  SHARKS . . .

The sparkling, fluffy stuff that turns everything white

in winter —SNOW . . . The adventure

of discovery when you go EXPLORING

. . . Special hunters who know

HOW TO CATCH A GIRAFFE . . .

Something we see inside our heads—

THE THINGS WE REMEMBER

A way to  LOOK AT THE LEAVES

and tell what season of the year it is . . . And

 BOOKS, the places where stories are stored.

Danger! Sharks!

This man is taking photographs of the beautiful, bright-colored fish that live in the ocean. Suddenly, he sees a giant shape. It looks at first like a long, dark shadow.

The man doesn't wait to see any more because he knows that this big shadow thing is really a shark. And some sharks eat people!

Because some sharks are dangerous, a wire net is stretched along the shore, out in the water, at beaches where sharks have been seen. This keeps the sharks away and makes it safe to swim there. Many large beaches have been made safe for swimming.

Sharks aren't everywhere in the ocean, and not all sharks are man-eaters. But these great white sharks are. They are so fierce that fishermen call them tigers of the sea.

It's hard for a man to fight them because they are such strong, fast swimmers and have bodies that are protected by a tough skin covered with tiny, toothlike bones. In their big mouths are rows and rows of sharp teeth that rip like the edge of a saw. White sharks make a quick meal out of almost anything!

This is another man-eating shark. You may think he looks too funny to be dangerous, but he's really too dangerous to be funny.

He's called the hammerhead shark. If you hold the book sideways, you can see why.

These small dogfish sharks can bite, but they are not likely to eat people. They are a big pest to a fisherman. The fish they don't eat, they scare away. Sometimes they even eat the fisherman's net.

It's only because they have faces that look a little like a dog's that they are named after man's friendliest pet.

The whale shark is a whale of a shark—the largest shark of all. But in spite of its size, it is one of the most harmless—unless you're a small fish. It eats small fish and doesn't attack large fish or people.

Some men work at catching sharks. They go hunting for them nearly every day. It is the way they make their money.

Just about every part of this big, dangerous fish is good for something.

The oil in a shark's liver contains vitamin A.

The skin of a shark makes a very tough leather
for belts and other things.

Some people collect shark teeth. You can find them in the sand on
many ocean shores. You can even make them into a necklace.

The meat of a shark is good to eat. But there are more sharks
caught than people want to eat, so some shark meat is made into
fertilizer. Farmers put fertilizer on their land to help things grow.

Even the fins of a shark are good for something. People in China
use them to make a soup.

Hello, Snow

You are looking out the window of your warm house. The sky is colorless and cold. It looks as if it would ring and clang if you could raise your fist and knock on it. The wind blows. The sun is hiding. What an unfriendly day! You turn away from the window.

An hour later your mother says, "Come look out the window!"

You wonder what there is to see that wasn't there before. You wonder why it's so quiet. The sounds of the city—voices, engines, alarms, wheels, horns—are hushed. When you look out the window, you see why. It's snowing. The snow has made a brand-new world, clean and soft and silent.

As snowflakes fall from the sky, they look like feathers, bits of lace, silvery spider webs, chips from a diamond. . . .

It's easy to catch a snowflake, but keeping one is harder. Snowflakes melt so fast. Take a piece of black paper or cloth outside with you to catch and hold a few snowflakes. And take a magnifying glass to get a really good look.

At first glance all snowflakes look the same. That's because they all have six sides. A closer look will show you that they are not the same—every one is different.

Aren't they pretty? How would you like to have your room wallpapered with pictures of snowflakes? Every night when you went to bed, you could have your own private snowstorm.

Can you imagine snow almost every night? That's a lot of snow. But there are places where there is that much snow. Eskimos, who live far north, toward the bitterly cold North Pole, have that much snow. They have so much they can even make houses of it!

Even if it doesn't snow enough where you live to build a snow-house, perhaps there will be enough snow to make a fort or a snowman.

When it's very, very cold, the snow is as dry and unstickable as sand. It won't pack in your hands to make a snowball. But just wait until the sun comes out and softens the snow a little.

Then . . .

Look out, boys and girls! Here come the snowballs!

Snowballs come from boys and girls. Snowflakes come from the sky—from the billions of tiny water droplets up there that form clouds.

Sometimes the wind blows these clouds from a warm place to a very cold place. If the wind stops blowing, it leaves the clouds hanging in the freezing cold. When that happens, the tiny droplets of water in the cloud freeze into tiny ice crystals. And these ice crystals make up snowflakes.

Down
    down
        down
            comes the downy snow.

Do You Want to Be an Explorer?

Maybe you want to know what's on the next street,
or in a cave,
or on an island where nobody lives,
or even in a locked closet in your own house.
Especially a locked closet!
If so, you know how an explorer feels.

Explorers are people who go to faraway places to find out what is there. They sail across oceans, climb mountains, and cut their way through forests where snakes and wild animals live.

Sometimes they become lost in icy blizzards, in hot and dry deserts, or in dark forests. Often they are hungry and thirsty and tired.

Then why do they go exploring?

Long ago—very, very long ago—
when there were no machines
in the world and everybody lived
in trees or caves, people went
exploring to find food and water.

After people learned how to
build houses, they went exploring
for other reasons, too. Some went
to look for gold and jewels and
furs and spices. Some went to find
new lands for their king or queen.
Some went to find slaves to do
their work for them. Some tried
to find a new way to get to the
other side of the world.

Perhaps the best reason of all
for people to go exploring is that
they are curious and want to go
somewhere new. Many men have
wanted to know what it was like
in some faraway place.

An explorer named Ferdinand Magellan and his sailors left Spain and sailed toward the setting sun to see how far they could go. After sailing week after week on the ocean, they ran out of food. They became so hungry that they ate sawdust and leather.

One of the sailors told of "great and awful things of the ocean"—ugly flying fish, sharks, sea lions, giant crabs, and fearful sea serpents.

Finally, they sighted an unknown land. Their ships sailed through a narrow path, or *channel,* of stormy water between high mountains and came to another ocean—the biggest ocean in the world. Magellan named it the Pacific Ocean, and the channel where his ships sailed was named the Strait of Magellan.

One of Magellan's ships was the first to sail all the way around the world.

In the mountains of Mexico an
explorer named Cortés discovered
the land of the Aztec Indians. It
was like discovering a new world.
Some of the Aztec houses were
on floating islands in a lake.
Many houses were almost buried
in flowers.

Strange buildings—pyramids
made of stones—pointed high into the sky. Around the pyramids
for many miles was a tall new plant, green and waving in the wind.
Some of the explorers had never seen it before. They didn't know
what it was.

Corn! The tall, green, waving plant was corn.

The Aztecs also had gold—a lot of gold. The explorers knew
what that was. Some explorers were cruel and greedy people. They
fought the Indians and took their gold.

"I will find a way or make one," said Robert E. Peary.

Peary wanted to be first to reach the North Pole—a faraway place of ice and snow where it is light day and night in the middle of the summer and dark day and night in the middle of the winter.

Peary learned that explorers must be patient, as well as brave. He broke his leg and had to wait. He froze his toes and had to wait again. Storms and icy fog and polar bears caused more waiting. The sunlit snow almost blinded him. Some of his men died, and others turned back.

Only one man who had started out with him, Matthew Henson, was still with him when, finally, he reached the North Pole.

Look on the globe. You'll see the South Pole, as well as the North Pole. Both are places of icy blizzards and are very cold. With snowshoes and dog teams, a man named Amundsen raced a man named Scott to be the first one to the South Pole. Amundsen was first. Scott reached it soon afterward, but he was so weak from hunger and cold that he died on the way home.

The first man to fly an airplane over both the North Pole and the South Pole was Admiral Byrd.

Today in an airplane an explorer can go farther in a minute than a dog team sometimes went in a whole day. And today, radio keeps explorers in touch with the rest of the world.

Do you like to read about faraway, hard-to-reach places? You can because of books about explorers who dared to go to these places. Now most of the land on the Earth has been explored. But the bottoms of the oceans haven't—or not very much. And today's explorers are just beginning to explore space. There will always be something new to be curious about.

How to Catch a Giraffe

How did the giraffes you see in this picture get to the zoo?
They weren't born in the zoo.
They didn't walk or run or swim to get to the zoo.
These giraffes had to travel many miles over mountains and rivers and even cross an ocean before they reached the zoo.
The story of their journey begins on the hot, dusty plains of Africa when these long-legged, long-necked fellows were only one year old.

The men who trap wild animals say this is just the right age for a giraffe to be captured. A one-year-old giraffe is small enough to be shipped to the zoo without getting hurt. And being fed and cared for by strange people doesn't seem to frighten it for very long.

Catching almost any wild animal is difficult and often dangerous. The giraffe is one of the fastest of all animals. Animal trappers can't run nearly so fast as a giraffe. So when they go hunting giraffes for a zoo, the hunters ride in a high-wheeled automobile that can go rolling over the grasslands where there are no roads.

When they get very close, the hunters act like cowboys— maybe we should call them giraffeboys. They stand up in the automobile and whirl a rope and try to drop the lasso loop over the giraffe's head.

Roping the giraffe is only the beginning of the job.

The giraffe is then herded into a high, open crate and taken by truck to an animal camp. It's kept there until the animal trainers and doctors who run the camp decide the giraffe is ready for the trip to the zoo.

Now, a giraffe is no ordinary animal. Its neck and legs are so long that it can't be shipped on an airplane. And so, with one of the trainers, the giraffe rides in a truck, on a train, and finally on a ship. The trainer makes sure that the giraffe eats the right foods and is kept safe and warm on the long journey.

After the ship lands, the giraffe gets one last ride on a truck and train—to the last stop. The zoo!

Except for fat, heavy animals like the rhinoceros, most wild animals are shipped to zoos by airplane. For animals that are used to living in deserts or jungles, the airplanes are heated.

The people who catch wild animals and take them to zoos have to know as much about taking care of animals as a zoo keeper does.

The Things We Remember

What can you remember?

Lots of things. Close your eyes. Now remember
  the smell of hot buttered toast,
  the taste of chocolate,
  the feel of a cat's fur,
  the sound of your mother calling your name,
  what a bicycle looks like.

What helps you remember these things?

The smell of hot buttered toast got in through your nose.

The taste of chocolate got in through your tongue.

The feel of a cat's fur got in through the skin on your fingers.

The sound of your mother calling your name got in through your ears.

What a bicycle looks like got in through your eyes. These things got in through smell, taste, feel, sound, and sight—which are called our *senses*.

Can you remember things that you didn't ever smell, taste, feel, hear, or see?

Close your eyes again. Now try to remember
        the smell of an eagle's egg,
        the taste of elephant meat,
        the feel of a newborn seal,
        the sound of a volcano shooting into the air,
        what it looks like under your sidewalk.

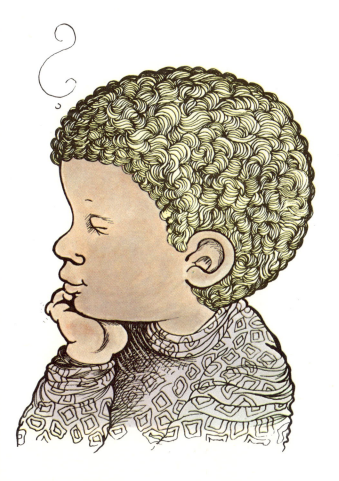

If you had ever smelled an eagle's egg, tasted elephant meat, touched a newborn seal, listened to a volcano shooting off, or lifted up a sidewalk and looked under it, then you *might* remember these things.

Of course, you might *not* remember them. Because sometimes you forget. Things that were in your memory get lost.

Sometimes if you sit and think about it for a while, you remember once more.

The things you remember best are things that you smell, taste, feel, hear, or see again and again.

Look at the Leaves

In some parts of the world it gets very cold in the winter and very warm in the summer. In these places you can tell what time of the year it is just by noticing two things: the kinds of things that children are doing and what's happening to the leaves on the broad-leaved trees.

Spring leaves—
March, April, May
leaves are light, bright
green. They look very, very
clean—as if each one had been
carefully washed and hung out to dry
in the sun. Some trees have blossoms
among their fresh green leaves. It's
time to fly kites in the fresh breezes
blowing up the hill. It's time to play
outdoors. Good-bye, walls and winter chills!

Summer leaves—
June, July, August
leaves are green, too; but
instead of being a light, sunny
green, they are dark and shaded. They
look as if they'd been colored by someone who
pressed down very hard on his crayon. There are
no blossoms among these leaves. They are so thick and
heavy that you wonder how the branches can hold them all. Now
it's time for bicycling, for swimming, or singing around a campfire.

Autumn leaves—
September, October,
November leaves are red
and yellow and gold. They
come drifting down from tree branches
like little airplanes floating. These bright,
fire-colored leaves warn us that we'd better light
the fire again. Cold weather is coming! It's time to
walk through the brown grass and fallen leaves—after school.

Winter leaves—
December, January, February
leaves are dull gray or dusty brown.
Most of them lie on the ground near the
tree on which they grew. They look tired and
sad. But wait! Look up at the branches of the tree!
Do you see all those little bumps? They are the buds.
From the buds tiny leaves and blossoms will grow for next year.
But now it's time to build a snowman, go Christmas shopping,
sit by the fire. And almost before you know it, the light,
bright green leaves will tell you that it's spring again!

Who's in the Library?

The books in your library were written by many different men and women from all over the world. Some lived long, long ago. Some are still alive today. Even those who are not alive can still tell you things—*in their books.*

If all of these writers could suddenly be in your library, they would fill all the rooms, hang out the windows, and cover the roof! They would fill the street and spread through the neighborhood!

Isn't it lucky that libraries are filled with books instead of writers? The writers couldn't be in all libraries at once.

But their books can.

In nearly every large town and city, people can go to libraries to read the wise and beautiful and exciting and funny things that have been written.